Visual C++ 2

Developer's Guide, Second Edition

Naba Barkakati

SAMS
PUBLISHING

201 West 103rd Street
Indianapolis, Indiana 46290

*This book is dedicated to my
wife Leha, and daughters
Ivy, Emily, and Ashley*

Trademarks

Overview

Contents

II Object-Oriented Programming

III Learning C++

V   Windows Programming

Preface

For years, C has been the language of choice among programmers, especially those developing software for Microsoft Windows. C has its limitations, however, and recently C++ has begun to gain a large and loyal following as the successor to C. Much of C++'s popularity comes from its support for object-oriented programming (OOP), which has become the new wave of programming technique. Because C++ evolved from C, most compilers of C++ (including Visual C++ 2.0) also compile C code—making the transition from C to C++ easier.

The combination of C++ and the Microsoft Foundation Class (MFC) Library (Version 3.0 comes with Visual C++ 2.0) gives you a set of powerful tools to create applications for Windows. With OOP you are able to organize your code into modules based on real-world objects. Although you can apply OOP techniques in any language (even C), C++ includes the necessary language constructs that make it easier to implement OOP techniques. The class libraries that compose MFC are needed because C++ provides only a small set of keywords for controlling program execution and defining new data types; all other tasks, such as input and output, string manipulations, and mathematical computations, are relegated to the library of functions and classes.

To utilize the power and flexibility of the Visual C++ environment, you must become familiar with three distinct subjects: C++, OOP concepts and techniques, and the tools and libraries that are part of Visual C++. Further, to create complete applications, you must gain some experience in the synergistic use of OOP, C++, and the libraries. Although many books are published on these topics, most suffer from one or more drawbacks:

- Books that cover object-oriented design principles do not pay much attention to C++.
- Books that are designed to teach C++ do not adequately describe how to implement OOP techniques in C++.
- Books designed as reference guides to the Visual C++ libraries do not cover C++ and OOP.
- The documentation that is included with Visual C++ has all the information you need—many, many thousands of pages—but it is too extensive to be an easy-to-use tutorial and developer's guide.

Due to these shortcomings, there is a definite need for a comprehensive source of information for all three topics: C++, OOP, and the MFC libraries. *Visual C++ 2 Developer's Guide,* Second Edition, is intended to answer the needs of intermediate-to-advanced programmers who are learning C++ and OOP in order to develop Windows applications using Visual C++ 2.0 and MFC 3.0. This book teaches C++ and OOP, and, at the same time, serves as a developer's guide to the MFC 3.0 libraries that are part of Visual C++ 2.0. Because C++ and OOP are likely to be new to many C programmers, the book includes in-depth tutorials that gently introduce C++ and the use of OOP concepts in C++ programs.

Visual C++ 2 Developer's Guide, Second Edition, features the following:

- A description of the Visual Workbench, which is the primary Windows-based interface between Visual C++ and the programmer
- A quick overview of ANSI standard C
- Extensive tutorials on the basic concepts of object-oriented programming
- A discussion of data abstraction, inheritance, and polymorphism
- A step-by-step introduction to the features of C++, such as classes and virtual functions that support OOP
- A discussion of how C++ differs from ANSI standard C
- Detailed examples showing how to use OOP techniques
- A description of the different approaches to building a library of reusable classes in C++
- Tutorial coverage of the Microsoft Foundation Class Version 3.0 (MFC 3.0) Library
- Coverage of the latest 32-bit Windows programming topics, including the following:
    - Dynamic Link Libraries (DLLs)
    - Dynamic Data Exchange (DDE)
    - OLE 2.0 programming
    - OLE Custom Controls (OCX)
    - ODBC (Open Data Base Connectivity) programming
    - Network programming with Windows Sockets
- A disk with the source code for all example programs appearing in the book

Visual C++ 2 Developer's Guide, Second Edition, uses short, simple example programs to illustrate the syntactical details of OOP techniques. Features of C++ are always presented in the context of an OOP concept that the feature supports.

Visual C++ 2 Developer's Guide, Second Edition, also includes coverage of the class and function libraries that are necessary for building real-world applications. Specifically, the book covers application development for the Windows environments using the MFC 3.0 libraries—a collection of over 130 classes designed to make Windows programming easier. The latter part of the book covers specific Windows programming topics including OLE 2.0 programming, OLE custom controls, database programming with ODBC, and network programming with Windows Sockets.

To make it easier for you to use the programs appearing in the book, *Visual C++ 2 Developer's Guide,* Second Edition, includes a bound-in disk that contains the source code for all example programs appearing in the book.

It is easy to get overwhelmed by the new syntax of C++, the details of how everything fits together in a program that uses an object-oriented design, and the large number of tools, functions, and classes that Visual C++ 2.0 offers. However, with a grasp of the fundamentals of OOP and with the help of the MFC 3.0 Library, you will find it relatively easy to employ OOP techniques in your Windows applications. *Visual C++ 2 Developer's Guide,* Second Edition, will get you started on your way to harnessing the full power of object-oriented techniques, C++, and the MFC 3.0 Library.

Acknowledgments

I am grateful to Greg Croy for getting me started on this book—a tutorial guide to Windows programming with Visual C++ 2.0 and the MFC 3.0 Library. Thanks to Grace Buechlein for subsequently taking care of the project and seeing it through to successful completion.

Thanks to Microsoft Corporation for providing copies of Visual C++ 2.0, Windows 95, and Windows NT 3.5. Thanks to Sams Publishing for making the necessary arrangements with Microsoft Corporation to get Beta copies of these products during the preparation of this book.

Thanks to everyone at Sams Publishing for transforming my manuscript into this well-edited and beautifully packaged book. In particular, I would like to thank Nancy Albright for the thorough copy and production editing, Keith Davenport for the development editing and for taking care of the companion disk, and Cindy Morrow for managing the production of the book.

Finally, I am most thankful to my wife Leha and my daughters, Ivy, Emily, and Ashley—it is their love and support that keeps me going.

About the Author

Naba Barkakati is an accomplished computer programmer and well-known author of computer programming books, including *Borland C++ 4 Developer's Guide* and *X Windows System Programming.*

Naba lives in North Potomac, Maryland, with his wife Leha and daughters Ivy, Emily, and Ashley.

Introduction

Visual C++ 2 Developer's Guide, Second Edition, is an intermediate-level book that introduces you to the basic concepts of object-oriented programming (OOP) and shows you how to apply OOP techniques using the C++ programming language. Additionally, the book is designed to serve as a tutorial to the Microsoft Foundation Class Libraries Version 3.0 (MFC 3.0) that accompanies Visual C++ 2.0. The book's goal is to get you, the C programmer, familiar with the terminology of OOP, to describe how various features of C++ support OOP, and to show you how to use the MFC 3.0 classes to develop Windows applications.

To this end, *Visual C++ 2 Developer's Guide,* Second Edition, focuses on the basic concepts of OOP, how OOP helps you handle changes in software requirements easily, and how C++ supports OOP. It also covers programming with the *iostream* I/O library and shows how to call C functions from C++, organize C++ class libraries, and use the MFC 3.0 Library. Once you master the basics of C++, OOP, and MFC 3.0, *Visual C++ 2 Developer's Guide,* Second Edition, moves on to the subject of developing Windows applications in C++. It includes sample graphics and imaging applications for Windows. Figures and screen shots are used extensively to illustrate concepts, show outputs of various applications, and show the inheritance hierarchies of classes.

Visual C++ 2 Developer's Guide, Second Edition, also covers specific 32-bit Windows programming topics, such as OLE 2.0 programming, OLE custom controls (OCX), database programming with Open Database Connectivity (ODBC), and network programming with Windows Sockets.

What You Need

To make the best use of this book, you should have access to a reasonably powerful computer with the Visual C++ 2.0 compiler. At a minimum, you need an 80486 or Pentium system with a large disk (at least 300M) and enough memory (at least 8M) to run Windows efficiently. Although most of the examples in this book should run under Windows 3.1 with Win32s, some examples require Windows NT.

All examples in this book were tested with Visual C++ 2.0 on a 486DX2/66 system with 16M RAM, a 256-color display, a SoundBlaster card, and a 1G hard disk running Windows 95 and Windows NT 3.5.

Notational Conventions

Visual C++ 2 Developer's Guide, Second Edition, uses a simple notational style. All listings are typeset in a monospace font for ease of reading. All command names, function names, variable names, and keywords appearing in text are also in the same monospace font. The first occurrence of new terms and concepts is in *italic.* Notes, typeset in boxes, are used to explain terms and concepts that appear in the text nearby.

How to Use This Book

If you are a newcomer to Visual C++, you should browse through Chapters 1 through 4 to see what Visual C++ 2.0 offers and how to set it up on your system. If you are starting to learn C++, you should read Chapters 5 through 16 in sequence. These chapters teach object-oriented programming (OOP), C++, and how to apply OOP techniques in C++. If you already know OOP and C++ and you want to learn how to develop Windows applications with Visual C++ 2.0 and MFC 3.0, you will be interested in Chapters 17 through 32.

This book is divided into seven parts, plus a bibliography:

- ■ Part I, "Getting Started with Visual C++ 2.0," includes four chapters that describe the Visual C++ 2.0 programming environment and give an overview of the C programming language.

- ■ Part II, "Learning Object-Oriented Programming," has two chapters that explain the basic concepts of object-oriented programming (OOP).

- ■ Part III, "Learning C++," is comprised of seven chapters that describe how to use the features of C++ that support OOP.

- ■ Part IV, "Applying OOP Techniques in C++," includes three chapters that show how to organize C++ class libraries and use the general-purpose classes in MFC 3.0.

- ■ Part V, "Windows Programming," has eight chapters that cover various aspects of Windows programming, from displaying graphics and text to writing multimedia applications with audio and video output.

- ■ Part VI, "Advanced Windows Programming," includes five chapters that cover DDE, DLL, OLE 2.0, OCX, and multimedia programming with Visual C++ 2.0 and MFC 3.0.

- ■ Part VII, "Extending Visual C++ 2.0," contains two chapters that cover database programming with Open Database Connectivity (ODBC) and network programming with Windows Sockets.

From this quick overview, you can decide how you want to use the book. For example, if you are already familiar with Visual C++ 2.0, you can skip Part I and go straight to Part II to learn the basic terminology of OOP. If you are a newcomer to C++, consult the chapters in Part III. On the other hand, if you know how C++ supports OOP and want to start using C++ in Windows applications, you can skip Parts I through III and read Chapters 17 through 32.

It's time to get started. You're on your way to mastering the basic concepts of object-oriented programming and applying OOP techniques using the latest enhancements available in Visual C++ 2.0.

I

Getting Started with
Visual C++ 2.0

1

The Visual C++ 2.0 Programming Environment

This book's major goal is to help you, the C programmer, learn the basic concepts of object-oriented programming (OOP) and C++ using the Microsoft Visual C++ 2.0 compiler. This book also serves as a guide to developing 32-bit Windows applications using the Microsoft Foundation Class library 3.0 (MFC 3.0). However, before you get into OOP, C++, and the MFC 3 classes, you need to know what tools Microsoft Visual C++ 2.0 offers to help you carry out the essential programming tasks of editing, compiling, linking, and debugging.

To help familiarize you with the Visual C++ 2.0 environment, this chapter provides an overview of the Microsoft Visual C++ 2.0 product, including what components it contains and how to set up and use it on a PC running Windows. Visual C++ is a Windows application. Although you can compile and link with commands entered at the command prompt in a command window, the best programmer's interface with Visual C++ is the Visual Workbench. This chapter introduces the interactive development environment called the Visual Workbench and includes a short look at CL, the command-line interface to the compiler and linker. Chapter 2, "Program Development Tools in Visual C++ 2.0," further describes the rest of the program development tools—such as LIB, LINK, and NMAKE—that help you manage the edit-compile-link-debug cycle of building applications. Of course, with the Visual Workbench, you don't have to concern yourself as much with the mechanics of actually creating an executable program. The Visual Workbench does most of the work for you. You learn more about the Visual Workbench in Chapter 17, "Windows Programming with Visual C++ 2.0 and MFC 3.0."

Chapter 3, "An Overview of ANSI Standard C," and Chapter 4, "Visual C++ 2.0 Extensions to Standard C," summarize the features of the C programming language. Although this book assumes that you already know C, you may want an overview of the C language as a refresher, especially to review the features of ANSI Standard C and the extensions to the language that are specific to Visual C++ 2.0. Another reason for reviewing ANSI C is that familiarity with ANSI C helps you learn the syntax of C++ because of the similarity between the two. Chapter 3 offers an overview of ANSI C, and Chapter 4 describes how Microsoft augments ANSI C with certain keywords that are necessary to utilize fully the capabilities of the Intel 80x86 microprocessors used in MS-DOS PCs.

NOTE

Microsoft Visual C++ 2.0 is used for developing 32-bit Windows applications that can run under 32-bit operating systems such as Windows NT (as well as Windows 3.1 with the Win32s extension).

A Quick Tour of Microsoft Visual C++ 2.0

Microsoft Visual C++ 2.0 is many products in one. It provides a complete programming environment for C and C++ and contains all the supporting tools and libraries necessary to write Microsoft Windows applications. As a programmer, you use the following tools primarily:

■ The Visual Workbench is a Windows-based interactive development environment used for editing source files and interfacing with many of the supplied utilities, including the C and C++ compiler. The Visual Workbench enables you to build applications—and debug them—without ever leaving the Visual Workbench. Normally, the Visual Workbench helps you in using other development tools—for example, running the compiler, linker, and resource compiler to create the executable application for you. In Visual C++ 2.0, the tools integrated into the Visual Workbench include the following:

   ■ AppWizard, a code generator that generates a skeleton Windows application using the MFC application framework

   ■ ClassWizard, a utility for creating and managing C++ classes (in programs developed using AppWizard)

   ■ AppStudio, a program for editing a Windows application's resources, such as menus, dialog boxes, bitmaps, icons, and cursors

   ■ A built-in debugger to track down errors in your applications

   ■ An incremental linker that reduces the time needed to link a program by linking only those object files that have changed since the last link

■ CL is the command-line interface to the C and C++ compiler for translating source files into object files.

■ LINK is the command-line interface to the linker for combining one or more object modules into an executable file.

■ LIB is the command-line-based library manager for managing collections of object modules in a single file.

■ NMAKE is the command-line-based make utility for automating program development.

NOTE

Through the Visual Workbench, Microsoft Visual C++ 2.0 provides nearly complete integration of all necessary tools for developing Windows applications.

There are a few more command-line based utilities that you may not use directly, but they are handy when you need their functionality. These utilities include the following:

■ CVPACK compresses the size of executable files that contain information needed by the debugger.

■ DUMPBIN is a utility for viewing the contents of object files in the Common Object File Format (COFF). DUMPBIN is new in Visual C++ 2.0.

■ EDITBIN is a binary file editor for editing object files in the Common Object File Format. EDITBIN is new in Visual C++ 2.0.

In addition, Microsoft Visual C++ 2.0 includes a number of Windows-based utilities that include the following:

■ Spy++ is a program that enables you to examine messages and message parameters being sent to a window.

■ DDESpy is a program that enables you to see Dynamic Data Exchange (DDE) between a DDE server and a client application.

■ MFC Trace Options is a utility that enables you to set the debug options that MFC uses.

■ WinDiff is a Windows file comparison utility.

■ Zoomin is a small application that enables you to zoom into a small part of the screen.

COMMAND PROCESSOR AND THE COMMAND LINE

All operating systems provide a *command processor* program—this is the program that prompts for and executes commands. Some examples of command processors are COMMAND.COM in MS-DOS and Windows 3.1 and CMD.EXE in Windows NT. The term *command line* refers to the input that you provide in response to the command prompt from the command processor.

How you use Visual C++ 2.0 depends on your needs. You can compile and link your program with one or more of the following approaches:

■ Accessing the compiler and linker from the Visual Workbench, using Project | Build and Project | Rebuild All menu selections

■ Running the compiler and linker from the command prompt in a command window

■ Using NMAKE to automate the compiling and linking process from the command prompt

NOTATION FOR MENU SELECTIONS

This book uses the notation *MenubarItem* | *PulldownItem* to denote a menu selection, where *MenubarItem* represents an item from the menu bar and *PulldownItem* is a selection from a pull-down menu. Thus, Project | Rebuild All indicates the Rebuild All menu item from the Project menu.

Using the Visual Workbench is the most efficient method of developing applications using Visual C++ 2.0. Running the compiler from a command window is possible. However, it is not efficient—you must run an editor to edit the source code and then compile (and link) the code using the CL command.

Generally, you will find the Visual Workbench's editor an effective programming tool. The editor can, to a limited extent, be configured to your liking. Using the Visual Workbench's tool bar, you can interactively access the compiler and linker. The Visual Workbench is a Windows application that presents workspace sporting a standard Windows Multiple Document Interface (MDI). You can go through the entire application development cycle—defining a project with multiple source files; editing the source files; creating the Windows resources (dialogs, menus, icons, and cursors); compiling, linking, and running the program; and debugging—without ever leaving the Visual Workbench.

For a large software project involving many source modules, using the Visual Workbench is a must. The Visual Workbench creates a project file (that is stored on the disk as NMAKE's .MAK file), which contains all the directives needed for the Visual Workbench to compile and link all necessary modules. With a project file, after you edit one or more source files, selecting the Visual Workbench's Project | Build menu compiles all affected files. For example, changing a header file requires compiling all source files that include the altered header file.

The project file describes the interdependence of source, object, and executable files. The Visual Workbench uses the knowledge of the interdependency to compile the appropriate files and build a new executable program.

You specify various options for the compiler and linker, both when a project is first created and after it has been created, using the Settings dialog displayed by the Project | Settings menu selection. Later in this chapter, summary descriptions demonstrate how to use the compiler and linker from the Visual Workbench and the command prompt. The next section briefly describes how to set up Microsoft Visual C++ 2.0. Following that section, you will find an overview of the Visual Workbench and CL, the command-line interface to the compiler and linker. Many other tools included with Visual C++ 2.0 are described in Chapter 2.

Setting Up Microsoft Visual C++ 2.0

Installing Microsoft Visual C++ 2.0 is straightforward with the SETUP program included with the product. SETUP decompresses files from the distribution compact disc (CD-ROM) and copies them to specific directories on your hard disk. You have the option of indicating the drive and the directory where you want Visual C++ 2.0 installed. Under Windows, there are three basic steps to install Visual C++ 2.0:

1. Insert the Visual C++ 2.0 CD-ROM into the CD-ROM drive.
2. Run the SETUP program from the \MSVC20 directory of the CD-ROM drive.
3. Once SETUP starts, you should read and respond to the screens that SETUP displays (see Figure 1.1). Help is available at any time by pressing the on-screen Help button (see Figure 1.2). By responding to the questions presented in SETUP's screens, you execute the following:

   ■ Select the drive and directory where you want to install Visual C++ 2.0
   ■ Select the type of installation you prefer (see Figure 1.2)

The Visual C++ 2.0 SETUP program also suggests several configuration commands in your system's CONFIG.SYS and AUTOEXEC.BAT files. If you agree with these default configuration commands, the SETUP program automatically makes the necessary changes to CONFIG.SYS and AUTOEXEC.BAT. However, you may prefer to let SETUP save the recommended changes in separate files and then make the actual additions and deletions after you examine what SETUP suggests.

FIGURE 1.1.

Opening screen of the Microsoft Visual C++ 2.0 SETUP program.

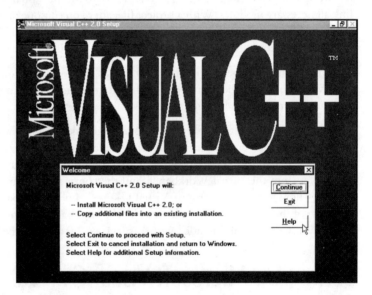

SETUP also creates icons for the programs, including Visual Workbench, Spy++, and WinDiff.

SETUP saves the definitions of a number of environment variables in the VCVARS32.BAT file in the BIN subdirectory where you installed Visual C++ 2.0. From your experience with MS-DOS, you already know that an environment variable, such as PATH, is basically a name for an arbitrary string and is defined using the SET command. Entering SET at the command prompt displays the current settings of the environment variables, and the following:

```
SET PATH=c:\msvc20\bin;%PATH%
```

defines PATH as the string c:\msvc20\bin concatenated to the current definition of PATH, thus replacing its previous definition. Here are two of the environment variables that SETUP defines:

INCLUDE   List of semicolon-separated directory names where the C and C++ include files (usually files with .H extension) are located. For example:

```
SET INCLUDE=C:\MSVC20\INCLUDE;C:\MSVC20\MFC\INCLUDE;%INCLUDE%
```

LIB   List of semicolon-separated directory names where the libraries are located. For example:

```
SET LIB=C:\MSVC20\LIB;C:\MSVC20\MFC\LIB;%LIB%
```

Microsoft Visual C++ 2.0 uses these environment variables to locate important files when using the command-line compiler.

FIGURE 1.2.

Types of installation offered by the Microsoft Visual C++ 2.0 SETUP program.

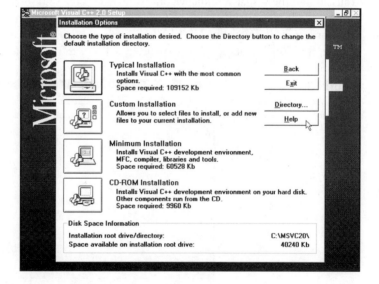

Using the Visual Workbench

After you successfully install Visual C++ 2.0, you can try out the C and C++ compiler from the Visual Workbench, an all-in-one C and C++ programming environment. Using the Visual Workbench, you can execute the following:

■ Edit one or more source files

■ Set up a project consisting of a number of source files

■ Define the resources (menus, dialogs, icons, and cursors) required by a Windows program

- Build the executable file for a project by compiling the source files and linking one or more object files
- Run the newly built program
- Use the built-in debugger to find any programming errors

Additionally, the Visual Workbench offers a voluminous amount of online help. In fact, the best way to learn the Visual Workbench is to start using it and browse through the online help. For your convenience, though, the next few sections briefly summarize some of the significant options offered in the Visual Workbench's menus—especially the options that are important for C and C++ programming.

Getting Started with the Visual Workbench

You can start the Visual Workbench only from Microsoft Windows. To start the Visual Workbench, merely select the Visual C++ 2.0 icon (see Figure 1.3). What appears on screen depends on your last session with the Visual Workbench. If you worked on a project during the last session, the Visual Workbench automatically starts with that project.

FIGURE 1.3.

The Visual Workbench in Microsoft Visual C++ 2.0.

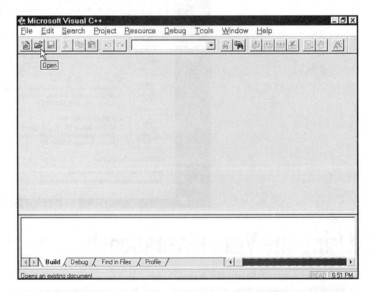

EXITING THE VISUAL WORKBENCH

As with most other Windows applications, to exit the Visual Workbench, press Alt+F4. Otherwise, bring up the File menu using the mouse or by pressing Alt+F, and then select the Exit option (using the mouse or pressing X).

Getting Help in the Visual Workbench

The Visual Workbench has so many features that it's going to take several chapters to document all of them. AppWizard and ClassWizard are covered in Chapter 17, "Windows Programming with Visual C++ 2.0 and MFC 3.0." Other parts of the Visual Workbench are covered throughout the book. The Visual Workbench does offer extensive online help, however, so you need only to know how to navigate the Windows help system. Once you discover how to get help in the Visual Workbench, you can learn the Visual Workbench's features as you need them.

There are two ways you can get help in the Visual Workbench:

- Select an item from the **H**elp menu by using the mouse or by pressing Alt+H followed by the underlined letter for the menu item.
- Place the cursor on a keyword and press F1 to get help for that keyword.

Figure 1.4 shows the result of pressing Alt+H to pop up the Help menu. As you can see, with the Help menu you can call up anything from a quick reference to Books Online, which gives you access to the entire Visual C++ 2.0 online documentation set.

KEYPRESS NOTATIONS

In the Visual C++ 2.0 documentation and in this book, you will often see references to key combinations, such as Alt+F, Shift+F1, and Ctrl+F4. This notation means that you have to press two keys simultaneously. Thus for Alt+F, keep the Alt key pressed down while you press the F key. Similarly, to execute Ctrl+F4, keep the Ctrl (Control) key pressed down and press the F4 key. Notice that Alt+F is the same as Alt+f; you don't need to press the Shift key for an uppercase F when you want the Alt+F key combination.

If you select the Books Online option from the Help menu, you see the screen shown in Figure 1.5.

As you can see from Figure 1.5, Books Online is organized as a number of books, each with one or more chapters. You can "open" a book by clicking on its icon and then continue to go through the chapters until you reach a "page" in a chapter (see a highlighted page in Figure 1.5). You can read a page by double-clicking on the page's icon. For example, if you select the page "How to Use Books Online," you get the screen shown in Figure 1.6.

FIGURE 1.4.

The Help menu in the Visual Workbench.

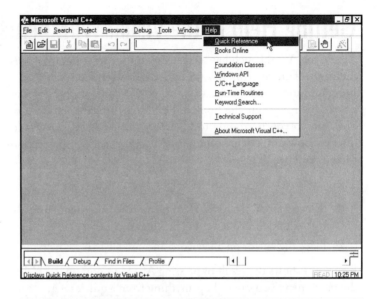

FIGURE 1.5.

The contents of Books Online in the Visual Workbench's help system.

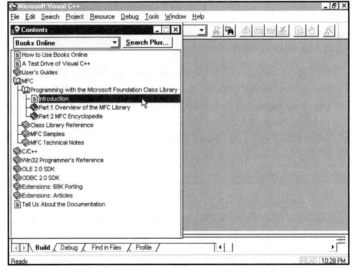

FIGURE 1.6.

Help on how to use Books Online.

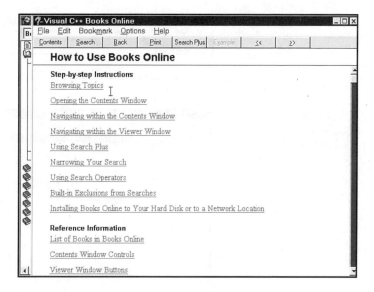

As you can see, this is a list of topics that describe various aspects of Books Online. You can get further information by clicking on any of these topics.

Using the Visual Workbench Menus

Because the Visual Workbench is a Windows application, almost all your interaction with it occurs through menus and the toolbar. As you can see in Figure 1.3, the main menu options appear on a menu bar at the top of the Visual Workbench's display. Below the menu bar is the Visual Workbench tool bar. The bottom of the Visual Workbench is a message area and a status bar. The Visual Workbench treats the rest of the display area as a workspace where you can open multiple overlapping windows showing project and source files.

The Visual Workbench's menu bar has nine items: **F**ile, **E**dit, **S**earch, **P**roject, **R**esource, **D**ebug, **T**ools, **W**indow, and **H**elp (see Figure 1.7). Each of these items leads to a pull-down menu. Through these pull-down menus, you can perform tasks such as opening and editing files, compiling and linking programs, running programs, and debugging programs. Table 1.1 summarizes the options offered in the Visual Workbench's pull-down menus.

The pushbuttons in the tool bar provide quick access to tasks you perform often. You can modify the contents of the tool bar by selecting **C**ustomize... from the **T**ools menu. Select the Toolbars tab in the resulting tab dialog box (see Figure 1.8).

FIGURE 1.7.

The menu bar in the Visual Workbench.

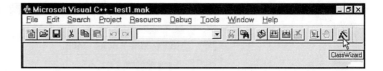

FIGURE 1.8.

Customizing the tool bar in the Visual Workbench.

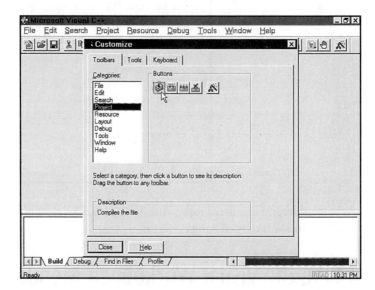

FIGURING OUT THE TOOL BAR

The tool bar gives you quick access to many functions in the Visual Workbench, but it can be difficult to guess the meaning of the icons on the buttons. Luckily, the Visual Workbench provides helpful hints called *tool tips* that appear in tiny pop-up windows when you position the mouse cursor over a button for a period of time. For example, Figure 1.7 shows the tool tip for the rightmost button on the tool bar. Use this feature of the Visual Workbench to find out what a button does before you click the button to initiate an action.

Table 1.1. The Visual Workbench's pull-down menus.

Title	Options
File	Create a new file or open an existing file. The file can be a source file, a project file, or one of many different types of resource files (such as bitmap, icon, or cursor). Close and save files. Print a file. Exit the Visual Workbench.
Edit	Edit a file: cut, copy, and paste a selected item; undo and redo the last editing command.
Search	Find and replace a text string or pattern. Find a string in a selected set of files. Move to a specific line in a file. Place a bookmark at a location in a file and move to a bookmark. Locate a source line with errors in case building an executable fails. (These errors are displayed in the message area.)
Project	Set up and edit a project (a list of modules and their interdependencies). Compile a C or C++ source file. Build an executable program. Run ClassWizard to define or edit classes generated by AppWizard.
Resource	Create resources, such as menus, dialogs, bitmaps, cursors, and icons needed by Windows applications.
Debug	Run and debug the current program.
Tools	Customize tool bars. Set options for the workspace and other aspects of the Visual Workbench. Run any available tool, such as Spy++, MFC Tracer, Control Wizard, and OLE Test Container.
Window	Manage the windows in the Visual Workbench's workspace. Arrange the windows in the Visual Workbench's workspace. Bring a hidden window to the top.
Help	Display a list of topics for online help information. Search for information on a specific keyword. Display the Visual C++ version number and copyright notice.

Menu Selections with the Mouse

Because the Visual Workbench is a Windows application, you usually interact with the Visual Workbench through the mouse. To activate a pull-down menu, move the mouse cursor to an item on the menu bar and click the left mouse button. The pull-down menu appears and remains on screen. Now you can move the mouse cursor to an item in the pull-down menu and click the left button to select it. To close the pull-down menu without making any selection, click anywhere outside the menu.

MOUSE ACTIONS

You can perform a number of actions with the mouse. Here are the six basic actions with which you can interact with the Visual Workbench (and other Windows applications):

- ■ *Press* a mouse button by holding the button down without moving the mouse.
- ■ *Release* a mouse button that you have previously held down. This usually initiates some action.
- ■ *Click* a mouse button by quickly pressing and releasing it.
- ■ *Double-click* a mouse button by clicking it twice in rapid succession without moving the mouse.
- ■ *Drag* the mouse cursor by pressing a mouse button and moving the mouse while keeping the button pressed.
- ■ *Move* the mouse cursor by moving the mouse without pressing any button.

In response to certain menu selections, the Visual Workbench displays dialog boxes. A *dialog box* is a window through which the Visual Workbench solicits input from (or sometimes provides information to) the user. Usually, the dialog box has checkboxes where you indicate your choices, lists from which you pick a selection, and text-entry fields where you enter text.

When interacting with a dialog box using a mouse, you move the mouse cursor to an item and click the left button. Clicking a checkbox turns on a selection. If you click in a text-entry area such as a box for entering a filename, you see another cursor in that area waiting for you to enter the requested information.

Menu Selections with the Keyboard

Although you normally don't use either Windows or the Visual Workbench without a mouse, it can be done. Here is a brief description of how to access the Visual Workbench's menus using the keyboard.

Press Alt to activate the menu bar. The **F**ile menu is highlighted because this is the current choice; if you press Enter, the File pull-down menu appears. You can activate the pull-down menu for a specific option in one of two ways:

- ■ Use the left and right arrow keys to select a main menu option and then press Enter.
- ■ Press the first character of the main menu option that you want, displaying the pull-down menu for that option.

Once a pull-down menu is displayed, you can use the left and right arrows to switch to other pull-down menus. Within a pull-down menu, use the up and down arrows to indicate the selection. As you press the up or down arrow, the selected item is highlighted. Pressing Enter activates the selection. If you do not want to make any selection from a pull-down menu, press Alt again or press Esc to get rid of the pull-down menu.

A faster way to access menu items is to press Alt and the first letter of one of the items on the menu bar. For example, to get the **H**elp menu, press Alt and H—this is commonly written as Alt+H. Once the Help menu appears (see Figure 1.4), you will notice an underlined character in each of the items in the menu . This character is called a *hot key* or *mnemonic key*. Pressing the underlined character activates that item. For example, when the **H**elp menu is visible, pressing A activates the **A**bout... menu item.

Next to some menu items, you will notice the names of keystrokes. These are the *shortcut keys* or *accelerator keys*. Pressing these key combinations activates that menu option even when the pull-down menu is not displayed. Thus, pressing Ctrl+N always brings up the **N**ew... dialog for the Visual Workbench's **F**ile menu. Table 1.2 summarizes the purposes of several shortcut keys and a number of other keys in the Visual Workbench.

Table 1.2. Shortcut keys in the Visual Workbench.

Keystroke	Function
<down arrow>	Moves one line down
<left arrow>	Moves one character to the left
<right arrow>	Moves one character to the right
<up arrow>	Moves one line up
Alt	Toggles main menu bar
Alt+1	Shows output window
Alt+2	Shows Watch window during debugging
Alt+3	Shows Locals window during debugging
Alt+4	Shows Register window during debugging
Alt+5	Shows Memory window during debugging
Alt+6	Shows Call Stack window during debugging
Alt+7	Shows Disassembly window during debugging
Alt+Backspace	Undoes effects of last editing action
Alt+Enter	Displays properties of currently selected item
Alt+Esc	Switches to next application's window (applies to any application running under Microsoft Windows)
Alt+F3	Opens Find dialog box
Alt+F4	Exits the Visual Workbench

continues

Table 1.2. continued

Keystroke	Function
Alt+F5	Ends debugging session
Alt+F8	Rebuilds (compiles and links) everything for current project
Alt+Hyphen	Opens System menu for a window
Alt+Print Screen	Copies image of active window to Clipboard
Alt+Spacebar	Opens System menu for an application window
Alt+Tab	Switches to next application
Backspace	Deletes one character to the left
Ctrl+<	Finds enclosing `#ifdef`
Ctrl+<down arrow>	Scrolls down one line at a time
Ctrl+<left arrow>	Moves one word to the left
Ctrl+<right arrow>	Moves one word to the right
Ctrl+<up arrow>	Scrolls up one line at a time
Ctrl+>	Finds `#endif`, `#else`, or `#elif`
Ctrl+]	Finds matching brace
Ctrl+A	Redoes last edit action
Ctrl+Alt+T	Toggles display of tab symbols
Ctrl+B	Opens Breakpoints dialog box
Ctrl+Backspace	Deletes word to the left
Ctrl+Break	Stops current build process
Ctrl+C or Ctrl+Insert	Copies selected text to Clipboard, without deleting it
Ctrl+End	Moves to end of file
Ctrl+Enter	Moves to first indentation of next line
Ctrl+Esc	Switches to Windows Task List
Ctrl+F11	Starts browser that displays structure of a program
Ctrl+F2	Toggles bookmark
Ctrl+F3	Searches forward for selected text
Ctrl+F4	Closes active window
Ctrl+F5	Executes current program
Ctrl+F8	Compiles selected source file
Ctrl+G	Jumps to specific line (prompts for line number)
Ctrl+Home	Moves to beginning of file
Ctrl+N	Opens New File dialog box

Keystroke	Function
Ctrl+Num Pad's *	Returns to original symbol location
Ctrl+Num Pad's +	Jumps to next reference in browse list
Ctrl+Num Pad's -	Jumps to previous reference in browse list
Ctrl+O	Brings up Open File dialog box
Ctrl+P	Prints current file
Ctrl+Page Down	Scrolls right one window width
Ctrl+Page Up	Scrolls left one window width
Ctrl+R	Creates new resource file
Ctrl+S	Saves current file
Ctrl+Shift+R	Records keystrokes
Ctrl+Shift+U	Changes selection to uppercase
Ctrl+U	Changes selection to lowercase
Ctrl+V or Shift+Insert	Inserts contents of Clipboard at current cursor position
Ctrl+W	Runs ClassWizard
Ctrl+X or Shift+Delete	Copies selected text to Clipboard, deleting it from current window
Ctrl+X or Shift+Delete	Deletes selected text and copies it to Clipboard
Ctrl+Y	Copies current line to Clipboard, deleting it
Ctrl+Z or Alt+Backspace	Undoes last edit action
Delete	Deletes one character to the right
End	Moves to end of line
F1	Provides help on selected topic
F10	Executes next statement, stepping over function calls
F11	Jumps to definition of a selected symbol
F12	Displays Save As dialog box
F2	Finds next bookmark
F3	Searches forward for next occurrence of a string
F4	Finds next error or output window item
F5	Continues execution of program from current statement onward
F7	Executes program up to cursor
F8	Executes next statement, stepping into function calls

continues

Table 1.2. continued

Keystroke	Function
Home	Moves to first indentation of current line
Insert	Toggles keyboard insert mode on or off
Page Down	Scrolls down one page at a time
Page Up	Scrolls up one page at a time
Print Screen	Copies image of display to Clipboard
Shift+<down arrow>	Selects current line if insertion point is home
Shift+<left arrow>	Selects character to the left
Shift+<right arrow>	Selects character to the right
Shift+<up arrow>	Selects line above if insertion point is home
Shift+Alt+Tab	Switches to previous application's window
Shift+Ctrl+<	Selects to enclosing `#endif`, `#else`, `#elif`
Shift+Ctrl+<left arrow>	Selects one word to the left
Shift+Ctrl+<right arrow>	Selects one word to the right
Shift+Ctrl+>	Selects to enclosing `#ifdef`
Shift+Ctrl+End	Selects to end of file
Shift+Ctrl+F3	Searches backward for selected text
Shift+Ctrl+Home	Selects to beginning of file
Shift+Ctrl+M	Selects to matching brace
Shift+Ctrl+N	Inserts carriage return at insertion point and moves cursor down one line
Shift+End	Selects to end of line
Shift+Esc	Hides output window
Shift+F11	Jumps to first reference of selected symbol
Shift+F2	Finds previous bookmark
Shift+F3	Searches backward for next occurrence of a string
Shift+F4	Finds previous error or output window item
Shift+F5	Starts program execution from beginning
Shift+F8	Builds executable file for current project
Shift+F9	Opens QuickWatch dialog box
Shift+Home	Selects to beginning of line
Shift+Page Down	Selects one screen down
Shift+Page Up	Selects one screen up

Keystroke	*Function*
Shift+Tab	Moves all selected lines one tab stop left
Tab	In editor, moves all selected lines one tab stop right

When a menu option ends in an ellipsis (...), selecting the menu option causes the Visual Workbench to display dialog boxes in which you have to enter some information. In such dialog boxes, you can use either the mouse or keystrokes to navigate through the options. First, you can get rid of a dialog box—or just about anything in the Visual Workbench—by pressing Esc. Pressing Tab moves the cursor from one group of options to another, and Shift+Tab moves the cursor from option to option in the reverse order. Once the cursor is on the item you want, you can select it by pressing Enter. In listboxes, you can select an item by using the up and down arrows. Most dialog boxes show three or four buttons, usually labeled OK, Cancel, and Help. You can get to these buttons by pressing Tab repeatedly. Navigating through a dialog box is tedious without a mouse, but it can be done.

Editing a Program

One of the first steps in writing a program is to prepare the source file. When writing Windows applications using MFC 3.0, you will probably start with a set of source files generated by the AppWizard (described in Chapter 17). However, you have to edit these files to add application-specific code. The Visual Workbench includes a text editor that you can use to edit the source files for your program.

To edit a source file, double-click on the file's icon in the project window. This causes the Visual Workbench to display the selected file in a window. Because the project window shows a list of all the files needed by your application, most of your editing sessions start with the selection of the file from the project window.

You also can choose a file for editing by selecting **O**pen... from the **F**ile menu. The Visual Workbench displays a dialog box with the list of files in the current directory. You either can type the name of a file in the text-entry area labeled File **N**ame: or pick a file from the list of files (by double-clicking with the mouse). You can change the directory or drive by making a selection from the list of drives and directories. Selecting a directory brings up the list of files in that directory. After selecting a file, select the OK button to load the file.

Editing a file is straightforward with a mouse. To enter text:

1. Move the mouse cursor to the desired position.
2. Click the left mouse button.
3. Begin typing the new text.

To select text for cut and paste operations:

1. Press the left mouse button at the starting location.
2. Drag the mouse cursor to the end of the text you want to select.

You then can select **C**opy or **C**ut from the **E**dit menu. Your selection goes into an internal buffer called Clipboard. Later, you can paste this text anywhere in the file (or in another file) by using the **P**aste option from the **E**dit menu.

As with menu selections, you can edit with the keyboard only. For example, to select and copy text:

1. Position the cursor at the start of the selection.
2. Press Shift and use the arrow keys to move the cursor to the end of the selected text.
3. Press Ctrl+C (or Ctrl+Insert) to copy the text into the Clipboard.

To paste, position the cursor where you want to insert the text and press Ctrl+V or Shift+Insert. Table 1.2 lists some of the keystrokes used to accomplish basic editing functions in the Visual Workbench.

Compiling, Linking, and Running a Program

Once the source files are ready, you have to compile and link them to create an executable program. In the Visual Workbench, the way to build a program is to define a project. To do this, follow these steps:

1. Select **N**ew... from the **F**ile menu. This brings up the New dialog box (see Figure 1.9).
2. Select Project from the list and click on OK. This brings up the New Project dialog box (see Figure 1.10).
3. Enter a name up to eight characters long for the project. The Visual Workbench appends a .MAK to the project name and stores information about the project as a makefile (that can be used by the NMAKE utility).
4. Select the type of project. Figure 1.10 shows a project that builds a Console Application—an application that uses console I/O through calls to the `printf()` function, for example.

After the project is created, you can add files to it. Once you define a project, you can build the executable program by selecting **R**ebuild All from the **P**roject menu. The Visual Workbench invokes CL, the program that compiles and links, with the appropriate options. The Visual Workbench displays in the output window any errors or warnings generated during the compile and link operations.

Once the executable file is successfully built, you can run it by selecting the E**x**ecute option from the **P**roject menu.

FIGURE 1.9.
The New dialog box.

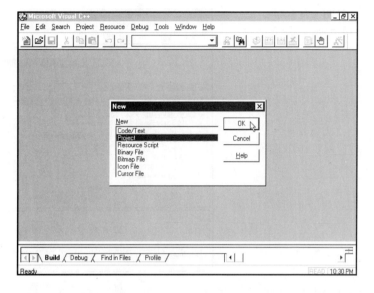

FIGURE 1.10.
The New Project dialog box.

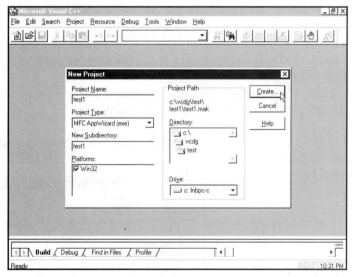

Browsing

Browse is a useful feature of the Visual Workbench that enables you to see how your program is organized; you can see information such as the order in which functions call each other, where a function or variable is defined, and the hierarchy of classes in C++ programs. The browser functions are accessible through the Browse option in the Search menu. By default, the Visual Workbench automatically generates the database used by the browser.

FIGURE 1.11.

The Browse dialog box.

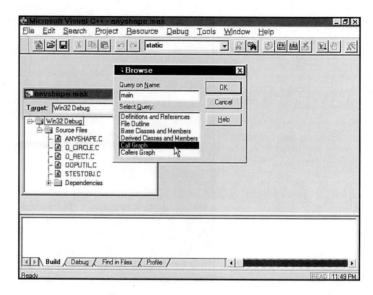

As an example, load and build the project for a sample program that appears in Chapter 5, "Basics of Object-Oriented Programming." Select the **B**rowse option from the **S**earch menu. Figure 1.11 shows the activated dialog box for a sample project file. From the Select **Q**uery list, select Call Graph and enter `main` in the text-entry area labeled Query on **N**ame. When you click on the OK button, the Visual Workbench displays the browser output window shown in Figure 1.12 for a sample project file. As you can see, the browser's output shows the call tree—the order in which the functions call each other.

FIGURE 1.12.

The Call Graph for a sample program.

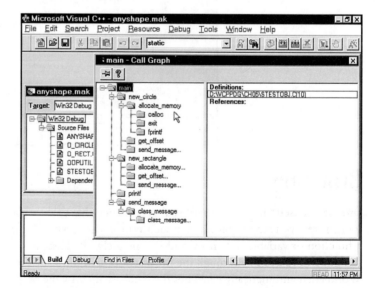

Specifying the Project Settings

You can control all aspects of a project through the project settings. These settings include items such as the compiler options, preprocessor directives, linker options, the processor for which object code is generated (80386, 80486, or Pentium), the levels of optimization, and whether information is generated for source-level debugging and browsing.

To specify the project settings, select the **S**ettings... item from the **P**roject menu. Selecting this item displays a tab dialog box (see Figure 1.13) from which you can specify various categories of settings. Suppose you want to set the options for the C or C++ compiler. Click on the C/C++ tab of the dialog box. Now you see the dialog box illustrated in Figure 1.13, in which you can specify the options for the Visual C++ 2.0 compiler.

FIGURE 1.13.

Specifying the project settings in the Visual Workbench.

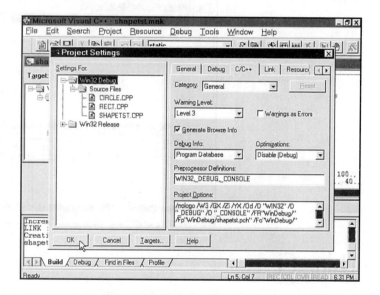

Debugging

In addition to compiling, linking, and running a program, you also can debug your program in the Visual Workbench. If you want to debug at the source code level—to see lines of the source file as you step through your program—you must build the project in debug mode.

After building a project in debug mode, you can debug the program. Typically, you set a breakpoint near the suspect source lines where you want the debugger to stop so that you can examine values of variables and look for clues. To designate a line of code as a breakpoint, position the cursor on that line and select **B**reakpoints... from the **D**ebug menu. Then click on the Add button of the resulting dialog box. After setting one or more breakpoints, if you select **G**o from the **D**ebug menu (or press F5), the debugger starts the program and runs up to the line designated as the first breakpoint. Once the debugger stops at a breakpoint, you can check values of variables in the W**a**tch window (see the lower-right corner of Figure 1.14) for a sample program.

Sometimes you may want to execute a program one statement at a time to pinpoint an erroneous statement. Press F8 to run the program by stepping into each function as your program calls it. Pressing F10 works similarly, but it treats each function call as a single statement and does not step through the statements in the function.

FIGURE 1.14.

Debugging in the Visual Workbench.

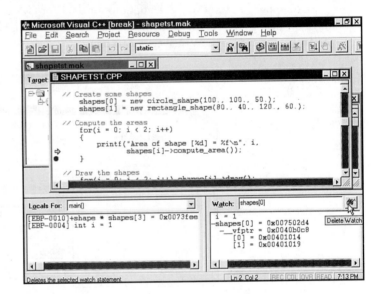

Using CL

Although the Visual Workbench's interactive environment is convenient and you can specify most compiler options through the graphical interface, sometimes you may have to enter an esoteric option directly in the Project **O**ptions field of the C/C++ tab in the Project Settings dialog box (see Figure 1.13). For this reason, you may want to be aware of the options that CL accepts.

The rest of this chapter briefly describes how to use CL and lists the options it offers.

Compiling and Linking with CL

Using CL to compile and link a program with a small number of source files is simple. For example, you can compile and link the C++ source files FORMFILL.CPP and

FORMPACK.CPP and create the executable program named FORMFILL.EXE with the following command issued at the command prompt:

```
CL FORMFILL.CPP FORMPACK.CPP
```

This command runs the C++ compiler with the default settings, links the resulting object files, and creates an executable program named FORMFILL.EXE.

CL determines how to process a file based on the filename extension. Table 1.3 lists the extensions CL understands.

Table 1.3. Interpretation of file extensions by CL.

Extension	How CL Processes a File
.C	C source file—compile using C compiler
.CPP or .CXX	C++ source file—compile using C++ compiler
.ASM	Assembly language file—assemble using MASM (Microsoft Macro Assembler)
.OBJ	Object file—pass to linker for use during linking
.LIB	Library file—pass to linker for use in linking
.DEF	Module definition file (used in Microsoft Windows programs)—pass name to linker
Other extensions	Object file—pass name to linker

However, more often than not, you want to use CL with certain options. Each option is a combination of letters and numbers preceded by a slash (/) that instructs CL to take some specific action. For example, you may want to generate code optimized for a Pentium processor, disable optimizations (because you want to debug), and include information for the debugger. To do this, you have to run CL with this command:

```
CL /G5 /Od /Zi FORMFILL.CPP FORMPACK.CPP
```

where /G5 generates Pentium code, /Od disables optimizations, and /Zi ensures inclusion of information needed for source-level debugging with the Visual Workbench debugger.

OPTIONS ARE CASE-SENSITIVE

All CL options, except for /HELP, are case-sensitive. At the command prompt, type **CL /HELP** to view detailed online help information for CL.

CL Options

CL accepts more than 80 command-line options so that it may offer you, the programmer, complete control over building an executable program or Windows Dynamic Link Library (DLL). Of course, you don't need to specify every option explicitly when using CL. In particular, if you use the Visual Workbench, the options are automatically set as you specify various project settings. In addition, most CL options have default settings. However, if you ever need them, the options are there.

Table 1.4 provides an alphabetical listing of the options that CL accepts.

COMMAND SYNTAX

Throughout this book, you will see descriptions of commands with arguments shown in square brackets ([...]) or angular brackets (<...>). The arguments enclosed in [...] are optional, the ones inside <...> are required. Also, arguments shown in *italic monospace* font are placeholders; you must enter a specific value when actually using the command. For example, in this command:

```
CL <filename>
```

`<filename>` is a placeholder. `CL` must be entered exactly as shown because it appears in regular monospace font.

Table 1.4. Alphabetic list of CL options.

Option	Interpretation by CL
/c	Compiles without linking
/C	Preserves comments during preprocessing (valid only with options /E, /P, or /EP)
/D*<name>*[=*text*]	Defines specified macro
/E	Preserves #line directives in listings of preprocessed files
/EP	Does not include #line directives in listings of preprocessed files
/F *<number>*	Sets program's stack size to the number of bytes specified by the number *<number>* (default stack size is 1M)
/FA	Generates assembly language listing with an .ASM extension
/Fa[*file*]	Uses specified name for assembly listing file (if name is missing, this option uses the source filename with an .ASM extension)

Option	Interpretation by CL
/Fd[*file*]	Uses specified name for program database (PDB) file
/Fe<*file*>	Uses specified name for executable file
/FI[*file*]	Causes preprocessor to include specified file
/Fm[*file*]	Uses specified name for linker map file (if name is missing, this option uses the source filename with a .MAP extension)
/Fo<*file*>	Uses specified name for object file (in the absence of this option, the compiler uses the source file's name with an .OBJ extension)
/Fp<*file*>	Uses specified name for precompiled header file (the default uses the source file's name with a .PCH extension)
/FR[*file*]	Uses specified name for extended source browser information file, a browser information file with local symbols (the default is the source filename with an .SBR extension)
/Fr[*file*]	Uses specified name for source browser information file, a browser information file without any local symbols
/G3	Optimizes generated code for the 80386 processor
/G4	Optimizes generated code for the 80486 processor
/G5	Optimizes generated code for the Pentium processor
/GB	Optimizes generated code for the 80486 processor, but includes many Pentium optimizations that do not seriously impact performance on the 80386 or 80486
/Gd	Uses C naming and function calling conventions (this option is on by default)
/Ge	Embeds calls to stack-checking function that tests for stack overflow
/Gf	Enables "string pooling" (only one copy of identical strings kept in memory)
/Gh	Embeds calls to function named __penter at start of every function (provides a hook for your use); __penter function should have the following prototype: `void __cdecl __penter( void );`
/Gr	Uses `fastcall` calling convention, whereby function arguments are passed in registers
/Gs	Does not include calls to stack-checking functions
/GX	Calls destructors for C++ objects when exceptions occur (use

continues

Table 1.4. continued

Option	Interpretation by CL
	the /GX- option to inhibit calls to destructors during exception-handling in C++ programs)
/Gy	Enables linking on a function-by-function basis rather than at a module level
/Gz	Uses standard-call (__stdcall) calling convention for all prototyped C functions that do not take a variable number of arguments and are not marked as __cdecl or __fastcall (code generated for __stdcall function pushes arguments onto stack from right to left, and called function pops these arguments from stack before it returns)
/H<number>	Assumes that external names are, at most, <number> characters long
/HELP	Displays listing of compiler options on standard output stream
/I<path>	Searches specified directory when attempting to find include files
/J	Changes default type of char data type from signed to unsigned
/LD	Creates dynamically linked library (DLL)
/link <options>	Provides specified options to linker (see Chapter 2 for a listing of linker options)
/MD	Uses multithreaded DLL version of runtime routines
/ML	Uses single-threaded version of runtime routines (this is the default)
/MT	Uses multithreaded version of runtime routines
/nologo	Does not display sign-on banner
/O1	Generates smallest code possible
/O2	Generates fastest code possible
/Oa	Assumes no *aliasing* (aliasing occurs when same memory location is accessed using more than one name—for example, through two pointers)
/Ob<n>	Controls inline expansion of functions (<n> is a single digit from 0 to 2: /Ob0 disables inline expansion; /Ob1 uses inline expansions for only those functions that you explicitly mark as candidates for inline expansion; /Ob2 enables compiler to generate inline expansions at its discretion)

Option	Interpretation by CL
/Od	Disables all optimizations
/Og	Eliminates duplicate expressions within functions
/Oi	Generates intrinsic (inline) functions
/Op	Improves consistency of tests for equality and inequality of floating-point values (use /Op- to turn this option)
/Os	Optimizes for space (small code)
/Ot	Optimizes for time (fast code)
/Ow	Assumes that aliasing can occur only across function calls (aliasing occurs when the same memory location is accessed using more than one name—for example, through two pointers)
/Ox	Uses maximum optimization
/Oy	Suppresses creation of frame pointers (frees up one more register) during function calls (use /Oy- to enable creation of frame pointers)
/P	Writes preprocessor output to a file (the default filename is the same as the source file's name but with an .I extension)
/Tc<file>	Assumes that specified file is a C source file regardless of its extension
/Tp<file>	Assumes that specified file is a C++ source file regardless of its extension
/u	Undefines all preprocessor macros
/U<name>	Undefines the specified preprocessor macro
/V<string>	Embeds the specified string in the object code (you can place version number in object file using this option)
/vd<n>	If <n> is 0, disables generation of constructor/destructor displacement members in C++ classes (use /vd1 to enable generation of these members)
/vmb	Controls representation of pointers to member functions (use this option if you always define a class before you declare a pointer to a member of the class)
/vmg	Controls representation of pointers to member functions (use this option if you need to declare a pointer to a member of a class before defining the class)
/vmm	Use this option with /vmg to indicate that you use both single- and multiple-inheritance classes

continues

Table 1.4. continued

Option	Interpretation by CL
/vms	Use this option with /vmg to indicate that you use only single-inheritance classes
/vmv	Use this option with /vmg to indicate that the pointers to member functions must be capable of representing pointers to members in any class
/w	Same as /W0 (turns off all warning messages)
/W<number>	Sets warning level to specified <number>, an integer from 0 to 5 (warning level 0 means no warning messages are generated; at level 5, compiler treats all warnings as fatal errors)
/WX	Same as /W5; treats all warnings as fatal
/X	Does not search standard directories for include files
/Yc	Generates precompiled header (.PCH) file
/Yd	Places information for debugger in precompiled header file
/Yu	Uses precompiled header file for faster compilation
/YX	Automatically creates precompiled header file
/Z7	Same effect as /Zi option in Microsoft C/C++ 7 (precursor to Microsoft Visual C++); is provided for compatibility
/Za	Disables Microsoft-specific extensions (Chapter 2 describes these extensions)
/Zd	Embeds line number information in the object file to support debugging
/Ze	Enables Microsoft-specific extensions
/Zg	Generates prototype declaration for each function but does not compile files
/Zi	Generates program database (PDB) that contains symbolic-debugging information for use with Visual C++ debugger
/Zl	Does not embed names of default libraries in object file
/Zn	Does not pack .SBR files generated by /FR or /Fr options
/Zp<number>	Packs structures on multiples of <number> bytes where <number> is 1, 2, 4, 8, or 16
/Zs	Checks syntax only without generating any object or executable file

Summary

Microsoft Visual C++ 2.0 is a combination of program development tools and utilities. Its most visible component is the Visual Workbench, through which you can access all program development tools, including the compiler, linker, resource editor and compiler, and the debugger. This chapter briefly describes how to use the Visual Workbench, summarizes the Visual Workbench's features, and points out that the best way to learn about all of Visual C++ 2.0's tools is through the extensive online help provided by the Visual Workbench. The last part of this chapter describes CL, the command-line interface to the Visual C++ 2.0 compiler and linker.

Although you can perform all the edit-compile-link-debug chores from the Visual Workbench, it helps to be familiar with the individual program development tools. That way, you can set up makefiles that invoke these tools and access such makefiles using NMAKE.

2

Program Development Tools in Visual C++ 2.0

Chapter 1, "The Visual C++ 2.0 Programming Environment," provides you with an overview—the tools it offers and how the Visual C++ compiler typically is used. Chapter 1 also describes the Visual Workbench and CL, the command-line interface to the compiler.

This chapter describes how to use a number of other program development tools: LINK, LIB, and NMAKE. (CL also invokes LINK to create executable programs, but Chapter 1 does not show LINK's options.)

Briefly, the LINK tool combines a number of object modules to create an executable file (an .EXE file) or a dynamic link library (DLL), whereas LIB enables you to store many object modules in a single library file (a .LIB file). NMAKE automates the use of the compiler, linker, and the other tools. This chapter presents a short description of how to use each of these tools and lists the options each offers.

This chapter is not advocating using any of the utilities described. Virtually all program development can (and should) be done using the Visual Workbench. Almost all features of the tools described here are available (and often are used automatically, without interaction on your part) from the Visual Workbench. Occasionally, however, you may have to use the command-line version of these utilities, so they are described here. This chapter does not cover these programming tools in great detail because all these tools provide complete and, more importantly, up-to-date online help.

GETTING HELP

Use the online help facility in Visual Workbench to find out more about the program development tools in Visual C++ 2.0—the tools described in this chapter (LINK, LIB, and NMAKE) as well as others, such as EDITBIN and DUMPBIN, that are not covered in this chapter. When running these tools from the command prompt, use the /? option to see a short list of all the command-line options that the tool accepts.

LINK, the Linker

The Microsoft linker is necessary because an operating system such as Microsoft Windows or Windows NT cannot execute .OBJ files, even if there is only a single source file for a program. The resulting .OBJ file must be converted to an .EXE format before Windows can load it into memory and run it. LINK performs this conversion from .OBJ format to .EXE.

Additionally, when a software project is broken down into a number of modules or source files, one source file might call functions that are defined in another file. When the compiler translates each source file into an object file, it embeds information about external functions and variables referenced in that source file. The linker then blends all the object files and ensures that all external functions and variables are found and referenced correctly in the executable program that it generates. LINK also can search through libraries (.LIB files) to resolve these references to external functions and variables.

Using LINK

Usually, the linker is called by the Visual Workbench; if you are using the command-line compiler (CL), the compiler calls the linker. Because the Visual Workbench offers such an integrated environment, it's unlikely that you'll have many opportunities to use the linker directly. However, LINK is often invoked directly in makefiles (described later in this chapter). Source files are first compiled into object files and then LINK is invoked to link the object files together with the required libraries. From the command prompt, you can invoke LINK in two ways:

■ Enter the LINK command with options and filenames on the command line. Here is the syntax:

```
LINK [options] <objfiles>
```

where [options] refers to one or more optional LINK options (listed later in Table 2.1) and <objfiles> denotes the required object filenames.

■ Place all LINK options and filenames in a text file and invoke LINK as follows:

```
LINK @<command_file>
```

where <command_file> is the name of the file containing the input commands meant for LINK. Notice that LINK does not assume any specific filename extension for the response file; you should provide the complete filename for the response file.

The simplest way to link a few object files is to invoke LINK as follows:

```
LINK windraw shapes winview;
```

In this case, LINK looks for the files WINDRAW.OBJ, SHAPES.OBJ, and WINVIEW.OBJ and automatically searches certain default libraries to complete the linking process and create an executable file named WINDRAW.EXE.

NOTE

Microsoft Visual C++ 2.0 supports *incremental linking*—a fast way to link by processing only those object files that have a timestamp that is more recent than the last link and updating only those parts of a program that have changed.

LINK Options

LINK accepts a number of options. When you compile and link using CL, you can pass these options to LINK through CL's /link option. Table 2.1 lists LINK's command-line options and their meanings.

Table 2.1. LINK Option

Option	*Interpretation by LINK*
/?	Displays the list of command-line options.
/ALIGN:*<number>*	Specifies the alignment of each section within the linear address space of the program. The *<number>* argument is in bytes and must be a power of two. The default alignment is at 4K boundaries.
/BASE:*<address¦@filename,key>*	Specifies the base address for the executable file or DLL. The linker rounds the address up to the nearest multiple of 64K. In place of the *<address>* argument, you may specify a filename prefixed with @ and place in that file the base addresses of all DLLs used in your program.
/COMMENT:["]*comment*["]	Inserts a comment string (optionally enclosed in double quotation marks) into the header of an executable file or DLL, after the array of section headers. You can use this option to embed copyright and version information in an executable file or DLL.
/DEBUG	Creates debugging information for the executable file or DLL.
/DEBUGTYPE:*<type>*	Specifies the type of debugging information generated by LINK. The *<type>* argument is one of the following: COFF, CV, or BOTH.
/DEF:*<filename>*	Specifies a module definition (.DEF) file, which is a text file that contains statements for defining an executable file or DLL. Because LINK provides equivalent command-line options for most module-definition statements, a typical program does not usually require a .DEF file.

Option	Interpretation by LINK
`/DEFAULTLIB:<lib1>[,lib2,...]`	Adds one or more libraries to the list of libraries that LINK searches when resolving references.
`/DLL`	Builds a dynamic link library (DLL) as output.
`/ENTRY:<function>`	Specifies the starting address for an executable or DLL. The starting address is specified in terms of the name of a function.
`/EXETYPE:<type>`	Used with the `/VXD` option to specify the type of the virtual device driver (VXD) to be built. The `<type>` can be `DEV386` or `DYNAMIC`.
`/EXPORT:<entryname>[=internalname][,@ordinal[,NONAME]][,DATA]`	
	Exports a function or data to enable other programs to call the function or use the data. The calling programs refer to the function or data as `<entryname>`. You can optionally specify `<internalname>`, which is how the function or data is known in the defining program; by default, `<internalname>` is the same as `<entryname>`. The `<ordinal>` is an index into the exports table in the range 1–65535; LINK assigns an index if you do not specify `<ordinal>`. If you use the `NONAME` argument, LINK exports the function or data only as an ordinal, without an `<entryname>`. Use the DATA argument to indicate that the exported item is a data item.
`/FIXED`	Requires the operating system to load the program only at its preferred base address. If the preferred base address is not available, the operating system will not load the file.
`/FORCE:[MULTIPLE|UNDEFINED]`	Forces LINK to generate a valid output file (.EXE or .DLL) even if there are errors. Use `/FORCE:MULTIPLE` to create an output file even if there are multidefined symbols. Use `/FORCE:UNDEFINED` to create an output file even if a symbol is undefined.

continues

Table 2.1. continued

Option	Interpretation by LINK
/HEAP:<reserve>[,commit]	Sets the size of the heap to <reserve> bytes of virtual memory where <reserve> is a decimal number (you may use the C language notation for hexadecimal numbers specified with a 0x prefix). The linker rounds the specified heap size up to the nearest 4 bytes. The default heap size is 1M. In Windows NT, the optional *commit* argument specifies the amount of physical memory to allocate at a time.
/IMPLIB:<filename>	Specifies the name of the import library that LINK creates when it builds a program that contains exported functions or data.
/INCLUDE:<symbol>	Adds the specified symbol to the symbol table. This forces linking with an object file that contains the specified symbol.
/INCREMENTAL:<YES¦NO>	Turns incremental linking (a fast way to link programs) on or off. Use /INCREMENTAL:YES to enable incremental linking.
/MAC<BUNDLE¦NOBUNDLE¦TYPE='*XXXX*'¦CREATOR='*XXXX*'>	Applies to Visual C++ Cross-Development Edition for Macintosh. Specifies whether the application has bundle resource (something that the Macintosh Finder uses) and sets the type and creator resources of the application.
/MACDATA:<filename>	Applies to Visual C++ Cross-Development Edition for Macintosh. Specifies the filename for the data fork. (A Macintosh file has two parts known as forks: data fork and resource fork.)
/MACHINE:<platform>	Specifies the target platform for the program. The <platform> argument can be one of IX86, MIPS, or M68K. Usually, LINK infers the machine type from the object files.
/MACRES:<filename>	Applies to Visual C++ Cross-Development Edition for Macintosh. Specifies the

Option	Interpretation by LINK
	filename for the resource fork. (A Macintosh file has two parts known as forks: data fork and resource fork.)
/MAP[:*filename*]	Generates a map file with the specified name. If you do not specify a name, LINK generates a map file whose name is derived from the program's name by adding a .MAP extension.
/NODEFAULTLIB:[*lib1*[,*lib2*...]]	Does not search the specified libraries when resolving external references. If you do not specify any library names, this option causes LINK to ignore all default libraries.
/NOENTRY	Creates a DLL that contains resources (dialogs, icons, and so forth) only.
/NOLOGO	Does not display the copyright notice and version number at startup.
/OPT:<REF¦NOREF>	Controls optimizations during linking. Use /OPT:NOREF to remove all unreferenced functions from the program.
/ORDER:<@*filename*>	Specifies a text file that describes the order in which certain functions are to be placed in the executable file.
/OUT:<*filename*>	Specifies the name of the output (executable or DLL) file.
/PDB:<*filename*¦NONE>	Controls how the linker produces debugging information. Use /PDB:NONE to suppress generation of program database (PDB). If you specify a filename rather than NONE, LINK generates a program database file with the specified name.
/PROFILE	Creates an output file that can be used for profiling, which enables you to gather information on function calls and the time it takes to execute each function. (To run the profiler, select Profile... from the Tools menu in the Visual Workbench.)

continues

Table 2.1. continued

Option	Interpretation by LINK
/RELEASE	Sets the checksum in the header of the executable file. (Use this option on the release version of your application.)
/SECTION:<name,attributes>	Sets the attributes of a section of code or data identified by <name>. The <attributes> option is a set of characters: E, R, W, or S with the following meanings:

E   Allows code to be executed
R   Allows data to be read
W   Allows data to be changed
S   Allows processes to share
       the section

Option	Interpretation by LINK
/STACK:<reserve>[,commit]	Sets the size of the stack to <reserve> bytes of virtual memory where <reserve> is a decimal number (you may use the C language notation for hexadecimal numbers specified with a 0x prefix). The linker rounds the specified heap size up to the nearest 4 bytes. The default stack size is 1M. In Windows NT, the optional *commit* argument specifies the amount of physical memory to allocate at a time.
STUB:<filename>	Attaches the specified stub program to a Windows program. The stub program is invoked when the program is executed under MS-DOS.
/SUBSYSTEM:<NATIVE¦WINDOWS¦CONSOLE¦POSIX>[,major[.minor]]	

Specifies how the operating system should run the executable file. The meaning of the arguments is as follows:

CONSOLE implies a Win32 character-mode application that runs in a console window provided by the operating system.

WINDOWS denotes a standard Windows application.

NATIVE applies to device drivers built for Windows NT.

Option	*Interpretation by LINK*
	POSIX specifies an application that runs under the POSIX subsystem in Windows NT.
	You can specify optional major and minor version numbers that indicate the minimum required version of the subsystem. Each of the major and minor version arguments is a decimal number in the range 0–65535. The default versions are 3.10 for CONSOLE and WINDOWS, 1.0 for NATIVE, and 19.90 for POSIX.
/VERBOSE	Displays details about the linking process.
/VERSION:<*major*>[.*minor*]	Inserts a version number in the header of the executable file or DLL. The *major* and *minor* arguments are decimal numbers in the range 0–65535. The default version is 0.0.
/VXD	Creates a virtual device driver (VXD). This is an advanced option for use by device driver writers. For more information on VXDs, consult the Microsoft Windows Device Driver Kit, which is available from Microsoft.
/WARN[:*level*]	Sets the level of LINK warnings. The *level* argument can be one of the following:

0	Suppresses all warnings
1	Displays most warnings
2	Displays additional warnings

If you do not specify a level, LINK assumes the option is /WARN:2.

LIB, the Library Manager

LIB, the Microsoft Library Manager, organizes one or more object modules into a single library file (with a .LIB extension). Rather than keeping a large number of object files and providing their names to the linker, you can use LIB to keep all the object files in a single library file and make the linker search the library file for any required object files. Use LIB to create a new library and modify an existing library file.

Using LIB

As with LINK, you can invoke LIB in two ways:

■ Enter a complete LIB command at the command prompt. Here is the full syntax:

```
LIB [options] [files]
```

where [options] denotes one or more optional LIB options (listed in Table 2.2) and [files] are the object files or libraries to be processed by LIB. The exact operation performed by LIB depends on the [options].

■ Place all LIB options and filenames in a text file and invoke LIB:

```
LIB @<command_file>
```

where <command_file> is the name of the file containing the input commands meant for LIB. Notice that LIB does not assume any specific filename extension for the response file; you should provide the complete filename for the response file.

The simplest example of using LIB is to create a new library. To create a library named AWIPS.LIB with the contents of the object file AWIPS.OBJ, enter the following command:

```
lib awips.obj
```

LIB assumes the extension .LIB and creates a library file named AWIPS.LIB. Now you can add object files to this library. For example, to add the modules DATAMGR.OBJ and SWINDOW.OBJ to the library AWIPS.LIB, you enter the following:

```
lib awips.lib datamgr.obj swindow.obj
```

Later, if you want to remove the DATAMGR.OBJ module from the AWIPS library, enter this:

```
lib /remove:datamgr.obj awips.lib
```

LIB Options and Commands

The command line for LIB has the following syntax:

```
LIB [options] [files]
```

This command creates a library from one or more input files, which can be object files or libraries. By default, LIB creates a new library containing the object modules from the specified files. LIB generates an output file whose name is constructed by appending .LIB to the base name of the first file. If you want a different name for the output filename, use the /OUT option to specify the name. The [options] field can be any one of the options listed in Table 2.2. You can view this list by entering LIB (or LIB /?) at the command prompt.

Table 2.2. LIB options.

Option	*Interpretation by LIB*
`/?`	Displays list of LIB options.
`/DEBUGTYPE:<type>`	Specifies the type of debugging information in a library. The `<type>` argument can be one of the following: `COFF`, `CV`, or `BOTH`.

`/DEF[:filename]`	Specifies a module definition file. Use to build an import library and an exports file, with the following syntax:
	
	`LIB /DEF[:deffile] [options]`
	`[objfiles] [libraries]`
	
	The options `/DEBUGTYPE`, `/EXPORT`, and `/INCLUDE` apply when building an import library.

`/EXPORT:<entryname>[=internalname][,@ordinal[,NONAME]][,DATA]`	
	Exports a function or data to enable other programs to call the function or use the data. For more information, see the `/EXPORT` option in Table 2.1.

`/EXTRACT:<object>`	Extracts the specified object module from the library. Use the `/OUT` option to specify the name of the file where the extracted object module is to be stored. To extract a copy of an object module, use the following command:
	
	`LIB library /EXTRACT:module`
	`/OUT:objfile`

`/INCLUDE:<symbol>`	Adds the specified symbol to the symbol table. This forces linking with an object file that contains the specified symbol.
`/LIST`	Displays the contents of an existing library without modifying it.
`/MACHINE:<IX86¦MIPS¦M68K>`	Indicates the target platform for the program. The machine type can be one of `IX86`, `MIPS`, or `68K`. Usually, LIB determines the machine type from the object files.

Table 2.2. continued

Option	Interpretation by LIB
/NOLOGO	Does not display the copyright message and version number at startup.
/OUT:<filename>	Specifies the name of the output file.
/REMOVE:<object>	Removes the specified object module from the output library.
/SUBSYSTEM:<NATIVE¦WINDOWS¦CONSOLE¦POSIX>[,major[.minor]]	
	Specifies how the operating system should run the executable file created by linking with the output library. For more information, see the /SUBSYSTEM option in Table 2.1.
/VERBOSE	Displays detailed information as LIB performs the specified operations.

NMAKE, the Program Maintenance Utility

Microsoft NMAKE is a program maintenance utility patterned after the UNIX MAKE utility. The following sections provide an overview of NMAKE. You should consult the online help (Books Online) for a detailed description of NMAKE.

You can pass a Visual Workbench project file (which has a .MAK extension) to NMAKE.

If you use the Visual Workbench for your projects, you may not have any need to learn about NMAKE. An understanding of NMAKE is helpful, however, in case you have to prepare a makefile or if you want to use NMAKE to build a project that already has a makefile.

The Makefile

NMAKE works by reading and interpreting a *makefile*, which is a text file that you have to prepare according to a specified syntax. By default, NMAKE expects the makefile to be named MAKEFILE. In fact, if you invoke NMAKE by entering the following:

NMAKE

at the command prompt, NMAKE searches for a text file named MAKEFILE. If the file exists, NMAKE interprets its contents and acts upon the commands contained in that file.

The makefile describes how NMAKE should maintain your program—how it should create the object files and which object files should be linked to create the executable program.

For a program that consists of several source and header files, the makefile indicates which items will be created by NMAKE—these usually are the .OBJ and .EXE files—and how these files depend on other files. For example, suppose you have a C++ source file named FORM.CPP containing the following statement:

```
#include "form.h"    // Include header file
```

FORM.OBJ clearly depends on the source file FORM.CPP and the header file FORM.H. In addition to these dependencies, you also must specify how NMAKE should convert the FORM.CPP file into FORM.OBJ. In this case, suppose you want NMAKE to use CL with the options /c /Zi /Od. This fact can be expressed by the following lines in the makefile:

```
# This is a comment in the makefile
# The following lines indicate how FORM.OBJ depends
# on FORM.CPP and FORM.H and how to build FORM.OBJ.

FORM.OBJ: FORM.CPP FORM.H
          CL /c /Zi /Od FORM.CPP
```

Here, FORM.OBJ is the *target* and FORM.CPP and FORM.H are the *dependent* files. The line following the dependency indicates how to build the target from its dependents.

The biggest benefit of using NMAKE is that it avoids unnecessary compilations. After all, you can invoke CL in a batch file to compile and link all the modules in your program, but the batch file compiles everything even if the compilations are unnecessary. NMAKE, on the other hand, builds a target only if one or more of its dependents has changed since the last time the target was built. It verifies this by examining the time of last modification stamped on the files.

One curious aspect of NMAKE is that it treats the target as the name of a goal to be achieved— the target does not have to be a file. For example, you can have a target such as the following:

```
clean:
        erase form.exe
        erase form.obj
```

which specifies an abstract target named clean that does not depend on anything. This dependency statement says that to make clean, NMAKE should invoke two commands: erase form.exe and erase form.obj. Thus, the net effect of creating the target named clean is to delete the files FORM.EXE and FORM.OBJ.

Macros

In addition to the basic service of building targets from dependents, NMAKE provides many nice features that make it easy for you to express the dependencies and rules for building a target from its dependents. For example, if you need to compile a large number of C++ files with the same CL options, it is tedious to type the options for each file. You can avoid this by defining a symbol or *macro* in NMAKE:

```
# Define macros for standard options for CL
CLFLAGS=/c /Zi /Od
# Define macro used to invoke CL
CL=cl $(CLFLAGS)
# Now define the rule for building FORM.OBJ
FORM.OBJ: FORM.CPP FORM.H
        $(CL) FORM.CPP
```

Notice how the CL options are defined as a macro named CLFLAGS and this symbol is used to define another macro named CL that uses CLFLAGS. To use a macro elsewhere in the makefile, start with a $ followed by the macro within parentheses. For example, NMAKE replaces all occurrences of $(CLFLAGS) with the definition of the macro CLFLAGS.

NMAKE has a number of predefined macros as well as some macros with special meaning (see Table 2.3). You can see a list of all NMAKE macros by entering the /P option when you run NMAKE. When you see the list of predefined macros that NMAKE displays, you will notice that NMAKE considers all environment variables to be predefined macros.

Table 2.3. Some predefined macros in NMAKE.

Macro	*Meaning*
$*	Name of target file without extension
$@	Complete name of target
$**	All names appearing in list of dependents
$<	Name of dependent file with later timestamp than current target (valid only in commands in inference rules)
$?	All dependent files that have later timestamp than current target
$(CC)	Command used to invoke C compiler—by default, CC = CL
$(CFLAGS)	Undefined, but used by NMAKE when invoking $(CC)—C compiler (you can pass options to C compiler by defining CFLAGS macro)
$(CPP)	Command used to invoke C++ compiler—by default, CPP = CL
$(CPPFLAGS)	Undefined, but used by NMAKE when invoking $(CPP)—C++ compiler (you can pass options to C++ compiler by defining CPPFLAGS macro)

Inference Rules

NMAKE also supports the definition of rules—known as *inference rules*—that define how a file with one extension is created from a file with another extension. Consider, for example, the rule for generating an object file (.OBJ file) from a C++ source (.CPP) file. Because this involves running CL with a specified set of options, this is a good candidate for an inference rule. You have to define an inference rule only once in a makefile. For example, to instruct NMAKE to build an .OBJ file from a .CPP file by using CL with the /c option, you write the following inference rule:

```
# Inference rule to make .OBJ file from .CPP file
.CPP.OBJ:
        $(CPP) /c $<
```

This rule utilizes the macro CPP, which is predefined in NMAKE as CL. Notice the use of another macro $< in this rule—you can also write this as $(<). As you can see from Table 2.4, this predefined macro represents the name of a dependent file that has a timestamp later than the target.

To help you set up makefiles, NMAKE already defines a number of inference rules, including the one that builds .OBJ files from .CPP files.

A Sample Makefile

You can easily write a makefile if you use NMAKE's predefined macros and its built-in inference rules. Consider, for example, a makefile that creates the executable WINDRAW.EXE from three C++ source files (WINDRAW.CPP, SHAPES.CPP, and WINVIEW.CPP) and a header file (WINDRAW.H). Assume that each source file includes the header file. Given this, NMAKE creates WINDRAW.EXE if you use the following makefile with NMAKE:

```
###################################################################
#  Sample makefile for Microsoft NMAKE
#  Comments start with '#'
#

# Macro to define flags for the C++ compiler

CPPFLAGS=/Od /Zi

# Define the target "all"--the first target (NMAKE builds this
# one by default).

all: windraw.exe

# Compile the files

windraw.obj: windraw.cpp windraw.h

winview.obj: winview.cpp windraw.h
```

```
shapes.obj: shapes.cpp windraw.h

# Invoke LINK to create the executable with support for debugging

windraw.exe:  windraw.obj shapes.obj winview.obj
    LINK /DEBUG $**
```

Notice that this makefile relies mostly on NMAKE's built-in inference rules. The conversion of .CPP files to .OBJ files uses the built-in rule. The flags to the C++ compiler are passed by defining the macro CPPFLAGS. The target named all is defined as the first target for a reason— if you invoke NMAKE without specifying any targets on the command line (see the syntax presented in the next section), it builds the first target it finds. By defining the first target as WINDRAW.EXE, you can ensure that NMAKE builds this executable file even if you do not explicitly specify it as a target. UNIX programmers traditionally use all as the name for the first target, but the target's name is immaterial—all that matters is that it is the first target in the makefile.

Running NMAKE

You may run NMAKE in two ways:

■ From the command prompt, invoke NMAKE using the following syntax:

NMAKE [*options*] [/f *makefile*] [/x *errfile*] [*macrodefs*] [*targets*]

where [*options*] is one or more options from Table 2.4, [*macrodefs*] is a macro definition of the form MACRO=STRING that is passed to NMAKE, and [*targets*] is the name of a target from the makefile you want built. The /f and /x options are explicitly shown because these options require you to provide filenames; you must provide the name of a makefile for the /f option and the name of a file to log errors for the /x option.

■ Place all NMAKE options and filenames in a text file and invoke NMAKE:

NMAKE @<*command_file*>

where <*command_file*> is the name of the file containing the command-line input meant for NMAKE. Notice that NMAKE does not assume any specific filename extension for the command file; you should provide the complete filename for the command file.

If you save the sample makefile from the previous section in a file named MAKEFILE, merely type NMAKE and press Enter to build the target—in this case, WINDRAW.EXE. However, if the makefile has a different name—WINDRAW.MAK, for example—you must use a command-line option to indicate this to NMAKE:

NMAKE /f windraw.mak

In fact, NMAKE accepts many more options on the command line. Table 2.4 shows a list of NMAKE's options.

Table 2.4. NMAKE options.

Option	Interpretation by NMAKE
/A	Builds all targets in makefile, including those with dependents that are not out of date with respect to target
/B	Builds target even if timestamps of target and dependents are equal
/C	Suppresses nonfatal errors or warning messages
/D	Displays timestamp of each file
/E	Overrides macro definitions in makefile with definitions of environment variables of the same name
/F<file>	Designates <file> as name of makefile
/I	Ignores exit codes from commands listed in makefile
/K	Continues to build unrelated targets even if error occurs when building a target
/N	Displays but does not execute makefile's commands (use to find out what a makefile might cause NMAKE to do before actually doing it)
/NOLOG	Suppresses NMAKE copyright message
/P	Displays all macro definitions and inference rules
/Q	Checks timestamps for specified targets but does not build any target (this command is useful when NMAKE is invoked from a batch file)
/R	Ignores predefined macros and inference rules
/S	Suppresses display of commands listed in makefile (with this option, NMAKE silently performs its job)
/T	Changes timestamp of specified targets, but does not build target
/X<file>	Sends all error messages to file named <file>
/?	Displays brief summary of NMAKE's command-line syntax and list of options

Summary

In addition to the C and C++ compilers, Visual C++ 2.0 includes a large assortment of programming tools and utilities. This chapter provides an overview of the following program development tools: LINK, the linker; LIB, the library manager; and the NMAKE program maintenance utility. By reading this chapter, you have gained an understanding of how to use each of these tools for program development. Consult the extensive online help in Visual Workbench for detailed information on these tools as well as others not described in this chapter.

3

An Overview of ANSI Standard C

In late 1989, the C programming language went through a significant transition. That's when the American National Standards Institute (ANSI) adopted a standard for C, referred to as the ANSI X3.159 1989, which defines not only the C language but also the standard header files, standard libraries, and the behavior of the C preprocessor. Prior to the ANSI standard, the C language as defined by Kernighan and Ritchie's book (*The C Programming Language*, published in 1978 by Prentice Hall, Englewood Cliffs, NJ) was the de facto standard—one that often goes by the name K&R C. The library de facto standard was the C library in UNIX. ANSI C changes this by clearly specifying all aspects of C: the language, the preprocessor, and the library.

One goal of this book is to provide you with complete details of the C++ programming language—explaining its syntax and showing how to use its features to write object-oriented programs. However, before getting into C++ in earnest, you should become familiar with the ANSI standard for the C programming language, because certain seemingly new features of C++ are already in ANSI C. Because C++ existed and continued to evolve as C was being standardized during the period from 1983 through 1989, many features that appear in C++ also found their way into ANSI C. Therefore, if you know ANSI C, you will find many C++ constructs familiar. This chapter briefly describes ANSI C.

The Structure of a C Program

As Figure 3.1 shows, a typical C program is organized into one or more *source files,* or *modules.* Each file has a similar structure with comments, preprocessor directives, declarations of variables and functions, and their definitions. You usually place each group of related variables and functions in a single source file.

Some files are merely a set of declarations that are used in other files through the #include directive of the C preprocessor. These files are usually referred to as *header files* and have names ending with the .H extension. In Figure 3.1, the file SHAPES.H is a header file that declares common data structures and functions for the program. Another file, SHAPES.C, defines the functions. A third file, SHAPETST.C, implements the main function—the function in which the execution of a C program begins. These files with names ending in .C are the source files wherein you define the functions needed by your program. Although Figure 3.1 shows only one function in each source file, in typical programs there are many functions in a source file.

You must compile and link the source files to create an executable program. The exact steps for building programs from C source files depends on the compiler and the operating system. You can find this information in your compiler's documentation.

DECLARATION VERSUS DEFINITION

A *declaration* determines how the program interprets a symbol. A *definition,* on the other hand, actually creates a variable or a function. Definitions cause the compiler to set aside storage for data or code, but declarations do not. For example, the following:

```
int x, y, z;
```

is a definition of three integer variables, but this:

```
extern int x, y, z;
```

is a declaration indicating that the three integer variables are defined in another source file.

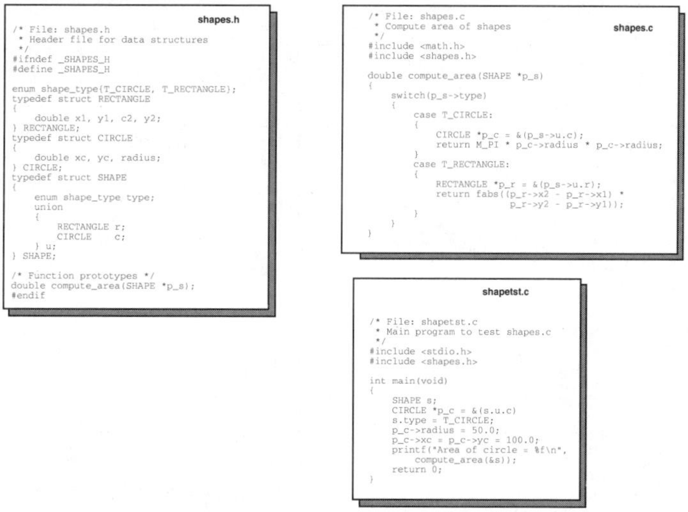

FIGURE 3.1.

Source files of a C program.

```
                                              shapes.h
/* File: shapes.h
 * Header file for data structures
 */
#ifndef _SHAPES_H
#define _SHAPES_H

enum shape_type{T_CIRCLE, T_RECTANGLE};
typedef struct RECTANGLE
{
    double x1, y1, c2, y2;
} RECTANGLE;
typedef struct CIRCLE
{
    double xc, yc, radius;
} CIRCLE;
typedef struct SHAPE
{
    enum shape_type type;
    union
    {
        RECTANGLE r;
        CIRCLE    c;
    } u;
} SHAPE;

/* Function prototypes */
double compute_area(SHAPE *p_s);
#endif
```

```
/* File: shapes.c
 * Compute area of shapes
 */                                        shapes.c
#include <math.h>
#include <shapes.h>

double compute_area(SHAPE *p_s)
{
    switch(p_s->type)
    {
        case T_CIRCLE:
        {
            CIRCLE *p_c = &(p_s->u.c);
            return M_PI * p_c->radius * p_c->radius;
        }
        case T_RECTANGLE:
        {
            RECTANGLE *p_r = &(p_s->u.r);
            return fabs((p_r->x2 - p_r->x1) *
                        p_r->y2 - p_r->y1)));
        }
    }
}
```

```
                                          shapetst.c
/* File: shapetst.c
 * Main program to test shapes.c
 */
#include <stdio.h>
#include <shapes.h>

int main(void)
{
    SHAPE s;
    CIRCLE *p_c = &(s.u.c)
    s.type = T_CIRCLE;
    p_c->radius = 50.0;
    p_c->xc = p_c->yc = 100.0;
    printf("Area of circle = %f\n",
           compute_area(&s));
    return 0;
}
```

Within each source file, the components of the program are laid out in a standard manner. As Figure 3.2 shows, the typical components of a C source file (in order) are as follows:

1. The file starts with some comments that describe the purpose of the module and that provide some other pertinent information, such as the name of the author and revision dates. In ANSI C, comments start with /* and end with */.

2. Commands for the preprocessor, known as *preprocessor directives,* follow the comments. The first few directives typically are for including header files and defining constants.

3. Declarations of variables and functions that are visible throughout the file come next. In other words, the names of these variables and functions may be used in any of the functions in this file. Here, you also define variables needed within the file. Use the static keyword as a prefix when you want to confine the visibility of the variables and functions to this module only. On the other hand, the extern keyword indicates that the items you declare are defined in another file.

4. The rest of the file includes definitions of functions. Inside a function's body, you can define variables that are local to the function and that exist only while the function's code is being executed.

FIGURE 3.2.

Layout of a typical C source file.

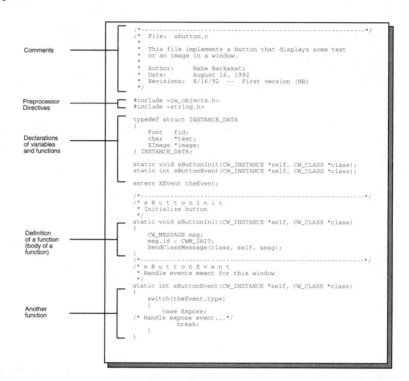

Comments

Preprocessor Directives

Declarations of variables and functions

Definition of a function (body of a function)

Another function

```
/*--------------------------------------------------------------*/
/*  File:  sbutton.c
 *
 *  This file implements a button that displays some text
 *  or an image in a window.
 *
 *  Author:    Naba Barkakati
 *  Date:      August 16, 1992
 *  Revisions: 8/16/92 -- First version (NB)
 */

#include <cw_objects.h>
#include <string.h>

typedef struct INSTANCE_DATA
{
    Font   fid;
    char   *text;
    XImage *image;
} INSTANCE_DATA;

static void sButtonInit(CW_INSTANCE *self, CW_CLASS *class);
static int sButtonEvent(CW_INSTANCE *self, CW_CLASS *class);

extern XEvent theEvent;

/*--------------------------------------------------------------*/
/* s B u t t o n I n i t
 * Initialize button
 */
static void sButtonInit(CW_INSTANCE *self, CW_CLASS *class)
{
    CW_MESSAGE msg;
    msg.id = CWM_INIT;
    SendClassMessage(class, self, &msg);
}
/*--------------------------------------------------------------*/
/* s B u t t o n E v e n t
 * Handle events meant for this window
 */
static int sButtonEvent(CW_INSTANCE *self, CW_CLASS *class)
{
    switch(theEvent.type)
    {
        case Expose:
/* Handle expose event...*/
            break;
    }
}
```

ANSI C KEYWORDS

The following is a list of all ANSI C keywords:

auto	double	int	struct
break	else	long	switch
case	enum	register	typedef
char	extern	return	union
const	float	short	unsigned
continue	for	signed	void
default	goto	sizeof	volatile
doif	static	while	

The keywords const, enum, void, and volatile are new in ANSI C.

ANSI C Escape Sequences and Trigraphs

In C, you can insert nonprintable characters, such as a tab, in strings by using an *escape sequence*—a sequence of characters that starts with a backslash (\). For example, a tab and a newline character are represented by \t and \n, respectively. ANSI C has enlarged the set of escape sequences. Table 3.1 lists the escape sequences supported in ANSI C.

Table 3.1. ANSI C escape sequences.

Sequence	Name	Interpretation or Action
\a	Alert	Rings bell
\b	Backspace	Moves backward one space
\f	Form feed	Moves to beginning of next page
\n	Newline	Moves to beginning of next line
\r	Carriage return	Moves to beginning of current line
\t	Horizontal tab	Moves to next tab position on this line
\v	Vertical tab	Moves to next vertical tab position
\\	Backslash	\
\'	Single quote	'
\"	Double quote	"
\?	Question mark	?
\<octal digits>	Octal constant	Depends on printer or terminal
\x<hexadecimal digits>	Hexadecimal	Depends on printer or terminal

ANSI C also introduces the concept of *trigraph sequences,* enabling programmers to enter certain important characters from their keyboard, even if their keyboards do not have that feature—for example, non-English keyboards may not have some characters that English keyboards have. Each three-character trigraph sequence begins with a pair of question marks (??) followed by a third character. For example, if a keyboard does not have a backslash (\), a programmer can use the trigraph ??/ to enter it in a C program. Table 3.2 lists the nine trigraph sequences available in ANSI C.

Table 3.2. ANSI C trigraph sequences.

Trigraph	Translation
??(	[
??/	\

continues

Table 3.2. continued

Trigraph	Translation
??)	]
??'	^
??<	{
??!	|
??>	}
??-	~
??=	#

Preprocessor Directives

Preprocessing refers to the first step in translating or *compiling* an ANSI C file into machine instructions. Traditionally, the C preprocessor has been used for this task. Although the ANSI standard does not require a separate preprocessor, most C compilers provide a distinct preprocessor.

The preprocessor processes the source file and acts on the commands, the preprocessor directives, embedded in the program. These directives begin with the pound sign (#). Usually, the compiler automatically invokes the preprocessor before beginning compilation, but most compilers give you the option of invoking the preprocessor alone. You can utilize three major capabilities of the preprocessor to make your programs modular, more readable, and easier to customize:

■ You can use the #include directive to insert the contents of a file into your program. With this, you can place common declarations in one location and use them in all source files through file inclusion. The result is a reduced risk of mismatches between declarations of variables and functions in separate program modules.

■ Through the #define directive, you can define macros that enable you to replace one string with another. You can use the #define directive to give meaningful names to numeric constants, thus improving the readability of your source files.

■ With directives such as #if, #ifdef, #else, and #endif, you can compile only selected portions of your program. You can use this feature to write source files with code for two or more systems, but compile only those parts that apply to the computer system on which you compile the program. With this strategy, you can maintain multiple versions of a program using a single set of source files.

Including Files

You can write modular programs by exploiting the `#include` directive. This is possible because the C preprocessor enables you to keep commonly used declarations in a single file that you can insert in other source files as needed. ANSI C supports three forms of the `#include` directive. As a C programmer, you should be familiar with the first two forms:

```
#include <stdio.h>
#include "winobj.h"
```

You use the first form of `#include` to read the contents of a file—in this case, the standard C header file STDIO.H from the default location where all the header files reside. You can use the second form, which displays the filename within double quotation marks, when the file being included (WINOBJ.H) is in the current directory. For locating the file that is being included, the exact conventions depend on the compiler.

ANSI C provides a third way of specifying the name of the file in the `#include` directive. You can now specify the name of the file through a macro. The following example illustrates how this might be done:

```
/* The following was introduced in ANSI C */

#ifdef WINDOWS
    #define  SYSTEM_DEFINES   "windef.h"
#else
    #define  SYSTEM_DEFINES   "dosdef.h"
#endif

#include SYSTEM_DEFINES
```

This example uses the `#ifdef` and `#define` directives (described in the Conditional Directives section later in this chapter) to set the symbol SYSTEM_DEFINES to the name of the file to be included, depending on the definition of the symbol WINDOWS.

Defining Macros

By defining a macro, you can define a symbol (a *token*) to be equal to some C code. You can then use that symbol wherever you want to use that code in your program. When the source file is preprocessed, every occurrence of a macro's name is replaced with its definition. A common use of this feature is to define a symbolic name for a numerical constant and then use the symbol instead of the numbers in your program. This improves the readability of the source code because with a descriptive name you are not left guessing why a particular number is being used in the program. You can define such macros in a straightforward manner using the `#define` directive:

```
#define PI         3.14159
#define GRAV_ACC   9.80665
#define BUFSIZE    512
```

Once these symbols are defined, you can use PI, GRAV_ACC, and BUFSIZE rather than the numerical constants throughout the source file.

The capabilities of macros, however, go well beyond replacing a symbol for a constant. A macro can accept a parameter and replace each occurrence of that parameter with the provided value when the macro is used in a program. Thus, the code that results from the expansion of a macro can change depending on the parameter you use when running the macro. For example, here is a macro that accepts a parameter and expands to an expression designed to calculate the square of the parameter:

```
#define square(x) ((x)*(x))
```

If you use square(z) in your program, it becomes ((z)*(z)) after the source file is preprocessed. This macro is essentially equivalent to a function that computes the square of its arguments, except that you don't call a function—the expression generated by the macro is placed directly in the source file.

SIDE EFFECTS OF MACROS

When the preprocessor expands a macro, it replaces each parameter with the one you provide when using the macro. If you are not careful when you define the macro, you may end up with code that does something completely different from what you intended. For example, if you define square(x) as x*x, a macro invocation of the form square(a+b) will expand to a+b*a+b, which is certainly not the square of a+b. However, with square(x) defined as ((x)*(x)), square(a+b) results in ((a+b)*(a+b)), which gives you the correct result. So, as a general rule, you should use parentheses liberally when defining a macro with parameters.

An interesting new feature of the ANSI C preprocessor is the *token-pasting* operator denoted by a pair of pound signs (##). With this operator, you can append one token to another and create a third valid token. The following scenario provides an example of where you might use this. Suppose you have two types of data files, and an integer at the beginning of each file identifies each type. File type 1 uses the hexadecimal constant 0x4d4d, and type 2 uses 0x4949 in the first 2 bytes. To read these files in your program, you want to refer to the type with a macro of the form Type(n) where n is either 1 or 2. Here is how you can use the token-pasting operator ## to define the Type(n) macro:

```
#define TYPE1    0x4d4d
#define TYPE2    0x4949
#define Type(n) TYPE##n
```

With this definition, when the preprocessor expands the macro Type(2), it replaces n with 2 and generates the string TYPE##2 that, upon interpretation of the token-pasting operator, becomes the token TYPE2. The preprocessor finds that TYPE2 is defined as 0x4949 and uses that as the replacement for the macro Type(2).

Another new feature of the ANSI C preprocessor is the *string-izing* operator, which creates a string out of any parameter with a # prefix by putting that parameter in quotes. Suppose you want to print the value of certain variables in your program. Rather than calling the printf() function directly, you can define a utility macro that will do the work for you. Here is how you might write the macro:

```
#define Trace(x)        printf(#x" = %d\n", x)
```

Then, to print the value of an integer variable named current_index for example, you can write it as follows:

```
Trace(current_index);
```

When the preprocessor expands it, it generates this statement:

```
printf("current_index"" = %d\n", current_index);
```

At this point, another new feature of ANSI C becomes relevant. ANSI C also stipulates that adjacent strings will be concatenated. Applying that rule, the macro expansion becomes the following:

```
printf("current_index = %d\n", current_index);
```

This is exactly what you would write to print the value of the current_index variable.

Conditional Directives

You can use the *conditional directives,* such as #if, #ifdef, #ifndef, #else, #elif, and #endif, to control which parts of a source file are compiled and under what conditions. With this feature, you maintain a single set of source files that can be selectively compiled with different compilers and in different environments. Another common use is to insert printf() statements for debugging that are compiled only if a symbol named DEBUG is defined. Conditional directives start with either #if, #ifdef, or #ifndef and may be followed by any number of #elif directives (or none at all). Next comes an optional #else, followed by an #endif directive that marks the end of that conditional block. Here are some common ways of using conditional directives. To include a header file only once, you can use this:

```
#ifndef _ _PROJECT_H
#define _ _PROJECT_H
/*  Declarations to be included once */
/* ... */

#endif
```

The following prints a diagnostic message during debugging (when the symbol DEBUG is defined):

```
#ifdef DEBUG
    printf("In read_file: bytes_read = %d\n", bytes_read);
#endif
```

The next example shows how you can include a different header file depending on the type of the system for which the program is being compiled. To selectively include a header file, you can use this:

```
#if CPU_TYPE == IX86
    #include <ix86\sysdef.h>
#elif CPU_TYPE == M68K
    #include <m68k\sysdef.h>
#else
    #error Unknown CPU type.
#endif
```

The #error directive is used to display error messages during preprocessing.

Other Directives

Several other preprocessor directives perform miscellaneous tasks. For example, you can use the #undef directive to remove the current definition of a symbol. The #pragma directive is another special purpose directive that you can use to convey information to the C compiler. You can use pragmas to access special features of a compiler, and as such, they vary from one compiler to another.

ANSI standard C compilers maintain several predefined macros (see Table 3.3). Of these, the macros _ _FILE_ _ and _ _LINE_ _ respectively refer to the current source filename and the current line number being processed. You can use the #line directive to change these. For example, to set _ _FILE_ _ to "file_io.c" and _ _LINE_ _ to 100, you write the following:

```
#line 100 "file_io.c"
```

Table 3.3. Predefined macros in ANSI C.

Macro	Definition
_ _DATE_ _	This is a string containing the date when you invoke the C compiler. It is of the form MMM DD YYYY (for example, Aug 16 1994).
_ _FILE_ _	This expands to a string containing the name of the source file.
_ _LINE_ _	This is a decimal integer with a value that is the line number within the current source file.
_ _STDC_ _	This macro expands to the decimal constant 1 to indicate that the C compiler conforms to the ANSI standard.
_ _TIME_ _	This string displays the time when you started compiling the source file. It is of the form HH:MM:SS (for example, 21:59:45).

Additionally, all C++ compilers including Microsoft Visual C++ 2.0 define the macro _cplusplus whenever a C++ module is being compiled.

Declaration and Definition of Variables

In C, you must either define or declare all variables and functions before you use them. The definition of a variable specifies three things:

- Its *visibility*, which indicates exactly where the variable can be used (is it defined for all files in a program, the current file, or only in a function)

- Its *lifetime*, which determines whether the variable exists temporarily (for example, a local variable in a function) or permanently (as long as the program is running)

- Its *type* and, where enabled, its *initial value*; for example, an integer variable x initialized to 1 is defined as the following:

```
int  x = 1;
```

If a variable that you are using is defined in another source file, you declare the variable with an extern keyword:

```
extern int message_count;
```

You must define this variable without the extern qualifier in at least one source file. When the program is built, the linker resolves all references to the message_count variable and ensures that they all use the same variable.

Basic Types

C has four basic data types: char and int are for storing characters and integers, and float and double are for floating-point numbers. The ANSI standard specifies only the minimum range of values that each type must be able to represent. The exact number of bytes used to store each data type may vary from one compiler to another. For example, ANSI C requires that the size of an int be at least 2 bytes, which is what most MS-DOS and Windows 16-bit C compilers provide. Most UNIX C compilers and 32-bit Windows compilers (such as Microsoft Visual C++ 2.0), on the other hand, use 4 bytes for an int. Most systems use a single byte for a char. Common sizes for float and double are 4 and 8 bytes, respectively. You can define variables for these basic data types in a straightforward manner:

```
char   c;
int    i, j, bufsize;
float  volts;
double mean, variance;
```

With C, you can expand the basic data types into a much larger set by using the long, short, and unsigned qualifiers as prefixes. The long and short qualifiers are size modifiers. For example, in ANSI C a long int is at least 4 bytes long, whereas a short int has a minimum size of only 2 bytes. The size of an int is system-dependent, but it will definitely be at least as large as a short.

The unsigned qualifier is reserved for int and char types only. Normally, each of these types holds negative as well as positive values. This is the default signed form of these data types. You can use the unsigned qualifier when you want the variable to hold positive values only. Here are some examples of using the short, long, and unsigned qualifiers:

```
unsigned char  mode_select, printer_status;
short          record_number; /* Same as "short int"          */
long           offset;         /* Same as "long int"           */
unsigned       i, j, msg_id;   /* Same as "unsigned int"       */
unsigned short width, height;  /* Same as "unsigned short int" */
unsigned long  file_pos;       /* Same as "unsigned long int"  */
long double    result;
```

Notice that when the short, long, and unsigned qualifiers are used with int types, you can drop the int from the declaration. Also, ANSI C enables you to extend the double data type with a long prefix.

The exact sizes of the various data types and the ranges of values they can store depend on the C compiler. ANSI C requires that these limits be defined in the header files LIMITS.H and FLOAT.H. You can examine these files in your system to determine the sizes of the basic data types that your C compiler supports.

Enumerations

ANSI C introduces the enum data type, which you can use to define your own *enumerated list*— a fixed set of named integer constants. For example, you can declare a Boolean data type named BOOLEAN using enum:

```
/* Declare an enumerated type named BOOLEAN */
    enum BOOLEAN {false = 0, true = 1, stop = 0, go = 1,
                  off = 0, on = 1};

/* Define a BOOLEAN called "status" and initialize it */
    enum BOOLEAN status = stop;
```

This example first declares BOOLEAN to be an enumerated type. The list within the braces shows the *enumeration constants* that are valid values of an enum BOOLEAN variable. You can initialize each constant to a value of your choice, and several constants can use the same value. In this example, the constants false, stop, and off are set to 0, and true, go, and on are initialized to 1. The example then defines an enumerated BOOLEAN variable named status, which is initially set to the constant stop.

Structures, Unions, and Bit Fields

In C, you use struct to group related data items together, and refer to that group by a name. For example, the declaration of a structure to hold variables of a queue might look like this:

```
/* Declare a structure */
struct QUEUE
{
    int   count;      /* Number of items in queue   */
    int   front;      /* Index of first item in queue */
    int   rear;       /* Index of last item in queue */
    int   elemsize;   /* Size of each element of data */
    int   maxsize;    /* Maximum capacity of queue  */
    char *data;       /* Pointer to queued data     */
};

/* Define two queues */
struct QUEUE rcv_q, xmit_q;
```

The elements inside the QUEUE structure are called its *members*. You can access these members by using the member selection operator (.). For example, rcv_q.count refers to the count member of the rcv_q structure.

A union is like a struct, but rather than grouping related data items together as struct does, a union allocates storage for several data items starting at the same location. Thus, all members of a union share the same storage location. You can use unions to view the same data item in different ways. Suppose you are using a compiler that supports 4-byte longs, and you want to access the 4 individual bytes of a long integer. Here is a union that enables you to accomplish this:

```
union
{
    long  file_type;
    char  bytes[4];
} header_id;
```

With this definition, header_id.file_type refers to the long integer, and header_id.bytes[0] is the first byte of that long integer.

In C, you can also define structures that contain groups of bits that are packed into an int. These *bit fields* are useful for manipulating selected bits of an integer and often are used when accessing hardware devices such as disk drive controllers and serial ports. Think of a bit field as a structure with bits as members. The declaration of a bit field is like any other structure except for the syntax used to indicate the size of each group of bits. For example, in the IBM PC, the text display memory uses a 16-bit cell for each character: the least significant 8 bits for the character's ASCII code and the other 8 bits for attributes such as foreground and background colors. A 16-bit bit field describing this layout might be written as follows:

```
struct TEXT_CELL
{
    unsigned  c:8, fg_color:4, bg_color:3, blink_on:1;
};
```

This bit field definition assumes that the compiler packs the bit fields from the least significant bit to the most significant bit. The exact order of the bits in a bit field depends on the compiler.

Arrays

An *array* is a collection of one or more identical data items. You can declare arrays of any type of data, including structures and types defined by typedef. For example, to define an array of 80 characters, you write the following:

```
char     string[80];
```

The characters in the string array occupy successive storage locations, beginning with location 0. Thus in this example, string[0] refers to the first character in this array, and string[79] refers to the last one. You can define arrays of other data types and structures similarly:

```
struct Customer                    /* Declare a structure      */
{
    int  id;
    char first_name[40];
    char last_name[40];
};

struct Customer customers[100]; /* Define array of structures */
int             index[64];      /* An array of 64 integers    */
```

You can also define multidimensional arrays. For example, to represent an 80-column by 25-line text display, you can use a two-dimensional array:

```
unsigned char text_screen[25][80];
```

Each item of text_screen is an array of 80 unsigned chars, and text_screen contains 25 such arrays. In other words, the two-dimensional array is stored by laying out one row after another in memory. You can use expressions such as text_screen[0][0] to refer to the first character in the first row and text_screen[24][79] to refer to the last character of the last row of the display screen. Higher dimensional arrays are defined similarly:

```
float coords[3][2][5];
```

This example defines coords as a three-dimensional array of three data items: each item is an array of two arrays, each of which, in turn, is an array of five float variables. Thus, you interpret a multidimensional array as an "array of arrays."

Pointers

A *pointer* is a variable that can hold the address of any type of data except a bit field. For example, if p_i is a pointer to an integer variable, you can define and use it as follows:

```
/* Define an int pointer and an integer */
   int *p_i, count;

/* Set pointer to the address of the integer "count" */
   p_i = &count;
```

In this case, the compiler allocates storage for an int variable count and a pointer to an integer p_i. The number of bytes necessary to represent a pointer depends on the underlying system's addressing scheme. You should not use a pointer until it contains the address of a valid object.

The example shows p_i being initialized to the address of the integer variable count using the & operator, which provides the address of a variable. Once p_i is initialized, you can refer to the value of count with the expression *p_i, which is read as "the contents of the object with its address in p_i."

Pointers are useful in many situations; an important one is the dynamic allocation of memory. The standard C libraries include functions such as malloc and calloc, which you can call to allocate storage for arrays of objects. After allocating memory, these functions return the starting address of the block of memory. Because this address is the only way to reach that memory, you must store it in a variable capable of holding an address—a pointer.

Suppose you allocate memory for an array of 50 integers and save the returned address in p_i. Now you can treat this block of memory as an array of 50 integers with the name p_i. Thus, you can refer to the last element in the array as p_i[49], which is equivalent to *(p_i+49). Similarly, ANSI C treats the name of an array as a pointer to the first element of the array. The difference between the name of an array and a pointer variable is that the name of the array is a constant without any explicit storage necessary to hold the address of the array's first element, whereas the pointer is an actual storage location capable of holding the address of any data.

In addition to storing the address of dynamically allocated memory, pointers are also commonly used as arguments to functions. When a C function is called, all of its arguments are *passed by value*—that is, the function gets a copy of each argument, not the original variables appearing in the argument list of the function call. Thus, a C function cannot alter the value of its arguments. Pointers provide a way out. To change the value of a variable in a function, you can pass it a pointer to the variable, and the function can alter the value through the pointer.

Type Definitions

Through the typedef keyword, C provides you with a convenient way of assigning a new name to an existing data type. You can use the typedef facility to give meaningful names to data types used in a particular application. For example, a graphics application might declare a data type named Point:

```
/* Declare a Point data type */
    typedef struct Point
    {
        short x;
        short y;
    } Point;

/* Declare PointPtr to be pointer to Point types */
    typedef Point *P_PointPtr;

/* Define some instances of these types and initialize them */
    Point    a = {0, 0};
    PointPtr p_a = &a;
```

As shown by the Point and PointPtr types, you can use typedef to declare complex data types conveniently.

Type Qualifiers: *const* and *volatile*

ANSI C introduces two new keywords, const and volatile, that you can use as qualifiers in a declaration. The const qualifier in a declaration tells the compiler that the particular data object must not be modified by the program. This means that the compiler must not generate code that might alter the contents of the location where that data item is stored. On the other hand, volatile specifies that the value of a variable may be changed by factors beyond the program's control. You can use both keywords on a single data item to mean that, although the item must not be modified by your program, it may be altered by some other process. The const and volatile keywords always qualify the item that immediately follows (to the right). The information provided by the const and the volatile qualifiers is supposed to help the compiler optimize the code it generates. For example, suppose the variable block_size is declared and initialized as follows:

```
const int block_size = 512;
```

In this case, the compiler does not need to generate code to load the value of block_size from memory. Instead, it can use the value 512 wherever your program uses block_size. Now suppose you add volatile to the declaration and change the declaration to the following:

```
volatile const int block_size = 512;
```

This says that the contents of block_size may be changed by some external process. Therefore, the compiler cannot optimize away any reference to block_size. You may need to use such declarations when referring to an I/O port or video memory because these locations can be changed by factors beyond your program's control.

Expressions

An *expression* is a combination of variables, function calls, and operators that results in a single value. For example, here is an expression with a value that is the number of bytes needed to store the null-terminated string str (an array of chars with a zero byte at the end):

```
(strlen(str) * sizeof(char) + 1)
```

This expression involves a function call, strlen(str), and the multiplication (*), addition (+), and sizeof operators.

ANSI C has a large number of operators that are an important part of expressions. Table 3.4 provides a summary of the operators in ANSI C.

Table 3.4. Summary of ANSI C operators.

Name of Operator	Syntax	Result
Arithmetic Operators		
Addition	x+y	Adds x and y
Subtraction	x-y	Subtracts y from x
Multiplication	x*y	Multiplies x and y
Division	x/y	Divides x by y
Remainder	x%y	Computes the remainder that results from dividing x by y
Preincrement	++x	Increments x before use
Postincrement	x++	Increments x after use
Predecrement	--x	Decrements x before use
Postdecrement	x--	Decrements x after use
Minus	-x	Negates the value of x
Plus	+x	Maintains the value of x unchanged
Relational and Logical Operators		
Greater than	x>y	Value is 1 if x exceeds y; otherwise, value is 0
Greater than or equal to	x>=y	Value is 1 if x exceeds or equals y; otherwise, value is 0
Less than	x<y	Value is 1 if y exceeds x; otherwise, value is 0
Less than or equal to	x<=y	Value is 1 if y exceeds or equals x; otherwise, value is 0
Equal to	x==y	Value is 1 if x equals y; otherwise, value is 0
Not equal to	x!=y	Value is 1 if x and y are unequal; otherwise, value is 0

continues

Table 3.4. continued

Name of Operator	*Syntax*	*Result*
Logical NOT	!x	Value is 1 if x is 0; otherwise, value is 0
Logical AND	x&&y	Value is 0 if either x or y is 0
Logical OR	x¦¦y	Value is 0 if both x and y are 0

Assignment Operators

Assignment	x=y	Places the value of y into x
Compound assignment	x O=y	Equivalent to x = x O y, where O is one of the following operators: +, -, *, /, %, <<, >>, &, ^, or ¦

Data Access and Size Operators

Subscript	x[y]	Selects the yth element of array x
Member selection	x.y	Selects member y of structure (or union) x
Member selection	x->y	Selects the member named y from a structure or union with x as its address
Indirection	*x	Contents of the location with x as its address
Address of	&x	Address of the data object named x
Size of	sizeof(x)	Size (in bytes) of the data object named x

Bitwise Operators

Bitwise NOT	~x	Changes all 1s to 0s and 0s to 1s
Bitwise AND	x&y	Result is the bitwise AND of x and y
Bitwise OR	x¦y	Result is the bitwise OR of x and y
Bitwise exclusive-OR	x^y	Result contains 1s where corresponding bits of x and y differ
Left shift	x<<y	Shifts the bits of x to the left by y bit positions; fills 0s in the vacated bit positions
Right shift	x>>y	Shifts the bits of x to the right by y bit positions; fills 0s in the vacated bit positions

Name of Operator	Syntax	Result
Miscellaneous Operators		
Function call	`x(y)`	Result is the value returned (if any) by function `x`, which is called with argument `y`
Type cast	`(type)x`	Converts the value of `x` to the `type` named in parentheses
Conditional	`z?x:y`	If `z` is not `0`, evaluates `x`; otherwise, evaluates `y`
Comma	`x,y`	Evaluates `x` first and then `y`

Operator Precedence

Typical C expressions consist of several operands and operators. When writing complicated expressions, you must be aware of the order in which the compiler evaluates the operators. For example, a program uses an array of pointers to integers defined as follows:

```
typedef int *IntPtr;  /* Use typedef to simplify declarations */
IntPtr  iptr[10];     /* An array of 10 pointers to int       */
```

Now, suppose that you encounter the expression `*iptr[4]`. Does this refer to the value of the `int` with the address in `iptr[4]`, or is this the fifth element from the location with the address in `iptr`? In other words, is the compiler going to evaluate the subscript operator (`[]`) before the indirection operator (`*`), or is it the other way around? To answer questions such as these, you need to know the *precedence* or order in which the program applies the operators.

Table 3.5 summarizes ANSI C's precedence rules. The table shows the operators in order of decreasing precedence. The operators with highest precedence—those that are applied first—are shown first. The table also shows the *associativity* of the operators—this is the order in which operators at the same level are evaluated.

Table 3.5. Precedence and associativity of ANSI C operators.

Operator Group	Operator Name	Notation	Associativity
Postfix	Subscript	`x[y]`	Left to right
	Function call	`x(y)`	
	Member selection	`x.y`	
	Member selection	`x->y`	
Unary	Postincrement	`x++`	Right to left
	Postdecrement	`x--`	

continues

Table 3.5. continued

Operator Group	Operator Name	Notation	Associativity
	Preincrement	`++x`	
	Predecrement	`--x`	
	Address of	`&x`	
	Indirection	`*x`	
	Plus	`+x`	
	Minus	`-x`	
	Bitwise NOT	`~x`	
	Logical NOT	`!x`	
	Sizeof	`sizeof x`	
	Type cast	`(type)x`	
Multiplicative	Multiply	`x*y`	Left to right
	Divide	`x/y`	
	Remainder	`x%y`	
Additive	Add	`x+y`	Left to right
	Subtract	`x-y`	
Shift	Left shift	`x<<y`	Left to right
	Right shift	`x>>y`	
Relational	Greater than	`x>y`	Left to right
	Greater than or equal to	`x>=y`	
	Less than	`x<y`	
	Less than or equal to	`x<=y`	
Equality	Equal to	`x==y`	Left to right
	Not equal to	`x!=y`	
Bitwise	Bitwise AND	`x&y`	Left to right
	Bitwise exclusive-OR	`x^y`	

Operator Group	Operator Name	Notation	Associativity
	Bitwise OR	x¦y	
Logical	Logical AND	x&&y	Left to right
	Logical OR	x¦¦y	
Conditional	Conditional	z?x:y	Right to left
Assignment	Assignment	x=y	Right to left
	Multiply assign	x *= y	
	Divide assign	x /= y	
	Remainder assign	x %= y	
	Add assign	x += y	
	Subtract assign	x -= y	
	Left shift assign	x <<= y	
	Right shift assign	x >>= y	
	Bitwise AND assign	x &= y	
	Bitwise XOR assign	x ^= y	
	Bitwise OR assign	x ¦= y	
Comma	Comma	x,y	Left to right

Returning to the question of interpreting *iptr[4], a quick look at Table 3.5 tells you that the [] operator has precedence over the * operator. Thus, when the compiler processes the expression *iptr[4], it evaluates iptr[4] first, and then it applies the indirection operator, resulting in the value of the int with the address in iptr[4].

Statements

You use statements to represent the actions C functions will perform and to control the flow of execution in the C program. A *statement* consists of keywords, expressions, and other statements. Each statement ends with a semicolon.

A special type of statement, the *compound statement,* is a group of statements enclosed in a pair of braces ({...}). The body of a function is a compound statement. Also known as *blocks,* such compound statements can contain local variables.

The following alphabetically arranged sections describe the types of statements available in ANSI C.

The *break* Statement

You use the break statement to jump to the statement following the innermost do, for, switch, or while statement. It is also used to exit from a switch statement. Here is an example that uses break to exit a for loop:

```
for(i = 0; i < ncommands; i++)
{
    if(strcmp(input, commands[i]) == 0) break;
}
```

The *case* Statement

The case statement marks labels in a switch statement. Here is an example:

```
switch (interrupt_id)
{
    case XMIT_RDY:
        transmit();
        break;

    case RCV_RDY:
        receive();
        break;
}
```

A Compound Statement or Block

A compound statement or block is a group of declarations followed by statements, all enclosed in a pair of braces ({...}). The body of a function and the block of code following an if statement are some examples of compound statements. In the following example, the declarations and statements within the braces constitute a compound statement:

```
if(theEvent.xexpose.count == 0)
{
    int i;
/* Clear the window and draw the figures
 * in the "figures" array
 */
    XClearWindow(theDisplay, dWin);
    if(numfigures > 0)
        for(i=0; i<numfigures; i++)
            draw_figure(theDisplay, dWin,
                        theGC, i);
}
```

The *continue* Statement

The continue statement begins the next iteration of the innermost do, for, or while statement in which it appears. You can use continue when you want to skip the execution of the loop. For example, to add the numbers from 1 to 10, excluding 5, you can use a for loop that skips the body when the loop index (i) is 5:

```
for(i=0, sum=0; i <= 10, i++)
{
    if(i == 5) continue;   /* Exclude 5 */
    sum += i;
}
```

The *default* Label

You use default as the label in a switch statement to mark code that will execute when none of the case labels matches the switch expression.

The *do* Statement

The do statement, together with while, forms iterative loops of the following kind:

```
do
  statement
  while(expression);
```

where the statement (usually a compound statement) executes until the expression in the while statement evaluates to 0. The expression is evaluated after each execution of the statement. Thus, a do-while block always executes at least once. For example, to add the numbers from 1 to 10, you can use the following do statement:

```
sum = 0;
do
{
    sum += i;
    i++;
}
while(i <= 10);
```

Expression Statements

Expression statements are evaluated for their side effects. Some typical uses of expression statements include calling a function, incrementing a variable, and assigning a value to a variable. Here are some examples:

```
printf("Hello, World!\n");
i++;
num_bytes = length * sizeof(char);
```

The *for* Statement

Use the for statement to execute a statement any number of times based on the value of an expression. The syntax is as follows:

```
for (expr_1; expr_2; expr_3) statement
```

where the *expr_1* is evaluated once at the beginning of the loop, and the statement is executed until the expression *expr_2* evaluates to 0. The third expression, *expr_3*, is evaluated after each execution of the statement. All three expressions are optional and the value of *expr_2* is assumed to be 1 if it is omitted. Here is an example that uses a for loop to add the numbers from 1 to 10:

```
for(i=0, sum=0; i <= 10; sum += i, i++);
```

In this example, the actual work of adding the numbers is done in the third expression, and the statement controlled by the for loop is a null statement (a lone ;).

The *goto* Statement

The goto statement transfers control to a statement label. Here is an example that prompts the user for a value and repeats the request if the value is not acceptable:

```
ReEnter:
    printf("Enter offset: ");
    scanf(" %d", &offset);
    if(offset < 0 ¦¦ offset > MAX_OFFSET)
    {
        printf("Bad offset: %d Please reenter:\n",
            offset);
        goto ReEnter;
    }
```

The *if* Statement

You can use the if statement to test an expression and execute a statement only when the expression is not zero. An if statement takes the following form:

```
if ( expression )   statement
```

The statement following the if is executed only if the expression in parentheses evaluates to a nonzero value. That statement is usually a compound statement. Here is an example:

```
if(mem_left < threshold)
{
    Message("Low on memory! Close some windows.\n");
}
```

The *if-else* Statement

The if-else statement is a form of the if statement together with an else clause. The statement has this syntax:

```
if ( expression )
    statement_1
else
    statement_2
```

where *statement_1* is executed if the expression within the parentheses is not zero. Otherwise, *statement_2* is executed. Here is an example that uses if and else to pick the smaller of two variables:

```
if ( a <= b)
    smaller = a;
else
    smaller = b;
```

The Null Statement

The null statement, represented by a solitary semicolon, does nothing. You use null statements in loops when all processing is done in the loop expressions rather than in the body of the loop. For example, to locate the zero byte marking the end of a string, you might use the following:

```
char str[80] = "Test";
int i;

for (i=0; str[i] != '\0'; i++)
                            ;   /* Null statement */
```

The *return* Statement

The return statement stops executing the current function and returns control to the calling function. Here is the syntax:

```
return expression;
```

where the value of the expression is returned as the value of the function. For a function that does not return a value, use the return statement without the expression:

```
return;
```

The *switch* Statement

The switch statement performs a multiple branch, depending on the value of an expression. It has the following syntax:

```
switch (expression)
{
    case value1:
        statement_1
        break;
    case value2:
        statement_2
        break;
            .
            .
            .
    default:
        statement_default
}
```

If the expression being tested by switch evaluates to *value1*, *statement_1* is executed. If the expression is equal to *value2*, *statement_2* is executed. The value is compared with each case label and the statement following the matching label is executed. If the value does not match any of the case labels, the block *statement_default* following the `default` label is executed. Each statement ends with a `break` statement that separates the code of one `case` label from another. Here is a `switch` statement that calls different routines depending on the value of an integer variable named `cmd`:

```
switch (cmd)
{
    case 'q':
          quit_app(0);

          case 'c':
          connect();
          break;

    case 's':
          set_params();
          break;

    case '?':
    case 'H':
          print_help();
          break;

    default:
          printf("Unknown command!\n");
}
```

The *while* Statement

The `while` statement is used in this form:

```
while (expression) statement
```

where the *statement* is executed until the *expression* evaluates to 0. A `while` statement evaluates the expression before each execution of the statement. Thus, a `while` loop executes the statement zero or more times. Here is a `while` statement for copying one array to another:

```
i = length;
while (i >= 0)   /* Copy one array to another */
{
    array2[i] = array1[i];
    i--;
}
```

Functions

Functions are the building blocks of C programs. A *function* is a collection of declarations and statements. Each C program has at least one function: the `main` function. This is the function where the execution of a C program begins. The ANSI C library also comprises mostly functions, although it contains quite a few macros.

Function Prototypes

In ANSI C, you must declare a function before using it. The function declaration tells the compiler the type of value that the function returns and the number and type of arguments it takes. Most C programmers are used to declaring functions only when they return something other than an int because that is how Kernighan and Ritchie's definition of C works. For example, in the old UNIX C library, the memory allocation function `calloc` returns a pointer to a char (as you will see soon, the ANSI C version of `malloc` returns a void pointer). Thus, an old-style C program that uses `calloc` includes this declaration:

```
char *calloc();
```

You can continue to use this in ANSI C, but you can also declare a function as a complete *function prototype*, showing the return type as well as a list of arguments. The `calloc` function in the ANSI C library returns a void pointer and accepts two arguments, each of type size_t, which is an unsigned integer type of sufficient size to hold the value of the sizeof operator. Thus, the ANSI C prototype for `calloc` is the following:

```
void *calloc(size_t, size_t);
```

which shows the type of each argument in the argument list. You can also include an identifier for each argument and write the prototype as follows:

```
void *calloc(size_t num_elements, size_t elem_size);
```

In this case, the prototype looks exactly like the first line in the definition of the function, except that you stop short of defining the function and end the line with a semicolon. With well-chosen names for arguments, this form of prototype can provide a lot of information about the function's use. For example, one look at the prototype of `calloc` should tell you that its first argument is the number of elements to allocate, and the second one is the size of each element.

Prototypes also help the compiler check function arguments and generate code that may use a faster mechanism for passing arguments. From the prototype, the compiler can determine the exact number and type of arguments to expect. Therefore, the prototype enables the compiler to catch any mistakes you might make when calling a function, such as passing the wrong number of arguments (when the function takes a fixed number of arguments) or passing a wrong type of argument to a function.

The *void* Type

What do you do when a function does not return anything or accept any parameters? To handle these cases, ANSI C provides the void type, which is useful for declaring functions that return nothing and for describing pointers that can point to any type of data. For example, you can use the void return type to declare a function such as exit that does not return anything:

```
void exit(int status);
```

On the other hand, if a function doesn't accept any formal parameters, its list of arguments is represented by a void:

```
FILE *tmpfile(void);
```

The void pointer is useful for functions that work with blocks of memory. For example, when you request a certain number of bytes from the memory allocation routine malloc, you can use these locations to store any data that fits the space. In this case, the address of the first location of the allocated block of memory is returned as a void pointer. Thus, the prototype of malloc is the following:

```
void *malloc(size_t numbytes);
```

Functions with a Variable Number of Arguments

If a function accepts a variable number of arguments, you can indicate this by using an ellipsis (...) in place of the argument list; however, you must provide at least one argument before the ellipsis. A good example of such functions is the printf() family of functions defined in the header file STDIO.H. The prototypes of these functions are as follows:

```
int fprintf(FILE *stream, const char *format, ...);
int printf(const char *format, ...);
int sprintf(char *buffer, const char *format, ...);
```

As you can see, after a list of required arguments, the variable number of arguments is indicated by an ellipsis.

The ANSI C Library

The ANSI standard for C defines all aspects of C: the language, the preprocessor, and the library. The prototypes of the functions in the library, as well as all necessary data structures and preprocessor constants, are defined in a set of standard header files. Table 3.6 lists the standard header files, including a summary of their contents.

Table 3.6. Standard header files in ANSI C.

Header File	Purpose
ASSERT.H	Defines the assert macro; used for program diagnostics
CTYPE.H	Declares functions for classifying and converting characters
ERRNO.H	Defines macros for error conditions, EDOM and ERANGE, and the integer variable errno where library functions return an error code
FLOAT.H	Defines a range of values that can be stored in floating-point types

Header File	Purpose
LIMITS.H	Defines the limiting values of all integer data types
LOCALE.H	Declares the `lconv` structure and the functions necessary for customizing a C program to a particular locale
MATH.H	Declares math functions and the `HUGE_VAL` macro
SETJMP.H	Defines the `setjmp` and `longjmp` functions that can transfer control from one function to another without relying on normal function calls and returns; also defines the `jmp_buf` data type used by `setjmp` and `longjmp`
SIGNAL.H	Defines symbols and routines necessary for handling exceptional conditions
STDARG.H	Defines macros that provide access to the unnamed arguments in a function that accepts a varying number of arguments
STDDEF.H	Defines the standard data types `ptrdiff_t`, `size_t`, `wchar_t`; the symbol `NULL`; and the macro `offsetof`
STDIO.H	Declares the functions and data types necessary for input and output operations; defines macros such as `BUFSIZ`, `EOF`, `NULL`, `SEEK_CUR`, `SEEK_END`, and `SEEK_SET`
STDLIB.H	Declares many utility functions, such as the string conversion routines, random number generator, memory allocation routines, and process control routines (such as `abort`, `exit`, and `system`)
STRING.H	Declares the string manipulation routines, such as `strcmp` and `strcpy`
TIME.H	Defines data types and declares functions that manipulate time; defines the types `clock_t` and `time_t` and the `tm` data structure

Summary

One quick way to grasp C++'s seemingly new syntax is to learn ANSI standard C, because many features of C++ have been incorporated into ANSI standard C (officially known as ANSI X3.159 1989). For example, function prototypes, as well as `void` and `enum` types, appear in both ANSI C and C++. Because many syntactical details of C++ are similar to those of ANSI C, a knowledge of ANSI C is helpful when you write programs in C++. This chapter provides a quick overview of ANSI C.

4

Visual C++ 2.0 Extensions to Standard C

As its title indicates, Chapter 3 provides an "Overview of ANSI Standard C." Microsoft Visual C++ 2.0, however, adds a number of keywords, global variables, and predefined macros to support the unique needs of the 32-bit Windows (Win32) operating systems such as Windows NT. In addition to the compiler options summarized in Chapter 1, "The Visual C++ 2.0 Programming Environment," Visual C++ 2.0 also includes many keywords and compiler directives (called *pragmas*) to support 32-bit Windows programming. This chapter describes the keywords, pragmas, and preprocessor macros unique to Visual C++ 2.0. Other compiler-specific information, such as limits on the values of various data types, is also described in this chapter.

NOTE

This chapter describes the keywords, pragmas, and preprocessor macros that are unique to the Visual C++ 2.0 compiler and not part of ANSI standard C. The C++ language itself can be thought of as an extension of ANSI standard C, but C++ is not covered in this chapter. Chapters 5 through 13 teach C++ from the viewpoint of object-oriented programming.

Keywords Unique to Visual C++ 2.0

In Chapter 3, you learned the reserved keywords of ANSI C. The ANSI standard requires that compiler-specific reserved words start with two leading underscores. Visual C++ 2.0 follows this rule and defines 20 additional reserved words, each with two leading underscores. Table 4.1 summarizes these Microsoft-specific reserved words. The sections following this table briefly describe some of these keywords.

NOTE

With support for 32-bit Windows programming, Visual C++ 2.0 provides a flat 32-bit address space. Unlike older versions of Visual C++, you no longer have to worry about special keywords, such as __far, __huge, and __near, that were used to specify *memory models*—the term for the various ways in which a program's code and data are organized in memory under the segmented memory architecture that is prevalent under MS-DOS and 16-bit Windows 3.1.

Table 4.1. Microsoft-specific keywords.

Keyword	Purpose
__asm	Used to insert assembly language code in a C or C++ source file.
__based	Used as an address qualifier when declaring a data item or a function to indicate that the address of that item is the 32-bit offset from a specified 32-bit base pointer.
__cdecl	Used to indicate that the function or variable that follows uses the C naming and calling conventions (during function calls, arguments are pushed on the stack from right to left; names are case-sensitive and an underscore prefix is added to each name).
__declspec	Used to extend the storage class attribute of a variable. The syntax for using __declspec is the following: `__declspec( `*`attribute`*` ) `*`variable-declaration`* where *attribute* is one of four special storage attributes: `dllexport`, `dllimport`, `thread`, or `naked`
__fastcall	Indicates that a function uses a calling convention that passes arguments in the registers for faster function calls.
__fortran	Used to indicate that a function or variable uses the FORTRAN and Pascal naming and calling conventions (during function calls, arguments are pushed on the stack from left to right and names are converted to all uppercase).
__huge	Used to indicate that a data item must be addressed using 32-bit segment:offset address and that it may exceed 64K.

__except	Used with the __try keyword to handle error conditions (called exceptions) in Win32 programs. The syntax is as follows:
	
	`__try`
	`{`
	`/* A block of code */`
	`}`
	`__except (`*`expression`*`)`
	`{`
	`/* Exception-handling code */`
	`}`
	
	If an exception occurs in the block of code following the __try, the code after the __except clause is executed. The value of `expression` determines how the exception is handled. There are three possible values:

continues

Table 4.1. continued

Keyword	Purpose
	EXCEPTION_CONTINUE_EXECUTION means continue execution at the point where the exception occurred.
	EXCEPTION_CONTINUE_SEARCH means that the exception is not recognized. Continue to search up the stack for a handler, first for containing try-except statements, then for handlers with the next highest precedence.
	EXCEPTION_EXECUTE_HANDLER means recognize the exception and transfer control to the exception handling code following the __except statement, then resume execution at the point where the exception occurred.
	In C++ programs, you should use the C++ exception handling mechanism supported by the try, catch, and throw statements.
__fastcall	Indicates that a function uses a calling convention that passes arguments in the registers for faster function calls.
__finally	Used with the __try keyword to handle the error condition that occurs when a block of code is interrupted in a Win32 program. The syntax is as follows:

```
__try
{
/* A block of code */
}
__finally
{
/* Handle termination condition */
}
```

Keyword	Purpose
	If the block of code following the __try keyword is interrupted, the code after the __finally clause is executed.
	In C++ programs, you should use the C++ exception handling mechanism supported by the try, catch, and throw statements.
__inline	Causes the compiler to insert a copy of a function's body wherever the function is called (such functions are called inline functions and are used in both C and C++).
__int8, __int16, __int32	Used to declare 8-bit, 16-bit, and 32-bit integer variables, respectively. Note that __int8, __int16, and __int32 are synonymous with the data types char, short, and int, respectively.

Keyword	Purpose
__leave	Used within a __try-__finally statement block to jump to the end of the __try-__finally block. The termination handler is immediately executed.
__stdcall	Used to specify that the arguments of a function are pushed right to left, an underscore prefix is added to the name, and the string @*nnn* is appended to the name (*nnn* are digits denoting the size of the function's arguments in bytes). For a __stdcall function that takes a fixed number of arguments, the compiler generates code to pop the arguments off the stack before the function returns.
__try	Used with the __except and __finally keywords to handle error conditions in Win32 programs. In C++ programs, you should use the C++ exception handling mechanism supported by the try, catch, and throw statements.

Embedding Assembly Language Code in C and C++

The __asm keyword enables you to place assembly language statements directly inside a C or C++ program. You can place a single line of assembly language in your program by prefixing the statement with the __asm keyword:

```
// Assembly language statements—one per line
    __asm push    ebp
    __asm mov     ebp, esp
    __asm sub     esp, 4
```

If you prefer, you also can place both statements on a single line:

```
// Multiple __asm statements on a single line
    __asm push ebp __asm mov ebp, esp __asm sub esp, 4
```

You can embed a block of assembly language statements by enclosing them inside a pair of braces ({...}) and prefixing the block with the __asm keyword. For example, the preceding statements could be written as follows:

```
__asm      // An __asm block
{
    push    ebp
    mov     ebp, esp
    sub     esp, 4
}
```

The inline assembler supports a large subset of assembly language statements and directives available under MASM, the Microsoft Macro Assembler. You can reference C and C++ symbols including constants, macros, variables, and function names inside __asm blocks.

Predefined Global Variables and Preprocessor Macros

Microsoft Visual C++ 2.0 includes a number of predefined global variables in the C library. These variables contain important information, such as the DOS version number, the current operating system (DOS or Windows), and a pointer to the environment variables. You can refer to these global variables if you include the header file where they are declared. These global variables are automatically initialized when your program starts up. Table 4.2 lists the predefined global variables in Visual C++ 2.0.

Table 4.2. Predefined global variables in Visual C++ 2.0.

Name	*Type, Declaration, and Purpose*
`_amblksiz`	Type: `unsigned` Declared in: MALLOC.H This variable controls how memory is obtained from the operating system for eventual allocation by the library functions such as `malloc` and `calloc`. The memory allocation functions request memory from the operating system in chunks of the size specified by the value of the `_amblksiz` variable. The default value is 8,192 bytes (or 8K).
`_daylight`	Type: `int` Declared in: TIME.H This variable has a nonzero value if a daylight saving time zone is specified in the TZ environment variable; otherwise, the variable has a zero value. This variable is used when converting local time to Greenwich Mean Time (also known as Universal Coordinated Time or by its French acronym, UTC).
`_doserrno`	Type: `int` Declared in: STDLIB.H This variable contains the error code returned by the last operating system I/O call.
`_environ`	Type: `char *_environ[];` Declared in: STDLIB.H This is an array of pointers to strings that constitute the environment of the current program. You can directly access the environment variables through this array. The library functions `getenv` and `_putenv` use the `_environ` array.
`errno`	Type: `int` Declared in: STDLIB.H This variable is set to an error code corresponding to the last error in a system level call.

Name	Type, Declaration, and Purpose
_fileinfo	Type: `int` Declared in: STDLIB.H This variable controls whether information about open files is passed to new processes. The default value of `_fileinfo` is zero, which means that information about open files is not passed to new processes.
_fmode	Type: `int` Declared in: STDLIB.H This variable controls the default file translation mode. The default value is `_O_TEXT`, which means files are translated in the text mode.
_osver	Type: `unsigned int` Declared in: STDLIB.H This value contains the build number of Windows NT.
_pgmptr	Type: `extern char *_pgmptr;` Declared in: STDLIB.H The `_pgmptr` variable is automatically initialized at startup to point to the drive, path, and filename of the program.
_sys_errlist	Type: `char *_sys_errlist[];` Declared in: STDLIB.H This variable comprises an array of strings, each corresponding to a system error message.
_sys_nerr	Type: `int` Declared in: STDLIB.H This variable contains the total number of strings in the `_sys_errlist` array.
_timezone	Type: `long` Declared in: TIME.H This variable contains the difference in seconds between Universal Coordinated Time and the local time.
_tzname	Type: `char *_tzname[2];` Declared in: TIME.H This is an array of two null-terminated strings, with `_tzname[0]` set to the three-letter time zone name (for example, EST or PST) and `_tzname[1]` set to the name of the daylight saving time zone.
_wenviron	Type: `wchar_t *_environ[];` Declared in: STDLIB.H This is a wide-character version of `_environ` that can be accessed through the library functions `_wgetenv` and `_wputenv`.

continues

Table 4.2. continued

Name	Type, Declaration, and Purpose
_winmajor	Type: `unsigned int` Declared in: STDLIB.H This variable contains the major version number of the operating system. For Windows NT 3.1, `_winmajor` is 3.
_winminor	Type: `unsigned int` Declared in: STDLIB.H This variable contains the minor version number of the operating system. For Windows NT 3.1, `_winminor` is 10 (because the minor version number is specified with a trailing zero).
_winver	Type: `unsigned int` Declared in: STDLIB.H This variable holds the value of `_winmajor` in high byte and the value of `_winminor` in low byte. For Windows NT 3.1, the value of `_winver` is 0x30A (value in the high-order byte is 3; value in the low-order byte is hexadecimal 0A, which is decimal 10).
_wpgmptr	Type: `extern wchar_t *_wpgmptr;` Declared in: STDLIB.H This variable is the wide-character counterpart of `_pgmptr` for programs that use `wmain` as its main function.

The Visual C++ 2.0 preprocessor also defines a number of macros (symbols) that you can use in your source files without defining them. As explained in Chapter 3, ANSI C also contains a number of preprocessor macros that are predefined. In addition to these ANSI standard preprocessor macros, Visual C++ 2.0 defines the additional macros listed in Table 4.3. You can use these macros to compile sections of code based on conditions, such as the processor type and the memory model being used.

Table 4.3. Microsoft-specific predefined preprocessor macros in Visual C++ 2.0.

Symbol	Purpose
_CHAR_UNSIGNED	Defined when the /J option is used. When this macro is defined, the default type of `char` is assumed to be `unsigned`.
__cplusplus	Defined when the compiler is compiling a C++ program.
_CPPUNWIND	Defined for code compiled with Enable Exception Handling (/GX).
_DLL	Defined when the /MD option is specified so that the program can use the multithreaded DLL version of the runtime library.

Symbol	Purpose
_M_IX86	Defined as 300 for the 80386 processor (/G3), 400 for the 80486 processor (/G4), and 500 for the Pentium processor (/G5). The default definition is 400, corresponding to the default option of /GB for Blend.
_MSC_VER	Defined as the version of the compiler. Defined as 900 for Microsoft Visual C++ 2.0. This macro is always defined. (Remember that Microsoft's C/C++ compiler prior to Visual C++ 1.0 was called Microsoft C/C++ 7.0. Thus, Visual C++ 1.0 should have been version 8.0 and Visual C++ 2.0, version 9.0).
_MT	Defined when command-line option /MD or /MT is specified to use multithreaded version of runtime libraries.
_WIN32	Always defined for Win32 applications.

Pragmas

You can use the `#pragma` preprocessor directive to instruct the C compiler to turn on or off specific features. Pragmas vary from one compiler to another. The following is a list of pragmas supported by the Microsoft Visual C++ 2.0. compiler:

◼ `#pragma alloc_text("`*sname*`",` *function1, function2,* `...)`

Instructs the compiler to place the functions *function1, function2,* and so on, in the code section named *sname.* The name of the code section should be enclosed in double quotes. The `alloc_text` pragma applies to C functions only.

◼ `#pragma auto_inline(on)` or `#pragma auto_inline(off)`

Turns on or off the inline expansion of functions.

◼ `#pragma check_stack(on)` or `#pragma check_stack(off)`

Turns on or off the generation of stack checking code; also see compiler option /Gs in Chapter 1.

◼ `#pragma code_seg([`"*sname*"`[,`"*sclass*"`]])`

Specifies the name of a code section where all subsequent functions are allocated.

◼ `#pragma comment(`*comment_type*`[,` *comment_string*`])`

Places a comment record in an object file. (Please consult the online help in the Visual C++ 2.0 compiler for more information.)

◼ `#pragma data_seg([`"*sname*"`[,`"*sclass*"`]])`

Specifies the name and, optionally, the class of a data section where all subsequent data are allocated.

■   `#pragma function(func1[, func2, ...])`

Instructs the compiler to generate function calls rather than using the intrinsic forms of the functions named `func1`, `func2`, and so on.

■   `#pragma hdrstop[("filename")]`

When used with the `/YX` or `/Yc` options, the compiler saves the state of the compilation up to the location of the `hdrstop` pragma in the specified file. The compiler does not save the compiled state of any code that follows the pragma.

■   `#pragma include_alias( "long_filename", "short_filename" )`

Specifies that `short_filename` be used as an alias for `long_filename`. Whenever the compiler encounters the `long_filename`, it substitutes `short_filename`, and looks for the header file named `short_filename` instead. This pragma must appear before any `#include` directives that use the `long_filename`.

■   `#pragma inline_depth(level)`

Controls the number of times inline expansion can occur when an inline function is called recursively. The argument `level` is a number between 0 and 255. This pragma takes effect with the `/Ob1` or `/Ob2` options only.

■   `#pragma inline_recursion(on)` or `#pragma inline_recursion(off)`

Turns on or off recursive expansion of inline functions. This pragma takes effect with the `/Ob1` or `/Ob2` options only.

■   `#pragma intrinsic(func1, [func2,...])`

Instructs the compiler to use the intrinsic forms of the functions named `func1`, `func2`, and so on. For intrinsic functions, the compiler places the function's code directly at the point where the function is called. This results in faster execution because you do not incur the overhead of a function call. This is also controlled by the `/Oi` option.

■   `#pragma message(message_string)`

Directs the compiler to display the `message string` to the standard output during compilation.

■   `#pragma optimize("optimization_flags", on)` or `#pragma optimize("optimization_flags", off)`

Turns on or off the specified optimization flags. This pragma must appear outside a function.

■   `#pragma pack(n)`

Packs structures for alignment at multiples of the number of bytes specified by the integer *n*, which can be 1, 2, 4, 8, or 16. Structure packing is also selected by compiler option `/Zp`.

■   `#pragma setlocale("locale_string")`

Defines the locale (country and language) to be used when translating wide-character constants and string literals. The default *locale_string* is "C".

■ `#pragma warning(warning_specifier:warning_numbers)`

Specifies how the compiler should treat warnings. The *warning_specifier* and their meanings are as follows:

`once`	Display only once
`default`	Apply the default behavior
`1, 2, 3, 4`	Apply the specified warning level
`disable`	Ignore the specified warnings
`error`	Treat the specified warnings as errors

warning_numbers is a list of warning numbers separated by whitespace.

Size and Capacity of Basic Data Types

The size and numerical limits of several standard C data types depend on the compiler. Following the ANSI standard requirement, Visual C++ 2.0 provides the numerical limits of integer and floating-point variables in the header files LIMITS.H and FLOAT.H, respectively. Table 4.4 provides a combined listing of the size and numerical limits of the standard C data types.

NOTE

In Microsoft Visual C++ 2.0, an `int` variable is 4 bytes. In earlier versions of Visual C++, an `int` variable is only 2 bytes.

Table 4.4. Sizes and numerical limits of basic data types in Visual C++ 2.0.

Type Name	Storage Size in Bytes	Range of Values
`char`	1	-128 to 127
`int`	4	-2,147,483,648 to 2,147,483,647
`short`	2	-32,768 to 32,767
`long`	4	-2,147,483,648 to 2,147,483,647
`unsigned char`	1	0 to 255
`unsigned`	4	0 to 4,294,967,295
`unsigned short`	2	0 to 65,535
`unsigned long`	4	0 to 4,294,967,295

continues

Table 4.4. continued

Type Name	Storage Size in Bytes	Range of Values
enum	4	-2,147,483,648 to 2,147,483,647
float	4	Approximately 3.4E-38 to 3.4E+38 with 7-digit precision
double	8	Approximately 1.7E-308 to 1.7E+308 with 15-digit precision
long double	10	Approximately 1.2E-4932 to 1.2E+4932 with 19-digit precision

Knowing the size and numerical limits of the data types can help you decide the type of variable you want for a specific purpose. For example, rather than using a 4-byte int for a variable with values between 0 and 255, you can use an unsigned char. Similarly, 4-byte float variables might be sufficient where you otherwise use an 8-byte double variable.

Note that the size of the int data type can be a problem for C or C++ code that might otherwise be portable. For instance, int used to be a 2-byte data type in earlier versions of Visual C++, but in Visual C++ 2.0, an int occupies 4 bytes and is the same as a long. This size difference can create subtle problems when you move Visual C++ 1.0 code to Visual C++ 2.0. One way to minimize these problems is to use short where you need 2-byte storage and long where you need a 4-byte data type.

Summary

To support 32-bit Microsoft Windows environments fully, Visual C++ 2.0 includes a number of reserved keywords in addition to those required by ANSI standard C. Many of these keywords are necessary to support the segmented memory-addressing scheme used by the Intel 80x86 microprocessors in MS-DOS systems.

This chapter also describes a number of predefined global variables, preprocessor macros, and compiler directives or pragmas that enable your programs to take full advantage of the capabilities of Visual C++ 2.0.

II

Object-Oriented Programming

5

Basics of Object-Oriented Programming

Part I, "Getting Started with Visual C++ 2.0," provided an overview of the tools that Visual C++ 2.0 offers for writing programs in C and C++. Part II covers object-oriented programming (OOP).

Object-oriented programming is not new; its underlying concepts—data abstraction, inheritance, and polymorphism—have been around for quite some time (for example, in languages such as Simula67 and Smalltalk). What's new is the increasing interest in OOP among programmers in general and C programmers in particular. One of the reasons for this growing appeal is the popularity of the C++ programming language, which improves C (the current language of choice among software developers) by introducing several new programming constructs that directly support object-oriented techniques. If you program in C, you will find it reasonably easy to learn the syntax of C++, but you need to reorient your thinking if you want to use object-oriented techniques in your programs.

The best way to learn C++ is to understand the basic concepts of OOP and see how C++ supports OOP. This book uses this approach, explaining OOP through examples, and at the same time, teaching the C++ programming language by explaining its features and their relationships to OOP. This chapter begins by exploring the basic terminology of OOP. Examples show how you can apply object-oriented techniques in C. Chapter 6, "C++ and Object-Oriented Programming," furnishes you with an overview of C++ with an emphasis on OOP. Chapter 6 also revisits the examples of this chapter rewritten in C++. Seeing the examples again illustrates how an object-oriented programming language such as C++ makes it easy to apply object-oriented methods.

What Is Object-Oriented Programming?

The term *object-oriented programming (OOP)* is widely used, but experts do not agree on its exact definition. However, most of them agree that OOP involves defining *abstract data types (ADTs)*, which represent complex real-world or abstract objects, and organizing your program around these ADTs with an eye toward exploiting their common features. The term *data abstraction* refers to the process of defining ADTs, whereas *inheritance* and *polymorphism* refer to the mechanisms that enable you to take advantage of the common characteristics of the ADTs (the *objects* in OOP). These terms are explored in this chapter.

The term abstract data type refers to a programmer-defined data type together with a set of operations that can be performed on that data. It is called abstract to distinguish it from the fundamental built-in C data types, such as int, char, and double. In C, you can define an ADT by using typedef and struct and implementing the operations with a set of functions. As you will soon learn, C++ has much better facilities for defining and using ADTs.

Remember these two points:

■ First, OOP is a method only of designing and implementing software. Use of object-oriented techniques does not add anything to a finished software product that the user can see. However, as a programmer implementing the software, you can gain a significant advantage by using object-oriented methods, especially in large software projects. Because OOP enables you to remain close to the conceptual, higher-level model of the real-world problem you are trying to solve, you can manage its complexity better than with approaches that force you to map the problem to fit the features of the language. You can take advantage of the modularity of objects and implement the program in relatively independent units that are easier to maintain and extend. You also can share code among objects through inheritance.

■ Second, OOP has nothing to do with any programming language, although a programming language that supports OOP makes it easier to implement the object-oriented techniques. As you will learn shortly, with some discipline you can use objects in C programs.

Procedure-Oriented Programming

Before you jump into OOP, take a look at conventional procedure-oriented programming in a language such as C. In the procedure-oriented approach, you view a problem as a sequence of things to do. You organize the related data items into C structs and write the necessary functions (procedures) to manipulate the data. In the process, you complete the sequence of tasks that solves your problem. Although the data may be organized into structures, the primary focus is on the functions. Each C function transforms data in some way. For example, one function may calculate the average value of a set of numbers, another may compute the square root of a number, and another may print a string. You don't need to look far to find examples of this kind of programming—C function libraries are implemented this way. Each function in a library performs a well-defined operation on its input arguments and returns the transformed data as a return value. Arguments may be pointers to data that the function directly alters, or the function may display graphics on a video monitor.

An Example in C

For a better understanding of procedure-oriented programming, suppose that you want to write a computer program that works with geometric shapes such as rectangles and circles. The program should be able to draw any shape and compute its area. This section takes a conventional approach to writing such a program.

As shown in Figure 5.1, you can break down the tasks of the program into two procedures: one to draw a shape and the other to compute its area. Call each function with a single argument—a pointer to a data structure that contains a shape's pertinent information, such as coordinates of a circle's center and its radius. For each geometric shape, it is easy to define an appropriate structure, but how do you reconcile these different structures into a single one? After all, the functions need a pointer to a *single* data structure. In such cases, a common technique is to combine the different structures into one using a C union with an additional integer flag to indicate the exact shape being handled by the union. In keeping with common C coding style, you should define these data types in a header file, CSHAPES.H, as shown in Listing 5.1. The resulting data type, SHAPE, is graphically illustrated in Figure 5.1.

FIGURE 5.1.

C data and procedures for handling geometric shapes.

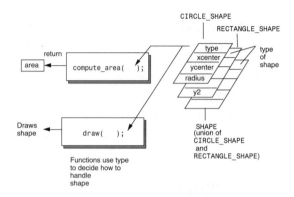

Listing 5.1. CSHAPES.H. Definition of data types for shapes.

```
/*------------------------------------------------------------*/
/*  File:  cshapes.h
 *
 *  Defines data types for manipulating geometric shapes
 *  in C
 */
#ifndef CSHAPES_H      /* Used to avoid including file twice */
#define CSHAPES_H

#include <math.h>      /* For declaration of fabs          */

#define M_PI        3.14159265358979323846 /* Value of "Pi" */

#define T_CIRCLE    1
#define T_RECTANGLE 2

/* Define each individual shape's data structure */

typedef struct CIRCLE_SHAPE
{
    short   type;    /* Type of shape (T_CIRCLE)    */
    double  x, y;    /* Coordinates of center       */
    double  radius;  /* Radius of circle            */
} CIRCLE_SHAPE;

typedef struct RECTANGLE_SHAPE
{
    short   type;    /* Type of shape (T_RECTANGLE) */
    double  x1, y1;  /* Coordinates of the corners  */
    double  x2, y2;
} RECTANGLE_SHAPE;

/* Now define a union of the two structures */

typedef union SHAPE
{
    short           type;      /* type of shape    */
```

```
    CIRCLE_SHAPE    circle;     /* data for circle   */
    RECTANGLE_SHAPE rectangle;  /* data for rectangle*/
} SHAPE;

/* Function prototypes */

double compute_area(SHAPE *p_shape);
void   draw(SHAPE *p_shape);

#endif   /* #ifndef CSHAPES_H   */
```

The data structure for each shape is essentially a block of memory. Because the members of a C union all share the same block of memory, you need a way to determine which member is valid at any time. This example does so by declaring the first field in the union SHAPE as a short integer denoting the type of the shape. Knowing the type, you can access the right structure in the union to extract information about the shape. The code in Listing 5.2 shows how the structures in the union SHAPE are used.

Once the data structures are defined, you can start writing the functions that operate on the data. In fact, as required by ANSI standard C, the CSHAPES.H header file already includes the prototypes for the functions compute_area and draw_shape. Listing 5.2 shows the implementation of these functions. The functions are straightforward; a switch statement is used to handle each shape individually.

Listing 5.2. CSHAPES.C. Functions for geometric shapes.

```
/*-------------------------------------------------------------*/
/*  File: cshapes.c
 *
 *  C functions to operate on geometric shapes.
 */
#include <stdio.h>
#include "cshapes.h"

/*-------------------------------------------------------------*/
/*  c o m p u t e _ a r e a
 *
 *  Compute the area of the shape and return the area
 */
double compute_area(SHAPE *p_shape)
{
    double area;

/* Handle each shape according to its type */

    switch(p_shape->type)
    {
        case T_CIRCLE:
            area = M_PI * p_shape->circle.radius
                        * p_shape->circle.radius;
            break;
```

continues

Listing 5.2. continued

```
        case T_RECTANGLE:
            area = fabs(
                (p_shape->rectangle.x2 - p_shape->rectangle.x1) *
                (p_shape->rectangle.y2 - p_shape->rectangle.y1));
            break;

        default:  printf("Unknown shape in 'compute_area'!\n");
    }
    return area;
}
/*-----------------------------------------------------------*/
/*  d r a w
 *
 *  "Draw" a shape (print information about shape)
 */
void draw(SHAPE *p_shape)
{
/* Handle each shape according to its type */
    printf("Draw: ");
    switch(p_shape->type)
    {
        case T_CIRCLE:
            printf("Circle of radius %f at (%f, %f)\n",
                    p_shape->circle.radius,
                    p_shape->circle.x, p_shape->circle.y);
            break;

        case T_RECTANGLE:
            printf("Rectangle with corners:"
                    " (%f, %f) at (%f, %f)\n",
                    p_shape->rectangle.x1,
                    p_shape->rectangle.y1,
                    p_shape->rectangle.x2,
                    p_shape->rectangle.y2);
            break;

        default:  printf("Unknown shape in 'draw'!\n");
    }
}
```

To keep the program simple, this example does not proceed with the steps that actually display the shapes on a particular graphics device. Rather, the draw function merely prints the name, location, and size of the shape. The compute_area function uses a standard formula to compute the area and return the result.

You can test these functions with the simple program STEST1.C, shown in Listing 5.3. This program defines an array of two shapes and initializes them. It then computes the area of each shape and "draws" it. In a more realistic implementation, you might include utility functions such as create_circle and create_rectangle to allocate and initialize a SHAPE union dynamically and return a pointer to it.

Listing 5.3. STEST1.C. Program to test shape-manipulation functions.

```c
/*-------------------------------------------------------------*/
/*  File:   stest1.c
 *
 *  Program to test shape handling functions of Listing 5.2.
 *  Compile and link with the file shown in Listing 5.1
 */
#include <stdio.h>
#include "cshapes.h"

int main()
{
    int i;
    SHAPE s[2];

/* Initialize the shapes */

/* A 40x20 rectangle with lower-left corner at (80,30) */
    s[0].type = T_RECTANGLE;
    s[0].rectangle.x1 = 80.0;
    s[0].rectangle.y1 = 30.0;
    s[0].rectangle.x2 = 120.0;
    s[0].rectangle.y2 = 50.0;

/* A circle at (200.0, 100.0) of radius 50.0 units */
    s[1].type = T_CIRCLE;
    s[1].circle.x = 200.0;
    s[1].circle.y = 100.0;
    s[1].circle.radius = 50.0;

/* Compute the areas... */
    for(i = 0; i < 2; i++)
        printf("Area of shape[%d] = %f\n", i,
                            compute_area(&s[i]));

/* Draw the shapes... */
    for(i = 0; i < 2; i++) draw(&s[i]);
    return 0;
}
```

You can build the STEST1.C program by compiling and linking the files shown in Listings 5.2 and 5.3. In the Visual WorkBench, create a new project (with Console Application as the project type) and add the files STEST1.C and CSHAPES.C to the project. Then select the Build option from the Project menu to create the executable file STEST1.EXE (for more information on Visual Workbench, consult Chapter 1, The Visual C++ 2.0 Programming Environment). Another way to build STEST1.EXE is to enter the following at the command prompt in a command window:

```
cl stest1.c cshapes.c
```

When you run STEST1.EXE (you can run it by entering stest1 in a command window), it produces the following output:

```
Area of shape[0] = 800.000000
Area of shape[1] = 7853.981634
Draw: Rectangle with corners: (80.000000, 30.000000) at (120.000000, 50.000000)
Draw: Circle of radius 50.000000 at (200.000000, 100.000000)
```

Even though this example is somewhat contrived, it does embody the general style of procedure-oriented programming in C. Programmers design data structures first, and then write procedures to manipulate the data. The usual practice is to handle different types of related data (such as the geometric shapes of circle and rectangle) by switch statements.

Adding a New Shape

Some problems do exist with conventional procedure-oriented programming. Consider what happens when you want your program to handle another type of geometric shape—a triangle, for example. To do this, you must follow these steps:

1. Define a data structure for triangles. If you choose to represent the triangle by the coordinates of its vertices, you might add the following structure to the CSHAPES.H file (Listing 5.1):

```
#define T_TRIANGLE  3


 typedef struct TRIANGLE_SHAPE
{
    short   type;    /* Type of shape (T_TRIANGLE)   */
    double  x1, y1;  /* Coordinates of the corners   */
    double  x2, y2;
    double  x3, y3;
} TRIANGLE_SHAPE;
```

2. Add a new member to the SHAPE union to reflect the addition of the new shape:

```
typedef union SHAPE
{
    short            type;      /* type of shape     */
    CIRCLE_SHAPE     circle;    /* data for circle   */
    RECTANGLE_SHAPE rectangle;  /* data for rectangle*/
    TRIANGLE_SHAPE   triangle;  /* data for triangle */
} SHAPE;
```

3. In the CSHAPES.C file (Listing 5.2), add code in the functions compute_area and draw to handle triangles. Specifically, you need to add additional case statements in the switch statement for each function, as in the following example:

```
/*  In the compute_area function  */
```

```
    double compute_area(SHAPE *p_shape)
{
    double area;

/* Handle each shape according to its type */
    switch(p_shape->type)
    {
        .

        .

        case T_TRIANGLE:
        {
            double x21, y21, x31, y31;

            x21 =  p_shape->triangle.x2 - p_shape->triangle.x1;
            y21 =  p_shape->triangle.y2 - p_shape->triangle.y1;
            x31 =  p_shape->triangle.x3 - p_shape->triangle.x1;
            y31 =  p_shape->triangle.y3 - p_shape->triangle.y1;

            area = fabs(y21 * x31 - x21 * y31) / 2.0;
        }

        break;
        .

        .

    }

/*------------------------------------------------------------*/
/* In function: draw() */
void draw(SHAPE *p_shape)
{
    printf("Draw: ");
    switch(p_shape->type)
    {
        .

        .

        case T_TRIANGLE:
            printf("Triangle with vertices: "
                    "(%f, %f) (%f, %f) (%f, %f)\n",
                    p_shape->triangle.x1, p_shape->triangle.y1,
                    p_shape->triangle.x2, p_shape->triangle.y2,
                    p_shape->triangle.x3, p_shape->triangle.y3);
            break;
```

.

.

```
        }
    }
```

4. Test operations on the triangle shape. For example, you can define a triangle shape and use it in STEST1.C by changing it as follows:

```
    SHAPE s[3];
    s[2].type = T_TRIANGLE;
    s[2].triangle.x1 = 100.0;
    s[2].triangle.y1 = 100.0;
    s[2].triangle.x2 = 200.0;
    s[2].triangle.y2 = 100.0;
    s[2].triangle.x3 = 150.0;
    s[2].triangle.y3 = 50.0;
/* Compute the area... */
    printf("Area of triangle = %f\n", compute_area(&s[2]));

/* Draw the triangle... */
    draw(&s[2]);
```

This exercise illustrates the types of changes you must make when a new data type—a new object—is added to an existing program that is written in conventional procedure-oriented style. Notice that you have to edit working code—the `switch` statements in the `compute_area` and `draw` functions—when you want to handle triangles in addition to the rectangles and circles that the program was originally designed to accept. If this were a realistic program with many files, a change such as this requires you to edit `switch` statements in most of the files. The object-oriented approach avoids this problem by keeping data structures together with the functions that operate on them. This effectively localizes the changes that become necessary when you decide to add a new object to your program. This is one of the benefits of OOP.

Object-Oriented Programming Terminology

As mentioned earlier, there are three basic underlying concepts in OOP:

- ■ Data abstraction
- ■ Inheritance
- ■ Polymorphism

Individually, these concepts have been known and used before, but their use as the foundation of OOP is new.

Data Abstraction

To understand data abstraction, consider the file I/O routines in the C runtime library. With these routines, you can view the file as a stream of bytes, and you also can perform various operations on this stream by calling the file I/O routines. For example, you can call `fopen` to open a file, `fclose` to close it, `fgetc` to read a character from it, and `fputc` to write a character to it. This abstract model of a file is implemented by defining a data type named `FILE` to hold all relevant information about a file. The C constructs `struct` and `typedef` are used to define `FILE`. You find the definition of `FILE` in the header file stdio.h. You can think of this definition of `FILE`, together with the functions that operate on it, as a new data type just like C's `int` or `char`.

To use the `FILE` data type, you do not have to know the C data structure that defines it. In fact, the underlying data structure of `FILE` can vary from one system to another. Yet, the C file I/O routines work in the same manner on all systems. This is possible because you never access the members of the `FILE` data structure directly. Rather, you rely on the functions and macros that essentially hide the inner details of `FILE`. This is known as *data hiding*.

Data abstraction combines the process of defining a data type, often called an abstract data type (ADT), with data hiding. The definition of an ADT involves specifying the internal representation of the ADT's data as well as the functions that other program modules use to manipulate the ADT. Data hiding ensures that you can alter the internal structure of the ADT without breaking the programs that call the functions operating on that ADT. Thus, C's `FILE` data type is an example of an ADT (see Figure 5.2).

FIGURE 5.2.
C's FILE data type as an example of an ADT.

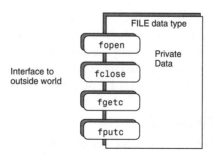

Objects, Classes, and Methods

In OOP, you create an object from an ADT. Essentially, an ADT is a collection of variables and the functions necessary to operate on those variables. The variables represent the information contained in the object, whereas the functions define the operations that can be performed on that object. You can think of the ADT as a template from which specific instances of objects can be created as needed. The term *class* is often used for this template; consequently, a class is synonymous with an ADT. In fact, C++ provides the `class` declaration precisely for defining an ADT—the template from which objects are created. The ADT is a template for objects in the sense that creating an object involves setting aside a block of memory for the variables of that object.

The functions that operate on an object are known as *methods*. This term comes from the object-oriented language Smalltalk. Methods define the behavior of an object. In C++, methods are called the *member functions* of the class.

Another common OOP concept also originated in Smalltalk—the idea of *sending a message* to an object, which directs it to perform an operation by invoking one of the methods. In C++, you do this by calling the appropriate member function of the object. For objects implemented in C, you can send a message by calling a function that accepts a pointer to a data structure representing the ADT's internal structure. Of course, the function must be capable of handling the operation you want. For example, C's file I/O routines accept a pointer to the FILE structure as an argument. The file I/O routines then use that pointer to identify the file on which the I/O operation will be performed.

Inheritance

Data abstraction does not cover one important characteristic of objects: real-world objects do not exist in isolation. Each object is related to one or more other objects. In fact, you can often describe a new kind of object by pointing out how the new object's characteristics and behavior differ from that of a class of objects that already exists. This is what you do when you describe an object with a sentence such as "B is just like A, except that B has...and B does...." Here, you are defining objects of type B in terms of those of type A.

This notion of defining a new object in terms of an old one is an integral part of OOP. The term inheritance is used for this concept because you can think of one class of objects inheriting the data and behavior from another class. Inheritance imposes a hierarchical relationship on classes wherein a child class inherits from its parent. In C++ terminology, the parent class is the *base class*, and the child class is the *derived class*.

Multiple Inheritance

A real-world object often exhibits characteristics that it inherits from more than one type of object. For example, you can classify a lion as a carnivore on the basis of its eating habits or as a mammal on the basis of its biological class. When modeling a corporation, you may want to describe a technical manager as someone who is an engineer as well as a manager. An example from the programming world is a full-screen text editor. It displays a block of text on-screen, and it also stores the text in an internal buffer so that you can perform operations (such as inserting a character, deleting a character, and so on). Thus, you may want to say that a text editor inherits its behavior from two classes: a *text buffer class* and a *text display class* that, for example, manages a text display area that is 80 characters by 25 lines.

These examples illustrate *multiple inheritance*—the idea that a class can be derived from more than one base class. Many object-oriented programming languages do not support multiple inheritance, but C++ does.

Polymorphism

In a literal sense, polymorphism means the quality of having more than one form. In the context of OOP, polymorphism means that a single operation can behave differently in different objects. In other words, different objects can react differently to the same message. For example, consider the operation of addition. For two numbers, addition should generate the sum. In a programming language that supports OOP, you should be able to express the operation of addition with a single operator: a plus sign (+). When this is supported, you can use the expression x+y to denote the sum of x and y for many different types of x and y: integers, floating-point numbers, and complex numbers, to name a few. You can even define the + operation to mean the concatenation of two strings.

Similarly, suppose a number of geometric shapes all respond to the message draw. Each object reacts to this message by displaying its shape on a display screen. Obviously, the actual mechanism for displaying the object differs from one shape to another, but all shapes perform this task in response to the same message.

Polymorphism helps by enabling you to simplify the syntax that performs the same operation on a collection of objects. For example, by exploiting polymorphism, you can compute the area of each geometric shape in an array of shapes with a simple loop such as this:

```
/* Assume "shapes" is an array of shapes (rectangles, circles,
 * etc.) and "compute_area" is a function that computes the
 * area of a shape
 */
for (i = 0; i < number_of_shapes; i++)
    area_of_shape = shapes[i].compute_area();
```

The program can do this because, regardless of the exact geometric shape, each object supports the compute_area function and computes the area in a way appropriate for that shape.

Object-Oriented Programming in C

Once you know the basic concepts of OOP, it isn't difficult to implement them in a C program, provided you have identified the objects and what they do. Deciding how to organize your software around objects—physical or abstract—falls under the topic of object-oriented analysis and design. The remainder of this chapter uses the geometric shapes as an example and shows one way to handle these shapes using object-oriented techniques.

Defining Objects in C

To illustrate the use of OOP techniques in C, consider the example of the geometric shapes introduced earlier in this chapter to explain procedural programming. The task is to write a computer program that handles geometric shapes such as rectangles and circles. The program should draw any shape and compute its area.

To implement the program using objects, you should first work out the details of how to support message handling and inheritance. Figure 5.3 gives an overview of the data structures you can use to implement the objects.

FIGURE 5.3.

Data structures for OOP in C.

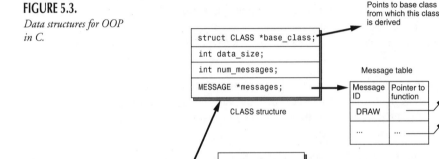

An easy way to handle messages is to assign each message an identifier (ID). You can associate each message ID with the pointer to a function that handles the message. To maintain this association, you can use a data structure such as this MESSAGE structure:

```
typedef struct MESSAGE
{
    int  message_id;          /* Message identifier        */
    int  (*message_handler)(); /* Function to handle message */
} MESSAGE;
```

With this definition of MESSAGE, a program can handle messages for a class by maintaining an array of MESSAGE structures (you can think of this as a table of messages). To exploit inheritance, each class data structure needs a pointer to the base class. This pointer will be NULL for any class not derived from anything. Thus, a possible declaration of the CLASS data structure is as follows:

```
typedef struct CLASS
{
    struct CLASS *base_class;  /* Pointer to "base" class */
    int          data_size;    /* Size of instance's data */
    int          num_messages; /* Number of messages      */
    MESSAGE      *messages;     /* Table of messages       */
} CLASS;
```

Later on, you will see a utility function that sends messages to objects. That function handles the messages by searching the `messages` array for an entry with a matching message ID and by calling the function with the pointer that is stored in that entry. You can implement inheritance by sending unprocessed messages to the base class through the `base_class` pointer.

Because the `CLASS` structure has only one base class, this implementation does not support multiple inheritance. If you want multiple inheritance, you must make room for more than one base class, perhaps through an array of pointers in place of the lone `base_class` pointer in the `CLASS` structure.

The `CLASS` structure can facilitate the handling of messages sent to an object, but it cannot accommodate the object's data. This is because each object has its own data. In other words, a single copy of the class structure can serve all the objects of that class, but each object must have room for its own data. You can handle this by defining a data structure specifically meant to hold the instance-specific data of an object:

```
typedef struct OBJECT
{
    void  *p_data;  /* Data for an instance of the object */
    CLASS *p_class; /* Pointer to the class structure     */
} OBJECT;
```

As you can see, this `OBJECT` data structure holds a pointer to its data and a pointer to its class so that messages can be processed by consulting the message table in the class. The function responsible for creating an object also allocates room for the object's data and saves the pointer in the p_data field of the `OBJECT` structure. The data_size variable in the `CLASS` structure represents the number of bytes of memory needed for an object's data.

The file SHAPEOBJ.H shown in Listing 5.4 declares the necessary data structures and functions in this scheme of implementing objects in C.

Listing 5.4. SHAPEOBJ.H. Definition of shapes in an example of OOP in C.

```
/*  File:   shapeobj.h
 *
 *  Header file with definitions of shapes for
 *  an example of object-oriented programming in C.
 *
 */

#if !defined(SHAPEOBJ_H)
#define SHAPEOBJ_H
```

continues

Listing 5.4. continued

```c
#include <stdio.h>
#include <stdlib.h>    /* For mem. alloc routines     */
#include <stdarg.h>    /* For variable no. of arguments */
#include <math.h>      /* For declaration of fabs     */

#define M_PI        3.14159265358979323846 /* Value of "Pi" */

typedef struct MESSAGE
{
    int  message_id;              /* Message identifier        */
    int  (*message_handler)(); /* Function to handle message */
} MESSAGE;

typedef struct CLASS
{
    struct CLASS *base_class;  /* Pointer to "base" class */
    int          data_size;    /* Size of instance's data */
    int          num_messages; /* Number of messages      */
    MESSAGE      *messages;     /* Table of messages       */
} CLASS;

typedef struct OBJECT
{
    void   *p_data;  /* Data for an instance of the object */
    CLASS  *p_class; /* Pointer to the class structure     */
} OBJECT;

/* Define some messages */
#define   ALLOCATE_DATA 1
#define   DRAW          2
#define   COMPUTE_AREA  3

/* Functions to create objects */

OBJECT *new_circle(double x, double y, double radius);
OBJECT *new_rectangle(double x1, double y1,
                      double x2, double y2);

/* Utility functions to handle messages */

int send_message(OBJECT *p_obj, int msgid, ...);
int class_message(CLASS *p_class, OBJECT *p_obj, int msgid,
                  va_list argp);
void *allocate_memory(size_t bytes);
int  get_offset(CLASS *p_class);

#endif /* #if !defined(SHAPEOBJ_H) */
```

Implementing Geometrical Shapes

To illustrate the use of these structures, implement two shapes: a circle and a rectangle. Because each shape must draw itself and compute its area, move these functions to a common base class called generic_shape. Figure 5.4 shows the inheritance hierarchy of shapes.

FIGURE 5.4.

Inheritance hierarchy of geometric shapes.

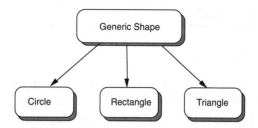

Listings 5.5, 5.6, and 5.7 show the implementation of the generic shape, the circle, and the rectangle, respectively. If you study the listings, you notice that each file includes a CLASS structure properly initialized with a message table, a pointer to the base class, if any, and the size of the data structure for each instance of that class. The circle and rectangle classes include functions that you can call to create an instance of each. For example, to create a circle, you call the new_circle function with the coordinates of the center and radius as arguments (see Listing 5.6). This function allocates an OBJECT structure, sends a message to the base class for allocating the instance data, and returns a pointer to the newly allocated OBJECT structure.

Listing 5.5. ANYSHAPE.C. Implementation of a generic shape class.

```
/*  File:  anyshape.c
 *
 *  This is the generic "shape" class.
 *  Data and functions common to all shapes appear here.
 *
 */
#include "shapeobj.h"

static int allocate_data(OBJECT *p_obj, va_list argp);

static MESSAGE messages[] =
{
    ALLOCATE_DATA,  allocate_data
};

/* The "class" data structure */

CLASS generic_shape =
{
    NULL,                           /* No base class     */
    0,                              /* No common data    */
    sizeof(messages)/sizeof(MESSAGE), /* How many messages */
    messages                        /* Message table     */
};

/*----------------------------------------------------------------*/
/*  a l l o c a t e _ d a t a
 *
 *  Allocate memory for an object's data.
 */
static int allocate_data(OBJECT *p_obj, va_list argp)
```

continues

Listing 5.5. continued

```c
{
    CLASS   *p_class;
    int     size = 0;

/* Determine sum of instance data sizes for each class in the
 * hierarchy of this object
 */
    for(p_class = p_obj->p_class, size = 0;
        p_class != NULL; p_class = p_class->base_class)
            size += p_class->data_size;

/* Allocate the necessary number of bytes */
    p_obj->p_data = allocate_memory(size);

    return 1;
}
```

Listing 5.6. O_CIRCLE.C. Implementation of the circle class.

```c
/*  File:  o_circle.c
 *
 *  This is the circle class of shapes
 */

#include "shapeobj.h"

typedef double *P_DOUBLE;

typedef struct CIRCLE_DATA
{
    double  x, y;     /* Coordinates of center */
    double  radius;   /* Radius of circle      */
} CIRCLE_DATA;

extern CLASS generic_shape; /* The base class */

static int compute_area(OBJECT *p_obj, va_list argp);
static int draw(OBJECT *p_obj, va_list argp);

static MESSAGE messages[] =
{
    COMPUTE_AREA,  compute_area,
    DRAW,          draw
};

/* The "class" data structure */

CLASS circle_class =
{
    &generic_shape,                       /* Ptr to base class   */
    sizeof(CIRCLE_DATA),                  /* Data for circles    */
    sizeof(messages)/sizeof(MESSAGE),     /* Number of messages */
    messages                              /* The message table   */
};
```

```c
static int circle_offset = -1;  /* Offset to circle's data  */
/*------------------------------------------------------------*/
/* n e w _ c i r c l e
 *
 * Create an instance of a circle and initialize it
 */
OBJECT *new_circle(double x, double y, double radius)
{
    OBJECT    *p_obj;
    CIRCLE_DATA *p_data;

    p_obj = (OBJECT *) allocate_memory(sizeof(OBJECT));
    p_obj->p_class = &circle_class;

/* Send message to allocate memory for data */
    send_message(p_obj, ALLOCATE_DATA, 0);

/* Get offset to circle-specific data */
    if(circle_offset < 0)
        circle_offset = get_offset(&circle_class);
    p_data = (CIRCLE_DATA *)((char *)p_obj->p_data +
                                    circle_offset);

    p_data->x = x;
    p_data->y = y;
    p_data->radius = radius;

    return(p_obj);
}
/*------------------------------------------------------------*/
/* c o m p u t e _ a r e a
 *
 * Compute area of circle. Arguments expected:
 *      pointer to a double where answer is returned.
 */
static int compute_area(OBJECT *p_obj, va_list argp)
{
    int            status = 0;
    double         *p_area;
    CIRCLE_DATA    *p_data;

/* Set up the pointer to circle's data */
    p_data = (CIRCLE_DATA *)((char *)p_obj->p_data +
                            circle_offset);
/* Get pointer to double where answer is to be returned */
    p_area = va_arg(argp, P_DOUBLE);
    if(p_area != NULL)
    {
        *p_area = M_PI * p_data->radius * p_data->radius;
        status = 1;
    }
    return(status);
}
/*------------------------------------------------------------*/
/* d r a w
 *
 * Draw the circle (for now, just print a message).
 * Does not expect any arguments
 */
```

continues

Listing 5.6. continued

```c
static int draw(OBJECT *p_obj, va_list argp)
{
    CIRCLE_DATA    *p_data;

/* Set up the pointer to circle's data */
    p_data = (CIRCLE_DATA *)((char *)p_obj->p_data +
                              circle_offset);
    printf("Draw: Circle of radius %f at (%f, %f)\n",
            p_data->radius, p_data->x, p_data->y);

    return 1;
}
```

Listing 5.7. O_RECT.C. Implementation of the rectangle class.

```c
/*  File:  o_rect.c
 *
 *  This is the rectangle class of shapes
 */

#include "shapeobj.h"

typedef double *P_DOUBLE;

typedef struct RECTANGLE_DATA
{
    double  x1, y1;  /* Coordinates of the corners   */
    double  x2, y2;
} RECTANGLE_DATA;

extern CLASS generic_shape; /* The base class */

static int compute_area(OBJECT *p_obj, va_list argp);
static int draw(OBJECT *p_obj, va_list argp);

static MESSAGE messages[] =
{
    COMPUTE_AREA,   compute_area,
    DRAW,           draw
};

/* The "class" data structure */

CLASS rectangle_class =
{
    &generic_shape,                     /* Ptr to base class  */
    sizeof(RECTANGLE_DATA),             /* Data for rectangles*/
    sizeof(messages)/sizeof(MESSAGE),   /* Number of messages */
    messages                            /* The message table  */
};

static int rectangle_offset = -1; /* Offset to rectangle's data*/
/*--------------------------------------------------------------*/
/*  n e w _ r e c t a n g l e
```

```
 *
 *   Create an instance of a rectangle and initialize it
 */
OBJECT *new_rectangle(double x1, double y1, double x2, double y2)
{
    OBJECT    *p_obj;
    RECTANGLE_DATA *p_data;

    p_obj = (OBJECT *) allocate_memory(sizeof(OBJECT));
    p_obj->p_class = &rectangle_class;

/* Send message to allocate memory for data */
    send_message(p_obj, ALLOCATE_DATA, 0);

/* Get offset to rectangle-specific data */
    if(rectangle_offset < 0)
        rectangle_offset = get_offset(&rectangle_class);
    p_data = (RECTANGLE_DATA *)((char *)p_obj->p_data +
                                    rectangle_offset);
    p_data->x1 = x1;
    p_data->y1 = y1;
    p_data->x2 = x2;
    p_data->y2 = y2;

    return(p_obj);
}
/*-----------------------------------------------------------------*/
/* c o m p u t e _ a r e a
 *
 *   Compute area of a rectangle. Arguments expected:
 *       pointer to a double where answer is returned.
 */
static int compute_area(OBJECT *p_obj, va_list argp)
{
    int            status = 0;
    double         *p_area;
    RECTANGLE_DATA    *p_data;

/* Set up the pointer to rectangle's data */
    p_data = (RECTANGLE_DATA *)((char *)p_obj->p_data +
                            rectangle_offset);
/* Get pointer to double where answer is to be returned */
    p_area = va_arg(argp, P_DOUBLE);
    if(p_area != NULL)
    {
        *p_area = fabs((p_data->x2 - p_data->x1) *
                        (p_data->y2 - p_data->y1));
        status = 1;
    }
    return(status);
}
/*-----------------------------------------------------------------*/
/* d r a w
 *
 *   Draw the rectangle (for now, just print a message).
 *   Does not expect any arguments
 */
static int draw(OBJECT *p_obj, va_list argp)
```

continues

Listing 5.7. continued

```
{
    RECTANGLE_DATA    *p_data;

/* Set up the pointer to rectangle's data */
    p_data = (RECTANGLE_DATA *)((char *)p_obj->p_data +
                                rectangle_offset);
    printf("Draw: Rectangle with corners: "
           "(%f, %f) at (%f, %f)\n",
            p_data->x1, p_data->y1,
            p_data->x2, p_data->y2);
    return 1;
}
```

Allocating an Object's Data

When developing a framework for OOP in C, one tricky problem involves the allocation of an object's data. Suppose you are allocating the data structure for an object with a class that inherits data from a base class. In the current implementation, the data for the base class and the derived class is laid out in a single block with one following the other. Each class can access its data, provided it knows the offset for the start of its data in this block of memory. Figure 5.5 illustrates the layout of data for a derived class and a base class.

FIGURE 5.5.

Layout of an object's data.

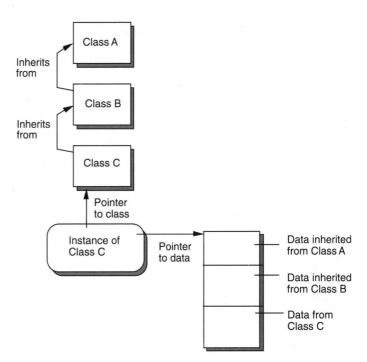

For the geometric shapes, the `allocate_data` function handles the allocation of the data block in the generic shape class (see Listing 5.5). This function figures the amount of storage needed by adding the sizes of data blocks for all classes in the hierarchy and then allocates the data. When an object needs to access its data—for example, in the `new_circle` function of Listing 5.6—it obtains the offset to its data structure by calling a utility function named `get_offset`.

Utility Functions

Because C does not directly support sending messages to objects, you must devise your own means of doing so. For the messaging scheme used in our approach, you can accomplish this by writing a set of utility functions that invoke the appropriate function in response to a message. Listing 5.8 presents the file OOPUTIL.C, which defines a number of utility functions to help implement OOP in C. You may want to study the `send_message` function to see how messages are dispatched to an object's class and how any message not handled by a class is passed up the class hierarchy (see Listing 5.8).

Listing 5.8. OOPUTIL.C. Utility functions for OOP in C.

```
/*-------------------------------------------------------------*/
/*  File: ooputil.c
 *
 *  Utility routines for example of OOP in C
 *
 */

#include "shapeobj.h"

/*-------------------------------------------------------------*/
/*  s e n d _ m e s s a g e
 *
 *  Process message sent to an object by passing it to its class
 */
int send_message(OBJECT *p_obj, int msgid, ...)
{
    int    status;
    va_list argp;
    va_start(argp, msgid);
    status = class_message(p_obj->p_class, p_obj, msgid, argp);
    va_end(argp);
    return(status);
}
/*-------------------------------------------------------------*/
/*  c l a s s _ m e s s a g e
 *
 *  Search through the message table for a specific message
 *  and call the "message handler" if found
 */
int class_message(CLASS *p_class, OBJECT *p_obj, int msgid,
                  va_list argp)
{
    int i, status;
```

Listing 5.8. continued

```
    if(p_class == NULL) return 0;

    if(p_class->messages != NULL)
    {
        for(i = 0; i < p_class->num_messages; i++)
            if(p_class->messages[i].message_id == msgid)
            {
                return ((*p_class->messages[i].message_handler)
                                                (p_obj, argp));
            }
/* If the message is not handled, send it to the base class */
        status = class_message(p_class->base_class, p_obj,
                                    msgid, argp);
    }
    return(status);
}
/*-------------------------------------------------------------*/
/*  a l l o c a t e _ m e m o r y
 *
 *  Allocate memory. Check for failure to allocate.
 */
void *allocate_memory(size_t numbytes)
{
    void *ptr;
    if((ptr = calloc(1, numbytes)) == NULL)
    {
     fprintf(stderr, "Error allocating %d bytes of memory."
            "Exiting...", numbytes);
        exit(1);
    }
    return(ptr);
}
/*-------------------------------------------------------------*/
/*  g e t _ o f f s e t
 *
 *  An instance's data is the concatenation of data of
 *  all classes in its hierarchy. This function computes
 *  the offset to the beginning of data for a specific class.
 */
int  get_offset(CLASS *p_class)
{
    CLASS *p_ct;
    int size = 0;
/* Traverse the class hierarchy up to the "root" class and add
 * up the sizes of data belonging to each class
 */
    for(p_class = p_class->base_class;
        p_class != NULL;
        p_class = p_class->base_class) size += p_class->data_size;

    return size;
}
```

Using the Shapes

Once the framework for C-based OOP is in place, you easily can create the shapes and use them. For example, to create a circle with a radius of 50 centered at the point (100,100), use the following:

```
OBJECT *circle1;

/* Create a circle at (100, 100) with radius = 50 */
    circle1 = new_circle(100.0, 100.0, 50.0);
```

You can compute the area of this circle by sending it a COMPUTE_AREA message and passing it the arguments expected by this message:

```
double area;
send_message(circle1, COMPUTE_AREA, &area);
printf("Area of circle = %f\n", area);
```

The file STESTOBJ.C in Listing 5.9 shows an example that uses the circle and rectangle shapes. To build the executable file for this example, you need to compile and link the following files:

- ■ STESTOBJ.C (Listing 5.9)
- ■ OOPUTIL.C (Listing 5.8)
- ■ ANYSHAPE.C (Listing 5.5)
- ■ O_CIRCLE.C (Listing 5.6)
- ■ O_RECT.C (Listing 5.7)

Create a Visual Workbench project with these files or use the following command line in a command window:

```
cl stestobj.c anyshape.c ooputil.c o_rect.c o_circle.c
```

to compile and link the STESTOBJ.EXE program.

Listing 5.9. STESTOBJ.C. Main function for testing the shape objects.

```
/*------------------------------------------------------------*/
/*  File:  stestobj.c
 *
 *  Test C-based OOP implementation of geometric shapes.
 */

#include "shapeobj.h"

int main(void)
{
    int    i;
    double area;
    OBJECT *shapes[3];

/* Create some shapes */
    shapes[0] = new_circle(100.0, 100.0, 50.0);
```

continues

Listing 5.9. continued

```
    shapes[1] = new_rectangle(100., 150., 200., 100.);

/* Compute the area of the shapes */
    for(i = 0; i < 2; i++)
    {
      send_message(shapes[i], COMPUTE_AREA, &area);
        printf("Area of shape [%d] = %f\n", i, area);
    }

/* "Draw" the shapes */
    for(i = 0; i < 2; i++)
        send_message(shapes[i], DRAW);

    return 0;
}
```

Adding a New Shape Object

Earlier, this chapter discussed a procedural implementation of the geometric shapes, showing the steps needed to handle a new shape such as a triangle. To see how OOP helps reduce the ripple effect of change, consider the addition of a triangle shape to the shape objects. Prepare a new file—call it O_TRIANG.C—that defines the data and functions for the triangle shape. Listing 5.10 shows a sample implementation of O_TRIANG.C.

That's it! All you do is write a single module implementing the new object. Once you do this, you can use the new shape in your programs (of course, you have to compile O_TRIANG.C and link with it to build the program). For example, you can create a triangle, compute its area, and draw it by making the following changes in the STESTOBJ.C file:

```
    OBJECT *shapes[3];
    double area;

/* Create a triangle */
    shapes[2] = new_triangle(100.,100., 200.,100., 150.,50.);

/* Now adjust the for loop in STESTOBJ.C to loop up to i < 3
```

Clearly, OOP techniques make it very easy to add new capabilities to the program, because you don't need to modify existing code, only those new modules with code necessary to support the new objects.

Listing 5.10. O_TRIANG.C. Implementation of a triangle shape.

```
/*------------------------------------------------------------*/
/*  File:  o_triang.c
 *
 *  This is the triangle class of shapes
 */
```

```
#include "shapeobj.h"

typedef double *P_DOUBLE;

typedef struct TRIANGLE_DATA
{
    double  x1, y1;  /* Coordinates of the corners  */
    double  x2, y2;
    double  x3, y3;
} TRIANGLE_DATA;

extern CLASS generic_shape; /* The base class */

static int compute_area(OBJECT *p_obj, va_list argp);
static int draw(OBJECT *p_obj, va_list argp);

static MESSAGE messages[] =
{
    COMPUTE_AREA,  compute_area,
    DRAW,          draw
};

/* The "class" data structure */

CLASS triangle_class =
{
    &generic_shape,                 /* Ptr to base class  */
    sizeof(TRIANGLE_DATA),          /* Data for triangles */
    sizeof(messages)/sizeof(MESSAGE), /* Number of messages */
    messages                        /* The message table  */
};

static int triangle_offset = -1;  /* Offset to triangle's data */
/*-------------------------------------------------------------*/
/*  n e w _ t r i a n g l e
 *
 *  Create an instance of a triangle and initialize it
 */
OBJECT *new_triangle(double x1, double y1, double x2, double y2,
                     double x3, double y3)
{
    OBJECT    *p_obj;
    TRIANGLE_DATA *p_data;

    p_obj = (OBJECT *) allocate_memory(sizeof(OBJECT));
    p_obj->p_class = &triangle_class;

/* Send a message to allocate memory for data */
    send_message(p_obj, ALLOCATE_DATA, 0);

/* Get the offset to triangle-specific data */
    if(triangle_offset < 0)
        triangle_offset = get_offset(&triangle_class);
    p_data = (TRIANGLE_DATA *)((char *)p_obj->p_data +
                                        triangle_offset);
    p_data->x1 = x1;
    p_data->y1 = y1;
    p_data->x2 = x2;
```

continues

Listing 5.10. continued

```
    p_data->y2 = y2;
    p_data->x3 = x3;
    p_data->y3 = y3;

    return(p_obj);
}
/*----------------------------------------------------------------*/
/*  c o m p u t e _ a r e a
 *
 *  Compute the area of triangle. Arguments expected:
 *      pointer to a double where answer is returned.
 */
static int compute_area(OBJECT *p_obj, va_list argp)
{
    int         status = 0;
    double      *p_area;
    TRIANGLE_DATA   *p_data;

/* Set up the pointer to triangle's data */
    p_data = (TRIANGLE_DATA *)((char *)p_obj->p_data +
                            triangle_offset);
/* Get the pointer to double where answer will be returned */
    p_area = va_arg(argp, P_DOUBLE);
    if(p_area != NULL)
    {
        double x21, y21, x31, y31;

        x21 =  p_data->x2 - p_data->x1;
        y21 =  p_data->y2 - p_data->y1;
        x31 =  p_data->x3 - p_data->x1;
        y31 =  p_data->y3 - p_data->y1;

        *p_area = fabs(y21 * x31 - x21 * y31) / 2.0;
        status = 1;
    }
    return(status);
}
/*----------------------------------------------------------------*/
/*  d r a w
 *
 *  Draw the triangle (for now, just print a message).
 *  Does not expect any arguments
 */
static int draw(OBJECT *p_obj, va_list argp)
{
    TRIANGLE_DATA   *p_data;

/* Set up the pointer to triangle's data */
    p_data = (TRIANGLE_DATA *)((char *)p_obj->p_data +
                            triangle_offset);
    printf("Draw: Triangle with vertices: "
                    "(%f, %f) (%f, %f) (%f, %f)\n",
                    p_data->x1, p_data->y1,
                    p_data->x2, p_data->y2,
                    p_data->x3, p_data->y3);
    return 1;
}
```

Problems with OOP in C

Although you can define data structures to implement objects in C, several problems occur when implementing OOP in C:

■ As a basic tenet of OOP, you must access and manipulate the object's data by calling the functions provided by that object. This ensures that the internal implementation details of the object stay hidden from the outside world, thus enabling you to change these details without affecting other parts of the program. Although object-oriented languages enforce this principle of data hiding, implementing object-oriented techniques in a C program requires discipline on the part of the programmer because C enables code that directly accesses members of an object's data structure.

■ You are responsible for ensuring that the data structures of an object are laid out properly to support data inheritance from base classes. You must write utility functions to enable an object to access its data properly.

■ The programmer must devise a scheme to invoke methods of objects in response to messages. Inheritance of behavior also requires support functions for properly dispatching messages.

In spite of these problems, the modularity and localization of change afforded by OOP is worth the trouble, even if you write your object-oriented programs in C. Of course, as you will see in Chapter 6, OOP becomes much easier if you use a programming language, such as C++, that supports the basic necessities of object-orientation: data abstraction, inheritance, and polymorphism.

Summary

Object-oriented programming, or OOP, relies on three basic concepts: data abstraction, inheritance, and polymorphism.

Data abstraction is the capability of defining abstract data types, or ADTs (essentially, user-defined data types), that encapsulate some data and a set of well-defined operations. Such user-defined data types can represent objects in software. Class refers to the template from which specific instances of objects are created. Objects perform specific actions in response to messages (which function calls may implement).

Inheritance is the mechanism that enables one object to behave the same way as another one, except for some modifications. Inheritance implies a hierarchy of classes, with derived classes inheriting behavior from base classes. In the context of software, inheritance promotes the sharing of code and data among classes.

Polymorphism occurs when different objects react differently to the same message. In particular, OOP is a new way of organizing your program, using a collection of objects with classes that are organized in a predefined hierarchy to share code and data through inheritance.

A comparison of two implementations of an example—one using a procedural approach and the other using OOP—shows that the object-based organization enhances the modularity of the program by placing related data and functions in the same module. Therefore, an object-based program can accommodate changes more easily than a procedural program. Although you can implement object-oriented techniques in a procedural programming language, such as C, you can do this more easily when the language has features that support OOP.

6

C++ and Object-Oriented Programming

Chapter 5, "Basics of Object-Oriented Programming," provides an overview of object-oriented programming (OOP) terminology and demonstrates how to implement the object-oriented techniques in a procedure-oriented language such as C. However, the example shown in Chapter 5 clearly illustrates several problems with using OOP in C:

■ The language does not enforce information hiding.

■ The programmer must implement message-passing.

■ The programmer must devise clever schemes to implement inheritance.

Consider, for example, C's FILE data type. Although you can think of it as an object, the file I/O functions are not closely tied to the FILE data type. In addition, the internal details of the FILE data type are not really hidden because C has no way of preventing you from accessing the members of the FILE data structure. When writing object-oriented software in C, you can achieve information hiding only through self-discipline—you and others working on the software must agree not to access directly the contents of data structures that should be hidden.

Basically, although it is possible to use OOP techniques in C, the lack of built-in support for OOP requires extra work to enforce the principles of data abstraction and to set up the mechanisms for inheritance and polymorphism. C++, on the other hand, was designed with OOP in mind. C++ was built by adding certain features to C that ease the task of implementing objects. This chapter describes these features and illustrates the ease of using OOP in C++ by reimplementing the first chapter's example of geometric shapes.

This chapter does not feature a complete description of all the C++ features. Rather, it provides an overview of the features necessary for object-oriented programming. In particular, this chapter does not delve into the syntactical details of C++. Part III, "Learning C++," covers all aspects of C++ in detail. Of course, you can supplement this book's coverage of C++ and OOP by consulting one or more of the references listed at the end of this book.

A BRIEF HISTORY OF C++

C++ was developed in the early 1980s by Bjarne Stroustrup of AT&T Bell Laboratories. He created C++ while adding features to C to support efficient event-driven simulation programs. His inspiration came from the language Simula67, which supported the concept of a class. AT&T made many improvements to this initial language before releasing it commercially in 1985. Since then, C++ has continued to evolve with AT&T controlling the releases.

In the beginning, AT&T supplied a translator called Cfront for converting C++ programs into C, which were then compiled using a C compiler. By the time Release 1.2 of AT&T's Cfront came out, C++ compilers were becoming available for PCs and workstations. (The release numbers of Cfront are used synonymously as release numbers of AT&T C++.) AT&T released C++ 2.0 in 1989 and followed it promptly with Release 2.1. In late 1991, AT&T released Cfront 3.0 with support for templates.

The X3J16 committee of the American National Standards Institute (ANSI) is currently in the process of drafting a standard specification for the C++ programming language based on the following documents:

- The ANSI C standard (ANSI X3.159-1989—Programming Language C)
- The AT&T C++ Language System Release 2.1 Reference Manual (also available as the Annotated C++ Reference Manual by Margaret A. Ellis and Bjarne Stroustrup, published by Addison-Wesley in 1990).

Microsoft Visual C++ 2.0 conforms to the specifications of AT&T C++ Release 3.0 together with additional features, such as exception handling, that have already been accepted by the ANSI C++ standards committee.

Object-Oriented Programming in C++

Chapter 5 mentioned three basic concepts that underlie OOP: data abstraction, inheritance, and polymorphism. To review, here is how these concepts help OOP:

- Data abstraction helps you tie data and functions together, which effectively defines a new data type with its own set of operations. Recall that such a data type is called an abstract data type (ADT), also referred to as a class.
- Inheritance helps you organize the classes in a hierarchy so that you can place common data and functions in a base class from which other classes can inherit them (see Figure 6.1).
- Polymorphism helps you keep your programs conceptually simple by enabling you to call the same function to perform similar tasks in all classes of a hierarchy.

C++ includes features that support each of these concepts.

Data Abstraction in C++

In C, an abstract data type such as FILE, for example, is declared with a construct such as this:

```
typedef struct
{
    char     *buf;    /* Buffer for file I/O      */
    unsigned flags;   /* Flags to indicate status */
        .             /* Other internal variables */
        .
} FILE;               /* This is the FILE data type */
```

The operations on FILE are separate functions that take a pointer to a FILE structure as an argument. C++ introduces the class construct to augment C's struct. Using class, you can define the File data type, equivalent to C's FILE, as shown in Listing 6.1.

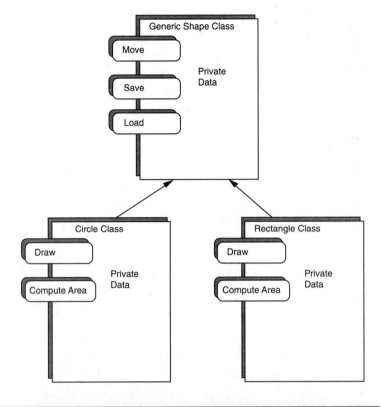

FIGURE 6.1.

Data abstraction,
inheritance, and
polymorphism in OOP.

THE MEANING OF const

The const keyword prefixing the name of a variable indicates that the variable is a constant and must not be modified by the program. Similarly, if a function's argument is a pointer and if that pointer is declared as a const, the function cannot modify the contents of the location referenced by that pointer.

Listing 6.1. FILE.H. A data type for file I/O.

```
/*  File: file.h
 *
 *  A File class for file I/O
 */
#if !defined(FILE_H)
#define FILE_H

#include <stdio.h>    // For C File I/O function declarations

class File
{
    FILE    *fp;    // C stream
```

```
// ...                    // Other internal variables

public:
    File(const char *name,         // Constructor
        const char *open_mode);
    ~File();                       // Destructor
    size_t read(const size_t howmany,    // Read from file
                const size_t elem_size,  //   into buffer
                void *buffer);
    size_t write(const size_t howmany,   // Write buffer to
                 const size_t elem_size, //   file
                 const void *buffer);
};                                 // Note the semicolon
#endif
```

C++ COMMENTS

C++ recognizes the standard C comments, which start and end with the /* characters. Additionally, C++ treats as a comment everything following the // characters up to the end of the line. You can use the C format for comments spanning multiple lines, and the new style is convenient for single-line comments.

As a C programmer (especially, if you know ANSI C), you should find most of Listing 6.1 familiar. Don't be concerned, however, if you understand little at first; the rest of this chapter explains much of it. Part III of this book covers the C++ features again, in detail. In particular, Chapter 7, "C++ and ANSI Standard C," provides an overview of ANSI C and compares it with C++.

Listing 6.1 assumes that the File class provides a higher level abstraction for file I/O, but that it uses C's file I/O functions for the actual work. That is why a pointer to a FILE exists in the class. As you will see later, the constructor of the File class sets up this FILE pointer when an instance of the File class is created.

If you examine the declaration of the File class in Listing 6.1, you see that it looks very similar to C's struct, except for the ANSI C-style declaration of several functions following the public: keyword. These member functions operate on the data items being encapsulated in the class. The data items in the class declaration are called *member variables*. The public: keyword is significant because all member functions and variables appearing after the keyword are accessible to other parts of the program. The initial members of the class—those that appear before the public: keyword—are considered private. Such private variables and functions are not accessible to any function other than those declared within the class. The C++ compiler enforces this rule and displays an error message if any outside function refers to the private members of any class.

When you define a class in C++, you are defining a new, possibly complex, data type. The compiler hides the internal details of this data type from the outside world. The only way the outside functions can access the data is through the public member functions. Therefore, the `class` construct enables you to implement data abstraction and promotes modularity.

---

class VERSUS struct

C++ continues to support ANSI C's struct keyword. In fact, C++ expands the definition of struct by enabling the inclusion of member functions. In C++, the only difference between a class and a struct is that the struct's contents are always public.

Defining the Member Functions for *File*

When declaring a class, you declare its member functions, but you don't define them. Typically, you define the member functions in a separate file. That way, you can think of the header file with the class declaration as a specification of the interface to the class, whereas the module with the function definitions is its implementation. Ideally, if the interface is defined clearly enough, programmers using the class don't need to know the details of the implementation. For the File class, plan to call standard C file I/O functions to implement the member functions. You can do this in a straightforward manner as shown in Listing 6.2.

THE C++ FILENAME EXTENSION

This book uses .cpp as the filename extension for C++ source files. Header files have the .h extension, as they do in C. Microsoft Visual C++ 2.0 accepts both .cpp and .cxx as extensions for C++ source files.

Listing 6.2. FILE.CPP. Definition of member functions of the File class.

```
/*------------------------------------------------------------*/
/*  File:  file.cpp
 *
 *  Illustrates data encapsulation in C++
 */
#include "file.h"
/*------------------------------------------------------------*/
// Constructor -- opens a file
File::File(const char *name, const char *open_mode)
{
    fp = fopen(name, open_mode);
}
/*------------------------------------------------------------*/
// Destructor -- closes a file
File::~File()
{
    if(fp != NULL) fclose(fp);
}
/*------------------------------------------------------------*/
```

```
size_t File::read(const size_t howmany,    // Read from file
                  const size_t elem_size,  //   into buffer
                  void *buffer)
{
    if(fp != NULL)
        return(fread(buffer, elem_size, howmany, fp));
    else
        return 0;
}
/*-------------------------------------------------------------*/
size_t File::write(const size_t howmany,   // Write buffer to
                   const size_t elem_size, //   file
                   const void *buffer)
{
    if(fp != NULL)
        return(fwrite(buffer, elem_size, howmany, fp));
    else
        return 0;
}
```

You do need to be aware of one operator—the scope resolution operator, denoted by a pair of colons (`::`). When defining the member functions, you use the scope resolution operator to indicate the class with which the function is associated. Therefore, the notation `File::read` identifies `read` as a member function of the `File` class. You also can use the scope resolution operator without a class name to indicate a globally defined function or variable. For example, the following code illustrates how you can differentiate between a globally defined `int` variable and a local one with the same name:

```
int AllDone;        //Variable visible throughout file

void AnyFunction(void)
{
    int AllDone;  // Local variable with same name
    AllDone = 1;  // Refers to local variable

    if(::AllDone) // This refers to the global "AllDone"
        DoSomething();
}
```

The same approach can be used to call a global function in a member function of the same name.

Constructors and Destructors

Notice that the `File` class contains a member function named `File` and another named `~File`. The two member functions are called the *constructor* and the *destructor* of the class, respectively. The C++ compiler calls a constructor, if one is defined, whenever an instance of a class is created. You can use the constructor to handle any specific requirements for initializing objects of a class. For example, if an object needs extra storage, you can allocate memory in the constructor. In the `File` class, the constructor calls `fopen` to open the file. Notice that the constructor function always has the same name as the class.

You also can define a destructor function for a class, if any need exists to clean up after an object is destroyed (for example, if you want to free memory allocated in the constructor). The C++ compiler calls the destructor function of a class whenever it needs to destroy an instance of that class. The destructor has the same name as the class except for a tilde (~) prefix. Therefore, the destructor function for the `File` class is `~File()`. Notice that in the `File` class, you merely close the file that the constructor opened.

Using the *File* Class

You can define an instance of the `File` class and access its member functions just as you would define a C `struct`. For example, to define an instance of the `File` class named `f1` and call its `read` function, you write the following:

```
// Open file named "test.dat" for reading
File   f1("test.dat", "rb");
char   buffer[128];
size_t bytes_read;
//...
bytes_read = f1.read(128, sizeof(char), buffer);
```

For a more meaningful example, consider the short program shown in Listing 6.3. It uses the `File` class to copy the contents of one file to another by reading from one and writing to the other.

Listing 6.3. FILE.CPP (second part). Program to copy from one file to another.

```
/*-------------------------------------------------------------*/
/*  Main function to copy file "test.dat" to "copy.out"
 */
void main(void)
{
// Open files...
    File f1("test.dat", "rb");
    File f2("copy.out", "wb");

    char   buffer[512];
    size_t count;

// Read a chunk from one file and write it to the other...
    while((count = f1.read(512, sizeof(char), buffer)) != 0)
    {
        f2.write(count, sizeof(char), buffer);
    }
}
```

Inheritance in C++ Classes

When declaring a class, you also can indicate whether it inherits from any other classes. On the first line of the `class` declaration, place a colon (:) followed by a list of base classes from which this class inherits. For example, suppose you want to declare the `circle_shape` class, which is derived from a generic shape class. In this case, the first line of the declaration of the `circle_shape` class looks like this:

```
class circle_shape: public shape
{

// Declare member variables and member functions...

}
```

Here, the `shape` class is the base class and `circle_shape` is the derived class. The `public` keyword preceding `shape` signifies that any public member variables and functions of `shape` are accessible to the `circle_shape` class.

Polymorphism and Dynamic Binding

C++ provides a way to override a function defined in a base class with a function defined in a derived class. Another feature of C++ is that you can use pointers to a base class to refer to objects of a derived class. With these two features you can implement polymorphic behavior in C++ classes.

Suppose you have a base class called `shape` that encapsulates data and functions common to other classes of shapes, such as `circle_shape` and `rectangle_shape`, which are derived from the shape class. One of the functions is `draw`, which draws the shape. Because each shape is drawn differently, the base class defines the `draw` function with the `virtual` keyword:

```
class shape
{
public:
    virtual void draw(void) const{ }
// Other member functions...
};
```

The `virtual` keyword tells the C++ compiler that the `draw` function defined in the base class should be used only if the derived classes do not define it. In this case, the base class defines `draw` as a "do nothing" function.

In a derived class, you can override this definition by supplying a function with the same name:

```
class circle_shape: public shape
{
// Private data...
public:
// Other member functions...
    virtual void draw(void) const;
};
```

Later, you must actually define the `draw` function for the `circle_shape` class. You can do the same for the `rectangle_shape` class. Once you do this, you can apply the same member function to instances of different classes, and the C++ compiler will generate a call to the correct draw function:

```
// Create instances of circle_shape and rectangle_shape
circle_shape c1(100.,100.,50.);
rectangle_shape r1(10.,20.,30.,40.);

c1.draw();    // "draw" from "circle_shape" class is called
r1.draw();    // "draw" from "rectangle_shape" class is called
```

Although this is polymorphic behavior, it is not an interesting example because the C++ compiler (and you) can determine, by studying the code, exactly which function should be called. In fact, this case is referred to as the *static binding* of virtual functions because the compiler can determine the function to be called at compile time.

The more interesting case is that of *dynamic binding*, which happens when a virtual function is invoked through a pointer to an object and the type of the object is not known during compilation. This is possible because C++ enables you to use a pointer to a base class when referring to an instance of a derived class. For example, suppose you want to create a number of shapes, store them in an array, and draw them. Here is how you might do it:

```
    int i;
    shape *shapes[2];    // Array of pointers to base class

// Create some shapes and save the pointers
    shapes[0] = new circle_shape(100., 100., 50.);
    shapes[1] = new rectangle_shape(80., 40., 120., 60.);

// Draw the shapes
    for(i = 0; i < 2; i++) shapes[i]->draw();
```

Notice how you can loop through the pointers to the shapes and call the draw member function of each object. Because draw is a virtual function, the actual draw function that is called at runtime depends on the type of shape that the shapes[i] pointer references. If shapes[i] points to an instance of circle_shape, the circle_shape::draw() function is called. On the other hand, if shapes[i] points to an instance of rectangle_shape, the draw function of rectangle_shape is called. At runtime, the pointers in the shapes array can point to any instance of the classes derived from the shape base class. Therefore, the actual function being called varies according to the pointer's type determined at runtime. That is why this style of virtual function call is called dynamic binding.

Geometric Shapes in C++

To illustrate how C++'s object-oriented features help you write object-oriented programs, consider the example of geometric shapes from Chapter 5 that presents a C-based implementation of the shape objects. Here, that example is rewritten in C++. Notice that the code is much more compact because you no longer need additional C utility routines to support the implementation of objects.

The *shape* Classes

The first step in implementing the geometric shapes in C++ is to define the classes. As in the C version of the program (see Chapter 5), you start with an abstract base class called shape. This class is abstract because you never create any instance of this class. You use it to encapsulate data and functions common to all derived classes, thus promoting inheritance and polymorphism (through the virtual keyword, which is explained later). As shown in Figure 6.2, all other shapes are derived from this base class. See the SHAPES.H file (Listing 6.4) for the actual declaration of the classes.

FIGURE 6.2.

A class hierarchy for geometric shapes

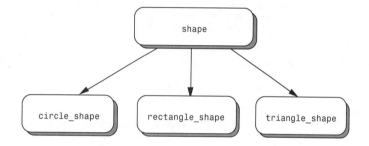

Listing 6.4. SHAPES.H. Classes of geometric shapes in C++.

```
/*-----------------------------------------------------------*/
/* File:  shapes.h
 *
 *  C++ header file with definitions of geometrical shapes
 */

#if !defined(SHAPES_H)
#define SHAPES_H

#include <stdio.h>
#include <math.h>

#define M_PI 3.141592653589793  //Value of "Pi"

// Define an abstract shape class--"abstract" because you
// do not create any instances of this class. It's there
// to encapsulate common data and functions that will be
// shared by all shapes

class shape
{
// In this case, you do not have any data,
// only member functions
public:
    virtual double compute_area(void) const
    {
        printf("Not implemented\n");
        return 0.0;
    }
```

continues

Listing 6.4. continued

```
    virtual void draw(void) const{ }
};

// Define the "circle" class

class circle_shape: public shape
{
private:
    double x, y;    // Coordinates of center
    double radius; // Radius of circle
public:
    circle_shape(double x, double y, double radius);
    virtual double compute_area(void) const;
    virtual void draw(void) const;
};

// Define the "rectangle" class

class rectangle_shape: public shape
{
private:
    double x1, y1;  // Coordinates of opposite corners
    double x2, y2;
public:
    rectangle_shape(double x1, double y1, double x2, double y2);
    double compute_area(void) const;
    void draw(void) const;
};

#endif   // #if !defined(SHAPES_H)
```

The SHAPES.H header file declares the member functions of the classes, but usually the definitions are placed in separate modules. For smaller functions, you can define a function directly in the body of the class, as you have done for the compute_area function in the shape class.

const MEMBER FUNCTIONS

Use the const keyword after the arguments in the declaration of a member function if that member function does not modify any member variable. This tells the compiler that it can safely apply this member function to a const instance of this class. For example, the following is permissible because compute_area is a const member function:

```
// Define a const circle
    const circle_shape c1(100.0, 100.0, 50.0);
    double area = c1.compute_area();
```

Circle and Rectangle Classes

Listings 6.5 and 6.6 show the implementation of the `circle_shape` and `rectangle_shape` classes, respectively. You implement each class in its own file, just as you do for a larger project. You implement a class by defining its member functions. In this example, each class has two member functions: `draw` and `compute_area`. The definition of each member function resembles a standard C function, except for the scope resolution operator (`::`), which indicates the class to which that function belongs. For example, the `compute_area` function of the `circle_shape` class is defined as follows:

```
double circle_shape::compute_area(void) const
{
    return (M_PI * radius * radius);
}
```

Listing 6.5. CIRCLE.CPP. C++ implementation of the `circle_shape` class.

```
/*-------------------------------------------------------------*/
/* File:  circle.cpp
 *
 * Definition of the "circle" class of shapes in C++
 */

#include "shapes.h"
/*-------------------------------------------------------------*/
circle_shape::circle_shape(double xc, double yc, double r)
{
    x = xc;
    y = yc;
    radius = r;
}
/*-------------------------------------------------------------*/
double circle_shape::compute_area(void) const
{
    return (M_PI * radius * radius);
}
/*-------------------------------------------------------------*/
void circle_shape::draw(void) const
{
    printf("Draw: Circle of radius %f centered at (%f, %f)\n",
           radius, x, y);
}
```

Listing 6.6. RECT.CPP. C++ implementation of the `rectangle_shape` class.

```
/*-------------------------------------------------------------*/
/* File:  rect.cpp
 *
 * Definition of the "rectangle" class of shapes in C++
 */

#include "shapes.h"
```

continues

Listing 6.6. continued

```
rectangle_shape::rectangle_shape(double xul, double yul,
                                 double xlr, double ylr)
{
    x1 = xul;
    y1 = yul;
    x2 = xlr;
    y2 = ylr;
}
/*-------------------------------------------------------------*/
double rectangle_shape::compute_area(void) const
{
    return fabs( (x1-x2) * (y1-y2) );
}
/*-------------------------------------------------------------*/
void rectangle_shape::draw(void) const
{
    printf("Draw: Rectangle with corners (%f, %f) (%f, %f)\n",
           x1, y1, x2, y2);
}
```

Using the *shape* Classes

Listing 6.7 shows a sample C++ program, SHAPETST.CPP, that creates instances of circle and rectangle shapes and tests their member functions. To build the executable file of this program, compile and link the following files in this order:

■ SHAPETST.CPP (Listing 6.7)

■ CIRCLE.CPP (Listing 6.5)

■ RECT.CPP (Listing 6.6)

Each of these files needs the SHAPES.H header file shown in Listing 6.4.

Listing 6.7. SHAPETST.CPP. A C++ program to test the shape classes.

```
/*-------------------------------------------------------------*/
/*  File:  shapetst.cpp
 *
 *  Program to test the "shape" classes
 */

#include "shapes.h"

int main(void)
{
    int i;
    shape *shapes[3];

// Create some shapes
    shapes[0] = new circle_shape(100., 100., 50.);
    shapes[1] = new rectangle_shape(80., 40., 120., 60.);
```

```
// Compute the areas
    for(i = 0; i < 2; i++)
    {
        printf("Area of shape [%d] = %f\n", i,
                shapes[i]->compute_area());
    }

// Draw the shapes
    for(i = 0; i < 2; i++) shapes[i]->draw();

// Destroy the shapes
    delete shapes[0];
    delete shapes[1];

    return 0;
}
```

The sample program uses dynamic binding of the `virtual` function by storing pointers to different types of shapes in an array and invoking the member functions of the appropriate class through the pointer. This is a good example of how dynamic binding and polymorphism are used in C++ programs.

Adding a New *shape* Class

How do you add a new shape such as a triangle to the classes that already exist? With an object-oriented program, it's easy to accomplish this. Here are the steps:

1. Insert the declaration of a `triangle_shape` class at the end of the SHAPES.H header file (Listing 6.4). Here is the definition:

   ```
   // Define the "triangle" class

   class triangle_shape: public shape
   {
   private:
       double x1, y1;   // Coordinates of the corners
       double x2, y2;
       double x3, y3;
   public:
       triangle_shape(double x1, double y1,
                       double x2, double y2,
                       double x3, double y3);
       double compute_area(void) const;
       void draw(void) const;
   };
   ```

2. Define the member functions of the `triangle_shape` class in a separate file. Listing 6.8 shows the file TRIANGLE.CPP that defines the functions.

Once you complete these two steps, you can begin using the `triangle_shape` class in your program. However, you do need to compile and link your program with the TRIANGLE.CPP file (Listing 6.8). For example, you can write code such as this:

```
    int i;
    shape *shapes[3];

// Create some shapes
    shapes[0] = new circle_shape(100., 100., 50.);
    shapes[1] = new rectangle_shape(80., 40., 120., 60.);
    shapes[2] = new triangle_shape(100.,100., 200.,100.,150.,50.);

// Compute the areas
    for(i = 0; i < 3; i++)
    {
        printf("Area of shape [%d] = %f\n", i,
                shapes[i]->compute_area());
    }
```

Listing 6.8. TRIANGLE.CPP. C++ implementation of the `triangle_shape` class.

```
/*------------------------------------------------------------*/
/*  File:   triangle.cpp
 *
 *  Definition of the "triangle" class of shapes in C++
 */

#include "shapes.h"

/*------------------------------------------------------------*/
triangle_shape::triangle_shape(double xa, double ya,
                    double xb, double yb, double xc, double yc)
{
    x1 = xa;
    y1 = ya;
    x2 = xb;
    y2 = yb;
    x3 = xc;
    y3 = yc;
}
/*------------------------------------------------------------*/
double triangle_shape::compute_area(void) const
{
    double area, x21, y21, x31, y31;
    x21 =   x2 - x1;
    y21 =   y2 - y1;
    x31 =   x3 - x1;
    y31 =   y3 - y1;
    area = fabs(y21 * x31 - x21 * y31) / 2.0;
    return (area);
}
/*------------------------------------------------------------*/
void triangle_shape::draw(void) const
{
    printf("Draw: Triangle with corners at\n"
           "       (%f, %f) (%f, %f) (%f, %f)\n",
            x1, y1, x2, y2, x3, y3);
}
```

Creating Objects at Runtime

There is one more important feature of C++: the capability of creating instances of a class at runtime. In C, you use memory allocation routines such as `calloc` or `malloc` to allocate data dynamically. These functions return a pointer to the allocated data. When you no longer need the data, you can reclaim the memory by calling `free` with the pointer as the argument. C++ provides the operators `new` and `delete` to create and destroy objects, respectively.

Listing 6.7 illustrates how to use the `new` operator to create the geometric shapes and how to use `delete` to destroy them. As with `calloc` or `malloc`, `new` returns a pointer to the newly created instance of the class. `malloc` returns a generic pointer (`void *`) that you must cast to the type of your data, whereas `new` returns a pointer to the correct data type. Additionally, `new` automatically calls the constructor of the class to initialize the new instance.

Summary

Object-oriented programming is easier to practice if the programming language supports the basic necessities of OOP: data abstraction, inheritance, and polymorphism. C++ was developed from C by adding precisely the kind of features that support OOP. C++ provides the `class` construct to define abstract data types, supplies the `virtual` keyword to permit polymorphic functions, and includes the syntax necessary to indicate the inheritance relationship between a derived class and one or more base classes. C++'s `class` construct is similar to C's `struct`, but it has many more features. In particular, with `class` you can define the operations on the object—instances of a class—by member functions and operators. A C++ program manipulates objects by calling the member functions only. This enhances the modularity of programs because you are free to change the internal representation of objects without affecting other parts of a program.

III

Learning C++

7

C++ and ANSI Standard C

In Chapter 6, "C++ and Object-Oriented Programming," you encounter a small but important subset of C++ that specifically supports object-oriented programming. C++ possesses many more features that may not directly support OOP, but nevertheless are needed to write complete programs. Many of these features match what is in ANSI C, but some small differences exist between the two. This chapter describes some major features of C++ and demonstrates how C++ differs from ANSI C. If you are accustomed to ANSI standard C, knowing the differences between C++ and ANSI C can help you avoid potential problems when writing C++ programs. Consult Chapter 4, "Visual C++ 2.0 Extensions to Standard C," for an overview of ANSI standard C.

Features of C++

The following sections provide a quick overview of C++ features that differ from those in ANSI C. The coverage of the topics in the following sections is sparse because these topics are covered again in Chapters 8 through 12.

New Features for Functions in C++

As with C, C++ programs contain functions. C++ introduces several new requirements that make functions efficient and safe to use. One helpful change is the use of prototypes for functions. Although you can use prototypes in ANSI C, they are not mandatory. You can use a prototype or define the function before it is called. In C++, you must declare a function before using it.

Default Arguments

As an additional improvement to functions in C++, you can specify the default values for the arguments when you provide a prototype for a function. For example, if you are defining a function named create_window that sets up a window (a rectangular region) in a graphics display and fills it with a background color, you may opt to specify default values for the window's location, size, and background color:

```
// A function with default argument values
// Assume that Window is a user-defined type

Window create_window(int x = 0, int y = 0, int width = 100,
                      int height = 50, int bgpixel = 0);
```

When create_window is declared in this way, you can use any of the following calls to create new windows:

```
Window w;

// The following is same as: create_window(0, 0, 100, 50, 0);
w = create_window();
```

```
// This is same as: create_window(100, 0, 100, 50, 0);
w = create_window(100);

// Equivalent to create_window(30, 20, 100, 50, 0);
w = create_window(30, 20);
```

As you can see from these examples, it is impossible to give a nondefault value for the height argument without specifying the values for x, y, and width, because height follows them and the compiler can match arguments only by position. In other words, the first argument you specify in a call to create_window always matches x, the second one matches y, and so on. Therefore, you can leave only trailing arguments unspecified.

Overloaded Function Names

In C++ you can have several functions with the same name if their argument lists differ. When this happens, the function's name is *overloaded.* You can use overloading to give a meaningful name to related functions that perform the same task. For example, if you are evaluating the absolute value of numbers, the ANSI C library includes three functions for this purpose: abs for int arguments, labs for long, and fabs for the absolute value of a double. In C++, you can use the abs name for all three versions and declare them as follows:

```
int    abs(int x);
long   abs(long x);
double abs(double x);
```

Then, you can use the functions:

```
int i, diff = -2;
long offset;
double x;

i = abs(diff);          // abs(int)    called
offset = abs(-21956L);  // abs(long)   called
x = abs(-3.55);         // abs(double) called
```

The C++ compiler selects the correct function by comparing the types of arguments in the call with those specified in the function's declaration.

When you overload functions in C++, you must ensure that the number and type of arguments of all overloaded versions are different. C++ does not permit overloading for functions that differ only in the type of return value. Thus, you cannot overload functions such as double compute(int) and float compute(int) because their argument lists are identical.

Inline Functions

Inline functions are like preprocessor macros because the compiler substitutes the entire function body for each inline function call. The inline functions are provided to support efficient implementation of OOP techniques in C++. Because the OOP approach requires the extensive use of member functions, the overhead of function calls can hurt the performance of a program. For smaller functions, you can use the `inline` specifier to avoid the overhead of function calls.

On the surface, inline functions look like preprocessor macros, but the two differ in a crucial aspect. Unlike macros, the compiler treats inline functions as true functions. To see how this can be an important factor, consider the following example. Suppose you define a macro named `multiply`:

```
#define multiply(x,y) (x*y)
```

If you use this macro such as this:

```
x = multiply(4+1,6);   // you want the product of 4+1 and 6
```

by straightforward substitution of the `multiply` macro, the preprocessor transforms the left side of this statement into the following code:

```
x = (4+1*6);
```

This evaluates to 10 rather than 30, the result of multiplying (4+1) and 6. Of course, you know that the solution is to use parentheses around the macro arguments, but consider what happens when you define an inline function exactly as you defined the macro:

```
#include <stdio.h>

// Define inline function to multiply two integers

inline int multiply(int x, int y)
{
    return(x * y);
}

// An overloaded version that multiplies two doubles

inline double multiply(double x, double y)
{
    return(x * y);
}

main()
{
    printf("Product of 5 and 6 = %d\n", multiply(4+1,6));
    printf("Product of 3.1 and 10.0 = %f\n",
        multiply(3.0+.1, 10.0));
}
```

When you compile and run this program, it correctly produces the following output:

```
Product of 5 and 6 = 30
Product of 3.1 and 10.0 = 31.000000
```

As you can see from this example, inline functions do not produce the kind of errors that plague ill-defined macros. Because inline functions behave like true functions, you can overload them and rely on the compiler to use the correct function-based argument types. However, because the body of an inline function is duplicated wherever that function is called, you should use inline functions only when the functions are small in size.

friend Functions

C++ introduces another new keyword to help you implement OOP techniques efficiently: the friend specifier. The rules of data encapsulation in a class are such that only member functions can access the private data of a class. Of course, a class can provide special member functions that can return the values of its private variables, but this approach may be too inefficient in some cases. In such instances, you may want to allow a function outside the class to access data that is private to the class directly. You can do this by declaring that outside function within the class with the friend access specifier. For example, suppose you want to define the non-member function add to add two complex numbers. The following program illustrates how you might use friend functions to accomplish this. Note that this is a simplistic definition of a complex class; it is intended to show you how friend functions work:

```c
#include <stdio.h>

class complex
{
    float real, imag;
public:
    friend complex add(complex a, complex b);
    friend void print(complex a);
    complex() { real = imag = 0.0;}
    complex(float a, float b) { real = a; imag = b;}
};

complex add(complex a, complex b)
{
    complex z;
    z.real = a.real + b.real;
    z.imag = a.imag + b.imag;
    return z;
}

void print(complex a)
{
    printf(" (%f + i %f)\n", a.real, a.imag);
}

main()
{
    complex a, b, c;
    a = complex(1.5, 2.1);
    b = complex(1.1, 1.4);

    printf("Sum of ");
    print(a);
    printf("and");
    print(b);
```

```
    c = add(a,b);

    printf(" = ");
    print(c);
}
```

This program uses the friend function add to add two complex numbers and the friend function print to display the results. When you execute the program, it generates this result:

```
Sum of  (1.500000 + i 2.100000)
and (1.100000 + i 1.400000)
 =  (2.600000 + i 3.500000)
```

Reference Types as Arguments

Unfortunately, the add function has a drawback stemming from the way C passes arguments to functions. C passes arguments by value—when you call a function with some arguments, the values of the arguments are copied to a special area of memory known as the *stack*, and the function uses these copies for its operation. To see the effect of *call by value*, consider the following code:

```
    void twice(int a)
    {
        a *= 2;
    }
    .

    .
    int x = 5;

// Call the "twice" function
    twice(x);

    printf("x = %d\n", x);
```

Note that this program prints 5, not 10, as the value of x, even though the twice function multiplies its argument by 2. This result (5) happens because the twice function receives a copy of x, and any change it makes to that copy is lost upon return from the function.

In C, the only way you can change the value of a variable through a function is by explicitly passing the address of the variable to the function. For example, to double the value of a variable, you can write the function twice:

```
    void twice(int *a)
    {
        *a *= 2;    // Double the value
    }
    .

    .
    int x = 5;

// Call "twice" with the address of x as argument
    twice(&x);

    printf("x = %d\n", x);
```

This time, the program prints 10 as the result. Therefore, you can pass pointers to alter variables through a function call, but the syntax is messy. In the function, you must dereference the argument with the * operator.

C++ provides a way of passing arguments by reference with the introduction of a *reference*, the defining of an alias or alternative name for any instance of data. Syntactically, you append an ampersand (&) to the name of the data type. For example, if you have the following:

```
int i = 5;
int *p_i = &i;  // a pointer to int initialized to point to i
int &r_i = i;   // a reference to the int variable i
```

you can use r_i anywhere you would use i or *p_i. In fact, if you write this:

```
r_i += 10;  // adds 10 to i
```

i changes to 15 because r_i is another name for i.

Using reference types, you can rewrite the function named twice to multiply an integer by 2 in a much simpler manner:

```
    void twice(int &a)
    {
        a *= 2;
    }
    .
    .
    .
    int x = 5;
// Call "twice." Argument automatically passed by reference
    twice(x);

    printf("x = %d\n", x);
```

As expected, the program prints 10 as the result, but it looks a lot simpler than trying to accomplish the same task with pointers.

When classes are passed by value, an overhead exists from copying objects to and from the stack—this is another reason for passing arguments by reference. Passing a reference to an object avoids this unnecessary copying and enables an efficient implementation of OOP. This brings us back to the example in the previous section. Now that you know about references, you can rewrite that small complex class:

```
#include <stdio.h>

class complex
{
    float real, imag;
public:
    friend complex add(const complex &a, const complex &b);
    friend void print(const complex &a);
    complex() { real = imag = 0.0;}
    complex(float a, float b) { real = a; imag = b;}
};
```

```
complex add(const complex &a, const complex &b)
{
    complex z;
    z.real = a.real + b.real;
    z.imag = a.imag + b.imag;
    return z;
}

void print(const complex &a)
{
    printf(" (%f + i %f)\n", a.real, a.imag);
}
```

You can use the class in the same manner as its old version. If you look carefully, you can see that to pass arguments by reference, you simply add an ampersand (&) after the data type of the argument, thus changing all complex types to complex&. (You can add a space between the type and &.) This example includes a const prefix to the arguments to emphasize that the functions add and print must not alter their arguments.

Overloaded Operators

C++ enables you to define several functions with the same name but with varying arguments, and it also enables you to redefine the meaning of operators such as +, -, *, /, %, +=, and -= for any class. In other words, you can overload the meaning of operators. Because a class is a new abstract data type, such overloaded operators provide you with the capability of defining operations on this data.

For example, instead of writing an add function to add two complex variables, you can define the + operator to perform addition for the complex class shown earlier. Using friend functions and const reference types, you might define the + operator as follows:

```
class complex
{
    float real, imag;
public:
    friend complex operator+(const complex &a, const complex &b);

    complex() { real = imag = 0.0;}
    complex(float a, float b) { real = a; imag = b;}
};

complex operator+(const complex &a, const complex &b)
{
    complex z;
    z.real = a.real + b.real;
    z.imag = a.imag + b.imag;
    return z;
}
```

As you can see from the example, defining the operator is like defining a function, except for a special syntax for the name of the function. This syntax is the symbol of the operator with the operator keyword as a prefix.

After you define a + operator for the complex class, you can use it as you normally use the + operator for other data types:

```
complex a, b, c;
a = complex(1.5, 2.1);
b = complex(1.1, 1.4);

c = a+b;     // Add two complex numbers a and b
```

Data Declarations in C++

In ANSI C, you cannot mix declarations with the statements of a program. You must declare all variables at the beginning of a block. C++ does not distinguish between a declaration and other statements, and it enables you to declare variables anywhere. Thus, in C++, you can write the following:

```
#include <stdio.h>
#include <string.h>
.
.
.
void convert_string(char *s)
{
    if(str == NULL) return;
    int length = strlen(s);
    .

    .
    for(int i = 0; i <= length; i++)
    {
// Convert characters in the string...
    }
}
```

This feature of C++ is handy because you can declare a variable and initialize it immediately. The program is more readable because the variable is declared and initialized close to where it actually is used.

Another interesting feature of C++ enables you to start using the name of a struct as soon as its definition is started. In C, when you define structures containing pointers to its own type, you typically use constructs such as this:

```
typedef struct node
{
    struct node *prev; /* Pointer to previous node */
    struct node *next; /* Pointer to next node     */
    void        *info; /* Other members of struct  */
} node;

node *top_node;        /* Define a node */
```

In C++, the same code becomes much simpler:

```
struct node
{
```

```
    node *prev; // Pointer to previous node
    node *next; // Pointer to next node
    void *info; // Other members of struct
} node;

node *top_node; // Define a node
```

As you can see, the name of a struct can be used inside the definition of the struct itself.

How C++ Differs from C

Although it often is casually stated that C++ is a superset of C, especially ANSI standard C, a small number of things in ANSI C do not work quite the same way in C++. The following sections describe the differences.

New Reserved Keywords

To support object-oriented programming, C++ introduces 16 new keywords in addition to those reserved by ANSI C. You should watch out for any C program that might use these reserved words:

asm	friend	private	this
catch	inline	protected	throw
class	new	public	try
delete	operator	template	virtual

You encounter most of these keywords in the rest of this book. Some of them, such as catch, template, and throw are not yet in widespread use because they are used in new features that were recently added to the language. The template keyword is used to enable the definition of families of data types or functions. C++'s exception-handling mechanism uses the catch, throw, and try keywords.

Function Prototypes

In ANSI C, if a function does not have a prototype, the compiler assumes that the function returns an integer. C++ strictly enforces the prototypes and generates an error if you use a function without first declaring it. Thus, C++ displays an error when compiling the following old-style C program:

```
main()
{
    printf("Hello, World!\n"); // Allowed in C, but not in C++
                               // C++ needs prototype before use
}
```

Of course, in ANSI C you can remedy this by including stdio.h, which declares the printf function. You also can get another type of error from old-style C code wherein functions are declared only when they do not return an int. For example, many C programs declare and use malloc as follows:

```
char *malloc();
int  *raw_data;

raw_data = (int *) malloc(1024);
```

This code generates an error in C++ because C++ interprets empty argument lists differently than ANSI C. In ANSI standard C, an empty argument list in a function's declaration means that the function takes zero or more arguments, but C++ considers a function declaration with an empty argument list to be equivalent to the following:

```
char *malloc(void);
```

When C++ encounters the call malloc(1024), it produces an error message because it finds an argument where it expects none.

const Variables

C++ requires you to initialize const variables when you declare them; ANSI C does not. Thus, you have the following:

```
const buflen;       // OK in ANSI C, but not in C++
const buflen = 512; // OK in C++ as well as ANSI C
```

Another interesting property of const variables in C++ is that const integers can be used as subscripts in any constant expression. This is possible because C++ requires const variables to be initialized during declaration. Thus, the compiler always knows the value of a const integer. This enables the following:

```
const buflen = 512;
char  buffer[buflen];  // Allowed in C++, but not in ANSI C
```

Because const integers declared this way are full-fledged variables, you should use them wherever you need constants. In other words, in C++, instead of writing this:

```
#define  EOF    -1
#define  maxlen 128
#define  Pi     3.14159

char one_line[maxlen];   // Define an array to hold a line
```

you should write the following:

```
const EOF = -1;           // This is a const int by default
const maxlen = 128;
const double Pi = 3.14159; // This is a floating-point constant


char one_line[maxlen];    // Define an array to hold a line
```

void Pointers

ANSI C permits pointers of the void * type to be assigned to any other pointer and vice versa—any pointer can be assigned to a pointer of the void * type. C++ does not permit the assignment of a pointer of the void * type to any other pointer without an explicit cast. The following example illustrates the difference:

```
void *p_void;
int  i, *p_i;

p_void = &i;          /* Allowed in both C and C++    */
p_i = p_void;         /* Allowed in C, but not in C++ */
p_i = (int *)p_void;  /* Cast makes it OK to use in C++ */
```

Initialization of Character Arrays

In ANSI C, you can initialize an array of three characters with the following:

```
char name[3] = "C++"; // Allowed in ANSI C, but not in C++
```

After the initialization, the array elements name[0], name[1], and name[2] are set to C, +, and +, respectively. However, C++ does not enable this type of initialization because the array has no room for the terminating null character. In C++, if you need to set up the name array as you did in C, you must rewrite the initialization:

```
char name[3] = {'C', '+', '+'}; // Allowed in both C and C++
```

Of course, the following initialization is valid in both C and C++, but this sets up a 4-byte array with the last byte set to a null character:

```
char name[] = "C++"; // Allowed in both C and C++
```

sizeof Operator

In ANSI C, the size of a character constant such as the expression sizeof('Q') evaluates to the same value as sizeof(int). C++ correctly evaluates this to sizeof(char), however. In ANSI C, the size of an enum variable is the same as sizeof(int). In C++, it is the size of an integral type, not necessarily sizeof(int).

Scope of *enum*

In ANSI C, the list of constants appearing in an enum variable are known throughout the file. C++ considers the constants in an enum to be local to a class or a struct and known only to member and friend functions of the class. For example, the following code is allowed in C++, but not in ANSI C:

```
struct finite_state_machine
{
    enum state{init, reset, end};
// ...
}

int init(int state);   // Allowed in C++, but not in ANSI C
```

If a class declares an enum variable, functions outside the class can refer to the enumerated constants by explicitly qualifying the name with the scope resolution operator. For example, suppose you want to refer to the enumerated constant scientific that is defined in the class named ios. You must use the notation ios::scientific to access this constant.

Restriction on *goto*

With ANSI C, you can jump into a block of code, skipping over the declarations and initializations that may appear at the beginning of the block. You cannot do this in C++. Here is an example:

```
    goto Start;    // OK in ANSI C, but not in C++
// ...
    {
        int  x = 4, y = 8;
        Node t1;            // This could be a class
        char buf[10];

    Start:
// ...
    }  // Class destructors are called before leaving block
```

Although jumping into a block is a questionable practice in C, such jumps are almost always bound to be fatal in a C++ program because C++ calls constructors for any class objects created at the beginning of a block, and it calls the corresponding destructors when the block ends. Jumping into the middle of a block means that calls might go to destructors for which there are no matching calls to constructors. Typically, this produces a fatal error for the program.

Summary

C++ was created by extending C with features designed to support object-oriented programming. C++'s support for OOP comes through the class and struct constructs, the concepts of overloading functions and operators, and virtual functions. Many features of the C++ language, such as function prototypes and the void and enum types, have been incorporated into ANSI standard C. Although C++ compilers accept most ANSI C programs, certain constructs in ANSI C behave differently in C++. You should watch out for the new reserved keywords and for the strict enforcement of the function prototypes in C++.

8

C++ Classes for Standard I/O

Chapter 7, "C++ and ANSI Standard C," provides you with an overview of the C++ programming language and how it relates to ANSI standard C. Before you start using C++ to define your own classes, this chapter gets you started with the iostream class library, which comes with most C++ compilers, including Visual C++ 2.0. This library is C++'s equivalent to C's stdio library, which includes the printf and scanf family. This chapter explains the structure of the classes that form the basis of the iostream library and shows you how to use these classes for various types of I/O.

C++ I/O Library

As with C, C++ contains no built-in facilities for I/O. Instead, you must rely on a library of functions for performing I/O. In ANSI C, the I/O functions are a part of the standard library (C++ does not yet have a standard library). Of course, you can call the ANSI C library routines in C++, but for I/O, Visual C++ 2.0 provides an alternative to printf and scanf. Visual C++ 2.0 includes the iostream library, which handles I/O through a class of objects. The following sections describe simple usage of the iostream library and explain the class hierarchy that constitutes it.

Stream I/O in C++

As a programmer learning OOP, you may want to study the details of the classes in the iostream library, but you do not need to know much about these classes to use the library for simple I/O. To begin, you should be familiar with the concept of a stream and know the names of the predefined streams. The idea of a *stream*—a sequence of bytes—figures prominently in UNIX and C. As a C programmer, you have heard the term stream in connection with ANSI C's file I/O functions that are prototyped in the stdio.h header file. A stream serves as an abstract model of I/O devices, such as a disk file, the keyboard, the video display, or even a buffer in memory. In ANSI C, each stream has an associated FILE structure that holds the state of the stream and such data items as the buffer used for buffered I/O.

BUFFERED I/O

Buffered I/O refers to the use of a block of memory as a temporary storage area for the bytes being read from or written to the stream. ANSI C's stream I/O routines and C++'s iostream library use a buffer to hold data in transit to and from a stream.

For example, in a buffered read operation from a disk file, a fixed-size byte chunk is read from the disk into a buffer of the same size. The routines requesting data from the file actually read from the buffer. When the buffer has no characters left, it is automatically refilled by a disk read operation. A similar sequence occurs when writing to a file.

Buffered I/O operations are efficient because they minimize time-consuming read/write operations with the disk. If needed, you can turn off the buffering.

Each ANSI C stream is identified by the pointer to its associated FILE structure. You get this pointer back when you open the stream by calling the fopen function. In OOP terminology, this is equivalent to creating the stream object. Not all streams need to be explicitly opened, however. When your C program starts up, three streams are already opened for you. These streams, identified as stdin, stdout, and stderr, are used to get input from the keyboard, display output, and display error messages, respectively. The scanf function reads from stdin, and the printf function sends its output to stdout. The fscanf and fprintf functions can handle I/O with streams that you open.

The C++ iostream library is an object-oriented implementation of a stream, viewed as a flow of bytes from a *source* (producer) to a *sink* (consumer). As you will see later, the iostream library includes input streams (the istream class), output streams (the ostream class), and streams that can handle both input and output operations (the iostream class). The istream class provides the functionality of scanf and fscanf, whereas the ostream class has capabilities similar to those of printf and fprintf. Like the predefined C streams stdin, stdout, and stderr, the iostream library includes four predefined streams:

- ■ cin, an input stream connected to the standard input (analogous to stdin in C)
- ■ cout, an output stream connected to the standard output (analogous to stdout in C)
- ■ cerr, an output stream set up to provide unbuffered output to the standard error device (analogous to stderr in C)
- ■ clog, a fully buffered stream like cin and cout (similar to cerr)

Later, you see how to assign other streams to these identifiers so that you can redirect I/O to a different file or device.

Using *iostream*

To use the iostream library, your C++ program must include the iostream.h header file. This file contains the definitions of the classes that implement the stream objects and provides the buffering. The iostream.h file is analogous to stdio.h in ANSI C.

Instead of defining member functions that perform I/O, the iostream library provides an operator notation for input and output. It uses C++'s capability for overloading operators and defines << and >> as the output and input operators, respectively. Figure 8.1 illustrates how these operators work with the cin and cout streams.

FIGURE 8.1.

Buffered I/O with streams
cin and cout.

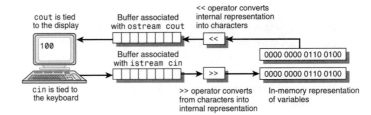

When you see the << and >> operators in use, you realize their appropriateness. For example, consider a program that prints some variables to the cout stream, which is usually connected to standard output:

```
#include <iostream.h>

void main()
{
    int    count = 2;
    double result = 5.4;
    char   *id = "Trying out iostream: ";

    cout << id;
    cout << "count = " << count << '\n';
    cout << "result = " << result << '\n';
}
```

When you run this program, it prints the following:

```
Trying out iostream: count = 2
result = 5.4
```

You can make three observations from this example:

- The << operator is a good choice to represent the output operation because it points in the direction of data movement that, in this case, is toward the cout stream.

- You can concatenate multiple << operators in a single line, all feeding the same stream.

- You can use the same syntax to print all the basic data types on a stream. The << operator automatically converts the internal representation of the variable into a textual representation. Contrast this with the need to use different format strings for printing different data types using printf.

Accepting input from the standard input is an easy process as well. Here is a small sample that combines both input and output:

```
#include <iostream.h>

void main()
{
    int    count;
    float  price;
    char   *prompt =
           "Enter count (int) and unit price (float): ";
```

```
// Display the prompt string and flush
// to force it to be displayed
    cout << prompt << flush;

// Read from standard input
    cin >> count >> price;

// Display total cost
    cout << count << " at " << price << " will cost: ";
    cout << (price * count) << endl;
}
```

When you run the program and enter the input, the program interacts as follows:

```
Enter count (int) and unit price (float): 5 2.5
5 at 2.5 will cost: 12.5
```

Ignoring, for the moment, items that you do not recognize, notice how easy it is to read values into variables from the cin stream—merely send the data from cin to the variables using the >> operator. As with the << operator, you can concatenate multiple >> operators. The >> operator automatically converts the strings into the internal representations of the variables according to their types. The simple syntax of input from cin is in sharp contrast with ANSI C's rather complicated scanf function, which serves the same purpose but needs proper format strings and addresses of variables as arguments.

Using Manipulators

Among the new items in the last example, you may have noticed the identifiers flush (in the first cout statement) and endl (in the last cout statement). These are special functions known as *manipulators*, which are written so that you can alter the state of the stream by placing a manipulator in the chain of << operators. The flush manipulator forces cout to display its output without waiting for its buffer to fill up—the buffer is flushed. The endl manipulator sends a newline character to the stream and also flushes the buffer. Table 8.1 summarizes some of the manipulators available in the iostream package. (The manipulators that take arguments are declared in the file iomanip.h; the rest are in iostream.h.)

Table 8.1. C++ iostream manipulators.

Manipulator	Sample Usage	Effect
dec	cout << dec << intvar; cin >> dec >> intvar;	Converts integers into decimal digits (similar to the %d format in C)
hex	cout << hex << intvar; cin >> hex >> intvar;	Hexadecimal conversion as in ANSI C's %x format

continues

Table 8.1. continued

Manipulator	Sample Usage	Effect
oct	`cout << oct << intvar;` `cin >> oct >> intvar;`	Octal conversion (%o format in C)
ws	`cin >> ws;`	Discards whitespace characters in the input stream
endl	`cout << endl;`	Sends a newline character to ostream and flushes the buffer
ends	`cout << ends;`	Inserts a null character into a string
flush	`cout << flush;`	Flushes ostream's buffer
resetiosflags(long)	`cout << resetiosflags(ios::dec);` `cin >> resetiosflags(ios::hex);`	Resets the format bits specified by the long integer argument
setbase(int)	`cout << setbase(10);` `cin >> setbase(8);`	Sets the base of conversion to the integer argument (must be 0, 8, 10, or 16); 0 sets the base to the default
setfill(int)	`cout << setfill('.');` `cin >> setfill(' ');`	Sets the fill character used to pad fields to the specified width
setiosflags(long)	`cout << setiosflags(ios::dec);` `cin >> setiosflags(ios::hex);`	Sets the format bits specified by the long integer argument
setprecision(int)	`cout << setprecision(6);` `cin >> setprecision(15);`	Sets the precision of floating-point conversions to the specified number of digits
setw(int)	`cout << setw(6) << var;` `cin >> setw(24) >> buf;`	Sets the width of a field to the specified number of characters

Using Manipulators for Formatted I/O

You can use manipulators for some simple formatted I/O. *Formatting* refers to the process of converting to and from the internal binary representation of a variable and its character string representation. For example, if a 16-bit integer variable holds the bit pattern 0000 0000 0110 0100, its character string representation is 100 in the decimal number system and 64 in hexadecimal. If the base of conversion is octal, the representation is 144. You can display all three forms on separate lines using these output statements:

```
#include <iostream.h>

void main()
{
    int i = 100;  // Integer initialized to 100 (decimal)

    cout << dec << i << endl;  // Displays 100
    cout << hex << i << endl;  // Displays 64
    cout << oct << i << endl;  // Displays 144
}
```

This produces the following output:

```
100
64
144
```

If you want to use a fixed field width of six characters to display each value, you can do this by using the setw manipulator:

```
#include <iostream.h>
#include <iomanip.h>
void main()
{
    int i = 100;  // Integer initialized to 100 (decimal)

// Set field widths to 6
    cout << setw(6) << dec << i << endl;
    cout << setw(6) << hex << i << endl;
    cout << setw(6) << oct << i << endl;
}
```

This changes the output to the following:

```
   100
    64
   144
```

Here, each variable is displayed in a six-character field aligned at the right and padded with blanks at the left. You can change both the padding and the alignment. To change the padding character, use the setfill manipulator. For example, just before the cout statements in the previous example, insert this line:

```
cout << setfill('.');
```

With that line in place, the output changes to the following:

```
...100
....64
...144
```

The spaces to the left are now padded with dots, the fill characters specified by the previous call to the setfill manipulator. The default alignment of fixed-width output fields pads on the left, resulting in right-justified output. The justification information is stored in a bit pattern called *format bits* in a class named ios, which forms the basis of all stream classes. You can set or reset specific bits with the setiosflags and resetiosflags manipulators, respectively. Here is a sample of how these manipulators work:

```cpp
#include <iostream.h>
#include <iomanip.h>

void main()
{
    int i = 100;   // Integer initialized to 100 (decimal)

    cout << setfill('.');

// Left-justified labels followed by right-justified values...

    cout << setiosflags(ios::left);
    cout << setw(20) << "Decimal";
    cout << resetiosflags(ios::left);
    cout << setw(6) << dec << i << endl;

    cout << setiosflags(ios::left);
    cout << setw(20) << "Hexadecimal";
    cout << resetiosflags(ios::left);
    cout << setw(6) << hex << i << endl;

    cout << setiosflags(ios::left);
    cout << setw(20) << "Octal";
    cout << resetiosflags(ios::left);
    cout << setw(6) << oct << i << endl;
}
```

This example generates the following output:

```
Decimal...............100
Hexadecimal...........64
Octal.................144
```

This output illustrates how the setiosflags and resetiosflags manipulators work and how they should be used. All you need to know are the names of the enumerated list of formatting flags so that you can use them as arguments to the setiosflags and resetiosflags manipulators. Table 8.2 lists the format bit flags and their meanings.

Table 8.2. Names of format flags in `iostream`.

Name of Flag	Meaning
`ios::skipws`	Skips whitespace on input
`ios::left`	Left-justifies output within the specified width of the field
`ios::right`	Right-justifies output
`ios::scientific`	Uses scientific notation for floating-point numbers (such as -1.23e+02)
`ios::fixed`	Uses decimal notation for floating-point numbers (such as -123.45)
`ios::dec`	Uses decimal notation for integers
`ios::hex`	Uses hexadecimal notation for integers
`ios::oct`	Uses octal notation for integers
`ios::uppercase`	Uses uppercase letters in output (such as F4 in hexadecimal, 1.23E+02)
`ios::showbase`	Indicates the base of the number system in the output (a `0x` prefix for hexadecimal and a `0` prefix for octal)
`ios::showpoint`	Includes a decimal point for floating-point output (for example, -123.)
`ios::showpos`	Shows a positive sign when displaying positive values
`ios::stdio`	Flushes all output streams after each character is inserted into an output stream
`ios::unitbuf`	Flushes all output streams after each output operation

To use any of the format flags shown in Table 8.2, insert the manipulator `setiosflags` with the name of the flag as the argument. Use `resetiosflags` with the same argument to revert to the format state prior to your using the `setiosflags` manipulator.

SCOPE OPERATOR (::)

The `ios::left` notation uses the scope resolution operator `::` to identify `left` as a member of the `ios` class. The names of the format flags are specified with an `ios::` pre-fix because they are defined in the `ios` class.

Controlling the Floating-Point Formats

You can control the floating-point format with the `setprecision` manipulator and three flags: `scientific`, `fixed`, and `showpoint`. To illustrate how these affect floating-point formatting, consider the following code that displays a floating-point value:

```
cout << "123.4567 in default format = ";
cout << 123.4567 << endl;

cout << "123.4567 in 2-digit precision = ";
cout << setprecision(2) << 123.4567 << endl;

// Set the precision back to 6
cout << setprecision(6);
cout << "123.4567 in scientific notation = ";
cout << setiosflags(ios::scientific) << 123.4567 << endl;
```

This code displays the following:

```
123.4567 in default format = 123.457
123.4567 in 2-digit precision = 1.2e+002
123.4567 in scientific notation = 1.234567e+002
```

The first line displays the value in the fixed format that is the default. The next line sets the precision to 2—that means you want no more than two digits after the decimal point. The floating-point number is rounded and printed. The last line shows the same number in scientific notation. If you set the `ios::uppercase` flag, the e in the exponent appears in uppercase.

Overloading <<

If you define a class for complex numbers and want to use the << operator to display the objects of your class, you want code that looks like this:

```
complex z(1.1, 1.2);
// ...
cout << z;
```

You can do this easily by overloading the << operator. To redefine this operator, you need to define the function `operator<<` for your class. Because the << operator is used with an `ostream` object on the left and a complex class object on the right, the prototype for the `operator<<` function is the following:

```
ostream& operator<<(ostream& s, const complex& x);
```

where the arguments are passed by reference for efficiency and the `const` prefix in the second argument directs the operator not to alter the complex number. When you learn more about references, you see that the `operator<<` function must return a reference to the stream—this is the key to concatenating the << operators. To illustrate an actual overloading of the << operator, the following sample program uses an abbreviated definition of a complex class and follows the steps necessary to define and use the << operator:

```
#include <iostream.h>

class complex            // a simple class for complex numbers
{
    float real, imag;
public:
    complex() { real = imag = 0.0;}
    complex(float a, float b) { real = a; imag = b;}
    void print(ostream& s) const;
};

// Need this function so that operator<< can do its job
// by calling this one
void complex::print(ostream& s) const
{
    s << real << " + " << imag;
}

// Overload the operator << for use with complex class

ostream& operator<<(ostream &s, const complex& z)
{
    z.print(s);
    return s;
}

// Test the overloaded << operator...

void main()
{
    complex a(1.5, 2.1);
    cout << " a = " << a << endl;
}
```

When compiled, linked, and run, this program produces the expected output:

```
a = 1.5 + 2.1
```

Note the following key points:

- ■ Define a member function that prints the class members the way you want.

- ■ Define the operator<< function with a reference to an ostream and a reference to your class as its first and second arguments, respectively. The function's return type should be ostream&. In the body of the function, call your class member function to print and to return the first argument, which happens to be the reference to the stream.

- ■ Now you can use the << operator to print objects of your class on a stream.

The *iostream* Class Hierarchy

Now that you know how to use the iostream library for simple I/O, take a look at Figure 8.2, which graphically illustrates the hierarchy of classes in a typical implementation of the iostream library. As shown in the figure, the streambuf class provides the buffer used by the streams. All the stream classes are derived from the ios base class, which stores the state of the stream and handles errors. The ios class has an associated streambuf object that acts as the buffer for the stream. The istream and ostream classes, derived from ios, are intended for input and output, respectively. The iostream class uses multiple inheritance to acquire the capabilities of both istream and ostream classes and, therefore, supports both input and output. The istream_withassign, ostream_withassign, and iostream_withassign classes are derived from istream, ostream, and iostream, respectively, by adding the definition of the assignment operator (=) so that you can redirect I/O by assigning one stream to another. The predefined streams cout, cerr, and clog are of ostream_withassign class, whereas cin is an instance of istream_withassign class.

FIGURE 8.2.

Classes in the C++ iostream library.

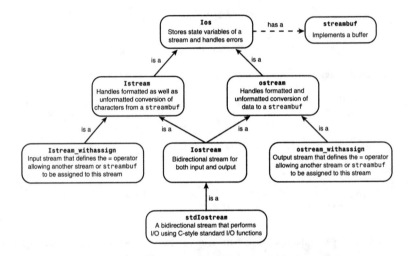

THE iostream CLASSES AND MULTIPLE INHERITANCE

The classes declared in iostream.h use inheritance to organize the classes in the library. The iostream classes illustrate an interesting consequence of multiple inheritance. In C++, an instance of a derived class contains a copy of all members of its base class. Thus, a class such as iostream that inherits from both istream and ostream, each with the same base class (ios), can end up with two copies of the members of ios. With C++, you avoid this by declaring istream and ostream with ios as a *virtual base class*:

```
class istream : virtual public ios { /* ... */ };
class ostream : virtual public ios { /* ... */ };
```

You can find further details of virtual base classes in Chapter 11, "Using Inheritance in C++," and Chapter 12, "Virtual Functions and Polymorphism."

File I/O

In ANSI C, file I/O is handled by functions such as `fopen` to open a file, `fclose` to close it, `fscanf` to read from it, and `fprintf` to write to it. In the `iostream` package, the classes intended for file I/O are defined in the fstream.h header file. Thus, for file I/O, you need to use the following:

```
#include <fstream.h>
```

There are three classes of interest in fstream.h:

- The `ifstream` class, which supports input
- The `ofstream` class, which supports output
- The `fstream` class, which supports both

The following sections explain how to use the file I/O facilities in `fstream.h`.

Simple File I/O

The easiest way to open a file for I/O is to create an instance of the `ifstream` or `ofstream` class:

```
#include <fstream.h>      // Defines classes ifstream and ofstream

// Open file named "infile" for input operations only and
// connect it to the istream "ins"
ifstream ins("infile");

// Open file named "outfile" for output operations only and
// connect it to the ostream "outs"
ofstream outs("outfile");

//...
```

As you can see, you can open a file and connect it to a stream when you create the stream. Two distinct streams exist for input and output—`ifstream` for input and `ofstream` for output. The ANSI C equivalent of connecting a file to an `ifstream` is to call `fopen` with the r mode; using `ofstream` with a file is similar to calling `fopen` with the w mode.

Before using the stream connected to a file, you should check whether the stream was successfully created. The logical NOT operator ! is overloaded for the stream classes so that you can check a stream using a test such as this:

```
// Open stream
   ifstream ins("infile");

// Check whether stream has been opened successfully...
   if(!ins)
     {
        cerr << "Cannot open: infile\n";
        exit(1);
     }
```

You do not have to attach an `ifstream` or `ofstream` to any file at the time of its creation. If you want, you can create the stream first, and open the file later using the `open` member function of the stream:

```
    ifstream ins;
//...
    ins.open("infile");
// Check whether file opened successfully...
    if(!ins)  // Open failed...
//...
```

You can disconnect the file from the stream by closing it. To do this, call the stream's `close` member function:

```
// Close file
    ins.close();
```

This does not destroy the stream. You can reconnect it to another file by calling `open` again.

Controlling the Stream Operating Modes

When you open a stream by supplying the name of a file to the stream's constructor, you are taking advantage of C++'s allowance for default argument values. When you call the following:

```
ifstream ins("infile");
```

the constructor invoked is declared as this:

```
ifstream(const char *, int = ios::in, int = filebuf::openprot);
```

The last two integer-valued arguments are used with the default values. The second argument to the constructor indicates the mode in which the stream operates. For `ifstream`, the default is `ios::in`, which means the file is open for reading. For an `ofstream` object, the default mode is `ios::out`, meaning that the file is open for writing. What if you want to open a file for output, but you want to append data to an existing file rather than destroy its current contents? You do this by specifying an operating mode of `ios::app`. Like the format flags shown in Table 8.2, the stream operating modes are also defined in the `ios` class—hence the `ios::` prefix for the names. Table 8.3 summarizes these modes.

Table 8.3. Stream operating modes.

Mode Name	Operation
ios::app	Appends data to the file
ios::ate	When first opened, positions the file at the end of the file (ate stands for "at end")
ios::in	Opens the file for reading
ios::nocreate	Fails to open the file if it does not already exist

Mode Name	Operation
ios::noreplace	If the file exists, open for output fails unless ios::app or ios::ate is set
ios::out	Opens the file for writing
ios::trunc	Truncates the file if it already exists

Notice that you can specify more than one mode for a file merely by using a bitwise OR of the required modes. For example, to open a file for output and to position it at the end, use the ios::out and ios::ate modes:

```
ofstream outs("outfile", ios::out | ios::ate);
```

Copying Files

As an example of file I/O in C++, consider a utility program that copies the contents of one file to another. Assume that the utility is named `filecopy` and that when you type this command:

```
filecopy in.fil out.fil
```

`filecopy` copies the contents of the file named in.fil to a second file named out.fil. Implementing such a program is straightforward: open the two files (one for input, another one for output), read characters from the input file, and write them to the output file. Listing 8.1 shows a sample implementation of the `filecopy` utility program.

Listing 8.1. FILECOPY.CPP. A utility program that copies the contents of one file to another.

```
//--------------------------------------------------------------
// FILE:  filecopy.cpp
// Copies contents of one file to another
//--------------------------------------------------------------

#include <stdlib.h>
#include <fstream.h>

void main(int argc, char **argv)
{
// Check if there are enough arguments
    if(argc < 3)
    {
        cerr << "Usage: filecopy infile outfile\n";
        exit(0);
    }

// Open the input file and connect it to stream "ins"
    ifstream ins(argv[1]);
    if(!ins)
    {
```

continues

Listing 8.1. continued

```
                cerr << "Cannot open: " << argv[1];
                exit(1);
        }

// Open the output file and connect it to stream "outs"
        ofstream outs(argv[2]);
        if(!outs)
        {
                cerr << "Cannot open: " << argv[2];
                exit(1);
        }

// Read from "ins" and write to "outs"
        char c;
        while(ins.get(c) && outs) outs.put(c);
}
```

Another way to implement the last while loop that does the actual copying between the files is to read and write one line at a time. To read a line, use the same get function but with the address of a buffer and the buffer's size as arguments:

```
const bufsize = 128;
char buf[bufsize];
//...
ins.get(buf, bufsize);
```

This call to get extracts up to bufsize-1 characters (or until a newline character is encountered) from the input stream to the specified buffer. Then get places a terminating null character in the buffer. By default, the get function stops at the newline character, but you can specify another delimiter as a third argument to the get function. Notice that this call to get is similar to the fgets function in C, except that unlike fgets, get does not copy the newline character to the buffer, nor does get skip over the newline character. Therefore, to read lines repeatedly from a file, you must extract the newline character separately after each line is read. Here is an example that does this:

```
#include <string.h>    // For prototype of "strlen"
#include <fstream.h>
//...
// Assume that streams "ins" and "outs" are already set up
// as shown in Listing 8.1

// Read lines from "ins" and write to "outs"

        const bufsize = 256;
        char buf[bufsize];
        char c;

        while(ins.get(buf, bufsize) && outs)
        {
// Write out buffer using the "write" function
                outs.write(buf, strlen(buf));
```

```
// Read leftover newline character and write that out also
    ins.get(c);
    outs.put(c);
  }
```

You can use this as the replacement for the last `while` loop of Listing 8.1. The actual writing of the buffer to the output file is done by the `write` function of the output stream. As shown, this function copies the specified number of characters from the buffer to the output stream.

Positioning in a File

Many times you have to read files containing binary data with a specific internal structure. For example, a 128-byte header might be followed by blocks of data. Information extracted from the file's header might tell you that the data you need is at a specific location inside the file. To read this data, you need to position the stream properly before reading from it. In ANSI C, you can use functions such as `fseek` and `ftell` to position streams. With the `iostream` library, you also can reposition streams, and, as expected, classes provide member functions that accomplish this.

You can position a stream in the `iostream` library by calling the `seekg` or `seekp` member functions of that stream. Because the same stream can be used for both input and output, the stream classes work with the concept of a *get* position and a *put* position which, respectively, indicate the location from which the next read or write occurs. Set the get position using `seekg`; set the put position using `seekp`. For example, to position the stream at the 513th byte in the `ins` input stream, you can use `setg`:

```
ins.seekg(512);     // next get will start at 513th byte
```

Specifying the Position: Relative Reference

You also can specify the position relative to some reference point, such as the end of the file. For example, to move eight bytes backward from the end of the stream, use the following:

```
ins.seekg(-8, ios::end);
```

There are three reference points identified by constants defined in the `ios` class:

- ■ `ios::beg`, representing the beginning of the stream
- ■ `ios::end`, representing the end of the stream
- ■ `ios::cur`, representing the current position

Getting the Current Position

You also can retrieve the current get or put position in a file. The `tellg` function returns the current location in an input stream, whereas the `tellp` function returns the corresponding item for an output stream. Both functions return a variable of the `streampos` type. You can save the returned value and use it with `seekg` or `seekp` to return to the old location in a file:

```
    streampos saved_pos = tellg();
// Other operations on stream...
// ...
// Get back to old location
    seekg(saved_pos);
```

Detecting Errors in File I/O

The `iostream` library provides several functions for checking the status of a stream. The `fail` function tells you whether something has gone wrong. Therefore, you can check for problems by calling `fail` for the stream:

```
    ifstream ins("infile");
    if(ins.fail())
    {
// Stream creation has failed. Take appropriate action.
// ...
    }
```

In fact, the logical NOT operator `!` has been overloaded to call `fail` for a stream so that the `if` test can be written more simply as the following:

```
    if(!ins)
    {
// Handle error...
    }
```

Detecting the End of the File

When reading from or writing to a file, you want to know whether the program has reached the end of the file. The `eof` function returns a nonzero value if the stream is at the end of the file. Once a stream has reached the end of the file, it does not perform any I/O (this is the case even if you attempt an I/O after moving the stream away from the end by using `seekg` or `seekp`), because the stream's internal state remembers the encounter with the end of the file. You have to call `clear` to reset the state before any further I/O can take place. Thus, sometimes `eof` and `clear` are used:

```
// "ins" is an istream. If the stream reached eof, clear the
// state before attempting to read from the stream
    if(ins.eof()) ins.clear();
// Reposition stream and read again...
    ins.seekg(-16, ios::cur); // Move back 16 bytes
    ins.get(buf, 8);          // Read 8 bytes into buffer
```

Using Good and Bad Conditions

Two other member functions, `good` and `bad`, indicate the general condition of a stream. As the names imply, `good` returns TRUE (a nonzero value) if no error has occurred in the stream, whereas `bad` returns TRUE if an invalid I/O has been attempted or if the stream has an irrecoverable failure. You can use `good` and `bad` in tests such as the following:

```
    if(ins.bad())
        {
// Invalid operation...
        }

    if(ins.good())
        {
// Everything ok. Continue using stream...
        }
```

String I/O

When your application uses a windowing system for I/O, you cannot readily use the cin and cout streams for I/O. With most windowing systems, you display a string (a null-terminated array of characters) in a window by calling a designated function from the windowing system's library. This is easy to do with plain strings, but how do you display the value of a variable? What you need is a way to send the formatted output to a string that you can then display by using the windowing system's text output functions. In ANSI C, you can use the sprintf function to prepare a formatted string. Similarly, you can use sscanf to extract variables from a string. The C++ iostream package also includes these capabilities in the form of the istrstream and ostrstream classes for reading from and writing to a string, respectively. These classes are declared in the strstrea.h file.

DEVIATION FROM AT&T C++

In UNIX systems and in AT&T C++, the strstrea.h header file is named strstream.h. Because MS-DOS permits only eight characters to be used in a filename, this header file is named strstrea.h in Microsoft Visual C++ 2.0.

Writing to a String

String I/O is commonly used to prepare formatted output to a string. You need an instance of an ostrstream class for this purpose. Typically, you have a buffer of fixed size in which to place the formatted output. To set up an ostrstream object connected to such a buffer, you can use the following code:

```
#include <strstrea.h>  // Defines the ostrstream class
// ...
    const buflen = 128;
    char buf[buflen];

// Set up an ostrstream connected to this buffer
    ostrstream s(buf, sizeof(buf));
```

This sets up an output stream connected to a buffer and assumes a stream operating mode of ios::out. As with file I/O, you can specify another mode, such as ios::app, to append data to an existing string. Sending output to this stream is as easy as writing to cout. Here is an example:

```
#include <strstrea.h>

void main()
{
    const buflen = 128;
    char buf[buflen];
    int   i = 100;
    float x = 3.1415;
// Open an output stream and connect to the buffer
    ostrstream s(buf, buflen);

// Write to the stream
    s << "i = " << i << " x = " << x << ends;

// Display the string on cout
    cout << buf << endl;
}
```

The program displays the following:

```
i = 100 x = 3.1415
```

Although here the program simply displays the buffer by sending it to cout, in practice, you prepare the output in a buffer because you need it for use by a function that cannot handle formatting.

Reading from a String

String I/O can also be used to convert characters from a string to internal representation of variables. The istrstream class is designed for reading from buffers. For example, if a string holds an integer and a floating-point number, you can extract the variables using the >> operator just as you would from cin. The following program illustrates the use of an istrstream class:

```
#include <strstrea.h>

void main()
{
    const buflen = 128;
    char  buf[buflen] = "120    6.432";  // A sample buffer
    int   i;
    float x;

// Open an input stream and connect to the buffer
    istrstream s(buf, buflen);

// Read from the stream
    s >> i >> x;
```

```
// Display the result on cout
    cout << "i = " << i << " x = " << x << endl;
}
```

The program displays the following:

```
i = 120 x = 6.432
```

This type of conversion from a string to variables is necessary when reading data from a text file to your program.

Summary

Although you can continue to use the ANSI C I/O routines (the `printf` and `scanf` family) in C++ programs, there is an alternative. The `iostream` I/O library included in Visual C++ 2.0 provides a cleaner, object-based mechanism for I/O. As with ANSI C's `stdin`, `stdout`, and `stderr`, the `iostream` package includes the following predefined streams: `cin`, `cout`, `cerr`, and `clog`, a buffered version of `cerr`.

The stream classes use a simple syntax for I/O: the `<<` and `>>` operators are used for output and input, respectively. The `iostream` library includes built-in support for I/O operations involving the basic data types, such as `int`, `char`, `float`, and `double`. Additionally, you can overload the `<<` and `>>` operators to handle I/O for your own classes. This enables you to use a consistent style for all I/O in your program.

The `iostream` package supports opening and closing files and performing I/O operations with files. The classes declared in fstream.h implement the file I/O capabilities similar to those provided by the C functions `fopen`, `fclose`, `fscanf`, and `fprintf`. Additionally, the I/O package includes several classes, declared in the strstrea.h header file, which can read from and write to arrays of characters as C's `sscanf` and `sprintf` do.

Using the `iostream` classes is easy, provided you know what classes are available and how to call their public member functions. Although you can learn some of this by browsing through the header files, to make proper use of the member functions, you need the documentation for the class. This chapter provides a reasonable amount of information about the `iostream` classes so you can begin using them for I/O in your C++ programs.

Apart from the I/O capabilities, the `iostream` package is also a good example of how C++'s support for OOP can be exploited in a class library. The classes in the library make extensive use of inheritance, including multiple inheritance and the virtual base class mechanism. Chapter 12 covers the details of these C++ language features.

9

Building Objects with Classes

Beginning with this chapter, you learn the details of C++'s syntax and see how its constructs support OOP. Rather than going through a litany of seemingly unrelated features, Chapters 9 through 12 explain the syntax of most C++ features in light of some well-defined needs that arise when you use object-oriented techniques in your programs. Small examples illustrate the need for a feature and show how a particular construct fulfills that need. This chapter focuses on the `class` and `struct` constructs that enable you to define new types of objects. It also provides general guidelines for implementing and using classes.

Classes as Objects

Before you manipulate objects, you need a way to create them. Defining an object involves describing a new data type and the functions that can manipulate that data type. How do you represent a new data type? You must declare the new data type in terms of some existing types. For instance, you can express a point in a two-dimensional plane by an x,y coordinate pair. If each coordinate is represented by an integer type, such as `int`, you can declare a point as a structure:

```
struct Point          // Declare a Point structure
{
    int x, y;
};

struct Point ul, lr;  // Define two Points
```

These are facilities already existing in C. If you prefer calling the new type `Point` (without the `struct` prefix), you can do so with the `typedef` facility:

```
typedef struct Point  // Declare a Point type
{
    int x, y;
} Point;

Point ul, lr;         // Define two Points
```

With this code segment, you can use `Point` as the name of a type, but this is far from being a new data type. For example, you might want to define the addition operator (+) for `Point`. This is not possible with C's `struct`. C enables you to group data items into a single entity, but it does not provide any way to declare the functions and operators inside the structure. Therefore, it is not a complete data type with well-defined operations. Of course, you can write functions that manipulate `Point` structures, but you don't receive any support from the compiler to help associate these functions more closely with `Points`.

User-Defined Data Types

To support the definition of a full-fledged data type, C++ needs to extend the syntax of `struct` by enabling you to include functions and operators as members of a `struct`. C++ also made the *structure tag* or *name*—the symbol following `struct`—a standalone name, meaning that you can use that name without the `struct` prefix. With these extensions to C's `struct`, C++ enables you to declare and use a `Point` type:

```
struct Point      // Declare a Point type
{
    int x, y;

// Define operations on Point
    void operator+(const Point& p) const
    {
        return Point(x+p.x, y+p.y);
    }
//...
};

Point ul, lr;    // Define two Points
```

For now, ignore the definition of the + operator; it is covered in Chapter 10, "Defining Operations on Objects." Notice that you can place function definitions inside a `struct` and that the name of a `struct` serves as a data type.

As an example of another user-defined type, suppose you want to create a `String` data type that provides the functionality of C's null-terminated strings but uses an object-oriented approach. What you essentially want is a pointer to an array of characters and the capability of storing C-style null-terminated strings in that array. Because the length of the string is needed often, you decide to store it as a member variable as well. Finally, suppose you plan to use the strings to store lines of text that are being edited. Because the number of characters in each line can fluctuate as characters are added or removed, you decide to allocate a slightly larger array than necessary. To manage the string's storage properly, you also need to store the size of the allocated array. Allowing, for the moment, a lone function that returns the length of the string, you end up with a preliminary definition of the `String`:

```
#include <stddef.h>    // For size_t type

struct String
{
    size_t length(void);
// Other member functions...

    char   *p_c;       // pointer to allocated space
    size_t _length;    // current length of string
    size_t _maxlen;    // number of bytes allocated
};
```

This appears clean enough, but a problem exists. By default, all members of the structure are accessible to any function that wants to use them. You don't want this because that goes against one of the basic principles of data abstraction, which advocates that you should define an abstract data type (a user-defined type) but hide the internal details of the new type. In particular, for `String` objects, you want to hide details, such as the way you decide to implement the string's internal storage. If programs come to rely on these details, you cannot change the implementation in the future, even if a change clearly makes manipulation of the `String` type more efficient.

Access Control for Class Members

For complete support of data abstraction, you need control over who can access what in a structure. C++ introduces a new keyword, `class`, which you can use exactly like `struct`. Unlike members of a `struct`, however, the members of a `class` are not accessible to any outside functions. In other words, a `struct` is wide open, but a `class` is totally hidden. Because neither of these is a good solution, C++ adds three new keywords to help specify access: `private`, `public`, and `protected`. You can explicitly mark sections of a `class` or a `struct` as `private`, `public`, or `protected`:

```
#include <stddef.h>   // For size_t type

class String          // Declare the String class
{
public:
    size_t length(void);
// Other publicly accessible member functions...

protected:
// Members accessible to derived classes only
// ...

private:
// Members accessible to other members of this class

    char   *p_c;      // pointer to allocated space
    size_t _length;   // current length of string
    size_t _maxlen;   // number of bytes allocated
};
```

The `public` section lists the members that are accessible to any function in the program. Only member functions of the class can access the `private` section. When you read about inheritance in Chapter 11, "Using Inheritance in C++," you learn why the `protected` section is needed. For now, remember that the members in the `protected` section of a class are accessible to classes derived from that class. Figure 9.1 illustrates how the access control keywords work.

Notice that you can include multiple `public`, `private`, and `protected` sections in a class. Each section label determines the access level of the members listed between that label and the next label or the closing right brace (`}`) that marks the end of the class declaration. If you don't provide any label at the beginning of a class, the compiler considers all members up to the next access control label as `private`. On the other hand, everything before the first access specifier is `public` in a `struct`.

public Functions Can Return *private* Values

The `private` section of a class usually declares all the member functions that can be invoked from anywhere in the program. You can think of these functions as the interface to the outside world. If you need to provide the value of a `private` variable to the outside world, you can write a `public` member function that returns the value. A good example is the `length` member

FIGURE 9.1.

Access control in C++ classes.

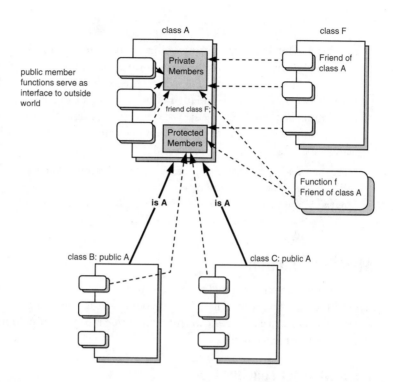

function of the rudimentary `String` class. The `private` variable `_length` holds the current length of the string. If you are working with a `struct`-based implementation of `String` without the `private` keyword, you might be tempted to access the length:

```
    String this_line;
//...
    if(this_line._length > 0)  // this refers to length of string
// ...
```

The principle of information hiding, enforced by the `private` keyword, prevents you from doing this. You can solve this problem by writing a `length` function that returns `_length`. In this case, any function can refer to the length of a string:

```
if(this_line.length() > 0)  // this refers to length of string
```

This simple example illustrates what you encounter in all class-based designs: `public` member functions provide access to `private` variables of the class. This insulates the users of the class from any changes to its internal variables.

LEADING UNDERSCORES IN NAMES OF MEMBER VARIABLES

You don't need the leading underscores in names of private member variables of a class; however, there is a reason for using names with leading underscores. Most private member variables require a corresponding public member function so that other classes can access the private variable. If you name the private member variable with a leading underscore, you can use the same name without the underscore for the access function. For instance, notice the private member variable named _length and the member function named length in the String class. By choosing the variable's name with a leading underscore (_length), you can provide an access function with a more logical name (length).

Note that many programmers prefer an alternate approach of using an underscore suffix in the names of private member variables. In this approach, you would use length_ as the variable name and provide an access function named length.

Member Functions

Member functions are designed to implement the operations enabled on the data type represented by a class. To declare a member function, place its prototype in the body of the class or struct. You don't need to define the function inside the class; the definition can be outside the class or even in a separate file.

Inline Member Functions

Defining a function inside the body of a class produces a special consequence. Such definitions are considered inline, and the entire body of an inline function is repeated whenever that function is called. Thus, if you have an inline function in a class and if you call that function often, you can use a large amount of memory for the program. The advantage of inline functions is that you avoid the overhead of a function call when executing the body of the function.

The previous argument implies that you should make a function inline only if the overhead of calling the function is a large proportion of the time needed to execute the body of the function. When you include a simple function such as length in the String class, you can safely define the entire function inside the body of the class, thus making it inline:

```
class String
{
public:
    size_t length(void) { return _length; }
// ...

private:
// ...
    size_t _length;
};
```

You don't need to define a function inside a class to make it inline. C++ provides the inline keyword that, when placed in front of a function's definition, makes it inline. Notice, however, that you can use an inline function only in the file in which it is defined. This is because the compiler needs the entire definition of an inline function so that it can insert the body of the function wherever the function is called. Therefore, you should place the definitions of inline functions in the same header file that declares a class to ensure that every program that uses the class can also use its inline functions.

INLINE FUNCTIONS AND PREPROCESSOR MACROS

Inline functions are like preprocessor macros without the pitfalls. For example, this macro:

```
#define  square(x)  x*x
```

provides the wrong answer when used to evaluate an expression such as square(a+b) because you didn't use parentheses around the macro's argument. However, if you define square as an inline function:

```
inline double square(x) { return x*x; }
```

you can safely use square(a+b) to evaluate the square of a+b because inline functions work as any C++ function.

Typical *public* Member Functions

The public member functions of a class are important because they are the outside world's gateway to a class. For a class to be useful, it must include a complete set of public member functions. A minimal set should include the following categories of functions:

- ■ *Class management functions* are a standard set of functions that perform chores, such as creating an instance of the class (constructor), destroying it (destructor), creating an instance and initializing it by copying from another instance (*copy constructor*), assigning one instance to another (*operator equals*), and converting an instance to some other type (*type conversion operator*). These functions have a standard declaration syntax. You will encounter these functions in this and the following chapter.

- ■ *Class implementation functions* implement the *behavior* of the data type represented by the class. They are the workhorses of the class. For a String class, these functions might include operator+, for concatenating strings, and comparison operators, such as operator==, operator>, and operator<. Chapter 10 explains how such functions are defined.

- ■ *Class access functions* return information about the internal variables of a class. The outside world can access the object's internal state through these functions. The length function in the String class is a good example of this type of member function.

- ■ *Class utility functions*, often declared to be private, are used internally within the class for miscellaneous tasks such as error handling.

const Member Functions

If a member function does not alter any data in the class, you should declare that member function as a const function. For example, the length function of the String class merely returns the value of a member variable. It is definitely a const function because it doesn't change any data of the String class. You can declare it as such by appending a const to the usual function prototype:

```
size_t length(void) const;
```

This informs the compiler that the length function should not alter any variable in the class. The compiler generates an error message if the definition of the length function includes any code that inadvertently assigns a value to any variable in the String class.

Implementing Classes

The difficult part of writing object-oriented programs is deciding which classes or abstract data types you need to solve your problem. Once you know the classes, their inheritance hierarchy, and their desired behavior, implementing the classes is straightforward. The following sections offer some general guidelines.

Header Files

When implementing a class, think of the class as a provider of some service that other classes or functions need. In other words, the class is a server that acts upon the requests of its clients. This is the idea behind the client-server architecture, and it works well when implementing classes in object-oriented programs. The clients of a class make requests by calling the member functions of that class. The *interface* to the class refers to the information that a client must have in order to use the facilities of a class. At a minimum, the client must know the following:

■ The names of the public member functions of the class
■ The prototypes of the member functions
■ The purpose of each member function

Ideally, if you want to use a class, you want a textual description of the class and how its facilities are intended for use. Without this information, you might have to manage with the header file that declares the class.

The header file describes the interface to a class. In fact, it shows you everything except the functions that are defined in another file, but your program can access only those members that appear in the public section. Because the public interface to the class is important to its clients, you should place these declarations at the very beginning of a class. The protected section can follow these declarations. The private members can come last because these members are visible only to the member functions of that class.

Assuming that a reasonable assortment of public member functions exists, a `String` class might include a header file STR.H as shown in Listing 9.1.

Listing 9.1. STR.H. Header file for the `String` class.

```
//------------------------------------------------------------
//   File:  str.h
//   Declares a "String" data type
//
//   Note: Couldn't use String.h as name because we include
//         ANSI C's string.h and some systems (such as MS-DOS)
//         do not differentiate between uppercase and lowercase
//         letters in filenames
//------------------------------------------------------------

#if !defined(__STR_H)  // Make sure file is included only once
#define __STR_H

// Include any other required header files...
// NOTE: The header files from the ANSI C library must enclose
//       all function declarations inside a block like this:
//              extern "C"
//              {
//                  ...
//              }
//       Microsoft Visual C++ compiler's header files do this.

#include <stddef.h>      // For "size_t" type
#include <iostream.h>    // For stream I/O
#include <string.h>      // For ANSI C string library

typedef int Boolean;     // For return type of operators

class String
{
public:
// Constructors with a variety of arguments
    String();
    String(size_t len);
    String(const char *str);
    String(const String &s);

// Destructor
    ~String();

// Overloaded operators
    Boolean operator==(const String& s) const;
//    Boolean operator<(const String& s) const;
//    Boolean operator>(const String& s) const;
//    Boolean operator<=(const String& s) const;
//    Boolean operator>=(const String& s) const;
//    Boolean operator!=(const String& s) const;

// Assignment operator
    String& operator=(const String& s);
```

continues

Listing 9.1. continued

```
// Type conversion operator
    operator const char*() const;

// Access operator
    char& operator[](int index);
    char& char_at_pos(int index);

// The + operator concatenates strings
    friend String operator+(const String& s1, const String& s2);
//    friend String operator+(const String& s1, const char *s2);
//    friend String operator+(const char *s1, const String& s2);

// Function giving access to internal variable
    size_t length(void) const;

// Function to print a String
    void print(ostream& os) const;

private:
// Internal data members of this class

    char   *p_c;      // pointer to allocated space
    size_t _length;   // current length of string
    size_t _maxlen;   // number of bytes allocated

};

// Stream I/O for String class


ostream& operator<<(ostream& os, String& s);
istream& operator>>(istream& is, String& s);

//-----------------------------------------------------------
//      I N L I N E    F U N C T I O N S
//-----------------------------------------------------------
//   l e n g t h
//   Returns the length of the String

inline size_t String::length(void) const
{
    return _length;
}

#endif
```

Notice that the #if !defined directive is used to ensure that the header file is included only once in any file. It also is good practice to make your header file complete by including all other header files required by your class. For example, the String class uses the size_t type, which is defined in <stddef.h>. Rather than forcing users of the String class to include <stddef.h> whenever they use the class, you should include that file in the header file for the String class. This way, a user of the String class needs only to remember to include STR.H, the header file that defines the interface to the String class.

C++ FILE NAMING CONVENTION

The file suffix or extension—the characters following the period in a filename—used for header files and other source files varies among C++ compilers. In UNIX systems, C++ source files generally use the .C extension, whereas C uses the .c extension. In UNIX, header files end with .h for both C and C++ languages. Under MS-DOS, this is not possible because MS-DOS does not distinguish between lowercase and uppercase letters in filenames. C++ compilers, including Visual C++ 2.0, that have to retain compatibility with the MS-DOS file naming convention use either .cpp or .cxx as the extension for C++ files. Header files often mirror this convention and use .hpp or .hxx as extensions rather than .h. This book uses .h for header files and .cpp for C++ source files.

Separate Implementation from Interface

The clients of a class do not need the definition of a class's member functions if they are adequately documented. Therefore, you can place the actual definitions of the member functions in a separate file. For a class such as String, define the interface to the class in the STR.H file. The member functions are implemented in a second file, such as STR.CPP. The general layout of STR.CPP looks like this:

```
//------------------------------------------------------------
//  File:  str.cpp
//  Implements the member functions of the "String" class

#include "str.h"    // For declaration of String class

// Other header files, if needed...
// Header files needed by String class should be included
// in str.h

const chunk_size = 8;  // Allocation unit for Strings

//------------------------------------------------------------
//  S t r i n g
//  Creates a String object and initializes it
//  from a null-terminated C string

String::String(const char *s)
{
    _length = strlen(s);
    _maxlen = chunk_size * (_length / chunk_size + 1);
    p_c = new char[_maxlen];
    strcpy(p_c, s);
}
//------------------------------------------------------------
//  p r i n t
//  Outputs the String on a specified output stream
```

```
void String::print(ostream& os) const
{
    os << p_c;
}
//-----------------------------------------------------------
//  o p e r a t o r < <
//  Stream insertion operator for String class

ostream& operator<<(ostream& os, String& s)
{
    s.print(os);
    return os;
}
//-----------------------------------------------------------
//  Definitions of other member functions...
//  ...
//-----------------------------------------------------------
```

When defining a member function outside the body of a class, you must associate each function with the class by explicitly using the scope resolution operator (::). For the String class, use a String:: prefix with each member function, as shown in the previous example. (The implementation of the other parts of the String class is covered in Chapter 10 and the STR.CPP file is shown in its entirety in Chapter 11, Listing 11.2.)

Using Classes

A well-designed C++ class should behave like one of the basic data types, such as int, char, or double, except that a class is likely to permit a much larger variety of operations than those enabled for the basic types. This is because the operations defined for a class include all its public member functions, which can be as diverse as the class's functionality warrants. As with the basic data types (such as int and float), to use a class in a program, you must proceed through the following steps:

1. Define one or more instances of the class. These are the objects of object-oriented programming. Just as you write this:

   ```
   double x, y, z;  // doubles named x, y, z
   ```

   to create three instances of double variables, you can create three String objects with the following:

   ```
   String s1, s2, s3; // Strings named s1, s2, s3
   ```

   For a class that provides all required interface functions, you should be able to create and initialize instances in a variety of ways:

   ```
   String s1 = "String 1";
   String s2("Testing.1..2...3");
   String s3 = s1;
   ```

   In each of these cases, the compiler calls the appropriate constructor and creates the String.

2. Call the member functions of the objects and use the available operators to manipulate the objects. For `String` objects, you can write code such as this:

```
#include "str.h"

void main()
{
    String title("Object-Oriented Programming in C++");

    cout << "title = " << title << endl;

    String first_name("Naba"), last_name("Barkakati");
    String full_name = first_name + " " + last_name;

    cout << "full_name = " << full_name << endl;

    cout << "Enter some text (end with a return):";
    String response;
    cin >> response;

    cout << "You typed: " << response << endl;
}
```

If you use this program with the full implementation of the `String` class shown in Listing 11.2 in Chapter 11, "Using Inheritance in C++," here is what you get when you run this program (user input is in boldface):

```
title = Object-Oriented Programming in C++
full_name = Naba Barkakati
Enter some text (end with a return):This is a test.
You typed: This is a test.
```

Creating Objects on the Fly

You can create instances of classes in two ways:

■ Define the objects just as you define `int` or `double` variables.

■ Create the objects dynamically as needed.

When you create objects through definition, the compiler can reserve storage space for the objects during compilation. To create objects dynamically, you need a way to acquire a chunk of memory for the object. In C, you can dynamically create variables or arrays by calling the functions, such as `malloc` or `calloc`, from the C library.

Although you often can create objects by defining instances of classes, dynamic allocation of objects is more interesting, because with this approach you can use as much memory as is available in a system.

Allocating Objects in the Free Store

You may have encountered the term *heap* in reference to dynamic memory allocation in C. The heap is the pool of memory from which standard C functions such as `malloc` and `calloc` parcel out memory. C++ books and manuals refer to the heap with the term *free store*. In C++, you gain the functionality of `malloc` and `calloc` by using the `new` operator, which allocates enough memory to hold all members of a `class` or `struct`.

In C, if you define a structure such as the following:

```
struct Opcode
{
    char    *name;
    void    (*action)(void);
};
```

you allocate space for an instance of this structure:

```
struct Opcode *p_code;
p_code = (struct Opcode *) malloc(sizeof(struct Opcode));
```

In C++, the equivalent code to create a new Opcode reduces to this:

```
Opcode *p_code;
p_code = new Opcode;
```

Apart from the cleaner syntax, the `new` operator also provides another advantage. If the Opcode structure contains a constructor that takes no arguments, the `new` operator automatically calls that constructor to initialize the newly created instance of Opcode.

In fact, you have the option of specifying other initial values for an object allocated by `new`. For example, you can write the following:

```
String *file_name = new String("cpphelp.doc");
int     *first_byte = new int(128);
```

to allocate and initialize a String and an int object. The String is initialized to cpphelp.doc, whereas the int is set to 128. The String is initialized by calling the String(const char*) constructor of the String class.

Destroying Objects in the Free Store

In C, when you no longer need memory that you previously allocated in the heap, you call the free function to release the memory. In C++, the `delete` operator serves the same purpose as C's free. Like free, the `delete` operator expects a pointer to an object as its operand. Thus, if p_code is the pointer to an instance of Opcode created by the new operator, you can destroy it with this statement:

```
delete p_code;  // Frees storage pointed to by p_code
```

In addition to freeing up storage used by the object, if that object's class has a defined destructor, `delete` calls it to ensure proper cleanup.

Allocating Arrays of Objects in the Free Store

One use of new is to allocate an array of objects. The syntax for this is very much like the syntax for defining arrays. For example, you can define an array of String objects by writing the following:

```
String edit_buf[128];
```

To create the same array on the free store, you use this:

```
String *edit_buf = new String[128];
```

You can use the array of Strings as you would any other array. The first String is edit_buf[0], the second one is edit_buf[1], and so on.

A special syntax exists for deallocating the array of objects on free store. Use the following syntax to indicate that you are deleting an array of objects:

```
delete[] edit_buf;
```

This ensures that the destructor of the String class is called for each element of the array. Each String object maintains an internal pointer to a character array that is allocated by the constructor and freed by the destructor. So a call to the destructor of each String in the array takes care of properly deallocating the internal char arrays used by the String objects.

Handling Errors in Memory Allocation

If you allocate many objects dynamically, chances are that sooner or later the free space will be exhausted and the new operator will fail. In ANSI C, when malloc and calloc fail, they return a NULL pointer (a pointer set to zero). C++ provides a way to intercept allocation errors. In Visual C++ 2.0, when the new operator fails, it calls a function that you install by calling the _set_new_handler function. You can handle memory allocation errors in a central function by writing the error handler and calling _set_new_handler with the pointer to the error handler as an argument. The advantage of handling errors this way is that you no longer need to test each use of the new operator for a return value of zero.

The _set_new_handler function is declared in the NEW.H header file. In Visual C++ 2.0, the pointer to the error handling function is of type _PNH, which is defined as a pointer to a function that takes a size_t argument and returns an int. The error handler should return a nonzero value to indicate that the memory allocation should be retried (in case the error handler can recover enough heap space); otherwise, it returns zero to indicate that allocation has failed.

Calling Member Functions

In C++, you build object-oriented programs by creating instances of classes (the objects) as necessary. The program does its work by calling the member functions of the objects. The syntax for calling the member functions is similar to the syntax used to call any other function, except that you use the . and -> operators to identify the member function within the object. For example, to use the `length` function of a `String` object named `s1`, use the . operator to specify the function:

```
String s1;
size_t len;
len = s1.length();
```

Apart from the use of the . operator to identify the function, the calling syntax is like other function calls. As with any function, you must know the member function's return type as well as the number and type of arguments that it takes. For dynamically allocated objects, use the -> operator:

```
String *p_s = new String("Hello, World!");
size_t len;
len = p_s->length();
```

Using *static* Member Variables

When you define member variables for a class, each instance of that class obtains its own unique copy of the member variables. However, sometimes you want a single variable for all instances of a class. C++ makes use of the `static` keyword to introduce this type of member variable. Here, `static` member variables are introduced in the context of a rather useful class.

Most C programmers agree that at some point in time they have debugged their program by inserting calls to `printf` or `fprintf` and printing messages and values from variables of interest. These messages can help you pinpoint where a program fails. Often programmers enclose these calls to `fprintf` in a `#if` directive:

```
#if defined(DEBUG)
    fprintf(stderr, "Loop ended. Index = %d\n", i);
#endif
```

so that such messages are printed only when the DEBUG preprocessor macro is defined. In C++, you can use a similar strategy for debugging, but rather than insert calls to `fprintf`, you accomplish the work with a Debug class. The class is designed so that whenever an instance of the Debug class is created, it prints a message, properly indented to make the sequence of function calls easier to follow. The Debug class also provides a member function called `print`, which can be used just like `printf`. Listing 9.2 shows the DEBUG.H header file, which declares the interface to the class and defines the inline functions.

Listing 9.2. DEBUG.H. Interface to the Debug class.

```
//-----------------------------------------------------------
//  File:  debug.h
//
//  A class for debugging C++ programs
//
//-----------------------------------------------------------
#if !defined(_ _DEBUG_H)
#define _ _DEBUG_H
```

```
#include <stdio.h>
#include <stdarg.h>

class Debug
{
public:
    Debug(const char *label = " ");
    ~Debug();
    void print(const char *format, ...);
private:
    unsigned int indent();
    void draw_separator();

    static unsigned int debug_level;
    static unsigned int debug_on;
    static unsigned int indent_by;
    static unsigned int line_size;
    enum {off = 0, on = 1};
};

//------------------------------------------------------------
//        I N L I N E   F U N C T I O N S
//------------------------------------------------------------
// ~ D e b u g
// Destructor for the Debug clss

inline Debug::~Debug()
{
    debug_level--;
    draw_separator();
}

#endif
```

At the end of the body of the Debug class, notice that a number of member variables are declared with the static keyword. These variables are static member variables, and the Debug class contains exactly one copy of them.

To understand the need for such static member variables, consider the debug_level member variable, which keeps track of how many instances of Debug class have been created up to that point. As you can see from Listing 9.3, this information is used to indent appropriately the messages printed by the print member function. You can't use debug_level to keep a count of the instances of the Debug class if each instance has its own copy of the debug_level variable. The solution is to have what you might call a *class-wide global variable*, which occurs when you place the static keyword in front of a member variable.

Listing 9.3. DEBUG.CPP. Implementation of the Debug class.

```
//------------------------------------------------------------
// File: debug.cpp
//
// Implementation of the "Debug" class
```

continues

Listing 9.3. continued

```cpp
//-----------------------------------------------------------
#include "debug.h"

//-----------------------------------------------------------
//  D e b u g
//  Constructor for Debug class

Debug::Debug(const char *label)
{
    if(debug_on)
    {
        int i;
        draw_separator();
        (void) indent();
        fprintf(stderr, "%s\n", label);
    }
    debug_level++;
}
//-----------------------------------------------------------
//  p r i n t
//  Uses ANSI C's vfprintf function to print debug message

void Debug::print(const char *format, ...)
{
    if(debug_on)
    {
        (void) indent();
        va_list argp;
        va_start(argp, format);
        vfprintf(stderr, format, argp);
    }
}
//-----------------------------------------------------------
//  i n d e n t
//  Indents line according to debug_level. Returns the
//  number of spaces indented

unsigned int Debug::indent()
{
    int i;
    unsigned int num_spaces = debug_level*indent_by;
    for(i = 0; i < num_spaces; i++)
        fputc(' ', stderr);
    return(num_spaces);
}
//-----------------------------------------------------------
//  d r a w _ s e p a r a t o r
//  Draws a separator using dashes (-) to identify debug levels

void Debug::draw_separator()
{
    if(debug_on)
    {
        unsigned int i;
        for(i = indent(); i < line_size; i++)
                        fputc('-', stderr);
```

```
            fputc('\n', stderr);
        }
}
//------------------------------------------------------------
```

Initializing *static* Member Variables

Listing 9.4 shows a test program that illustrates how the Debug class of Listings 9.2 and 9.3 might be used. At the beginning of this program, you can see the syntax that refers to the static member variables of the Debug class. To refer to the static member variable of a class, use the name of the class (not the name of the instance) as the prefix, followed by the scope resolution operator (::). Therefore, you can set the debug_level member of the Debug class to zero by writing this:

```
// Initialize static member "debug_level" of the Debug class
unsigned int Debug::debug_level = 0;
```

Except for the Debug:: prefix, this looks like the definition of any other variable in the program.

When you examine Listing 9.3, you notice that inside the member functions you can access the static member variables, such as debug_level, in the same way that you would access any other member variable of the class. So, you need the scope resolution prefix (Debug::) for the static member variables only when referring to them outside the scope of the class.

Listing 9.4. DBGTST.CPP. Program to test the Debug class.

```
//------------------------------------------------------------
//  File:  dbgtst.cpp
//
//  Test the "Debug" class
//------------------------------------------------------------
#include "debug.h"

// Initialize the debug_level to 0 and debug_on to "on"
unsigned int Debug::debug_level = 0;
unsigned int Debug::debug_on = Debug::on;

// Set number of characters per line to 55
unsigned int Debug::line_size = 55;

// Indent by 4 spaces for each level
unsigned int Debug::indent_by = 4;
//------------------------------------------------------------
//  f a c t o r i a l
//  Recursive function that evaluates factorial

unsigned long factorial(int n)
{
    Debug dbg("factorial");
    dbg.print("argument = %d\n", n);
```

continues

Listing 9.4. continued

```
    if(n == 1) return 1;
    else return n*factorial(n-1);
}
//-----------------------------------------------------------
//  m a i n
//  Main function to test 'Debug' class

void main()
{
    Debug dbg("main");
    unsigned long n = factorial(4);
    dbg.print("result = %ld\n", n);
}
```

To show the effects of `debug_level`, the sample program defines and calls a `factorial` function, which is a recursive function that evaluates the factorial of its integer argument. The `factorial` function creates an instance of the `Debug` class on each entry. The `Debug` class increases the indentation as the `debug_level` increases, and it draws dashed lines to show increases and decreases in `debug_level`. Therefore, you expect to see an indented list of calls to `factorial` in the output of this program. Indeed, when you run the program built by compiling and linking the files shown in Listings 9.3 and 9.4, it displays the following output:

```
---------------------------------------------------------
main
     ---------------------------------------------------
     factorial
         argument = 4
         -----------------------------------------------
         factorial
             argument = 3
             -------------------------------------------
             factorial
                 argument = 2
                 ---------------------------------------
                 factorial
                     argument = 1
                 ---------------------------------------
             -------------------------------------------
         -----------------------------------------------
     ---------------------------------------------------
     result = 24
---------------------------------------------------------
```

Here, the indentation of the dashed lines clearly shows the sequence of function calls and returns.

COUNTING CLASS INSTANCES

Declare a member variable `static` if you want a single copy of the variable for all instances of a class. You can count the number of instances of a class by incrementing a static member variable in the constructor of the class.

Using *static* Member Functions

You can work with `static` member functions as well as `static` member variables. In C programs, programmers often define `static` functions to confine the visibility of a function to a specific file. With the `static` keyword, you can place more than one function with the same name in different files. C++ advances one step further and enables you to place functions that are `static` within a class. You can invoke such functions without creating any instance of the class. You need only to add the scope resolution operator to the class name. As an example, suppose you want a `static` member function of the `Debug` class that sets `debug_on` a variable. You can declare such a function inside the body of the class:

```
class Debug
{
public:
//...
static void set_debug(int on_off);    // static member function
//...
private:
//...
}
```

The function is defined as any other member function. Notice that you don't need the `static` keyword in the definition:

```
void Debug::set_debug(int on_off)
{
    if(on_off) debug_on = on;
    else       debug_on = off;
}
```

Once defined, you can call this function as an ordinary function, but with a `Debug::` prefix:

```
// Turn debugging off
    Debug::set_debug(0);
//...
// Turn debugging on
    Debug::set_debug(1);
```

Notice that you don't need an instance of the `Debug` class to call the `set_debug` function. The scope resolution prefix (`Debug::`) is necessary to indicate which `set_debug` function you are calling. After all, another class also might have defined a static member function named `set_debug`.

Using Pointers to Class Members

Because of encapsulation of data and functions in a class, C++ includes a pointer to a class member in addition to ordinary pointers to class and functions. A pointer *to a class member* is actually the offset of the member from the beginning of a particular instance of that class. In other words, it is a relative address, whereas regular pointers denote the absolute address of an object. The syntax for declaring a pointer to a class member is `X::*`, where `X` is the name of the class. So, if you declare a class as follows:

```
class Sample
{
public:
    short step;           // Member variable
    void set_step(short s); // Member function
//...
private:
};
```

you can define and initialize a pointer to a short member variable of the Sample class like this:

```
short Sample::*p_s;  // Pointer to short in class Sample
p_s = &Sample::step; // Initialize to member "step"
```

Notice that to define and even initialize the pointer, you do not need an instance of the Sample class. Contrast this with the way you initialize a regular pointer to a short variable. With the regular pointer you have to define a short variable before you can assign its address to the pointer.

With pointers to class members, you need a concrete instance of the class only when using the pointers. Thus, you have to define an instance of the Sample class before you can use the pointer p_s. A typical use of p_s might be to assign a new value to the class member through the pointer:

```
Sample s1;
s1.*p_s = 5;
```

The syntax for dereferencing the pointer is of the form x.*p, where x is an instance of the class and p is a pointer to a class member. If, instead of a class instance, you have a pointer to an instance of a Sample class, the syntax for using p_s changes to the following:

```
Sample s1;
Sample *p_sample = &s1;
p_sample->*p_s = 5;
```

Pointers to Member Functions

The syntax for declaring a pointer to a member function of a class is similar to the syntax used for declaring a pointer to ordinary functions. The only difference is that you use the class name together with the scope resolution operator (::). Here is an example that defines a pointer to a member function of the class Sample. The definition says that the member function to which p_func points returns nothing but requires a short as argument:

```
void (Sample::*p_func)(short) = Sample::set_step;
```

The sample definition also initializes the pointer p_func to the address of the set_step function of the Sample class. You can call the function through the pointer:

```
Sample s1;
(s1.*p_func)(2);  // Call function through pointer
```

Here is another small program that illustrates how pointers to member functions are used:

```
//-------------------------------------------------------------
// Illustrates use of pointer to member function of a class
```

```
#include <iostream.h>

class CommandSet
{
public:
    void help(){cout << "Help!" << endl;}
    void nohelp(){cout << "No Help!" << endl;}
private:
//...
};

//  Initialize pointer to member function "f_help"

void (CommandSet::*f_help)() = CommandSet::help;

main()
{
    CommandSet set1;

// Invoke a member function through the "f_help" pointer
    (set1.*f_help)();

// Redefine the "f_help" pointer and call function again
    f_help = CommandSet::nohelp;
    (set1.*f_help)();
}
```

The example makes two calls to the function with the pointer. Between calls, it changes the pointer's value. When run, the program displays two messages:

```
Help!
No Help!
```

Pointers to *static* Members

Static members of a class are not covered by a syntax used for defining and using pointers to other members of a class. A pointer to a static member is treated as a regular pointer. For example, if you declare this class:

```
class Clock
{
public:
//...
    static double ticks_per_sec;
private:
//...
};
```

you can define a pointer to its static member variable:

```
double *p_tick = &Clock::ticks_per_sec;
```

This is just a regular pointer to double that has been initialized to the ticks_per_sec static member variable of the Clock class. Notice that you must use the class name with the scope resolution operator to identify the static variable ticks_per_sec. Use the p_ticks pointer as an ordinary pointer to `double`. For example, the following statement sets the `ticks_per_sec` static variable of the `Clock` class to 18.2:

```
*p_tick = 18.2; // Set 'ticks_per_sec' through pointer
```

Summary

C++ extends the syntax of C's `struct` and introduces the `class` construct. These enhancements enable the creation of user-defined data types that you can use just like the built-in types, such as `int`, `char`, `float`, and `double`. In the terminology of object-oriented programming, the `class` and `struct` mechanisms support data abstraction, which is one of the basic requirements for creating objects. The class declaration indicates how the object should behave, and the instances of the class refer to the objects being manipulated by the program.

A C++ class can include both data and functions as members. The data members represent the internal state of an object of that class, whereas the functions define the behavior of the object. By grouping the members into sections labeled `public`, `private`, and `protected`, you can control which members are accessible to the functions outside the class. The data members usually become `private`, and all interactions with the class are made through a set of `public` member functions. To implement a class, you must declare the class and define all its member functions. A good strategy for modular implementation is to declare the class in a header file and define the member functions in a separate implementation file.

Once a class is defined, you can create and use objects of that class just as you use built-in data types, such as `int`, `char`, and `double`. You either can define the objects like any other variable or create them dynamically by calling the `new` and `delete` operators, which are analogous to the C library's `malloc` and `free` functions.

10

Defining Operations on Objects

Chapter 9, "Building Objects with Classes," focuses on the use of class and struct constructs to encapsulate data with functions when defining a new data type with its own operators. You also learned the general strategy for implementing and using a class. The implementation includes two components: a header file with the declaration of the class and a source file with the actual definition of the member functions of the class.

This chapter shows you how to define the member functions and the operators for a class. Although the concept of creating objects with class is straightforward, many small details become important when implementing classes in C++. For example, you need to know when to pass arguments by reference and how to ensure that objects are initialized properly. This chapter addresses these questions.

Arguments and Return Values

In C++, you manipulate objects using member functions and operators defined for the class of which the object is an instance. As a C programmer, you know that functions accept one or more arguments and return a value. C employs the *pass-by-value* mechanism for providing a function with its arguments.

In pass-by-value, functions receive their argument in a special area of memory called the *stack*, a last-in-first-out (LIFO) data structure. Before calling a function, the calling program copies each argument's value to the stack and passes control to the function. The function retrieves the arguments from the stack and uses them in the body of the function. If necessary, the function can return a single value to the calling program. The net effect of this mechanism of passing arguments is that the function never accesses the actual storage locations of the arguments that its caller provides. Instead, it always works with local copies of the arguments, and the local copies are discarded from the stack when they are returned from the function.

This pass-by-value approach is a good choice for argument passing because it guarantees that a function never alters its arguments. However, pass-by-value is not always beneficial when you need to pass objects around.

Understanding Pointers and References

Although a function that receives its arguments by value cannot alter the arguments, what if an argument is the address of a variable or, in other words, a pointer to the variable? In this case, the function can clearly alter the value of the variable through that pointer. For example, if you want to swap the contents of two integer variables, one way to do this is to write a function that accepts pointers to the two int variables:

```
void swap_int(int *p_a, int *p_b)
{
    int temp;
    temp = *p_a;
    *p_a = *p_b;
```

```
    *p_b = temp;
}
```

You can use this function to swap integer variables:

```
int x = 2, y = 3;

swap_int(&x, &y);   /* Now x = 3 and y = 2 */
```

Although you can continue to use this type of function in C++ programs, C++ introduces a reference that makes it much easier to write this type of function. Recall that a reference is an alternate name for an object that you can use as you would the object itself. Think of a reference as the address of an item. Unlike a pointer, however, a reference is not a real variable. A reference is initialized when it is defined, and you cannot modify its value later. The syntax of a reference mimics that of a pointer, except a reference requires an ampersand (&) and the pointer declaration requires an asterisk (*). Thus, the following:

```
int *p_i;   // An unintialized pointer to integer
```

defines an int pointer, whereas this:

```
int &r_i = i;   // Reference to i (an int variable)
```

is a reference to an int variable named i.

As a practical example of the use of a reference, here is the swap_int function with arguments passed by a reference:

```
void swap_int(int &a, int &b)
{
    int temp;
    temp = a;
    a = b;
    b = temp;
}
```

Compare this version of the function with the one that uses pointers. You can see that the version that uses references looks cleaner—you no longer need to dereference pointers in each expression. The new version of the function is simpler to use because you do not need to provide the address of the integers that are being swapped as arguments. You call the function as if the arguments are being passed by value:

```
void swap_int(int&, int&);   // Prototype of function

int x = 2, y = 3;

swap_int(x, y);              // Now x = 3 and y = 2
```

The compiler knows from the function's prototype that it must pass references to the x and y variables.

As you can see from the examples in this section, you can think of a reference as a pointer with a constant value that the C++ compiler automatically dereferences whenever you use it. In other words, given the following:

```
int i;         // An integer variable
int &r_i = i;  // A reference to "i"
int *p_i = &i; // A pointer to "i"
```

you can think of r_i as equivalent to p_i, except that wherever you use the expression r_i, the compiler substitutes *p_i. Because the value of a reference cannot change from its initial assignment, the C++ compiler does not need to allocate storage for a reference. It needs only to implement the semantics of each reference.

Passing by Value Versus Passing by Reference

From the example of swapping integers, you might surmise that references are good for writing functions that need to alter the values of their arguments. Although this is certainly one of the uses of passing arguments by reference, there is another important reason for providing the reference mechanism in C++.

Consider what happens when an object is passed to a function by value. To implement the pass-by-value semantics, the compiler must copy the object to the stack before the function is called. For large class objects, copying involves a space and time penalty. You can avoid the overhead of copying by using a reference to the object (rather than the object itself) as an argument. If the function does not modify an argument, you can indicate this with the const qualifier for that reference argument. Thus, passing arguments by reference enhances the efficiency of object-based programming in C++.

Returning a Reference

In the same way that passing arguments by reference prevents unnecessary copying to the stack, you can return an object by reference to avoid copying the returned object. Watch what happens when you return an object by value. Suppose you return a String object from an add_strings function that returns the concatenation of two strings:

```
String add_strings(const String& s1, const String& s2)
{
// In function's body
    String s;
// Append s1 and s2 to s
//...
    return s;
}
```

In this case, the return statement must copy String s to an area of memory provided by the calling program. To do so properly, the return statement calls the copy constructor, which can create and initialize a new instance of an object from an existing one. After creating the copy, the return statement calls the destructor of the String class to destroy String s before returning to the calling program. This is a good example of the work done by the C++ compiler behind the scenes. You probably didn't realize that so much extra work was going into an innocuous return statement.

This example illustrates what happens when a function returns an object. Although returning by reference would save the time spent in copying the object, you cannot return a reference to String s because s is a temporary object that exists only within the add_strings function (s is destroyed when the function returns). Therefore, you should be careful what you return by reference. Because a reference is like a pointer, you cannot return a reference to anything that is temporary.

THE SIGNIFICANCE OF const ARGUMENTS

By qualifying an argument to a function with the const keyword, you can inform the C++ compiler that the function should not modify the argument. The compiler generates an error message if the function inadvertently tries to alter that argument. The const qualifier is significant only for arguments that are pointers or that are passed by reference, because changes made by a function to arguments passed by value cannot be seen in the calling program.

A common use of returning by reference is in an access function—a function that provides access to an internal element of an existing object. For example, if you want to write a member function named char_at_pos for the String class that provides access to the character at a specified location in an instance of String, you can safely return a reference to the character at the specified location. Thus, you might write the char_at_pos function as follows:

```
//-------------------------------------------------------------
// c h a r _ a t _ p o s
// Access a character in a String

char& String::char_at_pos(int index)
{
// Check whether index goes beyond allocated length.
// Return last element, if it does
    if(index > _maxlen-1) return p_c[_maxlen-1];
    else  return p_c[index];
}
```

Here is a typical use of the function:

```
    String s1 = "Test";
// ...

// Print the second character of String s1
    cout << "3rd char = " << s1.char_at_pos(2) << endl;

// Change the first character of s1
    s1.char_at_pos(0) = 'B';  // Now s1 = "Best"
```

Although you may expect the first use of the char_at_pos function to retrieve the character at a specific position in the string, you may not realize that you even can set a character to a new value. The second use of char_at_pos is possible only because the function returns a reference to a char. Because a reference is exactly like the variable itself, you can assign a new value to the returned reference.

If you already know C++, you may realize that a better solution for accessing a character in String is to overload the [] operator. A little later in this chapter you will see how to define such operators for a class.

Guidelines for Using References

You can follow several rules of thumb when deciding where to use references. You should pass arguments to a function by reference in the following situations:

- You want the function to modify the arguments.
- The function will not modify the arguments, but you want to avoid copying the objects to the stack. In this case, use the const qualifier to indicate that the argument being passed by reference should not be altered by the function.

As for return values, you should return a reference to an object whenever you want to use that return value as the left side of an assignment. Of course, you should return a reference to an object only when the object is guaranteed to exist after the function returns.

Creating and Destroying Objects

Basic data types, such as int and float, are merely chunks of memory that hold a single value, but a user-defined class can contain many more components, some of which may require additional work during creation besides setting aside a number of bytes of storage. Take, for instance, the String class. Internally, it stores a pointer to an array of characters that holds the null-terminated string. To function properly, a newly created String object must set this pointer to a properly allocated array of chars and, quite possibly, initialize that array to a specific string. After all, if you treat String like any other type of variable, you must be able to handle statements such as this:

```
String this_os = "Microsoft Windows";
String new_os = this_os;
```

For proper handling of this type of initialization, C++ enables each class to use the special constructor function, which has the same name as the class and does not have any return type. Thus, the constructor for the String class is a function named String. Of course, as with other functions, you can have more than one constructor, each with a unique list of arguments and each intended for a specific type of initialization.

A constructor for a class such as String allocates extra memory for the null-terminated string. This means that there must be a way to release this memory when the String is no longer needed. C++ handles this need through the destructor, a function with the same name as the class but with a tilde (~) as a prefix. Thus, the destructor of the String class is named ~String. Destructors do not take any argument—you cannot overload a destructor.

Constructors and Destructors for the *String* Class

Chapter 9 provides you with a brief description and the declaration of a String class that represents a text string data type with its own operators and string manipulation functions. The idea is to hold a pointer to an array of bytes that can hold a null-terminated array of characters, the standard way of representing strings in C and C++. The variables _maxlen and _length denote, respectively, the size of the allocated array and the length of the string stored in the array. To enable character insertion into the String, the size of the char array is rounded up to the next highest multiple of a specified chunk of bytes. For example, if the chunk is 8 bytes, the allocated size of the array to hold a 10-character string will be 16 bytes—the nearest multiple of 8 that exceeds 10. This idea is useful, for example, if you plan to use the String objects in a text editor where you must allow for the insertion of characters into a String.

Listing 9.1 in Chapter 9 shows the STR.H header file, which declares the String class. To refresh your memory, here is a skeleton declaration of the String class showing the private members, the constructors, and the destructor:

```
class String
{
public:
// Constructors with a variety of arguments
    String();
    String(size_t len);
    String(const char *str);
    String(const String &s);

// Destructor
    ~String();

// ...

private:
// Internal data members of this class

    char   *p_c;     // pointer to allocated space
    size_t _length;  // current length of string
    size_t _maxlen;  // number of bytes allocated

};
```

Which Constructor Is Called?

If a class defines constructors, the C++ compiler calls an appropriate constructor to initialize each instance of a class. The way you define the class instances controls the constructor that is called. The constructor with no arguments is called when you define an instance but do not specify any initial value. For other cases, the type of initial value determines the constructor that the C++ compiler calls. You can define and initialize a class instance in three ways:

■ Use the C-style syntax as illustrated by the following example for an instance of the String class:

```
String operating_system = "Microsoft Windows";
```

■ Use a function call syntax, such as the following:

```
String operating_system("Microsoft Windows");
```

■ Use the new operator to allocate on the free store:

```
String *lines = new String[25];
```

In the first two cases, the C++ compiler calls the `String(const char*)` constructor because you are initializing the `String` object with a null-terminated character array. Thus, the compiler calls the constructor that takes as an argument the type of value you are using to initialize the class instance. In the last case, the compiler calls the constructor that takes no arguments, and it calls this constructor for each of the 25 `String` objects being created.

Because the `String` class defines a constructor that accepts a string length as an argument, here is an initialization that is appropriate to use with the `String` class (even though this may look strange to C programmers):

```
String eight_blanks = 8;  // A string with 8 blanks
```

Based on the description of the `String(size_t)` constructor, this statement creates a `String` initialized with eight blank spaces.

Default Constructor

The *default constructor* is a constructor that takes no arguments. For the `String` class, you can define the default constructor as a function that allocates a single chunk of bytes and initializes it to a zero-length string:

```
//------------------------------------------------------------
//  S t r i n g
//  Creates a String and stores a zero-length string in it.

String::String()
{
    _maxlen = chunk_size;    // const chunk_size = 8;
    p_c = new char[_maxlen];
    _length = 0;
    p_c[0] = '\0';
}
```

In lieu of a constructor with no arguments, the upcoming ANSI standard for C++ plans to enable the compiler to use any constructor (with default values specified for all its arguments) as a default constructor. For a `Point` class that represents a point in the x-y plane, such a default constructor might appear as follows:

```
Point::Point(int x = 0, int y = 0)
{
// Copy x and y coordinates into internal variables of Point
}
```

The default constructor is called whenever you define an instance of the class without providing any explicit initial value. Here is an example where the default constuctor is called:

```
String s1;  // s1 is initialized by calling default constructor
```

The default constructor also plays an important role when you allocate an array of class instances. Here, the C++ compiler automatically calls the default constructor for each element of the array. If you write the following:

```
String edit_buf[24];  // Create an array of 24 Strings
```

the default constructor of `String` is called to initialize each element of the `edit_buf` array.

DEFINING A DEFAULT CONSTRUCTOR FOR EACH CLASS

If you define constructors for a class, you should always define a default constructor (a constructor that requires no arguments) as well. When you define an array of instances for a class, the C++ compiler initializes each instance in the array by calling the default constructor.

Defining Other *String* Constructors

The `String` class contains a few other constructors besides the default constructor. One of them takes a number of bytes as the argument and creates a blank string with that many bytes. Here is the definition of that constructor:

```
//--------------------------------------------------------------
//  S t r i n g
//  This version creates a blank string of size "len"

String::String(size_t len)
{
    _length = len;
// NOTE: const chunk_size = 8;
    _maxlen = chunk_size*(_length / chunk_size + 1);
    p_c = new char[_maxlen];
    int i;
    for(i = 0; i < len; i++) p_c[i] = ' ';
    p_c[i] = '\0';
}
```

First, the constructor computes _maxlen, the number of bytes to allocate. It then uses the `new` operator to allocate the array of `char`s and initialize the array to a null-terminated string that contains the specified number of space characters.

Another useful constructor for the `String` class is one that accepts a null-terminated character array and creates a `String` from it. You might define this constructor as follows:

```
//--------------------------------------------------------------
//  S t r i n g
```

```
//   Creates a String object and initializes it from a
//   null-terminated C string

String::String(const char *s)
{
    _length = strlen(s);
// NOTE: const chunk_size = 8;
    _maxlen = chunk_size*(_length / chunk_size + 1);
    p_c = new char[_maxlen];
    strcpy(p_c, s);
}
```

String Destructor

The destructor reverses anything done in the constructor. Usually, this means releasing memory that the constructor allocated when creating the object. For the String class, the constructor allocates the array that holds the null-terminated string. The pointer to this array is stored in the p_c private member variable. Thus, the ~String destructor frees up the memory allocated for the character array:

```
//-------------------------------------------------------------
//   ~ S t r i n g
//   Destroys a String

String::~String()
{
    delete[] p_c;
}
```

Copy Constructor

Recall that the copy constructor is capable of creating a replica of an object. To understand why a copy constructor is necessary, consider the following example. If you decide to pass a String object by value to an append_space function, which, presumably, adds a space to the end of the string, the function is declared and used as follows:

```
void append_space(String s);   // expects argument by value
String s1 = "Result is";
append_space(s1);              //  a sample call
```

To implement the call to append_space, the C++ compiler must make a copy of the String s1 on the stack. As shown in Figure 10.1, the body of a String object contains a pointer to the actual null-terminated string. The constructor of the String class takes care of allocating and initializing this memory.

To make a copy of String s1 on the stack, the compiler, by default, copies each member of String s1 to the stack. This, however, results in the situation shown in Figure 10.2. Both the copy and the original String point to the same null-terminated string because the character pointers are identical.

FIGURE 10.1.

An instance of the String *class.*

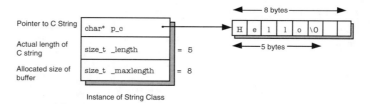

Instance of String Class

FIGURE 10.2.

Memberwise copy of one String *to another.*

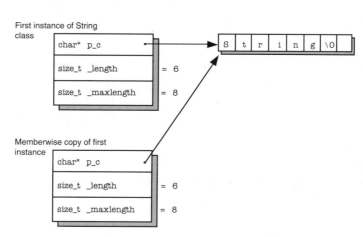

To create a complete copy, you must define a constructor for String that takes a String reference as the argument (in other words, a constructor that can create a copy of a String). For the String class, you might implement this copy constructor as follows:

```
#include "str.h"   // Header file that declares the String class

//------------------------------------------------------------
// String ( const String & )
// Creates a new String as a copy of another String
// This is called the "Copy Constructor"

String::String(const String &s)
{
    _length = s._length;
    _maxlen = s._maxlen;
    p_c = new char[_maxlen];
    strcpy(p_c, s.p_c);
}
```

Notice that the copy constructor allocates room for the null-terminated string and copies into it the C string from the String, which was passed to it as argument. When the copy constructor is used, you receive a complete copy of the String as shown in Figure 10.3.

The copy constructor also comes into play when you write the following:

```
String s1 = "Hello!";
String s2 = s1;
```

FIGURE 10.3.

Copying with the copy constructor.

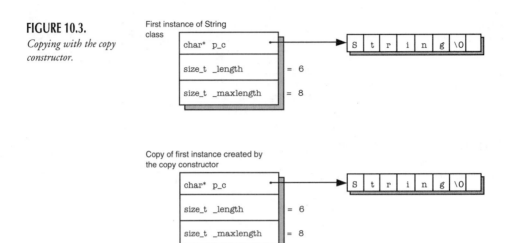

In this case, the C++ compiler must initialize s2 with the value of another String s1. To do this, the compiler looks for a copy constructor for the String class. The copy constructor for String is declared as follows:

```
String(const String&);
```

Because of the form of the declaration, books and manuals on C++ often refer to this as the X(const X&) constructor where X denotes any class.

When to Provide a Copy Constructor

If your class does not include any pointers that need to be properly initialized, you do not need to provide a copy constructor. The C++ compiler uses a default copy constructor that performs a memberwise copy of one class instance to another. You must provide a copy constructor only for classes with a pointer variable, such as the String class, for example. If you do not, the result of copying is as shown for the String objects in Figure 10.2. Both copies hold pointers to a single array of characters.

Even if you can accept the memberwise copy, you will run into another problem because of the destructor. If a String object created by a memberwise copy operation is no longer needed, the String destructor is called. The destructor frees the storage with the address in the character pointer of that String. This leaves the remaining copy of String with a *dangling pointer*— a pointer that does not point to any valid block of memory. When that remaining copy of String has to be destroyed, the delete operator is called with the address of memory that has already been freed. Worse yet, if that memory has been allocated to some other object, the destructor inadvertently frees memory belonging to some other object. To avoid such problems, you should always provide a copy constructor for any class that includes dynamically allocated members.

> **PROVIDING A COPY CONSTRUCTOR**
>
> Provide a copy constructor of the X::X(const X&) form for any class that allocates memory in its constructor. The copy constructor ensures that instances of that class are copied correctly.

Member Initializer List

How do you initialize a class that contains an instance of another class? If you decide to implement a Line class, which contains two instances of the Point class, each representing an endpoint of the line, your class declaration might look like this:

```
class Point
{
public:
    Point(double _x = 0.0, double _y = 0.0)
    {
        x = _x;
        y = _y;
    }
    Point(const Point& p) { x = p.x, y = p.y;}

private:
    double x,y;      // Coordinates of point
};

class Line
{
public:
    Line(const Point& b, Point& e) : p1(b), p2(e) {}
// ...
private:
    Point p1, p2;  // Endpoints of line
};
```

Notice the curious way of defining the constructor for the Line class. The constructor takes two Point references as arguments. It needs only to copy the points to the internal points p1 and p2. Of course, the obvious way is to write the following:

```
Line::Line(const Point& b, Point& e)
{
    p1 = b;
    p2 = e;
}
```

This works, but it sets up points p1 and p2, using the default constructor of the Point class, and then performs a memberwise copy of b to p1 and e to p2. A more efficient approach is to initialize p1 and p2 with the copy constructor. However, by the time you are inside the constructor of Line, the Point instances p1 and p2 are already constructed. C++ solves this problem by enabling the *member initializer list*—a list of member variable initializations of this form:

```
variable_name(value)
```

separated by commas. Here, `variable_name` refers to a member variable of the class, and the `value` within parentheses denotes the value with which that variable is initialized. The member initializer list appears between the function's argument list and its body and is guaranteed to be processed before the statements in the function's body are executed.

> **RESTRICTIONS ON INITIALIZER LIST**
>
> In the initializer list of a class's constructor, you can initialize only immediate base classes and member variables that are not inherited from a base class. This restriction ensures that base classes and inherited member variables are not initialized more than once.

Initializer List Versus Assignment

For another example of a member initializer list, consider a `Name` class that has two `String` members:

```
class Name
{
public:
    Name(const char *first, const char *last);
// Other public member functions...
private:
    String first_name;
    String last_name;
};
```

How do you define the constructor for this class? Most C programmers define it as follows:

```
Name::Name(const char *first, const char *last)
{
    first_name = first;
    last_name = last;
}
```

Although this looks straightforward, a lot of behind-the-scenes work is done to initialize the `first_name` and `last_name` members of the `Name` class. To be specific, the compiler takes the following steps:

1. It calls the default constructor of the `String` class to create the string's `first_name` and `last_name`. Note that the default constructor allocates some space for a character array.

2. It creates two temporary `String` objects from the `first` and `last` character arrays.

3. It calls the copy constructor of the `String` class to initialize `first_name` and `last_name` with the temporary `String`s of the preceding step. The copy constructor also allocates storage for the character array.

4. It generates code that destroys the temporary `String`s created in step 2.

Consider what happens if you rewrite the Name constructor using a member initializer list. The definition changes to this:

```
Name::Name(const char *first, const char *last)
          : first_name(first), last_name(last) {}
```

Now the compiler can construct an instance of Name in a single step by merely processing the initializer list. The compiler calls the String(const char*) constructor of the String class to create the String first_name out of first and the String last_name out of last. In this case, storage for character arrays is allocated only once for each String and no unnecessary temporary objects exist. For reasons of efficiency, you should use initializer lists to initialize member variables. Note that you can use the initializer list syntax for built-in types, such as int, double, and char* as well.

Initialization of *const* Member Variables and References

Even if you ignore the efficiency of initializer lists, some occasions occur when you must use member initializers to create an instance of a class. This occurs when the class in question has one of the following:

■ A const member variable
■ A reference member variable

Both of these, according to the rules of C++, must be initialized when defined. In other words, these member variables must contain a constant value as soon as the class instance is created. The following fictitious class illustrates how to do this:

```
class SampleClass
{
public:
// Constructor uses member initializer list
    SampleClass(int id) : obj_id(id), r_i(i) {}
//...
private:
    const int obj_id;
    int       i;
    int&      r_i;
};
```

Here, the integer argument to the constructor is used to initialize the const variable obj_id, whereas the int reference r_i is set to another integer variable within the class.

EFFICIENT INITIALIZATION WITH MEMBER INITIALIZER LISTS

Use member initializer lists efficiently to initialize class members that are instances of other classes. You must use member initializers to initialize nonstatic const and reference members of a class.

Nested Class Declarations

C++ enables you to nest one class declaration inside the body of another class. The name of such a nested class is local to the enclosing class. You can use nested classes to declare items with the same name but different types in several classes. For instance, you might declare a nested class named Attribute in several different classes:

```
class A
{
public:
    int command;
//     ...
    class Attribute
    {
    public:
        Attribute() : _id(0) {}
        id() { return _id;}
    private:
        int _id;
    };
private:
    int opcode;
};

class B
{
public:
    float speed;
//     ...
    class Attribute
    {
    public:
        Attribute() : _range(0) {}
    private:
        float _range;
    };
private:
    float fuel;
};
```

The first thing you should note is that declaring a class nested in another does not create an instance of the nested class. You have to define instances of the nested class explicitly to create the objects.

When you refer to a nested class outside the enclosing class, you have to qualify the nested class's name with a scope resolution operator. Thus, to define and use an instance of the nested class Attribute, declared in class A, you write the following:

```
A::Attribute attrib_a;
// ...
cout << "ID = " << attrib_a.id() << endl;
```

A nested class has to follow the usual access rules when accessing members of its enclosing class. Thus, the Attribute class, which is nested in A, cannot access A's private member variable opcode.

Member functions of the enclosing class obey similar rules; they can access only the public members of the nested class. In the example, A cannot access the _id member variable of Attribute except through Attribute's public function id.

Exploiting the Side Effects of Constructor and Destructor

You know that whenever an instance of a class is created, the C++ compiler automatically calls the constructor of that class. If the class instance is an automatic variable, the destructor is called when the instance goes out of scope and must be destroyed. This means that you can have classes that do all their work in the constructors and destructors.

There is nothing wrong with using classes only for the side effects of their constructors and destructors. In fact, they sometimes lead to an elegant solution of a problem. As an example, consider the dilemma of estimating the time taken to execute a block of code. Typically, you obtain the time at the start of the computation and perform the computations many times so that you can measure the elapsed time accurately. The ANSI C library includes functions such as time to obtain the current time and clock to get the clock ticks elapsed since the program started running; time has an accuracy of seconds, whereas clock is somewhat more accurate—each clock tick lasts approximately 55 milliseconds on MS-DOS systems.

A *Timer* Class

To perform the timing in a C++ program, write a Timer class with a constructor that calls clock to obtain the current clock ticks. In the destructor, call clock again and compute the difference of the starting and ending clock ticks. Report the elapsed time in seconds between construction and destruction of an instance of Timer. You can convert clock ticks to seconds using the preprocessor macro CLOCKS_PER_SEC, which supplies the number of clock ticks per second. This macro, as well as the prototype of the clock function, appears in the time.h ANSI C header file. Listing 10.1 shows the TIMER.H header file, which is a typical implementation of the Timer class.

Listing 10.1. TIMER.H. Implementation of a Timer class.

```
//------------------------------------------------------------------
//  File:  timer.h
//
//  Implements a timer that works solely through its
//  constructor and destructor.  Uses the "clock" function
//  of the ANSI standard C library.  The "clock" function
//  returns the number of clock ticks used by the current
//  process.  The preprocessor macro CLOCKS_PER_SEC tells us
//  how to convert clock ticks to seconds.
//------------------------------------------------------------------
#if !defined(__TIMER_H)
#define __TIMER_H

#include <time.h>       // For definition of the clock_t type
```

continues

Listing 10.1. continued

```
                        // and the CLOCKS_PER_SEC macro

#include <iostream.h> // For output to "cerr" stream

class Timer
{
public:
    Timer() { start = clock();}   // Constructor

    ~Timer()  // Destructor (compute and display elapsed time)
    {
        clock_t stop = clock();
        cerr << "Elapsed time = ";

        double et = (double)(stop - start)/
                            (double)CLOCKS_PER_SEC;

        cerr << et << " seconds" << endl;
    }
private:
    clock_t start;    // Store starting clock tick count
};

#endif
```

Using the *Timer* Class

Listing 10.2 shows the C++ program TIMERTST.CPP, which uses the Timer class to estimate the time taken to execute a set of computations. In Listing 10.2, the compute function performs all the work. It defines an instance of Timer that starts the clock ticking, so to speak. Then the function repeatedly executes the computations in a loop. When the loop ends and the function returns, the Timer object is destroyed. The C++ compiler automatically calls the destructor of the Timer class, and the destructor prints out the elapsed time.

Listing 10.2. TIMERTST.CPP. Sample use of the Timer class.

```
//-----------------------------------------------------------
//  File:  timertst.cpp
//
//  Use the Timer class to time a function
//-----------------------------------------------------------
#include "timer.h"

//-----------------------------------------------------------
//  c o m p u t e
//  A function that performs some computations

static void compute(unsigned long count)
{
    unsigned long i;
    double a, b, c, d;
    Timer t;                    // Create Timer to time function
```

```
    for(i = 0; i < count; i++)
    {
        a = (double)(i-1);
        b = (double)(i+1);
        c = (double)(i+i);
        d = a*b - c;
    }
}
//-----------------------------------------------------------------
//  m a i n
//  Main function that times the "compute" function

void main()
{
    unsigned long count;
    cout << "How many times? ";
    cin >> count;
    compute(count);
}
```

After building the TIMERTST program with optimizations turned off (/Od option for the Microsoft Visual C++ 2.0 compiler), the following is a typical output under Microsoft Windows NT 3.5 on a 66MHz Intel 80486DX2 PC/AT-compatible system (user's input is in boldface):

```
How many times? 1000000
Elapsed time = 2.134 seconds
```

As you can see from this example, you can have perfectly useful classes with instances used only for the side effects of their construction and destruction.

Defining Functions and Operators

The member functions and operators model the behavior of a class and define how you use the objects represented by a class. The functions are defined like any other functions, except that you must indicate the association of a function with a class by using the scope resolution operator (::). You have already seen the definition of several constructors for the String class. The following sections present a few other functions for the String class and describe how to define operators for a class.

The *this* Pointer

Before describing how member functions and operators are defined, you should know about the this keyword. Although a unique copy of member variables exists for each instance of a class, all instances share a single set of member functions. However, none of the member functions that you have seen so far have any way of indicating the class instance with member variables that are being used in the function. Take, for instance, the length function of the String class. If you write the following:

```
String s1 ("Hello"), s2("Hi");
len1 = s1.length();  // len1 = 5
len2 = s2.length();  // len2 = 2
```

each call to length returns a unique answer, yet the length function is defined as this:

```
inline size_t String::length(void) const
{
    return _length;
}
```

where _length is a member variable of the String class. How did the function know to return the correct length for each string? The answer is in this.

this Points to Instance of Class

The C++ compiler alters each member function in a class by making two changes:

■ It passes an additional argument named this, a pointer to the specific object for which the function is being invoked. Thus, the s1.length() call includes a this argument set to the address of the String instance s1.

■ It adds the this-> prefix to all member variables and functions. Thus, the _length variable in the length function becomes this->_length, which refers to the copy of _length in the class instance with an address in this.

Typically, you do not need to use this explicitly in a member function, but you can refer to this if needed. For example, if you need to return the object to a calling program, you can use the following statement to do the job:

```
return *this;
```

You can return a reference to the object with the same statement. As you will see in the following sections, you must return references when defining certain operators, such as the assignment operator (=).

If you are still wondering about the this keyword and its use, you may want to revisit the example of object-oriented programming in C that appears in Chapter 5, "Basics of Object-Oriented Programming." In that chapter, you were shown that the C functions implementing the OOP techniques need a pointer to the object as an argument. That need remains in C++, but the syntax of writing member functions is made more palatable to programmers by the behind-the-scenes handling of the pointer to the object through the this keyword.

Operators as Functions

Defining operators for a class is easy once you know how the application of an operator is translated to a function call. For a unary operator, such as &, when you write the following:

```
&X
```

where X is an instance of some class, the C++ compiler applies the operator by calling the function:

```
X.operator&()
```

The compiler automatically passes a pointer to the class instance to binary operators such as +. For an expression such as this:

```
X + Y
```

where X and Y are class instances, the compiler calls the function:

```
X.operator+(Y)
```

As you can see, the C++ compiler reduces the application of operators to function calls. Consequently, you can overload an operator by defining a function with a name that begins with the operator keyword followed by the symbolic notation of that operator.

Arguments to Operator Functions

Like all member functions, operator functions receive a pointer to the class instance in the hidden argument named this. Because this argument is implicit, unary operator functions are defined with no arguments at all. Binary operator functions that are members of the class take a single argument that is the right side of the operator expression. However, you can define an operator function as a friend rather than a member function of the class. As you will see next, sometimes you need to define friend operator functions. When declared as a friend, the operator function requires all arguments explicitly. This means that to declare operator+ as a friend function of class X you write the following:

```
friend X operator+(X&, X&);  // Assume X is a class
```

Then, to evaluate the expression x1 + x2 for two instances of class X, the C++ compiler calls the function operator(x1, x2).

SIGNIFICANCE OF THE this POINTER

Every member function of a class implicitly receives a pointer to the current instance of the class in a pointer named this. Inside the body of a member function, you can use this to refer to the address of the class instance upon which the function is to operate. If a function must return the instance or a reference to it, you can write the following:

```
return *this;
```

However, you do not need to use the this pointer explicitly in the member functions. The C++ compiler automatically uses it behind the scenes when accessing members of that instance of the class.

Operators You Can Overload

Table 10.1 lists the C++ operators that you can overload. As you can see, you can overload almost all predefined operators in C++. The only ones you cannot overload are the following:

Member access operator   x.y
Dereferencing a pointer to member   x.*y
Scope resolution operator   x::y
Conditional operator   x?y:z

Note that you can overload only the predefined operators. You cannot introduce any new operator notations. For example, FORTRAN uses ** to denote exponentiation. In FORTRAN, x**Y means X raised to the power Y. However, even with operator overloading, you cannot define a similar ** operator in C++ because C++ lacks a predefined ** operator.

Table 10.1. C++ operators that you can overload.

Type	*Name*	*Notation*	*Comments*
Unary	Preincrement	++x	Use operator++ for both
	Postincrement	x++	pre- and postincrement
	Predecrement	--x	Use operator-- for both
	Postdecrement	x--	pre- and postdecrement
	Address of	&x	
	Indirection	*x	
	Plus	+x	Define as operator+()
	Minus	-x	Define as operator-()
	Bitwise NOT	~x	
	Logical NOT	!x	
	Typecast	(type)x	Define as operator type()
Arithmetic	Multiply	x*y	
	Divide	x/y	
	Remainder	x%y	
	Add	x+y	Define as operator+(y) or as friend operator+(x,y)
	Subtract	x-y	Define as operator-(y) or as friend operator -(x,y)

Type	Name	Notation	Comments
Shift	Left shift	x<<y	
	Right shift	x>>y	
Relational	Greater than	x>y	
	Greater than or equal	x>=y	
	Less than	x<y	
	Less than or equal	x<=y	
	Equal to	x==y	
	Not equal to	x!=y	
Bitwise	Bitwise AND	x&y	
	Bitwise exclusive-OR	x^y	
	Bitwise OR	x¦y	
Logical	Logical AND	x&&y	
	Logical OR	x¦¦y	
Assignment	Assignment	x=y	
	Multiply assign	x *= y	
	Divide assign	x /= y	
	Remainder assign	x %= y	
	Add assign	x += y	
	Subtract assign	x -= y	
	Left shift assign	x <<= y	
	Right shift assign	x >>= y	
	Bitwise AND assign	x &= y	
	Bitwise XOR assign	x ^= y	
	Bitwise OR assign	x ¦= y	
Data Access	Subscript	x[y]	
	Member selection	x->y	
	Dereference Member Pointer	x->*y	
Function call	Function call	x(y)	
Comma	Comma	x,y	
Storage	new	x *p=new x or x *q=new x[10]	
	delete	delete p or delete[] q	

Operator Precedence Remains Unchanged

Although C++ enables you to redefine the meaning of most built-in operator symbols for a class, you cannot change the precedence rules that dictate the order in which operators are evaluated. C++ operators follow the same precedence as those of their ANSI C counterparts (see Table 3.5 in Chapter 3, "An Overview of ANSI Standard C"). Even if, for some class, you define + and * operators as something entirely different from addition and multiplication, in an expression such as the following, for example:

```
a + b * c    // a, b, c are some class instances
```

the C++ compiler still invokes the operator* function to evaluate b * c before calling opera-tor+.

Defining *operator+* for the *String* Class

As an example of operator overloading, consider the + operator—the binary version—for the String class. A good interpretation of this operator for the String class is to concatenate two String objects. In other words, a typical use of the + operator for String might be the following:

```
String s1("This "), s2("and that"), s3;
s3 = s1+s2;  // Now s3 should contain "This and that"
```

You can get this functionality by defining this function as a member of the String class:

```
//------------------------------------------------------------
//    o p e r a t o r +
//    Member function to concatenate two String objects

String String::operator+(const String& s)
{
    size_t len = _length + s._length;
    char *t = new char[len+1];
    strcpy(t, p_c);
    strcat(t, s.p_c);
    String r(t);
    delete[] t;
    return (r);
}
```

Because this version of operator+ is a member function of the String class, it takes only one argument—a reference to the String on the right side of the + operator. The function returns a new String object that is a concatenation of the two Strings being added. As you can see from the body of this operator+ function, if you use new to allocate temporary storage, you are responsible for freeing the storage by using the delete operator.

Although the operator+ member function works fine when adding Strings, it cannot handle another type of use for the operator. Because a String is intended to model a dynamic array of characters, it is natural to enable the use of the operator in expressions such as the following:

```
String s1 = "World!";
String s2 = "Hello," + s1; // s2 should be "Hello, World!"
```

In this case, the C++ compiler interprets the right side of the expression as this:

```
"Hello".operator+(s1)
```

This is an error because `"Hello"` is not an instance of a class, and, therefore, contains no member `operator+` function that can be applied to it. You might think that a solution would be to convert `"Hello"` to a String and then apply the `operator+` function of the `String` class. However, this does not happen because the C++ compiler does not automatically convert the left operand of any member operator functions. However, if you define a nonmember `friend` `operator+` function in the `String` class:

```
friend String operator+(const String& s1, const String& s2)
```

the compiler converts the expression `"Hello" + s1` to the function call:

```
operator+(String("Hello"), s1)
```

which automatically converts the left side of the + operator to a `String`. The definition of the `friend` `operator+` function is similar to the member function, except that it takes two `String` arguments, and the body of the function must refer to each argument explicitly. Here is a definition of the function:

```
//----------------------------------------------------------------
//   o p e r a t o r +
//   Nonmember function that concatenates two String objects
//   (Declare as "friend" in String class)

String operator+(const String& s1, const String& s2)
{
    size_t len = s1._length + s2._length;
    char *t = new char[len+1];
    strcpy(t, s1.p_c);
    strcat(t, s2.p_c);
    String s3(t);
    delete[] t;
    return (s3);
}
```

The `friend` version of the `operator+` function does not require the `String::` scope resolution prefix because it is not a member function of the `String` class.

Testing Strings for Equality

Another interesting operator is ==. You can use this operator with the `String` class to compare two `String` instances for equality. Because the `String` class internally maintains a C string, the easiest way to implement this operator is to call the `strcmp` function from the C library:

```
#include "str.h"  // Includes <string.h>
//...
```

```
//--------------------------------------------------------------
//  o p e r a t o r = =
//  String equality operator. Returns nonzero if strings are
//  equal

inline Boolean String::operator==(const String &s) const
{
// Use ANSI C's strcmp function to compare the strings
// Remember strcmp returns 0 if the strings match, but this
//  function has to return nonzero (true) for a match
    return(strcmp(s.p_c, p_c) == 0);
}
```

(You can similarly define other relational operators, such as `operator!=`, `operator >`, and `operator<`.)

Accessing and Altering Individual Characters in a String

Earlier in this chapter, you encountered a `char_at_pos` function that returned a reference to a character at a specific position in the character array inside an instance of a `String`. A better way to provide the functionality of the `char_at_pos` function is to overload the `[]` operator for the `String` class. Knowing the implementation of the `char_at_pos` function, you can define the `operator[]` function as follows:

```
//--------------------------------------------------------------
//  o p e r a t o r [ ]
//  Access a character in a String

char& String::operator[](int index)
{
// Check whether index goes beyond allocated length.
// Return last element, if it does
    if(index > _maxlen-1) return p_c[_maxlen-1];
    else  return p_c[index];
}
```

With the `[]` operator defined in this way, you can use it in statements such as this:

```
String s = "hello";
char c = s[4];     // c = 'o', the 5th character of "hello"
s[0] = 'H';        // Now String s contains "Hello"
```

Defining the Type Conversion Operator

The `String` class is an abstraction of a character string and suitable for use in places where C-style, null-terminated strings are required. Suppose you want to enable `String` instances to be used in calls to the C library's string manipulation functions—the ones defined in the string.h header file. An example might be an expression such as the following:

```
#include <string.h>
//...
String command;
//...
if(strcmp(command, "quit") == 0) exit(0);
```

Because the strcmp function is declared to accept two const char* arguments, the C++ compiler successfully makes this call, provided it can convert the String command to a const char*. You can help the C++ compiler do this by defining a type conversion operator of the following form:

```
String::operator const char*()
```

Of course, for the String class, you need only return the private char pointer member p_c. Because this function is so simple, you may want to define it as inline:

```
//---------------------------------------------------------------
//  o p e r a t o r   c o n s t   c h a r   *
//  Converts from String to char pointer

inline String::operator const char*() const
{
    return p_c;
}
```

Once this conversion operator is defined, calls to functions such as strcmp work even with a String as an argument.

Defining the Assignment Operator for the *String* Class

The = assignment operator is similar to the copy constructor, except that the copy constructor works with an uninitialized copy of an object, and the assignment operator copies an object to another that is already initialized. Thus, for a String object, the assignment operator must eliminate the existing character array and set up a new one with the new value. A typical implementation of this operator function looks like this:

```
//---------------------------------------------------------------
//  o p e r a t o r =
//  Assigns one String object to another

String& String::operator=(const String& s)
{
// Do nothing if left and right sides are the same
    if(this != &s)
    {
        _length = s._length;
        _maxlen = s._maxlen;
        delete[] p_c;
        p_c = new char[_maxlen];
        strcpy(p_c, s.p_c);
    }
    return *this;
}
```

If you compare this function with the copy constructor, you find the two to be very similar. One crucial difference, however, is the if statement at the beginning of the operator+ function. This test ensures that the assignment operator works properly even when the left and right sides of the assignment operator are identical. When this happens, the variables p_c and s.p_c refer to the same pointer. You cannot indiscriminately delete p_c and expect strcpy(p_c, s.p_c) to work. The correctness of the assignment operation is ensured by comparing the this keyword with the operator's right side, which is the argument of the operator= function.

Why *operator=* Returns a Reference

You may wonder why the operator= function for the String class returns String&. This is to enable assignments such as the following:

```
String s1, s2, s3;
s1 = s2 = s3 = "None";
```

where the second statement initializes all three strings to the same value. This statement is possible only because the operator= function of the String class returns a reference to a String object and thereby can be the left side of further assignments.

ASSIGNMENT AND INITIALIZATION IN C++

In C++, assignment and initialization are often denoted by similar statements. Consider the following definitions of String objects:

String s1 = "This is initialization";
String s2;
s2 = "This is assignment"

This defines String s1 and String s2. String s1 is initialized by calling the String(const char*) constructor, whereas String s2 is initially constructed by the default constructor String(). The third statement assigns a value to String s2. The definition of a class instance followed by an equal sign indicates *initialization,* whereas a previously defined class instance name appearing on the left side of an equal sign denotes *assignment.*

Overloading the Input and Output Operators

Chapter 8, "C++ Classes for Standard I/O," explores the iostream class, which defines the >> operator for input and the << operator for output. As defined in the iostream.h header file, these operators work with all predefined types, such as int, long, double, and char*. When you define your own classes, such as the String class, you might want to overload the definitions of the << and >> operators so that they work with your classes. For example, once you overload the >> operator, you can read characters from an input stream to a String by writing the following:

```
String user_input;
cin >> user_input;   // Accept user's input
```

Similarly, to display a String, you would write this:

```
String greetings = "Hello, World!";
cout << greetings << endl;
```

The Output Operator <<

These operators are easy to define. To overload the output operator <<, you need a public member function for the class that can handle the actual output. For the String class, you can define a print function that performs the output as follows:

```
#include "str.h"    // This includes <iostream.h>
//...
//------------------------------------------------------------
//  p r i n t
//  Outputs the String on a specified output stream

void String::print(ostream& os) const
{
    os << p_c;
}
```

Once the print function is defined, you can overload the << operator for a String argument:

```
//------------------------------------------------------------
//  o p e r a t o r < <
//  Stream insertion operator for String class

ostream& operator<<(ostream& os, String& s)
{
    s.print(os);
    return os;
}
```

As you can see, this operator function does its work by calling the member function named print from the String class. Note that the ostream class declares operator<< as a friend function.

The Input Operator >>

The stream extraction operator >> is also easy to implement. The following version assumes a maximum string length of 256 characters, including the null byte, and uses the get function of the input stream to read the characters into an internal array. Then it creates a new String object from that character array and returns the String:

```
//------------------------------------------------------------
//  o p e r a t o r > >
//  Stream extraction operator for String class

istream& operator>>(istream& is, String& s)
{
    const bufsize = 256;
    char buf[bufsize];
```

```
        if(is.get(buf, bufsize)) s = String(buf);
        return is;
}
```

Overloading Operators *new* and *delete*

The dynamic storage allocation operators new and delete are two more interesting operators that you also can overload. You can overload the new operator to use another method for allocating storage. For instance, it is inefficient to allocate many small objects on the free store using the new default operator. One way to improve the efficiency is to obtain a large chunk of memory and use that as the pool of memory from which an overloaded version of the new operator doles out storage for the objects. As with other operators, overriding new and delete for any class involves defining the functions operator new and operator delete.

Some Rules for *new* and *delete*

You should follow these rules when overriding new and delete:

- ■ The first argument of operator new must be of the size_t type (as defined in the stddef.h ANSI C header file), and it must return a void*. Consequently, a prototype for operator new is as follows:

    ```
    void* operator new(size_t numbytes);
    ```

- ■ The first argument to operator delete must be of the void* type, and it must not return a value. You also can have a second argument of the size_t type. Here is a typical prototype for operator delete:

    ```
    void operator delete(void *p);
    ```

Whenever you define the operator new and operator delete functions for a class, the C++ compiler automatically treats them as static member functions of that class. This is true even if you do not explicitly declare them as static. The C++ compiler must call new before the constructor and delete after the destructor. In other words, the compiler must be able to call these operators even when no instance of the class exists. To make this possible, the compiler treats operator new and operator delete as static.

The Placement Syntax for Operator *new*

There is an intriguing way of using the new operator to initialize objects in preallocated memory. This is done with the placement syntax of the new operator. The following example shows how you might initialize a buffer in place with instances of a fictitious my_widget class:

```
//-------------------------------------------------------------
//  Illustrates placement syntax of operator "new"

#include <iostream.h>
#include <stddef.h>
```

```
class my_widget
{
public:
    my_widget(int x, int y) : _x(x), _y(y){}

// Define default new operator.
// NOTE: This simply calls global copy of "operator new"
    void* operator new(size_t sz) { return ::operator new(sz);}

// Define "new" invoked with placement syntax
    void* operator new(size_t sz, void* p)
    {
        return (my_widget*)p;
    }

// Another member function
    int& getx(){ return _x;}

private:
    int _x, _y;
};

//-------------------------------------------------------------
// Test program

main()
{
    char buf[10*sizeof(my_widget)];
    int i=1;

// Initialize chunks of buf with instances of "my_widget"
    for(char *b=buf; b < buf+10*sizeof(my_widget);
        b += sizeof(my_widget), i++)
    {
        (void) new(b) my_widget(i, i);  // placement syntax
    }

// See whether it worked...
    my_widget* widget = (my_widget*) buf;

    for(i=0; i<10; i++)
        cout << widget[i].getx() << " ";

    cout << endl;
}
```

When run, this sample program generates the following output:

```
1 2 3 4 5 6 7 8 9 10
```

which is what you would expect because of the way the instances of my_widget are initialized.

This approach of placing a new object in a predefined area of memory has a purpose. Some environments, such as Microsoft Windows and Apple Macintosh, have their own memory-management scheme that good programs are supposed to follow. If you happen to use C++ to write application programs for such environments, you can allocate a block of memory by calling an environment-specific function, and you can use the placement syntax of operator new to initialize instances of objects in that block of memory.

Using *friend* Classes

Sometimes data-hiding rules of C++ classes can be too restrictive. If, for reasons of efficiency, you want to provide an A class access to all members of a B class, you can do so by embedding the following statement in the declaration of class B:

```
class A;
class B
{
    friend A;  // A can access all members of this class
//...
};
```

To see how friend classes are used, consider the example in the next section.

Using a File as an Array

If you want to treat a file as an array of characters, to be specific, you should create a File class and then use it as follows:

```
File f("sample.dat");  // Open a file
char c = f[10];        // Get byte at index 10
f[128] = ']';          // Store ']' into a byte in the file
```

This tells you that you need a File constructor that takes a file's name as an argument. In the constructor, you must open the file and remember the FILE pointer, assuming that you use the standard C file I/O functions to the actual I/O operations with the file. Additionally, you must overload operator[] to read from and write to the file. With the File class alone, it is difficult to define this operator. You can do this, however, by using a helper class called FileLoc. The idea is to define operator[] for the File class so that applying the operator to a File implies creation of a FileLoc object—as the name implies, this object keeps track of the position within the file. The FileLoc object positions the stream and defines appropriate operators to read from and write to the disk file. The File and FileLoc classes are declared as friends of each other so that the I/O operations can be as efficient as possible. Listing 10.3 shows the actual declarations of the classes as well as a small test program.

Listing 10.3. FARRAY.CPP. An illustration of classes that treat a disk file as an array of characters.

```
//--------------------------------------------------------------
// File:  farray.cpp
// Treats a file as an array of bytes
//--------------------------------------------------------------

#include <stdio.h>
#include <iostream.h>
```

```
//----------------------------------------------------------------
// Declare the "FileLoc" class--the helper of File class

class File;

class FileLoc
{
public:
    friend File;

    void operator=(char c);
    void operator=(const char* str);
    operator const char();

private:
    File* p_file;
    fpos_t file_loc;
    FileLoc(File& f, fpos_t loc): p_file(&f), file_loc(loc){}
};
//----------------------------------------------------------------
// Now declare the "File" class

class File
{
public:
    friend FileLoc;

// Constructor open file for read and write operations
    File(const char* name)
    {
        fp = fopen(name, "r+");  // open for read and write
    }

// Destructor closes file
    ~File() { fclose(fp);}

// operator[] positions file and creates an instance of FileLoc
    FileLoc operator[](fpos_t loc)
    {
        fseek(fp, loc, SEEK_SET);
        return FileLoc(*this,loc);
    }

private:
    FILE* fp;  // ANSI C stream pointer
};
//----------------------------------------------------------------
//      M e m b e r   F u n c t i o n s
//----------------------------------------------------------------
// o p e r a t o r = ( c h a r )
// Handles assignments of the form:
//      f[n] = c, where f[n] is a FileLoc and c is a char
// by storing the character in the file

void FileLoc::operator=(char c)
{
    if(p_file->fp != NULL)
    {
```

continues

Listing 10.3. continued

```
            putc(c, p_file->fp);
        }
}
//------------------------------------------------------------
//  o p e r a t o r = ( c h a r * )
//  Handles assignments of the form:
//       f[n]="string", where f[n] is a FileLoc object
//  This stores the string into the file

void FileLoc::operator=(const char* str)
{
    if(p_file->fp != NULL)
    {
        fputs(str, p_file->fp);
    }
}
//------------------------------------------------------------
//  o p e r a t o r   c o n s t   c h a r ( )
//  Handles assignments of the form:
//       c = f[n], where f[n] is a FileLoc and c is a char
//  This reads a character from the file.

FileLoc::operator const char()
{
    if(p_file->fp != NULL)
    {
        return getc(p_file->fp);
    }
    return EOF;
}
//------------------------------------------------------------
//  m a i n
//  A program to test the File and FileLoc classes
//  Before running program, create a file "test.dat"
//  with the following line:
//
//       Testing: File and FileLoc classes

void main()
{
    File f("test.dat");
    int i;
    char c;
    cout << "First 14 bytes = " << endl;
    for(i=0; i<14; i++)
    {
        c = f[i];
        cout << c;
    }
    cout << endl;

// Change first 7 bytes to ' ' (blank space)
    for(i=0; i<7; i++) f[i] = ' ';

// Display the first 14 characters again
    cout << "Now the first 14 bytes = " << endl;
    for(i=0; i<14; i++)
```

```
    {
        c = f[i];
        cout << c;
    }
    cout << endl;
// Store a string in the file
    f[0] = "Creating";

    cout << "After string insert: the first 25 bytes = " << endl;
    for(i=0; i<25; i++)
    {
        c = f[i];
        cout << c;
    }
    cout << endl;
}
```

If you prepare a file named TEST.DAT with the following line:

```
Testing: File and FileLoc classes.
```

and run the program shown in Listing 10.3, you should see the following output:

```
First 14 bytes =
Testing: File
Now the first 14 bytes =
        : File
After string insert: the first 25 bytes =
Creating File and FileLoc
```

When you write this:

```
char c = f[i];  // f is a File, i an integer
```

the expression f[i] results in a FileLoc object, which positions the file to the character at location i. The C++ compiler then applies FileLoc::operator const char() to this FileLoc object. As you can see from the definition of FileLoc::operator const char(), this reads a character from the file. On the other hand, when you write the following:

```
f[i] = c;  // f is a File, i an integer, c, a char
```

the expression f[i] again creates a FileLoc object that positions the file to the position i. The C++ compiler then invokes the function FileLoc::operator=(char), which writes the character to the file. This operator is overloaded for a string argument as well so that an entire string can be written to a file.

This is a good example of using a friend class as an intermediary when implementing a desired syntax of usage for a class. Here, as the sole purpose of the FileLoc class, you can use the File class not only to view a disk file as an array of characters, but you can even use the array-access syntax to read from and write to a file.

Summary

The class construct forms the basis of object-oriented programming in C++. The member functions of a class control how the class can be used. To make a class as easy to use as the built-in data types, you must define a complete assortment of member functions for each class. Constructors that the C++ compiler calls to initialize a newly created instance of a class are very important. At a minimum, you should provide the default constructor, which takes no arguments, and the copy constructor, which initializes a new instance of a class from an existing instance. When initializing a class that includes instances of other classes as members, you should use member initializer list syntax to initialize these class instances. The initializer list is the only way to initialize constant member variables.

To make classes easy to use, C++ enables you to redefine most operators so that they can be used with instances of a class to perform meaningful operations. For example, for a String class, the + operator can be defined to concatenate two Strings. Overloading operators involves defining functions with names that begin with the operator keyword followed by the symbol used for the operator.

Although C++ supports strict data hiding, you can use the friend keyword to declare one class or a function as a friend of another class. A friend can access all members of a class: public as well as private and protected. An example illustrates how you can use a friend class to implement a convenient syntax of usage for a class that enables you to treat a file as an array of bytes.

11

Using Inheritance
in C++

The last two chapters focused on data abstraction. This is only one ingredient, albeit an important one, of object-oriented programming. The other two components of OOP are inheritance and polymorphism. Although data abstraction helps you define a new data type, you need inheritance to exploit the common features of related data types or to extend the functionality provided by one or more existing classes.

Inheritance enables you to do the following:

■ Classify objects—for example, with inheritance you can categorize circles, rectangles, and triangles as different types of shapes and share everything the shapes have in common

■ Express the differences between related classes while sharing the functions and member variables that implement the common features

■ Reuse existing code from one or more classes by merely deriving a new class from them

■ Extend an existing class by adding new members to it

This chapter explains how to use inheritance in C++ classes.

Derived Classes

Suppose you have a C++ class that implements a specific data type and you need another data type that is similar to the first but has some additional member variables or functions. Rather than create the new data type from scratch, OOP techniques suggest that you inherit from the existing type and add the necessary capabilities to the inherited type. In C++, you can do this by deriving the new class from the existing class. You can add capabilities to the derived class by the following methods:

■ Defining new member variables

■ Defining new member functions

■ Overriding the definition of inherited member functions

Inheritance Can Represent the "is a" Relationship

One common use of inheritance is to express the "is a" relationship among various types of objects. The geometric shapes discussed in Chapter 6, "C++ and Object-Oriented Programming," are based on this idea. Because a circle *is a* shape and a rectangle *is a* shape, the `circle_shape` and `rectangle_shape` classes inherit from the `shape` class. In some object-oriented languages, such as Smalltalk, `circle_shape` is called a *subclass* of `shape`, which in turn is the *superclass* of `circle_shape`. In C++, the `circle_shape` and `rectangle_shape` classes are derived from the `shape` class, which is their base class. Figure 11.1 illustrates this concept. Notice that you may further specialize the `rectangle_shape` class by deriving from it a `rounded_rectangle_shape` class that represents rectangles with rounded corners.

As you can see, a base class can have more than one derived class, and a derived class can serve as the base class for others. Thus, you end up with a tree-structured hierarchy of classes in which the classes near the bottom (the leaves) are more specialized versions of the classes at the top.

FIGURE 11.1.

Inheritance in C++.

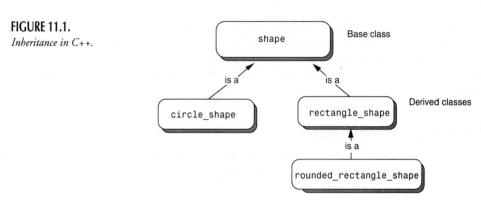

Inheritance Can Extend a Class

In addition to seeing inheritance as a mechanism for implementing the "is a" relationship among types of objects, you also can use inheritance to extend the functionality provided by one or more classes. Suppose you have a class named single_link that maintains a pointer to another instance of the same class. You plan to use the single_link objects in a linked list. You might declare the single_link as follows:

```
class single_link
{
public:
    single_link(): _next(0) {}

    single_link(single_link& sl) : _next(sl._next) {}

// Other member functions...

protected:
    single_link* _next;  // link to next "single_link"
};
```

Later, you might want a doubly linked list for which you need a double_link class with instances capable of holding two pointers—one to the next instance and the other to the previous one. Instead of defining from scratch, you can create the double_link class by merely deriving it from single_link and adding a new member variable:

```
// Include declaration of "single_link" class here

class double_link: public single_link
{
public:
    double_link() : single_link(), _previous(0){}
```

```
// Other member functions...

protected:
    single_link* _previous;  // Add another "link"
};
```

As you soon will learn, making the _next data item in the `single_link` class protected enables derived classes, such as `double_link`, to access the `next` pointer directly. This improves the speed with which a program can manipulate the items in linked lists that use these classes. Later in this chapter, you will see an example that uses these link classes to construct linked list data structures.

Syntax of a Derived Class

The `class` construct of C++ already includes the syntax necessary to indicate that a class is derived from another. For a base class, you declare the `class` the same way you declare a `struct`:

```
class shape
{
public:
// ...
};
```

For a derived class, you must list the name of its base class:

```
class circle_shape: public shape  // circle is derived from shape
{
public:
// ...
private:
    double x_center, y_center;
    double radius;
};
```

Access to the Base Class

The `public` keyword preceding the name of the base class indicates how `circle_shape` is derived from `shape`. In this case, `circle_shape` is publicly derived from `shape`; in other words, `shape` is a public base class of `circle_shape`. This means all `public` and `protected` members of `shape` are also `public` and `protected` members of `circle_shape`.

You also can specify a `private` keyword in front of the base class name. In this case, all `public` and `protected` members of the base class become `private` members of the derived class. As illustrated in Figure 11.2, the net effect is that if `rectangle_shape` is privately derived from `shape`, the `rounded_rectangle_shape` class derived from `rectangle_shape` can no longer access the `public` and `protected` members of `shape`. In effect, a privately derived class blocks any further access to members of its base class.

FIGURE 11.2.
Controlling access to members of base class.

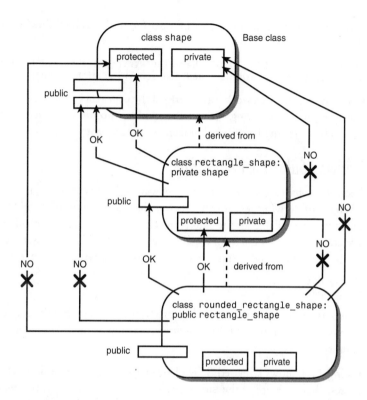

When you use the class keyword to define object types, the default derivation is private. In other words, if you forget the access specifier and write the following:

```
class rectangle_shape: shape
{
// rectangle_shape is privately derived from shape
// ...
};
```

you get a private derivation of shape. On the other hand, with the struct keyword, all derivations are public by default. Thus, the following code declares a rectangle_shape class with a public base class named shape:

```
struct rectangle_shape: shape
{
// rectangle_shape is publicly derived from shape
// ...
};
```

Using Inheritance to Build a *Substring* Class

Chapter 9, "Building Objects with Classes," and Chapter 10, "Defining Operations on Objects," use a String class as an example. Suppose you want to create a new class called Substring with which you can access a part of a String object. The following code should accomplish this:

```
String path_name(32); // 32-character string, set to all blanks
path_name(0,4) = "/bin"; // Replace substring with "/bin"
```

One way to make this work is to overload the operator() for the String class so that it returns a Substring. The C string /bin is then copied into the substring. The net result of this code should be to set the first four characters of String path_name to /bin.

Deriving *Substring* from *String*

Because a Substring is a String, an easy way to define Substring is to derive it from String. As a benefit of deriving it from the String class, all operations defined for the String class are immediately available for the Substring class. A Substring is a full-fledged String, but it holds a reference to the String from which it was derived. This is necessary so that the original String can be altered through a statement such as the following:

```
String path_name(32);
path_name(0,4) = "/bin";
```

This path_name(0,4) expression creates a Substring class and the Substring::operator=(const char*) function replaces four characters, starting at the first character of path_name with the /bin string.

Listing 11.1 shows a revised STR.H header file that declares both the String and Substring classes. Before defining the Substring class, change the private members of String to protected so that Substring objects can access the internal variables of the Strings.

Initializing the Base Class

As you can see from Listing 11.1, declaring the Substring class is a straightforward process. Notice how you initialize a base class from the constructor of the derived class. In Chapter 10, you learned how member initializer lists are used to initialize static members and member classes—that is, class instances that appear as a member of another class. You can use the same technique to initialize the base class in the constructor of a derived class. As an example, consider the following Substring constructor:

```
// Substring constructor
    Substring(String& s, const char *cs, size_t pos, size_t len) :
        String(cs, len), s_original(s), _pos(pos) { }
```

This creates a Substring by copying len characters starting at position pos of the specified String. As you can see, the body of this constructor is empty. All initializations are done through the initializer list, which invokes an appropriate String constructor and initializes the members of the newly created Substring.

Listing 11.1. Revised STR.H file with declaration of String and Substring classes.

```
//------------------------------------------------------------
//  File:  str.h
//  Declares a "String" class and a "Substring" class derived
//  from the "String" class
//------------------------------------------------------------

#if !defined(__STR_H)  // Be sure file is included only once
#define __STR_H

// Include other required header files...
// The ANSI C headers work because they are already enclosed
// in an extern "C"{...}
// Be sure your compiler does this.

#include <stddef.h>      // For "size_t" type
#include <iostream.h>    // For stream I/O
#include <string.h>      // For ANSI C string library

typedef int Boolean;     // For return type of operators

class Substring;

class String
{
public:
// Constructors with a variety of arguments
    String();
    String(size_t len);
    String(const char *str);
    String(const char *str, size_t len);
    String(const String &s);

// Destructor
    ~String() { delete[] p_c;}

// Overloaded operators
    Boolean operator==(const String& s) const
    {
        return(strcmp(s.p_c, p_c) == 0);
    }

// Assignment operator
    String& operator=(const String& s);

// Type conversion operator
    operator const char*() const { return p_c;}

// Access operator
    char& operator[](int index);

// Replace a portion of a string with another
// Used to insert or delete parts of a string
    String& replace(size_t pos, size_t len, const char* s);

//  o p e r a t o r ( )
//  Overload the function call operator to return a Substring
```

continues

Listing 11.1. continued

```
    Substring operator()(size_t pos, size_t len);

// The + operator concatenates strings
    friend String operator+(const String& s1, const String& s2);

// Function giving access to internal variable
    size_t length(void) const { return _length;}

// Function to print a String
    void print(ostream& os) const;

protected:    // so that derived classes can access these data

    char   *p_c;      // pointer to allocated space
    size_t _length;   // current length of string
    size_t _maxlen;   // number of bytes allocated

};

// Stream I/O for String class

#include <iostream.h>

ostream& operator<<(ostream& os, String& s);
istream& operator>>(istream& is, String& s);

//-------------------------------------------------------------
//  Declare the "Substring" class

class Substring: public String
{
public:
    friend String;  // Give the String class access to this one

// Substring operators...
    String& operator=(const char* str)
    {
        return s_original.replace(_pos, _length, str);
    }
    String& operator=(Substring& s)
    {
        return s_original.replace(_pos, _length, s.p_c);
    }

private:
    String& s_original;  // Reference to original String
    size_t _pos;         // Position of Substring in String

// Substring constructor
    Substring(String& s, const char *cs, size_t pos, size_t len) :
        String(cs, len), s_original(s), _pos(pos) { }

// Substring copy constructor
```

```
    Substring(const Substring& s) : String(s),
        s_original(s.s_original), _pos(s._pos) { }

};

#endif
```

Modifying the Original String Through a *Substring*

As I mentioned earlier, one reason to introduce the Substring class is to use it in statements such as the following that modify a portion of a String through an intermediate Substring created by the String::operator():

```
String hello = "Hello......";
hello(5,3) = " there";   // Now hello = "Hello there..."
```

To make this work, you must define Substring::operator=(const char*) and have a way to replace a number of characters in a String. To this end, I added a String::replace function, shown toward the end of Listing 11.2, which shows the STR.CPP file, an implementation of the String class. With the String::replace function in place, you can implement the opera-tor= function for the Substring class by merely calling String::replace:

```
String& operator=(const char* str)
{
// Invoke the original String's "replace" function
    return s_original.replace(_pos, _length, str);
}
```

The *String::operator()*

Substrings are created through the operator() function of the String class. This operator is invoked with two size_t arguments, the first denoting the starting position of the substring and the second indicating the substring's length. Once you have defined a constructor for the Substring class that can create a Substring from a String, you can define the String::operator():

```
Substring String::operator()(size_t pos, size_t len)
{
    return Substring(*this, &(p_c[pos]), pos, len);
}
```

This function returns a new Substring by calling the Substring constructor.

Listing 11.2. STR.CPP. Implementation of the *String* class.

```
//-----------------------------------------------------------
//  File:  str.cpp
//  Implements the member functions of the "String" class

#include "str.h"    // For declaration of String class

const chunk_size = 8;
```

continues

Listing 11.2. continued

```cpp
//--------------------------------------------------------------
// S t r i n g
// Creates a String object and initializes it
//  from a null-terminated C string

String::String(const char *s)
{
    _length = strlen(s);
    _maxlen = chunk_size*(_length / chunk_size + 1);
    p_c = new char[_maxlen];
    strcpy(p_c, s);
}
//--------------------------------------------------------------
// S t r i n g
// Creates a String object and initializes it using a
//  specified number of characters from a null-terminated
//  C string

String::String(const char *s, size_t len)
{
    _length = len;
    _maxlen = chunk_size*(_length / chunk_size + 1);
    p_c = new char[_maxlen];
    p_c[len] = '\0';
    strncpy(p_c, s, len);
}
//--------------------------------------------------------------
// S t r i n g
// Creates a String and stores a zero-length string in it.

String::String()
{
    _maxlen = chunk_size;
    p_c = new char[_maxlen];
    _length = 0;
    p_c[0] = '\0';
}
//--------------------------------------------------------------
// S t r i n g
// This version creates a blank string of size "len"

String::String(size_t len)
{
    _length = len;
    _maxlen = chunk_size*(_length / chunk_size + 1);
    p_c = new char[_maxlen];
    int i;
    for(i = 0; i < len; i++) p_c[i] = ' ';
    p_c[i] = '\0';
}
//--------------------------------------------------------------
// S t r i n g
// Creates a new String as a copy of another String
// This is often called the "Copy Constructor"
```

```
String::String(const String &s)
{
    _length = s._length;
    _maxlen = s._maxlen;
    p_c = new char[_maxlen];
    strcpy(p_c, s.p_c);
}
//---------------------------------------------------------------
// o p e r a t o r +
// Concatenates two String objects

String operator+(const String& s1, const String& s2)
{
    size_t len = s1._length + s2._length;
    char *t = new char[len+1];
    strcpy(t, s1.p_c);
    strcat(t, s2.p_c);
    String s3(t);
    delete[] t;
    return (s3);
}
//---------------------------------------------------------------
// o p e r a t o r =
// Assigns one String object to another

String& String::operator=(const String& s)
{
    if(this != &s)
    {
        _length = s._length;
        _maxlen = s._maxlen;
        delete[] p_c;
        p_c = new char[_maxlen];
        strcpy(p_c, s.p_c);
    }
    return *this;
}
//---------------------------------------------------------------
// p r i n t
// Outputs the String on a specified output stream

void String::print(ostream& os) const
{
    os << p_c;
}
//---------------------------------------------------------------
// o p e r a t o r < <
// Stream insertion operator for String class

ostream& operator<<(ostream& os, String& s)
{
    s.print(os);
    return os;
}
//---------------------------------------------------------------
// o p e r a t o r > >
// Stream extraction operator for String class
```

continues

Listing 11.2. continued

```
istream& operator>>(istream& is, String& s)
{
    const bufsize = 256;
    char buf[bufsize];

    if(is.get(buf, bufsize)) s = String(buf);
    return is;
}
//-------------------------------------------------------------
//  o p e r a t o r [ ]
//  Access a character in a String

char& String::operator[](int index)
{
// Check whether index goes beyond allocated length.
// Return last element , if it does
    if(index > _maxlen-1) return p_c[_maxlen-1];
    else   return p_c[index];
}
//-------------------------------------------------------------
//  r e p l a c e
//  Replace a portion of a string with another C string

String& String::replace(size_t pos, size_t len, const char* s)
{
    size_t new_len = strlen(s);

// Check whether there is enough room
    if(_length + new_len - len < _maxlen)
    {
// Move bytes around using ANSI C function "memmove"
        memmove(&(p_c[pos+new_len]), &(p_c[pos+len]),
                _length-pos-len);
        memmove(&(p_c[pos]), s, new_len);
    }
    else
    {
// Must reallocate string
        _maxlen = chunk_size * ((_length+new_len-len) /
                                chunk_size + 1);
        char *t = new char[_maxlen];
// Copy strings over...
        memmove(t, p_c, pos);
        memmove(&(t[pos]), s, new_len);
        memmove(&(t[new_len+pos]),
                &(p_c[pos+len]), _length-pos-len);
        delete[] p_c;
        p_c = t;
    }
// Adjust the length of the String
    _length += new_len - len;

// Terminate the new C string
    p_c[_length] = '\0';

    return *this;
}
```

```
//----------------------------------------------------------------
// operator()
// Overload the function call operator to return a Substring

Substring String::operator()(size_t pos, size_t len)
{
    return Substring(*this, &(p_c[pos]), pos, len);
}
```

Testing the *Substring* Class

Here is a short program that tries out the Substring class through operator() applied to a String variable named hello:

```
// Test Substring class
#include "str.h"

void main()
{
    String hello = "Hello......";
    cout << "Before: " << hello << endl;

    hello(5,3) = " there";
    cout << "After: " << hello << endl;

    hello(11,1) = " C++ Programmer";
    cout << "After another 'replace': " << hello << endl;
}
```

You must compile this program, as well as the STR.CPP file shown in Listing 11.2, and link them to create the executable file. When run, the program generates the following output:

```
Before: Hello......
After: Hello there...
After another 'replace': Hello there C++ Programmer..
```

Other Issues for Derived Classes

Now that you have seen how the Substring class is created by deriving from String, you should be aware of a few more details about derived classes that were not illustrated by the Substring class. The following sections briefly cover these issues.

Overriding Inherited Member Functions

Presumably, your reason for declaring a derived class is to model a new type of object in terms of one or more existing types or to extend the functionality of an existing class. Usually, this means that you add new member variables and member functions to complete the functionality of the derived class. Adding new members is a straightforward process: merely place any new member that you want to add to the definition of the derived class. Apart from adding new members, you also can redefine member functions that already appear in a base class. You can do so to improve efficiency or to alter the functionality of an existing function. Whatever the reason, you can redefine member functions of the base class freely, provided you keep in mind the following rule:

> *An overloaded member function in the derived class hides all inherited member functions of the same name.*

This means that, if a base class provides one or more versions of a member function, overloading that function in a derived class hides all inherited versions of the function. The following example clarifies this.

Suppose the String class defines two versions of a member function called insert—one to insert a single character at a specific position and the other to insert a C string. You could declare the functions as follows:

```
class String
{
public:
//...
    void insert(size_t pos, char c);
    void insert(size_t pos, char* str);

protected:
//...
}
```

After deriving the Substring class from String, you decide to add another version of the insert function, this one to insert the formatted representation of a float variable into a Substring. With this in mind, you declare the new insert function:

```
class Substring: public String
{
public:
//...
    void insert(size_t pos, float x);
private:
//...
};
```

The rule for overriding member functions of the base class says that the function Substring::insert hides the functions String::insert. In other words, once you define the new insert function for Substring, you lose access to the insert function that the Substring class inherits from the String class. Keep this in mind when overloading inherited member functions in a derived class.

Order of Initialization of Classes Under Single Inheritance

Another detail worth knowing is the order in which the C++ compiler initializes the base classes of a derived class. When the C++ compiler initializes an instance of a derived class, it must initialize all the base classes first. If you are working with a hierarchy of classes, it helps to know how C++ initializes the base classes so that you can track down problems that may occur from improper initialization of a class instance. For single inheritance, the C++ compiler uses the following basic rules during initialization:

■ Initialize the base class, if any.

■ Within the base class, initialize the member variables in the order in which they are declared in the class.

The only catch is that the compiler applies these rules recursively. Notice that the order in the initializer list does not affect the order in which member variables of a class are initialized. The best way to see the order of initialization is to run a simple example. The following example has a class hierarchy in which class C is derived from B, and B in turn is derived from A. Another class named Data is a member of A and B. Here is a sample implementation of the classes:

```
// Illustrate order of initialization
#include <iostream.h>

class Data
{
public:
    Data(int x = 0): _x(x)
    { cout << "Data::Data(" << x << ") ";}
private:
    int _x;
};

class A
{
    Data d1;
public:
    A(int x): d1(x-1) { cout << "A::A(" << x << ") ";}
};

class B: public A
{
    Data d2;
public:
    B(int x): d2(x-1), A(x-2)
    { cout << "B::B(" << x << ") ";}
};

class C: public B
{
public:
    C(int x): B(x-1) { cout << "C::C(" << x << ") ";}
};

void main()
{
    C(5);
}
```

When run, this program generates the following output:

```
Data::Data(1) A::A(2) Data::Data(3) B::B(4) C::C(5)
```

If you trace through the program's code, you see that the C++ compiler first initializes the Data member of A class, then follows with class A itself. Then it initializes the Data member of class B, then class B, and finally class C. All the base classes are initialized before the derived classes.

The order of initialization is more complicated when you use multiple inheritance.

Multiple Inheritance

The examples thus far show a derived class with a single base class—single inheritance. Recall that C++ also supports the notion of multiple inheritance, in which you can derive a class from several base classes. Support for multiple inheritance was introduced in AT&T C++ Release 2.0 to enable implementation of classes that need to share the data and function members of several classes at once. As you will see in the following sections, multiple inheritance is often used to reuse code from several base classes. Of course, you also can use multiple inheritance when you feel that a particular class truly manifests the characteristics of more than one class of objects. For example, suppose you have two classes: CollectorsItem and Cars. Perhaps the CollectorsItem class has member functions that can estimate the value of an object based on its age and rarity. You might decide to define a new class, AntiqueCars, that inherits from both Cars and CollectorsItem. In C++, you can do so by deriving AntiqueCars from two base classes:

```
class Cars;
class CollectorsItem;

class AntiqueCars: public Cars, public CollectorsItem
{
//...
};
```

Now the AntiqueCars class can use all public members of both Cars and CollectorsItem classes. If necessary, the AntiqueCars class can also add new member functions and variables. Additionally, the member functions of AntiqueCars can access all protected members of its base classes.

ostream Uses Multiple Inheritance

The iostream class library uses multiple inheritance. As discussed in Chapter 8, "C++ Classes for Standard I/O," and illustrated in Figure 8.2 in that chapter, the iostream library contains the istream class for input, the ostream class for output, and a bidirectional iostream class derived from both istream and ostream. Therefore, multiple inheritance enables the iostream class to support both input and output operations on a stream.

Virtual Base Class

A problem with inheriting from multiple base classes is that you may end up with more than one instance of a base class. As a concrete example, consider the following hierarchy of classes:

```
// Illustrates need for "virtual base class"

#include <iostream.h>

class device
{
public:
    device()
    { cout << "device: constructor" << endl;}
};

class comm_device: public device
{
public:
    comm_device()
    { cout << "comm_device: constructor" << endl;}
};

class graphics_device: public device
{
public:
    graphics_device()
    { cout << "graphics_device: constructor" << endl;}
};

class graphics_terminal: public comm_device,
                          public graphics_device
{
public:
    graphics_terminal()
    { cout << "graphics_terminal: constructor" << endl;}
};

void main()
{
    graphics_terminal gt;
}
```

Here, the device class models a generic UNIX-style device with functions to open and close the device and control it. The comm_device class models a communication device: it adds functions to set the communications parameters. The graphics_device class models a device capable of drawing graphics. Finally, the graphics_terminal class is derived from both comm_device and graphics_device classes. Notice what happens when an instance of the graphics_terminal class is created. The program prints the following:

```
device: constructor
comm_device: constructor
device: constructor
graphics_device: constructor
graphics_terminal: constructor
```

The constructor for the device base class is called twice because it appears twice in the inheritance hierarchy—once as the base class of comm_device and once as the base class of graphics_device.

Because the graphics_terminal class models a physical device, you do not want two instances of the device base class in every instance of graphics_terminal. You need a way to create a graphics_terminal class that inherits from both comm_device and graphics_device but has only one instance of the device class. You can do this with the virtual base class. Merely add the virtual keyword wherever the device class name appears in the inheritance list of a class. The new class definitions are as follows:

```
// Illustrates how "virtual base class" works

#include <iostream.h>

class device
{
public:
    device()
    { cout << "device: constructor" << endl;}
};

class comm_device: public virtual device
{
public:
    comm_device()
    { cout << "comm_device: constructor" << endl;}
};

class graphics_device: public virtual device
{
public:
    graphics_device()
    { cout << "graphics_device: constructor" << endl;}
};

class graphics_terminal: public comm_device,
                         public graphics_device
{
public:
    graphics_terminal()
    { cout << "graphics_terminal: constructor" << endl;}
};

void main()
{
    graphics_terminal gt;
}
```

This version of the test program produces the following output:

```
device: constructor
comm_device: constructor
graphics_device: constructor
graphics_terminal: constructor
```

Notice that the device class is constructed only once.

Restrictions on Virtual Base Classes

The virtual base class mechanism fills an important need, but beware of the following restrictions when you use virtual base classes:

■ You cannot initialize a virtual base class with an initializer list. For an example, look at the constructor of the `Substring` class in Listing 11.1. There, the `String` class is initialized through the initializer list. You can't do the same with a virtual base class. This implies that a class you plan to use as a virtual base class should have a default constructor, a constructor that takes no arguments.

■ You cannot cast a virtual base class pointer as a pointer to any class that is derived from it. Therefore, in the example, you cannot cast a `device*` pointer to a `graphics_terminal*` pointer.

Order of Initialization of Classes Under Multiple Inheritance

The rules for initializing classes in the presence of multiple inheritance are rather complicated. Generally speaking, the C++ compiler follows this order of initialization:

1. All virtual base classes are initialized. The constructor of each virtual base class is called exactly once.

2. Nonvirtual base classes are initialized by the order in which they appear in a class declaration.

3. Member variables are initialized, again by the order in which they appear in the class declaration.

The C++ compiler applies these rules recursively, just as it does under single inheritance. (For further details on this topic, consult *The Annotated C++ Reference Manual,* by Margaret Ellis and Bjarne Stroustrup, published by Addison-Wesley in 1990.)

Using Inheritance

You can use inheritance to create specialized versions of a general-purpose class. Suppose you have a class named `plain_window` that displays a rectangular area of screen wherein you can show text and graphics output. Typical members of such a class might include foreground and background colors, the font for text display, and a member function that refreshes the contents of the window.

Given the `plain_window` class, you can create a window that displays a text *label* in a window—a `static_text_window`—by deriving it from the `plain_window` class and adding a new member variable to store the text for the label. Furthermore, you can derive from `static_text_window` a `pushbutton_window` that displays a label; but unlike a `static_text_window`, it performs some action when a user selects the pushbutton with a pointing device such as a mouse. Figure 11.3 illustrates the inheritance hierarchy of these window classes. This is an example of specializing classes through inheritance.

FIGURE 11.3.
Inheritance hierarchy of window classes.

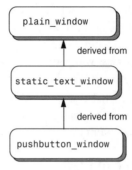

On the other hand, inheritance can extend the functionality of a class. Rather than specializing, use inheritance for even broader functionality than before. You can view the class construct in two ways:

- As a means for defining new data types
- As a module for packaging data and functions

When you use class to define a data type, inheritance is useful in creating more specialized types. When you think of a class as a means of packaging functions, you can use inheritance to add new functions, thus extending the capabilities of the module.

Linked Lists

Basic data structures (such as linked lists, queues, stacks, and trees) are popular targets for implementation as abstract data types because they can be easily implemented in the object-oriented style. Inheritance is often useful when defining such classes. A linked list, for example, can be the basis of several types of data structures including queues, stacks, and trees. Let's begin with an example of a single-linked list and show how you can use inheritance to create such a data structure.

Figure 11.4 represents a single-linked list of elements. The list consists of a number of data items, each capable of holding a pointer to another such item. In the single-linked list, each item points to the next one in the list so that you can start at the beginning and reach every element in the list by following these pointers.

In addition to these items, the list needs a pointer to the first element so that you know where to start looking for data stored in the list. Sometimes you may also want to maintain a pointer to what you might call the current element, which is the element being accessed at that time. Another item of interest is the number of elements in the list.

FIGURE 11.4.
A single-linked list data structure.

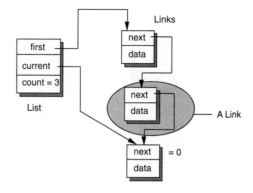

The Link and the List

As Figure 11.4 illustrates, one of the basic objects in a linked list is the link—an object with some data and a pointer to another link. The other object is the *list*, which holds information about the linked list, such as a pointer to the first item and the number of items. Having identified the basic objects, you can proceed to declare the C++ classes for them.

Making a Generic List

Before declaring the classes for the linked list, consider an important issue. You define data structures such as linked lists to store objects. What you really want is a linked list that can hold any type of object. If you can define a parameterized class with a parameter denoting the data type stored in each link, you can easily create linked lists capable of holding different data types by substituting an appropriate type for the parameter. As explained in Chapter 13, "Advanced Topics in C++," the template keyword of C++ is used to provide such a facility.

You also can simulate generic lists through inheritance. The idea is to create a list that can hold links of a class named single_link, for example. A single_link object does not contain any data other than a pointer to the next single_link object. If you want a single-linked list of String objects later, you can create a new type. Let's call it slink_string, which inherits from both single_link and String. Then objects of the slink_string class should be able to reside in the single-linked list you designed to hold single_link objects. Figure 11.5 illustrates the idea and the following sections demonstrate how this works. The major drawback of this approach is that you cannot have a list of built-in data types, such as int, char, and double, because they are not defined as classes and you therefore cannot create derived classes from these types.

FIGURE 11.5.
A single-linked list capable of holding String *objects.*

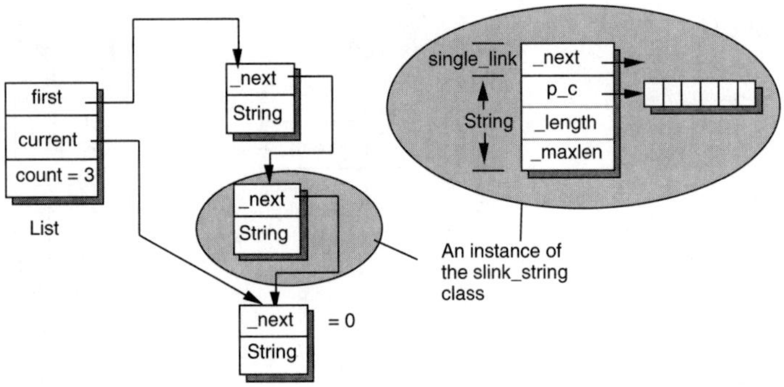

The *single_link* Class

Listing 11.3 shows the SLINK.H header file, which declares the single_link class. The class has only one protected data member, named _next, which is a pointer to the next single_link object. Therefore, you can string together instances of single_link class through their _next pointers.

Apart from the constructors, the single_link class also provides the next member function, which returns its _next pointer, and the set_next function, which sets the _next pointer to a new value.

The class also includes two virtual functions: clone and destroy. These functions ensure that you can correctly create and destroy instances of a class derived from single_link. The clone function makes a duplicate copy of an object, and destroy properly deletes objects derived from single_link. As you will learn in Chapter 12, "Virtual Functions and Polymorphism," these functions are declared as *pure virtual*. This is what the =0 assignment following the function's declaration does. As a side effect of this declaration, you can't create instances of the single_link class until you have derived another class from it and defined the functions clone and destroy.

Listing 11.3. SLINK.H. Declaration of the single_link class.

```
//------------------------------------------------------------
//  File: slink.h
//  Declares a "single link" class

#if !defined (__SLINK_H)
#define __SLINK_H

class single_link
{
public:
    single_link(): _next(0) {}
    single_link(single_link* next) : _next(next) {}
    single_link(single_link& sl) : _next(sl._next) {}

    single_link* next() { return _next; }
```

```
        void set_next(single_link *next) { _next = next;}

        virtual single_link* clone() = 0;
        virtual void destroy() = 0;

protected:
    single_link* _next;
};

#endif
```

The *singly_linked_list* Class

Now that you have defined the links, proceed to the list itself. Listing 11.4 shows the SLLIST.H
header file, which declares the `singly_linked_list` class. Listing 11.5 has the actual implementation of some of the member functions. As expected, the `singly_linked_list` class provides
member functions to traverse the list and to insert and remove elements from the list.

Listing 11.4. SLLIST.H. Declaration of the `singly_linked_list` class.

```
//--------------------------------------------------------------
//  File: sllist.h
//  Declares a "singly linked list" class

#if !defined (__SLLIST_H)
#define __SLLIST_H

#include "slink.h"

class singly_linked_list
{
public:
// Constructors
    singly_linked_list() : _first(0), _current(0), _count(0){}

    singly_linked_list(single_link& sl)
    {
     _first = sl.clone();
     _count = 1;
     _current = _first;
    }

// Destructor
    ~singly_linked_list();

//  Member-access functions...
    single_link* current() { return _current;}

    single_link* first()
    {
        _current = _first;
        return _current;
    }
}
```

continues

Listing 11.4. continued

```
    single_link* next()
    {
        single_link* t = _current->next();
        if(t != 0) _current = t;
        return t;
    }

    unsigned count(){ return _count;}
// List insertion and deletion
    void insert(single_link& sl);
    void remove();

protected:
    single_link *_first;
    single_link *_current;
    unsigned    _count;
};

#endif
```

The `insert` function in Listing 11.5 shows how the virtual function `clone` is used. Suppose you are inserting a `slink_string` object into the list. Remember that the `slink_string` class is derived from `String` and `single_link`. The `insert` function requires a reference to a `single_link` object as an argument. With C++, you can call `insert` with a reference to an instance of any class derived from `single_link`. When you call `insert` with a `slink_string` reference, `insert` calls the `clone` function through the reference to the `slink_string` object. Because `clone` is a virtual function, this invokes the `clone` function of the `slink_string` class, which, as you will see shortly, returns a pointer to a copy of that instance of `slink_string`. Consequently, you can obtain a proper copy of an object by using this mechanism. Chapter 12 provides further details on virtual functions.

Listing 11.5. SLLIST.CPP. Member functions of the `singly_linked_list` class.

```
//------------------------------------------------------------
//  File: sllist.cpp
//  Implements a singly linked list

#include "sllist.h"

//------------------------------------------------------------
//  ~ s i n g l y _ l i n k e d _ l i s t
//  Destructor for the list

singly_linked_list::~singly_linked_list()
{
    int         i;
    single_link *p_sl = _first, *t;
    if(_count > 0)
    {
        for(i = 0; i < _count; i++)
```

```
        {
            t = p_sl->next();
            p_sl->destroy();
            p_sl = t;
        }
    }
}
//----------------------------------------------------------------
//   i n s e r t
//   Insert a new item into the list

void singly_linked_list::insert(single_link& sl)
{
// Clone the element passed to the function and
// hook it up in the linked list
    single_link *t = sl.clone();
    if(_current != 0)
    {
        t->set_next(_current->next());
        _current->set_next(t);
    }
    else
    {
        _first = t;
    }

// Make this one the current item in the list
    _current = t;

// Increment of count of elements on the list
    _count++;
}
//----------------------------------------------------------------
//   r e m o v e
//   Removes the current element from the list

void singly_linked_list::remove()
{
// Locate element that points to current
    single_link *p_sl;
    int          i;

    if(_current == 0) return;

    for(i = 0, p_sl = _first;
        p_sl->next() != _current && i < _count;
        i++, p_sl = p_sl->next()) ;

    if(i != _count)
    {
        p_sl->set_next(_current->next());
        _current->destroy();
        _current = p_sl;
        _count--;
    }
}
```

The remove function uses the virtual function destroy in a similar manner to delete an item properly from the linked list.

A Linkable *String* Class

You saw the String class in Listings 11.1 and 11.2. If you want to store String objects in a singly_linked_list, you must create a new type of String that might be called a *linkable* String. To do this, use multiple inheritance to derive from String and from single_link. Listings 11.6 and 11.7 show this new class, which is called slink_string because these are String objects to which a single_link is added.

Notice how the clone and destroy functions are defined in Listing 11.6. The clone function creates a "clone" of the current slink_string and returns a pointer to the new copy. The destroy function calls the delete operator for the current slink_string. These functions ensure that objects stored in the singly linked list are properly initialized and destroyed.

Listing 11.6. SLSTR.H. Declaration of the slink_string class.

```
//-------------------------------------------------------------
//   File: slstr.h
//   Singly linkable string class

#if !defined(__SLSTR_H)
#define __SLSTR_H

#include "str.h"       // String class
#include "slink.h"     // single_link class

class slink_string: public single_link, public String
{
public:
    slink_string(const char *s): String(s), single_link(0){}

    slink_string(const slink_string& s) :
        String(s.p_c), single_link(s._next) {}

    slink_string(const String& s):
        String(s), single_link() {}

    slink_string& operator=(const slink_string& s);

    void destroy() { delete this;}

    single_link* clone()
    {
        slink_string* t = new slink_string(*this);
        return t;
    }

};

#endif
```

Listing 11.7. SLSTR.CPP. Implementation of the assignment operator for the `slink_string` class.

```
//------------------------------------------------------------
// File:  slstr.cpp

#include "slstr.h"

//------------------------------------------------------------
// o p e r a t o r =
// Assign one "slink_string" to another

slink_string& slink_string::operator=(const slink_string& s)
{
    if(this != &s)
    {
        _next = s._next;
        _length = s._length;
        _maxlen = s._maxlen;
        delete p_c;
        p_c = new char[_maxlen];
        strcpy(p_c, s.p_c);
    }
    return *this;
}
```

A *String* List Iterator Class

Now you possess all the equipment necessary to create a linked list of `string` objects, but one problem still exists. Specifically, the `singly_linked_list` class maintains a list of `single_link` objects. It knows nothing about `slink_string` objects. How do you traverse the list and process the `slink_string` objects in the list? You could use the `first`, `current`, and `next` member functions of the `singly_linked_list` class to traverse the list, but these return pointers to `single_link` objects. To treat them as pointers to `slink_string` objects, you must use an explicit cast. Rather than getting into details like this, it's best to create a helper class, commonly known as an *iterator* class, that provides access to the linked list of `string` objects. The class is called an iterator because it enables you to iterate or "loop over" the list.

Listing 11.8 shows the SLSITER.H header file, which implements the `sllist_iterator` class that acts as an iterator for the linked list of `string`s. The `sllist_iterator` class is quite simple. It holds a reference to the list over which it iterates, and it provides the same interface to the list as `singly_linked_list` does, but its member functions always return pointers to `slink_string` objects rather than pointers to `single_link` objects.

Listing 11.8. SLSITER.H. An iterator for a single-linked list of `string` objects.

```
//------------------------------------------------------------
// File: slsiter.h
// Iterator for single-linked list of strings
```

continues

Listing 11.8. continued

```
#if !defined(__SLSITER_H)
#define __SLSITER_H

#include "slstr.h"
#include "sllist.h"

class sllist_iterator
{
public:
    sllist_iterator(singly_linked_list& sl): sllist(sl){}

    slink_string* current()
    {
        return (slink_string*) sllist.current();
    }

    slink_string* next()
    {
        return (slink_string*) sllist.next();
    }

    slink_string* first()
    {
        return (slink_string*)sllist.first();
    }

private:
    singly_linked_list& sllist;
};

#endif
```

Trying Out a Single-Linked List of *Strings*

With all the equipment in place for working with single-linked lists of slink_string objects, you need only to try one out. Listing 11.9 shows a sample program that does this. It creates a linked list of slink_string objects and an iterator for the list. Then it inserts several slink_string objects into the list and displays what the list contains. Notice that you can display slink_string objects using the << operator because this operator is defined for the String class and the slink_string is derived from String. Finally, the program removes an item from the list and again displays the contents of the list.

Listing 11.9. A program to test a single-linked list of Strings.

```
//-------------------------------------------------------------
// File:  tstsls.cpp
// Test linked list of strings

#include "slsiter.h"
//-------------------------------------------------------------
```

```
//  m a i n
//  Program that exercises a singly linked list of Strings
void main()
{
// Create a String with a single link
    slink_string s1("One");

// Create a singly linked list with s1 as first element
    singly_linked_list strlist(s1);

// Create an iterator for this linked list
    sllist_iterator si(strlist);

// Insert another copy of s1 into the list
    strlist.insert(s1);

// Change the string value of s1 and insert it again
    s1 = "Two";
    strlist.insert(s1);
    strlist.insert(s1);
    s1 = "Three";
    strlist.insert(s1);

// Display what the list contains
    cout << "-----------------------------------" << endl;
    cout << "List contains:" << endl;
    slink_string* x;
    for(x = si.first(); x != 0; x = si.next())
        cout << *x << endl;

// Remove the current element from the list
// At this point, current element is the last element
    strlist.remove();

// Display the final contents of the linked list
    cout << "-----------------------------------" << endl;
    cout << "Now list contains:" << endl;
    for(x = si.first(); x != 0; x = si.next())
        cout << *x << endl;
}
```

To build this program, you need to compile and link the files from Listings 11.2, 11.5, 11.7, and 11.9. When run, the program displays the following output:

```
-----------------------------------
List contains:
One
One
Two
Two
Three
-----------------------------------
Now list contains:
One
One
Two
Two
```

A Double-Linked List

Now that you've created a single-linked list, you can extend this design to create a double-linked list. This data type is important because you can use it as the basis of other higher-level data structures such as queues and stacks. As Figure 11.6 illustrates, a double-linked list is like a single-linked list except that each link can point to the previous and the next link on the list. The list also contains a pointer to the last element because you can go backward and forward on the list.

FIGURE 11.6.
A double-linked list.

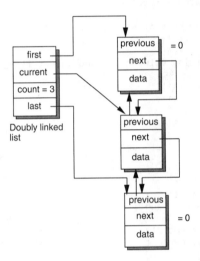

A *double_link* Class

You can create a class with two links by deriving from a class with a single link. Listing 11.10 shows the dlink.h header file, which declares the `double_link` class, derived from the `single_link` class. This serves as the base for a doubly linked list.

The `clone` and `destroy` virtual functions are still declared as purely virtual. This means that the `double_link` is still an abstract class, with its only purpose being to provide two links to some other data class so that the instances of the newly derived class can reside in a doubly linked list.

Listing 11.10. DLINK.H. Declaration of the `double_link` class.

```
//-----------------------------------------------------------
//  File: dlink.h
//  Declares a "double link" class

#if !defined (__DLINK_H)
#define __DLINK_H

#include "slink.h"
```

```
class double_link: public single_link
{
public:
    double_link(): single_link(0),_previous(0) {}
    double_link(double_link& dl) : single_link(dl._next),
        _previous(dl._previous) {}
    double_link(single_link* prev, single_link* next) :
        single_link(next), _previous(prev) {}

    single_link* previous() { return _previous; }

    void set_previous(single_link *previous)
    {
        _previous = previous;
    }

    virtual single_link* clone() = 0;
    virtual void destroy() = 0;

protected:
    single_link* _previous;
};

#endif
```

The *doubly_linked_list* Class

You also can exploit the existing `singly_linked_list` class (see Listings 11.4 and 11.5) when defining the `doubly_linked_list` class. As Listings 11.11 and 11.12 illustrate, you can derive the `doubly_linked_list` from the `singly_linked_list`.

The `doubly_linked_list` class provides the `insert_last` and `remove_first` functions for inserting and removing elements from the list. The insertion occurs at the front of the list, and the `remove_last` function always returns the last item in the list. These two functions are included so that you can use the `doubly_linked_list` as a queue. To use it as a stack, you must provide two more insert and remove functions, `insert_first` and `remove_last`, because a stack inserts at the top and removes from the bottom.

Listing 11.11. DLLIST.H. Declaration of the `doubly_linked_list` class.

```
//-----------------------------------------------------------
//  File: dllist.h
//  Declares a "doubly linked list" class

#if !defined (__DLLIST_H)
#define __DLLIST_H

#include "dlink.h"
#include "sllist.h"

class doubly_linked_list: public singly_linked_list
```

continues

Listing 11.11. continued

```
{
public:
// Constructor
    doubly_linked_list(double_link& dl) : singly_linked_list(dl)
    {
        _last = (double_link*)_current;
    }

    single_link* previous()
    {
        double_link* cur = (double_link*)_current;
        single_link* t = cur->previous();
        if(t != 0) _current = t;
        return t;
    }

    double_link* last() { return _last; }
// New list insertion and deletion functions
    void insert_last(double_link& sl);
    double_link* remove_first();

protected:
    double_link *_last;
};

#endif
```

If you examine the `remove_last` function in Listing 11.12, you'll notice that the function "unhooks" the last element from the list and returns a pointer to that element to the calling program. Because every item in the list is created on the free store, you need to somehow destroy the item when it is no longer needed. The idea is to have a queue class that provides the final interface to the programmer. The queue class calls `remove_last` to get an item, copies that item into a programmer-supplied variable, and then discards the item by calling its `destroy` function. (The get function of the `string_queue` class, defined in Listing 11.15 later in this chapter, illustrates how this is done.)

Listing 11.12. DLLIST.CPP. Implementation of the `doubly_linked_list` class.

```
//--------------------------------------------------------------
// File: dllist.cpp
// Implements "insert_last" and "remove_first" functions for a
// doubly linked list

#include "dllist.h"

//--------------------------------------------------------------
// i n s e r t _ l a s t
// Insert a new item at the end of the list
```

```
void doubly_linked_list::insert_last(double_link& dl)
{
// Clone the element passed to the function and
// hook it up in the linked list
    double_link *t = (double_link*)dl.clone();

    if(_last != 0)
    {
        _last->set_next(t);
        t->set_previous(_last);
        t->set_next(0);
    }
    else
    {
        _first = t;
        _current = t;
    }

// Make this one the last element in the list
    _last = t;
// Increment of count of elements on the list
    _count++;
}
//----------------------------------------------------------------
//    r e m o v e _ f i r s t
//    Removes the element from the beginning of the list

double_link* doubly_linked_list::remove_first()
{
    if(_count == 0) return 0;

    double_link* cp = (double_link*)_first;
    if(_current == _first) _current = _first->next();
    _first = _first->next();

    double_link* t = (double_link*)_first;
    if(t != 0) t->set_previous(0);

    if(_last == cp) _last = 0;
    _count--;

    return cp;
}
```

A Double-Linkable *String*

To show a real use of the doubly_linked_list class, you need a data item that can be stored in the list. As with the slink_string class of Listings 11.6 and 11.7, you can create a dlink_string class that is derived from String and double_link. Instances of this class include a String object with two links, _previous and _next, that come from the double_link class. Listings 11.13 and 11.14 show the DLSTR.H and DLSTR.CPP files, which implement the dlink_string class.

Listing 11.13. DLSTR.H. Declaration of the `dlink_string` class.

```
//------------------------------------------------------------
//  File: dlstr.h
//  Doubly linkable string class

#if !defined(__DLSTR_H)
#define __DLSTR_H

#include "str.h"        // String class
#include "dlink.h"      // double_link class

class dlink_string: public double_link, public String
{
public:
    dlink_string() : String(), double_link(0,0) {}
    dlink_string(const char *s): String(s), double_link(0,0){}

    dlink_string(const dlink_string& s) :
        String(s.p_c), double_link(s._previous, s._next) {}

    dlink_string(const String& s):
        String(s), double_link() {}

    dlink_string& operator=(const dlink_string& s);

    void destroy() { delete this;}

    single_link* clone()
    {
        dlink_string* t = new dlink_string(*this);
        return t;
    }
};

#endif
```

Listing 11.14. DLSTR.CPP. Implementation of the assignment operator for the `dlink_string` class.

```
//------------------------------------------------------------
//  File:  dlstr.cpp

#include "dlstr.h"

//------------------------------------------------------------
//  o p e r a t o r =
//  Assign one "dlink_string" to another

dlink_string& dlink_string::operator=(const dlink_string& s)
{
    if(this != &s)
    {
        _next = s._next;
        _previous = s._previous;
        _length = s._length;
        _maxlen = s._maxlen;
```

```
            delete p_c;
            p_c = new char[_maxlen];
            strcpy(p_c, s.p_c);
        }
        return *this;
}
```

A Queue of *String* Objects

In place of the iterator class used for the single-linked list, let's create a class that maintains a queue of `dlink_string` objects. This class, named `string_queue`, is defined in the SQUEUE.H file, which appears in Listing 11.15. With the `string_queue`, you can create a queue—actually a `double_linked_list`, for which `string_queue` provides a queuelike interface. The `get` and `put` functions, respectively, enable you to store `dlink_string` objects into the queue and retrieve them.

Think of `string_queue` as a class that knows how to use a `doubly_linked_list` class and that provides a first-in, first-out (FIFO) interface appropriate for a queue. It inserts objects at the end of the list and returns items from the beginning. You can similarly construct a stack class that provides a last-in, first-out (LIFO) interface to the `doubly_linked_list` class. In this case, the queue grows dynamically, but you easily can limit the size of the queue with some added code.

Listing 11.15. SQUEUE.H. Definition of the `string_queue` class.

```
//-------------------------------------------------------------
//  File: squeue.h
//  Interface for a queue of doubly linkable String objects

#if !defined(__SQUEUE_H)
#define __SQUEUE_H

#include "dlstr.h"
#include "dllist.h"

class string_queue
{
public:
    string_queue(dlink_string& ds)
    {
        my_queue = new doubly_linked_list(ds);
        created_here = 1;
    }

    string_queue(doubly_linked_list& q) :
        my_queue(&q), created_here(0) {}

    ~string_queue() { if(created_here) delete my_queue;}

    int get(dlink_string& dl)
```

continues

Listing 11.15. continued

```
    {
      dlink_string *p;
        p = (dlink_string*)my_queue->remove_first();

        if(p)
        {
// Copy the item and then destroy it
            dl = *p;
            p->destroy();
            return 1;
        }
        else
            return 0;
    }

    void put(dlink_string& dl)
    {
        my_queue->insert_last(dl);
    }

private:
    doubly_linked_list* my_queue;
    int                 created_here;
};


#endif
```

Testing the Queue

Listing 11.16 shows a small program that tests the queue of `dlink_string` objects defined by the `string_queue` class. The program first creates a queue and inserts three `dlink_string` objects into it. It then retrieves the items one by one and displays them. Because the `dlink_string` objects are also of the `String` type, you can use the `<<` operator with the `dlink_string` objects.

The program generates the following output:

```
Queue contains:
One
Two
Three
```

Listing 11.16. Sample program to exercise the `string_queue` class.

```
//-------------------------------------------------------------
// File:  tstsq.cpp
// Test queue of strings

#include "squeue.h"
//-------------------------------------------------------------
//  m a i n
//  Program that exercises a queue of Strings
```

```
void main()
{
// Create a String with a double link
    dlink_string ds1("One");

// Create a queue with ds1 as first element
    string_queue strq(ds1);

    ds1 = "Two";
    strq.put(ds1);

    ds1 = "Three";
    strq.put(ds1);

// Get entries from the queue and display them

    cout << "Queue contains:" << endl;
    cout << "--------------" << endl;

    while(strq.get(ds1))
    {
        cout << ds1 << endl;
    }
}
```

Summary

The first major component of OOP—data abstraction—enables you to introduce new data types from which you can create instances of objects. The second component, inheritance, defines new specialized data types in terms of existing ones or for extending the functionality of an existing type. C++'s class construct handles both of these needs: you can encapsulate data and functions with it and you can derive a class from one or more base classes. A derived class inherits all public and protected members of its base classes. Furthermore, you can differentiate the derived class from its base classes by one of the following methods:

■ Adding new member variables
■ Adding new member functions
■ Overriding the definition of functions inherited from the base classes

When the class construct is used to define an abstract data type, inheritance enables you to create specialized subtypes. On the other hand, when a class is merely a module that encapsulates some data and functions, you can use inheritance to extend the capabilities offered by the module. When defining functions in a derived class, be aware that any overloaded function hides all inherited versions of the same name.

C++ supports single and multiple inheritance. In single inheritance, each derived class has exactly one base class; multiple inheritance enables you to derive a class from more than one base class. You can use multiple inheritance to simulate generic classes, such as linked lists and queues.

This works by making the data structures capable of storing a link, for example, and then creating a linkable data type by inheriting from the link class as well as from your data type.

Another interesting feature of inheritance is that a pointer to an instance of the base class can hold the address of any of its derived class instances. The next chapter explains how this feature enables you to exploit polymorphism in C++ programs.

12

Virtual Functions and Polymorphism

This chapter focuses on polymorphism, the third basic component of object-oriented programming. Chapter 10, "Defining Operations on Objects," and Chapter 11, "Using Inheritance in C++," cover the other components of OOP—data abstraction and inheritance, respectively. Polymorphic functions work with many different argument types. C++ supports this kind of polymorphism through function overloading. The other type of polymorphism simplifies the syntax of performing the same operation with a hierarchy of classes. This is what enables you to use the same function name (draw, for example) to draw all types of shape objects, whether they are circle_shapes, rectangle_shapes, or triangle_shapes. You can therefore use polymorphism to maintain a clean interface to the classes because you don't need to define unique function names for similar operations on each derived class. This type of polymorphism goes hand in hand with inheritance and late or dynamic binding. This chapter explains the terminology and describes how the virtual keyword supports polymorphism.

Binding

Before you proceed, let's review the concept of binding that is explored in Chapter 6, "C++ and Object-Oriented Programming." Recall that binding refers to the connection between a function call and the actual code executed as a result of the call. The following sections explain how binding is determined and how it affects the style of code you write.

Static Binding

As with any new concept, the best way to explain binding is through an example. Suppose you want to process a one-character command and you have defined a number of functions that perform the tasks requested by various commands. Using a switch statement, you might handle the commands as follows:

```
#include <ctype.h>
#include <iostream.h>
//...
static void quit(), newparams() showparams();
char ch;
//...
// Respond to user command
// Assume 'ch' holds the command character

    int code = toupper(ch);
    switch (code)
    {
        case 'Q': quit();
        case 'P': newparams();
                  break;
        case '?': showparams();
                  break;
        default:  cout << "Unknown command:" << ch << endl;
    }
```

Of course, in this case the function invoked in response to each command is known when the program is compiling because each function is explicitly called by name. Recall that this is known as static binding because the compiler can figure out the function to be called before the program ever runs.

Dynamic Binding

Now consider an alternate implementation of this command-processing code. Start with a table of commands that can be implemented as an array of structures, each of which holds a command character and a pointer to the function to be called when the user types that character. The processing loop merely compares the input command character with the entries in the table and, if a matching entry is found, calls the function with the pointer that appears in that slot of the table. Here is a sample implementation of this schema:

```c
#include <ctype.h>
#include <iostream.h>

// Command-processing functions...
static void quit(), newparams(), showparams();

struct command
{
    char cmdchar;      // Each command is a character
    void (*action)(); // Function called to process command
};

command cmdtable[] =  // This is the table of commands
{
    'Q',   quit,
    'q',   quit,
    'P',   newparams,
    'p',   newparams,
    '?',   showparams
};

// Number commands in the command table
int cmdcount = sizeof(cmdtable) / sizeof(command);

char ch;
int  i;

//...
// Sample command-processing loop:
// Assume character 'ch' holds input character
// Search the command table for matching command

    for(i = 0; i < cmdcount; i++)
    {
        if(cmdtable[i].cmdchar == ch)
        {
// Found command...call the corresponding function
            (*cmdtable[i].action)();
            break;
        }
    }
```

```
    if(i == cmdcount)
        cout << "Unknown command: " << ch << endl;
```

Notice that this version of the command-processing loop differs from the previous one in two respects:

- ■ The `switch` statement is no longer needed.
- ■ A function call via a pointer is used to invoke the function that performs the task requested by each command. The content of the pointer determines the actual function called.

This is known as dynamic binding because the actual function called at runtime depends on the contents of the function pointer. This is also known as late binding because the connection between the function call and the actual code executed by the call is determined late—that is, during runtime rather than compile time.

Virtual Functions

Most of the examples you have seen thus far include classes with one or more `virtual` member functions. Consider, for example, the geometric `shape` classes introduced in Chapter 6. As you may recall, the `shape` class is the base class from which you derive several other classes, such as `rectangle_shape`, `circle_shape`, and `triangle_shape`. For the sample implementation, each shape was able to compute its area and draw itself. In this case, the `shape` class declares the following virtual functions:

```
class shape
{
public:
    virtual double compute_area(void) const;
    virtual void draw(void) const;

// Other member functions that define an interface to all
// types of geometric shapes
};
```

Here, the `virtual` keyword preceding a function signals the C++ compiler that the compiler may need to call the function indirectly through a pointer, if the function is defined in a derived class. Qualify a member function of a class with the `virtual` keyword only when there is a possibility that other classes may be derived from this one.

The `shape` class is an example of an *abstract base class*—a class that embodies a standard interface to a group of classes, but does not provide a concrete implementation for any of the member functions. A common use of virtual functions is in defining such an abstract base class.

Pure Virtual Functions

One problem in defining a base class with virtual functions is that you may not be able to provide appropriate implementation for all the functions. For example, you can't define a draw or a compute_area function for a generic shape. Programmers often solve this problem by providing a dummy function that prints an error message. For the compute_area function of the shape class, you might write the following:

```
virtual void draw()
{
    cerr << "Derived class must implement!" << endl;
}
```

In this case, if you forget to implement draw in a derived class such as circle_shape and the program calls draw for a circle_chape, it prints an error message. This is not so bad, but the situation is worse if you decide to call exit after printing the error message. A better way to handle this is to let the C++ compiler detect an unimplemented instance of a virtual class. That way, the error is detected before it's too late.

Recall from Chapter 11 that pure virtual functions are virtual functions that the base class cannot implement. You can indicate a pure virtual function by adding the =0 initializer following the declaration of the function. You gain two error-checking capabilities from pure virtual functions:

■ The C++ compiler does not enable creation of instances of a class containing pure virtual functions. Thus, if you write the following:

```
shape s1;
```

the compiler flags this as an error. This is good because you don't want anyone to create instances of an abstract base class anyway.

■ The compiler checks to be sure the pure virtual functions of a base class are implemented by one of its derived classes. If an immediate derived class cannot provide an implementation, it can merely pass the problem on to one of its derived classes by also declaring the function as pure virtual.

C++ includes the notion of pure virtual functions that you can use to indicate that certain member functions of an abstract base class are not implemented. For example, in the shape class, you can make draw and compute area pure virtual functions:

```
class shape
{
public:
// Make these "pure virtual functions"
    virtual double compute_area(void) const = 0;
    virtual void draw(void) const = 0;

// Other member functions
};
```

Concrete Implementation of *virtual* Functions

An abstract base class uses the virtual keyword to qualify the member functions that constitute the interface to all the classes derived from that class. Each specific derived class must define its own concrete versions of the functions that have been declared virtual in the base class.
Therefore, if you derive the circle_shape and rectangle_shape classes from the shape class,
you must define the compute_area and draw member functions in each class. For instance, the
definitions for the circle_shape class might appear like this:

```
class circle_shape: public shape
{
public:
    virtual double compute_area(void) const;
    virtual void draw(void) const;
// ...
private:
    double xc, yc;   // Coordinates of center
    double radius;   // radius of circle
};

#define M_PI 3.14159 // value of "pi"

// Implementation of "compute_area" function
circle_shape::compute_area(void) const
{
    return (M_PI * radius * radius);
}

// Implementation of "draw" function
circle_shape::draw(void) const
{
//...
}
```

When declaring the draw and compute_area functions in the derived class, you optionally can
add the virtual keyword to emphasize that these are indeed virtual functions. The function
definitions do not need the virtual keyword.

Dynamic Binding Through *virtual* Functions

You don't need to do anything special to use virtual functions. Treat them like any other member
function of a class. As an example, consider the following calls to the virtual functions draw and
compute_area:

```
circle_shape    c1;
rectangle_shape r1;
double area = c1.compute_area(); // Compute area of circle
r1.draw();                       // Draw a rectangle
```

When used in this manner, these functions are like any other member functions. In this case,
the C++ compiler can determine that you want to call the compute_area function of the
circle_shape class and the draw function of the rectangle_shape class. In fact, the compiler

makes direct calls to these functions, and the function calls are bound to specific code at link time. This is static binding.

An interesting case occurs when you make the function calls through a pointer to a shape:

```
shape*   s[10];  // Pointers to 10 shape objects
int      i, numshapes=10;
//... create shapes and store pointers in array "s"
// Draw the shapes
    for(i = 0; i < numshapes; i++) shape[i]->draw();
```

Because the individual entries in the array of `shape` pointers can point to any type of shape derived from the `shape` class, the C++ compiler cannot determine which specific implementation of the `draw` function to call. This is where dynamic binding and the `virtual` keyword comes in.

POINTER TO A DERIVED CLASS IS A POINTER TO THE BASE

In C++, you can use a reference or a pointer to any derived class in place of a reference or a pointer to the base class without an explicit type cast. So, if both `circle_shape` and `rectangle_shape` are derived from the `shape` class, you can call a function that requires a pointer to `shape` with a pointer to a `circle_shape` or a `rectangle_shape` as well. The opposite is not true; you cannot use a reference or a pointer to the base class in place of a reference or a pointer to an instance of a derived class.

Virtual Function Call Mechanism

As explained previously, an indirect function call (a function call through a pointer) provides dynamic binding. C++ compilers use this idea when calling virtual functions. The `virtual` keyword is a signal to the compiler that the member function qualified by the keyword may need to be called through a pointer.

A typical C++ compiler constructs an array of virtual function pointers for each class. This array goes by the name of *virtual table* or *vtable*. Each instance of the class has a pointer to its class-wide virtual table. Figure 12.1 illustrates the situation for the `circle_shape` class. Given this arrangement, the C++ compiler can achieve dynamic binding by transforming a call to a virtual function into an indirect call through a pointer in the class virtual table. For example, if the virtual table is laid out as shown in Figure 12.1, the compiler can implement this call:

```
circle_shape *c1 = new circle_shape(100.,100.,50.);
c1->draw();
```

by generating code for the following:

```
(*(c1->vtable[1]))(c1);  // c1 is "this"
```

where the second entry in the virtual table holds the pointer to the draw function of the circle_shape class. The pointer to the object is passed as the first argument of the function just as it is done implicitly for every member function of a class. This is the this pointer that a member function can use to refer to the current instance of the class.

FIGURE 12.1.

Virtual function implementation under single inheritance.

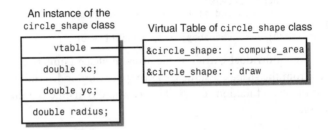

> **TIP**
>
> As a C++ programmer, you don't need to know how the compiler takes care of calling the correct virtual function, but you may find the knowledge helpful in understanding why a C++ program behaves the way it does. C++ compilers are not required to implement the virtual function call mechanism exactly as illustrated in Figure 12.1. However, most C++ compilers do follow the same techniques, partly because these ideas are outlined in *The Annotated C++ Reference Manual*, by Margaret Ellis and Bjarne Stroustrup (published by Addison-Wesley in 1990), which is the basis of the ongoing standardization of C++ by the ANSI X3J16 committee. If you are curious, you may want to consult this book for further information on how various features of C++ can be implemented. For example, with multiple inheritance, implementing a virtual function call is somewhat more complicated. For more information on this, see Ellis and Stroustrup.

Suppressing Virtual Function Calls

The virtual call mechanism is quite useful for implementing polymorphism, but occasions may arise when you want to call the function from the base class rather than the one from the derived class. For example, suppose you have a base class called BaseWindow with a virtual function called event_handler, which presumably processes events in a user interface. You are happy with the function, but you want a derived class called SpecialWindow with an event_handler that augments the processing done in the event handling function of its base class. In the event_handler of the SpecialWindow class, you want to catch a special type of event and process it there. For all other types of events, you want to call the event_handler of the BaseWindow class:

```
class BaseWindow
{
public:
    virtual void event_handler(int event_id);
// Other members...
};

class SpecialWindow: public BaseWindow
{
public:
    void event_handler(int event_id)
    {
        if(event_id == SPECIAL_EVENT)
        {
// process special event...
        }
        else
        {
// Call BaseWindow's event_handler
            BaseWindow::event_handler(event_id);
        }
    }

// Other members...
};
```

You can suppress the virtual call mechanism by explicitly qualifying a function with its class name. In this example, you can call the `event_handler` of the `BasicWindow` class by explicitly qualifying the function name with the `BasicWindow::` prefix.

Using Polymorphism

As you have seen from the examples in this chapter and Chapter 6, polymorphism eliminates the `switch` statement and generally simplifies the interface to a hierarchy of classes. The geometric shapes of Chapter 5, "Basics of Object-Oriented Programming," and Chapter 6 provide a good example of the use of polymorphism. Suppose you have a collection of `shape` objects in a storage structure, such as an array or a linked list. The array stores pointers to `shape` objects. These pointers could point to any type of shape, provided they are derived from the `shape` class. When operating on these shapes, you can loop through the array and invoke the appropriate member function via the pointer to the instance. Of course, for this to work, the member functions must be declared as `virtual` in the `shape` class, which happens to be the base class for all geometric shapes.

As you might gather from the examples, you must do the following to use polymorphism in C++:

1. Create a class hierarchy with the important operations defined by member functions declared as `virtual` in the base class. If the base class is such that you cannot provide implementations for these functions, you can declare them to be purely virtual. The `draw` function of the `shape` class is an example:

```
virtual void draw() const = 0;
```

2. Provide concrete implementations of the virtual classes in the derived classes. Each derived class can have its own version of the functions. For example, the implementation of the draw function varies from one shape to another.

3. Manipulate instances of these classes through a reference or a pointer. This is what causes the C++ compiler to use dynamic binding and call the functions using the virtual function mechanism described earlier.

The last item—invoking member functions through a pointer—is the essence of polymorphic use in C++. This is because you get dynamic binding only when virtual member functions are invoked through a pointer to a class instance and when you need dynamic binding for polymorphism.

Implications of Polymorphic Use of Classes

Because polymorphic use of class instances requires that you manipulate objects through pointers or references, you should be aware of certain problems that you may encounter when programming this way. The following sections briefly discuss some pitfalls.

Virtual Destructors

When you manipulate objects through pointers, you often tend to create them dynamically through the new operator and later destroy them with the delete operator. A typical situation might be as shown in the following example:

```
//  Illustrates why "virtual destructor" is needed

#include <iostream.h>

class Base
{
public:
    Base() { cout << "Base: constructor" << endl; }

//*** The destructor should be "virtual"
    ~Base() { cout << "Base: destructor" << endl; }
};

class Derived: public Base
{
public:
    Derived() { cout << "Derived: constructor" << endl; }
    ~Derived() { cout << "Derived: destructor" << endl; }
};

void main()
{
    Base* p_base = new Derived;
```

```
// Use the object...

// Now delete the object
    delete p_base;
}
```

This is a case in which the main function creates a copy of a derived class using the new operator and later destroys that instance using delete. When you compile and run this program, it displays the following:

```
Base: constructor
Derived: constructor
Base: destructor
```

The first two lines indicate the order in which the class constructors are called: the constructor for the base class followed by that for the derived class. This keeps with the order of initialization explained in Chapter 11. The third line of output, however, seems odd. Why isn't there a call to the destructor of the derived class?

The reason is that when you call the constructor, you use the derived class name with the new operator and, therefore, the C++ compiler correctly created the right type of object. You save the pointer in a p_base variable, which is declared as a pointer to the base class. Subsequently, when you write the following:

```
delete p_base;
```

the compiler can't tell that you are destroying a derived class instance.

Because delete does its job by calling the destructor for the class, you can solve the problem by declaring the destructor of the base class virtual. Then the destructor is invoked through the virtual function table and the correct destructor is called. Indeed, if you use the following for the base class destructor:

```
virtual ~Base() { cout << "Base: destructor" << endl; }
```

and rerun the program, you get the correct output:

```
Base: constructor
Derived: constructor
Derived: destructor
Base: destructor
```

Notice that the order of calls to the destructors is the opposite order in which the constructors were called. Therefore, the virtual destructor ensures that the object is properly destroyed.

How do you decide whether to declare a destructor virtual? If a class has any virtual function, chances are that instances of classes derived from this one will be manipulated through pointers to attain polymorphic behavior. In this case, you should declare a virtual destructor for the class.

Calling Virtual Functions in a Base Class Constructor

Another pitfall of using virtual functions is that at certain times they do not work as expected. One place where calling a virtual function may produce undesired results is in the constructor of a base class. You can see the problem from the following example program:

```cpp
//  Illustrates what happens when a virtual function
//  is called from the constructor of a base class

#include <iostream.h>

class Base
{
public:
    Base()
    {
        cout << "Base: constructor. Calling clone()" << endl;
        clone();
    }
    virtual void clone()
    {
        cout << "Base::clone() called" << endl;
    }
};

class Derived: public Base
{
public:
    Derived()
    {
        cout << "Derived: constructor" << endl;
    }

    void clone()
    {
        cout << "Derived::clone() called" << endl;
    }
};

void main()
{
    Derived x;
    Base *p = &x;

// Call "clone" through pointer to class instance
    cout << "Calling 'clone' through instance pointer";
    cout << endl;
    p->clone();
}
```

When you run this program, you get the following output:

```
Base: constructor. Calling clone()
Base::clone() called
Derived: constructor
Calling 'clone' through instance pointer
Derived::clone() called
```

You can go over the output to see what happened. When you create an instance of the derived class, as expected, the C++ compiler first calls the constructor of the base class. At this point, the derived class instance is only partially initialized. Therefore, when the compiler encounters the call to the `clone` virtual function, it cannot bind it to the version of `clone` for the derived class. Instead, the compiler calls the version of `clone` from the base class.

The last two lines of output show that once the object is created, you can correctly invoke the `clone` function for the derived class instance through a base class pointer, as is common in polymorphic use of virtual functions.

If you call a virtual function in a class constructor, the compiler invokes the base class's version of the function, not the version defined for the derived class.

Summary

The three features of object-oriented programming—data abstraction, inheritance, and polymorphism—go hand in hand. For realistic object-oriented programs, you need to use all these concepts in tandem. The data and functions are encapsulated into an object by a `class` or a `struct`. Inheritance enables you to implement the "is a" relationship among objects—as in "a circle is a shape." Finally, polymorphism enables you to use the same functional interface, such as member functions named `draw` and `compute_area`, to work with all kinds of shapes.

Several features of C++ work in concert to support polymorphism:

- You can use a pointer to a derived class anywhere a pointer to the base class is expected. The same rule applies to references.

- If a base class declares a member function with the `virtual` keyword, the compiler places the function in the class-wide virtual function table. Then it uses the base class's implementation of the function as a default that is used only if a derived class does not define the function.

- If a derived class redefines a `virtual` function and you call that function through a pointer to the class instance, the compiler invokes the function through the pointer stored in the virtual table. This invokes the version of the function from the derived class (dynamic binding).

Dynamic binding makes polymorphism possible. With polymorphism, you can control a particular behavior of a group of objects by calling the same member function. The `draw` function of `shape` classes provides a good illustration of polymorphic usage.

When you use virtual functions in C++, you need to watch out for some pitfalls. For example, if you call a virtual function from the constructor of a class, the compiler calls the version from itself or one of the bases, but not a version defined by derived classes. For correct destruction of objects, you may need to declare the destructor of the base class as virtual.

13

Advanced Topics in C++

The previous chapters have shown you how C++ supports object-oriented programming. Despite its well-known capabilities, C++ is relatively young (it was released commercially in late 1985). In fact, features such as multiple inheritance and the iostream library were not introduced until AT&T C++ Release 2.0 became available in 1989. The current release of AT&T C++ is 3.0, which includes a relatively new feature: templates (also known as parameterized types). AT&T is expected to include another important new feature in the next release of C++: exception handling.

Another ongoing development that affects the future of C++ is the work being done by the American National Standards Institute (ANSI) C++ Technical Committee, X3J16. The X3J16 committee is preparing a draft standard for the C++ programming language. Recall that the committee started with the following documents as the basis for its proposal:

- The ANSI C standard (*ANSI X3.159-1989—Programming Language C*)
- The *AT&T C++ Language System Release 2.1 Reference Manual* (also available as *The Annotated C++ Reference Manual* by Margaret A. Ellis and Bjarne Stroustrup, published by Addison-Wesley Publishing Company, 1990)

The X3J16 committee has already decided to include templates and exceptions in the C++ draft standard. The templates are based on the experimental design presented in Chapter 14 of *The Annotated C++ Reference Manual*, or the *ARM*, as it is popularly known. For exception handling, the design is derived from the material in Chapter 15 of the *ARM*.

This chapter gives you an overview of templates and exception handling based on information available in the *ARM* and some recent articles in the *C++ Report* and the *Journal of Object-Oriented Programming* (both published by SIGS Publications, New York). Templates enable you to define generic classes, and exception handling provides a uniform way to cope with errors in C++ programs. Microsoft Visual C++ 2.0 supports both templates and exception handling. The examples in this chapter that illustrate how you might use these features are based on the syntax for templates and exception handling as implemented in Visual C++ 2.0.

> **NOTE**
>
> Microsoft Visual C++ 2.0 supports templates and exception handling as required by the draft ANSI standard for C++.

Templates

A *template* defines a family of classes or functions. For example, with a class template for a Stack class, you can create stacks of various data types, such as int, float, and char*. Similarly, with a function template for a sort function, you can create versions of the sort function that sort, for example, an array of int, float, or char* data. When you create a class or function template, you essentially want to define a class or a function with a *parameter*—a data type, for example, that you can specify when the class or function is being used. This is why templates are often referred to as *parameterized types*.

Stacks for *int* and *float*

As an example of a class declaration with a parameter, consider the following simple declaration of a stack class, named `intStack`, which is capable of holding `int` variables:

```
const int MAXSIZE = 128;

class intStack            // Define a stack for int variables
{
public:
    intStack() { _stackptr = 0;}
    int push(int x) {return _array[_stackptr++] = x;}
    int pop() { return _array[_stackptr];}
    int empty() const { return (_stackptr == 0);}
private:
    int _array[MAXSIZE]; // Internally, an array stores the data
    int _stackptr;
};
```

The `intStack` class uses an array of `int` variables as the internal storage for the stack. You might use the `intStack` class in this way:

```
    intStack i_stack;

// Push an integer value
    i_stack.push(301);

// Pop a number off the stack
    int last_val = i_stack.pop();
```

If you want to define a stack of `floats` (a `floatStack` class) that uses the same internal mechanism as `intStack`, replace every `int` in the `intStack` class declaration with `float`. This tells you that if you were able to define a single `Stack` class that accepted a data type as a parameter, and if the C++ compiler enabled you to create new class definitions by invoking `Stack`'s definition with any data type, you could use a single definition to create stacks for any type of data. In other words, what you need is a way to define parameterized classes. With the C++ templates mechanism, you can define classes and functions with parameters.

Class Templates

In C++, the reserved `template` keyword is used to define class and function templates. The template for a generic `Stack` class looks like this:

```
const int MAXSIZE = 128;

template<class T> class Stack
{
public:
```

```
    Stack() : _stackptr(0) {}
    T push(const T x)
    {
        if(_stackptr < MAXSIZE)
            return _array[_stackptr++] = x;
        else
            return (T)0;
    }

    T pop()
    {
        if(_stackptr >0)
            return _array[-_stackptr];
        else
            return (T)0;
    }

    int empty() const { return (_stackptr == 0);}
private:
    T     _array[MAXSIZE];
    int   _stackptr;
};
```

The `template<class T>` prefix in the class declaration states that you will declare a class template and that you will use T as a class name in the declaration. Thus, Stack is a parameterized class with the T type as its parameter. With this definition of the Stack class template, you can create stacks for different data types:

```
Stack<int>    istack;   // A stack for int variables
Stack<float>  fstack;   // A stack for float variables
```

You can similarly define a generic Array class:

```
template<class T> class Array
{
public:
    Array(int n=16) { _pa = new T(_size = n);}
    ~Array() { delete[] _pa;}
    T& operator[](int i);
//...

private:
    T*    _pa;
    int   _size;
};
```

You then can create instances of different Array types:

```
Array<int>    iArray(128);  // A 128-element int array
Array<float>  fArray(32);   // A 32-element float array
```

Function Templates

Like class templates, function templates define a family of functions parameterized by a data type. For example, you can define a parameterized sort function for sorting any type of array:

```
template<class T> void sort(Array<T> a)
{
```

```
// Body of function (do the sorting)
// ...
}
```

This example essentially declares a set of overloaded sort functions, one for each type of Array. When defining the sort function, you need a comparison operator for the class T. One restriction on using the sort function template is that the class you provide in place of T must define a comparison operator.

You can invoke the sort function as you would any ordinary function. The C++ compiler analyzes the arguments to the function and calls the proper version of the function. For example, given iArray and fArray—the arrays of int and float, respectively—you can apply the sort function to each:

```
sort(iArray);   // Sort the array of int
sort(fArray);   // Sort the array of float
```

Member Function Templates

In the example, when declaring the Array class template, the operator[] member function is undefined. Each member function in a class template is also a function template. When defined inline, no special syntax is necessary for the member functions of a template class—use the template parameters as necessary in the function's body and in its argument list. When the member function of a class template is defined outside the body of the class, you must follow a specific syntax. For instance, you can define the operator[] function of the Array class template like this:

```
template<class T> T& Array<T>::operator[](int i)
{
    if(i < 0 || i >= _size)
    {
// Handle error condition. Assume that there is a function
// named "handle_error" available for this purpose.
        handle_error("Array: index out of range");
    }
    else
        return _pa[i];
}
```

Advantages of Templates

Templates help you define classes that are general in nature (generic classes). Even though generic classes already can be defined using macros, templates make the process simpler and safer.

Another approach to generic classes, explained in Chapter 11, "Using Inheritance in C++," presents a way of creating a generic singly_linked_list class. Start with a singly linked list of a base class called single_link, making sure that any data type that needs to be stored in the list is also derived from the single_link class. The only problem with this approach is that the member functions of the singly_linked_list class return pointers to single_link but not to the type of objects actually stored in the list. Thus, you must cast each pointer returned by the singly_linked_list class to your data type before using it. Such type casts defeat the type-checking facilities of C++ and increase the potential for errors. With class templates, you can eliminate the need for any type casts and define parameterized classes in a safe manner.

Exception Handling

Exceptions refer to unusual conditions in a program. They can be outright errors that cause the program to fail or conditions that can lead to errors. Typically, you can always detect when certain types of errors are about to occur. For instance, when implementing the subscript function (operator[]) of the Array class, you can detect whether the index is beyond the range of valid values. Such errors are called *synchronous exceptions* because they occur at a predictable time; an error caused by the array index going out of bounds occurs only after executing a statement in which that out-of-bounds index is used. Contrast this with *asynchronous exceptions*, which are caused by events beyond the control of your program; therefore, your program cannot anticipate their occurrence. The proposed exception handling mechanism for C++ is intended to cope with synchronous exceptions only.

Benefits of Exception Handling

Although it is easy to detect synchronous exceptions, such as failing to allocate memory or an array index going out of bounds, it is difficult to decide what to do when the exception occurs. Consider the malloc function in the ANSI C library. When you call malloc to allocate a block of memory, you get back a pointer to the allocated block. Recall that if malloc fails, it returns a NULL pointer (a zero address). The caller carries the burden of checking for this exceptional condition. As a C programmer, you are probably quite familiar with blocks of code such as this:

```
#define MAXCHR 80
char *line;


if((line = (char *) malloc(MAXCHR)) == NULL)
{
/* Failed to allocate memory. Print message and exit. */
    fprintf(stderr, "Failed to allocate memory.\n");
    exit(1);
}
```

Whenever you call malloc in your program, you essentially repeat similar blocks of code again and again.

Now consider an alternative. Suppose malloc is written so that whenever it fails, it jumps to a function that you specify, perhaps with an error code—a code that indicates what went wrong—as an argument. (ANSI C's setjmp and longjmp functions provide the capability of jumping from one function to another.) Such a function is typically called a *handler* or an *exception handler.* If you do not provide an exception handler, `malloc` can jump to a default handler that prints a message and exits. If you do provide a handler, you can handle the error condition any way you wish. In certain applications, you may not even need to terminate the application. Best of all, with such an exception handler installed, you can call `malloc` without worrying about an error return because you know that, in case of any allocation failure, `malloc` will jump to the exception handler. Thus, if you know there is an exception handler, you can eliminate all those extra lines of code that check whether `malloc` has returned a `NULL` pointer.

Like `malloc`, C++ class libraries have many functions that detect and handle error conditions. If exception handling is an integral part of C++, all class libraries can cope with all "exceptional conditions" uniformly—thus, the decision of the ANSI standards committee to provide exception handling in C++.

The Trouble with *setjmp* and *longjmp*

In ANSI C, the functions `setjmp` and `longjmp` enable you to jump back from many levels of function calls to a specific location in your program—you can abort what you were doing and return to your starting point. The `setjmp` function saves the state or the context of the process, and `longjmp` uses the saved context to revert to a previous point in the program. The *context* or *state* of a process refers to the information with which you can reconstruct the way the process is at a given point in its flow of execution. In ANSI C, an array data type named `jmp_buf` is available for storing information needed to restore a calling environment. This data type is defined in the setjmp.h header file.

To understand the exact mechanics of `setjmp` and `longjmp`, look at the following lines of code:

```
#include <setjmp.h>
jmp_buf saved_context;

main()
{
    if (setjmp(saved_context) == 0)
    {
// This is executed the first time set_jmp is called.
        process_commands();
    }
    else
    {
// This block is executed when longjmp is called.
        handle_error();
    }
}

process_commands()
{
    int error_flag = 0;
// When an error occurs, error_flag is set to 1
// ...
    if(error_flag) longjmp(saved_context, 1);
}
```

When you call the setjmp function, it saves the current context in the jmp_buf variable named saved_context and returns a zero. In this case, the first if statement in main is satisfied, and the process_commands function is called. If any error occurs in process_commands, the error_flag is set to a nonzero value, and you call longjmp with these arguments:

1. The first argument is the jmp_buf variable, which contains the context to which longjmp should return.

2. The second argument specifies the return value to be used during this return.

The longjmp function reverts the calling environment to this saved state. This amounts to *unrolling* or *unwinding* the stack to where it was when setjmp was originally called. After reverting to the saved context, longjmp returns. When the return statement in longjmp is executed, it is like returning from the call to setjmp, which originally saved the saved_context buffer, except that the returned value is provided by you as the second argument to longjmp. Calling longjmp causes the program to jump to the else block of the first if statement in main. In this way, setjmp and longjmp enable you to jump unconditionally from one C function to another without using conventional return statements. Essentially, setjmp marks the destination of the jump and longjmp acts as a nonlocal goto that executes the jump.

When you first look at it, the combination of setjmp and longjmp appears to be the ideal way to handle exceptions in C++. This is indeed true, and the proposed exception handling mechanism (to be described later) can be implemented using setjmp and longjmp, but only because the proposed design also provides a solution to another problem. In C++, class instances must be initialized by calling class constructors and destroyed by calling the corresponding destructors. Because longjmp abruptly jumps back to a previous point in the execution of the program, situations occur wherein a constructor has been called, but a jump occurs before calling the destructor. In such cases, any memory allocated by a constructor is not freed because the call to the destructor is skipped. Other problems may crop up as well, because the internal state of some objects may be left in an unknown condition. Thus, if setjmp and longjmp are used to handle exceptions, there must be a way to call the destructors of all relevant objects before calling longjmp. This chapter does not provide the details, but this is precisely what a setjmp/longjmp-based implementation of the exception handling mechanism must do in practice.

Exception Handling Mechanism for C++

Andrew Koenig and Bjarne Stroustrup have proposed an exception handling mechanism for C++ that they describe in their recent paper "Exception Handling for C++" (*Journal of Object-Oriented Programming*, Vol.3, No.2, July/August 1990, pages 16-33). In this paper, they even outline a portable implementation of the proposed design based on C's setjmp/longjmp mechanism. In particular, they describe a scheme to solve the problem of ensuring that the destructors are called correctly before unwinding the stack.

Consider a Forms software package that uses a Form class to represent a form. Form has a member function, read, to read the definition of a form from a file. Suppose you are rewriting read so that it uses the proposed exception handling mechanism to cope with the exception caused by the failure to open a specified file. Here is how you add exception handling to the read function of the Form class:

1. Define a class with a descriptive name; FormIOException for example, represents the exception that can occur when trying to read or write forms. You might declare it as follows:

```
class FormIOException
{
public:
        FormIOException(const char* fname) :
                _filename(fname) {}
        const char *filename() const { return _filename;}
private:
        const char* _filename;
};
```

2. In the Form::read function, when the file cannot be opened, throw a FormIOException such as this:

```
void Form::read(const char* filename)
{
// Open an input stream on the specified file
        ifstream fs1(filename, ios::in | ios::nocreate);
        if(!fs1)
        {
// Throw exception if file could not be opened
                throw FormIOException(filename);
        }
// Continue with normal processing
// ...
}
```

That's how you throw the exception. Using the Form class, the programmer provides the code that catches the exception. It looks like this:

```
// Create a form and read in its definition from a file
    Form invoice;

// Be prepared to catch any exceptions
    try
    {
// If an exception is "thrown" control will transfer to the
// catch block.
        invoice.read("invoice.def");
    }
    catch(FormIOException fio)
    {
```

```
        // You can display a message or display a dialog box informing
        // the user that the file could not be opened.
            cout << "Error opening " << fio.filename() << endl;
        }
```

This example illustrates the essential features of the proposed exception handling mechanism.

The general syntax of exception handling can be illustrated as follows:

```
// Exception classes
    class IOException;
    class MemAllocException;
    class MathError;

// Place inside a "try" block code that may throw exceptions
    try
    {
        process_commands();
    }

// Place the exception handling code inside "catch" blocks_one
// for each type of exception.

    catch(IOExecption io)
    {
// Errors in I/O
//...
    }
    catch(MemAllocException mem)
    {
// "Out of memory" errors
//...
    }
    catch(MathError math)
    {
// Handle math errors
//...
    }
    catch(...)   // Use ... to mean any exception
    {
// Handle all other exceptions here
//...
    }
```

As you can see, each `try` block can contain several associated `catch` blocks, which establish handlers for various exceptions. The `catch` blocks are executed in the order of appearance. You should place `catch(...)` at the end because this block is meant for any type of exception.

A function that detects errors and throws exceptions can indicate the specific exceptions that it might throw. Suppose a function named `setup_data` throws the exceptions `IOException` and `MemAllocException`. The function's declaration can indicate this:

```
void setup_data() throw(IOException, MemAllocException);
```

The list of possible exceptions is called the *exception specification* of the function.

Special Functions

Two special functions are reserved for handling exceptions that occur during the exception handling itself:

■ `void terminate();` is called when you do not provide an exception handler for a thrown exception or when an error occurs during the stack unwinding. The `terminate` function, by default, calls the `abort()` function from the ANSI C library. You can, however, direct `terminate` to call a function that you can set up by calling the `set_terminate` function, which is declared as follows:

```
typedef void (*terminate_function)();
terminate_function set_terminate(terminate_function);
```

If you write a function named `handle_termination` to handle the termination, `terminate()` can call it with the following:

```
terminate_function old_term_handler; // To save old handler
void handle_termination();    // New handler
old_term_handler = set_terminate(handle_termination);
```

■ `void unexpected();` is called if a function throws an exception that is not in its exception specification—the list of exceptions that the function is supposed to throw. As the default action of `unexpected()`, it calls `terminate()`, which in turn calls `abort()` to exit the program. Like `set_terminate`, a `set_unexpected` function enables you to specify a function that `unexpected()` should call. You use `set_unexpected` in the same manner as `set_terminate`:

```
typedef void (*unexpected_function)();
unexpected_function old_unexpected;  // To save old handler
void handle_unexpected();    // New handler
old_unexpected = set_unexpected(handle_unexpected);
```

In Visual C++ 2.0, the header file <eh.h> declares the prototypes of the functions `set_terminate` and `set_unexpected`.

Summary

Even though C++ is already proving to be useful in many practical problems, it is still evolving, as evidenced by the recent additions of new features such as exception handling and templates. Exception handling provides a uniform way to handle errors in C++ class libraries and programs, whereas templates support the definition of parameterized classes and functions. The American National Standards Institute's (ANSI) X3J16 committee, which is developing a draft standard for the C++ programming language, has added exception handling and templates to the C++ language. The X3J16 committee has defined these features using the experimental designs presented in Chapters 14 and 15 of *The Annotated C++ Reference Manual* (*ARM*) by Margaret Ellis and Bjarne Stroustrup (Addison-Wesley, 1990). This chapter provides an overview of templates and exception handling based on the designs presented in the *ARM*. Microsoft Visual C++ 2.0 supports both templates and exception handling.

IV

Applying OOP Techniques
in C++

14

Using C Libraries in C++

The first three parts of this book, Chapters 1 through 13, described the Visual C++ 2.0 compiler, explained the terminology of object-oriented programming, and introduced you to the C++ programming language. Chapters 7 through 12, in particular, focused on the features of C++ that support data abstraction, inheritance, and polymorphism—the concepts that form the basis of object-oriented programming.

This section of the book, Chapters 14 through 16, focuses on building and using C++ class libraries. Because there are no standard C++ libraries yet, they are still important functionality sources for C++ programmers. This chapter describes how you can use C libraries (the standard one as well as your own) in C++ programs. It also provides a summary description of the functions in the ANSI standard C library and shows some examples of these functions in C++ programs. Chapter 15, Building Class Libraries in C++, shows you how to build (and design) C++ class libraries. Chapter 16, "Using the General-Purpose Classes in MFC 3.0," details the general-purpose classes in the Microsoft Foundation Class 3.0 (MFC 3.0) class library that comes with Visual C++ 2.0.

Linkage Between C and C++

Suppose you have a library of functions that have been compiled into object code and stored in the library object code form. When you call a function from such a library in your program, the compiler marks the name of the function as an unresolved symbol in the object code of your program. To create an executable program, you must use a linker and make sure that the linker searches the right library for the code of that function. If the linker finds the function's object code in the library, it combines that code with your program's object code to create an executable file. To use C functions in C++ programs, you must be able to complete this process of linking. The following sections explain how you can do this by using the linkage specifier syntax of C++.

Type-Safe Linkage

To understand how C++ programs link with C functions, you must know how C++ resolves the names of functions. You can overload a function name in C++ so that you can declare the same function with different sets of arguments. To help the linker, the C++ compiler uses an encoding scheme that creates a unique name for each overloaded function. The general idea of the encoding algorithm is to generate a unique signature for each function by combining the following components:

- ■ The name of the function
- ■ The name of the class in which the function is defined
- ■ The list of argument types accepted by the function

You don't need to know the exact details of the encoding algorithm because they differ from one compiler to another. However, knowing that a unique signature is generated for each function in a class should help you understand how the linker can determine which of the many different versions of a function to call.

Effect of Function Name Encoding

How does function name encoding affect C++ programs? To see one benefit of name encoding, consider the following C program:

```
//  Illustrates effect of wrong argument type

#include <stdio.h>

void print(unsigned short x)
{
    printf("x = %u", x);
}

void main(void)
{
    short x = -1;
    print(x);
}
```

The print function expects an unsigned short integer argument, but main calls print with a signed short integer argument. You can see the result of this type of mismatch from the output of the program:

```
x = 65535
```

Even though print was called with a -1, the printed value is 65535 because the program was run on a system that uses a 16-bit representation for short integers. The bit representation of the value -1 happens to be 0xffff (all 16 bits are 1); when treated as an unsigned quantity, 0xffff produces the value 65535. In C++, you can avoid problems such as this by defining overloaded functions—one version of print for unsigned short type and another version for short. With this modification, the C++ version of the C program looks like this:

```
// C++ version avoids problem by overloading function

#include <stdio.h>

void print(unsigned short x)
{
    printf("x = %u", x);
}

void print(short x)
{
    printf("x = %d", x);
}

void main(void)
{
    short x = -1;
    print(x);
}
```

When you run this C++ program, you get the following output:

```
x = -1
```

This time, the result is correct because the C++ compiler uses function name encoding to generate a call to the version of print that takes a signed short argument. This feature of C++, the capability of distinguishing between overloaded functions based on argument types, is known as *type-safe* linkage because you cannot inadvertently call a function with the wrong types of arguments.

C Linkage Directive

Now that you know that C++ encodes all function names, you can understand the main problem with calling C functions from C++ programs. If a C++ program calls the C function strlen to get the length of a null-terminated string of characters:

```
// C++ program

#include <stddef.h>              // for definition of "size_t"

size_t strlen(const char* s); // prototype of "strlen"

//...
char str[] = "Hello";
size_t length = strlen(str);
```

when you compile and link the program containing this C++ code with the C library, the linker complains that the function named strlen is unresolved, even though you are linking with the C library that contains the code for strlen. This happens because the C++ compiler uses the function prototype strlen(const char*) to create a name that is very different from strlen, the name the C library uses to store the object code of the strlen function.

To link C object code with C++ programs successfully, you need some mechanism to prevent the C++ compiler from encoding the names of C functions. The linkage directive of C++ provides this escape mechanism. You can successfully link the C++ program that uses strlen, for example, if you qualify strlen as a C function by declaring it this way:

```
// Specify "C" linkage for the strlen function

extern "C" size_t strlen(const char* s);
```

Other Forms of Linkage Directive

To declare a number of functions with the "C" linkage, you can use the compound form of the linkage directive:

```
// Compound form of linkage directive

extern "C"
{
```

```
    int printf(const char* format, ...);
    void exit(int status);

/* Other functions... */
}
```

Typically, header files contain such linkage directives because that is where the functions are declared.

Sharing Header Files Between C and C++ Programs

Because of the close ties between C++ and C, you will often find the need to use C functions in C++ programs. In C++ programs, you declare the C functions with an extern "C" linkage. You can do this easily with the compound form of the linkage directive, but that leaves the declarations unacceptable to the C compiler because the extern "C" directive is not a standard C construct. You can solve this problem by using a conditional compilation directive of the C preprocessor:

```
/* Header file shared between C and C++ */

#ifdef __cplusplus
extern "C" {      /* if it's C++, use linkage directive */
#endif

/* Declare C functions here */
void clearerr(FILE *f);
FILE* fopen(const char* name, const char* mode);
int fclose(FILE* f);

/* ... */

#ifdef __cplusplus
}
#endif
```

The __cplusplus macro is predefined in every C++ compiler. Compilers that can handle C and C++ programs define this symbol when compiling a C++ program. Usually, these compilers provide header files that use the #ifdef __cplusplus construct to declare the C library functions with extern "C" linkage (you need only to include the header file in your C++ program). The programs in this book assume that the standard C header files such as stdio.h are designed to work with C++ programs.

If you are using C header files not conditioned to work with C++ compilers and you cannot alter the C header files, you can still specify the extern "C" linkage by surrounding the #include directive:

```
extern "C"
{
#include <stdio.h>
}
```

If you must do this, the best approach is to create a new header file with an extern "C" wrapper around the #include directive, as shown in the preceding example. This enables you to avoid cluttering the C++ programs with linkage directives that rightfully belong in header files. All source files that use C functions can do so with a consistent linkage directive.

Restrictions on Linkage Directive

You can specify the linkage directive for one instance of an overloaded function. If you declare the sqrt function for the complex and binary_coded_decimal classes as follows:

```
class complex;
class binary_coded_decimal;

extern complex  sqrt(complex&);
extern binary_coded_decimal sqrt(binary_coded_decimal&);
```

you also can use the standard C sqrt function if you declare it this way:

```
extern "C" double sqrt(double);
```

In this case, you have two instances of sqrt for C++ classes and one from the C library; however, only one version of sqrt can be defined in C.

You cannot place linkage specification restrictions because you cannot place them within a local scope—all linkage specifications must appear in the file scope. In particular, the C++ compiler flags the following as an error:

```
// This is an error: cannot have linkage specification in a
// function's scope

main()
{
extern "C" size_t strlen(const char*); // flagged as error
//...

}
```

You can correct this error by moving the linkage specification to the file scope:

```
// This is the right place for linkage specifications, in
// file scope (outside the body of functions)

extern "C" size_t strlen(const char*);

void main()
{
//...

}
```

Linkage to Other Languages

Although you have seen only the extern "C" linkage directive, the appearance of c within quotation marks should inform you that the linkage mechanism is intended to link C++ programs with functions written in other languages as well. Indeed, the linkage specification mechanism is designed for this purpose, but C++ compilers are required to support only two linkages: "C" and "C++". You have seen examples of C linkage; C++ is the default linkage for all C++ programs.

Using the ANSI Standard C Library

By now you know how to use C functions in C++ programs. If your C compiler's standard header files are designed to work with a C++ compiler, you can use the C functions by merely including the appropriate header files in your C++ program. If you are a C programmer, you also know that C relies on its library to provide capabilities such as I/O, memory management, and mathematical functions. Every C program of any significance uses functions such as `printf`, `scanf`, and `gets` that are declared in the stdio.h header file. In addition to the I/O functions, the standard C library has many more functions, such as those for string manipulation and those that return date and time in various formats. The following sections summarize the capabilities of the ANSI C library and demonstrate their use in sample C++ programs.

Overall Capabilities of the ANSI C Library

From Chapter 3, "An Overview of ANSI Standard C," you know that the standard defines not only the C programming language but the contents of the library as well. Even the header files and the prototypes of the functions are specified by the standard. Because most C compilers are beginning to conform to the ANSI standard for C, the standard C library is a good place to look for functions that may be useful in your C++ programs.

The ANSI standard specifies more than 140 functions for the C library, but many of these functions, not yet available in most C compilers, are for handling international character sets. Table 14.1 lists most of the functions in the standard C library, grouped according to capability. The following sections further describe each function category and how each might be used in C++ programs.

Table 14.1. Capabilities of the standard C library.

Category of Function	Function Names
Standard I/O	`clearerr, fclose, feof, ferror, fflush, fgetc,`
	`fgetpos, fgets, fopen, fprintf, fputc, fputs, fread,`
	`freopen, fscanf, fseek, fsetpos, ftell, fwrite,`
	`getc, getchar, gets, printf, putc, putchar, puts,`
	`remove, rename, rewind, scanf, setbuf, setvbuf,`
	`sprintf, sscanf, tmpfile, tmpnam, ungetc, vfprintf,`
	`vprintf, vsprintf`

continues

Table 14.1. continued

Category of Function	*Function Names*
Process control	abort, assert, atexit, exit, getenv, localeconv, longjmp, perror, raise, setjmp, setlocale, signal, system
Memory allocation	calloc, free, malloc, realloc
Variable-length argument list	va_start, va_arg, va_end
Data conversions	atof, atoi, atol, strtod, strtol, strtoul
Mathematical functions	abs, acos, asin, atan, atan2, ceil, cos, cosh, div, exp, fabs, floor, fmod, frexp, labs, ldexp, ldiv, log, log10, modf, pow, rand, sin, sinh, sqrt, srand, tan, tanh
Character classification	isalnum, isalpha, iscntrl, isdigit, isgraph, islower, isprint, ispunct, isspace, isupper, isxdigit, tolower, toupper
String and buffer manipulation	memchr, memcmp, memcpy, memmove, memset, strcat, strchr, strcmp, strcoll, strcpy, strcspn, strerror, strlen, strncat, strncmp, strncpy, strpbrk, strrchr, strspn, strstr, strtok
Search and sort	bsearch, qsort
Time and date	asctime, clock, ctime, difftime, gmtime, localtime, mktime, strftime, time

Standard I/O Functions

The standard I/O functions, declared in the stdio.h header file, include some of the most commonly used functions, such as printf and scanf, in the C library. Almost all C programs use at least one of these functions. You can continue to use these functions in C++. However, as explained in Chapter 8, "C++ Classes for Standard I/O," most C++ compilers include the iostream class library, which provides a cleaner, object-based mechanism for I/O in C++ programs.

Process Control Functions

This broad category of the standard C library includes the signal-handling functions that manage error conditions and utility functions that terminate a process, communicate with the operating system, and set up numeric and currency formats, depending on the locale for which your program is customized. These functions are declared in the following header files (a summary of these functions and their uses follows in the next section):

- LOCALE.H declares `localeconv` and `setlocale`.
- SIGNAL.H declares `raise` and `signal`.
- SETJMP.H declares `longjmp` and `setjmp`.
- STDLIB.H declares `abort`, `atexit`, `exit`, `getenv`, `perror`, and `system`.
- ASSERT.H declares `assert`.

Environment Variables

The term *process* refers to an executing program—when you run a program, you create a process. The *environment* of a process includes the information necessary to execute the process. The exact interpretation of the environment differs from one operating system to another. In UNIX or MS-DOS, the environment consists of an array of null-terminated strings, with each string defining a symbol of this form:

```
VARIABLE=value
```

where the symbol appearing on the left side of the equality is an environment variable. In a UNIX system, you can see the environment variables using either of the commands `printenv` or `env`. In MS-DOS, type `SET` at the DOS prompt to see a list of environment variables.

Environment variables are used to pass information to processes. For example, under UNIX, the full-screen editor vi uses the `TERM` environment variable to determine the type of terminal on which the text is to be displayed. You, the user, indicate the terminal type in the `TERM` environment variable, and the vi editor picks up this setting by determining the value of `TERM`. Your programs can exploit environment variables as well. For example, in UNIX systems, the `TZ` environment variable indicates your time zone. You can get the value of this environment variable by calling the `getenv` function, one of the utility routines defined in the stdlib.h header file.

Exception Handling Using *setjmp* and *longjmp*

In C, you can use `setjmp` and `longjmp` to handle exceptional conditions. You can save the state (or context) of the process by calling `setjmp` and then calling `longjmp` with the saved context to revert to a previous point in your program (recall that the terms state and context have the same meaning and refer to the information needed to reconstruct the process exactly as it is at a particular point in its flow of execution). ANSI C requires a compiler to define an array data type named `jmp_buf` that can hold the information needed to restore a calling environment. This data type is defined in the setjmp.h header file. To understand the mechanics of `setjmp` and `longjmp`, consider the following C code:

```
/*-----------------------------------------------------------*/
/*  Illustrates use of "setjmp" and "longjmp" to
 *  handle exceptions
 */

#include <setjmp.h>
```

```
jmp_buf last_context;

void process_commands(void);
/*-----------------------------------------------------------*/
void main(void)
{
/* Establish a context to which you can return */
    if (setjmp(last_context) == 0)
    {
        process_commands();
    }
    else
    {
/* This part executed when longjmp is called.
 * Place code for handling error here...
 */

    }
}
/*-----------------------------------------------------------*/
void process_commands(void)
{
    int error_flag;
/* ... */
/* In case of error, return to last context */
    if(error_flag) longjmp(last_context, 1);
}
```

The setjmp function saves the current context in the last_context variable and returns 0. In this case, the if statement in main is satisfied and process_commands() is called. Assume that the integer error_flag is set to 1 when any error occurs in the process_commands function. Then you can handle the error by testing this flag and by calling the longjmp function with two arguments. The first argument is the jmp_buf array, which contains the context to which you want to return. When the calling environment reverts to this saved state, and longjmp returns, it is the same as returning from the call to setjmp, which originally saved the last_context buffer. The second argument to longjmp specifies the value to be returned by the function. It should be nonzero so that the if statement in main branches to the else clause when the return is induced by a longjmp.

You can use the combination of setjmp and longjmp to jump unconditionally from one C function to another without using the conventional return statement. Essentially, setjmp marks the destination of the jump, and longjmp acts as a nonlocal goto that executes the jump.

It is tempting to use setjmp and longjmp to handle exceptions in C++, but the calls to constructors and destructors create some problems. All objects initialized up to the point of the error must be destroyed before calling longjmp to jump to an error handling section of the program. This can be done only if you keep track of all objects created in your program. Still, at least one major C++ class library, the *NIH Class Library* (NIH stands for National Institutes of Health), uses setjmp and longjmp to handle exceptions. Nevertheless, you may not have to devise your own exception handling scheme using setjmp and longjmp because the ANSI standard for C++ will include a well-defined method for handling exceptions in C++ programs. Refer to Chapter 13, "Advanced Topics in C++," for further details on this topic.

Customizing Programs to a Locale

The term *locale* refers to the locality, the geographic region, for which certain aspects of your program can be customized. ANSI C groups the locale-dependent aspects of a C program into six categories and defines macros to identify them. Table 14.2 summarizes the locale categories defined in the locale.h header file. You can use the setlocale function selectively to set each category shown in Table 14.2 to conform to a selected locale. The locale named "C" indicates the minimal environment for C programs. Most compilers support only the locale named "C", but future C compilers may support other locale names as well.

You can obtain the numeric and currency formatting style for the current locale by calling the localeconv function, which returns a pointer to a statically allocated lconv structure. You will find the lconv structure declared in the locale.h header file. This structure includes formatting information such as the decimal point character and the currency symbol for the current locale.

Table 14.2. Locale categories in ANSI standard C.

Locale Category	*Parts of Program Affected*
LC_ALL	The entire program's locale-specific parts (all categories that follow)
LC_COLLATE	Behavior of the strcoll and strxfrm functions, which use the collating sequence of the character set
LC_CTYPE	Behavior of the character classification functions
LC_MONETARY	Monetary formatting information returned by the localeconv function
LC_NUMERIC	Decimal point character for the formatted output functions (for example, printf) and the data conversion functions, and for the nonmonetary formatting information returned by the localeconv function
LC_TIME	Behavior of the strftime function, which formats time

You can use the locale mechanism to ensure that the output generated by your application program conforms to the standard representation of monetary and numeric information, as practiced in the locality where the program is being used. For example, you may use localeconv to get formatting information in a C++ class designed to represent currency. Unfortunately, most C compilers still support only the "C" locale, which does not include any information on formatting monetary information.

Memory Allocation

One advantage that C has over older languages such as FORTRAN is its capability of managing memory at runtime. In FORTRAN, there is no provision for requesting memory at runtime. All data items and arrays must be declared in the program. You must guess the maximum size of an array beforehand, and it is not possible to exceed the maximum without recompiling the program. This is inefficient because you often define large arrays, yet use only a small portion of each.

In C, you can request blocks of memory at runtime and release the blocks when your program no longer needs them. This enables your application to exploit all available memory in the system. Like most other capabilities in C, this comes in the form of four standard functions: `calloc`, `malloc`, `realloc`, and `free`, which are defined in the stdlib.h header file. `calloc` and `malloc` are used for allocating memory, `realloc` for adjusting the size of a previously allocated block, and `free` for releasing memory.

C++ not only retains C's capability of allocating memory at runtime but also makes it a part of the language by providing two built-in operators, `new` and `delete`, to handle allocation and deallocation of objects. Of course, many C++ compilers define `new` and `delete` in terms of `malloc` and `free`. If you need to overload the `new` and `delete` operators for one of your C++ classes, you can use `malloc` and `free` to define the overloaded versions of the operators.

Variable-Length Argument Lists

When writing C programs, you used functions (such as `printf` and `scanf`) that can take a variable number of arguments. In fact, their prototypes use an ellipsis in the argument list to reflect this:

```
int printf(const char *format_string, ...);
int scanf(const char *format_string, ...);
```

ANSI standard C includes the `va_start`, `va_arg`, and `va_end` macros, defined in the stdarg.h header file, that enable you to write functions capable of accepting a variable number of arguments. The only requirement of such functions is that they must accept at least one required argument. You can use these macros in C++ programs as well. As an example, consider a `menu_widget` class with a constructor that accepts a variable number of strings and creates a menu with those strings as labels. The following skeleton C++ program illustrates how you can use the ANSI standard approach to handle a variable number of arguments in a class member function:

```
//-----------------------------------------------------------
// Demonstrates the use of variable-length argument lists

#include <iostream.h>
#include <stdlib.h>      // For declaration of NULL
#include <stdarg.h>
```

```
#define MENU_BAR   1
#define PULL_DOWN 2

typedef char *P_CHAR;

class menu_widget
{
public:
    menu_widget(int style, ...);
// ...
private:
// ...
};

//-------------------------------------------------------------
menu_widget::menu_widget(int style, ...)
{
// Get the first optional parameter using "va_start"
    va_list  argp;        // Used to access arguments
    va_start(argp, style);

// Get items one by one
    char     *item_text;
    int      count = 0;

    cout << "------------------------------" << endl;
    while((item_text = va_arg(argp, P_CHAR)) != NULL)
    {
        cout << "Item " << count << " = " << item_text << endl;
        count++;
    }
}
//-------------------------------------------------------------
//  Test the use of variable-length argument lists

void main()
{
    menu_widget m1(MENU_BAR, "File", "Edit", "Utilities", NULL);
    menu_widget m2(PULL_DOWN, "Open", "Close", "New", "Save",
                             "Save As...", "Quit", NULL);
//...
}
```

If you run this program, you get the following output showing that the menu_widget constructor is processing a variable number of arguments:

```
------------------------------
Item 0 = File
Item 1 = Edit
Item 2 = Utilities
------------------------------
Item 0 = Open
Item 1 = Close
Item 2 = New
Item 3 = Save
Item 4 = Save As...
Item 5 = Quit
```

Data Conversions

The functions in this category—atof, atoi, atol, strtod, strtol, and strtoul—convert character strings into internal representations of variables. They are declared in the stdlib.h header file.

The conversion routines are ideal for converting command-line arguments from their string representation into the internal format. For example, in a small calculator program, you might want to process an input line of this form:

```
eval 12.43 + 17.52
```

where eval is the name of the program that accepts a command line of the form <value1> <operator> <value2> and prints the result of the operation. In this example, the program should print 29.95 as the answer. When implementing this program, you can use the atof function to convert the second and fourth command-line arguments (the first argument is always the name of the program) to double variables. The code for the addition operator might be written as the following:

```
#include <stdlib.h>
#include <iostream.h>

void main(int argc, char **argv)
{
    double op1, op2, result;

    op1 = atof(argv[1]);
    op2 = atof(argv[3]);

    switch(argv[2][0])
    {
// ...
        case '+':
            result = op1 + op2;
// ...
    }
    cout << result << endl;
}
```

This example assumes a decimal calculator. If you want a hexadecimal calculator so that all input and output is in hexadecimal, you can use the strtoul function to convert the input arguments to unsigned long integers. This is a typical use of the data conversion functions.

Mathematical Functions

Both C and C++ support the basic floating-point data types float and double and enable you to write arithmetic expressions using these data types. Additionally, the standard C library includes a set of mathematical functions that enables you to evaluate common functions such as sine and cosine. Most of these functions are declared in the math.h header file.

Basic Functions

The trigonometric functions—cos, sin, tan, acos, asin, atan, and atan2—evaluate the cosine, sine, and tangent of any angle in radian and compute the inverses of cosine, sine, and tangent. These functions are useful for the transformation of rectangular to polar coordinates that often occurs in graphics programs. The following are other commonly used mathematical functions:

sqrt to compute square roots

log to return the natural logarithm of an argument

log10 to return the base 10 logarithm of an argument

exp to compute exponentials

For example, you call exp(1.75) to evaluate $e^{1.75}$, fabs to return the absolute value of a floating-point value, ceil to return the nearest integer larger than a given floating-point number, and floor to return the nearest integer smaller than its floating-point argument.

Integer Arithmetic

Four functions, declared in stdlib.h, handle arithmetic using integer arguments: abs and labs return the absolute value of an integer and a long integer, respectively; div divides one integer by another and returns the integer quotient and an integer remainder; and ldiv operates similarly but with long integer arguments.

Generating Random Numbers

If you need to generate random numbers (for a random screen pattern, a game, or a statistical analysis problem, for example), the ANSI C library includes a function named rand that can generate a random positive integer in the range 0 to RAND_MAX, a constant defined in stdlib.h. The rand function generates random numbers by using a well-defined algorithm. Given the same starting number, rand always generates the same sequence of random numbers. In other words, rather than being truly random, the sequence generated by rand is a pseudorandom sequence. If the algorithm used to generate the random numbers is good, the sequence will not repeat frequently, and all numbers between 0 and RAND_MAX will appear with equal probability. A function named srand sets the starting point of the random sequence.

Sometimes you need to select a random sequence of random numbers. For example, you wouldn't want to be dealt the same hand in a card game again and again. ANSI C does not provide a routine to generate a random seed, but you can use the value returned by the time function as the argument to srand to set a new random seed for rand.

Character Classification

The C ctype.h header file contains several functions that are useful for classifying and converting characters. The behavior of these functions is affected by the LC_CTYPE category of the current locale. Table 14.3 shows a summary of ANSI C functions that can be used to classify and convert characters. These functions are useful when parsing strings. You can use the `isspace` function, for example, to locate a valid whitespace character in a string.

Table 14.3. Summary of ANSI C's character classification functions.

Name	Description
isalnum	Returns nonzero if character is alphanumeric
isalpha	Returns nonzero if character is alphabetic
iscntrl	Returns nonzero if character belongs to the set of control characters
isdigit	Returns nonzero if character is a numerical digit
isgraph	Returns nonzero if character is printable (excluding the space character)
islower	Returns nonzero if character is lowercase
isprint	Returns nonzero if character is printable (includes space)
ispunct	Returns nonzero if character belongs to the set of punctuation characters
isspace	Returns nonzero if character belongs to the set of whitespace characters, which includes space, formfeed, newline, carriage return, horizontal tab, and vertical tab
isupper	Returns nonzero if character is uppercase
isxdigit	Returns nonzero if character is a hexadecimal digit
tolower	Converts character to lowercase only if that character is an uppercase letter
toupper	Converts character to uppercase only if that character is a lowercase letter

String and Buffer Manipulation

You have already encountered some of ANSI C's string manipulation functions in the `String` class shown in Chapter 10, "Defining Operations on Objects," and Chapter 11, "Using Inheritance in C++." These functions, declared in string.h, are primarily for comparing two strings or buffers, copying one string or buffer into another, and searching for the occurrence of a character in a string.

> **NOTE**
>
> Recall that a buffer is a contiguous block of memory, and string refers to an array of characters. By convention, a string in C is marked by a null character—a byte with all zero bits. Because of this, C strings are known as null-terminated strings.

Strings in C and C++

Neither C nor C++ has any built-in data type for strings. Instead, strings are treated as an array of characters with a null character marking the end of the string. You can declare strings as you would any other array objects:

```
char line[81], filename[]="test.1";
```

Here, `line` is a string with room for 81 characters, but because of the terminating null character, `line` can hold no more than 80 characters. The second string, `filename`, is declared without a size, but the initial value of the string provides enough information about the size. The compiler reserves enough storage for the string and the terminating null character. As shown in Figure 14.1, the `filename` string requires 7 bytes of storage.

FIGURE 14.1.

A null-terminated string in C and C++.

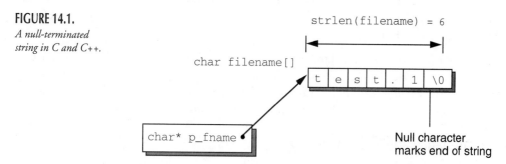

Because a string is an array of characters, you also can access a string through a `char*` pointer. For example, to access the `filename` string using a pointer named `p_fname`, you write the following:

```
char   filename[] = "test.1";
char *p_fname = filename;
```

Once the `p_fname` pointer is initialized, you can use it to access the `filename` string as you would through the array named `filename`. Of course, as shown in Figure 14.1, the `p_fname` pointer requires some additional storage space. You also can declare and initialize a `char*` pointer to a string in a single statement. For example, you write the following:

```
char *p_str = "Some string";
```

to initialize the p_str character pointer to the string constant Some string. You actually have initialized p_str to the address of the first character of the string Some string.

Length of a String

The length of a C string is the number of characters in the string up to, but not including, the terminating null character. For example, the filename string in Figure 14.1 is 6 bytes long, even though 7 bytes are needed to store the string. You can use the strlen function to get the length of a C string.

Comparing Strings and Buffers

The string and buffer manipulation category contains five functions for comparing strings and buffers: memcmp, strcmp, strncmp, strcoll, and strxfrm. Each function takes two arguments and returns a zero when the arguments match. The functions return a negative value if the first argument is less than the second and a positive value if the first argument is greater than the second. This means, for strings, that the first argument appears after the second in a dictionary of words in that character set.

The strcmp function is used for case-sensitive comparisons of two strings. The memcmp and strncmp functions behave like strcmp, but are used for comparing a specified number of characters from the beginning of each string.

The strcoll function is intended to be used for comparing strings using a collating sequence determined by the LC_COLLATE category of the locale. The strxfrm function is a utility routine that transforms a string into a new form so that, if strcmp is used to compare two transformed strings, the result is identical to that returned by strcoll applied to the original strings.

Concatenating and Copying Strings

The memcpy, memmove, strcat, strcpy, strncat, and strncpy functions are used for concatenating and copying strings and buffers. Each of these functions accepts two arguments. In all cases, the second argument is the source and the first is the destination. When copying or concatenating strings, you must ensure that there is enough room in the destination string to hold the source string. You can do this either by declaring an array of characters with enough room or by allocating memory at runtime.

The memcpy and memmove functions are used for copying one buffer into another. Of these two, the memmove function is guaranteed to work properly, even if the source and destination buffers overlap. Both memcpy and memmove work with nonoverlapping source and destination buffers.

The strcat function appends the second string argument to the first and produces a null-terminated string as the result. The strncat function is similar to strcat, but it copies only a specified number of characters from the second string to the first.

The `strcpy` function copies the second string argument onto the first one. `strcpy` copies the entire string, but `strncpy` copies only a specified number of characters. Because `strncpy` does not automatically append a null character to the destination string, you must be alert for instances wherein a null character is not included in the characters being copied.

Search and Sort

The standard C library also includes two very useful functions: `qsort` (for sorting an array of objects) and `bsearch` (for searching for an object in a sorted array). These sort and search functions are suitable for in-memory operations when the entire array fits into memory.

Using *qsort* and *bsearch*

Figure 14.2 shows a typical sorting scenario: you have an array of pointers to `String` objects (see Chapter 11 for the `String` class), each of which contains a C string, and you want to sort the array by rearranging the pointers so that the C strings appear in ascending order. Figure 14.2 shows the original array of pointers and the array after sorting. Although the pointers have been rearranged, the `String` objects have remained in their original positions. Because the pointers are usually much smaller than the objects, the result is faster sorting—it is faster to shuffle the pointers than to copy the objects. However, memory usage increases because the pointers require extra storage space.

FIGURE 14.2.
Sorting an array of `String` *objects.*

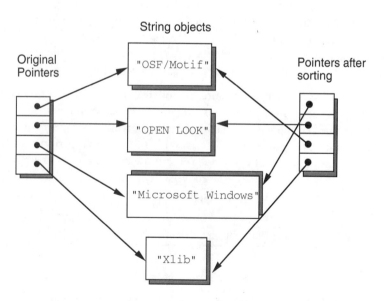

The `qsort` and `bsearch` functions are declared in stdlib.h as follows:

```
void *bsearch(const void *key, const void *base, size_t num,
        size_t width,
            int (*compare)(const void *elem1, const void *elem2));
```

```
void qsort(const void *base, size_t num, size_t width,
           int (*compare)(const void *elem1, const void *elem2));
```

As you can see from the prototype, the qsort function expects (as argument) the starting address of the array, the number of elements in it, the size (in bytes) of each element, and a pointer to a function that performs the comparison of any two elements in the array. The bsearch function, in addition, requires a pointer to the value being sought, and the array being searched must already be sorted in ascending order.

The key to using qsort and bsearch is to provide an appropriate comparison function, the last argument to either function. This function will receive, as argument, pointers to the two elements being compared. It must return one of the following integer values:

- A positive value if the first element is greater than the second one
- A zero if the two elements are equal
- A negative value if the first element is less than the second one

You determine the meanings of "less than," "greater than," and "equal." When sorting String objects, for example, you compare the C string field of the two objects and return a value based on the lexicographic ordering of the strings.

Sorting an Array of *String* Objects

As an example of using qsort, consider the problem of sorting an array of String objects. You must first define a StringArray class that holds an array of pointers to instances of the String class. As shown in Listing 14.1, the StringArray class provides member functions to add new String objects to the array, display the current contents of the array, and sort the array. The str.h file, which declares the String class, appears in Listing 11.1 in Chapter 11.

For this discussion, the interesting part of StringArray is the sort function. This function sorts by calling qsort from the ANSI C library. The final argument to qsort, the compare function, is the crucial component in making this scheme work. For the StringArray class, you can implement the compare function as a class static function that performs the comparison by calling strcmp from the ANSI C library. You can use String objects as arguments to strcmp because the String class provides a type-conversion operator that enables the C++ compiler to convert the String type to const char* type.

Listing 14.1. STRARRAY.H. Implementation of the StringArray class.

```
//------------------------------------------------------------
//   File:  strarray.h
//   Implements an array of String objects
//
//   NOTE: The "sort" function sorts the contents of the
//         array by calling the "qsort" function from the
//         standard C library

#if !defined(__STRARRY_H)
```

```
#define __STRARRAY_H

#include <stdlib.h>
#include "str.h"

const size_t default_capacity = 16;
    typedef String* StringPtr;

class StringArray
{
public:
// Constructor
    StringArray() : _count(0), _capacity(default_capacity)
    {
        _strp = new StringPtr[default_capacity];
    }

// Destructor
    ~StringArray();

    void add(const char* s)
    {
// If there is no more room, you should expand the capacity
// by allocating more space.  Here, simply return.
        if(_count == _capacity) return;
        _strp[_count] = new String(s);
        _count++;
    }

// Function to be used with "qsort"
    static int compare(const void* s1, const void* s2)
    {
        return strcmp(**(String**)s1, **(String**)s2);
    }

// The "sort" function simply calls "qsort"
    void sort()
    {
        qsort(_strp, _count, sizeof(String*),
            StringArray::compare);
    }

    void show();

private:
    String** _strp;
    size_t   _count;
    size_t   _capacity;
};

//------------------------------------------------------------
// ~StringArray
//  Destructor for the StringArray class

StringArray::~StringArray()
{
int i;
    for(i = 0; i < _count; i++)
```

continues

Listing 14.1. continued

```
        delete _strp[i];
    delete _strp;
}
//-------------------------------------------------------------
//  s h o w
//  Display the contents of the array

void StringArray::show()
{
    cout << "Contents of String array:" << endl;
    cout << "------------------------" << endl;
    int i;
    for(i = 0; i<_count; i++)
    {
        cout << *_strp[i] << endl;
    }
}

#endif
```

Listing 14.2 displays a sample program that tests the sorting operation of the StringArray class. The program sets up an instance of the StringArray class, adds some String objects to it, and sorts the array. After sorting the array, it displays the contents.

Listing 14.2. Sample sorting program.

```
//-------------------------------------------------------------
//  Sample program to create an array of String objects,
//   add some Strings, and sort the array
#include "strarray.h"

void main()
{
    StringArray sa;
// Add some strings to the array
    sa.add("OSF/Motif");
    sa.add("OPEN LOOK");
    sa.add("Microsoft Windows");
    sa.add("Xlib");
// Sort the array
    sa.sort();
// Display contents
    sa.show();
}
```

When you run this program, it displays the following as the contents of the sorted array:

```
Contents of String array:
------------------------
Microsoft Windows
OPEN LOOK
OSF/Motif
Xlib
```

As you can see, the array is sorted in ascending order. You can reverse the order of sorting by placing a minus sign in front of the strcmp function call in the body of the compare function of the StringArray class.

Date and Time

The ANSI C library includes a set of functions for obtaining, displaying, and manipulating date and time information. These functions are declared in the time.h header file. Figure 14.3 is a pictorial representation of the different formats of date and time in ANSI C and the functions that enable you to convert from one format to another. The core of these functions is the time function, which returns a value of the time_t type that is defined in the time.h header file. This time_t value represents the calendar time in encoded form (often called *binary time*). You can convert it to a tm structure with the gmtime and localtime functions. The gmtime function accepts a binary time and sets the fields in a tm structure to correspond to Greenwich Mean Time (GMT), or Universal Time Coordinated (UTC), as this standard time reference is now called. The localtime function sets the fields of the tm structure to local time. The mktime function converts time from a tm structure to a value of time_t.

FIGURE 14.3.

Different forms of time in ANSI C.

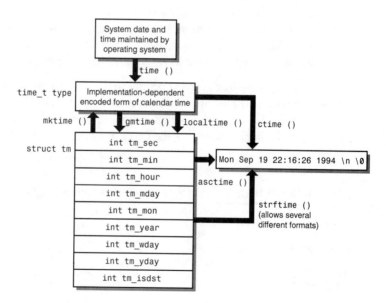

Printing Date and Time

The asctime function converts the value in a tm structure to a null-terminated C string that you can print. The ctime function converts the output of time directly to a string. Thus, you can print the current time from a C++ program as follows:

```
#include <iostream.h>
#include <time.h>

main()
{
    time_t tnow;
// Get the current time in binary form
    time(&tnow);
// Convert the time to a string and print it.
    cout << "Current time = " << ctime(&tnow) << endl;
}
```

Here is a sample output from this program:

```
Current time = Tue Sep 13 23:06:21 1994
```

A *DateTime* Class

A more concrete example of the time-manipulation functions in C++ is the DateTime class, which represents date and time information. As shown in Listing 14.3, the DateTime class maintains the calendar time in binary format. Its default constructor calls the time function to get the current time. The other interesting member of this class is the addition operator that advances the date by a specified number of days. The addition operator uses the mktime function to accomplish this task. The mktime function converts calendar time from a tm structure into a time_t format. Before making this conversion, mktime also adjusts all members of the tm structure to reasonable values. As you can see from the definition of the operator+ function in Listing 14.3, you can exploit this feature of mktime to advance the DateTime values by a number of days.

The DateTime class also overloads the << operator so that you can use << to print DateTime variables on an output stream. This overloading is done with the help of the print member function of the DateTime class that prints on an ostream. The print function, in turn, calls ctime from the standard C library. Note that the ctime function converts a binary time into a formatted C string.

Listing 14.3. DATETIME.H. Definition of the DateTime class for manipulating calendar time.

```
//--------------------------------------------------------------
//   File:  datetime.h
//
//   A date and time class

#if !defined(__DATETIME_H)
#define __DATETIME_H

#include <time.h>       // ANSI standard "Time" functions
#include <iostream.h>   // For stream I/O

class DateTime
{
public:
DateTime() { time(&_bintime); }
```

```
    DateTime(time_t t) : _bintime(t) { }

    friend DateTime operator+(DateTime d, int n)
    {
        struct tm *ltime = localtime(&d._bintime);
        ltime->tm_mday += n;
        time_t t = mktime(ltime);
        return DateTime(t);
    }

    friend DateTime operator+(int n, DateTime d)
    {
        return d+n;
    }

    DateTime operator+=(int n)
    {
        struct tm *ltime = localtime(&_bintime);
        ltime->tm_mday += n;
        _bintime = mktime(ltime);
        return *this;
    }

    void print(ostream& os) { os << ctime(&_bintime);}
private:
    time_t      _bintime;
};

// Stream output operator for DateTime class

ostream& operator<<(ostream& os, DateTime& d)
{
    d.print(os);
    return os;
}

#endif
```

Although the DateTime class is far from being complete (it is intended to serve as an example that illustrates how to use ANSI C's time-manipulation functions in a C++ class), you still can use the class for some useful work. Listing 14.4 presents a short program that displays the current date and time and illustrates the use of the addition operators.

Listing 14.4. Sample program to test the DateTime class.

```
//-------------------------------------------------------------
// Test the DateTime class

#include "datetime.h"

void main()
{
    DateTime d1;
```

Listing 14.4. continued

```
     cout << "Current date and time = " << d1 << endl;

// Advance by 45 days
     d1 += 45;
     cout << "45 days later, it will be = " << d1 << endl;

//  Try addition operator...(add another 5 days)
     cout << "50 days later, it will be = ";
     cout << d1+5 << endl;
}
```

Here is a sample output from this program:

```
Current date and time = Tue Sep 13 23:07:35 1994

45 days later, it will be = Fri Oct 28 23:07:35 1994

50 days later, it will be = Wed Nov 02 23:07:35 1994
```

Notice that an extra line feed appears after each line because the ctime function, called by the print member function of DateTime, formats the binary time into a string with a newline character at the end. This feature of ctime, together with the explicit use of the endl manipulator, is responsible for the extra blank lines. To format the time into a string without an extra newline character, you can call the strftime function, which is specifically intended for formatting time information.

Compiler-Specific Libraries

Although the standard C library is a good source of portable functions, you should also examine your C++ compiler's offering of nonstandard libraries. In particular, C++ compilers such as Visual C++ 2.0 include many additional functions in their libraries. Most notable among these functions are the ones for accessing the services of the MS-DOS operating system and those for graphics output.

If you are developing a program specifically for the MS-DOS environment and you do not mind being tied to a particular compiler's library, you should consider making use of the compiler-specific functions. These functions are as easy to use as the standard C functions. In all likelihood, the header files are probably conditioned to work with the C++ compiler. You need only to include the header file and call the function. However, you must know the overall capabilities of the additional functions. You can usually find this information in the documentation that comes with the C++ compiler. Another possible source of information is a book like this one that specifically covers your C++ compiler's library.

Summary

Like C, C++ is built around a sparse core, and all major functions are delegated to support libraries. The core of the language provides a small set of built-in data types, constructs such as `class` and `struct` to define new types, operators to build expressions, and control structures to manage the flow of execution of the program. You must rely on libraries for everything from I/O to string manipulations.

Because C++ is still in a state of evolution, it does not yet have a standard library like ANSI C. Typical C++ compilers include the `complex` class for complex arithmetic and the `iostream` library for I/O. You can, however, use the functions from the standard C library in your C++ programs. To link C++ programs with the C library, you must enclose the declaration of the C functions and data inside an `extern "C" { ... }` linkage specifier. Many C++ compilers, including Microsoft Visual C++ 2.0, already provide C header files with declarations enclosed in an `extern "C" { ... }` block. With such header files, using C functions is as easy as including the header files in a C++ program and making the function calls.

The standard C library includes a large assortment of functions that you are guaranteed to find in all standard conforming C compilers. Because C++ does not yet have a standard library, the ANSI C library is a good place to look for functions that may be useful in your C++ classes. This chapter provides a summary description of the ANSI C library and shows you how to use these capabilities in C++ programs and in C++ classes.

15

Building Class Libraries in C++

Chapter 14, "Using C Libraries in C++," explores how to use existing C libraries in C++ programs. This chapter examines the topics of designing, organizing, and building C++ classes that can provide specific functionality for use in C++ programs. When designing a class library, you must determine the inheritance hierarchy of the classes, the way one class uses the facilities of others, and the kinds of operations the classes will support.

Organizing C++ Classes

If a standard class library for C++ existed, deciding how to organize C++ classes would be easy—you would model your classes after the standard ones. Unfortunately, C++ does not yet have standard classes. The `iostream` class library (described in Chapter 8, "C++ Classes for Standard I/O"), which comes with most C++ compilers (including Visual C++ 2.0), may be the only standard class library currently available. Of course, the `iostream` class library provides only I/O capabilities. You need much more than the `iostream` classes when developing complete applications in C++. Additionally, even if many standard classes for C++ were available, your particular application still would require you to write new, customized classes. The point is that sooner or later you will face the task of organizing a library of classes that will form the basis of your application. Organization of C++ classes refers to their inheritance hierarchy, as well as to the way one class can use the facilities of another. First, consider the question of inheritance hierarchy.

Inheritance Hierarchy Under Single Inheritance

Before AT&T C++ Release 2.0, a class could inherit from only one base class. As shown in Figures 15.1 and 15.2, you can organize the inheritance tree of classes under single inheritance in two distinct ways:

■ A single class hierarchy with all classes in the library derived from a single root class (a base class, which is not derived from any other class). The Smalltalk-80 programming language provides this type of class hierarchy. Therefore, this organization of C++ classes is known as the *Smalltalk model* or a single *tree model*.

■ Multiple disjoint class hierarchies with more than one root class. This has been referred to as the *forest model* because the library contains multiple trees of class hierarchies.

FIGURE 15.1.

A typical single tree organization of C++ classes patterned after Smalltalk-80.

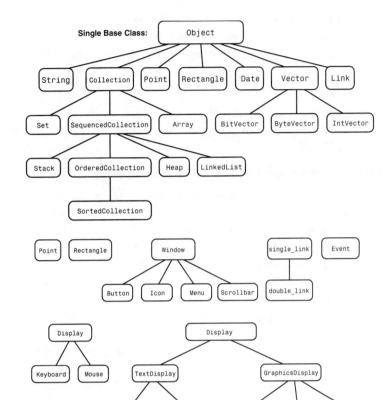

FIGURE 15.2.

A forest of C++ classes for building user interfaces.

Single Class Hierarchy

As Figure 15.1 shows, a library that uses a single class hierarchy starts with a base class, usually named `Object`, which declares a host of virtual functions that apply to all other classes in the library. These virtual functions handle standard operations, such as copying, printing, storing, retrieving, and comparing objects. Each derived class defines concrete versions of these functions and thereby provides a standard interface to the library. Several prominent C++ class libraries, including the NIH Class Library by Keith Gorlen, use this model of organization. Proponents of the single class hierarchy point out the following benefits of this approach:

■ The definition of a single root class ensures that all classes provide the same standard set of `public` interface functions. This enhances consistency and compatibility among classes.

■ When all classes are guaranteed to inherit from a single base class, capabilities such as persistence—storing and retrieving collections of objects in a disk file—are easier to provide. Prior to the support for exception handling in C++, some C++ class libraries (with a single root class) provided a library-wide exception handling mechanism by placing the exception handling code in the `Object` class.

■ Because every class in the library is an `Object`, you can easily define polymorphic data structures. For example, the following array of pointers:

```
Object *ArrayOfObjPtr[16];
```

can hold pointers to instances of any class in the library, so you can easily define data structures such as linked lists and stacks capable of holding instances of any class in the library.

However, a monolithic class hierarchy has these disadvantages:

■ The compiler cannot provide strict type checking because many objects in the library are of the `Object*` type, which can point to an instance of any class in the library. Such pointers to the base class are routinely used in polymorphic container classes that are capable of storing instances of any class in the library.

■ The root base class, `Object`, typically includes many virtual functions representing the union of all the virtual functions implemented by the derived classes. This is burdensome if you want to create a derived class because you must provide the definition of all the virtual functions, even though many may not be relevant to that derived class.

■ Although a single root `Object` class makes it easy to create a container class capable of storing any other object from the library, you cannot use these containers to store standard C++ data types, such as `float`, `int`, and `char`. If you want to store these types in a container, you must write your own classes that mimic the built-in types of C++. For example, you can define `Float` and `Integer` classes that model, respectively, C++'s `float` and `int` data types. (Template-based container classes are capable of storing all types of objects, including the built-in data types, such as `float`, `int`, and `char`.)

■ Because of the large monolithic class hierarchy, compiling a single program may require processing a large number of header files. This can be a slow compilation on systems with a limited amount of memory.

Multiple Class Hierarchies

In contrast to the monolithic, single class hierarchy of the Smalltalk-80 library, a C++ class library based on the forest model includes multiple class trees, with each tree providing a well-defined functionality. Figure 15.2, for example, shows several class hierarchies in a C++ class library that provide the objects needed to build window-based user interfaces. Different types of windows are grouped together in the class hierarchy with the `Window` class as the root. Each window has a rectangle represented by the `Rectangle` class, which, in turn, uses the `Point` class to represent the corners of the window. The `Event` class models user inputs that come from one of the devices shown in the class hierarchy whose root is the `Device` class. The stand-alone `String` class represents text strings that might appear in windows. You can model the physical display by a class hierarchy with a generic `Display` as the base class. From this generic display, you can further specialize to text or graphics displays. You might categorize text displays into ANSI-standard terminals or IBM PC-compatible displays. Graphics displays may be based on one of the following: the X Window System, Borland International's Borland Graphics Interface (BGI), or Microsoft Windows.

The following are the main advantages of the forest model of class libraries:

■ Because each class hierarchy is small, you can understand and use the classes easily.

■ Virtual functions declared in each root class are relevant to that class tree. It is not difficult, therefore, to implement the derived classes in each hierarchy.

On the other hand, the lack of an overall structure implies that you cannot create the elegant container classes of the Smalltalk model. Thus, the primary disadvantages of the forest model are the following:

■ Because there is no common base class, it is difficult to design container classes, such as linked lists, stacks, and queues, that can store any type of object. You must devise your own schemes for creating such data structures.

■ Anything that requires a library-wide discipline becomes difficult to implement. For example, persistence is more difficult to support under the forest model than under a single tree model.

Effects of Multiple Inheritance

The introduction of multiple inheritance in AT&T C++ Release 2.0 changed the implications of organizing C++ class libraries according to either the single tree model or the forest model. Because multiple inheritance enables a derived class to inherit from more than one base class, you can combine the capabilities of classes in unique ways to suit your needs. A good example is the singly linked list of String objects illustrated in Chapter 11, "Using Inheritance in C++." The linked list is constructed by linking instances of a new class named slink_string, which is defined from the String class and the single_link class:

```
class slink_string: public single_link, public String
{
//...
};
```

The single_link class is capable of holding a pointer to another instance of single_link. In this way, multiple inheritance enables you to combine the capabilities of two classes into a single class. Here are some ways of applying multiple inheritance to extend the capabilities of C++ class libraries:

■ You can derive a class from two or more classes in a library, even if the class library follows a single tree model of inheritance hierarchy. For example, the NIH Class Library includes a Link class and a String class. With multiple inheritance, you can combine these two classes to define a String with a Link just as you did to define the slink_string class in Chapter 11.

■ Even with a multiple-class hierarchy, you can add a standard capability such as persistence by defining a new base class and deriving other classes from it. You can do this, although it takes extra work to create a new set of derived classes that incorporate the capability defined in the new base class. With single inheritance, you do not have the opportunity of combining the behavior of two or more classes packaged in a library.

Client-Server Relationship Among Classes

In addition to the inheritance relationship among classes, a class can use the facilities of another class. This is called the *client-server* relationship among classes because the client class, in order to use the capabilities of the server class, calls the member functions of the server class. In C++, the client class needs an instance of the server class to call the member functions of the server. The client class can get this instance in one of the following ways:

■ One of the member functions of the client class receives an instance of the server class as an argument.

■ A member function of the client class calls a function that returns an instance of the server class.

■ An instance of the server class is available as a global variable.

■ The client class incorporates an instance of the server class as a member variable.

■ A member variable of the client class is a pointer to an instance of the server class.

The last two cases are of interest because they constitute the most common ways of expressing a client-server relationship between two classes. This approach—using a class by incorporating an instance or a pointer to an instance—has been referred to as *composition*. The following sections briefly describe these two approaches of composition.

Class Instance as a Member

In Chapter 6, "C++ and Object-Oriented Programming," Listing 6.4 shows the declaration of several classes intended to represent geometric shapes, such as triangles and rectangles. All geometric shapes are derived from an abstract shape class. In particular, the rectangle_shape class is declared as follows:

```
class shape
{
public:
    virtual double compute_area(void) const = 0;
    virtual void draw(void) const{ } = 0;
};

// Define the "rectangle" class

class rectangle_shape: public shape
```

```
{
private:
    double x1, y1;   // Coordinates of opposite corners
    double x2, y2;
public:
    rectangle_shape(double x1, double y1, double x2, double y2);
    double compute_area(void) const;
    void draw(void) const;
};
```

A better way to define the rectangle_shape class is to use the notion of a point in a plane. For example, you can first define a Point class:

```
//-----------------------------------------------------------
// File: point.h
// Define a point in two-dimensional plane

#if !defined(__POINT_H)
#define __POINT_H

#include <math.h>

typedef double Coord;

class Point
{
public:
    Point() : _x(0), _y(0) {}
    Point(Coord x, Coord y) : _x(x), _y(y) {}
    Point(const Point& p) : _x(p._x), _y(p._y) {}

    Point& operator=(const Point& p)
    {
        _x = p._x;
        _y = p._y;
        return *this;
    }

    Point operator-(const Point& p) const
    {
        return Point(_x-p._x, _y-p._y);
    }

    Coord xdistance() const { return fabs(_x);}
    Coord ydistance() const { return fabs(_y);}
private:
    Coord _x, _y;
};

#endif
```

Because a rectangle is uniquely defined by any two opposite corners, you can implement the rectangle_shape class using two instances of the Point class:

```
//-----------------------------------------------------------
// File:  rect.h
// C++ header file with definitions of a rectangle shape
```

```
#if !defined(__RECT_H)
#define __RECT_H

#include <stdio.h>
#include <math.h>

#include "point.h"  // For definition of the Point class

class shape
{
public:
    virtual double compute_area(void) const = 0;
    virtual void draw(void) const = 0;
};

// Define the "rectangle" class

class rectangle_shape: public shape
{
public:
    rectangle_shape(Point& c1, Point& c2) : _c1(c1), _c2(c2){}

    double compute_area(void) const
    {
        Point p = _c1 - _c2;
        return p.xdistance() * p.ydistance();
    }

    void draw(void) const { } // Not defined

private:
    Point _c1, _c2;   // Opposite corners of rectangle
};

#endif   // #if !defined(__RECT_H)
```

Point _c1 _c2 denotes two opposite corners of the rectangle. Here is a sample program that uses the rectangle_shape class:

```
#include <iostream.h>
#include "rect.h"

int main(void)
{
    Point p1(10,10), p2(30,40);
    rectangle_shape r(p1,p2);

    cout << "Area of rectangle = " << r.compute_area();
    cout << endl;

    return 0;
}
```

When you run the program, it displays the expected output:

```
Area of rectangle = 600
```

This is an example of the `rectangle_shape` class making use of the `Point` class. Member functions of the `rectangle_shape` class access the member functions of the `Point` class through `Point` instances _c1 and _c2.

Pointer to Class Instance as a Member

An alternative to incorporating `Point` instances in the `rectangle_shape` class is to define pointers to the `Point` class as members of `rectangle_shape`. Used carefully, this approach enables you to declare the `rectangle_shape` class without including the definition of the `Point` class. For example, you can rewrite the declaration of the `rectangle_shape` class:

```
//---------------------------------------------------------------
//  File:  rect_p.h
//  C++ header file with definitions of rectangle_shape class
//  This version uses pointers to Point class

#if !defined(__RECT_P_H)
#define __RECT_P_H

#include <stdio.h>
#include <math.h>

class Point;

class shape
{
public:
    virtual double compute_area(void) const = 0;
    virtual void draw(void) const = 0;
};

// Define the "rectangle" class

class rectangle_shape: public shape
{
public:
    rectangle_shape() : _p1(0), _p2(0) {}
    rectangle_shape(const Point& p1, const Point& p2);
    rectangle_shape(const rectangle_shape& r);
    ~rectangle_shape();

    void operator=(const rectangle_shape& r);

    double compute_area(void) const;

    void draw(void) const { } // Not defined

private:
    Point *_p1, *_p2;    // Pointers to Points
};

#endif  // #if !defined(__RECT_P_H)
```

Notice that this declaration of the `rectangle_shape` class does not include the complete declaration of the `Point` class. This effectively hides the specification of the `Point` class from the users of the `rectangle_shape` class. The trick is to not invoke any member functions of the `Point` class within the declaration of the `rectangle_shape` class.

You can place the actual definition of the member functions of `rectangle_shape` in another file and include the declaration of the `Point` class there. For example, here is the definition of the member functions of the revised `rectangle_shape`:

```
#include "rect_p.h"
#include "point.h"

double rectangle_shape::compute_area(void) const
{
    Point p = *_p1 - *_p2;
    return p.xdistance() * p.ydistance();
}

rectangle_shape::rectangle_shape(const Point& p1, const Point& p2)
{
    _p1 = new Point(p1);
    _p2 = new Point(p2);
}

rectangle_shape::rectangle_shape(const rectangle_shape& r)
{
    _p1 = new Point(*r._p1);
    _p2 = new Point(*r._p2);
}

void rectangle_shape::operator=(const rectangle_shape& r)
{
    if(this != &r)
    {
        if(_p1 != 0) delete _p1;
        if(_p2 != 0) delete _p2;
        _p1 = new Point(*r._p1);
        _p2 = new Point(*r._p2);
    }
}

rectangle_shape::~rectangle_shape()
{
        delete _p1;
        delete _p2;
}
```

Although `rectangle_shape` is now implemented differently, you can use it as you would use the preceding version. For example, to create a rectangle with corners at (30, 20) and (130, 60), you write the following:

```
Point p1(30,20), p2(130,60); // Define the corner points
rectangle_shape r1(p1,p2);   // Create a rectangle
```

This version of the `rectangle_shape` class is much more complicated than the previous one, which uses instances of the `Point` class as member variables. The following explains this complexity:

■ The C++ compiler automatically creates and destroys class instances that are member variables of another class. The compiler also handles copy and assignment operations for such class member instances.

■ On the other hand, when you use pointers to class instances, you are responsible for creating and destroying these class instances. You also must define the copy constructor and the assignment operator so that these operations work correctly. Therefore, the revised version of the `rectangle_shape` class requires several additional member functions, including a destructor, a copy constructor, and an assignment operator.

Chapter 12, "Virtual Functions and Polymorphism," points out that, despite the additional work involved, managing pointers to class instances is necessary when you want to use polymorphism.

Public Interface to C++ Classes

Public interface to the classes in a library is as important as the relationships among the classes. The term *public interface* refers to the public member functions that enable you to access the capabilities of a class. Just as there is no standard C++ class library, there is no standard interface to C++ classes. If you are designing a class library, however, it is good practice to provide a minimal set of member functions. Some member functions are needed to ensure proper operations, others to provide a standard interface to the library. The following sections briefly describe some of the functions needed in each class's interface.

Default and Copy Constructors

Each class in the library should have a default constructor—a constructor that takes no argument. The default constructor should initialize any data members that the class contains. For example, the following is the default constructor for the `rectangle_shape` class:

```
class rectangle_shape : public shape
{
public:
    rectangle_shape() : _p1(0), _p2(0) {}
//...
private:
    Point *_p1, *_p2;
};
```

This constructor sets the data members _p1 and _p2 to zero.

The default constructor is important because it is called when arrays of class instances are allocated or when a class instance is defined without an initial value. For example, the `rectangle_shape::rectangle_shape()` constructor is called to initialize the `rectangle_shape` objects in the following:

```
rectangle_shape rects[16];
rectangle_shape r;
```

Each class should also include a copy constructor of the form `X(const X&)`, in which `X` is the name of the class. The copy constructor is called in the following cases:

■ When an object is initialized with another of the same type, such as the following:

```
rectangle_shape r2 = r;// where r is a rectangle_shape
```

■ When an object is passed by value to a function
■ When an object is returned by value from a function

As explained in Chapter 10, "Defining Operations on Objects," the copy constructor is necessary for classes that contain pointers as members. If you do not define a copy constructor for a class, the C++ compiler defines one that uses memberwise copy. When a class has pointers as members, memberwise copy causes pointers in two objects to point to identical areas of the free store.

Copying Objects

Often, it is necessary to make a copy of an object. For example, Chapter 11 shows how to create a linked list capable of holding `String` objects. A new class, `slink_string`, is created by multiply deriving from `single_link` and `String` classes. This `slink_string` class has links that enable its instances to reside in a `singly_linked_list`. To insert elements into the list, you must be able to create a copy of the object. In the `slink_string` class, this is done by the virtual member function `clone` (see Listings 11.3 and 11.7 in Chapter 11). In the terminology of other C++ libraries, such as the NIH Class Library, the `clone` function is equivalent to what is known as the `deepCopy` function because `clone` makes a complete copy of a `slink_string` object, including a copy of the character string allocated by the `String` class. For a class `X`, you can define the `clone` function as follows:

```
X* X::clone() { return new X(*this); }
```

As long as all classes define appropriate copy constructors, the `clone` function will make a duplicate copy of the object on the free store and return a pointer to the copy. When using functions (such as `clone`) that return a pointer to a dynamically created object, you must destroy the object by using the `delete` operator. This deletes the object, provided appropriate destructors are defined for all classes with member variables that are pointers.

Destructors

Defining a destructor is important for classes that include pointers as member variables. The destructor should reverse the effects of the constructor. If the constructor allocates memory by calling `new`, the destructor should deallocate the memory by using the `delete` operator. As explained in Chapter 12, if the class contains any virtual member functions, you should declare the destructor as virtual.

Assignment Operator

You should define the assignment operator for each class because derived classes do not inherit the assignment operator from the base class. In addition, if you do not define the assignment operator, the C++ compiler provides a default one that merely copies each member of one class instance to the corresponding member of another. If a class has member variables that are pointers to other class instances, such memberwise copying results in multiple pointers that point to a single area of the free store. When defining the assignment operator, you must do the following:

■ Handle the special case in which an object is assigned to itself

■ Return a reference to the target of the assignment so that statements of the type `x=y=z;` work properly

For an example, see the definition of the `String::operator=` function in Listing 11.2 in Chapter 11.

Input and Output Functions

Each class should also define two functions for I/O:

■ An output function that prints a formatted text representation of each member of an object on an output stream

■ An input function that can read from an input stream the output generated by the output function and reconstruct the object

These functions enable you to define the `<<` and `>>` operators so that they can accept instances of any class in the library as arguments. For example, you might use the names `print_out` and `read_in`, respectively, for the output and input functions. Each of these functions should take a single argument—the reference to the stream on which the I/O operation occurs. Then, for a class `X`, you define the output `operator<<` as follows:

```
#include <iostream.h>
//...
ostream& operator<<(ostream& os, const X& x)
{
    x.print_out(os);
    return os;
}
```

Summary

Organizing a C++ class library involves deciding the inheritance hierarchy of the classes, how one class uses the facilities of other classes, and what public member functions each class supports. There are two trends in picking an inheritance hierarchy for the classes in a library: the single tree model, in which all classes are ultimately derived from a single base class, and the forest model, in which there are multiple disjoint hierarchies of classes. The single tree model of inheritance hierarchy is patterned after the basic classes of the Smalltalk-80 programming language, which does not support multiple inheritance, as does C++. With multiple inheritance, you can mix and match classes from one or more class hierarchies and create custom classes.

Inheritance is not the only relationship among classes. A class also may incorporate instances of other classes as member variables. Although inheritance models the "is-a" relationship among classes, inclusion of class instances captures the "has-a" relationship. The inclusion is in the form of a member variable that is either a class instance or a pointer to a class instance. Defining a class instance as a member variable is simpler than maintaining a pointer to an instance, but the pointer is necessary to exploit polymorphism.

In addition to these relationships among the classes, each class in the library should present a consistent set of member functions so that there is a standard public interface to the library. This makes the library easy to use.

16

Using the General-Purpose Classes in MFC 3.0

Developing an application in C++ can be easy provided you can get most of the functionality of the program from existing C++ classes. Programmers embarking on large-scale C++ programming efforts typically begin by designing and developing a library of classes. Then they build the final software products using these classes. Clearly, you can reduce the time spent on software development if an off-the-shelf class library meets the needs of a software project and if the programmers working on the project can easily use the library. This is where class libraries can be useful.

To help programmers reap the benefits of a class library, Microsoft Visual C++ 2.0 comes with the Microsoft Foundation Class Library version 3.0 (MFC 3.0)—a collection of over 130 classes in three broad categories:

■ General-purpose classes, such as a set of template-based collection classes, dynamic arrays, linked lists, files, and strings, including features to support exception handling and archiving objects in files

■ Classes for building Microsoft Windows applications, including classes that provide an application framework, simplify the use of the Windows Graphics Device Interface (GDI), and support Object Linking and Embedding 2.0 (OLE 2.0)

■ Classes that simplify database programming with the Open Database Connectivity (ODBC), which provides a call-level interface for writing programs to access data from any database that provides an ODBC driver

This chapter provides a tutorial introduction to the general-purpose classes in MFC 3.0. In Chapter 18, "Using the Windows Programming Classes in MFC 3.0," you will find a complete overview of the classes used for building Windows applications. Chapter 31, "Using MFC 3.0 Database Classes for ODBC Programming," covers the database classes.

Visual C++ 2.0 includes the full source code for the Microsoft Foundation Classes. If you want, you can always browse through the source code to see exactly how the classes are defined and implemented.

> **NOTE**
>
> The template-based collection classes are new in MFC 3.0.

Overview of the General-Purpose Classes in MFC 3.0

Figure 16.1 shows the general-purpose classes in MFC 3.0. Here are some highlights of these classes:

■ Counting CObject, there are 42 general-purpose C++ classes. Of the eight stand-alone classes, CString, CTime, and CTimeSpan represent dynamically allocated strings, time, and time-difference, respectively.

■ Of the classes derived from CObject, CFile is for file I/O (both disk-based and in-memory files), and CException provides a subhierarchy of classes intended for handling exceptions.

■ Twenty-three other classes, derived from CObject, provide the facilities necessary to manage collections of objects in three different ways: indexed arrays, linked lists, or keyed maps (associative arrays or dictionaries).

■ Of the collection classes, three template-based classes—CArray, CList, CMap—can be instantiated to build arrays, lists, and maps, respectively, and to hold any type of objects, including built-in data types such as int and float. (See Chapter 13, "Advanced Topics in C++," for a description of C++'s template mechanism.)

The inheritance hierarchy of the general-purpose classes, shown in Figure 16.1, gives you a feel for the organization of these classes. Table 16.1 lists the general-purpose classes organized by category. The following sections summarize most of these classes by category.

FIGURE 16.1.
General-purpose classes in the Microsoft Foundation Class Version 3.0 Library.

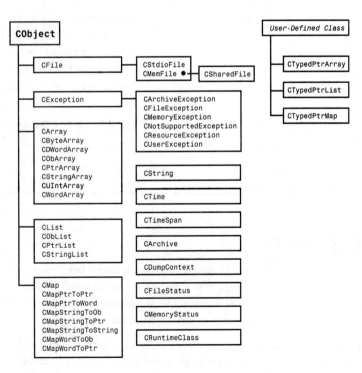

Table 16.1. General-purpose MFC classes listed by category.

Category	Classes
Strings	CString
Date and time	CTime, CTimeSpan
Arrays of objects	CByteArray, CWordArray, CDWordArray, CPtrArray, CObArray, CStringArray, CArray<Tstore,Taccess>, CTypedPtrArray<Tbase,Tstore>
Linked lists	CPtrList, CObList, CStringList, CList<Tstore,Taccess>, CTypedPtrList<Tbase,Tstore>
Mapping keys to values	CMapWordToPtr, CMapPtrToWord, CMapPtrToPtr, CMapStringToPtr, CMapStringToOb, CMapStringToString, CMapWordToOb, CMap<Tkey, TkeyRef, Tval, TvalRef>, CTypedPtrMap<Tbase, Tkey, Tvalue>
Exception handling	CException, CMemoryException, CArchiveException, CFileException, CResourceException, COleException, CNotSupportedException
File I/O operations	CFile, CStdioFile, CMemFile, CSharedFile, CFileStatus
Diagnostics support	CDumpContext, CMemoryState
Archiving objects	CArchive
Determining the class of an object at runtime	CRuntimeClass

Basic Data Types

The CString, CTime, and CTimeSpan classes represent basic data types: the CString class is reserved for character strings, CTime objects can store absolute dates and times, and CTimeSpan represents relative time (the difference between two times). These are stand-alone classes—unlike most other classes, they are not derived from the CObject class.

CString, CTime, and CTimeSpan classes are often used as members of other classes. For example, you might use CStrings to store the name and address of a customer in a Customer class:

```
class Customer: public CObject
{
// Various member functions...

protected:
    CString m_FirstName;
    CString m_LastName;
    CString m_Title;
    CString m_Company;
    CString m_Address1;
    CString m_Address2;
    CString m_City;
    CString m_State;
    CString m_PostalCode;
    CString m_Country;
};
```

Similarly, the CTime class can be used to store date and time information when needed.

The *CString* Class

The CString class represents a variable-length sequence of characters. The CString class essentially provides a complete replacement for C's null-terminated strings and the string manipulation functions of the standard C library. With CString, you need not worry about some common mistakes programmers make when they use C's string handling functions. For example, when you concatenate one string to another with strcat or copy one string to another with strcpy, you must ensure that the destination string has enough room to hold the result. With CString, copying is easy with the assignment operator (=) and you can concatenate two CStrings by "adding" them (adding the second to the first):

```
CString name = "GOES-8", ext = ".dat";
CString filename = name + ext; // filename = "GOES-8.dat"

CString new_name;              // An empty CString
new_name = filename;           // Copying...
```

With the CString class, you can manipulate arrays of characters without worrying about the capacity of the arrays.

With the CString class in the Microsoft Foundation Class Library, each CString object represents a unique value. For example, when you copy one CString to another, two unique sequences of characters exist, even though both sequences contain the same characters.

Because many functions require C-style null-terminated strings as arguments, CString maintains its string in a null-terminated format and provides the const char* operator that casts a CString as a const char*, thus enabling you to use a CString where a function expects a const char* argument. At the same time, you might want to use a C-style string (const char*) where a CString is expected. To handle this conversion, the CString class includes the constructor CString(const char*).

Using the CString class is straightforward. Listing 16.1 shows a short program that initializes a string and displays it.

Listing 16.1. TSTSTR.CPP. Sample program that demonstrates the CString class.

```
//------------------------------------------------------------
// File: tststr.cpp
// Example program showing how to use the "CString" class

#include <afx.h>
#include <iostream.h>

void main()
{
    try
    {
        CString s("Hello, ");

        char buf[256];
        cout << "Please enter your name: ";
        cin >> buf;

        s += buf;
        cout << s << "!" <<endl;
    }
    catch(CMemoryException *e)
    {
        cout << "Failed to allocate memory!" << endl;
    }
}
```

The program looks a bit longer because it includes the exception handling code to show how to catch exceptions raised by various member functions of the CString class.

There are three categories of some of the major capabilities of the CString class:

■ Constructors

■ Operators

■ Functions

There are over half a dozen constructors available to create a CString. A few interesting ones are the following:

■ Ctring();

creates a string of zero length.

■ CString(const CString& s);

is a copy constructor.

■ CString(TCHAR c, int n = 1);

creates a string with the character c repeated n times. (TCHAR is defined to be a data type capable of holding a character of the selected character set.)

■ `CString(LPCSTR lpsz);`

creates a string from a null-terminated C-style string.

Many string operations, such as copying and concatenating, that used to require function calls from the ANSI C library are now supported by operators. Here are some important operators:

■ `const CString& operator=(const CString& s);`

copies from `CString` s into this `CString` (the `CString` that appears on the left side of the assignment).

■ `const CString& operator+=(const CString& s);`

appends contents of s to this `Cstring`.

■ `const CString operator+=(LPCTSTR lpsz);`

appends the null-terminated C string `lpsz` to this `Cstring`.

■ `friend CString operator +(const CString& string1, const CString& string2);`

concatenates two `Cstrings`.

■ `friend CString operator +(const CString& string, LPCTSTR lpsz);`

creates a new `CString` by concatenating the `CString` s and the null-terminated C string `lpsz`.

■ `TCHAR operator[](int nIndex) const;`

returns a character at the specified position (index 0 means the first character).

■ `operator LPCTSTR() const;`

returns the null-terminated C string contained in the `Cstring`.

■ `BOOL operator==(const CString& s1, const CString& s2);`

returns a nonzero value (TRUE) if the `CStrings` s1 and s2 are equal (two strings are equal if they have the same length and if the character arrays contain the same sequence of characters); otherwise, it returns 0.

■ `BOOL operator<(const CString& s1, const CString& s2);`

returns a nonzero value (TRUE) if s1 is less than s2; it returns 0 otherwise.

■ `BOOL operator>(const CString& s1, const CString& s2);`

returns a nonzero value (TRUE) if s1 is greater than s2; it returns 0 otherwise.

Member functions of the `Cstring` class provide functionalities similar to those of the ANSI C library's string manipulation functions as well as some additional functionality required for Windows programming. Here are some of the member functions of `Cstring`:

■ `void AnsiToOem( );`
  `void OemToAnsi( );`

converts a string from ANSI character set to OEM character set and back (used in Windows programs; see Chapter 20, "Displaying Text in Windows," for a discussion of character sets).

■ `int Compare(LPCTSTR lpsz) const;`
`int CompareNoCase(LPCTSTR lpsz) const;`

compares this string with the null-terminated C string `lpsz` using `lstrcmp` or `lstrcmpi`.

■ `void Empty;`

makes this an empty string and frees the memory used to store the array of characters.

■ `int Find(TCHAR ch) const;`
`int Find(LPCTSTR lpszSub) const;`

locates the first occurrence of a character or a string and returns the starting position of that character or substring. Returns -1 if the search fails.

■ `TCHAR GetAt(int nIndex) const;`

returns a character at the specified position.

■ `int GetLength() const;`

returns a count of the characters (excluding the terminating null) in the current string.

■ `BOOL IsEmpty( ) const;`

returns a nonzero value if the `CString` object has zero length; otherwise, it returns `0`.

■ `CString Left(int n) const;`

returns a new `CString` containing the first `n` characters of this string.

■ `BOOL LoadString(UINT nID);`

loads up to 255 characters from a Windows string resource (identified by `nID`) into this string.

■ `void MakeLower();`
`void MakeUpper();`

converts the case of the string.

■ `CString Mid(int nFirst, int nCount) const;`

extracts a substring `nCount` characters long starting at index `nFirst`. (This function is similar to the `MID$` function in BASIC except that the indexes are zero-based in C++.)

■ `int ReverseFind(TCHAR ch) const;`

finds the last occurrence of the character `ch` in the string. Returns -1 if `ch` is not found.

■ `CString Right(int n) const;`

returns a new `CString` containing the last `n` characters of this string.

■ `void SetAt(int nIndex, TCHAR ch);`

inserts character `ch` into the location `nIndex`.

The *CTime* Class

The CTime class enables you to manipulate time in various ways. Listing 16.2 shows an example program that demonstrates how you can use CTime to display the current time. Note that the formatting of the time is controlled by a format string, which follows the formatting convention used by the ANSI C function strftime. The FormatGmt function converts the current time to Greenwich Mean Time (GMT) as dictated by the setting of the environment variable TZ, which indicates the time zone and the daylight saving time zone for use in converting a local time to GMT (GMT is now known as UTC or Universal Coordinated Time).

Listing 16.2. TSTTIME.CPP. Sample program that demonstrates the CTime class.

```
//---------------------------------------------------------------
// File: tsttime.cpp
// Sample program to illustrate the CTime class.

#include <afx.h>
#include <iostream.h>

void main()
{
// Create a CTime with today's time and display the time
// in local time as well as in GMT
    CTime now(time(NULL));
    cout << "Time now is: "
        << now.Format("%a %b %d, %Y %I:%M:%S %p ")
        << tzname[0] << tzname[1] << " ("
        << now.FormatGmt("%H:%M:%S") << " GMT)"
        << endl;

// Add 45 days to current time
// First create a CTimeSpan of 45 days (0 hours, 0 min., 0 sec)
    CTimeSpan duration(45, 0, 0, 0);
    now = now + duration;
    cout << "45 days from now it will be: "
        << now.Format("%a %b %d, %Y %I:%M:%S %p") << endl;
}
```

To compile and link this program, enter the following command at the command prompt:

```
cl /MT tsttime.cpp
```

The output of the program depends on the exact date and time when you run the program. Here is a typical output:

```
Time now is: Sat Sep 24, 1994 01:23:03 PM ESTEDT (17:23:03 GMT)
45 days from now it will be: Tue Nov 08, 1994 12:23:03 PM
```

Classes for File I/O

The CFile class supports unbuffered binary read and write operations to disk files. CFile offers a number of member functions for manipulating files. It also includes a number of static functions, such as GetStatus and Rename, that you can use to query the status of a file or rename it without opening the file.

The CFile class makes it easy to open a file, read a block of data from the file into a buffer, and write data from a buffer to a file. Listing 16.3 shows how to do this by copying the file c:\config.sys to another file.

Listing 16.3. TSTFILE.CPP. Sample program that demonstrates the CFile class.

```cpp
//-------------------------------------------------------------
// File: tstfile.cpp
// Sample program to illustrate the CFile class.

#include <afx.h>
#include <iostream.h>

const size_t BUFSIZE = 256;

void main()
{
    try
    {
// Open a CFile associated with a specific file
        CFile fin("c:\\config.sys", CFile::modeRead);

// Open another file
        CFile fout("junk.dat", CFile::modeWrite |
                               CFile::modeCreate);

// Read from one file and write to the other
        char buf[BUFSIZE];
        int n = fin.Read(buf, BUFSIZE);

        while (n > 0)
        {
            fout.Write(buf, n);
            n = fin.Read(buf, BUFSIZE);
        };

        fin.Close();
        fout.Close();
    }
    catch(CFileException *e)
    {
        cout << "File I/O Error: ";
        if(e->m_cause == CFileException::fileNotFound)
            cout << "File not found!" << endl;
        e->Delete();
    }
}
```

Another common use of a `CFile` object is to associate it with a `CArchive` object in archiving objects in a file:

```
// Open a file for writing. Use a try...catch block because
// file I/O exceptions may occur.

    try
    {
        CFile file(filename, CFile::modeCreate |
                            CFile::modeWrite);

// Now create an archive for storing objects.
// Once again use a try...catch pair.

        try
        {
            CArchive archive(&file, CArchive::store);

// Code to store objects in the archive,
//...
            archive.Close();
        }
        catch(CArchiveException *e)
        {
// Handle archiving errors,
// Close file and throw exception to caller,
            file.Close();
            throw;
        }
    }
    catch(CFileException *e)
    {
// Handle File I/O exceptions here,
        throw; // Send exception to caller
    }
```

A number of other classes are derived from `CFile` and are useful for specialized I/O:

■ `CStdioFile` represents a file opened for a buffered I/O using the C library function `fopen`.

■ `CMemFile` provides a block of memory that you can treat as a file.

■ `CSharedFile` is derived from `CMemFile` for use in Microsoft Windows OLE as a shared buffer.

A `CFileStatus` structure also stores status information about any `CFile` object, such as the creation date, modification date, size, attributes, and full pathname.

Collections of Objects

The Microsoft Foundation Class Library provides three distinct groups of classes to organize collections of objects:

- Arrays (CPtrArray, CObArray, CStringArray, CByteArray, CWordArray, CDWordArray, and two template-based classes: CArray<Tstore,Taccess>, CTypedPtrArray<Tbase,Tstore>). The array classes can store pointers to any user-defined objects, as well as void pointers, instances of CString, or other fixed-size objects such as 8-, 16-, and 32-bit values. Arrays store their contents in a sequential manner, and the contents are accessed through integer indexes.

- Linked lists (CPtrList, CObList, CStringList, and two template-based classes: CList<Tstore,Taccess>, CTypedPtrList<Tbase,Tstore>). The linked list classes (CPtrList, CObList, and CStringList) can hold void pointers, pointers to CObjects, and CStrings. Linked lists provide a fast method for inserting objects into the list.

- Maps with individual entries that associate a key object to a value object (CMapWordToPtr, CMapPtrToWord, CMapPtrToPtr, CMapStringToPtr, CMapStringToOb, CMapStringToString, CMapWordToOb, and two template-based classes: CMap<Tkey, TkeyRef, Tval, TvalRef>, CTypedPtrMap<Tbase, Tkey, Tvalue>). The map classes are essentially hash tables. You can use a key to access any value, and the access is fast compared to arrays or linked lists.

You should know about the MFC 3.0 container classes because your application might need containers, such as arrays, lists, and queues, capable of holding a variety of objects. When you need such containers, you can save yourself a lot of work by using the classes included in MFC 3.0.

Arrays

The array classes enable you to define one-dimensional arrays to store various types of data. MFC 3.0 includes the following array classes (the two template-based array classes are described in a later section):

- CByteArray is an array of bytes.
- CDWordArray is an array of 32-bit double-word values.
- CObArray is an array of CObject pointers (CObject*).
- CPtrArray is an array of void pointers (void*).
- CStringArray is an array of CString objects.
- CWordArray is an array of 16-bit words.

Each of these arrays can grow dynamically, if necessary. All the array classes— CByteArray, CDWordArray, CObArray, CPtrArray, CStringArray, and CWordArray—contain the same set of member functions. Only the data stored in the array elements varies.

The following is a summary of the member functions of the CObArray class. Because of the similarity among the array classes, you can use the documentation for the CObArray class to see how the member functions of any array class work. Of course, when using the documentation of the CObArray class for another array class such as CByteArray, you have to remember that CObArray stores pointers to CObject, but CByteArray stores the BYTE data type. Wherever you see the CObject* data type in CObArray, therefore, you have to replace it with BYTE.

Constructor and Destructor

```
CObArray();
```

Creates an empty array.

```
~CObArray();
```

Destroys the CObArray object. When a CobArray is destroyed, only the CObject pointers are gone. The actual CObjects still exist.

Attributes

```
int GetSize() const;
```

Returns the size—the number of elements in the array.

```
int GetUpperBound() const;
```

Returns the maximum array index (one less than the size because the first index is 0). GetUpperBound returns −1 if the array is empty.

```
void SetSize(int nNewSize, int nGrowBy = -1);
```

Sets the new size of the array and indicates the number of elements by which the array should grow.

Cleaning Up

```
void FreeExtra();
```

Releases any extra memory that was allocated when the array had grown.

```
void RemoveAll();
```

Removes all the pointers from the array.

```
void RemoveAt(int nIndex, int nCount = 1);
```

Removes nCount elements starting at the index nIndex, which should be between 0 and the value returned by GetUpperBound.

Accessing Elements

```
CObject*& ElementAt(int nIndex);
```

Returns a reference to the element at nIndex and is used internally to implement the access operators (operator[]).

```
CObject* GetAt(int nIndex) const;
```

Returns the CObject pointer at the specified index.

```
CObject* operator[](int nIndex) const;
```

Accesses the CObject pointer at the specified index and is a substitute for the GetAt function.

```
CObject*& operator[](int nIndex);
```

Gets or sets the element at a specified index.

```
void SetAt(int nIndex, CObject* newElement);
```

Sets the element at the specified index, nIndex, which should be between 0 and the value returned by GetUpperBound.

Growing the Array

```
int Add(CObject* newElement);
```

Adds the specified element to the end of the array and returns the index of the newly added element.

```
void InsertAt(int nIndex, CObject* newElement,
              int nCount = 1); // Insert nCount elements
void InsertAt(int nStartIndex, CObArray* pNewArray);
```

Inserts one or more elements into the CObArray starting at the specified index.

```
void SetAtGrow(int nIndex, CObject* newElement);
```

Sets the element at the specified index. Unlike SetAt, SetAtGrow grows the array automatically if necessary.

Lists

The list classes represent a doubly linked list data structure for storing various types of data. MFC 3.0 provides three list classes (the two template-based list classes are described in a later section):

- CObList is a doubly linked list of CObject pointers (CObject*).
- CPtrList is a doubly linked list of void pointers (void*).
- CStringList is a doubly linked list of CString objects.

All the linked-list classes—CObList, CPtrList, and CStringList—contain the same set of member functions; only the data stored in the list elements varies. Because of this similarity, you can use the documentation for one list class (such as the CObList class) to see how the member functions work for all the other linked-list classes. When you do, remember that CObList stores pointers to CObject, but the other classes store different data types.

The following is a summary of the member functions of the `CObList` class.

Constructor and Destructor

```
CObList(int nBlockSize=10);
```

Creates an empty `CObList` that grows by `nBlockSize` elements when necessary.

```
~CObList();
```

Destroys the pointers in the list and the `CObList` object. Note that this does not destroy the actual objects whose addresses are in the linked list.

Attributes

```
int GetCount() const;
```

Returns the number of elements in the list.

```
BOOL IsEmpty() const;
```

Returns `TRUE` if the list is empty; otherwise, it returns `FALSE`.

Peeking at Head or Tail

```
CObject*& GetHead();
CObject* GetHead() const;
```

Returns the element (or a reference to the element) at the head of the list.

```
CObject*& GetTail();
CObject* GetTail() const;
```

Returns the element at the end of the list.

Adding and Removing

```
POSITION AddHead(CObject* newElement); // Add this element
void AddHead(CObList* pNewList); // Add all elements from
                                 // pNewList to this list
```

Adds an element or all the elements in another `CObList` to the head of this list. When a single element is added, `AddHead` returns the `POSITION` of that element. This may throw a `CMemoryException`.

```
POSITION AddTail(CObject* newElement);
void AddTail(CObList* pNewList);
```

Adds an element or all the elements in another `CObList` to the end of this list. When a single element is added, `AddTail` returns the `POSITION` of that element. This may throw a `CMemoryException`.

```
void RemoveAll();
```

Removes all the elements from the list and frees the associated memory. The list is empty after you call RemoveAll. Remember that this removes the pointers to the CObjects but not the CObjects themselves. You must delete them before you call RemoveAll.

```
void RemoveAt(POSITION position);
```

Removes the element from the specified position.

```
CObject* RemoveHead();
```

Removes the element at the beginning of the list and returns that element.

```
CObject* RemoveTail();
```

Removes the element at the end of the list and returns that element.

Iterating Through the List

```
POSITION GetHeadPosition() const;
```

Returns the position of the element at the beginning of the list. The position returns NULL if the list is empty.

```
CObject*& GetNext(POSITION& rPosition);
CObject* GetNext(POSITION& rPosition) const;
```

Returns the element (or a reference to the element) at rPosition and updates rPosition to the next element in the list.

```
CObject*& GetPrev(POSITION& rPosition);
CObject* GetPrev(POSITION& rPosition) const;
```

Returns the element (or a reference to the element) at rPosition and updates rPosition to the previous element in the list.

```
POSITION GetTailPosition() const;
```

Returns the position of the element at the end of the list. The position returns NULL if the list is empty.

Accessing an Element

```
CObject*& GetAt(POSITION position);
CObject* GetAt(POSITION position) const;
```

Returns the element (or a reference to the element) at the specified position.

```
void SetAt(POSITION pos, CObject* newElement);
```

Sets the element at the specified position to newElement.

Inserting an Element

```
POSITION InsertAfter(POSITION position,
                     CObject* newElement);
```

Inserts an element after the specified position and returns the position of the newly added element.

```
POSITION InsertBefore(POSITION position,
                      CObject* newElement);
```

Inserts an element before the specified position and returns the position of the newly added element.

Finding an Element

```
POSITION Find(CObject* searchValue,
              POSITION startAfter = NULL) const;
```

Searches the list to find an element matching searchValue, starting at the position startAfter. This also returns the position of the matching element or NULL if no matching element exists.

```
POSITION FindIndex(int nIndex) const;
```

Returns the POSITION for an element at a specified index in the list.

Maps

The map classes enable you to define one-dimensional arrays to store various types of data. MFC 3.0 includes the following array classes (the two template-based array classes are described in a later section):

- CMapPtrToPtr maps a void pointer to another void pointer. (In other words, you can look up a void pointer using another void pointer as a key.)
- CMapPtrToWord class maps a void pointer (void*) to a 16-bit WORD.
- CMapStringToOb class maps a CString to a CObject pointer (CObject*). (In other words, you can look up a CObject pointer using a CString as a key.)
- CMapStringToPtr class maps a CString to a void pointer (void*).
- CMapStringToString class maps one CString to another CString.
- CMapWordToOb class maps a 16-bit WORD to a CObject pointer (CObject*).
- CMapWordToPtr class maps a 16-bit WORD to a void pointer (void*).

All the map classes—CMapPtrToPtr, CMapPtrToWord, CMapStringToOb, CMapStringToPtr, CMapStringToString, CMapWordToOb, and CMapWordToPtr—contain the same set of member functions; only the data types of keys and values vary. Because of this similarity, you can use the documentation for one class (such as the CMapStringToOb class) to see how the member functions work in the other map classes. Remember that CMapStringToOb maps CStrings to CObject pointers, but the key and value types of the other map classes vary.

The following is a summary of the member functions of the CMapStringToOb class with the member functions grouped by similar functionality.

Constructor and Destructor

```
CMapStringToOb(int nBlockSize=10);
```

Constructs a `CMapStringToOb` collection that grows `nBlockSize` entries at a time.

```
~CMapStringToOb();
```

Destroys the `CMapStringToOb` collection, including all `CString` objects used as keys in the map. However, the `CObject` objects are not destroyed.

Attributes

```
int GetCount() const;
```

Returns the total number of key-to-value associations in the map.

```
BOOL IsEmpty() const;
```

Returns `TRUE` if the map is empty.

Operations

```
UINT GetHashTableSize() const;
```

Returns the size of the internal hash table used to map a key to a value.

```
void GetNextAssoc(
    POSITION& rNextPosition, // Get key-value at this position
                             // and update position afterward
    CString& rKey,           // Retrieved key goes here
    CObject*& rValue) const; // Retrieved value goes here
```

Retrieves the key-value pair at the `POSITION` indicated by `rNextPosition` and updates `rNextPosition` to the next pair. The retrieved key and value are in `rKey` and `rValue`, respectively.

```
POSITION GetStartPosition() const;
```

Returns a `POSITION` value that you can use with the `GetNextAssoc` function to iterate all the key-value pairs in the map.

```
UINT HashKey(LPCTSTR key) const;
```

Returns the result when applying the hash function to the key.

```
void InitHashTable(UINT hashSize, BOOL bAllocNow = TRUE);
```

Initializes a new hash table of the specified size and deletes the old hash table.

```
BOOL Lookup(LPCTSTR key, CObject*& rValue) const;
```

Retrieves the value corresponding to the specified key. The retrieved value is in `rValue`. It returns `TRUE` if the search succeeds; otherwise, it returns `FALSE`.

```
CObject*& operator[](LPCTSTR key);
```

Sets the value corresponding to a key:

```
CMapStringToOb map;
// Assume Widget is a class derived from CObject
map["Item 1"] = new Widget(1);
```

Operator serves as a convenient substitute for the SetAt function.

```
void RemoveAll();
```

Removes all key-value pairs in the map and destroys the keys only.

```
BOOL RemoveKey(LPCTSTR key);
```

Removes the key-value pair corresponding to a specified key. If the entry is found and removed, RemoveKey returns TRUE; otherwise, it returns FALSE.

```
void SetAt(LPCTSTR key, CObject* newValue);
```

Sets the value corresponding to a key. If that key is not found, SetAt inserts the key-value pair as a new entry to the map.

Template-Based Collection Classes

Prior to version 3.0, the Microsoft Foundation Class library included only the non-template-based container classes that were derived from the CObject base class. The problem with these container classes is that they can hold only specific types of data and items derived from CObject. For example, you cannot store any of the built-in data types, such as float, int, or double, in the older, non-template container classes. The template keyword, which is part of the proposed ANSI C++ standard and supported by Visual C++ 2.0, provides a much better method of defining container classes that can hold any type of objects, including char, float, double, and int.

MFC 3.0 includes a number of new container classes that use the template mechanism to define flexible container classes that can store anything from built-in C++ types, such as int and double, to your own class types. Class templates are class definitions parameterized by a data type. Although the older, non-template containers are supported for compatibility with existing code, Microsoft recommends that you use the template-based classes in new programs.

MFC 3.0 provides three types of template-based container classes:

■ Array: CArray<Tstore,Taccess> and CTypedPtrArray<Tbase,Tstore> classes

■ List: CList<Tstore,Taccess> and CTypedPtrList<Tbase,Tstore> classes

■ Map: CMap<Tkey, TkeyRef, Tval, TvalRef> and CTypedPtrMap<Tbase, Tkey, Tvalue> classes

These classes are declared in the header file <afxtempl.h>.

Array Template Classes

The array template class CArray<Tstore,Taccess> enables you to declare an array capable of storing any type of data. The parameter Tstore denotes the type of data stored as elements of the array. The second parameter, Taccess, specifies how the elements of the array are passed to and returned from member functions of the Array class, such as Add and GetAt. Thus, if you want to define an array to hold objects of a class named CPerson, you write the following:

```
CArray<CPerson, CPerson&> persons;
```

This means that you want to store CPerson objects in the array named persons but you want each element of the array to be accessed as a reference to CPerson. For a simpler data type such as int, you might store and access the objects directly. Thus, you might define arrays of int variables as follows:

```
CArray<int,int> ia1;
CArray<int,int> ia2;
CArray<int,int> ia2;
```

However, a better way is to define a new type name using typedef and then use that name in subsequent definitions:

```
// Define a type name for a list of integers
typedef CArray<int,int> IntegerArray;
// ...
// Use the type name to declare arrays of integers
IntegerArray ia1;
//...
IntegerArray ia2;
IntegerArray ia3;
```

With this scheme, you can have a more readable name for each new type of list and also can change the implementation of the list to another type by changing the typedef statement. For example, if you write your own class template for an array and call it MyArray<T>, you can use that as the basis for the array of integers by simply rewriting the typedef statement:

```
typedef MyArray<int> IntegerArray;
```

without changing any of the array declarations that use the type name IntegerArray.

SET AN INITIAL ARRAY SIZE FOR EFFICIENCY

To avoid frequent "growth" of the array through memory reallocation, you should call the SetSize member function to establish an initial size before using the array. If you do not set an initial size, adding elements to the array causes it to grow through an inefficient process of memory reallocation and copying.

Listing 16.4 shows a simple program that illustrates the use of the CArray template class. Use the following command at a command prompt to compile and link this example:

```
cl /MT iarray.cpp
```

When you run the program shown in Listing 16.4, it produces the following output:

```
ivec[0] = 10
ivec[1] = 9
ivec[2] = 8
After removing second element:
ivec[0] = 10
ivec[1] = 8
ivec[2] = 0
```

As you can see, after the second element is removed, the array is automatically compacted (that means the third element moves into the second position, the fourth one goes to the third place, and so on).

Listing 16.4. IARRAY.CPP. Test program to demonstrate the CArray class.

```cpp
//--------------------------------------------------------------
// File: iarray.cpp
// Sample program that illustrates the Array template class.

#include <afx.h>
#include <afxtempl.h>
#include <iostream.h>

typedef CArray<int,int> IntegerVector;

void main()
{
    IntegerVector ivec;

// Set initial size to 16 and let it grow by 8 elements at
// a time
    ivec.SetSize(16,8);

    int i;
    for(i = 0; i < 3; i++)
        ivec[i] = 10-i;

// Display the elements
    for(i = 0; i < 3; i++)
        cout << "ivec[" << i << "] = " << ivec[i] << endl;

// Remove the second element
    ivec.RemoveAt(1);

// Display elements again
    cout << "After removing second element: " << endl;
    for(i = 0; i < 3; i++)
        cout << "ivec[" << i << "] = " << ivec[i] << endl;
}
```

The CTypedPtrArray<Tbase,Tstore> class is a template class designed to provide type-safe storage and access for objects of class CPtrArray or CObArray. The Tbase parameter should be one of CPtrArray or CObArray, and Tstore denotes the type of objects being stored in the Tbase array.

Usually, when you use the CObArray class to store pointers to objects derived from CObject, you have to cast each retrieved pointer before use. For example, suppose you store, in a CObArray, pointers to objects of a class named Command (derived from CObject). When you access these pointers from the array, you have to cast them as shown in the following code fragment:

```
class Command : public CObject
{
public:
    Command(const char *s);
//...
};
//...
    CObArray cmd_array;
    cmd_array.SetSize(10);
    cmd_array[0] = new Command("help");
// Access the first command (notice the type cast)
    Command *p_cmde = (Command*)x.GetAt(0);
```

If you use the CTypedPtrArray<Tbase,Tstore> template class, you can avoid the type cast and write this simple example as follows:

```
// Define an array type that stores pointers to
// Command objects in a CobArray container
typedef CTypedPtrArray<CObArray,Command*> CommandArray;
//...
    CommandArray cmd_array;
    cmd_array.SetSize(10);
    cmd_array[0] = new Command;
// Get the first element (no type cast needed)
    Command *p_cmd = cmd_array.GetAt(0);
```

As you can see, when you use CTypedPtrArray rather than CPtrArray or CObArray, you avoid the explicit type casts and eliminate errors caused by mismatched pointer types.

List Template Classes

The template version of the list class, CList<Tstore,Taccess>, enables you to declare a doubly linked list to store any type of data you want. Listing 16.5 shows an example program that illustrates how to use the CList class to store objects of a class named Command (that is not derived from CObject). The steps in defining and using a list of these objects are illustrated by the following code fragment:

```
typedef CList<Command, Command&>   CommandList;

CommandList   cl;     // A command list

// Create a Command
    Command quit("quit", 0);
```

```
// Add the Command to the list
    cl.AddTail(quit);
```

You can compile and link the program shown in Listing 16.5 with the following command (enter the command at a command prompt):

```
cl /MT lists.cpp
```

When run, the program generates the following output:

```
------ Command List ------
0    quit
2    create_new_anim
1    load_file
4    refresh
3    play_sound_file
```

Listing 16.5. LISTS.CPP. Test program to demonstrate the CList template class.

```
//-------------------------------------------------------------
// File: lists.cpp
// Sample program that illustrates the CList template class.

#include <afx.h>
#include <afxtempl.h>
#include <iostream.h>
#include <string.h>

const short CMDLEN = 16;

class Command
{
public:
    Command() : code(0) { cmd[0] = '\0';}
    Command(const char* cs, short _code) : code(_code)
    {
        short len = strlen(cs);
        if(len < CMDLEN)
            strcpy(cmd, cs);
        else
        {
            strncpy(cmd, cs, CMDLEN-1);
            cmd[CMDLEN-1] = '\0';
        }
    }

    void print(ostream& os) const
    {
        os << code << "     " << cmd;
    }

private:
// Internal details of the command
    char        cmd[CMDLEN];
    short       code;
};
```

```
// Prototype for stream insertion operator for commands
ostream& operator<< (ostream& os, const Command& c);

typedef CList<Command, Command&>   CommandList;

CommandList   cl;     // A command list
//-----------------------------------------------------------
// m a i n

void main()
{
// Create a few Commands
    Command quit("quit", 0);
    Command anim("create_new_animation", 2);
    Command load("load_file", 1);
    Command refresh("refresh", 4);
    Command sound("play_sound_file", 3);

// Add the Commands to the list
    cl.AddTail(quit);
    cl.AddTail(anim);
    cl.AddTail(load);
    cl.AddTail(refresh);
    cl.AddTail(sound);

// Go through the command list and display the items
    POSITION pos = cl.GetHeadPosition();

    cout << "------ Command List ------" << endl;

    while(pos != NULL)
    {
        cout << cl.GetNext(pos) << endl;
    }
}
//-----------------------------------------------------------
// ostream&  o p e r a t o r < < ( ostream&,  const Command& )
// Stream insertion operator for the Command class

ostream& operator<< (ostream& os, const Command& c)
{
    c.print(os);
    return os;
}
```

Like the `CTypedPtrArray<Tbase,Tstore>` template class, the `CTypedPtrList<Tbase,Tstore>` class provides a wrapper around the `CObList` and `CPtrList` classes. For example, consider the problem of storing objects of type `Field` (assume this to be a class derived from `CObject`) in a `CObList`. One approach to building a type-safe list `classn` for `Field` objects is to derive a new class, `FieldList`, from `CObList` and add member functions that provide access to the contents of the list as pointers to `Field` objects. Here is a sample declaration of such a `FieldList` class:

```
class Field : public CObject
```

```
{
public:
    Field() {};
//...
};

class FieldList : public CObList
{
public:
    FieldList();

// Return pointer to first Field
    Field* first()
    {
        pos = GetHeadPosition();
        return (Field*) GetNext(pos);
    }

// Return pointer to last field (notice type cast)
    Field* last()
    {
        pos = GetTailPosition();
        return (Field*) GetPrev(pos);
    }
// Other member functions...
//...
private:
    POSITION  pos; // Current item's position
};
```

As you can see, the member functions `first` and `last` are essentially type-safe wrapper functions that do their job by properly type casting the results of calls to GetNext and GetPrev, which are member functions of the base class, CObList.

The `CTypedPtrList` template class enables you to define such type-safe wrapper classes with minimal effort. For example, to create a class that stores Field pointers in a CObList class and enables you to access them conveniently, you write the following:

```
typedef CTypedPtrList<CObList, Field*> FieldList;

FieldList flist;

// Save Field pointers in the list
// Call GetNext or GetPrev to retrieve elements from list
```

As you can see from the example code, to instantiate a CTypedPtrList<Tbase,Tstore>, you have to provide two parameters:

- ■ Tbase is either CObList or CPtrList.

- ■ Tstore is the type of item being stored in the Tbase class that was specified as the first parameter.

Map Templates

The CMap<Tkey, TkeyRef, Tval, TvalRef> template class is useful for defining any types of maps—associations of keys to values—where the key and value can be of any data type. For example, an identifying number, such as a driver's license number, could be a key and the name of a person could be the associated value. Alternatively, a person's name could be the key and the associated value could be a structure containing pertinent information about that person.

To use a type of object used as the key, you should define a HashKey function with the following prototype:

```
UINT HashValue(KeyType) const;
```

where *KeyType* denotes the type of objects being used as a key.

The operator == also must be defined for the key objects. The reason for requiring the HashKey function is that the key-value associations are stored in a hash table. The HashKey function maps a key to a hash value that serves as an index for the hash table. The equality operator == is needed because keys are used to look up values from the associations stored in a map, and this requires comparing keys to one another.

Listings 16.6 and 16.7 illustrate the use of the CMap class template. Listing 16.6 shows the definition of a class named ID that is used as a key. Essentially, ID is a four-character identifier. The HashKey function for ID is shown in Listing 16.7, which defines a map to store IDs associated with an integer value. Notice that the HashKey function evaluates the exclusive-OR of all four characters in ID to generate the hash value. The program stores a number of key-value associations in the map. It also illustrates how to look up values using a key.

Listing 16.6. ID.H. A data type used as a key in a map.

```
//---------------------------------------------------------------
// File: id.h
// A class that defines a 4-character identifier

#if !defined (__ID_H)
#define __ID_H

const short IDLEN = 4;
struct ID
{
    ID() { ids[0] = ids[1] = ids[2] = ids[3] = 'X';}

    ID(const char* s)
    {
        short len = strlen(s);
        if(len <= IDLEN)
            strcpy(ids, s);
        else
            strncpy(ids, s, IDLEN);
        ids[IDLEN] = '\0';
    }
```

```
    operator==(const ID& id) const
    {
        return (strcmp(id.ids, ids) == 0);
    }

    void print(ostream& os) const
    {
        os << ids;
    }

// Data for IDs
    char ids[5];
};

ostream& operator<<(ostream& os, const ID& id)
{
    id.print(os);
    return os;
}

#endif
```

Listing 16.7. TSTMAP.CPP. Test program to demonstrate the CMap class.

```
//--------------------------------------------------------------
// File: tstmap.cpp
// Sample program that illustrates the CMap template class

#include <afx.h>
#include <afxtempl.h>
#include <stdio.h>
#include <iostream.h>
#include "id.h"

typedef CMap<ID,ID&,int,int> IdInfo;

UINT HashKey(struct ID id);

//--------------------------------------------------------------
void main()
{
    IdInfo info;
    info.InitHashTable(128);

    info[ID("Naba")] = 1;
    info[ID("BOOK")] = 15;
    info[ID("OOPC")] = 8;
    info[ID("XWSP")] = 7;
    info[ID("MSVC")] = 2;
    info[ID("ABCD")] = 4;

// Display contents of the map
    cout << "There are " << info.GetCount() << " items." << endl;
```

```
        POSITION pos = info.GetStartPosition();
        ID key;
        int value;

        while(pos != NULL)
        {
            info.GetNextAssoc(pos, key, value);
            cout << "Key = " << key  << " "
                << "Value = " << value << endl;
        }
        cout << endl;

// Retrieve a value using a key
        char input[80];

        while(1)
        {
            cout << "Enter key (or 'quit' to exit): ";
            cin >> input;

            if(strnicmp(input, "quit", 4) == 0) break;

            if(info.Lookup(ID(input), value))
            {
                cout << "Value for " << input
                    << " = " << value << endl;
            }
            else
            {
                cout << "Key: " << input << " not found!" << endl;
                cout << "Enter integer value for this key: ";

                cin >> value;
                info[ID(input)] = value;

                cout << input << " : " << value
                    << " <- added." << endl;
            }
        }
        info.RemoveAll();
}
//-------------------------------------------------------------
// H a s h K e y

UINT HashKey(struct ID id)
{
    return id.ids[0]^id.ids[1]^id.ids[2]^id.ids[3];
}
```

You can compile and link this program with the following command at a command prompt:

```
cl /MT tstmap.cpp
```

Here is a sample output of the program (user's input shown in bold):

```
There are 6 items.
```

```
Key = ABCD Value = 4
Key = BOOK Value = 15
Key = MSVC Value = 2
Key = XWSP Value = 7
Key = OOPC Value = 8
Key = Naba Value = 1

Enter key (or 'quit' to exit): Leha
Key: Leha not found!
Enter integer value for this key: 10
Leha : 10 <- added.
Enter key (or 'quit' to exit): NOAA
Key: NOAA not found!
Enter integer value for this key: 100
NOAA : 100 <- added.
Enter key (or 'quit' to exit): Leha
Value for Leha = 10
Enter key (or 'quit' to exit): quit
```

Common Functionality from *CObject*

As you can see from Figure 16.1, most of the classes in the Microsoft Foundation Class Library inherit from the `CObject` base class, which provides support for the following activities:

- Identifying an object's type at runtime
- Storing objects in and retrieving them from a file
- Printing diagnostic messages at runtime

All classes derived from `CObject` inherit these capabilities. If you derive a class from `CObject`, your class also can take advantage of `CObject`'s capabilities through inheritance. As you will see, the Microsoft Foundation Class Library provides a number of macros and a step-by-step approach for using these capabilities.

RUN-TIME TYPE INFORMATION IN ANSI STANDARD C++

The ANSI C++ standards committee has accepted for inclusion in C++ the Run-Time Type Information (RTTI) feature that enables you to determine the type of an object at runtime. The new feature introduces two new operators: `dynamic_cast` and `typeid`. MFC 3.0 provides its own runtime class identification mechanism, but you should expect Microsoft to support these new features in future versions of Visual C++ and MFC.

Runtime Class Identification

Runtime class identification enables you to determine an object's type at runtime. For example, consider a hierarchy of classes representing graphics shapes. The shapes start with a base class shape from which you derive classes, such as `circle` and `rectangle`, which represent specific shapes. If you derive the shape class hierarchy from `CObject` and follow a cookbook approach to enable the runtime class identification feature, you can write code like this:

```
    shape *p_s;
// ...

// Assume that p_s points to a "shape" object (that
// may be any one of the shapes derived from the
// "shape" class). Assuming that the shape class hierarchy
// includes support for "runtime class identification,"
// here's how you would test the exact type of the shape
// object.

    if(p_s->IsKindOf(RUNTIME_CLASS(circle)))
    {
// OK to cast base class pointer p_s as a pointer to a "circle."
        circle *p_c = (circle*)p_s;
// ...
    }
```

The `IsKindOf` member function returns the `TRUE` constant if the object is of the class that its argument specifies or if the object derives from the specified class. The argument to the `IsKindOf` function is specified in terms of the `RUNTIME_CLASS` macro.

To include support for runtime class identification in a class, follow these steps:

1. Derive the class from `CObject`.

2. Include the `DECLARE_DYNAMIC` macro in the class declaration. For example, you declare the `shape` and the `circle` classes as follows:

```
#include <afx.h>

class shape : public CObject
{
    DECLARE_DYNAMIC(shape)
public:
// Other members...
};


class circle: public shape
{
    DECLARE_DYNAMIC(circle)
public:
// Other members...
};
```

3. Include the `IMPLEMENT_DYNAMIC` macro for each class in the source file (the .cpp file) where you define the member functions of the class:

```
IMPLEMENT_DYNAMIC(shape, CObject)
IMPLEMENT_DYNAMIC(circle, shape)
```

Once you follow these steps, you can use the IsKindOf member function and the RUNTIME_CLASS macro to compare the class of any shape object at runtime.

NOTE

The runtime class identification feature of the Microsoft Foundation Class Library works properly in single inheritance hierarchies only.

Persistence

Recall that persistence is the capability of storing objects in a file and retrieving them later. You can use persistence to store complex objects in disk files with minimal effort.

The Microsoft Foundation Class Library supports persistence through a process that Microsoft calls *serialization* —the process by which an object writes its current state to a CArchive object that represents the persistent (permanent) storage. When your program retrieves an object, the object is also responsible for reading its state back from the CArchive object. You can add the serialization functionality to any class derived from CObject or one of its derived classes with the following steps:

1. Include the DECLARE_SERIAL macro in the class declaration.
2. Provide a default constructor—a constructor that takes no arguments—for the class.
3. Include the IMPLEMENT_SERIAL macro in the C++ source file that implements the member functions of the class.
4. Define the Serialize member function for the class.

The DECLARE_SERIAL macro has the following syntax:

```
DECLARE_SERIAL(class_name)
```

Include DECLARE_SERIAL in the declaration of any class (derived from CObject) that you plan to archive (serialize). The *class_name* argument is the name of the class that will have serialization capability.

Including the DECLARE_SERIAL macro automatically incorporates the DECLARE_DYNAMIC macro as well, because runtime type determination is a necessary part of the scheme used by the Microsoft Foundation Class Library to archive and restore objects.

As an example, consider a class named shape that you plan to serialize. You must declare the shape class as follows:

```
#include <afx.h>

class shape : public CObject
{
    DECLARE_SERIAL(shape)
public:
// Member functions...

// Declare the Serialize function
    void Serialize(CArchive& archive);

private:
    CString name;    // a sample member
// Other members...
};
```

In the class body, you include the DECLARE_SERIAL macro as shown and specify a member function named Serialize. In the file implementing the shape class, include an IMPLEMENT_SERIAL macro and define the Serialize function:

```
IMPLEMENT_SERIAL(shape, CObject, 100)
void shape::Serialize(CArchive& archive)
{
// First call the "Serialize" function of the base class
    CObject::Serialize(archive);

// Now store this object in archive (one data member
// at a time). Here you show only one member being archived.
    if(archive.IsStoring())
        archive << name;
    else
        archive >> name;
}
```

As you can see, the first two arguments to the IMPLEMENT_SERIAL macro are the names of the class being serialized and its base class. The third argument is a called a *schema number*—this serves as a version number for the object. When loading an object from an archive, the Microsoft Foundation Class Library's serialization code checks this schema number against the schema number of the object in the file and throws an exception if the numbers do not match.

The actual archiving or restoration of an object requires a CArchive object. You first create a CFile object by opening a file and associating a CArchive with that CFile. For example, you serialize a shape object as follows:

```
    shape s1;

// Archive an object. First open a file and associate
// an archive with the file
    cout << "Archiving..." << endl;
    CFile file("shapes.sav", CFile::modeWrite |
                        CFile::modeCreate);
    CArchive archive(&file, CArchive::store);

    archive << &s1;
    archive.Close();
    file.Close();
```

To reload the shape from the file to an object, use the following code:

```
// Now restore a shape.
    cout << "Restoring..." << endl;

    CFile f2("shapes.sav", CFile::modeRead);
    CArchive ar(&f2, CArchive::load);

    shape *p_s = new shape;
    ar >> p_s;
    ar.Close();
    f2.Close();
```

Diagnostic Services

If you examine <afx.h>, the main header file of the Microsoft Foundation Class Library, you find functions and macros defined within #ifdef _DEBUG ... #endif blocks. Additionally, most classes contain member functions and operators defined inside #ifdef _DEBUG ... #endif blocks. These functions and macros are useful for displaying the contents of objects at runtime. The idea behind these diagnostic facilities is similar to inserting calls to printf in C programs to display information that might help pinpoint errors.

Because these diagnostic operators and functions are enclosed in #ifdef _DEBUG ... #endif blocks, you can use them only if you compile your programs with the _DEBUG macro defined. A convenient way to define the _DEBUG macro is to use the /D command-line option of the Visual C++ 2.0 compiler. Just include the /D_DEBUG flag when you invoke the compiler.

Besides defining the _DEBUG macro, you also must link with the debug version of the Microsoft Foundation Class Library. This step happens automatically if you either enable debugging in the Visual Workbench or use the /Zi option with the command-line compiler.

Dumping an Object's Contents

The Dump member function, defined when you compile your program with the /D_DEBUG flag, is useful for dumping the contents of an object—sending the textual representation of the object to an I/O stream. To use this feature, call the Dump function with a CDumpContext object as argument. The CDumpContext class serves as the I/O stream where the output of Dump appears. The Microsoft Foundation Class Library includes a predefined CDumpContext object named afxDump that you can use for diagnostic output. For example, if you derive a class named Customer from CObject, you can use its Dump function:

```
// Assume that the Customer's constructor takes two string arguments.
    Customer p_cust = new Customer("Naba", "Barkakati");

// Dump the contents... only when DEBUG is defined.

#ifdef _DEBUG
    p_cust->Dump(afxDump);
#endif
```

DUMPING TO afxDump IN WINDOWS NT

In Windows NT, calling the Dump function with afxDump as the argument causes output to be sent to the debugger, if present. Otherwise, nothing happens when you dump to afxDump.

Although you will get a display of a limited amount of fixed information from the default Dump function inherited by the Customer class, you should override the Dump function to display useful information about the Customer class. For the Customer class, the following code fragment illustrates how to override Dump:

```
class Customer: public CObject
{
public:

    Customer(const char* first, const char* last) :
        m_FirstName(first), m_LastName(last) {}

#ifdef _DEBUG
    virtual void Dump(CDumpContext& d) const;
#endif

private:
    CString m_FirstName;
    CString m_LastName;
};

// Define the Dump function...only when _DEBUG is defined.

#ifdef _DEBUG
void Customer::Dump(CDumpContext& d) const
{
// Call the Dump function of the base class first.
    CObject::Dump(d);

// Now "dump" the contents of this object....
// Use the << operator.
    d << "First name: " << m_FirstName << "\n";
    d << "Last name:  " << m_LastName  << "\n";
}
#endif
```

The *TRACE* and *ASSERT* Macros

The TRACE and ASSERT macros provide yet another set of debugging tools. If you compile your program with the /D_DEBUG flag, TRACE prints its string argument to the afxDump diagnostic output. When the _DEBUG macro is not defined, TRACE does nothing. TRACE is useful for printing status messages such as the following:

```
    TRACE("About to load form...\n");
// Code to load form....
    TRACE("Form loaded\n");
```

The ASSERT macro is similar to the assert macro in ANSI standard C. ASSERT evaluates its argument and, if that argument is zero, prints a message and terminates the program. Like TRACE, ASSERT works only when the _DEBUG macro is defined. Therefore, you can make liberal use of TRACE and ASSERT in your programs and use their diagnostic services by compiling the programs with the /D_DEBUG flag. When the programs are debugged, you can release them to the outside world by recompiling the programs without the /D_DEBUG flag.

ASSERT is useful for testing the validity of function arguments and object types. For example, to ensure that a pointer argument to a function is not NULL, you write the following:

```
void func(shape* s)
{
    ASSERT(s != NULL);  // Exit if s is a NULL pointer
//...
}
```

Other Diagnostic Support

As you have seen from the previous sections, classes derived from CObject inherit the capability of dumping the contents of an instance to an I/O stream. Macros such as TRACE and ASSERT can also help debug your programs. In addition to these diagnostic capabilities, the Microsoft Foundation Class Library includes the CMemoryState class to detect errors in memory allocation and deallocation. One common error with dynamic memory allocation occurs when you allocate memory (by using the new operator) and forget to delete the memory. This error is commonly referred to as a *memory leak*. You can use CMemoryState objects to detect memory leaks and obtain information about memory. The following code fragment illustrates the basic approach for using CMemoryState objects:

```
    CMemoryState first, second, diff;

// Take a "snapshot" of memory.
    first.Checkpoint();

// Code that allocates and deallocates memory goes here.
//...

// Take a second snapshot.
    second.Checkpoint();

// If there is any difference between the two snapshots,
// there must be some memory leak.

    if(diff.Difference(first, second))
    {
        TRACE("Memory leaked");
        diff.DumpStatistics();
    }
```

The DumpStatistics function displays useful information about blocks of memory that still remain allocated and about the total memory used between the two snapshots of memory.

> **NOTE**
>
> MFC 3.0 uses the standard C++ exception handling mechanism with the try, catch, and throw reserved keywords. Earlier versions of MFC relied on a set of macros for exception handling.

Exception Handling in MFC 3.0

As explained in Chapter 13, the ANSI X3J16 Committee is working on standardizing C++, and one of the Committee's additions to C++ will be a standard mechanism for exception handling (recall that exceptions refer to error conditions in your program). The ANSI C++ standard will use the reserved keywords throw, catch, and try for exception handling. Chapter 13 explains the proposed syntax for exception handling. Prior to version 3.0, the Microsoft Foundation Class Library provided support for exception handling with the TRY, CATCH, AND_CATCH, and END_CATCH macros that mimic the ANSI C++ syntax. MFC 3.0 supports the standard C++ exception handling mechanism that relies on the reserved keywords throw, catch, and try. Although the old macros (with uppercase names) are still supported, Microsoft recommends that you use the standard C++ keywords for exeception handling.

> **ENABLING C++ EXCEPTION HANDLING IN VISUAL C++ 2.0**
>
> By default, C++ exception handling is disabled in Visual C++ 2.0. To enable C++ exception handling, select Enable Exception Handling in the C++ Language category of the C/C++ tab of the Project Settings dialog box. An equivalent way is to use the /GX compiler option.

Catching Exceptions

The following code fragment shows an example of exception handling in code that uses MFC 3.0 classes:

```
#include <afx.h>
#include <iostream.h>

//...

    try
    {
// In this block, place code that might cause an
// exception

// For example, try "archiving" an object to a file
//...
    }
```

```
    catch(CFileException* e)
    {
// Test e->m_cause for exact cause of error.
        cerr << "Error opening file!" << endl;
        exit(1);
    }
    catch(CArchiveException* e)
    {
        cerr << "Error archiving!" << endl;
        exit(2);
    }
```

In this example, the operation performed in the TRY block is expected to cause two types of exceptions, CFileException and CArchiveException—classes derived from the CException base class (see Figure 16.1). If an exception occurs, the program jumps to the block that handles the appropriate exception. Each CATCH block should include code to handle that specific exception.

Each exception is represented by an object of a class derived from CException:

- CArchiveException represents errors during serialization.
- CDBException represents errors occurring in the database classes.
- CFileException represents file I/O errors.
- CMemoryException represents memory allocation errors.
- CNotSupportedException represents a request made for unsupported services.
- COleException represents errors that occur during Object Linking and Embedding (OLE) operations under Windows.
- COleDispatchException represents errors occurring in OLE automation operations under Windows.
- CResourceException represents Windows resource-allocation errors.
- CUserException represents a generic error that alerts the user with a message box.

Notice that even though this chapter is supposed to describe general-purpose classes, several classes in the CException hierarchy—COleException, COleDispatchException, and CResourceException—are specific to Microsoft Windows applications.

LOCAL SCOPE OF try AND catch BLOCKS

Variables declared within a try block are local variables and are not accessible outside the block. Thus, the following code fails to compile because the variable named count is defined within the try block only:

```
    try
    {
        int count;
```

```
        CFile f("test.dat", CFile::modeRead ¦
                          CFile::typeBinary);
// Read count from file.
        (void)f.Read(&count, sizeof(count));


    }
    catch(CFileException* e)
    {
        throw;   // Throw the same exception again
    }
    return count; // ERROR: count is not defined anymore
```

Determining the Cause of an Exception

In MFC 3.0, the argument in catch represents a pointer to an exception object. Depending on the type of exception, you can obtain further information about it from the data members of the exception object. For example, the CFileException exception contains a member variable named m_cause that indicates the cause of the file I/O error. To check the cause, compare the m_cause member variable with certain enumerated constants declared in the CFileException class in the following manner:

```
try
{
// Code that might throw a file I/O exception.
//...
}
catch(CFileException* e)
{
// Handle file errors here.
// Test e->m_cause for the exact cause of error.

    if(e->m_cause == CFileException::accessDenied)
        TRACE("Access denied");

    if(e->m_cause == CFileException::fileNotFound)
        TRACE("File not found");
//...
}
```

Throwing Exceptions

In addition to catching exceptions with the try and catch blocks, the Microsoft Foundation Class Library provides a number of global functions with which you can throw exceptions of specific types. For example, you can throw a file I/O error with a specific cause by calling AfxThrowFileException:

```
#include <fstream.h>

//...
{
    ifstream ifs("test.dat", ios::in | ios::nocreate);
// Throw an exception if the file could not be opened successfully.
    if(!ifs)
    {
        AfxThrowFileException(CFileException::generic);
    }

// Okay to use ifs here....
//...
}
```

Here, you throw a file I/O exception with the cause set to an unspecified (generic) error.

The following are other utility functions for throwing exceptions:

- `AfxThrowMemoryException`
- `AfxThrowNotSupportedException`
- `AfxThrowArchiveException`
- `AfxThrowDBException`
- `AfxThrowOleException`
- `AfxThrowOleDispatchException`
- `AfxThrowResourceException`
- `AfxThrowUserException`

As you can see, a function corresponds to each type of exception. Consult the online documentation in Visual C++ 2.0 for further information on these functions.

Summary

You can reduce the time needed to develop C++ programs by using C++ class libraries if the following statements are true:

- The library includes the classes that match your needs.
- The public interface to the classes is well documented.

Visual C++ 2.0 includes the Microsoft Foundation Class Library version 3.0 (MFC 3.0)—a collection of over 130 classes that provides a large number of general-purpose classes as well as a framework for building Microsoft Windows applications. Most of the general-purpose classes are for organizing objects in collections, with a few classes for modeling data (such as strings and time) and for supporting file I/O. The library includes support for handling exceptions and for archiving objects in files and restoring them later. This chapter summarizes the collection classes and provides a number of example programs to illustrate how you might use these classes.

Another large set of classes in MFC 3.0 is geared toward making Windows programming easier. These classes are described in Chapter 18 after an introduction to Windows programming in Chapter 17, "Windows Programming with Visual C++ 2.0 and MFC 3.0."

V

Windows Programming

17

Windows Programming with Visual C++ 2.0 and MFC 3.0

Windows applications are easy to use and they have a rich graphical user interface; unfortunately for software developers, the ease of use comes at the expense of a complex *Application Programming Interface (API)*—the collection of functions that programmers use to write Windows applications. For example, the Windows API contains over 600 functions. Although you can get by with a small fraction of these, you are never quite sure whether you are overlooking some function that does exactly what your application needs to do. In addition to the sheer volume of information, you have to follow an entirely different approach when you write Windows applications. Despite these drawbacks, there are advantages to writing applications for Windows:

■ Windows offers *device independence*. The same Windows application should display its output on any monitor from VGA to Super VGA and print on any printer from dot-matrix to laser.

■ For the developer, Windows offers a variety of predefined user interface components, such as pushbuttons, menus, dialog boxes, lists, and edit windows.

■ Windows includes an extensive interface to any graphics device (called *Graphics Device Interface* or *GDI*) for drawing graphics and text. In particular, the GDI enables you to draw in your own coordinate system.

Until recently, C has been the programming language of choice for writing Windows applications. Although C++ has been steadily gaining in popularity, calling Windows functions from a C++ program is not as simple as calling, for example, functions from the standard C library. This is because the compiler has to generate special object code when calling Windows functions, and Windows uses a different method of passing arguments to its functions. In other words, the C++ compiler has to support the requirements imposed by Windows. Like most C++ compilers for PCs, Microsoft Visual C++ 2.0 supports Windows programming. In particular, Visual C++ 2.0 comes with MFC 3.0—a library of C++ classes that makes it easier to write Windows applications.

This chapter is designed as a quick introduction to writing Windows programs with Visual C++ 2.0 and MFC 3.0. This will not be a complete tutorial. This chapter assumes that you are already familiar with the basics of object-oriented programming, C++, and some Windows programming, and that you have browsed through Microsoft's documentation. If you need further information on object-oriented programming or Windows programming, you should consult one of the books listed in the bibliography that appears at the end of this book.

The chapter starts with a small example program—the Windows version of the classic "Hello, World!" program—that illustrates the basics of Windows programming with MFC 3.0. Following the example, I describe AppWizard and ClassWizard—two tools that are designed to handle some routine chores in writing Windows applications.

ISN'T MICROSOFT WINDOWS ALREADY OBJECT-ORIENTED?

The Microsoft Windows environment was promoted as having an object-oriented architecture, so what do programmers gain by accessing the Windows environment through a layer of C++ classes such as those in the MFC 3.0 Library?

Although Windows supports the concept of certain objects, the data encapsulation and inheritance rely on the programmer's discipline. When you write Windows programs in C, you can access and modify all parts of the structures that represent the objects. Additionally, anyone who has written a Windows program in C knows that the programmer must attend to many details in order for the application and its windows to look and behave properly.

An object-oriented layer in an object-oriented programming language such as C++ can help tremendously, merely by hiding many unnecessary details. Basically, that's what you get when you use C++ classes that support Windows programming. The Windows environment has an underlying object-oriented architecture, but the Windows programming interface is procedural. Using a properly designed set of C++ classes makes the programming interface more object-oriented.

Windows Programming with MFC 3.0

The primary purpose of the MFC 3.0 is to provide a complete *application framework* for building Microsoft Windows applications. The collection of classes in MFC 3.0 are referred to as a framework because they essentially provide all the components for skeletal programs that can be easily fleshed out into complete Windows applications.

APPLICATION FRAMEWORK IN MFC 3.0

MFC 3.0 provides a complete application framework for building Microsoft Windows applications. When you study MFC 3.0, you will notice that many functions and macros in the MFC 3.0 library start with one of the following prefixes: afx, Afx, or AFX, each of which stands for *Application Frameworx*—derived from a slight mutation of the term *Application Frameworks*.

Model-View-Controller (MVC) Architecture

Even though MFC 3.0 includes most classes necessary to build the user interface and represent various data types, it is easier to build an application if you follow a well-defined architecture (*structural model*) for the application. The *Model-View-Controller (MVC) architecture* prevalent in the Smalltalk-80 programming language is a good candidate for Windows applications architecture.

As Figure 17.1 shows, the MVC architecture separates the application into three separate layers:

■ *Model* refers to the *application layer* where all application-dependent objects reside. For example, in a drawing program, this is the layer that maintains the graphics objects.

■ *View* is the *presentation layer* that presents the application's data to the user. This layer extracts information from the model and displays the information in windows. In a drawing program, this layer gets the list of graphics objects from the model and renders them in a window. The view provides the windows in the application's graphical user interface.

■ *Controller* is the *interaction layer,* which provides the interface between the input devices (such as keyboard and mouse) and the view and model layers.

FIGURE 17.1.

MVC architecture of Smalltalk-80.

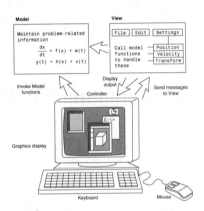

The MVC architecture does an excellent job of separating the responsibilities of the objects in the system. The application-specific details are insulated from the user interface. The user interface itself is broken down into two parts, with the presentation handled by the view and the interaction by the controller.

When building Windows applications using the Microsoft Foundation Classes, you do not have to follow the MVC model strictly. For example, when you use the MFC classes, you will find it difficult to separate the view and controller layers. As shown in Figure 17.2, your application consists of a model and an associated view-controller pair. Figure 17.2 also shows the usual interactions in Smalltalk-80's MVC architecture. The controller accepts the user's input and invokes the appropriate function from the model to perform the task requested by the user. When the work is done, the function in the model sends messages to the view and controller. The view updates the display in response to this message, accessing the model for further information, if necessary. Thus, the model has a view and a controller, but it never directly accesses any of them. The view and controller, on the other hand, accesses the model's functions and data, when necessary.

> **MVC ARCHITECTURE AND MFC 3.0**
>
> MFC 3.0 supports the MVC architecture through its document-view model (the term is used here to mean a representation) of applications. MFC's CDocument class corresponds to the model of MVC architecture and the CView class is the view-controller pair. The CDocument class provides the storage for a document's data and the CView class provides the means to view and manipulate the document. The AppWizard tool, described later in this chapter, can automatically generate the code for an application that uses a document-view model.

FIGURE 17.2.

Interactions among model, view, and controller in the MVC architecture.

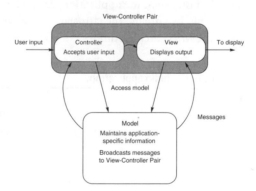

As you will see in the example that follows, most of the MFC 3.0 classes contribute to the view and controller pair. You typically use your own classes as well as the general-purpose classes, such as strings, lists, and arrays, in the application's model layer.

A Windows Application Using MFC 3.0

A simple example is the best way to understand the basic capabilities of the Microsoft Foundation Class Library. Because MFC 3.0 provides a framework for Windows applications, you will create an application using MFC 3.0 that displays Hello, World! in a window. Even with the Microsoft Foundation Classes, you must attend to many details when writing a Microsoft Windows application. This discussion provides the steps.

The *CHelloApp* Class

Because MFC 3.0 provides an application framework, all MFC-based Microsoft Windows applications rely on a class derived from the CWinApp class that models the entire application.

Listing 17.1 shows the file HELLO.CPP, which implements the CHelloApp class that models your sample application. In the CHelloApp class, you define the member function named InitInstance in which all initializations are performed. If you employ the MVC architecture, the basic steps for your application are as follows:

1. Create a model for the application. For this application, the model is a class named HelloModel, defined in the HELLOMDL.H header file (Listing 17.2).

2. Create a view and store a pointer to the model in the view. In this case, the View class is named CHelloView and is declared in the HELLOVW.H header file (Listing 17.3). You will see later that the CHelloView class is derived from the CFrameWnd class of the MFC Library.

3. Derive an application class from CWinApp and, in the InitInstance function of the application class, perform all necessary initializations, including the creation of the model and the view.

4. Create a global instance of the application class. This step is enough to get the application going. Essentially, the CWinApp class provides the functionality of the controller in the MVC architecture.

Listing 17.1. HELLO.CPP. The hello application.

```
//--------------------------------------------------------------
// File:  hello.cpp
//
// A Windows application that uses the Microsoft Foundation
// Class library

#include "hellovw.h"
#include "hellomdl.h"

class CHelloApp: public CWinApp
{
public:
    BOOL InitInstance();
    virtual int  ExitInstance();

private:
    CHelloModel *m_pModel;
};
//--------------------------------------------------------------
BOOL CHelloApp::InitInstance()
{
    Enable3dControls();

    m_pModel = new CHelloModel();
    m_pMainWnd = new CHelloView(m_pModel);

// Note that m_pMainWnd is a member variable of the CWinApp
// class (declared in the header file "afxwin.h")

    m_pMainWnd->ShowWindow(m_nCmdShow);
    m_pMainWnd->UpdateWindow();
```

```
    return TRUE;
}
//------------------------------------------------------------
int CHelloApp::ExitInstance()
{
    if(m_pModel) delete m_pModel;
    return 0;
}
//------------------------------------------------------------
// Creating an instance of the application is enough to
// get it going.

CHelloApp HelloWorld;
```

As you will see later in this chapter, you also can use AppWizard to create your application. AppWizard even gives you an MVC-like application architecture with the document-view model. Using AppWizard probably is the easiest way to create a C++ Windows application. For now though, let's continue writing the Hello program using the MVC model.

The *CHelloModel* Class

An application's model is supposed to store data unique to the application. In this case, the application is simple enough that the Hello, World! string could have been displayed directly from the view class. However, a model class is used here to illustrate how to build a realistic application using the MVC architecture. This application's model, the CHelloModel class (Listing 17.2), contains the string to be displayed in the window. The string is stored in an instance of a CString class (from the MFC 3.0 library and declared in the header file <afx.h>) that is created in the constructor of the CHelloModel class. The view class uses the member function named GetString to obtain a pointer to this CString instance.

Listing 17.2. HELLOMDL.H. Definition of the CHelloModel class.

```
//------------------------------------------------------------
//  File:  hellomdl.h
//
//  The "model" for the "hello" application.  In this case,
//  the model simply stores a string to be displayed in a window

#if !defined(__HELLOMDL_H)
#define __HELLOMDL_H

#include <afx.h>

class CHelloModel
{
public:
    CHelloModel() { m_pString = new CString("Hello, World!");}

    ~CHelloModel() { delete m_pString;}
```

continues

Listing 17.2. continued

```
    CString* GetString() { return m_pString;}

private:
    CString *m_pString;
};

#endif
```

The *CHelloView* Class

The CHelloView class, declared in the file HELLOVW.H (Listing 17.3) and implemented in HELLOVW.CPP (Listing 17.4), provides the view for this application. The CHelloView class is responsible for displaying the message (stored in the CHelloModel class) in a window. CHelloView, derived from the CFrameWnd class, serves as the main window of the application. The view class stores a pointer to the model; through this pointer the view can access the model as needed.

The most important function of the HelloView class is called OnPaint. The Microsoft Foundation Class Library automatically calls the OnPaint function for a window whenever the window needs repainting. (You will soon see how the painting is done.) Notice how the OnPaint function is declared with an afx_msg prefix in Listing 17.3. This is one of the steps you need to follow to ensure that messages intended for a window get handled properly. The inclusion of the DECLARE_MESSAGE_MAP() macro is another required step.

Listing 17.3. HELLOVW.H. Declaration of the CHelloView class.

```
//-------------------------------------------------------------
// File:  hellovw.h
//
// The "view" for the "hello" application.  In this case,
// the view is a window where the string from the model
// is displayed.

#if !defined(__HELLOVW_H)
#define __HELLOVW_H

// Include necessary header files
#include <afxwin.h>
#include "hellores.h"  // Resource identifiers for application

class CHelloModel;

class CHelloView : public CFrameWnd
{
public:
    CHelloView(CHelloModel* pModel);
```

```
    void InitView();
// Declare functions for handling messages from Windows
    afx_msg void OnPaint();
    afx_msg void OnAbout();

private:
    CHelloModel* m_pModel;

    DECLARE_MESSAGE_MAP()
};
```

```
#endif
```

The `OnAbout` function also is declared as a message handler (indicated by the `afx_msg` prefix). This function displays a dialog box with information about the application (see Listing 17.4).

WINDOWS MESSAGE HANDLING IN MICROSOFT FOUNDATION CLASSES

Microsoft Windows works by sending messages to the windows that constitute an application's user interface. The Microsoft Foundation Class Library provides a unique way to map one or more of these messages to functions that you write. You declare the message handling functions with an `afx_msg` prefix in your application's main window class—usually a class derived from the `CFrameWnd` class. Next, you include the `DECLARE_MESSAGE_MAP()` macro in the declaration of the window class. Finally, you associate each message handling function to a Windows message through a message map enclosed in the `BEGIN_MESSAGE_MAP()` and `END_MESSAGE_MAP()` macros.

Listing 17.4 shows the implementation of the `CHelloView` class. In Listing 17.4, you see another required step of Windows programming with the Microsoft Foundation Class Library: the definition of a message map—the association of a function with a Windows message so that Windows calls the specified function in response to the associated message. Because `CHelloView` has two message handlers, `OnPaint` and `OnAbout`, the message map is defined as follows:

```
// Define the "message map"

    BEGIN_MESSAGE_MAP(CHelloView, CFrameWnd)
        ON_WM_PAINT()
        ON_COMMAND(IDM_ABOUT, OnAbout)
    END_MESSAGE_MAP()
```

You start the message map with a `BEGIN_MESSAGE_MAP` macro that takes two arguments, the name of the class for which the message map is being defined and the name of its base class. An `END_MESSAGE_MAP()` macro marks the end of the message map.

Listing 17.4. HELLOVW.CPP. Implementation of the `CHelloView` class.

```cpp
//-------------------------------------------------------------
// File:  hellovw.cpp
//
// The "view" layer for the "hello" application
//-------------------------------------------------------------
#include "hellovw.h"
#include "hellomdl.h"


//-------------------------------------------------------------
// Define the "message map"

    BEGIN_MESSAGE_MAP(CHelloView, CFrameWnd)
        ON_WM_PAINT()
        ON_COMMAND(IDM_ABOUT, OnAbout)
    END_MESSAGE_MAP()


//-------------------------------------------------------------
// I n i t V i e w
// Initialize this view

void CHelloView::InitView()
{
    VERIFY(LoadAccelTable("MainAccelTable"));
    VERIFY(Create(NULL, "Hello", WS_OVERLAPPEDWINDOW,
            rectDefault, NULL, "MainMenu"));
}
//-------------------------------------------------------------
// C H e l l o V i e w
// Constructor for CHelloView class

CHelloView::CHelloView(CHelloModel* pModel) : m_pModel(pModel)
{
    InitView();
}
//-------------------------------------------------------------
// O n P a i n t
// Draw contents of window

void CHelloView::OnPaint()
{
// Set up device context (DC) for drawing
    CPaintDC dc(this);
    dc.SetTextAlign(TA_BASELINE | TA_CENTER);
    dc.SetBkMode(TRANSPARENT);

// Get the message
    CString* pString = m_pModel->GetString();

// Get window size
    CRect r;
    GetClientRect(r);

    int w = r.right - r.left;
    int h = r.bottom - r.top;

// Get number of characters in string
    int len = pString->GetLength();
```

```
// Display string roughly at the center of window
    int xpos = w/2;
    if(xpos < 0) xpos = 0;
    dc.TextOut(xpos, h/2, *pString, len);
}
//-------------------------------------------------------------
//   O n A b o u t
//   Display the "About..." box

void CHelloView::OnAbout()
{
    CDialog About("ABOUTHELLO", this);
    About.DoModal();
}
```

In the message map's body, you list the Windows messages for which this class provides handlers. Each message name is defined by a macro, an ON_ prefix followed by the standard Windows term for that message. Consequently, ON_WM_PAINT() indicates that this class handles WM_PAINT messages sent by Windows when a window needs repainting. The name of the message handling function is implicit in this case—it is OnPaint.

The next entry, ON_COMMAND(IDM_ABOUT, OnAbout), ensures that the OnAbout function is called when the menu item identified by the constant IDM_ABOUT is selected. The OnAbout message handling function must be explicitly associated with a menu item because you, the programmer, may choose to associate any function with a message generated by a menu selection. IDM_ABOUT is a constant defined in the HELLORES.H header file shown in Listing 17.5.

Because your application is supposed to display a message in its window, the code for displaying the message is embedded in the OnPaint function (Listing 17.4). In the OnPaint function, you receive the message string from the model by calling the GetString function of the CHelloModel class:

```
void CHelloView::OnPaint()
{

// Get the message
    CString* pString = m_pModel->GetString();

// Display the message ...
}
```

The actual rendering of the string is performed by calling member functions of the CPaintDC class, which provides a *device context* (or, in Windows terminology, *DC*) for drawing in a window. The DC holds information that controls the appearance of drawings created by Windows drawing functions. In MFC 3.0, you can obtain the DC by creating an instance of the CPaintDC class. Because a DC is created for a specific window, the constructor for CPaintDC requires the pointer to the window with which the DC is associated. In OnPaint, the DC for the window associated with the CHelloView class is created and used as follows:

```
// Set up device context (DC) for drawing
    CPaintDC dc(this);
```

```
    dc.SetTextAlign(TA_BASELINE | TA_CENTER);
    dc.SetBkMode(TRANSPARENT);
//...

// Draw the string
    dc.TextOut(xpos, h/2, *pString, len);
```

Member functions of the CPaintDC object set graphics attributes, such as alignment of text and the background mode. The text string is displayed by calling the TextOut function. In that call to TextOut, xpos denotes the x-coordinate of the location in the window where the text output originates, h denotes the height of the window, and len is the number of characters in the text string being displayed. You can obtain the size (width and height) of the window and the length of a CString object with the following:

```
// Get window size
    CRect r;
    GetClientRect(r);

    int w = r.right - r.left;
    int h = r.bottom - r.top;

// Get number of characters in string
    int len = pString->GetLength();
```

If you want to draw other graphics in the window, you can call other member functions of the CPaintDC class. Because the CPaintDC class is derived from the CDC class (the generic DC class), the documentation of the CDC class includes information on these graphics output functions. Chapter 18, "Using the Windows Programming Classes in MFC 3.0," summarizes the MFC 3.0 classes for user interface, Chapter 19, "Graphics Programming with MFC 3.0," discusses the drawing functions from the CDC class, and Chapter 20, "Displaying Text in Windows," covers the text output functions in detail.

Building the Application

Once you ready the header files and source files, compile and link them to create a Microsoft Windows application. You can use the Visual Workbench's File | New option to create a new project file. The project file has a name with a .MAK extension (which is similar to the files that NMAKE uses).

The companion disk has the project file (HELLO.MAK) that you need to build the example program. The disk also includes all the files needed to build the executable HELLO.EXE. In particular, here are two of the text files that you need:

■ HELLORES.H (Listing 17.5). This file defines constants that identify resources such as menu item numbers.

■ HELLO.RC (Listing 17.6). This file is known as the *resource file* and is a text file that specifies the layouts and contents of menus and dialog boxes. The Microsoft resource compiler (invoked by the RC command) compiles this file into binary form and appends it to the executable file. You can create and edit the resource file directly from the Visual Workbench.

Given the project file HELLO.MAK, you can build the HELLO.EXE file by selecting the Rebuild All option from the Project menu of the Visual Workbench. Once the program is successfully built, you can add it to the Windows Program Manager by selecting New... from the Program Manager's File menu. Once installed in this way, you can run HELLO.EXE by double-clicking on its icon in the Program Manager window.

Listing 17.5. HELLORES.H. Resource identifiers for HELLO.EXE.

```
//---------------------------------------------------------------
// File: hellores.h
//
// Declare the resource IDs for the Hello application
// In this case, we have only one.

#define IDM_ABOUT 100
```

Listing 17.6. HELLORES.RC. Resource file for HELLO.EXE.

```
//Microsoft Visual C++ generated resource script.
//
#include "resource.h"

#define APSTUDIO_READONLY_SYMBOLS
/////////////////////////////////////////////////////////////////////////////
//
// Generated from the TEXTINCLUDE 2 resource.
//
#include "hellores.h"
#include "afxres.h"


/////////////////////////////////////////////////////////////////////////////
#undef APSTUDIO_READONLY_SYMBOLS


/////////////////////////////////////////////////////////////////////////////
//
// Menu
//

MAINMENU MENU DISCARDABLE
BEGIN
    POPUP "&Help"
    BEGIN
        MENUITEM "&About Hello...\tF1",          IDM_ABOUT
    END
END


/////////////////////////////////////////////////////////////////////////////
//
// Accelerator
//
```

continues

Listing 17.6. continued

```
MAINACCELTABLE ACCELERATORS MOVEABLE PURE
BEGIN
    VK_F1,            IDM_ABOUT,                VIRTKEY
END


///////////////////////////////////////////////////////////////////////
//
// Icon
//

AFX_IDI_STD_FRAME      ICON    DISCARDABLE     "hello.ico"

///////////////////////////////////////////////////////////////////////
//
// Dialog
//

ABOUTHELLO DIALOG DISCARDABLE  22, 17, 144, 75
STYLE DS_MODALFRAME ¦ WS_CAPTION ¦ WS_SYSMENU
CAPTION "About Hello"
FONT 8, "System"
BEGIN
    CTEXT          "Hello, World! from",IDC_STATIC,37,2,107,8
    CTEXT          "Microsoft Foundation Classes",IDC_STATIC,36,12,108,8
    CTEXT          "(MFC 3.0)",IDC_STATIC,37,22,107,8
    DEFPUSHBUTTON  "OK",IDOK,58,52,32,14,WS_GROUP
    ICON           AFX_IDI_STD_FRAME,IDC_STATIC,9,4,18,20
END


#ifdef APSTUDIO_INVOKED
///////////////////////////////////////////////////////////////////////
//
// TEXTINCLUDE
//

1 TEXTINCLUDE DISCARDABLE
BEGIN
    "resource.h\0"
END

2 TEXTINCLUDE DISCARDABLE
BEGIN
    "#include ""hellores.h""\r\n"
    "#include ""afxres.h""\r\n"
    "\0"
END

3 TEXTINCLUDE DISCARDABLE
BEGIN
    "\r\n"
    "\0"
END
```

```
/////////////////////////////////////////////////////////////////////////
#endif    // APSTUDIO_INVOKED


/////////////////////////////////////////////////////////////////////////
//
// Bitmap
//

IDB_BITMAP1              BITMAP  DISCARDABLE      "BITMAP1.BMP"

#ifndef APSTUDIO_INVOKED
/////////////////////////////////////////////////////////////////////////
//
// Generated from the TEXTINCLUDE 3 resource.
//


/////////////////////////////////////////////////////////////////////////
#endif    // not APSTUDIO_INVOKED
```

Testing HELLO.EXE

Once you successfully compile and link the sample application HELLO.EXE, you can run it under Visual Workbench, either by selecting Go from the Debug menu or by pressing F5. Additionally, outside of the Visual Workbench, you can run HELLO.EXE from the Run option in the File menu of the Program Manager.

Figure 17.3 shows the program's output. If you resize the window, Hello, World! should appear centered in the window. Note that the About Hello... dialog also appears in Figure 17.3.

FIGURE 17.3.
Hello, World! from
MFC-based HELLO.EXE.

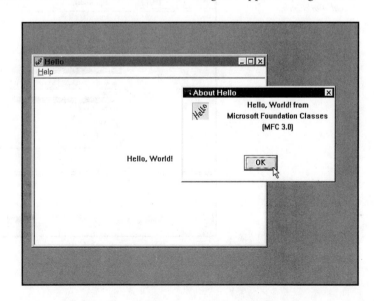

Tools for Building Applications

Now that you have seen an example of a Microsoft Windows application built manually using MFC 3.0 classes, let's look at two tools that make it easy to build the entire application's framework automatically. The AppWizard and ClassWizard tools, built into the Visual Workbench, are meant to reduce the programmer's burden by providing a way to generate much of the code that almost all Windows applications share. AppWizard generates the code for a standard set of classes that are necessary for a Windows application employing a document-view model. ClassWizard enables you to add member variables, member functions, and Windows message map functions to the existing classes as well as to declare and define any new classes that your application might need. The best way to learn about AppWizard and ClassWizard is to try out them out yourself. The following sections provide an overview of these two tools.

Building an Application with MFC AppWizard

The Visual Workbench in Visual C++ 2.0 runs AppWizard automatically when you create a new AppWizard EXE or DLL project. To create the project, select New from the File menu in Visual Workbench. A dialog box appears with a list showing the types of files you can create (see Figure 17.4). Select Project from this list. This brings up the New Project dialog where you can specify the project's name, directory, and type (see Figure 17.5). If you provide a project name and click on the Create... button to indicate that you accept the default project type of MFC AppWizard (exe), the Visual Workbench starts the AppWizard tool.

FIGURE 17.4.

Creating a new project in Visual Workbench.

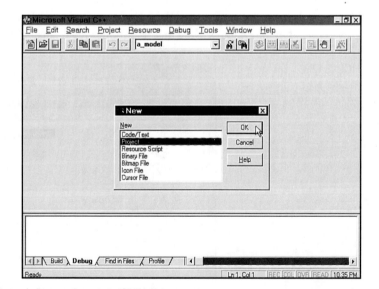

FIGURE 17.5.

Entering a project name for the application to be generated by MFC AppWizard.

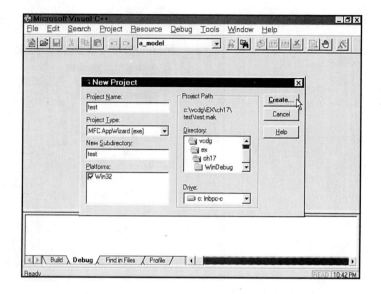

MFC AppWizard essentially conducts an interview by presenting a sequence of six major dialog boxes, each offering a host of options through which you can control the features of the application that AppWizard will generate. There are six steps AppWizard uses to gather information needed to generate the application:

1. Figure 17.6 shows the first dialog box that enables you to specify the type of user interface you want. As you can see, the three options are the following:

   ■ Single document interface (SDI), where the main frame window allows only one child window in which the user can view and manipulate a document (document means any type of data).

   ■ Multiple document interface (MDI), where the main frame window can have many child windows, each displaying a document. This is the type of interface you find in most Windows applications, such as Visual Workbench, Microsoft Excel, and Microsoft Word for Windows. In these applications, each open document appears in its own window, but all these windows are managed by a single main window that contains them.

   ■ Dialog-based interface where the user interacts with the application through a dialog. This type of interface is ideal for form-based data entry.

2. As shown in Figure 17.7, the dialog box for this step requires you to specify whether your application will require any database support. Let's use the database support in Chapter 31, "Using MFC 3.0 Database Classes for ODBC Programming."

FIGURE 17.6.

Specifying the interface type for an AppWizard-generated application.

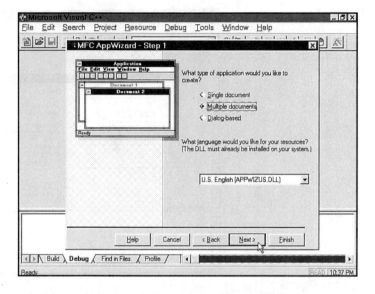

FIGURE 17.7.

Dialog box inquiring whether the AppWizard-generated application requires database support.

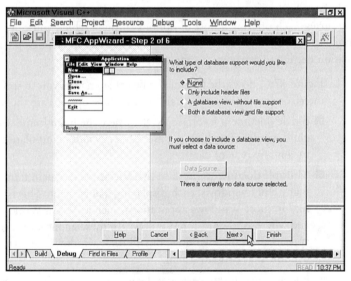

3. The purpose of this step is to select the type and level of support for Object Linking and Embedding version 2.0 (OLE 2.0) (see Figure 17.8). You will explore the options shown in this step in Chapter 28, "OLE 2.0 Programming with MFC 3.0."

FIGURE 17.8.

Specifying type and level of OLE 2.0 support for the AppWizard-generated application.

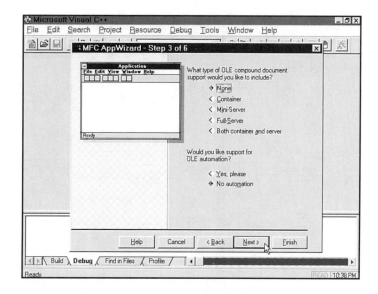

4. With the dialog box in step 4 you can enable a number of features, including tool bar, status bar, and controls with 3-D appearance (Figure 17.9). You can also enable support for context-sensitive help by turning on the Context Sensitive Help checkbox. Additionally, you can access another set of options by clicking on the Advanced... pushbutton. When you do, the Visual Workbench displays the tabbed dialog box of Figure 17.10 where you can indicate a number of other options such as the styles of the main frame and the child frame windows (for MDI applications).

FIGURE 17.9.

Enabling certain application features for the AppWizard-generated application.

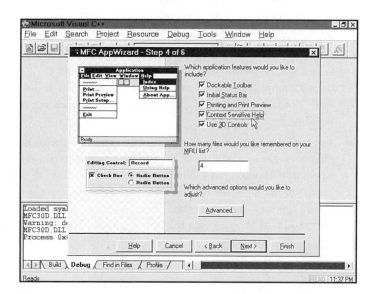

FIGURE 17.10.

Dialog box for setting advanced application features.

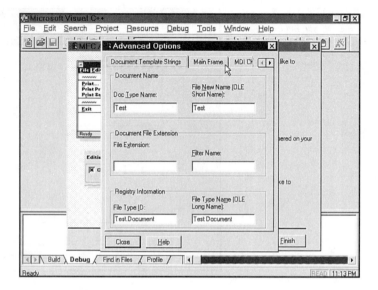

5. Through the dialog box shown in Figure 17.11, MFC AppWizard queries you about the type of makefile and MFC Library to be used for the application. You can also enable or disable the inclusion of special comments that show you where you must add functionality to the AppWizard-generated application. These comments take the following form:

```
void CTestView::OnDraw(CDC* pDC)
{
        CTestDoc* pDoc = GetDocument();
        ASSERT_VALID(pDoc);
        // TODO: add draw code for native data here
}
```

In this example, the comment line (in bold type) tells you where to add code to draw your "document's" data. The OnDraw function is called as part of processing the Windows WM_PAINT message.

6. The dialog box for the final step shows you a list of the classes that AppWizard will generate for your applications (Figure 17.12). For certain classes, you can change the names of the source and header files. For the view class (the class with name ending in View), you are given the opportunity to change the base class from the default of CView. You may want to use one of the other view classes: CEditView, CFormView, or CScrollView as the base class for your application's view.

FIGURE 17.11.

Selection of type of makefile and MFC Library for AppWizard-generated applications.

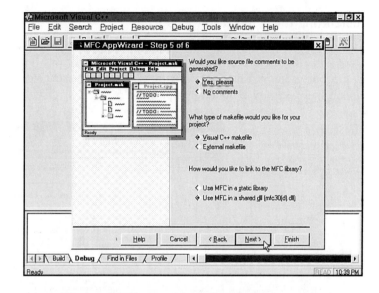

FIGURE 17.12.

Dialog box showing the list of classes to be generated by MFC AppWizard.

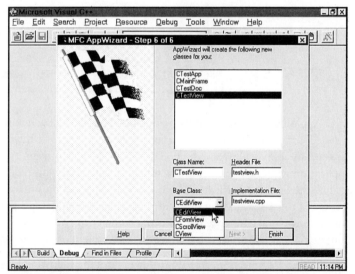

NOTE

MFC AppWizard automatically uses a document-view model for the applications it generates.

Generating the Application's Code

After you set all the options to customize the application, MFC AppWizard displays a final dialog box with information about the project that it will create (Figure 17.13). If you click on the OK button in the dialog box of Figure 17.13, AppWizard generates all source, header, and support files necessary to build the application.

FIGURE 17.13.

Information about the new project to be created by MFC AppWizard.

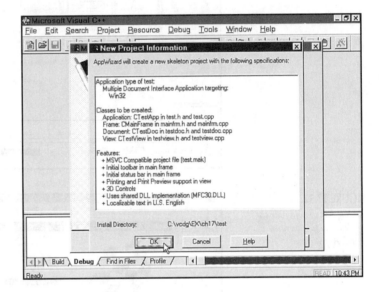

After AppWizard finishes generating the files, you will be back in the Visual Workbench with a project set up for the new application. Figure 17.14 shows the contents of the project window for an application named TEST that was generated using AppWizard. This is an MDI application with the document-view model. It uses a view object derived from CEditView that enables the user to enter text in a window. The application's main frame window has a status area and a tool bar with a set of buttons that facilitate opening a file, saving a file, cutting and pasting, searching and replacing, printing, and getting help. AppWizard also generates a standard help file if you select the Context Sensitive Help option in step 4 (Figure 17.9).

For the TEST application, AppWizard generates the following files:

■ TEST.MAK is the application's project file that you can use to build the application from within Visual Workbench, the Visual C++ development environment. This project file is also compatible with the NMAKE program that comes with Visual C++ 2.0.

■ TEST.CLW is a file used by the ClassWizard tool (described later in this chapter) to store information about the application's classes. ClassWizard uses this information to edit existing classes and add new classes to the application.

■ TEST.CPP and TEST.H are the source and header files for the application class (CTestApp) derived from the MFC 3.0 class CWinApp.

■ MAINFRM.CPP and MAINFRM.H are the source and header files for the application's main frame window class (`CMainFrame`), which is derived from the MFC 3.0 class `CFrameWnd`. This is the window where the tool bar, the status bar, and the child windows appear.

■ TESTDOC.CPP and TESTDOC.H are the source and header files for the application's document class (`CTestDoc`) class derived from the MFC 3.0 class `CDocument`. This class represents your application's data. You have to edit these files to add code that saves and restores data.

■ TESTVIEW.CPP and TESTVIEW.H are the source and header files for the application's view class (`CTestView`) derived from the MFC 3.0 class `CEditView` (this choice is made in the dialog box shown in Figure 17.12).

■ STDAFX.CPP and STDAFX.H are the source and header files used to create the precompiled header for standard include files for MFC applications. The STDAFX.CPP file includes the STDAFX.H header.

■ TEST.RC is the application's resource file.

■ RESOURCE.H is the header file for the application's resources. This file is included by TEST.RC, the application's resource file.

■ TEST.HPJ is the help project file used by the Microsoft Help compiler to create the application's help file.

■ MAKEHELP.BAT is the batch file used to create the application's help files. This file invokes the help compiler with TEST.HPJ as the help project. The source files for the help compiler are located in the HLP subdirectory.

■ README.TXT is a text file that contains some helpful information for the programmer.

FIGURE 17.14.

The new project for a test application created by MFC AppWizard.

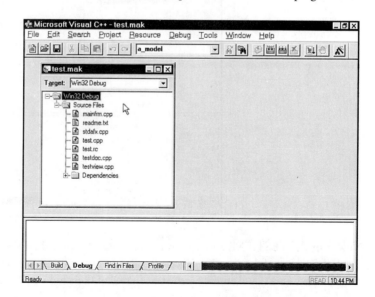

Additionally, AppWizard also generates a large number of support files in the following subdirectories:

- A HLP subdirectory with a few Rich Text Format files (.RTF) with the help information. The HLP subdirectory also includes several bitmap files (.BMP) that are used in the help file.
- A RES subdirectory with two icon files (.ICO): one icon is used for the application and the other is used when an MDI child window is minimized. The RES subdirectory also has the bitmap file TOOLBAR.BMP that is used for the pushbuttons displayed in the tool bar that appears underneath the application's menu bar.

Building the Application

The next logical step is to modify the generated source files to suit your need and build the application by compiling and linking the files. To see what AppWizard provides as is (without any additional code from the programmer), try selecting Rebuild All from the Project menu after AppWizard finishes generating the files. Figure 17.15 shows the completion of the compiling and linking process. To build the help files, enter the following command from a command window (such as a DOS window):

```
makehelp
```

FIGURE 17.15.

Building the test application.

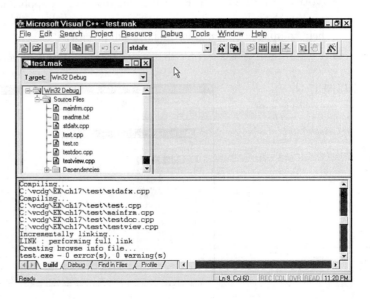

Now, run the TEST.EXE application by selecting Go from the Debug menu. Figure 17.16 shows the output of the test application after the user has created three child windows, iconified one of the windows, and entered some text in one of the windows. Notice that the application

gets a default menu bar, a status bar, and a tool bar with pushbuttons that offer "tool tips"—
tiny help windows that pop up when the cursor rests on the button.

FIGURE 17.16.

*Sample session with
the test application.*

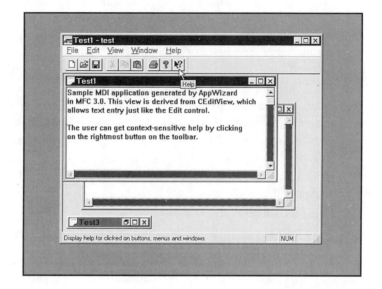

The bottom line is that AppWizard can generate the shell for a full-fledged MDI application
without any effort on your part. The idea behind AppWizard is that you generate the shell or
framework for your application and then add code to one or more of the generated files. You
also may define new classes that you need for your application. The tool that helps you with
these tasks is called ClassWizard.

Customizing the Application with ClassWizard

Although AppWizard can help by generating much of the code that a Windows application
needs, you still have to write additional code specific to your application. Usually, this means
that you have to add code to the classes generated by AppWizard as well as create new classes
that your application needs. ClassWizard is the tool that makes it easy to take care of these
customizations.

ClassWizard Dialog

You can start ClassWizard by selecting the ClassWizard... item from the Project menu (see
Figure 17.17). This brings up a tabbed dialog box organized into five tabs (Figure 17.18):

■ The Message Maps tab enables you to modify the message maps—the association
between a Windows message and the function that handles the message. As Figure
17.18 shows, you select the class from the combo box labeled Class Name. Two lists,
Object IDs and Messages, respectively show the objects and the associated messages

for the selected object. For example, when you select the CTestView object, you see a list of all the messages for the CTestView class. Underneath the Object ID and Messages lists, there is another list—this one showing the member functions of the currently selected class (items marked V are virtual functions, those marked W are called in response to Windows messages). The buttons along the right side of the page enable you to add a new class, add or delete a function, and edit the code of a selected function.

■ The Member Variables tab is for adding or editing member variables associated with a dialog box or a form view. For example, if you have a dialog box through which the user enters some information, you use this page of the ClassWizard dialog to add the member variables that should store the values entered by the user.

■ The OLE Automation tab is meant for adding or editing the OLE automation capabilities of the application. OLE programming is covered in Chapter 28.

■ The OLE Events tab enables you to define the OLE events that various objects in your program support.

■ The Class Info tab is for browsing and editing certain characteristics of a selected class.

FIGURE 17.17.

Activating ClassWizard from the Project menu.

Editing a Class

To edit or view specific member functions of a class, you should first select the class name from the Class Name combo box in the Message Maps tab of the ClassWizard dialog. To edit a member function of the selected class, merely double-click on the member function's name from the Member Functions list. At the next step, you are editing the source file (.CPP) of the selected class.

FIGURE 17.18.

The ClassWizard tab dialog.

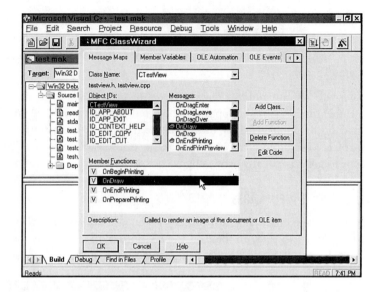

As an example, consider adding some code to the OnDraw member function of the CTestView class. After you select the class, a double-click on the OnDraw function's name brings up an edit window with the TESTVIEW.CPP file loaded in the window (see Figure 17.19). Begin entering the code necessary to display the data stored in your application's document. In this example, code is added to display a message in the window. If you build the TEST program after the editing and run it, each newly created window will display the message shown in the call to the TextOut function in Figure 17.19.

FIGURE 17.19.

Editing a member function with ClassWizard.

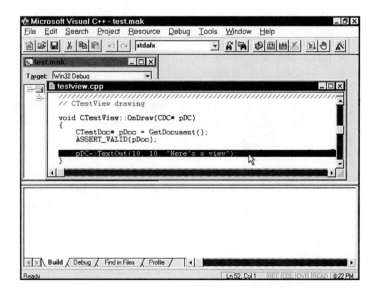

In addition to editing an existing member function, you also can add new member functions to customize a class. To do this, click on a message in the Messages list for which you want to add a handler. Now, click on the Add Function button on the left side of the tab dialog (see Figure 17.18).

After you add a handler, a mark appears next to the selected message and the newly added member function's name appears in the Member Functions list. You can edit the new member function by double-clicking on the name. If you edit the member function, you will notice that ClassWizard inserts a comment at the location where you are expected to add your own code to take care of any processing needs specific to your application.

Creating a New Class

In addition to modifying existing classes, you also can add new classes using ClassWizard. To add a new class, click on the Add Class... button on any tab in ClassWizard's tabbed dialog box. This action brings up the dialog shown in Figure 17.20.

FIGURE 17.20.

Dialog for adding a new class with ClassWizard.

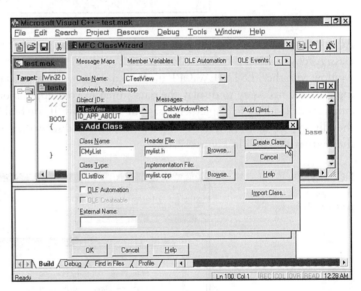

After specifying the class name and the base class, click on the Create Class button to create the new class. Once the class is created, you can use ClassWizard's tabbed dialog box to add the necessary member functions and member variables for the new class (Figure 17.18). Then you can fill in the body of the various member functions of the class to complete its implementation.

Summary

Visual C++ 2.0 includes the Microsoft Foundation Class Library Version 3.0 (MFC 3.0)—a collection of over 130 classes that provides a framework for building Microsoft Windows applications. This chapter includes a simple example program to illustrate how you use the MFC 3.0 classes to create Windows programs.

Visual C++ 2.0 also includes two labor-saving tools: AppWizard and ClassWizard. AppWizard can automatically generate the source and header files for a Windows application with a selected set of features, such as support for printing and multiple document interface. ClassWizard enables you to customize existing classes and define new classes in a convenient manner. This chapter also provides an overview of AppWizard and ClassWizard.

The MFC 3.0 classes are summarized in Chapter 18 and are used extensively in the sample applications presented in Chapters 19 through 25.

18

Using the Windows Programming Classes in MFC 3.0

In addition to the general-purpose classes described in Chapter 16, "Using the General-Purpose Classes in MFC 3.0," the Microsoft Foundation Class Library (MFC 3.0) offers a large collection of classes that help you write applications for the Microsoft Windows environment. An example in Chapter 17, "Windows Programming with Visual C++ 2.0 and MFC 3.0," illustrates how to use these classes as a framework for Windows programs. This chapter provides an overview of the MFC 3.0 classes for Windows programming together with a tutorial introduction to some of the more useful classes.

Note that Visual C++ 2.0 includes the full source code for the MFC 3.0 classes. Therefore, if you want, you can browse through the source code of the MFC 3.0 classes to see exactly how the classes are defined and implemented.

WHAT'S IN A NAME? WINDOWS VERSUS WINDOWS

This book uses the term *Windows* with an uppercase *W* to refer to *Microsoft Windows*, the graphical operating environment. The *windows* with a lowercase *w* refers to the rectangular areas of the screen in which applications display their output. Like all graphical operating environments, Windows uses windows extensively.

MFC 3.0 Windows Programming Classes at a Glance

Figure 18.1 shows the inheritance hierarchy of the Windows programming classes in the MFC 3.0 library. You should study the figure to familiarize yourself with the organization of the classes.

In Figure 18.1, you will see several major subhierarchies. The CWnd classes, derived from the CCmdTarget class, represent windows of various types: frame windows that are meant to manage one or more child windows, windows where the application displays its graphical or text output, dialog windows that prompt the user for input, and control window objects through which the user controls the application. To support graphics and text output through the Windows Graphics Device Interface (GDI is described further in Chapter 19, "Graphics Programming with MFC 3.0"), MFC 3.0 provides the CGdiObject class hierarchy. Additionally, MFC 3.0 includes the CDC classes that represent the various types of device contexts needed to display output on a device.

Other major class subhierarchies include: classes for building applications with the document-view model; classes to represent menus and tool bars; classes for scrolling and printing; and a large number of classes for supporting Object Linking and Embedding 2.0 (OLE 2.0). MFC 3.0 also includes classes such as CPoint, CRect, and CSize that represent Windows data types such as POINT, RECT, and SIZE, respectively.

FIGURE 18.1.

Classes for Windows programming in MFC 3.0.

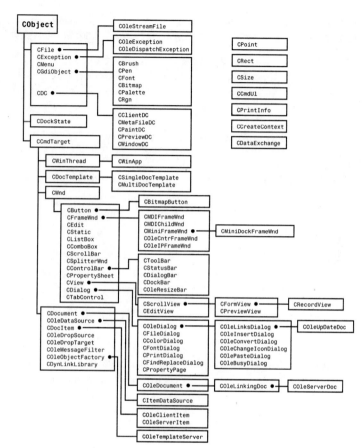

For another view of the Windows programming classes in MFC 3.0, consult Table 18.1, which lists the classes by category; Table 18.2 lists them alphabetically. The purpose of these tables is to give you an overall picture of the Windows programming capabilities offered by MFC 3.0. The following sections briefly describe the different categories of Windows programming classes in MFC 3.0. The latter part of this chapter provides example programs illustrating the use of some of the common Windows programming classes (except the OLE 2.0 classes—these are covered in Chapter 28, "OLE 2.0 Programming with MFC 3.0"). When you begin to use these MFC 3.0 classes in your applications, consult Table 18.2 to determine which header file you have to include when you use a specific class. Note that all include files are in the MFC\INCLUDE subdirectory of the directory where you installed Visual C++ 2.0. Classes internal to MFC are not shown in Table 18.2.

MFC 3.0 CLASSES FOR OLE 2.0 PROGRAMMING

MFC 3.0 provides over 25 classes for including OLE 2.0 capabilities in your Windows applications. These classes are summarized in Chapter 28.

Table 18.1. Windows programming classes by category.

Category	Classes
Application framework	CDocTemplate, CDocument, CEditView, CFormView, CMultiDocTemplate, CPreviewView, CScrollView, CSingleDocTemplate, CView, CWinApp, CWinThread
Message map	CCmdTarget, CCmdUI
Control windows	CBitmapButton, CButton, CControlBar, CComboBox, CDialogBar, CEdit, CListBox, CScrollBar, CStatic, CStatusBar, CToolBar
Dialogs	CColorDialog, CDataExchange, CDialog, CFileDialog, CFindReplaceDialog, CFontDialog, CPrintDialog, CPropertyPage, CPropertySheet
Various window types	CFrameWnd, CMDIChildWnd, CMDIFrameWnd, CMiniFrameWnd, CSplitterWnd, CWnd
Device contexts	CClientDC, CDC, CMetaFileDC, CPaintDC, CWindowDC
GDI objects	CBitmap, CBrush, CFont, CGdiObject, CPalette, CPen, CRgn
Menus	CMenu
OLE 2 classes	CDocItem, COleBusyDialog, COleChangeIconDialog, COleClientItem, COleCntrFrameWnd, COleConvertDialog, COleDataObject, COleDataSource, COleDialog, COleDocument, COleDropSource, COleDropTarget, COleInsertDialog, COleIPFrameWnd, COleLinkingDoc, COleLinksDialog, COleMessageFilter, COleObjectFactory, COlePasteSpecialDialog, COleResizeBar, COleServerDoc, COleServerItem, COleStreamFile, COleTemplateServer, COleUpdateDialog, CRectTracker
Windows data types	CPoint, CRect, CSize

Table 18.2. Alphabetical listing of Windows programming classes in MFC 3.0.

Class	Base Class	Include File
CBitmap	CGdiObject	AFXWIN.H
CBitmapButton	CButton	AFXEXT.H
CBrush	CGdiObject	AFXWIN.H
CButton	CWnd	AFXWIN.H
CClientDC	CDC	AFXWIN.H
CCmdTarget	CObject	AFXWIN.H
CCmdUI	—	AFXWIN.H
CColorDialog	CDialog	AFXDLGS.H
CComboBox	CWnd	AFXWIN.H
CControlBar	CWnd	AFXEXT.H
CDataExchange	—	AFXWIN.H
CDC	CObject	AFXWIN.H
CDialog	CWnd	AFXWIN.H
CDialogBar	CControlBar	AFXEXT.H
CDocItem	CCmdTarget	AFXOLE.H
CDocTemplate	CCmdTarget	AFXWIN.H
CDocument	CCmdTarget	AFXWIN.H
CEdit	CWnd	AFXWIN.H
CEditView	CView	AFXEXT.H
CFileDialog	CDialog	AFXDLGS.H
CFindReplaceDialog	CDialog	AFXDLGS.H
CFont	CGdiObject	AFXWIN.H
CFontDialog	CDialog	AFXDLGS.H
CFormView	CScrollView	AFXEXT.H
CFrameWnd	CWnd	AFXWIN.H
CGdiObject	CObject	AFXWIN.H
CListBox	CWnd	AFXWIN.H
CMDIChildWnd	CFrameWnd	AFXWIN.H
CMDIFrameWnd	CFrameWnd	AFXWIN.H
CMenu	CObject	AFXWIN.H

continues

Table 18.2. continued

Class	Base Class	Include File
CMetaFileDC	CDC	AFXEXT.H
CMiniFrameWnd	CFrameWnd	AFXWIN.H
CMultiDocTemplate	CDocTemplate	AFXWIN.H
COleBusyDialog	COleDialog	AFXODLGS.H
COleChangeIconDialog	COleDialog	AFXODLGS.H
COleClientItem	CDocItem	AFXOLE.H
COleConvertDialog	COleDialog	AFXODLGS.H
COleDataObject	—	AFXOLE.H
COleDataSource	CCmdTarget	AFXOLE.H
COleDialog	CDialog	AFXODLGS.H
COleDocument	CDocument	AFXOLE.H
COleDropSource	CCmdTarget	AFXOLE.H
COleDropTarget	CCmdTarget	AFXOLE.H
COleInsertDialog	COleDialog	AFXODLGS.H
COleIPFrameWnd	CFrameWnd	AFXOLE.H
COleLinkingDoc	COleDocument	AFXOLE.H
COleLinksDialog	COleDialog	AFXODLGS.H
COleMessageFilter	CCmdTarget	AFXOLE.H
COleObjectFactory	CCmdTarget	AFXDISP.H
COlePasteSpecialDialog	COleDialog	AFXODLGS.H
COleResizeBar	CControlBar	AFXOLE.H
COleServerDoc	COleLinkingDoc	AFXOLE.H
COleServerItem	CDocItem	AFXOLE.H
COleStreamFile	CFile	AFXOLE.H
COleTemplateServer	COleObjectFactory	AFXDISP.H
COleUpdateDialog	COleLinksDialog	AFXODLGS.H
CPaintDC	CDC	AFXWIN.H
CPalette	CGdiObject	AFXWIN.H
CPen	CGdiObject	AFXWIN.H
CPoint	tagPOINT	AFXWIN.H
CPrintDialog	CDialog	AFXDLGS.H
CPropertyPage	CDialog	AFXDLGS.H
CPropertySheet	CWnd	AFXDLGS.H

Class	Base Class	Include File
CRect	tagRECT	AFXWIN.H
CRectTracker	—	AFXEXT.H
CRgn	CGdiObject	AFXWIN.H
CScrollBar	CWnd	AFXWIN.H
CScrollView	CView	AFXWIN.H
CSingleDocTemplate	CDocTemplate	AFXWIN.H
CSize	tagSIZE	AFXWIN.H
CSplitterWnd	CWnd	AFXEXT.H
CStatic	CWnd	AFXWIN.H
CStatusBar	CControlBar	AFXEXT.H
CToolBar	CControlBar	AFXEXT.H
CView	CWnd	AFXWIN.H
CWinApp	CWinThread	AFXWIN.H
CWindowDC	CDC	AFXWIN.H
CWinThread	CCmdTarget	AFXWIN.H
Cwn	CCmdTarget	AFXWIN.H

Application Framework Classes

As explained in Chapter 17, Smalltalk-80's Model-View-Controller (MVC) architecture provides a good way to organize applications into distinct parts consisting of the application's data, the presentation of that data in windows, and interaction with the user (through the events that are generated when the user uses the mouse and the keyboard).

Many commercially available programming environments and libraries have been influenced by Smalltalk-80's MVC architecture. For example, the MVC architecture was used by Apple Computer in the MacApp class library that provides all the components necessary to build a standard user interface for any Macintosh application. MacApp's TApplication class is the controller that manages interactions with the user, TView is responsible for displaying the view, and TDocument provides the hooks for implementing the application's model. The TDocument class is also responsible for reading the application's data from the disk and writing it to the disk.

MFC 3.0's document-view architecture is also patterned after Smalltalk-80's MVC architecture. The CWinApp class handles the user interaction, the CDocument classes manage the application's data, and the CView classes display the application's data in one or more windows.

The CWinApp class supplies the shell of an application that you can expand to create your own Windows application. As shown in the example in Chapter 17, to build a Windows application you need to derive your application class from CWinApp and override the InitInstance member function to create the main window of your application.

You also derive a window class from one of the predefined window types, such as CFrameWnd, and create an instance of that window in the InitInstance member function of the application class. Once the window is displayed, the window's message handling mechanism takes over the interaction with the user. You must follow a cookbook approach (see Chapter 17 for an example) to handle specific Windows messages.

PRIOR EXPERIENCE WITH WINDOWS API IS HELPFUL

You can follow a cookbook approach and use the Windows programming classes to develop Microsoft Windows applications. However, to exploit fully the capabilities that these classes offer, you should familiarize yourself with the basics of Windows programming. For example, experience with writing Windows programs in C with the Microsoft Windows Application Programming Interface (API) is helpful, because the MFC 3.0 Library provides classes that mimic the organization and the programming interface of the Windows API. This chapter does not cover the Windows API in detail but points out similarities between the Windows programming classes and the API. Consult the online documentation that accompanies the Visual C++ 2.0 compiler for more information.

Documents

In MFC 3.0, the term *document* refers to the data that the user accesses with the File Open command and saves with the File Close command. The CDocument class provides the basic support for managing documents, which involves tasks such as the following:

- Creating a document
- Loading a document
- Saving a document

An application that uses the document-view model manipulates documents using the interface defined by CDocument. Usually, you derive your own document class from CDocument so that you can provide the appropriate interface to manipulate the data that represents your document.

Views

Users see and manipulate a document through one or more CView objects associated with it. As the name implies, the CView object associated with a CDocument displays the document in a frame window and interprets user input as operations on the document. A document can have several views associated with it. MFC 3.0 offers the following view classes derived from CView:

- CEditView provides a text editor that supports printing, find and replace operations, and text editing functions such as cut, copy, paste, clear, and undo. CEditView is similar to a Windows edit control, and a CEditView object can store only a limited amount of text.

- CFormView is for displaying controls such as buttons, static text, and edit controls as a "form." For example, an application might use CFormView to display information about a customer from its database. The layout of the controls in a CFormView is specified by a dialog template in the application's resource.

- CPreviewView provides a view that displays the document as it would appear when printed. CPreviewView is used to implement the "print preview" feature of applications.

- CScrollView provides a view with scrolling capabilities.

Document Templates

The document template classes, dervied from the CDocTemplate class, provide the mechanism for specifying what type of view and frame window are used to display each type of document. A typical Windows application uses one of the two CDocTemplate-derived classes provided by MFC 3.0:

- CSingleDocTemplate specifies a single document interface (SDI) where a view of the document is displayed in the main frame window and only one document can be opened at a time.

- CMultiDocTemplate implements a multiple document interface (MDI) that treats the display area of the main frame window as a workspace in which one or more documents can be viewed simultaneously.

In addition to specifying the view and frame window types for a document, a document template also specifies what resources (for example, menu, icon, or accelerator table) are used for that type of document. Each document contains a pointer to its associated CDocTemplate object.

Menus

The CMenu class represents the menu bar in a window. Generally, you define menus in resource files, and you can initialize a CMenu object from the definitions in the resource file using the LoadMenu member function of the CMenu class.

Microsoft Windows Window Types

The classes in the CWnd hierarchy represent different types of windows. CWnd is a general-purpose window that can be the main, pop-up, or child windows of an application. The CWnd class encapsulates a window handle (the HWND type from the Windows API) and provides the member functions necessary to manipulate the window.

The main window of MFC-based Windows applications is typically CFrameWnd or a CMDIFrameWindow; both are derived from the CWnd class. CWnd serves as the base class of several useful window classes:

■ CFrameWnd is a standard frame window. You can derive your application's main window class from CFrameWnd.

■ CMDIFrameWnd is derived from CFrameWnd and is used to provide an MDI wherein several child windows are managed by an outer frame window. If your application requires an MDI, you can derive a class from CMDIFrameWnd and use that derived class as the work area where the multiple child windows appear.

■ CMDIChildWnd is also derived from CFrameWnd. The CMDIChildWnd class represents the child windows that are managed by CMDIFrameWnd.

■ CMiniFrameWnd represents a half-height frame window typically used for floating tool bars. These mini-frame windows are like normal frame windows, except that they do not have the minimize and maximize buttons or menus, and a single-click on the system menu closes the window.

■ CSplitterWnd class provides a window that contains multiple panes, where each pane is usually an application-specific object derived from CView, but it can be any CWnd object with an appropriate child window ID. *Splitter windows* are usually embedded in a parent CFrameWnd or CMDIChildWnd.

Think of these classes in the CWnd hierarchy as C++ data types that represent the window types in Microsoft Windows.

In addition to the CWnd classes described so far, two major categories of classes, dialog boxes and controls, are derived from the CWnd class.

When you define a CWnd object, the CWnd constructor does not automatically create the window. You must call the Create member function that produces the window and saves its handle in the CWnd object's public member variable, m_hWnd. Therefore, a CWnd can exist without a valid window.

The CWnd class contains a virtual destructor that destroys the window as well as the CWnd object. You can destroy just the window by calling the DestroyWindow member function.

THE CWnd CLASSES AND THE WINDOWS IN MICROSOFT WINDOWS

The CWnd class and the Windows window associated with a CWnd object illustrate the relationship between the C++ classes and the Windows API. A window in Windows, represented by a *window handle,* HWND, is an internal data structure that corresponds to an area of the screen where an application's output appears. The Windows API provides many functions that manipulate windows and that accept a window handle as an argument. MFC 3.0 encapsulates a window handle, HWND, in the CWnd class and defines all necessary member functions to provide the functionality for all window manipulation functions of the Windows API.

Dialog Boxes

Dialog boxes are used in a *graphical user interface* (GUI) to display messages to the user and prompt for information. A simple dialog box is the window that you see when you select the About... option from the Help menu in a Microsoft Windows application. Another example of a dialog box is the window that appears when you select the Open... option from the File menu in many Windows applications. MFC 3.0 includes a hierarchy of C++ classes that provide several predefined dialog boxes.

The CDialog class, which is derived from CWnd, serves as the base class of the dialog class hierarchy. A dialog can be either *modal* (user must complete interaction with the dialog before performing other tasks) or *modeless* (user does not have to respond to the dialog prior to performing other tasks). You can define both modal and modeless dialogs by deriving your own dialog class from CDialog. MFC 3.0 provides the following dialog classes:

- CFindReplaceDialog is derived from CDialog and provides a *modeless dialog box* that prompts the user for a string and its replacement. Because this is a modeless dialog box, the user can continue to interact with other menu items in the application while CFindReplaceDialog is displayed.

- CFileDialog is derived from CDialog and displays a list of files and directories from which the user can select a file. This modal dialog box is based on the COMMDLG.DLL dynamic link library.

- CFontDialog is derived from CDialog and provides a modal dialog box from which the user can select a font.

- CPrintDialog is another modal dialog box, derived from CDialog, that prompts the user for information and displays a message during printing.

- CColorDialog is derived from CDialog. Users employ this modal dialog box as a convenient way to pick a color.

■ CPropertyPage is derived from CDialog and represents a "page" in a tabbed dialog box of the type used in many new Windows applications. For example, the Visual Workbench's Project Settings dialog (this style of dialog box is known as a *tabbed dialog*) uses such property pages.

The dialog classes make it very easy to display and use a dialog. For example, with the CDialog class, here is what you have to write to display the About box in the sample application shown in Chapter 17:

```
CDialog about("ABOUTHELLO", this);
about.DoModal();
```

ABOUTHELLO is the name of the dialog box, as defined in the application's resource file. The DoModal function displays the dialog in a modal manner—the user has to close the dialog box before interacting with the rest of the application. To display a modeless dialog, you have to call the Create function of the dialog class.

Control Classes

Controls refer to user-interface items, such as buttons and scrollbars, that the user manipulates with the mouse to supply input to the application. Controls usually appear inside dialog windows, but you can also place controls such as buttons in your own windows. The following are the control classes in MFC 3.0:

■ CBitmapButton is a pushbutton control labeled with a bitmap image in place of text.

■ CButton represents a Windows button control, which is used extensively in Windows applications—especially in dialog boxes.

■ CControlBar provides a window that can hold other controls, such as bitmap buttons to initiate actions or text items to display status information. The CControlBar class serves as the base class for the CToolBar, CStatusBar, and CDialogBar classes.

■ CComboBox is equivalent to a Windows combo box control, which consists of a static control or edit control together with a drop-down listbox for making selections. Usually, the listbox is hidden and a button with an arrow appears next to the edit window. The list appears when the user selects the drop-down arrow. The edit window shows the current selection from the list.

■ CDialogBar is a specialized version of CControlBar that is defined through a dialog template in a resource file and that acts like a dialog box organized in the form of a control bar (so named because the controls are usually organized in a row or column). A CDialogBar can contain any type of controls.

■ CEdit is a C++ class corresponding to the predefined edit control in Windows that provides a window wherein the user can enter and edit text.

■ CListBox represents a Windows listbox where the application can display a list of items, such as names of files. The user can view the list and select one or more items from it.

- ■ CScrollBar is a Windows scrollbar control that you can orient horizontally or vertically.

- ■ CStatic provides the functionality of Windows *static controls*, which are text fields used as labels or boxes used as decorative items. The text displayed in a Windows static control cannot be edited by the user.

- ■ CStatusBar is a type of CControlBar that provides a row of text output panes. These text output panes are used to indicate status (such as ths status of the Caps Lock key) and display messages (such as hints or one-line help messages). Many Windows applications (including the Visual Workbench in Visual C++ 2.0) sport a status bar at the bottom edge of the main window.

- ■ CToolBar is derived from CControlBar and it provides a row of bitmapped buttons and optional separators. The buttons can act like pushbuttons, checkbox buttons, or radio buttons. In the Visual Workbench, a tool bar appears below the menu bar.

Graphics Device Interface Objects

Recall that the GDI refers to the device-independent set of functions that the Microsoft Windows API provides for graphics output. These GDI functions can use a number of drawing tools to produce different graphics outputs. MFC 3.0 includes a number of C++ classes that represent these drawing tools. The CGdiObject class, which is derived from CObject, serves as the base class for the following drawing tool classes:

- ■ CBitmap represents a bitmap.

- ■ CBrush is the C++ class that models a GDI brush that you can use to fill graphics shapes.

- ■ CFont is a font that you can use to display text.

- ■ CPalette is a GDI color palette.

- ■ CPen represents a GDI pen object. You can use a pen to draw the outline of graphics shapes.

- ■ CRgn represents a *region*—a combination of elliptical, rectangular, and polygonal areas that you can use for drawing or clipping.

To use these GDI objects, you also need another important item—a device context, described in the next section.

Device Context Classes

In Windows, you must obtain a device context (DC) before you can use the GDI functions to display output on a device. Recall that the device context is an internal data structure that stores graphics attributes, such as background and foreground colors, the pen, and the font. The appearance of graphics and text is controlled by these attributes. Each GDI drawing function in the Windows API requires a handle to a DC as an argument. In MFC 3.0, the DC is encapsulated in the CDC class with the drawing functions defined as member functions of the CDC class.

For specific uses, MFC 3.0 includes the following classes derived from CDC:

■ CClientDC represents a device context associated with the *client area* of a window (the area of a window inside the frame or the area where output appears).

■ CMetaFileDC provides a device context for use with a *metafile*—a file used to store GDI graphics operations in a specific format.

■ CPaintDC is a device context for use in redrawing a window's contents in response to a WM_PAINT message. The CPaintDC class encapsulates the calls to BeginPaint and EndPaint that typically enclose calls to any graphics functions in Windows programs that are developed using the API.

■ CWindowDC provides a device context for the entire window, including the frame.

Basic Windows Data Types

Three classes—CPoint, CRect, and CSize—operate as basic data types in Windows applications:

■ CPoint represents a two-dimensional point with x,y coordinates.

■ CRect represents a rectangle.

■ CSize represents relative coordinates.

If you have programmed with the Microsoft Windows API, you should recognize CPoint, CRect, and CSize as classes that are similar to their respective POINT, RECT, and SIZE structures.

Exploring the Windows Programming Classes

Previous sections provided an overview of the MFC 3.0 classes for writing Windows applications. You have already seen how to use the application framework classes (CWin, CDocument, and CView) in Chapter 17. The following sections explain the usage of some of the other classes through short example programs.

Using the Control Classes

The control classes provide the basic user interface objects, such as buttons, edit controls, and listboxes, that normally appear in a dialog window. However, you also can use these controls in other windows.

The *CStatic* Class

The CStatic class is commonly used to display a text string in a dialog window. You can create an instance of a CStatic control by calling the Create member function of a CStatic object. The CStatic::Create function has the following syntax:

```
BOOL Create(
    LPCTSTR lpszText,      // Text to be displayed
    DWORD dwStyle,         // Style of the Static control
    const RECT& rect,      // Position and size
    CWnd* pParentWnd,      // Parent window
    UINT nID = 0xffff );   // Control ID
```

The first argument of the function is the null-terminated text string to be displayed in the CStatic control.

Listing 18.1 shows a sample program that uses a CStatic control to display the coordinates of the location where the user last pressed the left mouse button. The program uses another CStatic control as a label. Notice how the text displayed in the CStatic control is changed in the OnLButtonDown function, which Windows calls whenever the user presses the left mouse button with the cursor inside the program's window.

Figure 18.2 shows the program of Listing 18.1 displaying the position of the mouse cursor in a CStatic control.

FIGURE 18.2.

Displaying text with a CStatic control.

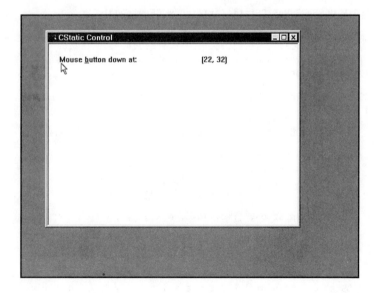

Listing 18.1. STEXT.CPP. Sample program to illustrate the use of `CStatic` control.

```cpp
//------------------------------------------------------------
// File: stext.cpp
//
// Demonstrate the use of the CStatic objects to display
// static text
//------------------------------------------------------------
#include <afx.h>
#include <afxwin.h>

class CStaticTextWindow : public CFrameWnd
{
public:
    CStaticTextWindow();
    ~CStaticTextWindow();

    afx_msg void OnLButtonDown(UINT nFlags, CPoint point);

private:
    int     m_x, m_y;
    CStatic m_ClkPos;
    CStatic m_Lbl;
    char    m_szPos[16];

    DECLARE_MESSAGE_MAP()
};

// Define the "message map"
BEGIN_MESSAGE_MAP(CStaticTextWindow,CFrameWnd)
    ON_WM_LBUTTONDOWN()
END_MESSAGE_MAP()
//------------------------------------------------------------
// CStaticTextWindow:: C S t a t i c T e x t W i n d o w
// Constructor

CStaticTextWindow::CStaticTextWindow() : m_x(0), m_y(0)
{
// Create the frame window
    Create(NULL, "CStatic Control");

// Set up the CStatic objects in the frame window
    m_Lbl.Create("Mouse &button down at: ",
                WS_CHILD | WS_VISIBLE | SS_LEFT,
                CRect(20, 20, 270, 44), this);

    wsprintf(m_szPos, "(%d, %d)", m_x, m_y);
    m_ClkPos.Create(m_szPos,
                    WS_CHILD | WS_VISIBLE | SS_CENTER,
                    CRect(260, 20,   360, 44), this);
}
//------------------------------------------------------------
// CStaticTextWindow:: ~ C S t a t i c T e x t W i n d o w
// Destructor

CStaticTextWindow::~CStaticTextWindow()
{
    m_Lbl.DestroyWindow();
    m_ClkPos.DestroyWindow();
```

```
}
//-----------------------------------------------------------
// CStaticTextWindow:: O n L B u t t o n D o w n
// Process WM_LBUTTONDOWN events

void CStaticTextWindow::OnLButtonDown(UINT, CPoint point)
{
// Display the location of "mouse button down" in the CStatic
// control
    m_x = point.x;
    m_y = point.y;
    wsprintf(m_szPos, "(%d, %d)", m_x, m_y);
    m_ClkPos.SetWindowText(m_szPos);
}
//-----------------------------------------------------------
class CStaticTextApp : public CWinApp
{
public:
    CStaticTextApp() : CWinApp() {}
    BOOL InitInstance()
    {
        m_pMainWnd = new CStaticTextWindow;
        m_pMainWnd->ShowWindow(m_nCmdShow);
        m_pMainWnd->UpdateWindow();
        return TRUE;
    }
};
//-----------------------------------------------------------
// Create an instance of the application

    CStaticTextApp App;
```

Pushbuttons, Checkboxes, Radio Buttons, and Group Boxes

Pushbuttons are commonly used to enable the user to initiate some action. For example, a dialog window might have a pushbutton labeled OK that the user can press to indicate acceptance of the settings that the dialog window offers. When the user presses the left mouse button with the cursor on a pushbutton, the button is pushed in, but the button reverts to its original state as soon as the user releases the mouse button. In MFC 3.0, the CButton class, declared in the header file <afxwin.h>, represents pushbuttons.

Checkboxes and radio buttons are specialized versions of pushbuttons. Unlike pushbuttons, these buttons can remain in one of two states: on (set) and off (reset). A mouse click on a checkbox or a radio button toggles its state.

The label for a checkbox appears next to a square box. When the checkbox is turned "on" (or checked), a small checkmark appears in the box. A radio button has a small circle next to its label. A dot appears in that circle when that radio button is set.

Checkboxes and radio buttons are used in groups—placed in a group box control (a CButton with a BS_GROUPBOX style). The difference in behavior between checkboxes and radio buttons becomes apparent when they are arranged in a group box. From a group of checkboxes, the user can click and select more than one checkbox. However, the user can select only one radio button from a group of radio buttons inside a group box. Thus, you should use checkboxes to accept multiple selections and radio buttons when only one item from a group of related items can be selected. As an example, if you are preparing a dialog box through which an employee selects health insurance coverage, you use a group of radio buttons to present the health insurance companies because the employee is allowed to choose only one health insurance provider. However, the dialog box might display a number of checkboxes showing several specific medical benefits from which the employee can pick one or more.

Listing 18.2 shows a sample program that enables the user to order a serving of ice cream. Figure 18.3 shows the output of the program after the user has selected the items and clicked on the button labeled Order. As you can see from Listing 18.2, one group box displays the flavors as radio buttons, and another group box shows the available toppings in a number of checkboxes. The common practice is to use a dialog box to prompt for this type of user input. Typically, a dialog box is initialized from the resource file. This example places the group boxes and the buttons directly in a window.

You can create a button by calling the Create function of the CButton class, which has the following syntax:

```
BOOL Create(
    LPCTSTR lpszCaption,   // Label of button
    DWORD   dwStyle,       // Button style
    const RECT& rect,      // Position and size
    CWnd*   pParentWnd,    // Parent window
    UINT    nID );         // Control ID
```

If the button has the BS_DEFPUSHBUTTON style, the button is drawn with a heavy border and the user can select this button by pressing the Enter key. Usually, a pushbutton has an associated control identifier (the nID argument in the constructor) because pushbuttons are used to initiate some action and this requires having a message response function that can be called in response to the message generated by the pushbutton. For example, in Listing 18.2, the button labeled Order is tied to the TakeOrder function as follows:

1. Assign an identifier when creating the button:

   ```
   const int ID_ORDER    = 1;
   //...
       m_Order.Create("Order", WS_CHILD ¦ WS_VISIBLE ¦
                   WS_TABSTOP ¦ BS_DEFPUSHBUTTON,
                   CRect(CPoint(50, 200), CSize(80, 24)),
                   this, ID_ORDER);
   ```

2. Declare the TakeOrder function as a member function of the window that contains the button:

   ```
   afx_msg void  TakeOrder();
   ```

3. Include the `take_order` function in the definition of the message map with an `ON_COMMAND` macro:

```
// Define the message map
BEGIN_MESSAGE_MAP(CButtonTestWindow, CFrameWnd)
     ON_COMMAND(ID_ORDER, TakeOrder)
//...
END_MESSAGE_MAP()
```

FIGURE 18.3.

Prompting for ice cream flavors and toppings with checkboxes and radio buttons.

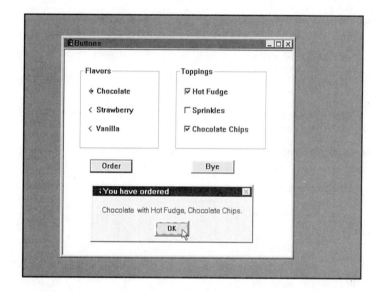

Listing 18.2. BUTTONS.CPP. Sample program to illustrate the use of pushbuttons.

```
//---------------------------------------------------------------
// File: buttons.cpp
//
// Sample program to illustrate the use of button, checkbox,
// radio buttons, and group box.
//---------------------------------------------------------------

#include <afx.h>
#include <afxwin.h>

const int ID_ORDER    = 1;
const int ID_BYE      = 2;

const int FWIDTH      = 150;
const int FHEIGHT     = 150;
const int TWIDTH      = 170;
const int THEIGHT     = 150;

static char* aszFlavorNames[3] =
{
```

continues

Listing 18.2. continued

```
    "Chocolate", "Strawberry", "Vanilla"
};

static char* aszToppingNames[3] =
{
    "Hot Fudge", "Sprinkles", "Chocolate Chips"
};

class CButtonTestWindow : public CFrameWnd
{
public:
    CButton m_aFlavors[3];
    CButton m_aToppings[3];
    CButton m_FlvrGrp;
    CButton m_TpngGrp;
    CButton m_Order;
    CButton m_Bye;

    CButtonTestWindow();
    ~CButtonTestWindow();

// Message handlers for the buttons

    afx_msg void  TakeOrder();
    afx_msg void  Quit()
    {
        DestroyWindow();
    }

    DECLARE_MESSAGE_MAP()
};

// Define the message map

BEGIN_MESSAGE_MAP(CButtonTestWindow, CFrameWnd)
      ON_COMMAND(ID_ORDER, TakeOrder)
      ON_COMMAND(ID_BYE, Quit)
END_MESSAGE_MAP()
//-------------------------------------------------------------
CButtonTestWindow::CButtonTestWindow() : CFrameWnd()
{
// Create the main frame window
    Create(NULL, "Buttons");

// Create the group boxes to display flavor and topping
// selections.
    m_FlvrGrp.Create("Flavors", WS_CHILD | WS_VISIBLE |
                      BS_GROUPBOX,
                      CRect(CPoint(30, 30),
                            CSize(FWIDTH, FHEIGHT)),
                      this, 0xffff);

    m_TpngGrp.Create("Toppings", WS_CHILD | WS_VISIBLE |
                      BS_GROUPBOX,
                      CRect(CPoint(FWIDTH+60, 30),
                            CSize(TWIDTH, THEIGHT)),
                      this, 0xffff);
```

```
// Set up the other buttons
    int i;
    DWORD style = WS_CHILD | WS_VISIBLE | WS_TABSTOP |
                    BS_AUTORADIOBUTTON;
    for(i = 0; i < 3; i++)
    {
        if(0 == i) style |= WS_GROUP;
        m_aFlavors[i].Create(aszFlavorNames[i],
                                style,
                                CRect(CPoint(46, 30+34*(i+1)),
                                    CSize(FWIDTH-30, 24)),
                                this, 0xffff);
        if(0 == i) style &= ~WS_GROUP;
    }
    style = WS_CHILD | WS_VISIBLE | WS_TABSTOP |
                    BS_AUTOCHECKBOX;
    for(i = 0; i < 3; i++)
    {
        if(0 == i) style |= WS_GROUP;
        m_aToppings[i].Create(aszToppingNames[i],
                                style,
                                CRect(CPoint(FWIDTH+76,
                                            30+34*(i+1)),
                                    CSize(TWIDTH-30, 24)),
                                this, 0xffff);
        if(0 == i) style &= ~WS_GROUP;
    }

    m_Order.Create("Order", WS_CHILD | WS_VISIBLE |
                    WS_TABSTOP | BS_DEFPUSHBUTTON,
                    CRect(CPoint(50, 200), CSize(80, 24)),
                    this, ID_ORDER);

    m_Bye.Create("Bye", WS_CHILD | WS_VISIBLE |
                    WS_TABSTOP,
                    CRect(CPoint(FWIDTH+90, 200),
                        CSize(80, 24)),
                    this, ID_BYE);
}
//----------------------------------------------------------------
CButtonTestWindow::~CButtonTestWindow()
{
// Destroy all button windows
    m_FlvrGrp.DestroyWindow();
    m_TpngGrp.DestroyWindow();

    int i;
    for(i = 0; i < 3; i++)
    {
        m_aFlavors[i].DestroyWindow();
        m_aToppings[i].DestroyWindow();
    }
    m_Order.DestroyWindow();
    m_Bye.DestroyWindow();
}
//----------------------------------------------------------------
void CButtonTestWindow::TakeOrder()
```

continues

Listing 18.2. continued

```
{
    char buf[256];
// Check which flavor was ordered
    int i, n = 0;
    for(i = 0; i < 3; i++)
    {
        if(m_aFlavors[i].GetCheck() == 1)
        {
            n = wsprintf(buf, "%s   ",
                            aszFlavorNames[i]);
            break;
        }
    }
    if(i >= 3)
    {
        MessageBeep(MB_ICONEXCLAMATION);
        return;
    }

// Now pick the selected toppings
    int with = 0;
    for(i = 0; i < 3; i++)
    {
        if(m_aToppings[i].GetCheck() == 1)
        {
            if(with == 0)
            {
                n += wsprintf(&buf[n], "with ");
                with = 1;
            }
            n += wsprintf(&buf[n], "%s, ",
                                aszToppingNames[i]);
        }
    }
    wsprintf(&buf[n-2], ".");

// Display the order in a message box...
    MessageBox(buf, "You have ordered", MB_OK);
}
//----------------------------------------------------------------
class CButtonTestApp : public CWinApp
{
public:
    CButtonTestApp() : CWinApp() {}
    BOOL  InitInstance();
};
//----------------------------------------------------------------
BOOL CButtonTestApp::InitInstance()
{
// Enable Microsoft's 3-D Controls
    Enable3dControls();
    m_pMainWnd = new CButtonTestWindow;
    m_pMainWnd->ShowWindow(m_nCmdShow);
    m_pMainWnd->UpdateWindow();
    return TRUE;
```

```
}
//--------------------------------------------------------------------
// Create an instance of the application

    CButtonTestApp app;
```

Listbox

The CListBox class encapsulates the Windows listbox control. Use this control to display a list of items together with a scrollbar to enable the user to scroll through the list.

Listing 18.3 shows a sample program that uses a listbox to display the names of all Windows programming classes in MFC 3.0. Figure 18.4 shows the resulting listbox with one of the items selected.

FIGURE 18.4.

A listbox showing the Windows programming classes in MFC 3.0.

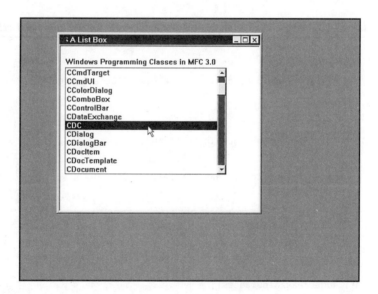

Like other controls, listboxes are most often used in dialog boxes, and their layout is defined in the resource file. In the example program shown in Listing 18.3, the listbox is created as a child of the CListBoxWindow class, which is derived from the MFC class CFrameWnd. The CListBox object is created and initialized in the constructor of the CListBoxWindow class by calling the Create member function of the CListBox object:

```
// Create the listbox
    m_ListBox.Create(WS_CHILD | WS_VISIBLE | WS_VSCROLL |
                     LBS_STANDARD,
                     CRect(CPoint(10, 40), CSize(300, 200)),
                     this, 0xffff);
```

Once the listbox is created, you can insert items into it by calling the AddString function of the CListBox class. For example, to insert the string "MFC 3.0", write the following:

```
m_ListBox.AddString("MFC 3.0");
```

By default, the listbox control sorts its contents in alphabetical order. The default behavior of the listbox is controlled by the setting of the first argument of the CListBox::Create function. Use the LBS_STANDARD style to get a listbox with standard behavior. The constant LBS_STANDARD (defined in <windows.h>) is part of the Windows API and it specifies the following behavior for the listbox:

1. Display a border (LBS_BORDER).
2. Sort the contents (LBS_SORT).
3. Notify the parent window when the user clicks on any item (LBS_NOTIFY).

Listing 18.3. LISTBOX.CPP. Sample program to illustrate the use of the CListBox class.

```cpp
//---------------------------------------------------------------
// File: listbox.cpp
//
// Sample program to demonstrate the use of CListBox control
//---------------------------------------------------------------
#include <afx.h>
#include <afxwin.h>

class CListBoxWindow : public CFrameWnd
{
public:
    CListBoxWindow(const char *title);
    ~CListBoxWindow();

private:
    CListBox    m_ListBox;
    CStatic     m_Title;
};

// Items for the listbox
static char* aszWinClasses[] =
{
    "CWinApp", "CWinThread", "CCmdTarget", "CCmdUI",
    "CDocTemplate", "CDocument", "CMultiDocTemplate",
    "CSingleDocTemplate", "CEditView", "CFormView",
    "CPreviewView", "CScrollView", "CView",
    "CBitmapButton", "CButton", "CControlBar",
    "CComboBox", "CDialogBar", "CEdit", "CListBox",
    "CScrollBar", "CStatic", "CStatusBar", "CTabControl",
    "CToolBar", "CColorDialog", "CDataExchange", "CDialog",
    "CFileDialog", "CFindReplaceDialog", "CFontDialog",
    "CPrintDialog", "CPropertyPage", "CPropertySheet",
    "CFrameWnd", "CMDIChildWnd", "CMDIFrameWnd",
    "CMiniFrameWnd", "CSplitterWnd", "CWnd", "CClientDC",
    "CDC", "CMetaFileDC", "CPaintDC", "CWindowDC",
    "CBitmap", "CBrush", "CFont", "CGdiObject", "CPalette",
    "CPen", "CMenu", "CDocItem", "COleBusyDialog",
```

```
        "COleChangeIconDialog", "COleClientItem", "COleCntrFrameWnd",
        "COleConvertDialog", "COleDataObject", "COleDataSource",
        "COleDialog", "COleDocument", "COleDropSource", "COleDropTarget",
        "COleInsertDialog", "COleIPFrameWnd", "COleLinkingDoc",
        "COleLinksDialog", "COleMessageFilter", "COleObjectFactory",
        "COlePasteSpecialDialog", "COleResizeBar", "COleServerDoc",
        "COleServerItem", "COleStreamFile", "COleTemplateServer",
        "COleUpdateDialog", "CRectTracker", "CPoint", "CRect",
        "CRgn", "CSize"
};
static int nNumCls = sizeof(aszWinClasses) /
                        sizeof(aszWinClasses[0]);

//-----------------------------------------------------------------
// CListBoxWindow Constructor

CListBoxWindow::CListBoxWindow(const char *title)
{
// Create the frame window
    Create(NULL, title);

// Create the label (a static control)
    m_Title.Create("Windows Programming Classes in MFC 3.0",
                WS_CHILD | WS_VISIBLE | SS_LEFT,
                CRect(10, 20, 310, 44), this);

// Create the listbox
    m_ListBox.Create(WS_CHILD | WS_VISIBLE | WS_VSCROLL |
                        LBS_STANDARD,
                        CRect(CPoint(10, 40), CSize(300, 200)),
                        this, 0xffff);
// Add items to the listbox
    int i;
    for(i = 0; i < nNumCls; i++)
    {
        m_ListBox.AddString(aszWinClasses[i]);
    }

}
//-----------------------------------------------------------------
// CListBoxWindow Destructor

CListBoxWindow::~CListBoxWindow()
{
    m_Title.DestroyWindow();
    m_ListBox.DestroyWindow();
}
//-----------------------------------------------------------------
class CListBoxApp : public CWinApp
{
public:
    BOOL InitInstance();
};
//-----------------------------------------------------------------
BOOL CListBoxApp::InitInstance()
{
    Enable3dControls();
    m_pMainWnd = new CListBoxWindow("A List Box");
```

continues

Listing 18.3. continued

```
    m_pMainWnd->ShowWindow(m_nCmdShow);
    m_pMainWnd->UpdateWindow();
    return TRUE;
}
//------------------------------------------------------------
// Create an instance of the application

    CListBoxApp app;
```

Combo Box

A combo box is a listbox together with an edit control or a static control that displays the current selection from the listbox. A combo box can keep the listbox hidden, showing only the current selection in the edit control. The list appears when the user clicks on a button next to the edit control. Thus, it is convenient to use a combo box to enable the user to pick one of many items without using a lot of space to display the complete list. Many Windows applications use combo boxes. For example, many Windows word processors use a combo box to enable the user to select a font.

The MFC class `CComboBox`, derived from `CWnd`, encapsulates the functionality of a Windows combo box control.

Listing 18.4 shows a sample program, similar to that for listbox, that displays the names of the MFC 3.0 Windows programming classes. Figure 18.5 shows the output of the program. In the figure, the drop-down listbox is shown in its visible state. Normally, only the selected item is visible next to the button with an arrow pointing down.

FIGURE 18.5.

A combo box with its drop-down listbox showing the Windows programming classes in MFC 3.0.

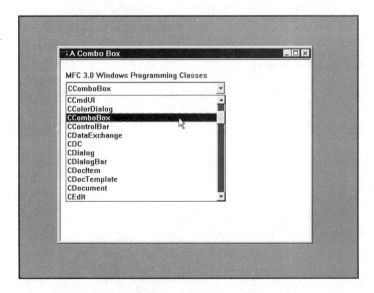

The example program creates the combo box by calling the following member function of the CComboBox class:

```
BOOL Create(
    DWORD dwStyle,     // Style constants (CBS_xxx)
    const RECT& rect,  // Position and size of combo box
    CWnd* pParentWnd,  // Pointer to parent window
    UINT nID );        // Control identifier
```

The appearance of the combo box is controlled by the dwStyle argument that you provide to the Create function. The following are some of the constants denoting the style of a combo box:

■ WS_VSCROLL adds vertical scrolling capability to the listbox in the combo box.

■ WS_HSCROLL adds horizontal scrolling capability to the listbox in the combo box.

■ CBS_AUTOHSCROLL automatically scrolls the text in the edit control when the user types one or more characters at the end of the line. If this style is not set, only text that fits within the rectangular boundary is allowed.

■ CBS_DROPDOWN creates a combo box that is similar to that specified by CBS_SIMPLE, except that the listbox is not displayed unless the user clicks on the button next to the edit control.

■ CBS_DROPDOWNLIST creates a combo box similar to that created for CBS_DROPDOWN, except that the current selection is displayed in a static control rather than an edit control.

■ CBS_SIMPLE creates a combo box that displays the listbox at all times. The edit control displays the current selection in the listbox.

■ CBS_SORT automatically sorts strings entered into the listbox.

You should use a bitwise OR of one or more of these constants to specify the style of the combo box.

Once the combo box is created, you can add the strings to its listbox by calling the AddString member function.

Listing 18.4. COMBOBX.CPP. Sample program to illustrate the use of the CComboBox class.

```
//--------------------------------------------------------------
// File: combobx.cpp
//
// Sample program to demonstrate the use of CComboBox control
//--------------------------------------------------------------
#include <afx.h>
#include <afxwin.h>

class CComboBoxWindow : public CFrameWnd
{
public:
    CComboBoxWindow(const char *title);
    ~CComboBoxWindow();
```

continues

Listing 18.4. continued

```
private:
    CComboBox    m_ComboBox;
    CStatic      m_Title;
};

// Items for the combo box
static char* aszWinClasses[] =
{
    "CWinApp", "CWinThread", "CCmdTarget", "CCmdUI",
    "CDocTemplate", "CDocument", "CMultiDocTemplate",
    "CSingleDocTemplate", "CEditView", "CFormView",
    "CPreviewView", "CScrollView", "CView",
    "CBitmapButton", "CButton", "CControlBar",
    "CComboBox", "CDialogBar", "CEdit",
    "CStatic", "CStatusBar", "CTabControl",
    "CToolBar", "CColorDialog", "CDataExchange", "CDialog",
    "CFileDialog", "CFindReplaceDialog", "CFontDialog",
    "CPrintDialog", "CPropertyPage", "CPropertySheet",
    "CFrameWnd", "CMDIChildWnd", "CMDIFrameWnd",
    "CMiniFrameWnd", "CSplitterWnd", "CWnd", "CClientDC",
    "CDC", "CMetaFileDC", "CPaintDC", "CWindowDC",
    "CBitmap", "CBrush", "CFont", "CGdiObject", "CPalette",
    "CPen", "CMenu", "CDocItem", "COleBusyDialog",
    "COleChangeIconDialog", "COleClientItem", "COleCntrFrameWnd",
    "COleConvertDialog", "COleDataObject", "COleDataSource",
    "COleDialog", "COleDocument", "COleDropSource", "COleDropTarget",
    "COleInsertDialog", "COleIPFrameWnd", "COleLinkingDoc",
    "COleLinksDialog", "COleMessageFilter", "COleObjectFactory",
    "COlePasteSpecialDialog", "COleResizeBar", "COleServerDoc",
    "COleServerItem", "COleStreamFile", "COleTemplateServer",
    "COleUpdateDialog", "CRectTracker", "CPoint", "CRect",
    "CRgn", "CSize"
};
static int nNumCls = sizeof(aszWinClasses) /
                     sizeof(aszWinClasses[0]);

//-------------------------------------------------------------
// CComboBoxWindow Constructor

CComboBoxWindow::CComboBoxWindow(const char *title)
{
// Create the frame window
    Create(NULL, title);

// Create the label (a static control)
    m_Title.Create("MFC 3.0 Windows Programming Classes",
                WS_CHILD | WS_VISIBLE | SS_LEFT,
                CRect(10, 20, 310, 44), this);

// Create the combo box
    m_ComboBox.Create(WS_CHILD | WS_VISIBLE | WS_VSCROLL |
                    WS_GROUP | WS_TABSTOP | CBS_SORT |
                    CBS_AUTOHSCROLL | CBS_DROPDOWNLIST,
                    CRect(CPoint(10, 40), CSize(300, 200)),
```

```
                        this, 0xffff);
// Add items to the combo box
    int i;
    for(i = 0; i < nNumCls; i++)
    {
        m_ComboBox.AddString(aszWinClasses[i]);
    }

}
//--------------------------------------------------------------
// CComboBoxWindow Destructor

CComboBoxWindow::~CComboBoxWindow()
{
    m_Title.DestroyWindow();
    m_ComboBox.DestroyWindow();
}
//--------------------------------------------------------------
class CComboBoxApp : public CWinApp
{
public:
    BOOL InitInstance();
};
//--------------------------------------------------------------
BOOL CComboBoxApp::InitInstance()
{
    m_pMainWnd = new CComboBoxWindow("A Combo Box");
    m_pMainWnd->ShowWindow(m_nCmdShow);
    m_pMainWnd->UpdateWindow();
    return TRUE;
}
//--------------------------------------------------------------
// Create an instance of the application

    CComboBoxApp app;
```

Using Dialogs

Windows applications use dialog boxes to prompt the user for input. For example, many Windows applications display a dialog enabling you to select a file to be opened or enter the name of a file where data will be saved. Dialog boxes are child windows that contain a variety of controls. Most dialog boxes use listboxes, edit controls, checkboxes, radio buttons, and pushbuttons to enable the user to enter input and specify options. You have already seen examples of these controls in the previous sections. This section presents a sample program that displays a standard dialog for color selection. This dialog is implemented by the CColorDialog class, which is part of a set of five commonly used dialog classes that are derived from the CDialog class (these dialogs rely on the COMMDLG.DLL file that accompanies Windows versions 3.1 and later):

- ■ CColorDialog to enable the user to select a color
- ■ CFileDialog to enable the user to select a filename
- ■ CFindReplaceDialog to enable the user to enter strings for a find or replace operation
- ■ CFontDialog to enable the user to select a font
- ■ CPrintDialog to enable the user to provide information for a print job

Figure 18.6 shows the appearance of the color selection dialog implemented by the CColorDialog class. Listing 18.5 shows the program that displays the dialog. The entire operation of setting up the dialog and retrieving the user's selection appears in the body of the CmColor function in Listing 18.5.

When displaying the dialog, you have to use the CColorDialog constructor to set up the dialog. The constructor has the following function prototype:

```
CColorDialog(
    COLORREF clrInit = 0,// Initial color, default is RGB(0,0,0)
    DWORD dwFlags = 0,   // Flags to customize the function
                         // and appearance of the dialog box.
                         // Meaning of flags same as that for
                         // the CHOOSECOLOR structure in the
                         // Windows API documentation.
    CWnd* pParentWnd = NULL); // Parent window
```

You also can access the m_cc member variable directly, which is a CHOOSECOLOR structure used to store characteristics and values for the color dialog box. After setting up the dialog, you can display it by calling the DoModal member function. After the user specifies the color and clicks on the OK button, you should use the GetColor function to retrieve the user-selected color. Here is how the color dialog is set up and displayed in the example program:

```
    CColorDialog ColorDlg(RGB(0,0,0), CC_FULLOPEN, m_pMainWnd);
    ColorDlg.m_cc.lpCustColors = m_aCustomColors;

    if(ColorDlg.DoModal() == IDOK)
    {
// Display information about selected color
        COLORREF ColorSel = ColorDlg.GetColor();
        char    msg[128];
        wsprintf(msg, "RGB intensities:\r\n\r\n Red: %d\r\n "
                    "Green: %d\r\n Blue: %d",
                    GetRValue(ColorSel), GetGValue(ColorSel),
                    GetBValue(ColorSel));
        m_pMainWnd->MessageBox(msg, m_pszAppName, MB_OK);
    }
```

You will see examples of other standard dialogs in the example programs in the rest of this book. For example, Chapter 20, "Displaying Text in Windows," uses a CFontDialog to enable the user to select a font.

FIGURE 18.6.

The color selection dialog box.

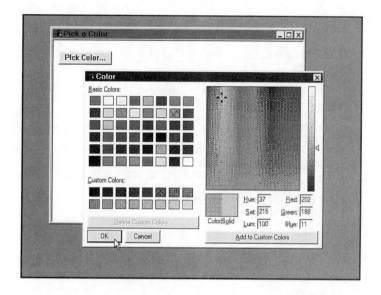

Listing 18.5. COLORDLG.CPP. Sample program to illustrate the use of the `CColorDialog` class.

```cpp
//--------------------------------------------------------------
// File: colordlg.cpp
//
// Sample program that demonstrates how to use the
// CColorDialog class.
//--------------------------------------------------------------
#include <afx.h>
#include <afxwin.h>
#include <afxdlgs.h>

#define CM_COLOR 101

class CColorDlgApp : public CWinApp
{
public:
    BOOL    InitInstance();
    virtual int ExitInstance();
    void    CmColor();

private:
    CButton    m_PickColor;
    DWORD      m_aCustomColors[16];

    DECLARE_MESSAGE_MAP()
};

// Define the message map
BEGIN_MESSAGE_MAP(CColorDlgApp, CWinApp)
  ON_COMMAND(CM_COLOR, CmColor)
END_MESSAGE_MAP()
//--------------------------------------------------------------
BOOL CColorDlgApp::InitInstance()
```

continues

Listing 18.5 continued

```
{
    Enable3dControls();

    CFrameWnd *Frame = new CFrameWnd;
    Frame->Create(NULL, "Pick a Color");
    m_pMainWnd = Frame;

// Create the button that the user can press to bring up the
// color selection dialog
    m_PickColor.Create("Pick Color...", WS_CHILD | WS_VISIBLE |
                        WS_TABSTOP,
                        CRect(CPoint(10, 20), CSize(100, 24)),
                        m_pMainWnd, CM_COLOR);
    m_pMainWnd->ShowWindow(m_nCmdShow);
    m_pMainWnd->UpdateWindow();

// Define the array of custom colors
    int i;
    for(i = 0; i < 16; i++)
        m_aCustomColors[i] = RGB(15*i, 15*i, 15*i);

    return TRUE;
}
//----------------------------------------------------------------
// CColorDlgApp:: E x i t I n s t a n c e
// Clean up before exiting application

int CColorDlgApp::ExitInstance()
{
    m_PickColor.DestroyWindow();
    return 0;
}
//----------------------------------------------------------------
// CColorDlgApp:: C m C o l o r
// Called when user presses the "Pick Color..." button

void CColorDlgApp::CmColor()
{
    CColorDialog ColorDlg(RGB(0,0,0), CC_FULLOPEN, m_pMainWnd);
    ColorDlg.m_cc.lpCustColors = m_aCustomColors;

    if(ColorDlg.DoModal() == IDOK)
    {
// Display information about selected color
        COLORREF ColorSel = ColorDlg.GetColor();
        char   msg[128];
        wsprintf(msg, "RGB intensities:\r\n\r\n Red: %d\r\n "
                      "Green: %d\r\n Blue: %d",
                      GetRValue(ColorSel), GetGValue(ColorSel),
                      GetBValue(ColorSel));
        m_pMainWnd->MessageBox(msg, m_pszAppName, MB_OK);
    }
}
//----------------------------------------------------------------
// Create an instance of this application

    CColorDlgApp app;
```

Using a Tool Bar and a Status Bar

Recall that a tool bar is a collection of pushbuttons, usually appearing at the top of an application's main window, that enables the user to initiate an action quickly. Many Windows applications, including the Visual C++ development environment, have a tool bar. Most include a button that enables the user to bring up the File Open dialog box quickly. Similarly, there is usually a bitmap button on the tool bar to print the document being displayed by the application. The user can perform each of these actions from the menus, but having the buttons on the tool bar makes it faster to do these tasks.

A status bar is another common decoration that appears in the main window of many Windows applications. This is an area at the bottom of a main window where the application displays short help messages as well as the status of specific keys, such as Caps Lock, Num Lock, and Insert.

MFC 3.0 makes it easy to create tool bars and status bars and associate specific message processing functions that are called when the user clicks on the buttons in the tool bar. MFC 3.0 provides the CToolBar and CStatusBar classes that you can use to implement a tool bar and a status bar, respectively.

The program in Listing 18.6 demonstrates the ease with which you can add a tool bar and a status bar to your application's main window. Figure 18.17 shows the main window created by the program of Listing 18.6. Listing 18.7 shows the resource identifiers used by the TOOLBAR.EXE program.

FIGURE 18.7.

A tool bar and a status bar in a main window.

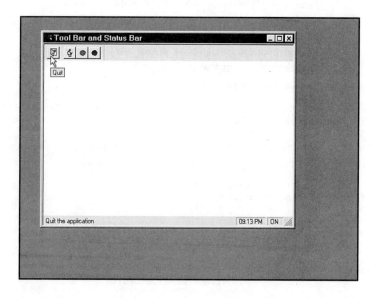

To create the tool bar, you need a bitmap file (TBAR.BMP, in this case) that provides an image for each button. The resource file TOOLBAR.RC (in the companion disk) references the bitmap file and assigns an ID to the bitmap. Here are the steps you use to create a main window with a tool bar:

1. Create the main frame window by calling the `Create` member function in the window class constructor.

2. After creating the frame, create a `CToolBar` as a child of the frame window:

```
// Create the tool bar (m_TBar is a member variable of
// type CToolBar)

    m_TBar.Create(this);
```

3. Load the tool bar bitmap. Here is how the example program does it:

```
// Load the tool bar bitmap (IDR_TBAR_BMP is the ID of the
// bitmap resource as defined in the resource file)

    m_TBar.LoadBitmap(IDR_TBAR_BMP);
```

4. Associate the tool bar buttons with the images in the bitmap file by calling the `SetButtonInfo` function of the `CToolBar` class.

5. Make the tool bar "dockable" if you want. For example, to enable the tool bar to be docked (attached) to any edge of the parent window, you write the following:

```
// In the constructor of the frame window class...

// Make the tool bar dockable
    m_TBar.EnableDocking(CBRS_ALIGN_ANY);
    EnableDocking(CBRS_ALIGN_ANY);
    DockControlBar(&m_TBar);
```

6. Enable the "tool tip" feature, if you want. When enabled, a small help window appears whenever the cursor rests on a tool bar button.

Creating the status bar is also straightforward. You need to define an array for the status indicators, create the status bar, and set the status indicators:

```
// Define the status indicators
static UINT aIndicators[] =
{
    ID_SEPARATOR,
    ID_SB_TIME,
    ID_SB_ONOFF
};
static int nIndicators = sizeof(aIndicators) /
                         sizeof(aIndicators[0]);
//...

// In constructor for the main frame window...
```

```
// Create the status bar (m_SBar is a member variable
// of type CStatusBar)

    m_SBar.Create(this);
    m_SBar.SetIndicators(aIndicators, nIndicators);
```

The example program in Listing 18.6 also illustrates how to use a timer to update the status bar—one of the indicators in the status bar displays the current time using this approach.

Listing 18.6. TOOLBAR.CPP. Sample program to illustrate the use of the CToolBar and CStatusBar classes.

```
//----------------------------------------------------------------
// File: toolbar.cpp
//
// Sample program to illustrate how to use a CToolBar and
// a CStatusBar
//----------------------------------------------------------------
#include <afx.h>
#include <afxwin.h>
#include <afxext.h>
#include "tbres.h"

const int PROG_TIMER = 1;

class CMainWnd : public CFrameWnd
{
public:
    CMainWnd();

    afx_msg void DisableButton(CCmdUI* pCmdUI)
    {
        pCmdUI->Enable(bExitBtnOn);
        if(!bExitBtnOn) OnClose();
    }
    afx_msg void TurnOn(CCmdUI* pCmdUI)
    {
        pCmdUI->Enable(TRUE);
    }
    afx_msg void Start();
    afx_msg void Stop();
    afx_msg void MakeSound();
    afx_msg void Exit()
    {
        KillTimer(PROG_TIMER);
        bExitBtnOn=FALSE;
    };

    afx_msg void OnTimer(UINT nTimerEvent);

private:
    CToolBar   m_TBar;
    CStatusBar m_SBar;
    BOOL       bExitBtnOn;
    BOOL       bOn;
```

continues

Listing 18.6. continued

```
    DECLARE_MESSAGE_MAP()
};

class CToolBarApp : public CWinApp
{
public:
    BOOL InitInstance();
};


// Define the tool bar buttons
struct ButtonInfo
{
    ButtonInfo(int nb, UINT id, UINT style, int ni) :
        nButton(nb), nID(id), nStyle(style), nImage(ni) {}

    int  nButton;
    UINT nID;
    UINT nStyle;
    int  nImage;
};

static ButtonInfo aButtons[] =
{
    ButtonInfo(0, CM_EXIT, TBBS_BUTTON, 0),
    ButtonInfo(1, 0xffff, TBBS_SEPARATOR, 8),
    ButtonInfo(2, CM_SOUND, TBBS_BUTTON, 1),
    ButtonInfo(3, CM_START, TBBS_BUTTON, 2),
    ButtonInfo(4, CM_STOP, TBBS_BUTTON, 3)
};

static int nButtons = sizeof(aButtons) / sizeof(aButtons[0]);

// Define the status indicators
static UINT aIndicators[] =
{
    ID_SEPARATOR,
    ID_SB_TIME,
    ID_SB_ONOFF
};
static int nIndicators = sizeof(aIndicators) /
                         sizeof(aIndicators[0]);

// Define the message map

BEGIN_MESSAGE_MAP(CMainWnd, CFrameWnd)
    ON_WM_TIMER()
    ON_COMMAND(CM_EXIT,  Exit)
    ON_COMMAND(CM_START, Start)
    ON_COMMAND(CM_STOP,  Stop)
    ON_COMMAND(CM_SOUND, MakeSound)
    ON_UPDATE_COMMAND_UI(CM_EXIT, DisableButton)
    ON_UPDATE_COMMAND_UI(ID_SB_TIME, TurnOn)
    ON_UPDATE_COMMAND_UI(ID_SB_ONOFF, TurnOn)
END_MESSAGE_MAP()


//-------------------------------------------------------------
```

```
CMainWnd::CMainWnd() : CFrameWnd(), bExitBtnOn(TRUE), bOn(FALSE)
{
// Create this window
    Create(NULL, "Tool Bar and Status Bar");

// Create the tool bar
    m_TBar.Create(this);

// Load the tool bar bitmap
    m_TBar.LoadBitmap(IDR_TBAR_BMP);
    m_TBar.SetButtons(NULL, nButtons);

// Associate buttons with images
    int i;
    for(i = 0; i < nButtons; i++)
    {
        m_TBar.SetButtonInfo(aButtons[i].nButton,
                             aButtons[i].nID,
                             aButtons[i].nStyle,
                             aButtons[i].nImage);
    }

// Make the tool bar dockable
    m_TBar.EnableDocking(CBRS_ALIGN_ANY);
    EnableDocking(CBRS_ALIGN_ANY);
    DockControlBar(&m_TBar);

// Enable "tool tips"
    m_TBar.SetBarStyle(m_TBar.GetBarStyle() |
                       CBRS_TOOLTIPS | CBRS_FLYBY);

// Create the status bar
    m_SBar.Create(this);
    m_SBar.SetIndicators(aIndicators, nIndicators);

// Create a timer (to update the time on the status bar)
    if(!SetTimer(PROG_TIMER, 1000, NULL))
    {
        MessageBox("Failed to start timer!", "Tool Bar App",
                   MB_OK | MB_ICONEXCLAMATION);
    }
}
//----------------------------------------------------------------
void CMainWnd::OnTimer(UINT nTimerEvent)
{
    if(nTimerEvent != PROG_TIMER) return;

    CTime CurTime(time(NULL));
    m_SBar.SetPaneText(1, CurTime.Format(" %I:%M %p "));
}
//----------------------------------------------------------------
BOOL CToolBarApp::InitInstance()
{
    m_pMainWnd = new CMainWnd;

    m_pMainWnd->ShowWindow(m_nCmdShow);
    m_pMainWnd->UpdateWindow();
```

continues

Listing 18.6. continued

```
    return TRUE;
}
//-------------------------------------------------------------
// CMainWnd:: S t a r t

void CMainWnd::Start()
{
    if(bOn) return;
    bOn = TRUE;
    m_SBar.SetPaneText(2, " ON ");
    MessageBox("Started...", "Tool Bar", MB_OK);
}
//-------------------------------------------------------------
// CMainWnd:: S t o p

void CMainWnd::Stop()
{
    if(!bOn) return;
    bOn = FALSE;
    m_SBar.SetPaneText(2, " OFF ");
    MessageBox("Stopped...", "Tool Bar", MB_OK);
}
//-------------------------------------------------------------
// CMainWnd:: S o u n d

void CMainWnd::MakeSound()
{
    MessageBeep(MB_ICONEXCLAMATION);
}
//-------------------------------------------------------------
// Create an instance of the application

    CToolBarApp App;
```

Listing 18.7. TBRES.H. Header file with the resource identifiers used by the TOOLBAR.EXE program.

```
//-------------------------------------------------------------
// File: tbres.h
// Resource IDs for the toolbar example program.

#if !defined(__TBRES_H)
#define __TBRES_H

#define IDR_TBAR_BMP  100

#define ID_SB_TIME    100
#define ID_SB_ONOFF   200

#define CM_START 1
#define CM_STOP  2
#define CM_SOUND 3
#define CM_EXIT  4

#endif
```

Using MDI Window Classes

Although you have not seen any explicit examples of frame windows, almost all example programs in this chapter use a frame window to display their output. Frame windows serve as containers where the application's windows appear. This section briefly describes a specific frame window: the CMDIFrameWnd class that provides the main window for an MDI application.

Currently, most Windows applications support the MDI that displays multiple child windows within a main frame window. An MDI application's main window serves as a frame. All other child windows, known as MDI child windows, appear inside the MDI frame window. MFC 3.0 provides two window classes that you can use in an MDI application:

■ CMDIFrameWnd for the frame window that holds the MDI child windows

■ CMDIChildWnd for the MDI child windows

Listing 18.8 presents a simple MDI application that shows how to use these two classes of windows (the resource identifiers are in Listing 18.9). Figure 18.8 shows the appearance of the program's main window after two MDI child windows have been created. The menus are defined in a resource file (MDITEST.RC on the companion disk). As you can see, this simple program provides all the features of a complete MDI application. This ease of programming is possible because all the work is done by the MFC classes CMDIFrameWnd and CMDIChildWnd.

FIGURE 18.8.

The framework of an MDI application.

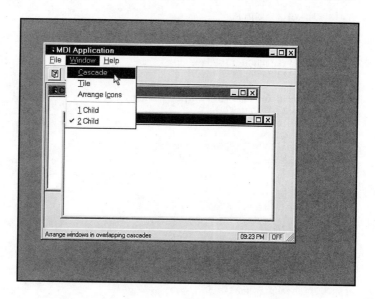

Listing 18.8. MDITEST.CPP. Sample program to illustrate the use of the CMDIFrameWnd class.

```
//------------------------------------------------------------
// File: mditest.cpp
//
```

continues

Listing 18.8. continued

```cpp
// Sample program to illustrate the use of MDI frame and MDI
// child window classes.
//-----------------------------------------------------------------
#include <afx.h>
#include <afxwin.h>
#include <afxext.h>
#include "resource.h"
#include "mdres.h"

const int PROG_TIMER = 1;

class CMainWnd : public CMDIFrameWnd
{
public:
    CMainWnd();

    afx_msg void DisableButton(CCmdUI* pCmdUI)
    {
        pCmdUI->Enable(bExitBtnOn);
        if(!bExitBtnOn) OnClose();
    }
    afx_msg void TurnOn(CCmdUI* pCmdUI)
    {
        pCmdUI->Enable(TRUE);
    }
    afx_msg void Start();
    afx_msg void Stop();
    afx_msg void MakeSound();
    afx_msg void Exit()
    {
        KillTimer(PROG_TIMER);
        bExitBtnOn=FALSE;
    }
    afx_msg void OnTimer(UINT nTimerEvent);
    afx_msg void MakeNew();
    afx_msg void About()
    {
        CDialog(IDD_DIALOG1).DoModal();
    }

private:
    CToolBar    m_TBar;
    CStatusBar  m_SBar;
    BOOL        bExitBtnOn;
    BOOL        bOn;

    DECLARE_MESSAGE_MAP()
};

class CMDITestApp : public CWinApp
{
public:
    BOOL InitInstance();
};
```

```
// Define the tool bar buttons
struct ButtonInfo
{
    ButtonInfo(int nb, UINT id, UINT style, int ni) :
        nButton(nb), nID(id), nStyle(style), nImage(ni) {}

    int   nButton;
    UINT  nID;
    UINT  nStyle;
    int   nImage;
};

static ButtonInfo aButtons[] =
{
    ButtonInfo(0, CM_EXIT,  TBBS_BUTTON,    0),
    ButtonInfo(1, 0xffff,   TBBS_SEPARATOR, 8),
    ButtonInfo(2, CM_SOUND, TBBS_BUTTON,    1),
    ButtonInfo(3, CM_START, TBBS_BUTTON,    2),
    ButtonInfo(4, CM_STOP,  TBBS_BUTTON,    3)
};

static int nButtons = sizeof(aButtons) / sizeof(aButtons[0]);

// Define the status indicators
static UINT aIndicators[] =
{
    ID_SEPARATOR,
    ID_SB_TIME,
    ID_SB_ONOFF
};
static int nIndicators = sizeof(aIndicators) /
                         sizeof(aIndicators[0]);

// Define the message map

BEGIN_MESSAGE_MAP(CMainWnd, CMDIFrameWnd)
    ON_WM_TIMER()
    ON_COMMAND(CM_EXIT,  Exit)
    ON_COMMAND(CM_START, Start)
    ON_COMMAND(CM_STOP,  Stop)
    ON_COMMAND(CM_SOUND, MakeSound)
    ON_UPDATE_COMMAND_UI(CM_EXIT, DisableButton)
    ON_UPDATE_COMMAND_UI(ID_SB_TIME, TurnOn)
    ON_UPDATE_COMMAND_UI(ID_SB_ONOFF, TurnOn)
    ON_COMMAND(ID_FILE_NEW, MakeNew)
    ON_COMMAND(ID_HELP_ABOUTMDITEST, About)
END_MESSAGE_MAP()

//-------------------------------------------------------------
CMainWnd::CMainWnd() : CMDIFrameWnd(), bExitBtnOn(TRUE), bOn(FALSE)
{
// Create this window
    Create(NULL, "MDI Application", WS_OVERLAPPEDWINDOW,
           CRect(CW_USEDEFAULT, CW_USEDEFAULT, 0, 0), NULL,
           MAKEINTRESOURCE(IDR_MENU1));
```

continues

Listing 18.8. continued

```
// Create the tool bar
    m_TBar.Create(this);

// Load the tool bar bitmap
    m_TBar.LoadBitmap(IDR_TBAR_BMP);
    m_TBar.SetButtons(NULL, nButtons);

// Associate buttons with images
    int i;
    for(i = 0; i < nButtons; i++)
    {
        m_TBar.SetButtonInfo(aButtons[i].nButton,
                             aButtons[i].nID,
                             aButtons[i].nStyle,
                             aButtons[i].nImage);
    }

// Make the tool bar dockable
    m_TBar.EnableDocking(CBRS_ALIGN_ANY);
    EnableDocking(CBRS_ALIGN_ANY);
    DockControlBar(&m_TBar);

// Enable "tool tips"
    m_TBar.SetBarStyle(m_TBar.GetBarStyle() |
                       CBRS_TOOLTIPS | CBRS_FLYBY);

// Create the status bar
    m_SBar.Create(this);
    m_SBar.SetIndicators(aIndicators, nIndicators);

// Create a timer (to update the time on the status bar)
    if(!SetTimer(PROG_TIMER, 1000, NULL))
    {
        MessageBox("Failed to start timer!", "Tool Bar App",
                   MB_OK | MB_ICONEXCLAMATION);
    }
}
//----------------------------------------------------------------
void CMainWnd::OnTimer(UINT nTimerEvent)
{
    if(nTimerEvent != PROG_TIMER) return;

    CTime CurTime(time(NULL));
    m_SBar.SetPaneText(1, CurTime.Format(" %I:%M %p "));
}
//----------------------------------------------------------------
void CMainWnd::MakeNew()
{
    CMDIChildWnd *c = new CMDIChildWnd;
    c->Create(NULL, "Child");
}
//----------------------------------------------------------------
BOOL CMDITestApp::InitInstance()
{
    m_pMainWnd = new CMainWnd;

    m_pMainWnd->ShowWindow(m_nCmdShow);
```

```
    m_pMainWnd->UpdateWindow();

    return TRUE;
}
//----------------------------------------------------------------
// CMainWnd:: C m S t a r t

void CMainWnd::Start()
{
    if(bOn) return;
    bOn = TRUE;
    m_SBar.SetPaneText(2, " ON ");
    MessageBox("Started...", "Tool Bar", MB_OK);
}
//----------------------------------------------------------------
// CMainWnd:: C m S t o p

void CMainWnd::Stop()
{
    if(!bOn) return;
    bOn = FALSE;
    m_SBar.SetPaneText(2, " OFF ");
    MessageBox("Stopped...", "Tool Bar", MB_OK);
}
//----------------------------------------------------------------
// CMainWnd:: C m S o u n d

void CMainWnd::MakeSound()
{
    MessageBeep(MB_ICONEXCLAMATION);
}
//----------------------------------------------------------------
// Create an instance of the application

    CMDITestApp App;
```

Listing 18.9. MDRES.H. Header file with resource identifiers for the MDITEST.EXE program.

```
//----------------------------------------------------------------
// File: mdres.h
// Resource IDs for the toolbar example program.

#if !defined(__MDRES_H)
#define __MDRES_H

#define IDR_TBAR_BMP  100

#define ID_SB_TIME    100
#define ID_SB_ONOFF   200

#define CM_START 1
#define CM_STOP  2
#define CM_SOUND 3
#define CM_EXIT  4

#endif
```

Manipulating Menus

MFC 3.0 provides the CMenu class to represent menus. An interesting example is to manipulate the system menu of a window by creating an instance of the CMenu class and using the member functions of that class. This section shows a program (Listing 18.10) that accesses the system menu and replaces the Close menu item with a small bitmap. Listing 18.11 shows the header file SMNURES.H with the resource identifiers used by the SYSMENU.EXE sample program. Figure 18.9 shows the resulting look of the system menu after the modification.

FIGURE 18.9.

Modifying the Close menu item in the system menu using the CMenu *class.*

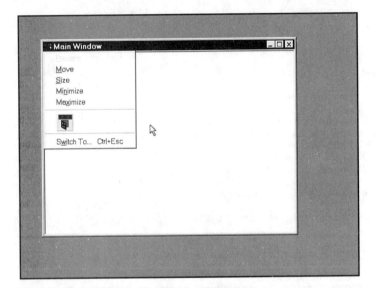

To replace the text in the menu entry with a bitmap, you need a bitmap from a resource file. This example uses a bitmap from the SYSMENU.RC resource file (you will find the file on the companion disk). As Listing 18.10 shows, you modify the menu entry using the following steps:

1. Create a CBitmap object from the bitmap resource and load the bitmap resource into the CBitmap object. You need the resource ID of the bitmap for the LoadBitmap function of the CBitmap class. Here is how the example program does this:

```
// m_BmpExit is a member variable of the application's
// main frame window class (derived from CFrameWnd)

    CBitmap   *m_BmpExit;
//...

    m_BmpExit = new Cbitmap;
    m_BmpExit->LoadBitmap(IDR_EXIT_BITMAP);
```

2. Access the system menu by using the `GetSystemMenu` function of the application's main frame window object:

```
CMenu *sysmnu = GetSystemMenu(FALSE);
```

3. Modify the specific menu entry with the `CBitmap` created earlier:

```
sysmnu->ModifyMenu(6, MF_BYPOSITION¦MF_BITMAP,
                     sysmnu->GetMenuItemID(6),
                     m_BmpExit);
```

The menu item in position 6 is being modified because that is the location of the `Close` menu item in the system menu.

You can access the text string of a menu item by calling the `GetMenuString` function. For example, you call the text string of the `Close` menu item with the following:

```
char buf[80];
sysmnu->GetMenuString(6, buf, 70, MF_BYPOSITION);
```

If you merely want to disable the `Close` item in the system menu, you can do so by calling `EnableMenuItem`:

```
sysmnu->EnableMenuItem(6, MF_BYPOSITION¦
                          MF_DISABLED¦MF_GRAYED);
```

Listing 18.10. SYSMENU.CPP. Sample program that modifies a system menu entry with the `CMenu` class.

```cpp
//-------------------------------------------------------------
// File: sysmenu.cpp
//
// Sample program that shows how to change the "Close" item
// in the system menu
//-------------------------------------------------------------
#include <afx.h>
#include <afxwin.h>
#include "smnures.h"
#include "resource.h"

class CTestApp : public CWinApp
{
public:
    BOOL InitInstance();
};

class CMyFrameWnd : public CFrameWnd
{
public:
    CMyFrameWnd() :  m_BmpExit(NULL), CFrameWnd() {}

    ~CMyFrameWnd() { if(m_BmpExit) delete m_BmpExit;}

    afx_msg int OnCreate(LPCREATESTRUCT);
```

continues

Listing 18.10. continued

```cpp
    CBitmap   *m_BmpExit;

DECLARE_MESSAGE_MAP()
};

// Define message map for the frame window
BEGIN_MESSAGE_MAP(CMyFrameWnd, CFrameWnd)
    ON_WM_CREATE()
END_MESSAGE_MAP()
//----------------------------------------------------------------
// CMyFrameWnd:: O n C r e a t e
// Handles WM_CREATE messages

int CMyFrameWnd::OnCreate(LPCREATESTRUCT lpCS)
{
    CFrameWnd::OnCreate(lpCS);

// Change the "Close" item of the System menu into a bitmap
// First create a CBitmap using a bitmap from a resource file

    m_BmpExit = new CBitmap;
    m_BmpExit->LoadBitmap(IDR_EXIT_BITMAP);

// Access and modify the system menu
    CMenu *sysmnu = GetSystemMenu(FALSE);

    sysmnu->ModifyMenu(6, MF_BYPOSITION¦MF_BITMAP,
                       sysmnu->GetMenuItemID(6),
                       m_BmpExit);

    return 1;
}
//----------------------------------------------------------------
BOOL CTestApp::InitInstance()
{
    CMyFrameWnd *pFrame = new CMyFrameWnd;
    pFrame->Create(NULL, "Main Window");

    m_pMainWnd = pFrame;

// Now display the main window
    m_pMainWnd->ShowWindow(m_nCmdShow);
    m_pMainWnd->UpdateWindow();

    return TRUE;
}
//----------------------------------------------------------------
// Start the application

    CTestApp App;
```

Listing 18.11. SMNURES.H. Header file with resource identifiers for the SYSMENU.EXE program.

```
//--------------------------------------------------------------
// File: smnures.h
// Resource IDs

#if !defined(__SMNURES_H)
#define __SMNURES_H

#define IDR_EXIT_BITMAP 100

#endif
```

Summary

Visual C++ 2.0 includes the Microsoft Foundation Class Library Version 3.0 (MFC 3.0) that provides a rich set of C++ classes for developing Microsoft Windows applications. MFC 3.0 organizes the classes into several hierarchies and exploits multiple inheritance to combine the capabilities of multiple base classes. Most MFC 3.0 classes represent user interface elements, such as controls and dialogs. These classes are derived from two base classes, TEventHandler and TStreamableBase. TEventHandler provides the event handling support, and TStreamableBase enables you to store objects in a file and retrieve them later.

One major MFC class hierarchy is the CWnd classes. These classes represent windows of various types: frame windows that are meant to manage one or more child windows, windows where the application displays its graphical or text output, dialog windows that prompt user for input, and control window objects through which the user controls the application. To support graphics and text output through the Windows Graphics Device Interface (GDI), MFC 3.0 provides the TGdiBase class hierarchy with the TGdiObject classes. The TGdiBase hierarchy includes the TDC classes that represent the various types of device contexts needed to display output on a device.

Other major MFC class hierarchies include: classes for building applications with a document-view model; classes to represent menus and provide clipboard support; and classes for scrolling, printing, and generating exceptions when errors occur in an MFC class. MFC 3.0 also provides classes that represent Windows data types, such as POINT, RECT, SIZE, PALETTEENTRY, RGBQUAD, and RGBTRIPLE.

This chapter briefly describes the different categories of MFC classes. The latter part of this chapter provides example programs demonstrating some commonly used MFC classes. The next chapter further describes the GDI functions and device contexts.

19

Graphics Programming
with MFC 3.0

Chapter 17, "Windows Programming with Visual C++ 2.0 and MFC 3.0," shows an example of building a Windows application using the MFC 3.0 classes, and Chapter 18, "Using the Windows Programming Classes in MFC 3.0," summarizes the MFC 3.0 classes used to build the graphical user interface in Windows applications. To display graphics in your application's window, you have to use functions from the Windows Graphics Device Interface (GDI), which you can access through the `CGdiObject` subhierarchy of classes in MFC 3.0. This chapter briefly describes the GDI functions for drawing graphics. Chapter 20, "Displaying Text in Windows," covers the text output functions.

Windows Graphics Device Interface

Recall that GDI refers to the graphics output functions of Windows. GDI is designed to isolate a Windows program from the physical output device such as the display or the printer. The basic idea is that you call GDI functions for all graphics output, and the GDI functions access specific device drivers for the actual graphics output. In addition to producing output on physical devices, GDI also supports output to two pseudodevices:

■ Bitmaps, rectangular arrays of pixels

■ Metafiles, stored collections of GDI function calls

Bitmaps are useful for displaying and animating images—tasks that are commonly needed in many Windows applications. Chapter 21, "Displaying Bitmaps in Windows," further describes how images are displayed using bitmaps.

Many GDI functions can be important to you when writing Windows software. In particular, you need the following categories of GDI functions:

■ Vector drawing functions that can draw graphical objects, such as lines, rectangles, and ellipses

■ Bitmap manipulation functions to display and manipulate images

■ Text output functions to display text in a window

■ Palette management functions to exploit the colors supported by a display adapter

The palette is useful in systems with Super-VGA-or-better display adapters that support more than the 16 colors available with standard VGA.

The following sections provide an overview of these functions, but before you can proceed, you have to understand the device context.

Device Context

The device context (DC) is the key to the GDI's support for device-independent graphics in Windows. All GDI functions require a *handle*—an integer identifier—to a DC as an argument.

You can think of the DC as a generalized model of a graphics output device. In reality, the DC is a data structure that holds all information needed to generate graphics output. For example, the DC contains graphics attributes, such as background color, pen, fill style, and font, that control the appearance of graphics and text.

Because a DC represents a graphics device, you have to treat it as a shared resource. When using a DC for graphics output, you should first call an appropriate GDI function to access the DC, use that DC to draw, then immediately release the DC.

WINDOWS ALLOWS A MAXIMUM OF FIVE DCS

Windows allows five DCs at most to be open at any one time—that's five DCs for the entire Windows system, not per application.

DC in MFC 3.0

In MFC 3.0, the CDC class encapsulates the Windows DC. The handle to the DC (HDC) is a public member variable (named m_hDC) of the CDC class. Specialized versions of the CDC class are available for drawing in a variety of devices and screen areas, such as the CClientDC for drawing in the client area of a window, CWindowDC for drawing anywhere in a window including the client area and the frame area, CMetaFileDC for creating a Windows metafile, and CPaintDC for drawing in response to a WM_PAINT message.

All GDI functions appear as member functions of the CDC class. The names of these member functions are the same as the corresponding GDI functions, but the member functions do not need an HDC as an argument. The CDC class also includes overloaded versions of the drawing functions that accept several different forms of arguments. As an example, consider the GDI functions MoveTo and LineTo that you can use to draw a line between two points. To draw a line from (x1,y1) to (x2,y2) with the GDI functions, you write the following:

```
    HDC hdc;
// Assume that the handle to the DC, hdc, is properly set up
    MoveTo(hdc, x1, y1);
    LineTo(hdc, x2, y2);
```

When using MFC 3.0 classes, you change the calls to the following form:

```
    CClientDC dc(this);
// Assume that the CClientDC is being created in the member
// function of a window class derived from CWnd
    dc.MoveTo(x1, y1);
    dc.LineTo(x2, y2);
```

Additionally, the CDC class in MFC 3.0 also enables you to write these function calls with CPoint objects as argument (CPoint represents a point in the x-y plane):

```
// Assume that the CClientDC is being constructed in the
```

```
// member function of a TWindow class
   CClientDC dc(this);
   CPoint start, end;
// Assume that the CPoint objects are appropriately initialized
   dc.MoveTo(start);
   dc.LineTo(end);
```

As you can see, the CDC class offers several flexible ways to call the GDI functions.

The following sections describe the DC as a data type in Windows API. However, the example code shows how to use the DC through the CDC classes in MFC 3.0.

Contents of a DC

The DC contains drawing objects, such as brush, pen, and bitmap, and drawing attributes, such as background color, text color, and font. Table 19.1 summarizes the contents of the DC and provides the default value of each item in it. Note that the constants appearing in the default values column are defined in an include file.

Table 19.1. Items in a DC and their default values.

Item Name	Default Value	Comments
Background color	White	
Background mode	OPAQUE	Background areas in drawings are filled with the background color as opposed to being left untouched
Bitmap	No default	Used when selecting a bitmap into a memory device context
Brush	WHITE_BRUSH	Defines a fill style
Brush origin	(0,0)	
Clipping region	Entire client area	Drawing operations affect the area within the clipping region only
Color palette	DEFAULT_PALETTE	
Current pen position	(0,0)	
Device origin	Upper-left corner	
Drawing mode	R2_COPYPEN	Specifies how to combine the pen's color with the color that already exists on the drawing surface
Font	SYSTEM_FONT	
Intercharacter spacing	0	

Item Name	Default Value	Comments
Mapping mode	MM_TEXT	One logical unit equals one pixel
Pen	BLACK_PEN	
Polygon fill mode	ALTERNATE	
Stretching mode	BLACKONWHITE	Used by StretchBlt when copying bitmaps from one device to another
Text alignment	TA_LEFT, TA_TOP, and TA_NOUPDATECP	
Text color	Black	
Viewport extent	(1,1)	Viewport refers to a rectangle in the device coordinate system
Viewport origin	(0,0)	
Window extent	(1,1)	Window refers to a rectangle in the logical coordinate system (the mapping mode maps the window to the viewport)
Window origin	(0,0)	

Getting a DC

Your Windows application will, most likely, acquire a DC in response to the WM_PAINT message because that's when an application's window has to be redrawn. If you use MFC classes and you derive your application's main window from the CWnd class, you can handle all graphics output in a member function named OnPaint, which MFC calls whenever Windows sends a WM_PAINT message to the window.

Inside the OnPaint function, you should get a DC by creating an instance of the CPaintDC class:

```
CPaintDC dc(this);
```

The CPaintDC class calls the Windows API function BeginPaint in the constructor—this is a necessary step that prepares the window for painting by filling a PAINTSTRUCT structure with information about the painting. The CPaintDC destructor calls the EndPaint function as required by the Windows API.

If you need a DC to draw in the window as soon as possible without waiting for a WM_PAINT message, you can create an instance of the CClientDC class to get a DC. When the CClientDC object is destroyed, the DC is automatically released. By the way, you also can force an immediate WM_PAINT event by calling the UpdateWindow function.

Saving and Restoring a DC

When you get the handle to a DC and make changes to the attributes, these changes are lost as soon as you release the DC. If you need to store a DC temporarily (perhaps to change some attributes, do some drawing with the changed attributes, and revert back to the original attributes), you can do so by calling SaveDC:

```
    CClientDC dc(this);
//...
    int nId;
    nId = dc.SaveDC();
// Make changes to DC and use it...
// After you are through using the changed DC, restore the DC
    dc.RestoreDC(nId);
```

If you merely want to revert a DC back to the state that existed before the last call to SaveDC, call the following:

```
dc.RestoreDC(-1); // Use -1 as ID
```

Using a DC for Graphics Output

The primary use of a DC is to draw graphics output. In fact, each GDI function is a member function of the CDC class. Here is the typical sequence to follow when using a CDC object for graphics output:

1. Create the appropriate CDC object. For example, to draw in the client area of a window, create a CClientDC object. To draw in response to a WM_PAINT message, create a CPaintDC object.

2. Set up the graphics attributes.

3. Call GDI drawing functions that are member functions of the CDC class.

4. If you created CDC object by using the new operator, destroy the CDC object with the delete operator.

Setting up the graphics attributes involves selecting drawing objects into the DC. A DC has the following graphics objects:

- *Pen* controls the appearance of lines and borders of rectangles, ellipses, and polygons.

- *Brush* provides a fill pattern used to draw filled figures.

- *Font* specifies the shape and size of textual output.

- *Palette* is an array of colors—the array index identifying each color. For display adapters that can display more than 16 colors, Windows uses a palette to pick the current selection of displayable colors out of the millions of colors that a display can represent.

- *Bitmap* is used to draw images.

- *Region* is a combination of rectangles, ellipses, and polygons that you can use for drawing or for clipping.

At any time, the DC can have one copy of each type of graphics object. Use the SelectObject function to select a graphics object into a DC. For example, to draw a rectangle filled with a specific fill pattern, you might write the following:

```
// Assume that this code is in the body of the OnPaint
// function of the application's window.

// Create a DC
   CPaintDC dc(this);

// Draw a filled rectangle with specific pen and brush

   CPen *pOldPen = (CPen*)dc.SelectStockObject(WHITE_PEN);

   CBrush hatch_brush;
   hatch_brush.CreateHatchBrush(HS_DIAGCROSS,
                                     RGB(0, 255, 255));
   CBrush *pOldBrush = (CBrush*)dc.SelectObject(&hatch_brush);

   dc.Rectangle(20, 10, 80, 50);

// Restore the original objects
   dc.SelectObject(pOldPen);
   dc.SelectObject(pOldBrush);
//...
```

Notice how the call to SelectStockObject selects a stock pen—one of the predefined graphics objects that are always available (see Table 19.2 for a list of available stock objects). The brush, hatch_brush, is created by calling CreateHatchBrush. Once you finish using the graphics objects, you have to restore the original objects by calling the SelectObject function again—this time with the pointers to the original GDI objects.

Table 19.2. Stock GDI objects.

Value	*Meaning*
BLACK_BRUSH	Black brush
DKGRAY_BRUSH	Dark gray brush
GRAY_BRUSH	Gray brush
HOLLOW_BRUSH	Hollow brush (same as NULL_BRUSH)
LTGRAY_BRUSH	Light gray brush
NULL_BRUSH	Null brush
WHITE_BRUSH	White brush
BLACK_PEN	Black pen
NULL_PEN	Null pen
WHITE_PEN	White pen
ANSI_FIXED_FONT	ANSI fixed system font

continues

Table 19.2. continued

Value	*Meaning*
ANSI_VAR_FONT	ANSI variable system font
DEVICE_DEFAULT_FONT	Device-dependent font
OEM_FIXED_FONT	OEM-dependent (OEM stands for original equipment manufacturer) fixed font; basically, a vendor-specific font
SYSTEM_FONT	System font that Windows uses to draw menus, dialog box controls, and other text
SYSTEM_FIXED_FONT	Fixed-width system font used in Windows version 3.0 and earlier
DEFAULT_PALETTE	Default color palette of 20 fixed colors in the system palette

Determining Device Capabilities with a DC

In addition to drawing with a DC, you also can determine the capabilities of a device through the DC. Specifically, you can call the GetDeviceCaps function to get a value for a specified capability code. For example, to determine the number of color planes available in the display device, call GetDeviceCaps with the handle to a display device context:

```
int nplanes = dc.GetDeviceCaps(PLANES);
```

where PLANES denotes the capability that you are querying.

You also can use GetDeviceCaps to determine whether a device supports enough colors or specific types of graphic operations, such as copying bitmaps or drawing curves for circles and ellipses. For example, in a Windows application you might want to use as many colors as the display adapter supports. If a display adapter supports 256 colors, the DC will support a logical palette. To determine whether a DC supports a logical palette, you write the following:

```
    if(dc.GetDeviceCaps(RASTERCAPS) & RC_PALETTE)
    {
// Yes, device supports logical palette
//...
    }
```

You can test whether the device driver associated with a DC is written for Windows 3.0 or later with the following:

```
// For Windows 3.1, the following function returns 0x030a

    if(dc.GetDeviceCaps(DRIVERVERSION) >= 0x300)
    {
// Yes, device driver is for Windows 3.0 or later.
//...
    }
```

GDI Coordinate Systems

The GDI supports the notion of two coordinate systems: *physical coordinates* and *logical coordinates*. The physical or device coordinate system is fixed for a device. For a window on the display screen, the physical coordinate system's origin is at the upper-left corner of a window's client area with the positive x-axis extending to the right and the positive y-axis going down.

The logical coordinate system can be one of several, and Windows maps each onto the physical one before displaying any graphics output. All GDI drawing functions accept logical coordinates as arguments. The mapping mode—the way a logical coordinate system is scaled to the physical one—identifies the types of logical coordinate systems that Windows supports. Table 19.3 lists the mapping modes available in Windows GDI.

Table 19.3. Mapping modes in Windows GDI.

Mapping Mode Identifier	*Meaning*
MM_ANISOTROPIC	Logical units along x- and y-axes can be set independently. Use SetViewportExt (set viewport extent) and SetWindowExt (set window extent) to set up the x- and y-ratios of logical-to-physical units. Note that, in this context, a viewport is a rectangular area in physical coordinate space and a window is a rectangle in logical coordinates. The viewport extent is the width and height of the viewport. The scaling along x- and y-axes is set so that the specified window in logical coordinates is mapped to the viewport in physical coordinates.
MM_HIENGLISH	Each logical unit is 0.001 inch with the positive x-axis extending to the right and the positive y-axis going up.
MM_HIMETRIC	Each logical unit is 0.01 millimeter; the x-axis is increasing to the right and the positive y-axis is extending upward.
MM_ISOTROPIC	This mapping mode is like MM_ANISOTROPIC except that the x- and y- scalings must be the same.
MM_LOENGLISH	This is like MM_HIENGLISH except each logical unit is 0.01 inch.
MM_LOMETRIC	This is like MM_HIMETRIC except each logical unit is 0.1 millimeter.
MM_TEXT	This is the default mapping mode in which the logical coordinate system is the same as the

continues

Table 19.3. continued

Mapping Mode Identifier	Meaning
	physical one—each logical unit is one pixel, with the x-axis increasing to the right and the y-axis increasing downward.
MM_TWIPS	Each logical unit is 1/20 of a point where a point is 1/72-inch. Thus, in MM_TWIPS mode, each logical unit is 1/1440-inch. The positive x-axis extends to the right and the y-axis increases upward.

UNDERSTANDING THE VIEWPORT, WINDOW, AND MAPPING MODE

The terms *viewport* and *window* possess a special meaning in a DC. Here, window does not mean an area of the screen where an application's output appears. Rather, a window is a rectangular area in a logical coordinate space with arbitrary units such as one-hundredth of an inch. A viewport, on the other hand, is another rectangular area in the display screen. Therefore, the viewport's units are device units such as pixels.

The term *mapping mode* refers to the way a window in logical coordinates is mapped to a viewport in the device coordinate space.

Setting a Mapping Mode

Use the SetMapMode function to set a mapping mode. At any time, you can get the current mapping mode with GetMapMode. For example, to set the mapping mode to MM_TWIPS, you write the following:

```
int old_mapmode = dc.SetMapMode(MM_TWIPS);
```

Specifying the mapping mode may not be enough to draw in a window. After setting a mapping mode such as MM_TWIPS, you have the situation shown in Figure 19.1. As you can see from the figure, a portion of the lower-right quadrant from the logical coordinate space is mapped to the display screen (or the device's work area, in case of devices other than the display). This means that drawings with positive x- and negative y-coordinates are the only ones that get displayed. The reason for this effect is that the logical frame's y-axis increases upward and the physical frame's y-axis increases downward. This is true for all mapping modes except MM_TEXT.

If you want to work with positive logical coordinates, you have to move the origin of the logical coordinate frame to an appropriate location in the physical space. This way, the positive quadrant (the quadrant where both x- and y-coordinates are positive) of the logical frame is mapped to the visible quadrant of the physical coordinate frame. You can use the `SetViewportOrg` to relocate the origin of the logical frame. Figure 19.2 illustrates the effect of changing the origin of the logical coordinate axes.

FIGURE 19.1.

Default mapping from logical to physical coordinates.

FIGURE 19.2.

Effect of aligning the window origin with a point in the viewport.

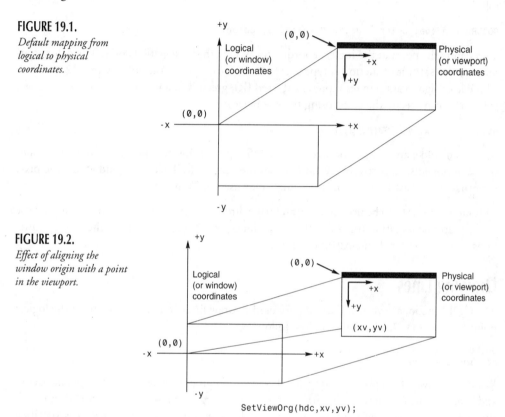

`SetViewOrg(hdc,xv,yv);`

You have to follow these steps whenever you are using one of the device-independent modes: `MM_HIENGLISH`, `MM_HIMETRIC`, `MM_LOENGLISH`, `MM_LOMETRIC`, or `MM_TWIPS`. We call these mapping modes device-independent because they express the logical units in absolute measurements, such as millimeters or inches.

Drawing with GDI Functions

The GDI provides a large number of drawing functions, including functions to draw individual pixels, lines, rectangles and polygons, and ellipses. The next few sections briefly summarize the drawing functions.

Drawing Points

You can draw a single point in a specified color with the SetPixel function, which you call as follows:

```
COLORREF actual_color = dc.SetPixel(x, y, color);
```

This paints the point at the logical coordinates (x,y) with the specified color. The color argument to the SetPixel function is type COLORREF. You can specify the color with a 32-bit value whose least significant 3 bytes represent the red (R), green (G), and blue (B) components of a color. You can specify the color using the RGB macro:

```
dc.SetPixel(x, y, RGB(r, g, b));
```

where r, g, and b are integers between 0 and 255 representing the intensity of red, green, and blue components, respectively. Windows uses the nearest available color and paints the pixel with that color. SetPixel returns the actual color used by Windows.

Although SetPixel can be used to draw an image directly on the display screen, you should use the bitmap manipulation functions to display images in Windows, because the bitmap functions are much faster than SetPixel.

Drawing Lines

The GDI functions MoveTo and LineTo are used to draw lines. To draw a line from the logical point (x1, y1) to (x2, y2), you write the following:

```
dc.MoveTo(x1, y1);
dc.LineTo(x2, y2);
```

Windows draws all the pixels starting at (x1, y1) up to, but not including, (x2, y2). The MoveTo and LineTo functions draw lines with the currently selected pen—the MoveTo function moves the pen to a new location without drawing anything, and LineTo draws a line to a specified point with the pen. The pen determines the appearance of the line being drawn. You can either call SelectObject to select a predefined pen into the device context or call CreatePen to create a new pen with a specific style, color, and width. To use the pen, you have to select it into the DC and, when you no longer need the pen, you must call the SelectObject function to restore the original pen (this is the pointer returned by the previous call to SelectObject that set the pen) back into the DC.

To draw multiple line segments, you use the Polyline function. You have to store the endpoints of all the line segments in an array. For example, to join the points (x1, y1), (x2, y2), and (x3, y3) with line segments, you write the following:

```
POINT aPoints[3] =
    {CPoint(x1, y1), CPoint(x2, y2), CPoint(x3, y3)};
dc.Polyline(aPoints, 3);
```

Note that to draw a closed polygon using Polyline, you have to close the figure by specifying the same coordinates for the first and the last point in the array of points. However, as you will see later, the `Polygon` function automatically draws a closed figure by connecting the last point to the first.

In addition to straight lines, the `CDC` class includes the `Arc` function to draw a curved line that is part of an ellipse. `Arc` requires four sets of x-y coordinates as its arguments:

```
// Prototype of Arc
BOOL Arc(
    short x1, short y1, // Upper-left corner of bounding box
    short x2, short y2, // Lower-right corner of bounding box
    short x3, short y3, // Defines startpoint of arc
    short x4, short y4);// Defines endpoint of arc
```

The points (x1, y1) and (x2, y2) are the opposite corners of a rectangle that encloses the ellipse to which the arc belongs. The starting point of the arc is where a line joining the center of the ellipse and (x3, y3) intersects the ellipse's boundary. The endpoint is defined similarly by the line joining the ellipse's center and (x4, y4). The arc is drawn counterclockwise from the starting point up to, but not including, the endpoint.

Another form of the `Arc` function takes a `RECT` structure with two `POINT` objects as arguments:

```
BOOL Arc(
    LPCRECT lpRect, // Pointer to bounding rectangle
                    // of ellipse
    POINT ptStart,  // Startpoint of arc
    POINT ptEnd);   // Endpoint of arc
```

Figure 19.3 illustrates two ways of specifying an arc drawn by the `Arc` function.

FIGURE 19.3.
Specifying an elliptical arc drawn by the `Arc` *function.*

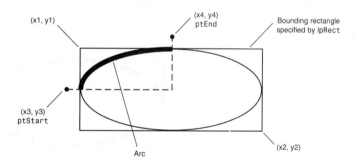

Drawing Closed Figures

The `CDC` class provides the following member functions to draw closed figures (each function returns `TRUE` if successful; otherwise, it returns `FALSE`):

■ `BOOL Rectangle(int x1, int y1, int x2, int y2);`

draws a rectangle whose upper-left corner is (x1, y1) and lower-right corner is (x2, y2). Note that the right and bottom edges of the rectangle are 1 pixel less than the corner (x2, y2).

■ `BOOL RoundRect(int x1, int y1, int x2, int y2, int x3, int y3);`
draws a rectangle with rounded corners. The rectangle's bounding box is specified by the upper-left corner (x1, y1) and lower-right corner (x2, y2). As shown in Figure 19.4, each corner is rounded by drawing a small ellipse whose width and height are x3 and y3, respectively.

FIGURE 19.4.

Drawing a rounded rectangle.

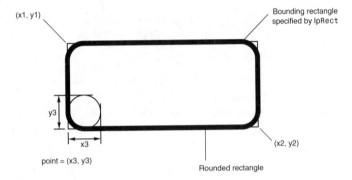

■ `BOOL Ellipse(int x1, int y1, int x2, int y2);`

draws an ellipse bounded by the rectangle whose opposite corners are (x1, y1) and (x2, y2). The following is another form of the function:

`BOOL Ellipse(LPCRECT lpRect);`

Figure 19.5 illustrates the meaning of the arguments.

FIGURE 19.5.

Specifying an ellipse.

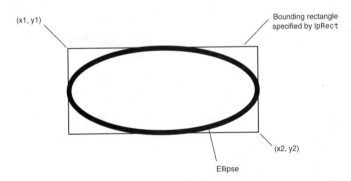

■ `BOOL Pie(int x1, int y1, int x2, int y2, int x3, int y3, int x4, int y4);`

or

`BOOL Pie(LPCRECT lpRect, POINT ptStart, POINT ptEnd);`

draws a pie-shaped wedge whose curved edge is a segment of the ellipse bounded by the rectangle defined by the corners (x1, y1) and (x2, y2). The two straight edges of the pie are defined by the line joining the center of the ellipse and the points (x3, y3) and (x4, y4). The pie slice starts at the point where the line from the center to (x3, y3) intersects the ellipse and continues counterclockwise to the point where the line from the center to (x4, y4) cuts the ellipse. Figure 19.6 shows the meaning of the arguments that Pie needs.

FIGURE 19.6.

Specifying a pie-shaped wedge.

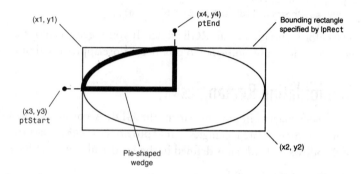

■ BOOL Chord(int x1, int y1, int x2, int y2, int x3, int y3, int x4, int y4);

or

BOOL Chord(LPCRECT lpRect, POINT ptStart, POINT ptEnd);

draws a segment of ellipse just like Pie, but unlike Pie, Chord joins the endpoints of the arc with a straight line (see Figure 19.7).

FIGURE 19.7.

A figure drawn by Chord.

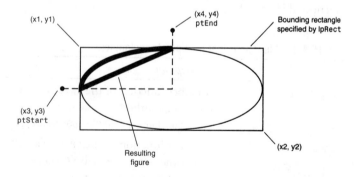

■ BOOL Polygon(LPPOINT lpPoints, int nCount);

draws a polygon by joining the nCount points in the array lpPoints. Polygon automatically joins the first and the last points in the array to form a closed figure.

Note that all drawing functions expect logical coordinates. For each of these closed figures, the Windows GDI draws the outline with the current pen style and fills the inside of the figures with the current brush. There are seven stock brush objects. You create an instance of the brush by calling GetStockObject with one of the following as the argument: BLACK_BRUSH, DKGRAY_BRUSH, GRAY_BRUSH, HOLLOW_BRUSH, LTGRAY_BRUSH, NULL_BRUSH, or WHITE_BRUSH.

You can create your own brush objects by using one of these member functions of the CBrush class: CreateBrushIndirect, CreateDIBPatternBrush, CreateHatchBrush, CreatePatternBrush, or CreateSolidBrush. CreateSolidBrush particularly is useful for creating a brush of a specified color:

```
CBrush RedBrush;
RedBrush.CreateSolidBrush(RGB(255, 0, 0));
```

The color is specified by an RGB triplet. If you specify a color that is not supported by hardware, Windows uses *dithering* to produce a close approximation to the requested color.

Manipulating Rectangles

Rectangles play an important part in the GDI. Accordingly, the GDI includes several functions that manipulate rectangles. MFC provides the CRect class to represent the RECT structure of Windows API, which is defined in the header file <windef.h> as the following:

```
typedef struct tagRECT
{
    LONG    left;    // Upper-left corner of rectangle
    LONG    top;
    LONG    right;   // Lower-right corner of rectangle
    LONG    bottom;
} RECT;
```

You have already seen the functions Rectangle and RoundRect for drawing rectangles. Table 19.4 lists several other rectangle functions. These are member functions of CDC or CRect classes as identified in the table.

Table 19.4. GDI functions that manipulate rectangles.

Name	Description
CopyRect	Member function of the CRect class that copies from one RECT object to another: void CopyRect(LPCRECT lpSrcRect);
EqualRect	Member function of the CRect class that returns TRUE if two RECT structures are equal: if(rectA.EqualRect(rectB)) { /* Rectangles are equal */ }
FillRect	Member function of the CDC class that fills a rectangle, up to but not including the right and bottom coordinates, with the specified brush: dc.FillRect(rect, &brush);
FrameRect	Member function of the CDC class that uses the specified brush (not the pen) to draw a rectangular frame: dc.FrameRect(rect, brush);
InflateRect	Member function of the CRect class that increases or decreases the size of a rectangle: rect.InflateRect(dx, dy);

Name	Description
InvertRect	Member function of the CDC class that inverts all the pixels in a rectangle: `dc.InverCRect(rect);`
OffsetRect	Member function of the CRect class that moves the rectangle along x- and y-axes: `rect.OffsetRect(dx, dy);`
PtInRect	Member function of the CRect class that returns TRUE if a point is in the rectangle: `if(rect.PtInRect(point)) { /* Point is in rectangle */ }`
SetRect	Member function of the CRect class that sets the fields of the RECT structure: `rect.SetRect(left, top, right, bottom);`
SetRectEmpty	Member function of the CRect class that sets the fields of the RECT structure to zero: `rect.SetRectEmpty(&rect);`
UnionRect	Member function of the CRect class that sets the fields of the RECT structure to be the union of two other rectangles: `rectA.UnionRect(rectB, rectC);`

Regions

Recall that regions are areas of the drawing surface. The GDI enables you to define a region as a combination of rectangles, polygons, and ellipses. You can use a region to draw—by filling the region with the current brush—or use it as the *clipping region*—the area where the drawing appears. Table 19.5 lists the GDI functions meant for defining and using regions. Note that to use a region, you must have a handle to it. You can create a region with one of the Windows API functions or through the MFC class CRgn, which represents a region. When using a region as a clipping region, you have to call SetClipRgn to select the region into the DC.

The functions listed in Table 19.5 are member functions of the CDC class and CRgn class.

Table 19.5. GDI functions that manipulate regions.

Name	Description
CreateRectRgn	Member function of the CRgn class that creates a rectangular region using specified coordinates for the opposite corners of the rectangle: `rgn.CreateRectRgn(left, top, right, bottom);`
CreateRectRgnIndirect	Member function of the CRgn class that creates a rectangular region using the fields of a RECT structure: `rgn.CreateRectRgnIndirect(rect);`

continues

Table 19.5. continued

Name	Description
CreateRoundRectRgn	Member function of the CRgn class that creates a rectangular region with rounded corners, specified the same way as the RoundRect function
CreateEllipticRgn	Member function of the CRgn class that creates an elliptic region: rgn.CreateEllipticRgn(left, top, right, bottom);
CreateEllipticRgnIndirect	Member function of the CRgn class that creates an elliptic region using the fields in a RECT structure: rgn.CreateEllipticRgnIndirect(rect);
CreatePolygonRgn	Member function of the CRgn class that creates a polygon region: rgn.CreatePolygonRgn(points, npoints, fill_mode); where fill_mode is ALTERNATE to WINDING
CreatePolyPolygonRgn	Member function of the CRgn class that creates a region out of multiple polygons
CombineRgn	Member function of the CRgn class that combines two regions into one according to a specified combining mode (which can be one of: RGN_AND, RGN_COPY, RGN_DIFF, RGN_OR, RGN_XOR): rgn.CombineRgn(pRgn1, pRgn2, combine_mode);
EqualRgn	Member function of the CRgn class that returns TRUE if two regions are equal: if(RgnA.EqualRgn(pRgnB)) { / * regions are equal */}
FillRgn	Member function of the CDC class that fills a region with the specified brush: dc.FillRgn(&rgn, &brush);
FrameRgn	Member function of the CDC class that draws a frame around a region with the specified brush: dc.FrameRgn(&rgn, &brush, width, height);
GetRgnBox	Member function of the CRgn class that returns the bounding box (largest rectangle enclosing the region) of the region: rgn.GetRgnBox(&rect);
InvalidateRgn	Member function of the CWnd class that marks the specified region for repainting: wnd.InvalidateRgn(&rgn, bErase);
InvertRgn	Member function of the CDC class that inverts the pixels in a region: dc.InvertRgn(rgn);

Name	Description
OffsetRgn	Member function of the CRgn class that moves the region by a specified x- and y-offset: `rgn.OffsetRgn(x, y);`
PaintRgn	Member function of CDC that fills the region with the current brush: `dc.PaintRgn(&rgn);`
PtInRegion	Member function of the CRgn class that returns TRUE if the specified point is in the region: `if(rgn.PtInRegion(50, 50)) { /* Point (50,50) is in the region) */ }`
RectInRegion	Member function of the CRgn class that returns TRUE if any part of the specified rectangle is in the region: `if(rgn.RectInRegion(rect)) { /* All or part of rectangle rect is in the region. */ }`
SelectClipRgn	Member function of the CDC class that sets the specified region as the clipping region: `dc.SelectClipRgn(&rgn);`
SetRectRgn	Member function of the CRgn class that changes the region to a rectangular shape specified by the CRect argument: `rgn.SetRectRgn(rect);`
ValidateRgn	Member function of the CWnd class that removes the region from the area to be repainted: `ValidateRgn(hrgn);`

Drawing Mode

When you are drawing lines and filled figures, the drawing mode controls the way the pen color is combined with the existing colors. This is referred to as a *raster operation (ROP)*. The GDI defines sixteen ROPs, identified by symbols that start with the R2_ prefix. The default ROP is R2_COPYPEN, which means that the pen overwrites whatever exists on the drawing surface. Table 19.6 lists the names of the ROP codes that apply to drawing with the GDI functions. Note that there is another set of ROP codes that applies when copying a bitmap to a DC.

Use the SetROP2 function to specify a new drawing mode:

```
int previous_ROP = dc.SetROP2(R2_XORPEN);
```

In this case, SetROP2 sets the ROP code to R2_XORPEN and returns the old ROP code, which is stored in the variable named previous_ROP.

Table 19.6. Drawing modes in Windows GDI.

Mode Name	Boolean Operation	Comments
R2_BLACK	All bits zero	Draws in black ignoring pen color and existing color
R2_COPYPEN	Pen	Draws with pen color (the default drawing mode)
R2_MASKNOTPEN	(NOT pen) AND dest	Inverts the bits in pen color and performs a bitwise AND with existing color
R2_MASKPEN	Pen AND dest	Performs bitwise AND of pen color and existing color
R2_MASKPENNOT	Pen AND (NOT dest)	Inverts existing color and performs bitwise AND with pen color
R2_MERGENOTPEN	(NOT pen) OR dest	Inverts pen color and performs bitwise OR with existing color
R2_MERGEPEN	Pen OR dest	Performs bitwise OR of pen color and existing color
R2_MERGEPENNOT	Pen OR (NOT dest)	Inverts existing color and performs bitwise OR with pen color
R2_NOP	Dest	Leaves existing color unchanged (hence the name NOP for "no operation")
R2_NOT	NOT dest	Inverts existing color
R2_NOTCOPYPEN	NOT pen	Draws with inverted pen color
R2_NOTMASKPEN	NOT (pen AND dest)	Performs bitwise AND of pen and existing color and inverts the result
R2_NOTMERGEPEN	NOT (pen OR dest)	Performs bitwise OR of pen and existing color and inverts the result
R2_NOTXORPEN	NOT (pen XOR dest)	Performs bitwise exclusive-OR of pen and existing color and inverts the result
R2_WHITE	All bits 1	Draws in white color
R2_XORPEN	Pen XOR dest	Performs bitwise exclusive-OR of pen color and existing color

Handling Color

Prior to Windows 3.0, the only way to represent a color was to express it in terms of the RGB intensities of the color. To represent the RGB value, the Windows API defines the COLORREF type, which is a 32-bit integer value with the RGB intensities stored in the low-order bytes (see Figure 19.8). The most significant byte of the COLORREF type indicates whether to interpret the value as a color or a palette entry—a topic that is discussed in the next section.

FIGURE 19.8.
Interpreting the contents of a COLORREF value.

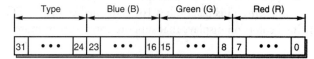

```
Type = 0  explicit RGB color
       1  logical palette index
       2  RGB from palette
```

You can use the RGB macro to represent an RGB color. For example, RGB(255, 0, 0) denotes a full-intensity red color. Because each intensity is an 8-bit value, the intensity can range from 0 to 255.

DITHERED COLORS

Windows uses dithering to display colors that may not be supported by the display hardware. The process of dithering displays neighboring pixels in different colors to create unique shades. Because dithering requires a collection of pixels to work, Windows uses dithering only when filling an area—Windows cannot use dithering when drawing points, lines, and text.

System Palette

Display adapters such as VGA, Super VGA, XGA, and 8514/A can generate the necessary signals to display a large number of colors on a color display, but only a small number of these colors are available at any one time. The number of colors that can be displayed at a time is determined by the number of bits of storage allocated for each pixel. In a standard VGA, each pixel has 4 bits of storage—this means the standard VGA can display $2^4 = 16$ simultaneous colors. On the other hand, a super VGA adapter with enough memory may support a graphics mode in which each pixel can have an 8-bit value. In this case, the display adapter can show $2^8 = 256$ simultaneous colors.

Although the number of simultaneous colors is limited, the display adapter represents each color in terms of the RGB intensities of the color and uses several bits to represent the R, G, and B components. For example, a VGA display adapter that uses 6 bits per R, G, and B component allows up to 2^6 x 2^6 x 2^6 = 262,144 distinct colors. From these you can display any 16 colors if the display adapter supports 4 bits per pixel, or any 256 colors if the adapter supports 8 bits per pixel. The display adapter converts each pixel's contents into a color by interpreting the pixel's value as an index into a table. This table is the *color palette,* whose entries are RGB values.

In keeping with the hardware palette in display adapters, Windows also defines a palette called the *system palette.* This palette has 16 predefined colors for EGA and VGA displays, and 20 predefined colors on displays that support 256 colors or more.

Logical Palette

Starting with version 3.0, Windows supports the notion of a *logical palette* that enables applications to take advantage of the large number of colors available in a system. Provided the display hardware supports more than 20 colors, Windows provides an extended system palette that mimics the hardware palette. Windows automatically sets aside 20 entries in the extended system palette—these are the 20 default colors. When you define a logical palette, Windows maps each color in the logical palette to the extended system palette:

■ If a color in the logical palette already exists in the system palette, that color is mapped to the matching color index in the system palette.

■ A logical palette color with no match in the system palette is added to the system palette, provided there is room.

■ When the system palette becomes full, a logical palette color is mapped to the closest matching color in the system palette.

When there are several applications with logical palettes, Windows maps the logical palette of the topmost window into the system palette.

If you write a Windows application and want to use all 256 colors in a super VGA adapter, you have to use a logical palette; otherwise, you can use only the 20 default colors in the system palette.

Creating and Using Logical Palettes

Like a hardware palette, a logical palette is merely a table of RGB colors. Each entry in the table is a PALETTEENTRY structure, defined in <wingdi.h> as the following:

```
typedef struct tagPALETTEENTRY
{
    BYTE    peRed;
    BYTE    peGreen;
    BYTE    peBlue;
    BYTE    peFlags;
} PALETTEENTRY;
```

The logical palette itself is a LOGPALETTE structure, declared in <wingdi.h> as the following:

```
typedef struct tagLOGPALETTE
{
    WORD         palVersion;      // Windows version
    WORD         palNumEntries;   // Number of palette entries
    PALETTEENTRY palPalEntry[1];  // Array of palette entries
} LOGPALETTE;
```

You use these steps to create and use a logical palette:

1. Check whether the display driver supports logical palettes:

```
if((dc.GetDeviceCaps(RASTERCAPS) & RC_PALETTE) &&
   (dc.GetDeviceCaps(DRIVERVERSION) >= 0x0300))
{
// Supports logical palettes.
}
else
{
// Does not support logical palettes.
}
```

2. Allocate room for a palette and define the palette entries. For example, here is the C++ code to allocate a logical palette with 16 entries (defined to be shades of red):

```
const int ncolors = 16;
LPLOGPALETTE lpal = (LPLOGPALETTE) new char[sizeof(LOGPALETTE) + (ncolors -
1) * sizeof(PALETTEENTRY)];

lpal->palVersion = 0x0300;
lpal->palNumEntries = ncolors;

int i;
for(i = 0; i < ncolors; i++)
{
    lpal->palPalEntry[i].peRed   = 16*i;
    lpal->palPalEntry[i].peGreen = 0;
    lpal->palPalEntry[i].peBlue  = 0;
    lpal->palPalEntry[i].peFlags = 0;
}
```

The peFlags field in each palette entry can be one of the following:

Value	Meaning
0	The entry is a normal palette entry.

PC_EXPLICIT   Treat the low-order 16-bit word as an index to the hardware palette.

PC_NOCOLLAPSE   Do not map this entry to any existing color in the system palette.

PC_RESERVED   This entry will be used for palette animation (this means the entry will be changed often). Do not map colors from other logical palettes with this entry.

3. Create a CPalette object using the constructor that accepts a pointer to the LOGPALETTE structure as argument:

```
CPalette *pal = new Cpalette;

pal->CreatePalette(lpal);
```

4. Call the SelectPalette function of the CDC class to select the new palette into the device context:

```
CPalette *oldPal = dc.SelectPalette(pal, FALSE);
```

Note that a FALSE for the last argument to SelectPalette specifies that the palette is to be used as a foreground palette; otherwise, the palette is used for background.

5. Before using the colors in the palette, call the RealizePalette member function of the CDC class to install the logical palette into the system palette and make the colors available:

```
dc.RealizePalette();
```

6. Before exiting the program, free the memory allocated for the logical palette and restore the original palette by calling SelectPalette with the previous palette as argument:

```
delete lpal;
dc.SelectPalette(oldPal);
delete pal;
```

You may want to do this cleanup in the handler for the WM_DESTROY event that Windows sends when a window is being closed.

Manipulating Logical Palettes

The Windows GDI provides a number of functions for manipulating logical and system palettes. Table 19.7 summarizes these functions. Most of these GDI functions are available as member functions of the CDC or CPalette classes.

Table 19.7. Windows functions that manipulate palettes.

Name	*Description*
AnimatePalette	Member function of the CPalette class that changes entries in a logical palette, resulting in instant changes to colors on the display: `pal.AnimatePalette(start_indx, count, pal_entries);`
CreatePalette	Member function of the CPalette class that creates a CPalette from a specified logical palette.
GetNearestPaletteIndex	Member function of the CPalette class that returns the index of the palette entry that most closely matches a specified COLORREF: `UINT p_indx = pal.GetNearestPaletteIndex(color);`
GetPaletteEntries	Member function of the CPalette class that retrieves the color values for a specified number of entries in a logical palette: `pal.GetPaletteEntries(start_indx, count, pal_entries);`
RealizePalette	Member function of the CDC class that maps the entries of the currently selected logical palette into the system palette: `dc.RealizePalette();`
ResizePalette	Member function of the CPalette class that enlarges or reduces the size of a logical palette after it has been created: `pal.ResizePalette(num_entries);`
SetPaletteEntries	Member function of the CPalette class that changes the color values of a specified number of entries in the logical palette: `pal.SetPaletteEntries(start, count, pal_entries);`
UpdateColors	Member function of the CDC class that updates the color of the pixels in the client area of a window to reflect the current entries in the system palette: `dc.UpdateColors();`

Handling Palette Messages

If your application uses a logical palette, it should handle three palette-specific Windows messages to ensure that the colors are displayed correctly in the application's windows. First of all, whenever your application's window becomes active, Windows sends a WM_QUERYNEWPALETTE message to offer an opportunity to realize the logical palette. The reason is that other applications that also use logical palettes may have loaded different colors into the system palette, and your application needs to reload its colors. The function that handles the WM_QUERYNEWPALETTE message should call the RealizePalette function to map the logical palette to the system palette. In an MFC program, you declare the message handler for WM_QUERYNEWPALETTE as follows:

```
afx_msg BOOL OnQueryNewPalette();
```

In addition to declaring this member function in the window class, you also have to add the following line to the window's message map:

```
// Assuming window is derived from CFrameWnd
BEGIN_MESSAGE_MAP(CMyWnd, CFrameWnd)
    ON_WM_QUERYNEWPALETTE()
END_MESSAGE_MAP()
```

Then you might implement the OnQueryNewPalette function:

```
    short changed = 0;

// Assume that "pal" is the CPalette object representing your
// application's logical palette (the one you want to use).

    CClientDC dc(this);
    dc.SelectObject(pal, FALSE);
    int changed = dc.RealizePalette();
    dc.RestorePalette();
    if(changed)
    {
        Invalidate(TRUE);
        UpdateWindow();
    }
```

The RealizePalette function returns the number of colors that were changed to accommodate the specified logical palette. You should redraw the contents of the window if any colors change.

The other two palette-related Windows messages are WM_PALETTEISCHANGING and WM_PALETTECHANGED. These messages matter to an application only if you want to display the best possible colors even when the application's windows are not active. Windows sends the WM_PALETTEISCHANGING message to the top-level windows of all applications when the system palette is about to change; the WM_PALETTECHANGED message is sent after the system palette has changed. Applications that do not use logical palettes can ignore these messages safely.

If your application has to display the best possible colors when it does not have the input focus, the application should handle the WM_PALETTECHANGED message by providing the OnPaletteChanged function in the window class. The first step in this function is to ensure that the palette change was not caused by an earlier call to RealizePalette made by your application. Here is a code fragment for a function that handles the WM_PALETTECHANGED message:

```
// Assume the window class is called CMyWnd
void CMyWnd::OnPaletteChanged(CWnd* pFocusWnd)
{
    if(pFocusWnd == this) return;
//...
```

```
// Assume that "pal" is the CPalette object representing your
// application's logical palette (the one you want to use).

    CClientDC dc(this);
    dc.SelectObject(pal, FALSE);
    int changed = dc.RealizePalette();
    if(changed)
    {
        dc.UpdateColors();
    }
    dc.RestorePalette();
}
```

In this case, too, you first realize the logical palette and, if any colors in the system palette change, call UpdateColors to refresh the colors quickly in your application's window. Of course, if you want, you also can redraw the contents of the window by invalidating the client area.

Bitmaps

Each pixel in an image corresponds to one or more bits in a bitmap. In a monochrome bitmap, corresponding to a black-and-white image, each bit in the bitmap represents a pixel in the image. For color images, each pixel requires more than one bit in the bitmap to indicate the color of the pixel. Additionally, the mapping of the bits in a pixel to a specific color depends on a color map.

Recall that Windows supported a single bitmap format prior to version 3.0, now known as the device-dependent bitmap (DDB). The DDB made certain assumptions about the display device. Windows 3.0 introduced a new version, called the device-independent bitmap (DIB) that stores the bitmap information in a device-independent manner—primarily by adding a color palette to the old DDB format. MFC 3.0 provides the CBitmap class to represent a DDB.

You can think of a bitmap as a canvas in memory where you can draw images. The Windows GDI includes functions such as BitBlt and StretchBlt that can copy a bitmap to the display device quickly. Bitmaps are very useful in applications that require animating images. For example, if you have to move a small image around on the display screen, you can store that image in a bitmap and use BitBlt to copy the image to the display screen as and when needed. The following sections summarize the bitmap formats and the bitmap manipulation functions. Chapter 21 further describes how to interpret image file formats and animate images.

The DDB

The simplest bitmap corresponds to a monochrome image. In this case, each bit in the bitmap represents one pixel in the image. You can derive the bitmap directly from the image by assigning a 1 to each white pixel and 0 to the black ones. Figure 19.9 shows how to write the hexadecimal values representing an 8x8 image. Note that Windows requires that the width (in pixels) of each row of an image be a multiple of 16—each row must have an even number of bytes. Thus, in the example of Figure 19.9, each row is padded with a null byte.

FIGURE 19.9.
Monochrome bitmap format.

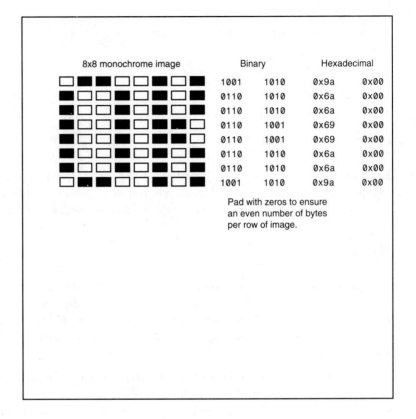

Displaying a Bitmap

Once you have the bitmap data, you can display it using the following steps:

1. Define an array of bytes with the bitmap data; write down the hexadecimal values row by row:

```
static BYTE image1[] = //This is the image from Figure 19.9
{
    0x9a, 0x00,  // Pad with zeros to get an even
    0x6a, 0x00,  // number of bytes per row of image
    0x6a, 0x00,
    0x69, 0x00,
    0x69, 0x00,
    0x6a, 0x00,
    0x6a, 0x00,
    0x9a, 0x00
};
```

2. Create a `CBitmap` object representing a monochrome bitmap from the bitmap data:

```
// Create the bitmap from the image data

    CBitmap bm;
    bm.CreateBitmap(8,        // Width of bitmap (in pixels)
                    8,        // Width of bitmap (in pixels)
                    1,        // Number of planes
                    1,        // Bits per pixel
                    image1);  // Bitmap data
```

3. Create a memory DC that is compatible with the device where you plan to display the bitmap, and select the bitmap into the memory DC:

```
// Create a memory device context compatible with
// the display device context (represented by the CDC
// object dc)

    CDC memdc;
    memdc.CreateCompatibleDC(&dc);


// Select bitmap into memory device context
    CBitmap *pOldBitmap = memdc.SelectObject(&bm);
```

4. Transfer the bitmap from the memory DC to the display device context by calling `BitBlt`:

```
// Copy bitmap into the display device context
// (assume that dc is a CClientDC)
    dc.BitBlt(
        10, 10, // Copy to this logical x,y coordinate
        8, 8,   // Width, height of destination
        &memdc, // Copy from this device context
        0, 0,   // Copy from this logical x,y
        SRCCOPY // One of 256 raster operation codes
        );
```

Stretching a Bitmap

The `BitBlt` function copies a bitmap from one DC to an identical rectangle in another DC. The `StretchBlt` function is another block transfer function that can shrink or stretch a bitmap to fit a specified rectangle in the destination DC. For example, if you want to stretch the 8x8 bitmap of Figure 19.9 to 64x64, you can do so with the following call to `StretchBlt`:

```
dc.StretchBlt(
    100, 10, // Copy to this logical x,y coordinate
    64, 64,  // Width, height of destination rectangle
```

```
&memdc,   // Copy from this device context (source)
0, 0,     // Copy from this logical x,y coordinate
8, 8,     // Width and size of source rectangle
SRCCOPY   // One of 256 raster operation codes
);
```

Drawing on a Bitmap

Sometimes you may want to prepare a drawing in memory before copying it to a device for displaying or printing. One good time to do this is when you are repeating the same figure. Keeping the drawing in memory and copying it to the device with a call to BitBlt is much faster than drawing everything directly on the device. You will find this technique useful for animation as well—the animation looks smoother when you prepare the animated drawing offscreen in memory and copy the drawing to the display.

To prepare a drawing in memory, you have to create a bitmap of a specified size, select it into a memory DC, and draw using that memory DC. The bitmap must be compatible with the device where you plan to display it. Here are the steps to follow:

1. Create a bitmap compatible with the display DC. You have to specify the size of the bitmap:

   ```
   CBitmap bm1;
   bm1.CreateCompatibleBitmap(&dc, // compatible with this DC
                        64, 64); // width and height in pixels
   ```

2. Select the bitmap into a memory DC that is compatible with the display DC:

   ```
   pOldBitmap = memdc.SelectObject(&bm1);
   ```

3. Fill the bitmap with a background color (otherwise, the bitmap will have a random bit pattern):

   ```
   // Fill the bitmap with white color
   pOldBrush = (CBrush*)memdc.SelectStockObject(WHITE_BRUSH);

   memdc.PatBlt(
       0, 0,      // Copy to this logical x,y
       64, 64,    // Width and height of rectangle to
                  // be filled with pattern
       PATCOPY);

   // Reset the brush
   memdc.SelectObject(pOldBrush);
   ```

4. Draw in the bitmap using GDI drawing functions:

   ```
   // Draw in the bitmap with GDI drawing functions
   memdc.Rectangle(4, 4, 40, 20);
   memdc.TextOut(10, 40, "Hello", 5);
   ```

5. Display the bitmap by calling BitBlt as shown in earlier sections.

ROP Codes

The last argument to the block transfer functions BitBlt, StretchBlt, and PatBlt, is a raster operation (ROP) code that specifies how the source bitmap is combined with the brush pattern and the destination pixels. There are 256 possible ROP codes. The 15 most common are listed in Table 19.8; the logical operations between the source (S), destination (D), and pattern (P) are expressed using the C++ bitwise logical operators: invert (~), AND (&), OR (¦), and exclusive-OR (^).

Table 19.8. Some raster operation codes used by the block transfer functions.

Constant	Operation	Meaning
BLACKNESS	0	Sets all destination pixels to zero (black)
DSTINVERT	~D	Inverts destination pixels
MERGECOPY	P&S	Performs bitwise AND of source bitmap and brush pattern
MERGEPAINT	~S¦D	Performs bitwise OR of the inverted source bitmap and the destination pixels
NOTSRCCOPY	~S	Copies inverted source bitmap to the destination
NOTSRCERASE	~(S¦D)	Inverts result of bitwise OR of the source and destination
PATCOPY	P	Copies brush pattern to the destination
PATINVERT	P^D	Performs exclusive-OR of the pattern and the destination
PATPAINT	P¦(~S)¦D	Inverts source bitmap and performs bitwise OR of the result with the pattern and the destination
SRCAND	S&D	Performs bitwise AND of source bitmap and destination
SRCCOPY	S	Copies source bitmap to the destination
SRCERASE	S&(~D)	Performs bitwise OR of the source and the inverted destination
SRCINVERT	S^D	Performs exclusive OR of the source and the destination
SRCPAINT	S¦D	Performs bitwise OR of the source and the destination
WHITENESS	1	Sets all bits of the destination pixels to 1 (white)

The *BITMAP* Structure

Device-dependent bitmaps are represented in memory by a BITMAP structure, which is defined in <wingdi.h> as the following:

```
typedef struct tagBITMAP
{
    LONG     bmType;        // Always set to zero
    LONG     bmWidth;       // Width of bitmap (in pixels)
    LONG     bmHeight;      // Height of bitmap (in pixels)
    LONG     bmWidthBytes;  // Bytes per row of bitmap data
                            //    (must be even)
    WORD     bmPlanes;      // Number of bit planes
    WORD     bmBitsPixel;   // Number of bits per pixel
    LPVOID   bmBits;        // Array of bitmap data
} BITMAP;
```

For color bitmaps, each pixel requires multiple bits of data, which may be stored as a number of planes or as groups of bits per pixel. The fields bmPlanes and bmBitsPixel determine how the bitmap data bmBits is interpreted.

When the data is organized as planes, bmBitsPixel is set to 1 and the bmPlanes field has the number of planes. The bmBits array starts with the first line of the image: all the bits of the first plane for the first line followed by the bits for that line from the second plane, and so on.

On the other hand, if the bitmap is meant for a device that stores all bits for a pixel contiguously, the bmPlanes field of the BITMAP structure is 1, but the bmBitsPixel is set to the number of bits used for each pixel. The bmBits array then stores the data for the image line by line, with each group of bmBitsPixel bits representing the color of consecutive pixels on a line.

The exact storage format for color bitmaps depends on the type of device in which the bitmap is to be displayed. Apart from the device-dependent manner of storing the image data, the BITMAP structure has no provision for indicating how the pixel values are mapped to actual colors. The DIB format, described next, corrects this shortcoming of the DDB format.

The DIB

The device-independent format, introduced in Windows 3.0, solves some of the device dependencies of the old-style bitmap format. Here are the specific differences:

■ The internal representation of bitmap data is standardized—color bitmaps are stored as multiple bits per pixel with only one plane per pixel. The number of bits per pixel can be one of the following:

1 for monochrome bitmaps

4 for 16-color bitmaps

8 for 256-color bitmaps

24 for 16,777,216 or 16 million color bitmaps

■ The array of bits stores the image data from the bottom row to the top (in DDB format, the data starts from the top row).

■ The DIB format includes information about the resolution of the image.

■ The bitmap data for 16- and 256-color bitmaps may be compressed using a run-length encoding (RLE) algorithm.

The DIB format is useful for storing images in files. The Windows PaintBrush application stores bitmaps in DIB format (with the .BMP file extension). Chapter 21 covers the DIB file format and shows how to read and display a device-independent bitmap.

Summary

Windows Graphical Device Interface (GDI) provides the data structures and functions necessary for displaying graphics, text, and images in your application's windows. This chapter provides an overview of the GDI functions. The device context, or DC, is the key to device-independent graphics in Windows. The DC holds drawing tools and attributes, such as pen, brush, background color, and font, that affect all graphics and text output.

The Windows GDI also supports drawing to bitmaps. You can define a memory DC with an associated bitmap and either load images or draw in the bitmap with GDI drawing functions. The GDI includes several block transfer functions, such as `BitBlt` and `StretchBlt`, that can efficiently copy bitmaps from memory to a device.

There are two types of bitmaps: the device-dependent bitmaps (DDB) from Windows versions prior to 3.0 and the device-independent bitmaps (DIB) introduced in Windows 3.0. The DIB format is used to store images in files—the .BMP files created by Windows PaintBrush use the DIB format. Chapter 21 describes how to interpret and display image files of various formats, including the DIB format.

MFC 3.0 provides the `CGdiObject` subhierarchy of classes that represents all data structures, such as DC, bitmap, font, brush, and pen, needed by the GDI functions. Most of the GDI functions appear as member functions of an appropriate class in the `CGdiObject` subhierarchy. In particular, all drawing functions are members of the `CDC` class, which represents a device context.

20

Displaying Text in Windows

Chapter 19, "Graphics Programming with MFC 3.0," describes the graphics output functions available in the Windows GDI. This chapter covers another important category of output functions—text output. Text output is important because text is an integral part of many Windows applications. Although you can get by with MFC classes that provide text editing capabilities, some Windows applications might use text in captions, annotations, and instructions. With the fonts available in Windows, you can customize the appearance of the text depending on the function. For example, you might want to use large bold characters for captions but smaller letters for the annotations. This chapter shows you how to display text in a Windows application.

Simple Text Output

The MFC class CDC provides several member functions for displaying text. These functions are similar to the Windows GDI functions with the same names. Here are the four prominent text output functions in the CDC class:

■ DrawText draws a text string inside a rectangle. You specify the positioning and format of the text in the nFormat argument. Consult the Visual C++ 2.0 online documentation for a list of possible values for nFormat. DrawText returns the height of the line of text:

```
int    DrawText(
    LPCTSTR lpszString, // Text string to be drawn
    int     nCount,     // Number of characters in the string
                        // (Use -1 if lpszString is
                        //null-terminated)
    LPRECT lpRect,      // Place text in this rectangle
    UINT   nFormat);    // Specifies how text is positioned
```

■ TabbedTextOut displays a string after expanding any embedded tabs according to the array of tab positions specified in lpnTabStopPositions. TabbedTextOut returns the height and width (in logical units) of the displayed string in a CSize object:

```
CSize TabbedTextOut(
    int    x,                // Logical x,y coordinates of the
    int    y,                // starting point of string
    LPCTSTR lpszString,      // Display this string
    int    nCount,           // Number of characters in string
    int    nTabPositions,    // Number of tab positions
    LPINT  lpnTabStopPositions, // Array of tab positions
    int    nTabOrigin);      // Start tab expansion from this point
```

■ TextOut displays a string at a specified location. It returns TRUE if successful; otherwise, it returns FALSE:

```
BOOL TextOut(int x, int y, const CString& str);
BOOL TextOut(int x, int y, LPCSTR lpString, int nCount);
```

■ ExtTextOut displays a string in a rectangular region using the current font. It returns TRUE if successful; otherwise, it returns FALSE:

```
BOOL ExtTextOut(
    int     x,          // Logical x,y coordinate of the
    int     y,          // first character's location
    UINT    nOptions,   // One or both of these:
                        // ETO_CLIPPED (clip to rectangle)
                        // ETO_OPAQUE (fill with current background)
    LPCRECT lpRect,     // Rectangle where string appears
    LPCTSTR lpszString, // String being displayed
    UINT    nCount,     // Number of characters
    LPINT   lpDxWidths);// Array of separations between chars
```

The positioning of the characters with respect to the text output location depends on the current text alignment specified by the SetTextAlign function.

You specify the text alignment by calling the SetTextAlign function of the CDC class. For a CDC object named dc, a typical call to SetTextAlign is as follows:

```
dc.SetTextAlign(TA_BOTTOM | TA_LEFT);
```

where the second argument is a bitwise OR of flags indicating the location of the text string with respect to the output position. In this case, the text output position is at the upper-left corner of the string. The vertical alignment can be one of the following:

TA_BASELINE	Baseline of text is aligned with the y-coordinate of the output position.
TA_BOTTOM	Bottom of text is aligned with the y-coordinate of the output position.
TA_TOP	Top of text is aligned with the y-coordinate of the output position.

The horizontal alignment can be one of the following:

TA_CENTER	Horizontal center of text is aligned with the x-coordinate of the output position.
TA_LEFT	Left side of text is aligned with the x-coordinate of the output position.
TA_RIGHT	Right side of text is aligned with the x-coordinate of the output position.

The default alignment is TA_TOP | TA_LEFT. Additionally, by default TextOut does not update the current position after the text output. If you want the current position updated, include the TA_UPDATECP flag with a bitwise OR operator in the call to SetTextAlign.

In addition to the text alignment, several other attributes in the DC affect text output. By default, the text color is black, but you can set the text color to any RGB value:

```
dc.SetTextColor(RGB(255, 0, 0)); // Set text color to red.
```

The background mode determines whether the spaces between the characters are filled in with the current background color. By default, the background mode is OPAQUE, which means Windows uses the background color to fill in the spaces between the character strokes. You can set the background mode to TRANSPARENT and display the characters without affecting the pixels between:

```
dc.SetBkMode(TRANSPARENT);
```

Of course, the font is another important attribute that determines the appearance (shape and size) of the text output. By default, Windows displays the text in the system font. As you will see in the next section, however, you can create and use many other fonts. The easiest way to display text is to use one of the six stock fonts. Like other stock objects, such as brush and pen, the fonts are identified by names. Here are the names of the six stock fonts in Windows:

ANSI_FIXED_FONT	This is a fixed-width ANSI character set font (usually Courier).
ANSI_VAR_FONT	This is a variable width ANSI character set font (usually MS Sans Serif).
DEVICE_DEFAULT_FONT	This is a font that is most suitable for the current device.
OEM_FIXED_FONT	This is a fixed-width font that contains the IBM-PC compatible character set. Windows uses this font in all windowed DOS character-mode applications (including COMMAND.COM).
SYSTEM_FIXED_FONT	This is a fixed-pitch ANSI character set font that Windows versions prior to 3.0 used for menus, dialog boxes, message boxes, and captions.
SYSTEM_FONT	This is a proportionally spaced ANSI character set font that Windows uses in menus, dialog boxes, message boxes, and captions.

You can use any of these stock fonts just as you use other stock objects: by selecting it into the DC with a call to the SelectStockObject function. For example, to use the ANSI_FIXED_FONT in an MFC program, you write the following:

```
// Assume that dc is the device context
    CFont *pOldFont = (CFont*)
                        dc.SelectStockObject(ANSI_FIXED_FONT);

// Display text using this font
    char msg[] = "Hello, World!";
    dc.TextOut(20, 50, msg, strlen(msg));

// Restore the old font
    dc.SelectObject(pOldFont);
```

The next few sections discuss how to select and use other fonts.

Using Fonts

The choice of typeface is limited when you use the stock fonts. Windows offers many more typefaces that you can use to create impressive text displays. Before beginning to use the font creation functions, you should know a few terms related to the use of fonts in Windows.

In Windows, the term *typeface* refers to the appearance of a specific set of characters regardless of size. A typeface is characterized by features such as serifs that are shared by all characters from the set. A *font*, on the other hand, is a complete set of characters from a typeface with a specific size and style, such as bold or italic. Thus, Helvetica is a typeface and 12-point Helvetica Bold is a font. Another important characteristic of a font is its character set.

Character Set

The *character set* of a font determines the character shape corresponding to each 8-bit character code. The American Standard Code for Information Interchange (ASCII) specifies the characters corresponding to the first 128 character codes. MS-DOS systems define a number of special and line-drawing characters for the last 128 of the 256 character codes that can be represented by an 8-bit value. Unfortunately, the American National Standards Institute (ANSI) defines different characters for the last 128 character codes. Windows primarily supports the ANSI character set in its fonts. However, Windows also supports the extended DOS character set in what is known as an OEM (Original Equipment Manufacturer) font for use in non-Windows applications. Because some characters in the ANSI font are also in the OEM font and vice versa, the Windows API includes two functions for converting from one character set to another: AnsiToOem and OemToAnsi. The ANSI font also includes special accented characters in the last 128 character codes. You have to call AnsiUpper and AnsiLower to ensure that the case conversions work properly with these characters in the ANSI font.

Font Types

Windows provides two font families: *fixed-width* and *variable-width*. In a fixed-width font, all characters occupy exactly the same width. In a variable-width font, each character takes up only as much space as it needs.

Windows supports three types of fonts: *raster, vector,* and *TrueType*. In a raster font, each character is defined by a bitmap image. Windows can display these fonts easily because displaying a character involves merely copying the bitmap to the screen.

A vector or *stroke* font defines each character's shape in terms of a series of line segments. Vector fonts can be rotated and scaled easily.

TrueType is a much more sophisticated way of representing fonts. Like fonts in the page-description language PostScript, a TrueType font contains a detailed description of each character. TrueType expresses the character's outline in terms of lines and curves. The font even contains information, known as hints, on displaying each character on various resolution devices. These hints ensure that characters are rendered legibly at all resolutions and in all sizes.

Windows includes many fonts—the older vector and raster fonts and a substantial number of new TrueType fonts. To view the available fonts, run the Character Map application (CHARMAP.EXE) that comes with Windows. Figure 20.1 shows the window that CHARMAP displays. If you click on the font selection box (or on the arrow next to it), a listbox appears with the names of available fonts. In Figure 20.1, you can see the character set of the System font.

FIGURE 20.1.

Displaying a font with the Character Map application.

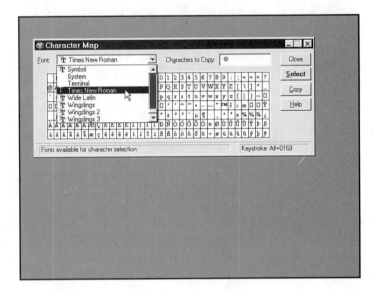

Font Families

Windows groups all available typefaces into a number of font families. All typefaces with the same general appearance belong to the same family. Here are the characteristics that determine the appearance of a font family:

Stroke width	This refers to the width of the lines that make up the shape of each character. The stroke width can be fixed or variable.
Pitch	This is the separation between characters in a line of text and is controlled by the width of the characters. If all characters in a typeface have the same width, the typeface is said to be of *fixed pitch* (or *monospace*). A typeface with a variable pitch is also called *proportionally spaced typeface.*
Serif	The serifs are the small lines that embelish the characters in some typefaces. For example, look at any character (such as S and A) in

the Times Roman font. You will notice the serifs at the end of the lines in the character. Fonts without serifs are referred to as *sans serif* fonts.

Table 20.1 summarizes the font families by names that are defined in the header file WINDOWS.H.

Table 20.1. Font family names.

Name	*Description*
FF_DONTCARE	This name is used by a program when it wants to use a font but it does not care or does not know the font's family.
FF_ROMAN	These typefaces have serifs and variable stroke width. Typical examples are Times New Roman, Century Schoolbook, and MS Serif.
FF_SWISS	These typefaces have variable stroke width and do not have any serifs (sans serif). Typical members of this family are Arial, Helvetica, MS Sans Serif, and System.
FF_MODERN	These fonts have constant stroke width. This family includes fonts with or without serifs. Typical examples are Courier, Courier New, and Terminal.
FF_SCRIPT	These fonts resemble cursive handwriting. Examples are Script and Zapf Chancery.
FF_DECORATIVE	These are decorative fonts. Many fonts in this family have characters that do not correspond to any alphabet. Typical examples are Monotype Sorts, WingDings, and Zapf Dingbats.

Getting Information on a Font

When displaying text output, Windows draws each character by painting the pixels in a rectangle matching the size of that character's bitmap. Because you have to specify where Windows should start drawing the characters, you need to know the size of each character's bitmap (at the very least, the maximum width and height of the character bitmaps in a font). The Windows API includes functions that enable you to obtain such information.

To get aggregate information about a font, call the GetTextMetrics member function of a device context object with a TEXTMETRIC structure as argument. GetTextMetric fills in the fields of the TEXTMETRIC structure with information about the font. The TEXTMETRIC structure's definition depends on whether you are using Unicode or plain ASCII character set. When the UNICODE macro is not defined, the TEXTMETRIC structure is the same as the TEXTMETRICA structure, which is defined in the <wingdi.h> header file:

```
typedef struct tagTEXTMETRICA
{
    LONG    tmHeight;          // Height of character(logical unit)
    LONG    tmAscent;          // Height above baseline
    LONG    tmDescent;         // Height below baseline
    LONG    tmInternalLeading; // Space for diacritical marks
    LONG    tmExternalLeading; // Extra space between lines
    LONG    tmAveCharWidth;    // Average width of characters
                               // in logical units
    LONG    tmMaxCharWidth;    // Width of the widest character
    LONG    tmWeight;          // A value between 0 and 999 that
                               // denotes whether font is bold or normal
    LONG    tmOverhang;        // Extra width added when creating
                               // an italic version of the font
    LONG    tmDigitizedAspectX;// These denote the aspect ratio
    LONG    tmDigitizedAspectY;// for which font is appropriate
    BYTE    tmFirstChar;       // Character code of first character
    BYTE    tmLastChar;        // Character code of last character
    BYTE    tmDefaultChar;     // Character that Windows uses to
                               // display nonexistent characters
    BYTE    tmBreakChar;       // Character that marks word breaks
    BYTE    tmItalic;          // Nonzero if font is italic
    BYTE    tmUnderlined;      // Nonzero if font is underlined
    BYTE    tmStruckOut;       // Nonzero if a line is to be drawn
                               // through every character
    BYTE    tmPitchAndFamily;  // Lower 2 bits indicate pitch
                               // Next 4 bits indicate family
    BYTE    tmCharSet;         // Character set of font (usually
                               // ANSI_CHARSET or OEM_CHARSET)
} TEXTMETRICA;
```

Figure 20.2 illustrates the meaning of some of the members of the TEXTMETRIC structure. Keep in mind that the dimensions returned in the TEXTMETRIC structure are in logical units. Thus, these dimensions are in pixel units only if you are using the MM_TEXT mapping mode.

FIGURE 20.2.

Character size information in TEXTMETRIC structure.

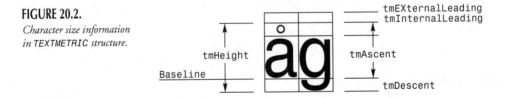

Windows 3.1 introduced a new structure, NEWTEXTMETRIC, with four additional fields appended to the older TEXTMETRIC structure. The new fields are meant to hold information about the TrueType fonts. The new structure is used by the EnumFontFamilies function. Because TrueType fonts have many more attributes than the older raster and vector fonts, Windows 3.1 also added another function, GetOutlineMetrics, and another structure, OUTLINETEXTMETRIC, to provide additional information about the TrueType fonts. The OUTLINETEXTMETRIC structure includes a TEXTMETRIC structure and a large number of other fields with detailed information about a TrueType font. You can look up detailed information on the new structure and the GetOutlineMetrics function in the online help of Visual C++ 2.0.

As an example of using the information returned by `GetTextMetrics`, consider the problem of displaying lines of text in a specific font. You need the height of characters to position the lines. Here is how you might set the height of a line of text:

```
TEXTMETRIC tm;

// Assume dc is the device context
    dc.GetTextMetrics(&tm);

    short line_height = tm.tmHeight + tm.tmExternalLeading;
```

Although the `GetTextMetrics` function provides information about the height of the characters in a font, you need another function to determine the width of a string displayed in a certain font. Unless the font is monospaced, the width of each character varies; you cannot find the width of a line of text with the general information from `GetTextMetrics`. You have to call `GetTextExtent` to determine the width of a string displayed in the current font. Here is how you use the `GetTextExtent` function to determine the height and width of the string `"Hello"` in logical units:

```
    int slen = strlen("Hello");

// Assume that dc is the device context
    CSize txtsz = dc.GetTextExtent("Hello", slen);
    int line_width = txtsz.cx;
    int line_height = txtsz.cy;
```

These sample code fragments assume that you are going to display the text in the currently selected font. If you want to use a specific font, you can follow the procedure outlined in the next section to create and use a font.

Creating a Font

To use a font (other than the stock fonts) in an MFC program, start by creating a CFont object that represents a Windows *logical font*—a description of the font you want. This description includes the name of the typeface as well as the font's height, weight, pitch, and family, among several other features.

There are two ways to create a CFont object. For both approaches, you have to first define a CFont object. The first way to construct the CFont object is similar in syntax to the CreateFont function in the Windows API. Here is an example that creates a bold Helvetica font with characters 60 logical units tall:

```
CFont font;
font.CreateFont(
                60,                     // height (logical units)
                0,                      // width (0 means
                                        // Windows chooses width)
                0,                      // escapement
                0,                      // orientation
                FW_BOLD,                // weight
                0,                      // italic - off
```

```
        0,                      // underline - off
        0,                      // strikeout - off
        ANSI_CHARSET,           // character set
        OUT_DEFAULT_PRECIS,     // output precision
        CLIP_DEFAULT_PRECIS,    // clipping precision
        PROOF_QUALITY,
        VARIABLE_PITCH,         // pitch and family
        "Helv");                // name of font face
```

Notice that creating the CFont object this way requires 14 arguments just as the CreateFont function does. You can set many of the arguments to zero, but you do have to specify all 14 of the arguments.

If you do not want to specify all these arguments when creating the CFont object, you can use another member function that relies on the Windows API function CreateFontIndirect, which requires only one argument: a pointer to a LOGFONT structure. The LOGFONT structure has exactly 14 members, one for each of the 14 arguments that CreateFont requires. Thus, you are still going to have to specify many parameters, but you can use the second form of the CFont creation as many times as you need, each time changing the fields of a single LOGFONT structure.

As with the TEXTMETRIC structure, the definition of the LOGFONT structure depends on whether you are using Unicode or the ASCII character set. When the UNICODE macro is defined, LOGFONT is defined as the LOGFONTW structure; otherwise, it is the same as the LOFONTA structure, which is declared in <wingdi.h>:

```
typedef struct tagLOGFONTA
{
    LONG       lfHeight;
    LONG       lfWidth;
    LONG       lfEscapement;
    LONG       lfOrientation;
    LONG       lfWeight;
    BYTE       lfItalic;
    BYTE       lfUnderline;
    BYTE       lfStrikeOut;
    BYTE       lfCharSet;
    BYTE       lfOutPrecision;
    BYTE       lfClipPrecision;
    BYTE       lfQuality;
    BYTE       lfPitchAndFamily;
    CHAR       lfFaceName[LF_FACESIZE];
} LOGFONTA;
```

Here is a brief description of each of the fields of the LOGFONT structure:

LONG lfHeight;	This is the height (in logical units) of the characters—what you want as the tmHeight field of the font's TEXTMETRIC structure. If you set this field to zero, Windows selects a font of default height.
LONG lfWidth;	This is the width of characters in logical units. If this field is zero, Windows selects the font based on the height.

`LONG lfEscapement;`	This is an angle measured in tenths of a degree in a counterclockwise direction from the horizontal. It specifies the direction along which `TextOut` is to draw a string of characters. Only certain devices can display text along any arbitrary direction. Most of the time, you can display text only along the horizontal or vertical axes. However, Windows can display TrueType fonts along any direction.
`LONG lfOrientation;`	This specifies the orientation of the characters with respect to the baseline. The value is an angle, in tenths of a degree, measured counterclockwise from the character's baseline.
`LONG lfWeight;`	This is the thickness of the lines used to draw the characters. The value can be anywhere between `0` and `1000`. Although there are a large number of defined symbols to specify many different weights, most fonts support only `FW_NORMAL` and `FW_BOLD` weights. You can set this field to `FW_DONTCARE` if you want Windows to choose a default weight.
`BYTE lfItalic;`	A nonzero value indicates that the font should be italic.
`BYTE lfUnderline;`	A nonzero value indicates that the font should be underlined.
`BYTE lfStrikeOut;`	A nonzero value indicates that the font should be struck out (a horizontal line drawn through the middle of each character).
`BYTE lfCharSet;`	This is the character set of the font. It can be one of `ANSI_CHARSET`, `UNICODE_CHARSET`, `SYMBOL_CHARSET`, `SHIFTJIS_CHARSET`, `HANGEUL_CHARSET`, `CHINESEBIG5_CHARSET`, or `OEM_CHARSET`.
`BYTE lfOutPrecision;`	This field specifies how Windows should attempt to pick an available font that matches the characteristics of the logical font. Here are a few of the possible values for this field (defined in wingdi.h):
`OUT_TT_PRECIS.`	In case of several matching fonts, this selects the matching TrueType font.

OUT_TT_ONLY_PRECIS.	This selects a TrueType font only.
OUT_DEVICE_PRECIS.	In case of several matching fonts, this selects a font belonging to a specific device (such as printer).
BYTE lfClipPrecision;	This specifies how Windows should deal with characters that lie at the edge of the clipping region of the DC. Use CLIP_DEFAULT_PRECIS for default clipping, which displays only those parts of the character that lie inside the clipping region.
BYTE lfQuality;	This field tells Windows what is more important when selecting a font matching the logical font. If you use the constants DEFAULT_QUALITY or DRAFT_QUALITY, Windows tries to synthesize any font it can. If you set this to PROOF_QUALITY, Windows selects a font closest in size but ensures that size does not exceed the request dimensions.
BYTE lfPitchAndFamily;	This field specifies both the pitch and the font family. Use a bitwise OR of two constant names, one specifying the pitch and the other specifying the font family. The pitch can be one of DEFAULT_PITCH, VARIABLE_PITCH, or FIXED_PITCH. The font family can be one of FF_DONTCARE, FF_ROMAN, FF_SWISS, FF_MODERN, FF_SCRIPT, or FF_DECORATIVE.
char lfFaceName[LF_FACESIZE];	This is the name of the typeface you want. Use names such as Helv, Courier, and Times New Roman. In Windows 3.1, the name can be up to 31 characters long (LF_FACESIZE is defined to be 32 but that includes room for the terminating null character).

After you create a CFont object, you have to select it into the device context before you can use it. This is where Windows selects, from the available set of fonts, one that best matches the parameters of the logical font. Here is how you would use a CFont identified by the name font:

```
// Assume that dc denotes the device context object.
   CFont *pOldFont = dc.SelectObject(&font);

// Now display the text string using the selected font.
   dc.TextOut(100, 100, "Test", strlen("Test"));

// Reset font in DC
   dc.SelectObject(pOldFont);
```

Once a font is selected into a DC, you can call the `GetTextFace` function to find out the name of the actual font being used. And you would call `GetTextMetrics` to find out the relevant size information of the selected font.

Listing All Available Fonts

If you are writing a "drawing program" that enables the user to draw graphics and text, you probably want to offer a way for the user to select a font for the text. You might want to do this through a dialog box wherein the fonts appear in a combo box. Recall that a combo box is a listbox next to a single-line edit window. (To see an example of this, select the Fonts... item from the Text menu in the PaintBrush application.) To construct that type of dialog box, you need the names of all the fonts available under Windows. You can get this information by calling the `EnumFontFamilies` function, which was introduced in Windows 3.1 to supersede the older `EnumFonts` function.

When calling the `EnumFontFamilies` function, you have to provide, as an argument, a pointer to one of your own functions. `EnumFontFamilies` calls this function for each available font; the callback function should include code to do whatever you want to do with the font information (usually add the information to a listbox). The callback function's prototype is the following:

```
int CALLBACK EnumFontFamProc(
    const ENUMLOGFONT FAR   *lpelf,    // Information about font
    const NEWTEXTMETRIC FAR *lpntm,    // Font dimensions
    int                     FontType,  // Font type
    LPARAM                  lParam);   // This is whatever you pass
                                       // as last argument to EnumFontFamilies
```

Given a callback function, here is the general syntax of the call to `EnumFontFamilies`:

```
// Assume that dc is the device context (CDC object)
    ::EnumFontFamilies(dc.m_hDC, // Handle to device context
                       "Arial",  // Font name or NULL
                       enumf_cb, // Callback function (you provide)
                       lparam);  // Last argument to enumf_cb
```

You can call `EnumFontFamilies` in two ways:

■ To get information on all fonts (of all styles and sizes) of a specific typeface, call `EnumFontFamilies`, with the second argument set to the name of the typeface.

■ To enumerate the names of the typefaces, call `EnumFontFamilies`, with the second argument set to `NULL`.

FontSee—An Example of Enumerating Fonts

This section presents the FontSee application. This application displays a dialog box that enables the user to pick a font and see some sample text displayed in that font. To display a list of fonts in the dialog box, you have to call the `EnumFontFamilies` function. This example takes the easy way out and uses a predefined dialog box offered by the MFC class `CFontDialog`.

Declaring the Classes for FontSee

The FontSee application has a simple structure. The CFontSeeApp class represents the application itself and is derived from the MFC class CWinApp. The CFontSeeWnd class, derived from CFrameWnd, represents the main window of the application. Listing 20.1 shows the file FONTSEE.H that declares these classes. Listing 20.2 shows the file FSRES.H with the resource identifiers used by the FontSee application.

The FontSee application relies on the CFontDialog class to display the dialog that enables the user to select a font. The CFontDialog constructor takes the following form:

```
CFontDialog(
    LPLOGFONT lplfInitial = NULL, // Pointer to LOGFONT structure
                                  // with initial font characteristics
    DWORD dwFlags = CF_EFFECTS ¦ CF_SCREENFONTS, // Flags that
                                  // control look and feel of dialog
    CDC* pdcPrinter = NULL,   // Identifies printer whose fonts
                                  // are listed (used if dwFlags has
                                  // the CF_PRINTERFONTS bit set).
    CWnd* pParentWnd = NULL);// Pointer to parent or owner window
```

The dwFlags argument of the CFontDialog constructor controls several features of the dialog displayed by the CFontDialog object. This field is a bitwise OR combination of one or more of the following constants (defined in the header file <commdlg.h>):

CF_APPLY	This enables the Apply button.
CF_ANSIONLY	This allows only the selection of fonts using the Windows character set. (If you specify this flag, the user cannot select a font that contains only symbols.)
CF_BOTH	This lists the available printer and screen fonts.
CF_TTONLY	This enumerates and allows the selection of TrueType fonts only.
CF_EFFECTS	This enables strikeout, underline, and color effects.
CF_FIXEDPITCHONLY	This lists only fixed-pitch fonts.
CF_FORCEFONTEXIST	This indicates an error condition if the user attempts to select a font or style that does not exist.
CF_INITTOLOGFONTSTRUCT	This uses the LOGFONT structure specified by the lplfInitial argument of the constructor to initialize the dialog box controls.
CF_LIMITSIZE	This limits font selections to only those with font sizes within the range specified by the SizeMin and SizeMax members.
CF_NOOEMFONTS	This is the same as CF_NOVECTORFONTS.
CF_NOFACESEL	This does not allow font selections.
CF_NOSTYLESEL	This does not allow style selections.

CF_NOSIZESEL	This does not allow size selections.
CF_NOSIMULATIONS	This does not allow graphics device interface (GDI) font simulations.
CF_NOVECTORFONTS	This does not allow the user to select vector fonts.
CF_PRINTERFONTS	This lists only the fonts supported by the printer associated with the device context (or information context) identified by the pdcPrinter argument of the CFontDialog constructor.
CF_SCALABLEONLY	This allows only the selection of scalable fonts, which include: vector fonts, scalable printer fonts, and TrueType fonts.
CF_SCREENFONTS	This lists only the screen fonts supported by the system.
CF_SHOWHELP	This causes the dialog box to show the Help button.
CF_USESTYLE	This specifies that the Style member points to a buffer that contains style data that should be used to initialize the Font Style selection. When the user closes the dialog box, the user-selected style data is returned in this buffer.
CF_WYSIWYG	This allows only the selection of fonts available on both the printer and the display. If this flag is set, the CF_BOTH and CF_SCALABLEONLY flags should also be set.

Of the arguments to the CFontDialog constructor, the first one specifying a LOGFONT structure is the most important because, after the dialog is displayed by calling the DoModal member function, the LOGFONT structure holds information about the font selected by the user through the font dialog.

Listing 20.1. FONTSEE.H. Declaration of the classes used in the FontSee program.

```
//------------------------------------------------------------
// File: fontsee.h
//
// Declares the classes used in the FontSee sample program
// that displays some sample text in a font selected by the user.
//------------------------------------------------------------
#if !defined(__FONTSEE_H)
#define __FONTSEE_H

#include <afx.h>
#include <afxwin.h>
#include <afxdlgs.h>

#include <string.h>


#include "fsres.h"    // Defines resource IDs
```

continues

Listing 20.1. continued

```
// Declare the main window class

class CFontSeeWnd : public CFrameWnd
{
public:
    CFontSeeWnd();

// Declare functions for handling messages from Windows
    afx_msg void OnPaint();
    afx_msg void Quit();
    afx_msg void About();
    afx_msg void CMSelFont();

private:
    LOGFONT    m_LogFont;
    COLORREF   m_FontColor;

    DECLARE_MESSAGE_MAP()
};

// Declare the application class

class CFontSeeApp : public CWinApp
{
public:

    BOOL InitInstance();
};

#endif
```

Listing 20.2. FSRES.H. Resource identifiers for the FontSee program.

```
//----------------------------------------------------------------
// File: fsres.h
//
// Resource IDs for FontSee

#if !defined(__FSRES_H)
#define __FSRES_H

// Resource identifiers

#define IDM_EXIT      101
#define IDM_ABOUT     301
#define IDM_SELFONT   201

#endif
```

Implementing the Classes in FontSee

Listing 20.3 shows the file FONTSEE.CPP that implements the member functions of CFontSeeApp and CFontSeeWnd. These functions constitute the FontSee application.

You might want to study two member functions in detail:

- CMSelFont is called when the user wants to select a new font (the user indicates this through the Font menu). Notice how this function displays the font selection dialog by calling the ChooseFont function.

- OnPaint handles WM_PAINT messages that Windows sends when the main window has to be redrawn. In OnPaint, you can see how to create fonts of various sizes and use these fonts to display sample text.

Listing 20.3. FONTSEE.CPP. Implementing the FontSee application.

```
//----------------------------------------------------------------
// File: fontsee.cpp
//
// Implements the classes used in the FontSee sample program
// that displays some sample text in a font selected by the user.
//----------------------------------------------------------------
#include "fontsee.h"

//----------------------------------------------------------------
// Define the "message map"

    BEGIN_MESSAGE_MAP(CFontSeeWnd, CFrameWnd)
        ON_WM_PAINT()
        ON_COMMAND(IDM_EXIT,    Quit)
        ON_COMMAND(IDM_ABOUT,   About)
        ON_COMMAND(IDM_SELFONT, CMSelFont)
    END_MESSAGE_MAP()

//----------------------------------------------------------------
// CFontSeeApp:: I n i t I n s t a n c e
// Initialize the main window of the FontSee application

BOOL CFontSeeApp::InitInstance()
{
    Enable3dControls();

    m_pMainWnd = new CFontSeeWnd;

    m_pMainWnd->ShowWindow(m_nCmdShow);
    m_pMainWnd->UpdateWindow();

    return TRUE;
}
//----------------------------------------------------------------
```

continues

Listing 20.3. continued

```
// CFontSeeWnd:: F o n t S e e W i n d o w
// Constructor for the CFontSeeWnd

CFontSeeWnd::CFontSeeWnd() : m_FontColor(RGB(0,0,0))
{
    VERIFY(LoadAccelTable("MainAccelTable"));
    VERIFY(Create(NULL, "FontSee", WS_OVERLAPPEDWINDOW,
            rectDefault, NULL, "MainMenu"));

// Initialize the LOGFONT structure m_LogFont
// First zero out the entire structure
    memset(&m_LogFont, 0, sizeof(LOGFONT));

// Now set the needed fields
    m_LogFont.lfHeight = 12;
    m_LogFont.lfWeight = FW_NORMAL;
    m_LogFont.lfCharSet = ANSI_CHARSET;
    m_LogFont.lfOutPrecision = OUT_DEFAULT_PRECIS;
    m_LogFont.lfClipPrecision = CLIP_DEFAULT_PRECIS;
    m_LogFont.lfQuality = PROOF_QUALITY;
    m_LogFont.lfPitchAndFamily = VARIABLE_PITCH;
    strcpy(m_LogFont.lfFaceName, "Helvetica");
    m_FontColor = GetSysColor(COLOR_WINDOWTEXT);
}
//-------------------------------------------------------------
// CFontSeeWnd:: C M S e l F o n t
// Display the Font Selection dialog and get
// the user's choice of font.

void CFontSeeWnd::CMSelFont()
{
// Activate "choose font" dialog...
    CFontDialog fd(&m_LogFont,
                    CF_INITTOLOGFONTSTRUCT | CF_BOTH |
                    CF_EFFECTS);
    fd.m_cf.rgbColors = m_FontColor;

    if(fd.DoModal() == IDOK)
    {
// Yes, user has chosen a font.
// Make sure window gets redrawn with new font.
        m_FontColor = fd.m_cf.rgbColors;
        Invalidate(TRUE);
    }
}
//-------------------------------------------------------------
// CFontSeeWnd:: O n P a i n t
// Draw the window's content

void CFontSeeWnd::OnPaint()
{
    short   len, x, y, points;
    char    str[256];
    CSize   txtsz;
    int     old_mapmode;
    LOGFONT tmpfont;
```

```
    x = 10;
    y = 0;

    CPaintDC dc(this);

    tmpfont = m_LogFont;
    dc.SetTextColor(m_FontColor);
    dc.SetBkColor(GetSysColor(COLOR_WINDOW));

// Set graphics mapping mode to MM_TWIPS. In this mode,
// 1 unit = 1/1440 inch, or 1/20 of a typesetter's point,
// which is approximately equal to 1/72 inch.

    old_mapmode = dc.SetMapMode(MM_TWIPS);

// Display a sample string for point sizes 8, 10, ..., 32
    points = 8;
    while (points <= 32)
    {

// Compute height in twips (20 twips = 1 point)
// Note negative value means height is based on actual
// character height
        tmpfont.lfHeight = -points * 20;
        CFont font;
        font.CreateFontIndirect(&tmpfont);
        CFont *pOldFont = dc.SelectObject(&font);

// Prepare the string to be displayed
        wsprintf(str, "ABCabc 123 - %s %d pt",
                 m_LogFont.lfFaceName, points);
        len = strlen(str);
        txtsz = dc.GetTextExtent(str, len);
        y = y + txtsz.cy + 5;
        dc.TextOut(x, -y, str, len);

// Restore previous font
        dc.SelectObject(pOldFont);
        points += 2;
    }
// Restore previous mapping mode
    dc.SetMapMode(old_mapmode);
}
//-----------------------------------------------------------
//  CFontSeeWnd:: A b o u t
//  Display the "About..." box

void CFontSeeWnd::About()
{
    CDialog About("ABOUTFONTSEE", this);
    About.DoModal();
}
//-----------------------------------------------------------
// CFontSeeWnd:: Q u i t
// Quit application

void CFontSeeWnd::Quit()
{
```

continues

Listing 20.3. continued

```
    OnClose();
}
//------------------------------------------------------------
// Create an instance of the application.

    CFontSeeApp App;
```

FIGURE 20.3.

The font selection dialog box.

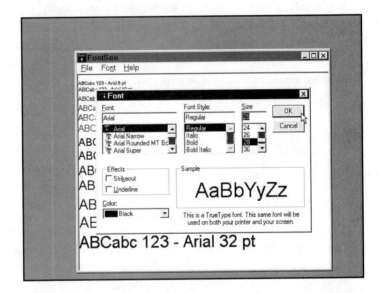

FIGURE 20.4.

Sample text in Arial font at various point sizes.

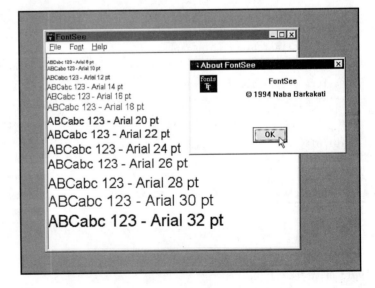

Running FontSee

All the files needed to build the FontSee program are in the disk bound into this book. To run the program, start Visual C++ 2.0 under Windows and load the project file FONTSEE.MAK from the CH20 directory.

Press Shift+F8 to compile and run the FontSee program. You can pick a new font through the Select Font... menu item in the Font menu. Figure 20.3 shows the font dialog box that appears when you try to a pick a new font. Figure 20.4 shows some sample text displayed in the Arial font at several point sizes.

Summary

The Windows Graphics Device Interface (GDI) includes a number of functions for text output. In the Microsoft Foundation Class (MFC) Library, these functions are available as member functions of the CDC class that represents a device context. With these text output functions, you can set the location of text output, the justification of the text, and the font used to display the text. It is simple to display text with the default system font, but you probably want a variety of fonts in any application that uses imaging and animation. The font is like any other Windows object, such as pen or brush. To use a font, you have to create it and select it into the device context before displaying any text in that font. Use the MFC class CFont to create and use a font.

Prior to version 3.1, Windows offered a limited selection of fonts, but the number of available fonts has increased dramatically with the introduction of TrueType fonts in Windows 3.1. TrueType is a sophisticated way of representing fonts, where each character's outline is expressed in terms of lines and curves. When you use a TrueType font for text output, bitmaps for the characters are prepared on the fly. Fortunately for us, all pre-Windows 3.1 font manipulation and text output functions work with TrueType fonts. However, Windows now offers many new functions to deal with TrueType fonts.

This chapter provides an overview of the text display functions and describes how to use fonts in Windows. The sample program, FontSee, enables the user to select a font and see sample output in that font at various point sizes. The FontSee program uses the font selection dialog provided by the MFC class CFontDialog.

21

Displaying Bitmaps
in Windows

Many Windows applications, especially multimedia applications, need images, because images are used as the central elements of a multimedia graphics application. To use an image in an application, you need the image in an electronic form. You can prepare the images in a paint or drawing program. For conventional hard copy drawings, you have to use a scanner to convert the images into electronic form. Whether drawn with a paint program or scanned from a hard copy, the image is stored in a disk file with its file contents interpreted before you use it in your application. This chapter presents a number of C++ classes that can read image files (in a number of popular formats such as BMP, PCX, and TIFF) and display the images in Windows. These image classes are used in a Windows application, ImageView, that enables you to open image files and view them.

Animation is another important aspect of some Windows applications—especially multimedia applications. Animation is the process of bringing an image to life. We usually associate animation with movement of images and the good examples pioneered by The Walt Disney Company. The last half of this chapter includes several C++ classes to model and animate small images known as *sprites*. These sprite animation classes rely on the Image classes developed earlier in this chapter. This chapter ends with a Windows program that animates a number of sprites on a background image.

Understanding Image File Formats

An image is a two-dimensional array of pixels, often called a raster. Each horizontal line is called a *scan line* or *raster line*. In the computer, the color of each pixel is represented in one of the following ways:

- If the image is monochrome, the color of each pixel is expressed as a 1-bit value—a 1 or a 0.

- For a true color image, each pixel's color is expressed in terms of red (R), green (G), and blue (B) intensities that make up the color. Typically, each component of the color is represented by a byte—thus providing 256 levels for each color component. This approach requires 3 bytes for each pixel and allows up to 256 x 256 x 256 = 16,777,216 or 16 million distinct combinations of RGB values (colors).

- For a palette-based image, each pixel's value is interpreted as an index into a table of RGB values known as a color palette or colormap. For each pixel, you are supposed to display the RGB value corresponding to that pixel's contents. The number of bits needed to store each pixel's value depends on the number of colors in the color palette. The common sizes of color palettes are 16 (needs 4 bits per pixel) and 256 (needs 8 bits per pixel).

Figure 21.1 shows some of the components of an image. The width and height of the image are expressed in terms of number of pixels along the horizontal and vertical directions, respectively.

FIGURE 21.1.
Elements of an image.

Width

Height

Pixel array

Common Characteristics of Image Files

When storing an image in a file, you have to make sure that you can interpret and display the image later. To ensure that you can read, interpret, and display a stored image, the image file must, at a minimum, contain the following information:

- Dimensions of the image—the width and the height
- Number of bits per pixel
- Type of image—whether pixel values should be interpreted as RGB colors or indexes to a color palette
- Color palette (also known as colormap), if the image uses one
- Image data, which is the array of pixel values

Almost all image files contain this set of information, but each specific file format organizes the information in a different way. Figure 21.2 shows the layout of a typical image file. The file starts with a short header—anywhere from a few to 128 or so bytes. The header contains any information besides the image data and the color palette. Next comes a color palette if the pixel values in the image require a palette. The *image data*—the array of pixel values—appear after the palette. Usually, the pixel array is stored line by line.

The array of pixels constitutes the bulk of the image file. For example, a 256-color 640x480 image requires 640x480 = 307,200 bytes of storage because each pixel's value occupies 1 byte. Of course, the storage requirements of the image data can be reduced by compressing the data either by run-length encoding or some other compression scheme.

Note that even though most image files have a layout similar to the one shown in Figure 21.2, there still is room for many possible variations:

- The order of information in the header can vary from one file format to another.

■ Some display-dependent image file formats skip the color palette entirely and store only the pixel array.

■ The pixel array might be stored from top to bottom or bottom to top.

■ If the pixel values are RGB components, the order of red, green, and blue may vary.

■ The pixel values may be stored in packed format or as bit planes. In the packed format, all bits belonging to a pixel are stored contiguously. When the image is stored according to bit planes, the bits for each pixel are split according to the bit position—the least significant bits of all pixels are stored line by line, then come the bits for the next bit position, and so on.

■ The pixel values may be stored in a compressed format.

FIGURE 21.2.

Typical image file format.

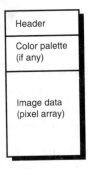

Some Common Image File Formats

As you can see, there are several ways to store an image in a file, which is why you find so many different types of image file formats. Here are some of the popular image file formats:

■ PCX format, originally used by ZSoft's PC PaintBrush, is a popular image file format that many drawing programs and scanners support. PCX files use a run-length encoding (RLE) scheme to store the image in a compressed form.

■ Windows BMP format stores an image as a device-independent bitmap, or DIB, a format introduced in Microsoft Windows 3.0. The DIB format includes a color palette and stores the image data in a standard manner to make the image file device-independent. The Windows BMP format can store images with 1 (monochrome), 4 (16-color), 8 (256-color), or 24 (16-million-color) bits per pixel. The BMP format is not as efficient as PCX and other formats, but it is relatively easy to interpret a BMP file.

■ The 24-bit Truevision Targa file format originated with Truevision's high-performance display adapters for PCs. There are several different types of Targa files; the most popular one is the 24-bit/pixel version that uses 8 bits for each of the R, G, and B components. This format can store image files with up to 16 million colors. However, the file size for a 24-bit image is very large—a 640x480 24-bit image requires 3x640x480 = 921,600 bytes or almost 1M.

■ TIFF or Tagged Image File Format was developed jointly by Microsoft Corporation and Aldus Corporation as a flexible, system-independent file format to store monochrome through 24-bit color images. Most desktop publishing and word processing software can read and use TIFF images. Additionally, all scanners provide control software that can save images in TIFF.

■ GIF (Graphics Interchange Format, pronounced "jif") was developed by CompuServe for compact storage of images with up to 256 colors. GIF files store images using the LZW (named after the scheme's authors, Lempel-Ziv and Welsh) compression scheme.

The next part of this chapter describes these five image file formats and shows sample code to interpret and display the images. The description of the image file formats is presented in the context of a C++ class hierarchy designed to represent different types of images.

C++ Classes for Handling Image Files

Because all images have a common set of information, the starting point of the C++ class hierarchy is an abstract base class named `Image`. The `Image` class stores the image in a standard internal format and provides pure virtual functions `write` and `read` to transfer an image to and from disk files, respectively. Note that a pure virtual function refers to a virtual function that is set equal to zero:

```
// Functions to load and save images
    virtual int read(const char* filename) = 0;
    virtual int write(const char* filename) = 0;
```

The C++ compiler does not enable you to create instances of a class with pure virtual functions. Thus, to actually use the `Image` class, you have to derive a class from `Image` and define the `read` and `write` functions in that class first. In this design, each class responsible for handling a specific image type is derived from `Image`. For example, a PC Paintbrush image file (which usually has a .PCX file extension) will be handled by the `PCXImage` class, which would include concrete implementations of the `read` and `write` member functions to load and save a PCX image. Similarly, classes such as `TIFImage` and `BMPImage` can handle TIFF and Windows BMP images, respectively. Figure 21.3 shows the `Image` class hierarchy for the classes needed to handle PCX, Windows BMP, and TIFF images.

FIGURE 21.3.
Image class hierarchy to handle PCX, BMP, and TIFF images.

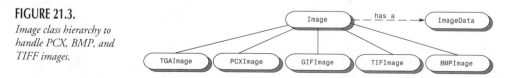

Additionally, in this design, the `Image` class is dependent on Microsoft Windows. This is accomplished by selecting the Windows device-independent bitmap (DIB) format for the internal representation of an image in the `Image` class. This design decision makes it easy to display the image, because the Image class itself can include a member function that accepts a device context as an argument, converts the internal DIB into a device-dependent bitmap (DDB), and displays the bitmap by calling Windows API functions. Details are explained in subsequent sections.

Another important design decision is to use an ImageData class to encapsulate the image's pixel array and then use a pointer to an ImageData object in each Image class (see Figure 21.3). This decision is based on the following: The DIB format, used for internal representation of images, requires a considerable amount of memory for any reasonably sized color image. When equating one image to another, you do not want to make a complete copy of the image's pixel array; rather, you want to copy a pointer to the pixel array and keep count of how many Image class instances are sharing a specific pixel array. When an Image is destroyed, the destructor decrements the pixel array's count and destroys the array only when the count is zero, which indicates that the pixel array is not referenced by any Image object. This scheme is known as *reference counting*.

The *ImageData* Class

The ImageData class represents all data necessary to represent an image—the pixel array as well as other pertinent information about the image. Because this example uses a Windows DIB format to represent the image, the definition of the ImageData class is simple (see Listing 21.1). The most important data in ImageData is the pointer (declared with the type LPVOID) p_dib. This is a pointer to a Windows device-independent bitmap—a block of memory that has the layout shown in Figure 21.4. The BITMAPINFOHEADER, a structure at the beginning of the DIB, contains all relevant information, such as image dimensions and number of bits per pixel, that you need to interpret the image's pixel array. You will see more about the fields of the BITMAPINFOHEADER in the PCXImage class. In this class, the read member function initializes the fields after reading an image in the PCX format and converting it to the internal DIB format.

FIGURE 21.4.
Layout of a DIB in memory.

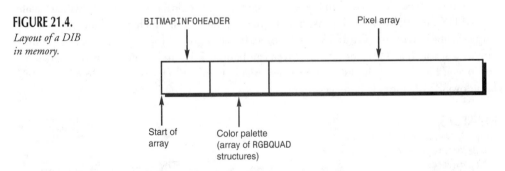

Listing 21.1. IMAGE.H. Header file for the ImageData and Image classes.

```
//-----------------------------------------------------------
// File: image.h
//
```

```
//   Defines the Image class.
//
//------------------------------------------------------------------
#if !defined(__IMAGE_H)
#define __IMAGE_H

#include <fstream.h>
#include <windowsx.h>

class CDC;
class Image;
class BMPImage;
class PCXImage;
class TIFImage;

// This class represents the data for an image
class ImageData
{
friend Image;
friend BMPImage;
friend PCXImage;
friend TIFImage;

protected:
    ImageData() : p_dib(0), count(1), hpal(0), hbm_ddb(0),
                  bytes_per_line(0), w(0), h(0) {}

    ~ImageData();

// This points to a BITMAPINFOHEADER followed by the
// image data.
    LPVOID          p_dib;    // Device-independent bitmap
    HPALETTE        hpal;     // Color palette
    HBITMAP         hbm_ddb;  // Device-dependent bitmap

    unsigned short w, h;      // Width and height
    unsigned short bytes_per_line;

    unsigned short count;
};

// Abstract base class for all images
class Image
{
public:
// Constructors
    Image()
    {
        imdata = new ImageData;
    }
    Image(HBITMAP hbm, unsigned short w, unsigned short h)
    {
        imdata = new ImageData;
        imdata->hbm_ddb = hbm;
        imdata->w = w;
        imdata->h = h;
    }
```

Listing 21.1. continued

```cpp
    Image(HDC hdc, Image *img, short x, short y,
        unsigned short w, unsigned short h);

// Copy Constructor
    Image(const Image& img);

    virtual ~Image()
    {
        if(--imdata->count <= 0) delete imdata;
    }

// Operators
    Image& operator=(const Image& img);

// Copy the imdata pointer from another image
    void image_data(const Image* img);

// Functions to load and save images
    virtual int read(const char* filename){ return 0;}
    virtual int write(const char* filename){ return 0;}
    virtual int read(ifstream& ifs){ return 0;}
    int write_dib(ofstream& ofs);

// Returns pointer to the Windows Device-Independent
// Bitmap (DIB).
    LPVOID get_dib() { return imdata->p_dib;}

// Function to return the handle to the device-dependent
// bitmap
    HBITMAP get_ddb() { return imdata->hbm_ddb;}

    unsigned short width()
    {
        if(imdata->p_dib != 0)
            return((LPBITMAPINFOHEADER)imdata->p_dib)->biWidth;
        return imdata->w;
    }
    unsigned short height()
    {
        if(imdata->p_dib != 0)
            return ((LPBITMAPINFOHEADER)imdata->p_dib)->biHeight;
        return imdata->h;
    }

    int image_loaded()
    {
        if(imdata->p_dib == 0) return 0;
        else return 1;
    }

    void detach()
    {
        if(--imdata->count == 0) delete imdata;
        imdata = new ImageData;
    }
```

```
// Functions to make palette and convert to DDB
    void make_palette();
    void DIBtoDDB(HDC hdc);
    void DDBtoDIB();

// Function that displays the DIB on a Windows device
// specified by a device context

    void show(HDC hdc, short xfrom = 0, short yfrom = 0,
                       short xto = 0,   short yto = 0,
                       short width = 0, short height = 0,
                       DWORD ropcode = SRCCOPY);

    void show(CDC *pDC, short xfrom = 0, short yfrom = 0,
                       short xto = 0,   short yto = 0,
                       short width = 0, short height = 0,
                       DWORD ropcode = SRCCOPY);

    unsigned int numcolors();
    HPALETTE palette() { return imdata->hpal;}

protected:
    ImageData* imdata;
};

#endif
```

The ImageData class also includes two important member variables:

■ HPALETTE hpal; is a handle to a Windows color palette—an array of PALETTEENTRY structures (defined in <wingdi.h>) that associate an index with an RGB color. The make_palette member function of the Image class creates the palette.

■ HBITMAP hbm_ddb; is the handle to the device-dependent bitmap (DDB) corresponding to the DIB. The DIBtoDDB member function of the Image class creates the DDB (for a specified device) from the DIB.

Encapsulating the image's data in the ImageData class enables sharing of the data between images, but you do not want to give up the capability of accessing and manipulating the image's pixel array directly from other image classes. One way to provide this access is to declare as friend all classes that have to manipulate the private and protected member variables of ImageData. In this case, Image and its derived classes, such as PCXImage, BMPImage, and TIFImage, are declared with the friend keyword in the ImageData class.

CHECK THE COMPANION DISK FOR COMPLETE SOURCE FILES

Because of limited space, all source files are not shown in printed form in this book. However, the companion disk includes the source files for all programs. After installing the code from the companion disk, you will find the source files for this chapter's programs in the CH21 subdirectory. The text mentions these files by name.

The *Image* Class

The Image class, declared in the file IMAGE.H (Listing 21.1), is an abstract base class that encapsulates the common features of all images. Because all images are internally maintained in the Windows DIB format, the Image class can take care of displaying the image rather than delegating that responsibility to the derived classes. The show member function of Image displays the image on a device specified by a device context. The Windows API provides a function, SetDIBitsToDevice, that enables you to display a DIB on a device directly, but this function is comparatively slow. A faster approach is to convert the DIB into a device-dependent bitmap (DDB) and use the BitBlt function to display the DDB. The drawback is that creating the DDB requires memory. Consult the listing of the show function (Listing 21.2) for complete details of how to display a DIB. The following are the general steps needed to convert the DIB to a DDB and display the DDB:

1. Set up a color palette if the image needs one. DIBs with 1, 4, or 8 bits per pixel use color palettes. The make_palette function in Listing 21.2 illustrates how to create a palette. Before converting a DIB to a DDB, you have to realize the color palette.

2. Call the CreateDIBitmap function to get back a handle to a DDB created from the DIB for a specified device. The DIBtoDDB function performs this task by calling CreateDIBitmap:

```
// Note: imdata is a pointer to an ImageData object
//       hbm_ddb is a handle to a bitmap (HBITMAP)
imdata->hbm_ddb = CreateDIBitmap(
                hdc,        // Device context handle
                p_bminfo,   // Pointer to BITMAPINFOHEADER
                CBM_INIT,   // Initialize DDB from DIB
                p_image,    // Pointer to image data
                (LPBITMAPINFO)p_bminfo, // Pointer to a
                            // BITMAPINFO structure
                DIB_RGB_COLORS); // Interpret palette
                            // entries as RGB colors
```

As indicated by the comments, the DIB is specified by three pointers: a pointer to the BITMAPINFOHEADER, a pointer to the image's pixel array, and a pointer to a BITMAPINFO structure with the color palette. In this case, the BITMAPINFO and BITMAPINFOHEADER structures overlap and the image data follows the BITMAPINFOHEADER.

3. Call CreateCompatibleDC to get back a handle to a memory device context (DC) compatible with a specified DC.

4. If the compatible DC is created successfully (the handle is nonzero), select the DDB into the DC by calling the Windows API function named SelectBitmap.

5. Call BitBlt to copy the bitmap from the memory DC to the actual device. Here is a sample call:

```
BitBlt(hdc, xto, yto, wdth, hght,
        memdc, xfrom, yfrom, ropcode);
```

This copies from the memdc device context to hdc. The wdth and hght represent the width and height of the bitmap being copied to the screen.

6. Clean up by deleting the memory DC. The DDB should be deleted also—this is done by the destructor of the ImageData class when the image is no longer needed.

Listing 21.2. IMAGE.CPP. Member functions of the Image class.

```cpp
//------------------------------------------------------------
//   File: image.cpp
//
//   Image manipulation functions
//------------------------------------------------------------
#include <afx.h>
#include <afxwin.h>
#include <fstream.h>
#include <string.h>
#include "image.h"

const size_t maxwrite = 30*1024; // Write 30K at a time
//------------------------------------------------------------
//   I m a g e D a t a : : ~ I m a g e D a t a
//   Destructor for an Image.

ImageData::~ImageData()
{
// If a DIB exists, delete it.
    if(p_dib != 0) GlobalFreePtr(p_dib);

// If a palette exists, free it also.
    if(hpal != 0) DeletePalette(hpal);

// If a DDB exists, destroy it.
    if(hbm_ddb != 0) DeleteBitmap(hbm_ddb);
}
//------------------------------------------------------------
//   I m a g e : : I m a g e
//   Copy constructor

Image::Image(const Image& img)
{
    img.imdata->count++;
    if(--imdata->count <= 0) delete imdata;
    imdata = img.imdata;
}
//------------------------------------------------------------
//   I m a g e : : i m a g e _ d a t a
//   Copy the ImageData pointer from another image

void Image::image_data(const Image* img)
{
    img->imdata->count++;
    if(--imdata->count <= 0) delete imdata;
```

continues

Listing 21.2. continued

```
    imdata = img->imdata;
}
//------------------------------------------------------------
// I m a g e : : o p e r a t o r =
// Assignment operator

Image& Image::operator=(const Image& img)
{
    img.imdata->count++;
    if(--imdata->count <= 0) delete imdata;
    imdata = img.imdata;
    return *this;
}
//------------------------------------------------------------
// I m a g e : : n u m c o l o r s
// Returns the number of colors used. Returns 0 if image uses
// 24-bit pixels.

unsigned int Image::numcolors()
{
    if(imdata->p_dib == 0) return 0;
    LPBITMAPINFOHEADER p_bminfo =
                (LPBITMAPINFOHEADER)(imdata->p_dib);

// If the biClrUsed field is nonzero, use that as the number of
// colors
    if(p_bminfo->biClrUsed != 0)
        return (unsigned int)p_bminfo->biClrUsed;

// Otherwise, the number of colors depends on the bits per pixel
    switch(p_bminfo->biBitCount)
    {
        case 1: return 2;
        case 4: return 16;
        case 8: return 256;
        default: return 0; // Must be 24-bit/pixel image
    }
}
//------------------------------------------------------------
// I m a g e : : m a k e _ p a l e t t e
// Create a color palette using information in the DIB

void Image::make_palette()
{
// Set up a pointer to the DIB
    LPBITMAPINFOHEADER p_bminfo =
                            (LPBITMAPINFOHEADER)(imdata->p_dib);
    if(p_bminfo == 0) return;

// Free any existing palette
    if(imdata->hpal != 0) DeletePalette(imdata->hpal);

// Set up the palette, if needed
    if(numcolors() > 0)
    {
        LPLOGPALETTE p_pal = (LPLOGPALETTE) GlobalAllocPtr(GHND,
```

```
                              sizeof(LOGPALETTE) +
                    numcolors() * sizeof(PALETTEENTRY));

        if(p_pal != NULL)
        {
            p_pal->palVersion = 0x0300;
            p_pal->palNumEntries = numcolors();

// Set up palette entries from DIB
            LPBITMAPINFO p_bi = (LPBITMAPINFO)p_bminfo;
            unsigned int i;
            for(i = 0; i < numcolors(); i++)
            {
                p_pal->palPalEntry[i].peRed =
                        p_bi->bmiColors[i].rgbRed;
                p_pal->palPalEntry[i].peGreen =
                        p_bi->bmiColors[i].rgbGreen;
                p_pal->palPalEntry[i].peBlue =
                        p_bi->bmiColors[i].rgbBlue;
                p_pal->palPalEntry[i].peFlags = 0;
            }
            imdata->hpal = CreatePalette(p_pal);
            GlobalFreePtr(p_pal);
        }
    }
}
//-----------------------------------------------------------
// I m a g e : : D I B t o D D B
// Create a device dependent bitmap from the DIB

void Image::DIBtoDDB(HDC hdc)
{
// Set up a pointer to the DIB
    LPBITMAPINFOHEADER p_bminfo =
                      (LPBITMAPINFOHEADER)(imdata->p_dib);
    if(p_bminfo == 0) return;

// If a DDB exists, destroy it first.
    if(imdata->hbm_ddb != 0) DeleteBitmap(imdata->hbm_ddb);

// Build the device-dependent bitmap.

// Set up pointer to the image data (skip over BITMAPINFOHEADER
// and palette).
    LPSTR p_image = (LPSTR)p_bminfo +
                    sizeof(BITMAPINFOHEADER) +
                    numcolors() * sizeof(RGBQUAD);

// Realize palette, if there is one. Note that this does not do
// anything on the standard 16-color VGA driver because that
// driver does not allow changing the palette, but the new palette
// should work on Super VGA displays.

    HPALETTE hpalold = NULL;
    if(imdata->hpal)
    {
        hpalold = SelectPalette(hdc, imdata->hpal, FALSE);
        RealizePalette(hdc);
```

continues

Listing 21.2. continued

```
    }

// Convert the DIB into a DDB (device-dependent bitmap) and
// block transfer (blt) it to the device context.

    imdata->hbm_ddb = CreateDIBitmap(hdc,
                                 p_bminfo,
                                 CBM_INIT,
                                 p_image,
                                 (LPBITMAPINFO)p_bminfo,
                                 DIB_RGB_COLORS);

// Don't need the palette once the bitmap is converted to DDB
// format.
    if(hpalold)
        SelectPalette(hdc, hpalold, FALSE);
}
//-----------------------------------------------------------------
// I m a g e : : D D B t o D I B
// Create a device-independent bitmap from the DDB
// specified by imdata->hbm_ddb

void Image::DDBtoDIB()
{
// Do nothing if the DDB does not exist or if the DIB exists
    if(imdata->hbm_ddb == 0) return;
    if(imdata->p_dib != NULL) return;

    BITMAP bm;
    GetObject(imdata->hbm_ddb, sizeof(bm), (LPSTR)&bm);

// Set up a BITMAPINFOHEADER for the DIB
    BITMAPINFOHEADER bh;
    bh.biSize         = sizeof(BITMAPINFOHEADER);
    bh.biWidth        = bm.bmWidth;
    bh.biHeight       = bm.bmHeight;
    bh.biPlanes       = 1;
    bh.biBitCount     = (WORD)(bm.bmPlanes * bm.bmBitsPixel);
    bh.biCompression  = BI_RGB;

    imdata->w = bm.bmWidth;
    imdata->h = bm.bmHeight;

// Compute bytes per line, rounding up to align at a 4-byte
// boundary
    imdata->bytes_per_line = ((long)bh.biWidth *
                        (long)bh.biBitCount + 31L) / 32 * 4;

    bh.biSizeImage    = (long)bh.biHeight *
                        (long)imdata->bytes_per_line;

    bh.biXPelsPerMeter = 0;
    bh.biYPelsPerMeter = 0;

// Determine number of colors in the palette
    short ncolors = 0;
```

```
    switch(bh.biBitCount)
    {
        case 1:
            ncolors = 2;
            break;
        case 4:
            ncolors = 16;
            break;
        case 8:
            ncolors = 256;
            break;
        default:
            ncolors = 0;
    }

    bh.biClrUsed        = ncolors;
    bh.biClrImportant   = 0;

// Compute total size of DIB
    unsigned long dibsize = sizeof(BITMAPINFOHEADER) +
                            ncolors * sizeof(RGBQUAD) +
                            bh.biSizeImage;

// Allocate memory for the DIB
    imdata->p_dib = GlobalAllocPtr(GHND, dibsize);
    if(imdata->p_dib == NULL) return;

// Set up palette
    HDC hdc = GetDC(NULL);

// Copy BITMAPINFO structure bh into beginning of DIB.
    _fmemcpy(imdata->p_dib, &bh, (size_t)bh.biSize);

    LPSTR p_image = (LPSTR)imdata->p_dib +
                    (WORD)bh.biSize +
                    ncolors * sizeof(RGBQUAD);

// Call GetDIBits to get the image and fill the palette indices
// into a BITMAPINFO structure
    GetDIBits(hdc, imdata->hbm_ddb, 0, (WORD)bh.biHeight,
            p_image,(LPBITMAPINFO)imdata->p_dib,
            DIB_RGB_COLORS);

// All done. Clean-up and return.
    ReleaseDC(NULL, hdc);
}
//--------------------------------------------------------------
// I m a g e : : s h o w (H D C, ... )
// Display a DIB on a Windows device specified by a
// device context

void Image::show(HDC hdc, short xfrom, short yfrom,
                          short xto,    short yto,
                          short wdth,   short hght,
                          DWORD ropcode)
{

// Set up a pointer to the DIB
```

continues

Listing 21.2. continued

```
        LPBITMAPINFOHEADER p_bminfo =
                            (LPBITMAPINFOHEADER)(imdata->p_dib);
        if(p_bminfo != NULL)
        {
// Set up the palette, if needed
            if(imdata->hpal == 0 && numcolors() > 0) make_palette();

// Convert to DDB, if necessary
            if(imdata->hbm_ddb == 0) DIBtoDDB(hdc);
        }

// "Blit" the DDB to hdc
        if(imdata->hbm_ddb != 0)
        {
            HDC memdc = CreateCompatibleDC(hdc);
            if(memdc != 0)
            {
                HBITMAP hbm_old = SelectBitmap(memdc,
                                            imdata->hbm_ddb);
// If width or height is zero, use corresponding dimension
// from the image.
                if(wdth == 0) wdth = width();
                if(hght == 0) hght = height();

                BitBlt(hdc, xto, yto, wdth, hght,
                        memdc, xfrom, yfrom, ropcode);
                SelectBitmap(memdc, hbm_old);
                DeleteDC(memdc);
            }
        }
}
//----------------------------------------------------------------
// I m a g e : : s h o w ( C D C *, ... )
// Display a DIB on a Windows device specified by a
// device context

void Image::show(CDC *pDC, short xfrom, short yfrom,
                          short xto,    short yto,
                          short wdth,   short hght,
                          DWORD ropcode)
{

// Set up a pointer to the DIB
        LPBITMAPINFOHEADER p_bminfo =
                            (LPBITMAPINFOHEADER)(imdata->p_dib);
        if(p_bminfo != NULL)
        {
// Set up the palette, if needed
            if(imdata->hpal == 0 && numcolors() > 0) make_palette();

// Convert to DDB, if necessary
            if(imdata->hbm_ddb == 0) DIBtoDDB(pDC->GetSafeHdc());
        }

// "Blit" the DDB to hdc
        if(imdata->hbm_ddb != 0)
```

```
    {
        CDC memdc;
        memdc.CreateCompatibleDC(pDC);

        if(memdc.GetSafeHdc() != 0)
        {
            CBitmap *pOldBitmap = memdc.SelectObject(
                        CBitmap::FromHandle(imdata->hbm_ddb));

// If width or height is zero, use corresponding dimension
// from the image.
            if(wdth == 0) wdth = width();
            if(hght == 0) hght = height();

            pDC->BitBlt(xto, yto, wdth, hght,
                        &memdc, xfrom, yfrom, ropcode);
            memdc.SelectObject(pOldBitmap);
        }
    }
}
//--------------------------------------------------------------
// Image::I m a g e
// Construct an image by copying a portion of the bitmap from
// another image

Image::Image(HDC hdc, Image *img, short x, short y,
            unsigned short w, unsigned short h)
{
    imdata = new ImageData;
    if(img == NULL) return;

    unsigned short iw = img->width();
    unsigned short ih = img->height();

    if(x < 0) x = 0;
    if(y < 0) y = 0;

// If width or height is 0, adjust them
    if(w == 0) w = iw;
    if(h == 0) h = ih;

// Make sure width and height are not too large
    if((w+x) > iw) w = iw - x;
    if((h+y) > ih) h = ih - y;

// Save width and height
    imdata->w = w;
    imdata->h = h;

// Create a new bitmap for the new image
    imdata->hbm_ddb = ::CreateCompatibleBitmap(hdc, w, h);

    if(imdata->hbm_ddb != 0)
    {
        HDC memdcn = ::CreateCompatibleDC(hdc);
        HDC memdco = ::CreateCompatibleDC(hdc);
        if(memdcn != 0 && memdco != 0)
        {
```

continues

Listing 21.2. continued

```
            HBITMAP ohbm = SelectBitmap(memdco, img->get_ddb());
            HBITMAP nhbm = SelectBitmap(memdcn, imdata->hbm_ddb);
            BitBlt(memdcn, 0, 0, w, h, memdco, x, y, SRCCOPY);
            SelectBitmap(memdco, ohbm);
            SelectBitmap(memdcn, nhbm);
            DeleteDC(memdco);
            DeleteDC(memdcn);
        }
    }
}
//--------------------------------------------------------------
// Image:: w r i t e _ d i b
// Write out the DIB starting at the current location in
// a stream (assumed to be opened with ios::out ¦ ios::binary)

int Image::write_dib(ofstream& ofs)
{
// If there is no image, return without doing anything
    if(imdata->p_dib == NULL) return 0;

// Check whether file is ok
    if(!ofs) return 0;

// Set up BMP file header
    BITMAPFILEHEADER bfhdr;

    bfhdr.bfType = ('M' << 8) ¦ 'B';
    bfhdr.bfReserved1 = 0;
    bfhdr.bfReserved2 = 0;
    bfhdr.bfOffBits = sizeof(BITMAPFILEHEADER) +
                      sizeof(BITMAPINFOHEADER) +
                      numcolors() * sizeof(RGBQUAD);
    bfhdr.bfSize = (long) height() *
                   (long) imdata->bytes_per_line +
                            bfhdr.bfOffBits;

// Write the file header to the file
    ofs.write((unsigned char*)&bfhdr, sizeof(BITMAPFILEHEADER));

// Save the file in big chunks.

// Allocate a large buffer to be used when transferring
// data to the file

    unsigned char *wbuf = new unsigned char[maxwrite];
    if(wbuf == NULL) return 0;

    unsigned char *data =
                (unsigned char*)imdata->p_dib;
    unsigned int chunksize;
    long bmpsize = bfhdr.bfSize - sizeof(BITMAPFILEHEADER);

    unsigned int i;
    while(bmpsize > 0)
    {
        if(bmpsize > maxwrite)
            chunksize = maxwrite;
```

```
        else
            chunksize = bmpsize;
// Copy image from DIB to buffer
        for(i = 0; i < chunksize; i++) wbuf[i] = data[i];
        ofs.write(wbuf, chunksize);
        bmpsize -= chunksize;
        data += chunksize;
    }
    delete wbuf;
    return 1;
}
```

The *BMPImage* Class

The BMPImage class handles Windows DIB images—these images are usually stored in files with the .BMP file extension and thus go by the name of BMP images. A BMP image file is the same as the in-memory representation of a DIB, shown in Figure 21.4, with a file header prefix added to the DIB. The header is represented by a BITMAPFILEHEADER structure defined in <wingdi.h>:

```
typedef struct tagBITMAPFILEHEADER
{
    WORD    bfType;         // File type. Should be 'BM'
    DWORD   bfSize;         // Size of file in bytes
    WORD    bfReserved1;    // 0
    WORD    bfReserved2;    // 0
    DWORD   bfOffBits;      // Offset to the start of image data
} BITMAPFILEHEADER;
```

A BITMAPINFOHEADER structure follows the file header. The color palette, if any, and the image's pixel array come after the BITMAPINFOHEADER.

Listing 21.3 shows the declaration of the BMPImage class. As you can see, the BMPImage class provides the read and write member functions and defines one additional member variable: BITMAPFILEHEADER bmphdr; is an instance of a BITMAPFILEHEADER structure that is used when reading or writing a BMP image file.

Listing 21.4 shows the file BMPIMAGE.CPP that implements the member functions read and write of the BMPImage class.

Listing 21.3. BMPIMAGE.H. Declaration of the BMPImage class.

```
//-------------------------------------------------------------
//  File: bmpimage.h
//
//  Defines the BMPImage class representing a Windows BMP image.
//
//-------------------------------------------------------------
#if !defined(__BMPIMAGE_H)
#define __BMPIMAGE_H

#include "image.h"
```

continues

Listing 21.3. continued

```
class BMPImage: public Image
{
public:
    BMPImage() {}

    ~BMPImage() {}

    virtual int read(const char* filename);
    virtual int write(const char* filename);
    virtual int read(ifstream& ifs);

private:
    BITMAPFILEHEADER bmphdr;
};

#endif
```

Reading a BMP Image

Listing 21.4 shows the file BMPIMAGE.CPP that implements the member functions read and write of the BMPImage class. Reading a BMP image into a BMPImage object is straightforward because the internal data format of the Image class hierarchy is the DIB and because a BMP image file is a file header followed by a DIB. As you can see from the read function, reading the BMP image file requires the following steps:

1. Read the file header into the bmphdr member of the BMPImage class. If ifs represents the input file stream, you can read the header as follows:

   ```
   // Read the file header
       ifs.read((unsigned char*)&bmphdr,
                   sizeof(BITMAPFILEHEADER));
   ```

2. Check that the bfType field of the header contains the characters BM, which indicates that this is a BMP image.

3. Determine the number of bytes remaining in the file—these are the bytes that make up the DIB stored in the BMP image file. You can position the file pointer at the end of the file and read the byte offset to determine the file size. Subtracting the size of the file header from the length of the file gives you the number of bytes in the DIB that you want to read:

   ```
   // Determine size of DIB to read
   // (that's file length - size of BITMAPFILEHEADER)
       ifs.seekg(0, ios::end);
       long bmpsize = ifs.tellg() - sizeof(BITMAPFILEHEADER);
   // Reset file pointer...
       ifs.seekg(sizeof(BITMAPFILEHEADER), ios::beg);
   ```

4. Allocate memory for the DIB by calling the `GlobalAlloc` function:

```
// Allocate space for the bitmap
    imdata->p_dib = GlobalAllocPtr(GHND, bmpsize);
```

5. Read the bytes from the file into this memory. For efficient file I/O, you should read from the file in large chunks. The `BMPImage::read` function reads the image in blocks that are up to 30K, as defined by the constant `maxread` declared at the beginning of the BMPIMAGE.CPP file (Listing 21.4).

Listing 21.4. BMPIMAGE.CPP. Member functions of the `BMPImage` class.

```
//------------------------------------------------------------------
//  File: bmpimage.cpp
//
//  Image manipulation functions for Windows BMP images.
//------------------------------------------------------------------
#include <fstream.h>
#include "bmpimage.h"

const size_t maxread  = 30*1024; // Read 30K at a time
const size_t maxwrite = 30*1024; // Write 30K at a time
//------------------------------------------------------------------
//  B M P I m a g e : : r e a d
//  Read and interpret a Windows .BMP image (Device-Independent
//  Bitmap).

int BMPImage::read(const char* filename)
{
// If there is an existing image, detach the image data
// before reading a new image
    if(imdata->p_dib != 0) detach();

// Open file for reading
    ifstream ifs(filename, ios::in | ios::binary);

// Call BMPImage::read(ifstream& ifs) to read in image
    return read(ifs);
}
//------------------------------------------------------------------
//  B M P I m a g e : : r e a d ( i f s t r e a m & )
//  Read image information from an open file

int BMPImage::read(ifstream& ifs)
{
    if(!ifs)
    {
// Error reading file. Return 0.
        return 0;
    }

// Read the file header
    ifs.read((unsigned char*)&bmphdr, sizeof(BITMAPFILEHEADER));

// Check whether image file format is acceptable (the type
// must be 'BM'
```

continues

Listing 21.4. continued

```
    if(bmphdr.bfType != (('M' << 8) ¦ 'B')) return 0;

// Determine size of DIB to read -- that's the file size (as
// specified by the bfSize field of the BITMAPFILEHEADER
// structure) minus the size of the BITMAPFILEHEADER
    long bmpsize = bmphdr.bfSize - sizeof(BITMAPFILEHEADER);

// Allocate space for the bitmap
    imdata->p_dib = GlobalAllocPtr(GHND, bmpsize);

// If memory allocation fails, return 0
    if(imdata->p_dib == 0) return 0;

// Load the file in big chunks. We don't have to interpret
// because our internal format is also BMP.

// Allocate a large buffer to read from file
    unsigned char *rbuf = new unsigned char[maxread];
    if(rbuf == NULL)
    {
        detach();
        return 0;
    }

    unsigned char *data =
                (unsigned char*)imdata->p_dib;
    unsigned int chunksize;
    unsigned int i;

    while(bmpsize > 0)
    {
        if(bmpsize > maxread)
            chunksize = maxread;
        else
            chunksize = bmpsize;
        ifs.read(rbuf, chunksize);

// Copy into DIB
        for(i = 0; i < chunksize; i++) data[i] = rbuf[i];
        bmpsize -= chunksize;
        data += chunksize;
    }
    delete rbuf;

// Compute bytes per line, rounding up to align at a 4-byte
// boundary
    LPBITMAPINFOHEADER p_bi = (LPBITMAPINFOHEADER)imdata->p_dib;
    imdata->bytes_per_line = ((long)p_bi->biWidth *
                        (long)p_bi->biBitCount + 31L) / 32 * 4;

// Ignore OS/2 1.x bitmap files. These files have a header
// size of 12 bytes whereas a Windows 3.1 DIB has a 40-byte
// header.
    if(p_bi->biSize == 12) return 0;

    return 1;
}
```

```
//-------------------------------------------------------------
// B M P I m a g e : : w r i t e
// Write a Windows .BMP image to a file (in Device-Independent
// Bitmap format)

int BMPImage::write(const char* filename)
{
// If there is no image, return without doing anything
    if(imdata->p_dib == 0) return 0;

// Open file for binary write operations.
    ofstream ofs(filename, ios::out | ios::binary);
    if(!ofs) return 0;

// Set up BMP file header
    bmphdr.bfType = ('M' << 8) | 'B';
    bmphdr.bfReserved1 = 0;
    bmphdr.bfReserved2 = 0;
    bmphdr.bfOffBits = sizeof(BITMAPFILEHEADER) +
                       sizeof(BITMAPINFOHEADER) +
                       numcolors() * sizeof(RGBQUAD);
    bmphdr.bfSize = (long) height() *
                    (long) imdata->bytes_per_line +
                                bmphdr.bfOffBits;

// Write the file header to the file
    ofs.write((unsigned char*)&bmphdr, sizeof(BITMAPFILEHEADER));

// Save the file in big chunks.

// Allocate a large buffer to be used when transferring
// data to the file

    unsigned char *wbuf = new unsigned char[maxwrite];
    if(wbuf == NULL) return 0;

    unsigned char *data =
                (unsigned char*)imdata->p_dib;
    unsigned int chunksize;
    long bmpsize = bmphdr.bfSize - sizeof(BITMAPFILEHEADER);

    unsigned int i;

    while(bmpsize > 0)
    {
        if(bmpsize > maxwrite)
            chunksize = maxwrite;
        else
            chunksize = bmpsize;
// Copy image from DIB to buffer
        for(i = 0; i < chunksize; i++) wbuf[i] = data[i];
        ofs.write(wbuf, chunksize);
        bmpsize -= chunksize;
        data += chunksize;
    }
    delete wbuf;
    return 1;
}
```

Writing a BMP Image

To save a DIB in a BMP format image file requires that you first prepare a header by initializing the fields of the bmphdr member variable, which is a BITMAPFILEHEADER structure. As shown in the write function in Listing 21.4, you can initialize the file header as follows:

```
// Set up BMP file header
    bmphdr.bfType = ('M' << 8) ¦ 'B';
    bmphdr.bfReserved1 = 0;
    bmphdr.bfReserved2 = 0;
    bmphdr.bfOffBits = sizeof(BITMAPFILEHEADER) +
                       sizeof(BITMAPINFOHEADER) +
                       numcolors() * sizeof(RGBQUAD);
    bmphdr.bfSize = (long) height() *
                    (long) imdata->bytes_per_line +
                              bmphdr.bfOffBits;
```

Once the file header is set up, save the header in the file:

```
// Write the file header to the file
    ofs.write((unsigned char*)&bmphdr, sizeof(BITMAPFILEHEADER));
```

Then you can write to the file the entire DIB from imdata->p_dib in large chunks.

The *PCXImage* Class

The PCX file format was developed by ZSoft to store images created by the PC PaintBrush paint program. The name PCX comes from the file extension .PCX that is used for PC PaintBrush files. Here is the PCX file format:

■ The file starts with a 128-byte header (described later). The header is followed by encoded scan lines of the image.

■ Each scan line in the PCX file is created by first laying out the scan lines of individual bit planes one after another. Then the entire line is encoded using a run-length encoding scheme that works like this: if the 2 highest-order bits of a byte are set, the low-order 6 bits indicate how many times the following byte must be repeated. If the 2 highest-order bits are not both 1, the byte represents the bitmap data.

Examine the read function (see the file PCXIMAGE.CPP on the companion disk) of the PCXImage class to understand this better.

PCX File Header

As you can see from the declaration of the PCXImage class in Listing 21.5, the PCX file's header is represented by the following PCXHeader structure:

```
struct PCXHeader
{
    unsigned char   manufacturer;
    unsigned char   version;
    unsigned char   encoding;
```

```
    unsigned char    bits_per_pixel_per_plane;
    short            xmin;
    short            ymin;
    short            xmax;
    short            ymax;
    unsigned short   hresolution;
    unsigned short   vresolution;
    unsigned char    colormap[48];
    unsigned char    reserved;
    unsigned char    nplanes;
    unsigned short   bytes_per_line;
    short            palette_info;
    unsigned char    filler[58];    // Header is 128 bytes
};
```

Here are the meanings of some of the important fields of the PCX file header:

- unsigned char manufacturer; is always set to 0x0a for a valid PCX file. You can use this information to verify that a file contains a PCX format image.

- unsigned char version; indicates the version of PC PaintBrush that created the image file. Note that if version is greater than 5 and bits_per_pixel_per_plane*nplanes is 8, the file has a 256-entry color palette (consisting of 256 RGB bytes occupying 256x3 = 768 bytes) appended at the end of the image.

- unsigned char encoding; should always be 1 to indicate that the image is stored using run-length encoding.

- unsigned char bits_per_pixel_per_plane; is the number of bits for each pixel in each bit plane. For example, a 256-color image has 1 bit plane with 8 bits per pixel per plane.

- short xmin, ymin, xmax, ymax; specify the dimensions of the image. The width is (xmax - xmin + 1) and the height is (ymax - ymin + 1).

- unsigned char colormap[48]; is a 16-entry colormap with a 3-byte RGB value per entry. This colormap is valid if bits_per_pixel_per_plane*nplanes is less than or equal to 4.

- unsigned char nplanes; is the number of bit planes.

Note that the PCX file header is always 128 bytes long; so you have to pad the structure with enough bytes to make the total size 128 bytes.

Listing 21.5. PCXIMAGE.H. Declaration of the PCXImage class.

```
//-------------------------------------------------------------
//  File: pcximage.h
//
//  Defines the PCXImage class representing PCX images.
//
//-------------------------------------------------------------
#if !defined(__PCXIMAGE_H)
```

continues

Listing 21.5. continued

```
#define __PCXIMAGE_H

#include "image.h"

class PCXImage: public Image
{
public:
    PCXImage() {}
    PCXImage(Image& img) : Image(img) {}

    ~PCXImage() {}

    virtual int read(const char* filename);
    virtual int read(ifstream& ifs){ return 0;}
    virtual int write(const char* filename)
    { return 1;} // Do nothing for now

private:
// A structure for the file header
    struct PCXHeader
    {
        unsigned char   manufacturer;
        unsigned char   version;
        unsigned char   encoding;
        unsigned char   bits_per_pixel_per_plane;
        short           xmin;
        short           ymin;
        short           xmax;
        short           ymax;
        unsigned short  hresolution;
        unsigned short  vresolution;
        unsigned char   colormap[48];
        unsigned char   reserved;
        unsigned char   nplanes;
        unsigned short  bytes_per_line;
        short           palette_info;
        unsigned char   filler[58];    // Header is 128 bytes
    };
    PCXHeader hdr;

};
#endif
```

Reading a PCX File

Conceptually, reading the PCX file is simple—you merely read one byte at a time and repeat the following byte a specified number of times when the byte indicates run-length encoding. The early part of the `read` function in the PCXIMAGE.CPP file shows the loop that unpacks the PCX image by undoing the effect of run-length encoding. Written in C++-like pseudocode, the loop looks like this:

```
while (file has not ended)
{
```

```
    read a byte
    if(byte & 0xc0) // Are 2 high bits set?
    {
        count = byte & 0x3f;
        copy the byte count number of times
    }
    else
        copy the byte once
}
```

Decoding the run-length encoding is the easy part of reading a PCX image. Because of the design of our Image class hierarchy, you also have to convert the PCX image from its bit plane structure to a packed format Windows device-independent bitmap. The code to this conversion is somewhat messy because to store as a DIB, you have to combine bits from each bit plane of the PCX image into a packed format representing a pixel's value. Figure 21.5 illustrates the process of converting a PCX image into a Windows DIB format.

FIGURE 21.5.

Converting a PCX image into a Windows DIB.

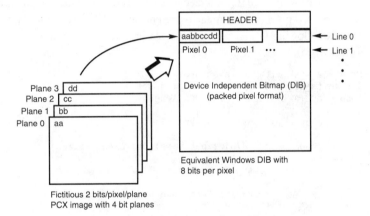

The first step in converting the image to a DIB is to initialize the BITMAPINFOHEADER that precedes the image in a DIB. The BITMAPINFOHEADER structure is defined in <wingdi.h> as the following:

```
typedef struct tagBITMAPINFOHEADER
{
    DWORD   biSize;          // Size of this structure
    LONG    biWidth;         // Width in pixels
    LONG    biHeight;        // Height in pixels
    WORD    biPlanes;        // Number of planes (always 1)
    WORD    biBitCount;      // Bits per pixel
    DWORD   biCompression;   // One of: BI_RGB, BI_RLE4 or
                             //         BI_RLE8
    DWORD   biSizeImage;     // Number of bytes in image
    LONG    biXPelsPerMeter; // Horizontal resolution
    LONG    biYPelsPerMeter; // Vertical resolution
    DWORD   biClrUsed;       // Number of colors used
    DWORD   biClrImportant;  // How many colors important?
} BITMAPINFOHEADER, FAR *LPBITMAPINFOHEADER, *PBITMAPINFOHEADER;
```

The read function of the PCXImage class intializes these fields of the BITMAPINFOHEADER with information derived from the header of the PCX file.

After setting the BITMAPINFOHEADER, the read function initializes the color palette that follows the BITMAPINFOHEADER in a DIB. The color palette consists of an array of RGBQUAD structures, each with the following fields:

```
typedef struct tagRGBQUAD
{
    BYTE    rgbBlue;    // Intensity of blue component (0-255)
    BYTE    rgbGreen;   // Intensity of green component (0-255)
    BYTE    rgbRed;     // Intensity of red component (0-255)
    BYTE    rgbReserved;// Reserved (set to zero)
} RGBQUAD;
```

Each RGBQUAD structure defines an RGB color for an entry in the color palette.

Once the color palette is initialized, the read function proceeds to convert the PCX bit planes into a packed pixel format image representing a DIB. The pseudocode for this operation looks like the following (a *mask* is a bit-pattern used to extract selected bits from an 8-bit byte or a 16-bit word):

```
Create a mask with the high-order
    "bits_per_pixel_per_plane" bits set
Loop over (all lines in the PCX image)
{
    Loop over (all bytes in each plane)
    {
        Loop over ("8/bits_per_pixel_per_plane" times)
        {
            Loop over (all planes)
            {
                Pack bits from each plane into a byte
                If all 8 bits are filled, copy byte to
                appropriate location in DIB
            }
            Shift mask to right by
            "bits_per_pixel_per_plane" bits
        }
    }
}
```

To understand this operation, you should carefully study the corresponding loops in the read function shown in the PCXIMAGE.CPP file. As you can see from the sample programs in the companion disk, the conversion from the PCX format to DIB works for monochrome, 4-, 8-, and even 24-bit color images.

The *TIFImage* Class

The Tagged Image File Format (TIFF) was jointly developed by Aldus Corporation and Microsoft Corporation as a versatile and extensible format for storing raster images. TIFF can handle black-and-white, greyscale, and color images well, and TIFF supports a variety of data compression schemes for the pixel values of an image.

The versatility of TIFF contributes to one of its major problems—very few TIFF readers (including the one shown in the TIFImage class) have the capability of decoding all the fields of a TIFF file. Thus, it is quite common for TIFF files created by one application to be nearly useless when loaded into another unrelated application. One reason for the problem in portability of TIFF images is the lack of support for some fields in the TIFF reader. The other reason is that TIFF allows proprietary data field formats, and many vendors exploit this feature.

Despite these problems, TIFF is widely supported by desktop publishing and graphics software. Additionally, almost all scanner vendors support the TIFF format.

TIFF File Structure

Like GIF files, a TIFF file uses tagged fields to store the information. The file starts with a header and at least one directory called an Image File Directory (IFD). An IFD contains a number of 12-byte directory entries, each with information on a tagged field. The directory entry for a tagged field identifies the field with a tag (an integer value such as 256 for the ImageWidth tag), a constant identifying the data type, the length of the data, and the location of that field's data expressed as an offset from the beginning of the file. If a field's data fits in 4 bytes, the data is placed in the directory entry. Figure 21.6 shows the layout of a TIFF file.

FIGURE 21.6.

TIFF file structure.

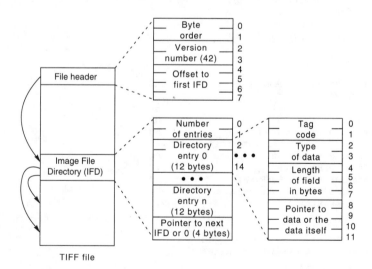

The TIFF file header occupies 8 bytes. The first 2 bytes of the file control the interpretation of the data in the rest of the file—these 2 bytes indicate the byte order. These 2 bytes contain the ASCII characters MM or II to indicate Motorola or Intel byte order, respectively. The Intel byte order is often referred to as the *little-endian byte order,* where the bytes comprising a 16- or 32-bit value are stored in the least-to-most significant byte order. The Motorola or *big-endian byte order* stores the bytes for multibyte integers in the opposite order—from most significant to least significant.

The IFD starts with a 2-byte value that indicates the total number of entries in the directory. The directory entries come next. Each directory entry is a 12-byte structure with information about a tagged field (see Figure 21.6). The IFD ends with a 4-byte value that is either a pointer to the next IFD or a zero marking the end of the last IFD.

Listing 21.6 shows the file TIFIMAGE.H that declares the `TIFImage` class designed to read and interpret a TIFF file. The header file also defines symbolic names for a number of TIFF tags.

Listing 21.6. TIFIMAGE.H. Declaration of the `TIFImage` class.

```
//------------------------------------------------------------
//   File: TIFimage.h
//
//   Defines the TIFImage class representing TIFF images.
//
//------------------------------------------------------------
#if !defined(__TIFIMAGE_H)
#define __TIFIMAGE_H

#include "image.h"

#define BYTE_TYPE       1
#define ASCII_TYPE      2
#define SHORT_TYPE      3
#define LONG_TYPE       4
#define RATIONAL_TYPE   5

// TIFF tag types

#define BitsPerSample              258
#define ColorMap                   320
#define Compression                259
#define ImageLength                257
#define ImageWidth                 256
#define PhotometricInterpretation  262
#define PlanarConfiguration        284
#define RowsPerStrip               278
#define SamplesPerPixel            277
#define StripByteCounts            279
#define StripOffsets               273


class TIFImage: public Image
{
public:
    TIFImage();
    TIFImage(Image& img) : Image(img) {}

    ~TIFImage();

    virtual int read(const char* filename);
    virtual int read(ifstream& ifs){ return 0;}
    virtual int write(const char* filename)
    { return 1;} // Do nothing for now

// Utility functions to read short and long integers
```

```
// from a TIFF file.
    unsigned short get_short(ifstream &ifs)
    {
        if(byteorder[0] == 'I')
            return((ifs.get() & 0xff) |
                   ((ifs.get() & 0xff) << 8));
        else
            return(((ifs.get() & 0xff) << 8) |
                    (ifs.get() & 0xff));
    }

    unsigned long get_long(ifstream &ifs)
    {
        if(byteorder[0] == 'I')
            return((unsigned long)(ifs.get() & 0xff)       |
                   ((unsigned long)(ifs.get() & 0xff) <<  8) |
                   ((unsigned long)(ifs.get() & 0xff) << 16) |
                   ((unsigned long)(ifs.get() & 0xff) << 24));
        else
            return((unsigned long)(ifs.get() & 0xff) << 24) |
                   ((unsigned long)(ifs.get() & 0xff) << 16) |
                   ((unsigned long)(ifs.get() & 0xff) <<  8) |
                   ((unsigned long)(ifs.get() & 0xff));
    }

// Function to read a row from the image file
    unsigned short read_row(ifstream &ifs);

private:

// This array is used to store the decoded TIFF image
    unsigned char *TIF_image;

    char           byteorder[2]; // "MM" or "II"
    short          version;      // Always decimal 42
    unsigned long  ifd;          // Offset to directory
    unsigned short tag;          // Tag code
    unsigned short type;         // Data type
    unsigned long  length;       // Number of bytes of data
    unsigned long  offset;       // Offset to data (or data)
    RGBTRIPLE      *ctbl;        // Color table
    unsigned short image_width;
    unsigned short image_height;
    unsigned short rows_per_strip;
    unsigned long  byte_count;
    unsigned long  strip_offset;
    unsigned short numstrips;
    unsigned short samples_per_pixel;
    unsigned short bits_per_sample;
    unsigned short planar_config;
    unsigned short compression;
    unsigned short palettesize;
    unsigned short bits_per_pixel;
    unsigned long  pos;
    unsigned short bytes_per_line;
    unsigned short bytes_per_strip_row;
    unsigned short photometric;
};
#endif
```

Reading a TIFF File

The strategy for reading a TIFF file is to start with the first 2 bytes of the file header. These 2 bytes tell you the byte order, which controls how you interpret the 16- and 32-bit integer values in the TIFF file. The read function in the TIFIMAGE.CPP file (on the companion disk) follows this strategy.

Once you know the byte order, you can read the rest of the header and locate the first IFD from the offset stored in the header. Next, you should read all the directory entries in the IFD and gather information about each tagged field.

After you have read and collected information on all directory entries in an IFD, you can read the image data. The data is stored in strips of a specified number of rows. The value of the Compression tag determines how to decipher the image data. Here are some of the common values for the Compression tag:

```
1 = No compression, but the bits are packed tightly into arrays of bytes.
5 = LZW compression as in a GIF file.
32773 = Macintosh PackBits compression (a run-length encoding scheme).
```

The read function in the TIFIMAGE.CPP file can handle Compression tags 1 and 32773 only.

As you can see from the read function in the TIFIMAGE.CPP file, the pseudocode for unpacking the PackBits encoded data is the following:

```
Loop until all bytes are read
{
    Read a byte
    if(byte & 0x80)  // Is most significant bit set?
    {
        if(byte != 0x80) // Byte is not equal to 128
        {
            n = - byte + 1;
            Copy the next byte n times.
        }
        else
        {
            n = byte + 1;
            Copy the next byte n times.
        }
    }
}
```

Once the image data from the TIFF file is available, you have to copy the data into a Windows DIB format. At this point, the steps are identical to those used in copying an unpacked PCX image to a DIB. Thus, for this task, the read function of the TIFImage class uses the same code fragments as the read function of the PCXImage class.

ImageView—A Windows Image Viewer

Now that you have seen an `Image` class hierarchy for handling BMP, PCX, and TIFF image files, it's time for an application that uses these classes. The next few sections present ImageView, a Windows MDI application that enables the user to open one or more image files for viewing. ImageView uses the `Image` class hierarchy developed in an earlier part of this chapter. You can view BMP, PCX, and TIFF files with ImageView.

This book's companion disk includes the complete source code for ImageView together with necessary auxiliary files, such as the resource file (IMAGEVW.RC) and the project file (IMAGEVW.MAK). Before reading any more about ImageView, you should run the program and see how it works. Then you can read the following descriptions and study the source files to understand how the program is implemented.

Running ImageView

If you have added a new program item for the ImageView application in Windows Program Manager, you can start the program by double-clicking on its icon. Otherwise, you have to start the program by selecting Run from the File menu in the Program Manager and specifying the application's name (IMAGEVW.EXE). To view an image, select Open from ImageView's File menu. You will see a file selection dialog box from which you can select an image file. Each image appears in its own window inside ImageView's main window. Figure 21.7 shows the basic features of ImageView including a number of images shown in different windows.

FIGURE 21.7.

Viewing images with ImageView.

The *ImageViewApp* Class

The ImageView application is built using Microsoft Visual C++ 2.0 and the MFC 3.0 classes. As you can see from Listing 21.7, the main source file IMAGEVW.CPP looks very much like the main source file of any MFC-based application.

The `ImageViewApp` class, derived from `CWinApp`, models the ImageView application. Its `InitInstance` function creates an instance of an `ImageViewFrame` window, which is the main window of the ImageView application. The images are displayed in child windows of `ImageViewFrame`.

Listing 21.7. IMAGEVW.CPP. The main source file of ImageView.

```
//------------------------------------------------------------
// File:  imagevw.cpp
//
// A Windows application for viewing images in a variety of
// formats such as Windows bitmap (.BMP), PC PaintBrush (.PCX),
// and the Tagged Image File Format (.TIF).
//------------------------------------------------------------
#include "imvwwin.h"

class ImageViewApp: public CWinApp
{
public:
// Define function to initialize application's main window
    BOOL InitInstance();
};
//------------------------------------------------------------
// I m a g e V i e w A p p : : I n i t I n s t a n c e

BOOL ImageViewApp::InitInstance()
{
    Enable3dControls();
    m_pMainWnd = new ImageViewFrame();

    m_pMainWnd->ShowWindow(m_nCmdShow);
    m_pMainWnd->UpdateWindow();

    return TRUE;
}
//------------------------------------------------------------
// Create an instance of the application and "run" it.

    ImageViewApp ImageView;
```

The *ImageViewFrame* and *ImageViewWindow* Classes

Listing 21.8 shows the declarations of the `ImageViewWindow` and `ImageViewFrame` classes. The `ImageViewWindow` class has a member variable, `image`, which is a pointer to the `Image` object that it displays. The `ImageViewFrame` class represents the MDI frame window, inside of which one or more `ImageViewWindow` objects display images. As such, the `ImageViewFrame` class does not have any member variables—it provides only member functions, such as `OpenFile` and `About`, that handle menu messages.

Listing 21.8. IMVWWIN.H. Declaration of the window classes in ImageView.

```
//----------------------------------------------------------------
// File: imvwwin.h
//
// Classes for an MFC application that enables you to open an image
// file and view the image in a window.
//----------------------------------------------------------------
#if !defined(__IMVWWIN_H)
#define __IMVWWIN_H

#include <afx.h>
#include <afxwin.h>
#include <afxdlgs.h>

#include <strstrea.h>
#include <string.h>

#include "image.h"
#include "bmpimage.h"
#include "pcximage.h"
#include "tifimage.h"


#define IDM_ABOUT      200
#define IDM_OPENFILE   101
#define IDM_SAVE       102
#define IDM_SAVEAS     103

class ImageViewWindow : public CMDIChildWnd
{
public:
    ImageViewWindow(CMDIFrameWnd *parent, const char *title,
                    CString fname);

    ~ImageViewWindow()
    {
        if(image != NULL) delete image;
    }
    BOOL PreCreateWindow(CREATESTRUCT& cs);

    Image *current_image() { return image;}

    void Save();

    afx_msg void OnPaint();

private:
    CString filename;
    Image   *image;

    DECLARE_MESSAGE_MAP()
```

continues

Listing 21.8. continued

```
};

class ImageViewFrame: public CMDIFrameWnd
{
public:
    ImageViewFrame();

// Declare functions for handling messages from Windows
    afx_msg BOOL OnQueryNewPalette();
    afx_msg void OnPaletteChanged(CWnd *pFocusWnd);

    afx_msg void OpenFile();
    afx_msg void SaveFile();
    afx_msg void SaveAsFile();
    afx_msg void About();

    DECLARE_MESSAGE_MAP()
};

#endif
```

Remember, the `ImageViewWindow` class contains information about the image it is displaying—in the form of a pointer to an `Image` object as a member variable. The `ImageViewWindow` constructor expects as an argument the name of an image file, which it uses to create and initialize the image. The image file's extension is used to decide what type of image is created: .BMP implies a Windows device-independent bitmap file, .PCX means PC PaintBrush files, and .TIF specifies TIFF files. Consult Listing 21.9 for further details of the `ImageViewWindow` constructor.

You should note that the image is displayed in the window by the `OnPaint` function of the `ImageViewWindow` class. Listing 21.9 shows the simplicity of the `ImageViewWindow::OnPaint` function—it merely calls the `show` member function of the image object. This shows the benefits of developing a C++ class hierarchy to handle a specific task for managing and displaying images. (You can see the benefits even more clearly with the image animation program ANIMATE.EXE presented later in this chapter.)

Listing 21.9. IMVWWIN.CPP. Implementation of the window classes in ImageView.

```
//-----------------------------------------------------------------
// File: imvwwin.cpp
//
// Member functions of the ImageViewFrame and ImageViewWindow
// classes.
//
//-----------------------------------------------------------------
#include "imvwwin.h"
//-----------------------------------------------------------------
// Define the message map for ImageViewFrame

BEGIN_MESSAGE_MAP(ImageViewFrame, CMDIFrameWnd)
```

```
    ON_COMMAND(IDM_ABOUT,      About)
    ON_COMMAND(IDM_OPENFILE,   OpenFile)
    ON_COMMAND(IDM_SAVE,       SaveFile)
    ON_COMMAND(IDM_SAVEAS,     SaveAsFile)
    ON_WM_QUERYNEWPALETTE()
    ON_WM_PALETTECHANGED()
END_MESSAGE_MAP()

// Define the message map for ImageViewWindow

BEGIN_MESSAGE_MAP(ImageViewWindow, CMDIChildWnd)
    ON_WM_PAINT()
END_MESSAGE_MAP()

//----------------------------------------------------------------
// I m a g e V i e w W i n d o w
// Constructor for the ImageViewWindow class

ImageViewWindow::ImageViewWindow(CMDIFrameWnd *parent,
    const char *title, CString fname) : CMDIChildWnd()
{
    image = NULL;

// Open the image file. We will decide the file type from
// the file extension:
//   .BMP = Windows bitmap file
//   .PCX = PC PaintBrush file
//   .TIF = TIFF file

    filename = fname;

// Convert filename to uppercase
    filename.MakeUpper();

// Extract the file extension
    char *ext = strrchr(filename, '.');

// Load file
    if(strcmp(ext, ".BMP") == 0)
    {
        image = new BMPImage;
        if(!image->read(filename))
        {
        // Error reading file
            delete image;
            image = NULL;
        }
    }

    if(strnicmp(ext, ".PCX", 4) == 0)
    {
        image = new PCXImage;
        if(!image->read(fname))
        {
            delete image;
            image = NULL;
        }
    }
```

continues

Listing 21.9. continued

```
    if(strnicmp(ext, ".TIF", 4) == 0)
    {
        image = new TIFImage;
        if(!image->read(fname))
        {
            delete image;
            image = NULL;
        }
    }

// Display a message if image format is unknown
    if(image == NULL)
    {
    MessageBox("Unknown image format!",
                "ImageView",
                MB_OK | MB_ICONEXCLAMATION);
    }
    else
    {
// Create the window
        Create(NULL, title);
    }
}
//------------------------------------------------------------
// ImageViewWindow:: P r e C r e a t e W i n d o w
//
// Calls AfxRegisterWndClass to set icon for child window

BOOL ImageViewWindow::PreCreateWindow(CREATESTRUCT& cs)
{
    cs.lpszClass = AfxRegisterWndClass(
                        CS_HREDRAW | CS_VREDRAW,
                        LoadCursor(NULL, IDC_ARROW),
                        ::CreateSolidBrush(
                                GetSysColor(COLOR_WINDOW)),
                        LoadIcon(AfxGetInstanceHandle(),
                                    "IMAGEVIEWWIN_ICON"));
    return TRUE;
}
//------------------------------------------------------------
// ImageViewWindow:: O n P a i n t
// Draw image in the window

void ImageViewWindow::OnPaint()
{
    if(image != NULL)
    {
        CPaintDC dc(this);
        image->show(&dc);
    }
}
//------------------------------------------------------------
// ImageViewFrame:: I m a g e V i e w F r a m e ( )
// Constructor for the ImageViewFrame class

ImageViewFrame::ImageViewFrame()
{
```

```
    VERIFY(LoadAccelTable("MainAccelTable"));
    VERIFY(Create(NULL, "ImageView", WS_OVERLAPPEDWINDOW,
                  rectDefault, NULL, "MAINMENU"));
}
//------------------------------------------------------------
// ImageViewFrame:: A b o u t
// Display the "About..." box

void ImageViewFrame::About()
{
    CDialog About("ABOUTIMAGEVIEW", this);
    About.DoModal();
}
//------------------------------------------------------------
// ImageViewFrame:: O p e n F i l e
// Display file dialog and open requested image file

void ImageViewFrame::OpenFile()
{
    int status = IDCANCEL;

// Create and display file selection dialog...

    CFileDialog FileDlg(
                    TRUE,  // This is a "File Open" dialog
                    NULL,  // Do not append default extension
                    "*.*", // Initial name in filename box
                    OFN_HIDEREADONLY |   // Flags controlling
                    OFN_FILEMUSTEXIST |  // dialog content and
                    OFN_PATHMUSTEXIST,   // behavior
        // Next comes the file filters that select listed files
        "All Files (*.*)|*.*|BMP Files (*.bmp)|*.bmp|"
        "PCX Files (*.pcx)|*.pcx|TIF Files (*.tif)|*.tif|",
                    this); // Parent or owner of dialog box

    status = FileDlg.DoModal();

 // Load selected image file in an ImageViewWindow
    if(status == IDOK)
    {
        CString pathname = FileDlg.GetPathName();

// Change to an hourglass cursor
        SetCapture();
        HCURSOR hOldCursor = ::SetCursor(
                            LoadCursor(NULL, IDC_WAIT));

        ImageViewWindow* iw = new ImageViewWindow(this,
                            pathname, pathname);
// Reset cursor to arrow
        ::SetCursor(LoadCursor(NULL, IDC_ARROW));
        ReleaseCapture();
    }
}
//------------------------------------------------------------
// ImageViewFrame:: O n Q u e r y N e w P a l e t t e
// Realize palette for the currently active child window
```

continues

Listing 21.9. continued

```
BOOL ImageViewFrame::OnQueryNewPalette()
{
    ImageViewWindow *w = (ImageViewWindow*)MDIGetActive();
    if(w == NULL) return 0;

    if(w->current_image == NULL) return 0;

    HPALETTE hpal = w->current_image()->palette();
    short changed = 0;
    if(hpal)
    {
        CClientDC dc(w);
        CPalette *pPal = CPalette::FromHandle(hpal);
        CPalette *pOldPal = dc.SelectPalette(pPal, FALSE);

        changed = dc.RealizePalette();
        dc.SelectPalette(pOldPal, FALSE);

        if(changed)
        {
            w->Invalidate(TRUE);
            w->UpdateWindow();
        }
    }
    return changed;
}
//--------------------------------------------------------------
// ImageViewFrame:: O n P a l e t t e C h a n g e d
// Handle a change in system palette

void ImageViewFrame::OnPaletteChanged(CWnd *pFocusWnd)
{
    ImageViewWindow *w = (ImageViewWindow*)MDIGetActive();
    if(w == NULL) return;

    if(pFocusWnd == w) return;
    if(w->current_image == NULL) return;

    HPALETTE hpal = w->current_image()->palette();
    short changed = 0;
    if(hpal)
    {
        CClientDC dc(w);
        CPalette *pPal = CPalette::FromHandle(hpal);
        CPalette *pOldPal = dc.SelectPalette(pPal, FALSE);

        changed = dc.RealizePalette();
        if(changed)
        {
            dc.UpdateColors();
        }
        dc.SelectPalette(pOldPal, FALSE);
    }
}
//--------------------------------------------------------------
```

```
// ImageViewFrame:: S a v e  F i l e
// Saves image (being displayed in currently active child window)
// in .BMP format in a file with the same name as the original,
// except for a .BMP extension.

void ImageViewFrame::SaveFile()
{
    ImageViewWindow *w = (ImageViewWindow*)MDIGetActive();
    if(w != NULL) w->Save();
}
//----------------------------------------------------------------
// ImageViewWindow:: S a v e
// Save image in BMP format

void ImageViewWindow::Save()
{
    char *ext = strrchr(filename, '.');
    if(strcmp(ext, ".BMP") != 0)
    {
// Change to an hourglass cursor
        SetCapture();
        HCURSOR hOldCursor = SetCursor(LoadCursor(NULL, IDC_WAIT));

        char bmpfilename[128];
        strcpy(bmpfilename, filename);
        ext = strrchr(bmpfilename, '.');
        strcpy(ext, ".BMP");
        BMPImage ibmp;
        ibmp.image_data(image);
        ibmp.write(bmpfilename);
// Reset cursor to arrow
        SetCursor(hOldCursor);
        ::ReleaseCapture();
    }
}
//----------------------------------------------------------------
// ImageViewWindow:: S a v e A s F i l e
// Display file dialog and save image in a selected format
// (Nothing happens for now)

void ImageViewFrame::SaveAsFile(){}
```

Building ImageView

You should use the Windows-based interactive development environment of Visual C++ 2.0 to build the ImageView application. The companion disk has the project file (IMAGEVW.MAK) that lists the files necessary to build the application. The companion disk includes all files needed to build the executable, IMAGEVW.EXE. After you install the code from the companion disk, you should be able to build IMAGEVW.EXE by selecting Rebuild All from the Project menu. Once the program is successfully built, you can run it directly from within Visual C++ by pressing F5 or Ctrl+F5.

Sprite Animation

Sprites are used in interactive video games to represent characters and fixtures that are part of the game. When the player moves an input device, such as a joystick, trackball, or mouse, the sprite moves over a background. Essentially, the player plays the video game by manipulating the sprites. Video game machines usually have graphics hardware with built-in support for sprites. In IBM-compatible PCs, the display hardware does not support sprites, so you have to rely on software techniques.

Erase and Redraw Technique

The obvious way to move an image is to erase it at the old location and redraw it at the new location. In a Windows program, you can use the BitBlt function for this. If you erase and redraw repeatedly, the image appears to move across the screen. However, a major drawback of this approach is that the display flickers as the image is erased and redrawn.

One way to avoid flickers in erase-and-redraw animation is to use video page flipping, provided the display hardware supports more than one video page. With multiple video pages, you draw the entire screen in the hidden video page while the active page is being displayed. Then you swap the active and hidden video pages to display the updated image. To continue the animation, you simply repeat this process in a loop. Many high-end graphics workstations (Silicon Graphics workstations, for example) support animation through page flipping—or *buffer swapping* as the technique is known in the workstation world.

Unfortunately, most PC display adapters do not support multiple video pages in the high-resolution video modes. More importantly, Microsoft Windows does not support multiple video pages. So you need some other approach to create flicker-free animation in Windows.

Offscreen Bitmap Technique

Screen flickers occur with the erase and redraw animation because all screen drawing operations are visible. As an image is erased, you see it vanish from the screen. Then the image appears again at a new location. When two video pages are used, the flicker goes away because the screen updates are always done in the hidden page. The fully updated screen appears instantaneously when the video pages are swapped. By this logic, you should be able to avoid the flicker as long as the images are prepared offscreen and the updated screen is redrawn quickly. Luckily, Windows supports drawing on an offscreen bitmap, which can serve as an ideal canvas for preparing the display screen. Then a single call to BitBlt can transfer the updated images to the display screen quickly. Of course, you have to attend to a myriad of details to prepare the image properly in the offscreen bitmap, but this basic idea works remarkably well for image animation under Windows.

To see how well the offscreen bitmap animation works, all you need to do is run the ANIMATE application (ANIMATE.EXE), which should be in the CH21 subdirectory after you install the code from the companion disk.

C++ Classes for Sprite Animation

To support a Windows application that animates sprites using an offscreen bitmap, you need C++ classes to represent the sprites and to animate them. The animation consists of a fixed background image and zero or more sprites that can be moved around on the background. The following sections define a Sprite class to model a sprite and a SpriteAnimation class to maintain the sprites and the background image.

The *Sprite* Class

Listing 21.10 shows the declaration of the Sprite class. A Sprite has two Image objects:

- The Sprite's image against a black background
- A black silhouette of the Sprite's image against a white background (a mask)

As you can see in the animate function of the SpriteAnimation class (in the SPRANIM.CPP file), both the image and the mask are needed to enable drawing the Sprite's outline without affecting the background on which the Sprite is drawn. In addition to the image and the mask, a Sprite has an x- and y-position and several other variables to keep track of its motion on the background.

A Sprite object also has a display priority associated with it. This is an integer, stored in the member variable disp_priority, that determines the order in which overlapping sprites are drawn—a Sprite with a higher priority is drawn over one with a lower priority. (The current version of the sprite animation program does not use this priority.)

Another interesting member variable is dproc of type DRAWPROC, which is declared with this typedef statement:

```
typedef void (CALLBACK *DRAWPROC)(HDC hdc, short x, short y,
                        LPVOID data);
```

As you can see, dproc is a pointer to a function. The function specified by dproc is called whenever the Sprite's image needs to be drawn. You can draw objects—such as a line, rectangle, ellipse, or text—so that a sprite can have much more than a bitmapped image. The moving text in the sample application ANIMATE (in the companion disk) is displayed using this feature of a Sprite.

Listing 21.10. SPRITE.H. Declaration of the Sprite class.

```
//-------------------------------------------------------------
// File: sprite.h
//
// Declares a Sprite class representing a small image that
// can be animated.
//-------------------------------------------------------------
#if !defined(__SPRITE_H)
```

continues

Listing 21.10. continued

```c
#define __SPRITE_H

#include <string.h>
#include "image.h"

const unsigned short SPRITE_ACTIVE      = 1;
const unsigned short SPRITE_UPDATE      = 2;
const unsigned short SPRITE_OVERLAP     = 4;
const unsigned short SPRITE_ERASE       = 8;


typedef void (CALLBACK *DRAWPROC)(HDC hdc, short x, short y,
                                  LPVOID data);


class Sprite
{
public:
    Sprite() : image(NULL), mask(NULL), disp_priority(1),
            dproc(NULL), dpdata(NULL), status(0), sid(-1),
            image_filename(NULL), mask_filename(NULL)
    {
        curpos.x = curpos.y = 0;
        lastpos.x = lastpos.y = 0;
    }

    Sprite(HDC hdc, LPSTR imagefilename,
        LPSTR maskfilename, short priority = 1);

    Sprite(Image *img, Image *msk, short priority = 1);

    ~Sprite();

// Read in an image and a mask
    void load_images(HDC hdc, LPSTR imagefilename,
            LPSTR maskfilename);

    operator==(const Sprite& s) const
    {
        return (disp_priority == s.priority());
    }
    operator<(const Sprite& s) const
    {
        return (disp_priority < s.priority());
    }

    void printOn(ostream& os) const
    {
        os << "Sprite : " << *image_filename << endl;
    }

    short priority() const { return disp_priority;}
    void priority(short dp) { disp_priority = dp;}

    unsigned short width() { return w;}
    unsigned short height() { return h;}
    void width(unsigned wdth) { w = wdth;}
```

```
    void height(unsigned hght) { h = hght;}

    short xpos() { return curpos.x;}
    short ypos() { return curpos.y;}
    void xpos(short x)
    {
        lastpos.x = curpos.x;
        curpos.x = x;
    }
    void ypos(short y)
    {
        lastpos.y = curpos.y;
        curpos.y = y;
    }
    void newpos(short x, short y)
    {
        lastpos.x = curpos.x;
        lastpos.y = curpos.y;
        curpos.x = x;
        curpos.y = y;
        reset_moves();
    }

    short lastxpos() { return lastpos.x;}
    short lastypos() { return lastpos.y;}

    void reset_moves()
    {
      xdelta = ydelta = 0;
    }
    short xmove() { return xdelta;}
    short ymove() { return ydelta;}

    void move(short x, short y)
    {
        xdelta += x;
        ydelta += y;
// Mark sprite for update
        status |= SPRITE_UPDATE;
    }

// Functions to manipulate the status of a sprite
    unsigned short needs_update()
    { return status & SPRITE_UPDATE;}
    unsigned short is_active()
    { return status & SPRITE_ACTIVE;}
    unsigned short is_overlapping()
    { return status & SPRITE_OVERLAP;}
    unsigned short to_be_erased()
    { return status & SPRITE_ERASE;}
    void active() { status |= SPRITE_ACTIVE | SPRITE_UPDATE;}
    void update() { status |= SPRITE_UPDATE;}
    void erase() { status |= SPRITE_ERASE;}
    void overlaps(){ status |= SPRITE_OVERLAP;}
    void update_done(){ status &= ~SPRITE_UPDATE;}
    void unerase() { status &= ~SPRITE_ERASE;}
    void inactive() { status &= ~SPRITE_ACTIVE;}
    void no_overlap() { status &= ~SPRITE_OVERLAP;}
```

continues

Listing 21.10. continued

```
// Convert the device-independent bitmaps to device-
// dependent bitmaps
    void make_ddb(HDC hdc)
    {
        if(image != NULL) image->DIBtoDDB(hdc);
        if(mask != NULL) mask->DIBtoDDB(hdc);
    }

    void drawproc(DRAWPROC dp, LPVOID data)
    {
        dproc = dp;
        dpdata = data;
    }
    DRAWPROC drawproc() { return dproc;}
    LPVOID data() { return dpdata;}

    HBITMAP hbm_image()
    {
        if(image != NULL) return image->get_ddb();
        else return NULL;
    }
    HBITMAP hbm_mask()
    {
        if(mask != NULL) return mask->get_ddb();
        else return NULL;
    }

    Image* sprite_image() { return image;}
    Image* sprite_mask() { return mask;}

    void id(short _id) { sid = _id;}
    short id() { return sid;}

    static Image* init_image(LPSTR fname);

protected:
    Image          *image;  // The sprite's image
    Image          *mask;   // The mask: a silhouette of image
    unsigned short w, h;    // Width and height of sprite
    short          disp_priority;
    POINT          curpos;
    POINT          lastpos;
    short          xdelta;
    short          ydelta;
    unsigned short status;
    DRAWPROC       dproc;   // Pointer to user-supplied
                            // function to draw
    LPVOID         dpdata;  // Argument for drawproc
    char           *image_filename;
    char           *mask_filename;

    short          sid; // Normally unused, but may be
                        // used to identify Sprite
};

#endif
```

Listing 21.11 shows the file SPRITE.CPP with several member functions of the Sprite class. A typical way to create and initialize a Sprite is to use the constructor that accepts the names of image and mask files as arguments:

```
Sprite::Sprite(HDC hdc, LPSTR imagefilename,
               LPSTR maskfilename, short priority);
```

This constructor calls the init_image function to load the bitmaps corresponding to the image and the mask. The constructor also requires the handle to a device context. This is necessary because the image and mask bitmaps are converted to a device-dependent format and this step needs a DC.

The init_image function (Listing 21.11) loads an image from a file. It uses the filename extension to determine the type of image. The following are the extensions it accepts:

- ■ .BMP for Windows DIB files
- ■ .PCX for PC PaintBrush files
- ■ .TIF for TIFF files

Listing 21.11. SPRITE.CPP. Implementation of the Sprite class.

```
//----------------------------------------------------------------
// File: sprite.cpp
// Member functions of the Sprite class.
//----------------------------------------------------------------
#include <string.h>
#include <afx.h>
#include <afxwin.h>

#include "sprite.h"
#include "bmpimage.h"
#include "pcximage.h"
#include "tifimage.h"


//----------------------------------------------------------------
// S p r i t e : : S p r i t e
// Constructor for a Sprite

Sprite::Sprite(HDC hdc, LPSTR imagefilename,
               LPSTR maskfilename, short priority):
    disp_priority(priority)
{
    image_filename = mask_filename = NULL;

// Read the image and the mask bitmaps
    image = init_image(imagefilename);
    size_t len;
    if(image != NULL)
    {
        w = image->width();
        h = image->height();
        len = strlen(imagefilename);
        image_filename = new char[len+1];
```

continues

Listing 21.11. continued

```cpp
        strcpy(image_filename, imagefilename);
    }

    mask = init_image(maskfilename);
    if(mask != NULL)
    {
        len = strlen(maskfilename);
        mask_filename = new char[len+1];
        strcpy(mask_filename, maskfilename);
    }

// Convert the image and the mask into device-dependent bitmaps
    make_ddb(hdc);

// Initialize other member variables
    curpos.x = curpos.y = 0;
    lastpos.x = lastpos.y = 0;
    dproc = NULL;
    dpdata = NULL;
    status = SPRITE_UPDATE | SPRITE_ACTIVE;
}
//--------------------------------------------------------------
// Sprite::S p r i t e ( I m a g e * , I m a g e * ...)
// Construct a Sprite from an image and a mask.

Sprite::Sprite(Image *img, Image *msk, short priority):
    disp_priority(priority)
{
    image_filename = mask_filename = NULL;

    image = img;
    if(image != NULL)
    {
        w = image->width();
        h = image->height();
    }
    mask = msk;

// Initialize other member variables
    curpos.x = curpos.y = 0;
    lastpos.x = lastpos.y = 0;
    dproc = NULL;
    dpdata = NULL;
    status = SPRITE_UPDATE | SPRITE_ACTIVE;
}
//--------------------------------------------------------------
// S p r i t e : : ~ S p r i t e
// Destructor for a Sprite

Sprite::~Sprite()
{
    if(image_filename != NULL) delete[] image_filename;
    if(mask_filename != NULL) delete[] mask_filename;
    if(image != NULL) delete image;
    if(mask != NULL) delete mask;
}
//--------------------------------------------------------------
```

```
// S p r i t e : : l o a d _ i m a g e s
// Read in image and mask from files

void Sprite::load_images(HDC hdc, LPSTR imagefilename,
                         LPSTR maskfilename)
{
// Read the image and the mask bitmaps
    image = init_image(imagefilename);
    size_t len;
    if(image != NULL)
    {
        w = image->width();
        h = image->height();
        len = strlen(imagefilename);
        strcpy(image_filename, imagefilename);
    }

    mask = init_image(maskfilename);
    if(mask != NULL)
    {
        len = strlen(maskfilename);
        strcpy(mask_filename, maskfilename);
    }

// Convert the image and the mask into device-dependent bitmaps
    make_ddb(hdc);

// Mark sprite as active and in need of update
    status = SPRITE_UPDATE | SPRITE_ACTIVE;
}
//-----------------------------------------------------------------
// S p r i t e : : i n i t _ i m a g e
// Read an image from a file

Image* Sprite::init_image(LPSTR fname)
{
    Image *img = NULL;
    if(fname == NULL) return img;

// Read the image file. We will decide the file type from
// the file extension:
//    .BMP  = Windows bitmap file
//    .PCX  = PC PaintBrush file
//    .TIF  = TIFF file

// Locate filename extension
    char *ext = strrchr(fname, '.');
    if(ext == NULL) return img;

// Load file
    if(strnicmp(ext, ".BMP", 4) == 0)
    {
        img = new BMPImage;

        if(!img->read(fname))
        {
            delete img;
            img = NULL;
        }
```

continues

Listing 21.11. continued

```
    }

    if(strnicmp(ext, ".PCX", 4) == 0)
    {
        img = new PCXImage;
        if(!img->read(fname))
        {
            delete img;
            img = NULL;
        }
    }

    if(strnicmp(ext, ".TIF", 4) == 0)
    {
        img = new TIFImage;
        if(!img->read(fname))
        {
            delete img;
            img = NULL;
        }
    }

    return img;
}
```

The *SpriteAnimation* Class

The SpriteAnimation class, declared in the file SPRANIM.H (Listing 21.12), manages a number of sprites and a background and provides the capability of animating the sprites. Its main data members are the following:

■ SpriteArray *sprites; is an array of pointers to sprites that are part of the animation. SpriteArray is an instance of the MFC 3.0 template class CArray<Tstore,Taccess> declared as an array that maintains an array of pointers to Sprite objects. (See Chapter 16, "Using the General-Purpose Classes in MFC 3.0," for more information on the template-based container classes in MFC 3.0.)

■ Image *background; is the background image that serves as the canvas on which the sprites are animated.

■ HBITMAP hbm_bg; is the device-dependent bitmap of the background image.

■ HBITMAP hbm_scratch; is a bitmap that serves as the scratch area where images are prepared before copying to the onscreen window (to be described later).

Additionally, there are a number of handles to device contexts that are kept ready for copying bitmaps to and from various components of the animation.

Listing 21.12. SPRANIM.H. Declaration of the `SpriteAnimation` class.

```
//---------------------------------------------------------------
// File: spranim.h
//
// Classes for animating sprites.
//---------------------------------------------------------------
#if !defined(__SPRANIM_H)
#define __SPRANIM_H

#include <afx.h>
#include <afxtempl.h>
#include <afxwin.h>

#include "sprite.h"

// A sorted, indirect array of sprites
typedef CArray<Sprite*,Sprite*> SpriteArray;

// A class that manages the animation
class SpriteAnimation
{
public:
    SpriteAnimation(HDC hdc, unsigned short w,
                    unsigned short h,
                    LPSTR filename);
    SpriteAnimation(HDC hdc, unsigned short w,
                    unsigned short h, Image* bg);
    ~SpriteAnimation();

    void init_animation(HDC hdc, unsigned short w,
                                 unsigned short h);
// Add a sprite to the animation
    void add(Sprite* s)
    {
        if(sprites != NULL && s != NULL)
        {
            sprites->SetAt(numsprites, s);
            numsprites++;
        }
    }

// Animate the images
    void animate(HDC hdc, short x, short y);

    void draw_bg(HDC hdc, short x, short y);

    void redisplay_all(HDC hdc, short x, short y);

    void set_refresh(BOOL flag) { refresh = flag;}

// Utility functions
    BOOL rects_overlap(short x1, short y1, short w1, short h1,
                       short x2, short y2, short w2, short h2)
    {
        if((x2 - x1) > w1) return FALSE;
        if((x1 - x2) > w2) return FALSE;
        if((y2 - y1) > h1) return FALSE;
```

continues

Listing 21.12. continued

```
            if((y1 - y2) > h2) return FALSE;
            return TRUE;
        }

    void set_priority(Sprite* s, short prio)
        {
            if(sprites != NULL && s != NULL)
            {
                if(prio != s->priority())
                {
// remove the sprite and add it again...***TO BE DONE***
                    s->priority(prio);
                    sprites->Add(s);
                }
            }
        }
// Returns sprite of highest priority that encloses point (x,y)
    Sprite* sprite_at(short x, short y);

    Image* bgimage() { return background;}
    HBITMAP bg_bitmap() { return hbm_bg;}

// Function to scroll the bitmap by changing top and left
    void xbmp_origin(short x) { left = x;}
    void ybmp_origin(short y) { top = y;}
    short xbmp_origin() { return left;}
    short ybmp_origin() { return top;}

// Functions that draw on the background bitmap
    void bg_rect(short x1, short y1, short x2, short y2)
    { Rectangle(hdc_bg, x1, y1, x2, y2);}
    void bg_line(short x1, short y1, short x2, short y2)
    {
        MoveToEx(hdc_bg, x1, y1, NULL);
        LineTo(hdc_bg, x2, y2);
    }

protected:
    SpriteArray    *sprites;
    short          numsprites;
    Image          *background; // The background image
    HBITMAP        hbm_bg;      // Bitmap from "background"
    HBITMAP        hbm_bg_saved;// A copy of hbm_bg
    HBITMAP        hbm_scratch; // Images prepared here before
                                // copying to window
    short          top, left;   // Top-left corner and
    short          width;       // dimensions of background
    short          height;      // being displayed
    short          ws, hs;      // Dimensions of scratch
                                // bitmap
    short          bg_image;
    HBITMAP        hbm_sprite;
    HDC            hdc_bg;
    HDC            hdc_sprite;
    HDC            hdc_scratch;
    HBITMAP        old_hbm_bg;
```

```
    HBITMAP         old_hbm_sprite;
    HBITMAP         old_hbm_scratch;
    BOOL            refresh;
};
#endif
```

Setting Up a *SpriteAnimation* Object

A SpriteAnimation object is designed to manage animation of a number of sprites on a background image. To use SpriteAnimation, you have to use this constructor:

```
SpriteAnimation::SpriteAnimation(HDC hdc,
                                 unsigned short w,
                                 unsigned short h,
                                 LPSTR filename);
```

The constructor expects a DC, the width and height of the scratch bitmap, and the name of an image file to be used as the background of the animation. As you can see from the file SPRANIM.CPP, the constructor loads the background image, sets up a number of bitmaps and DCs, and creates a SpriteArray to hold the Sprite objects.

Once the SpriteAnimation object is created, you can add Sprites to the animation by calling the add member function of the SpriteAnimation class. You have to move the Sprites by calling the move function of each Sprite. To update the display, call the animate function of the SpriteAnimation class. A sample application that uses the SpriteAnimation class appears later in this chapter.

Animating Sprites

The animate member function (see the SPRANIM.CPP file) of the SpriteAnimation class is at the heart of animating sprites on a background image. Before looking into the problem of updating the screen image in an efficient way, consider the problem of redrawing the entire window. If you look at the beginning of the animate function in SPRANIM.CPP, you see this line:

```
if(refresh) redisplay_all(hdc, x, y);
```

When the refresh flag is set, the animate function calls redisplay_all to update the entire window. The next section describes how the sprites are drawn on the background.

Updating the Entire Window

In the SPRANIM.CPP file, you find the source code for the function redisplay_all that draws the background and sprites. In a C++-like pseudocode notation, the steps involved in updating the animation are the following:

```
Copy designated portion of background into scratch bitmap
    using BitBlt.
```

```
for(all Sprite objects in the animation)
{
    Copy the Sprite's mask to the scratch bitmap using
        BitBlt in the SRCAND mode.

    Copy the Sprite's image to the scratch bitmap using
        BitBlt in the SRCPAINT mode.

    if(Sprite has a dproc)
        Call dproc.
}

Copy the scratch bitmap into the window using BitBlt
    in the SRCCOPY mode.
```

Thus, the basic idea is to copy the background into a scratch bitmap and draw all the sprites on the background. Because the SpriteAnimation class stores the sprites ordered by display priority, this step draws the sprites in the correct order.

Figure 21.8 illustrates the process of drawing a sprite on a background. Here are the steps:

1. Combine the sprite's mask bitmap with the background image using a bitwise AND operation. Remember that the mask is a silhouette of the sprite's image—it is black (all bits 0) on a white (all bits 1) background. This step essentially punches a hole the shape of the sprite in the background image.

2. Combine the sprite's image with the modified background image using a bitwise OR operation. Because the image is on a white (all bits 1) background, this step fills the hole created in the previous step.

FIGURE 21.8.

Drawing a sprite on a background.

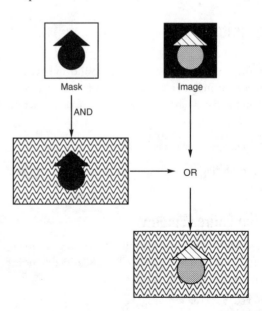

Efficient Animation of Overlapping Sprites

When the whole window does not need to be updated, the animate function draws the sprites using an algorithm that updates the window in an efficient manner. Here is the basic algorithm for efficient updates:

1. For a sprite s that needs updating, determine all other sprites that touch sprite s and are also in need of update. Determine the smallest rectangle that encloses all sprites that satisfy these conditions.
2. Find all stationary sprites that also touch the rectangle and mark them as overlapping.
3. Copy from the background image to the scratch bitmap an area corresponding to the rectangle determined in step 1.
4. Draw all overlapping sprites in the scratch bitmap. Set the status of the sprites as updated so that they are not included again.
5. Copy the rectangle from the scratch bitmap to the window.
6. Repeat steps 1 through 5 for all sprites.

These steps are implemented in the animate function in SPRANIM.CPP. Figure 21.9 depicts the update process for sprite animation.

FIGURE 21.9.

Updating the display to animate sprites.

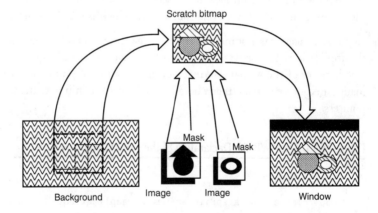

Sprite bitmaps

A Sample Animation Program

This section describes a sample MFC-based Windows program that makes use of the Sprite and SpriteAnimation classes to animate a number of sprites on a background image. The program is in the companion directory—it should be in the CH21 directory after you install the code on your system. When you run the ANIMATE application, you can see a number of sprites, including one with a text message animated on a complex background image. Figure 21.10 shows a sample output of the program (after you select the About item from the Help menu).

FIGURE 21.10.
Output of the sample animation program.

The *AnimationWindow* Class

The ANIMATE program uses an AnimationWindow as its main window. Listing 21.13 shows the declaration of the AnimationWindow class, which is derived from CFrameWnd.

AnimationWindow has a pointer to the SpriteAnimation object that manages the animation for the application. The SpriteAnimation object is created and initialized in the WM_CREATE message handler of the AnimationWindow class. An array of pointers to the Sprite objects is also maintained in AnimationWindow because we have to manipulate the Sprite objects using these pointers.

Listing 21.13. ANIMWIN.H. Declaration of the AnimationWindow class.

```
//----------------------------------------------------------------
// File: animwin.h
//
// Window classes for a sprite animation application.
//----------------------------------------------------------------
#if !defined(__ANIMWIN_H)
#define __ANIMWIN_H

#include "spranim.h"  // Sprite animation class

#define IDM_ABOUT 200

#define SPRITE_ANIMATE 1 // ID of timer for moving and
                         // drawing sprites

const short AnimBGWidth = 640;
const short AnimBGHeight = 480;
```

```
class AnimationWindow : public CFrameWnd
{
public:
    AnimationWindow(const char far *title);

    ~AnimationWindow();

    afx_msg void OnPaint();

    afx_msg int OnCreate(LPCREATESTRUCT lpcs);
    afx_msg void OnClose()
    {
        KillTimer(SPRITE_ANIMATE);
        CFrameWnd::OnClose();
    }
    afx_msg void OnTimer(UINT timer_id);
    afx_msg BOOL OnQueryNewPalette();
    afx_msg void OnPaletteChanged(CWnd *pFocusWnd);
    afx_msg void About();

private:
    SpriteAnimation  *anim;
    Sprite           **s;
    short            top;    // The point where the background
    short            left;   // is displayed
    short            width;
    short            height;

    void move_sprites();

    DECLARE_MESSAGE_MAP()
};
#endif
```

Sprites in the Sample Animation

For this sample application, the file ANIMWIN.CPP includes the definition of the sprites. A SpriteInfo structure is defined to hold the information needed to define a Sprite. A static array of SpriteInfo structures, called sprite_data, defines all the sprites for this application. Notice that the last SpriteInfo structure in the sprite_data array does not provide any filenames for the image and mask bitmaps. This Sprite is used to illustrate the use of a drawing procedure (the dproc member variable of a Sprite). I use the function draw_text (Listing 21.14) to display a text message that can be animated like a bitmapped sprite.

Initializing the Animation

The entire animation is set up in the OnCreate function (Listing 21.14) that handles the WM_CREATE message sent by Windows to the AnimationWindow when the window is created. The initialization involves creating a SpriteAnimation object and an array of Sprite objects and adding each Sprite object to the SpriteAnimation.

Animation Strategy

The strategy for this animation is to use a Windows timer event to move the sprites and update the display. Thus, you call SetTimer to set up a 50-millisecond timer in the OnCreate function.

The WM_TIMER events are handled by the OnTimer function (Listing 21.14). OnTimer first checks to ensure that the timer ID matches the one used when the timer was started. Then the sprites are moved. Finally, the display is updated by calling the animate function of the SpriteAnimation object that manages this animation.

In Listing 21.14, the sprites merely bounce back and forth within the confines of the animation's background. The move_sprites function handles the details of the movement algorithm.

Listing 21.14. ANIMWIN.CPP. Implementation of the AnimationWindow class.

```
//----------------------------------------------------------------
// File: animwin.cpp
//
// Member functions for the AnimationWindow class.
//----------------------------------------------------------------
#include <stdlib.h>
#include <string.h>
#include "animwin.h"

struct SpriteInfo
{
    SpriteInfo(char* imgfname, char* mskfname,
               short xp, short yp, short xv, short yv,
               short prio) :
               imagefilename(imgfname), maskfilename(mskfname),
               xpos(xp), ypos(yp), xvel(xv), yvel(yv),
               priority(prio) {}

    char* imagefilename;
    char* maskfilename;
    short  xpos, ypos;     // Initial x-y position
    short  xvel, yvel;     // Initial x- and y-velocity
    short  priority;
};
// Declare an array of sprites to be loaded from image files
static SpriteInfo sprite_data[] =
{
    SpriteInfo("face1.bmp",  "face1m.bmp", 10, 10, 3, 2, 4),
    SpriteInfo("ring.bmp",   "ringm.bmp", 200, 10, -3, 2, 5),
    SpriteInfo("car.bmp",    "carm.bmp",  10, 200, -1, -1, 2),
    SpriteInfo("strange.bmp","strangem.bmp",100, 100, 1, 1, 1),
    SpriteInfo(NULL, NULL, 100, 50, 1, 0, 99)
};
// Total number of sprites
static int numsprites = sizeof(sprite_data) /
                        sizeof(sprite_data[0]);

void CALLBACK draw_text(HDC hdc, short x, short y,
                        LPVOID data);
```

```
struct TEXT_DATA
{
    LPSTR   text;
    size_t numchars;
};
static TEXT_DATA dt;
static LPSTR msg = "Hello, There!";
//-------------------------------------------------------------
// Define the message map for AnimationWindow

BEGIN_MESSAGE_MAP(AnimationWindow, CFrameWnd)
    ON_WM_CREATE()
    ON_WM_CLOSE()
    ON_WM_TIMER()
    ON_WM_PAINT()
    ON_WM_QUERYNEWPALETTE()
    ON_WM_PALETTECHANGED()
    ON_COMMAND(IDM_ABOUT, About)
END_MESSAGE_MAP()
//-------------------------------------------------------------
// AnimationWindow:: A n i m a t i o n W i n d o w ( ... )
AnimationWindow::AnimationWindow(const char *title) :
                    CFrameWnd(),
                    anim(0), top(0), left(0),
                    width(AnimBGWidth), height(AnimBGHeight)
{
    VERIFY(LoadAccelTable("MainAccelTable"));
    VERIFY(Create(NULL, title, WS_OVERLAPPEDWINDOW,
                rectDefault, NULL, "MAINMENU"));

}
//-------------------------------------------------------------
// A n i m a t i o n : : O n C r e a t e
// Initialize everything for the animation

int AnimationWindow::OnCreate(LPCREATESTRUCT lpcs)
{
    if(CFrameWnd::OnCreate(lpcs) == -1) return -1;

// Get a DC for this window
    HDC hdc = ::GetDC(GetSafeHwnd());

// Set timers for moving sprites and displaying them
    SetTimer(SPRITE_ANIMATE, 50, NULL);

// Create an instance of the SpriteAnimation class and
// load the images (background plus the sprites)

    anim = new SpriteAnimation(hdc, width, height, "animbg.bmp");

// Create the array of sprites
    s = new Sprite*[numsprites];
    int i;
    for(i = 0; i < numsprites; i++)
    {
        s[i] = new Sprite(hdc, sprite_data[i].imagefilename,
                    sprite_data[i].maskfilename);
        s[i]->priority(sprite_data[i].priority);
```

continues

Listing 21.14. continued

```cpp
        s[i]->newpos(sprite_data[i].xpos, sprite_data[i].ypos);
// Add sprite to animation
        anim->add(s[i]);
    }

// The last sprite is used to display a text string
    s[numsprites-1]->width(100);
    s[numsprites-1]->height(16);
    dt.text = msg;
    dt.numchars = strlen(msg);
    s[numsprites-1]->drawproc(draw_text, &dt);
    s[numsprites-1]->active();
    s[numsprites-1]->update();

// Release the DC
    ::ReleaseDC(GetSafeHwnd(), hdc);

    return 0;
}
//-------------------------------------------------------------
//  ~ A n i m a t i o n W i n d o w
//  Destructor for the animation window.

AnimationWindow::~AnimationWindow()
{
    if(anim != NULL) delete anim;
    if(s != NULL) delete[] s;
}
//-------------------------------------------------------------
// A n i m a t i o n W i n d o w : : O n T i m e r
// Handle WM_TIMER ONents

void AnimationWindow::OnTimer(UINT timer_id)
{
    switch(timer_id)
    {
        case SPRITE_ANIMATE:
            {
                HDC hdc = ::GetDC(GetSafeHwnd());
// Move the sprites
                move_sprites();
                anim->animate(hdc, top, left);
                ::ReleaseDC(GetSafeHwnd(), hdc);
            }
            break;

        default:
            break;
    }
}
//-------------------------------------------------------------
//  AnimationWindow:: O n P a i n t
//  Draw everything in the window

void AnimationWindow::OnPaint()
{
```

```
        if(anim != NULL)
        {
            CPaintDC dc(this);
            anim->set_refresh(TRUE);
            anim->animate(dc.GetSafeHdc(), top, left);
        }
}
//------------------------------------------------------------
// AnimationWindow:: O n Q u e r y N e w P a l e t t e
// Realize palette for the animation's background

BOOL AnimationWindow::OnQueryNewPalette()
{
    if(anim == NULL) return 0;
    if(anim->bgimage() == NULL) return 0;

    HPALETTE hpal = anim->bgimage()->palette();
    short changed = 0;
    if(hpal)
    {
        CClientDC dc(this);
        CPalette *pPal = CPalette::FromHandle(hpal);
        CPalette *pOldPal = dc.SelectPalette(pPal, FALSE);

        changed = dc.RealizePalette();
        dc.SelectPalette(pOldPal, FALSE);

        if(changed)
        {
            Invalidate(TRUE);
            UpdateWindow();
        }
    }
    return changed;
}
//------------------------------------------------------------
// AnimationWindow:: O n P a l e t t e C h a n g e d
// Handle a change in system palette

void AnimationWindow::OnPaletteChanged(CWnd *pFocusWnd)
{
    if(pFocusWnd == this) return;
    if(anim == NULL) return;
    if(anim->bgimage() == NULL) return;

    HPALETTE hpal = anim->bgimage()->palette();
    short changed = 0;
    if(hpal)
    {
        CClientDC dc(this);
        CPalette *pPal = CPalette::FromHandle(hpal);
        CPalette *pOldPal = dc.SelectPalette(pPal, FALSE);

        changed = dc.RealizePalette();

        if(changed)
        {
            dc.UpdateColors();
```

continues

Listing 21.14. continued

```
        }
        dc.SelectPalette(pOldPal, FALSE);
    }
}
//-----------------------------------------------------------
// A n i m a t i o n W i n d o w :: A b o u t
// Display the "About..." box

void AnimationWindow::About()
{
    CDialog About("ABOUTANIMATION", this);
    About.DoModal();
}
//-----------------------------------------------------------
// m o v e _ s p r i t e s
// Move the sprites

void AnimationWindow::move_sprites()
{
    int i;
    for(i = 0; i < numsprites; i++)
    {
        if(s[i]->xpos() <= 0 ¦¦ s[i]->xpos() >= width)
            sprite_data[i].xvel = -sprite_data[i].xvel;

        if(s[i]->ypos() <= 0 ¦¦ s[i]->ypos() >= height)
            sprite_data[i].yvel = -sprite_data[i].yvel;

        s[i]->move(sprite_data[i].xvel, sprite_data[i].yvel);
    }
}
//-----------------------------------------------------------
void CALLBACK draw_text(HDC hdc, short x, short y,
                        LPVOID data)
{
    TEXT_DATA *td = (TEXT_DATA*)data;
    SetBkMode(hdc, TRANSPARENT);

    SetTextColor(hdc, RGB(255,255,0));
    TextOut(hdc, x, y, td->text, td->numchars);
}
```

The ANIMATE Application

Listing 21.15 shows the main program of the ANIMATE application. Like all MFC-based Windows programs, the ANIMATE application creates an instance of its main window, an `AnimationWindow` object, which automatically starts the program. All application-specific work is done in the `AnimationWindow` class, described in previous sections.

Listing 21.15. ANIMATE.CPP. Main program of the animation application.

```
//------------------------------------------------------------
//  File:  animate.cpp
//
//  A Windows application that animates a number of sprites
//  over a background image. Also enables user to move an
//  image around using the mouse.
//------------------------------------------------------------

#include "animwin.h"

//------------------------------------------------------------
class AnimationApp: public CWinApp
{
public:

// Define function to initialize application's main window
    BOOL InitInstance();
};
//------------------------------------------------------------
//  A n i m a t i o n A p p : : I n i t I n s t a n c e

BOOL AnimationApp::InitInstance()
{
    Enable3dControls();
    m_pMainWnd = new AnimationWindow("Sprite Animation");

    m_pMainWnd->ShowWindow(m_nCmdShow);
    m_pMainWnd->UpdateWindow();

    return TRUE;
}
//------------------------------------------------------------
//
//  Create an instance of the application and "run" it.

    AnimationApp Animation;
```

Building ANIMATE.EXE

Use Visual C++ 2.0 to build the ANIMATE application. The companion disk has all the files needed to build the executable, ANIMATE.EXE. In particular, the project file, ANIMATE.MAK, lists the files necessary to build the application. You should be able to build ANIMATE.EXE by selecting Rebuild All from the Project menu. Once the program is successfully built, you can run it directly from Visual C++ or by selecting the Run option from the program manager.

One of the files that you need to build ANIMATE.EXE is the resource file, ANIMATE.RC, which is included on the companion disk.

Summary

Images are an integral part of many Windows applications and you need lots of images to create interesting applications. Whether you draw images in a paint program or scan from a hard copy, the images are ultimately stored in image files that you have to interpret and use. The basic information in an image file is the same—the dimensions of the image and the pixel array that makes up the image—but there are many ways to organize this information in a file. There are many popular image file formats, such as PCX, GIF, TIFF, Windows BMP, and Truevision Targa. This chapter describes three popular file formats (BMP, PCX, and TIFF) and presents a C++ class hierarchy that helps you read image files and display images in Microsoft Windows.

The latter part of this chapter uses the image classes to define small images known as sprites that can be animated—moved smoothly—over a background image. Sprite animation is one of the common tasks in many multimedia applications. The obvious approach of erasing and redrawing sprites produces an undesirable flicker. One way to get around this problem is to draw the images on an offscreen bitmap and copy the final image to the screen using the Windows API function BitBlt. The last part of this chapter shows the Sprite and SpriteAnimation classes that enable you to animate sprites over a background image using the offscreen bitmap technique. A sample application, ANIMATE, illustrates how to use the sprite animation classes.

22

Handling Mouse and Keyboard Events

Chapters 19 through 21 cover the topics of graphics, text, and image output in Windows. Almost all Windows applications also require some input from the user in the form of mouse button presses and keystrokes. The mouse is important for the point-and-click parts of the Windows graphical user interface; the keyboard is indispensable for text entry. Whether it is annotating a figure or typing in a document, most Windows programs have to handle keyboard input to get the job done. This chapter briefly describes how to handle mouse and keyboard inputs under Windows.

Keyboard Messages

Like any other hardware device, Windows handles the keyboard through a device driver. When the user presses and releases a key, the keyboard driver decodes the key and passes the information to Windows. Windows provides the information in the form of keyboard messages to the program currently designated to receive keyboard input. Unlike the mouse, which has a cursor to indicate the window to which the mouse input is directed, Windows needs the concept of the input focus to deliver keyboard input to a specific window.

Input Focus

Windows can send mouse input to a specific window by noting which window contains the mouse cursor. There is no similar way to decide which window should receive keyboard inputs. To solve this problem, Windows uses the concept of *input focus*. The window with the input focus receives all keyboard messages, regardless of the cursor's location. The concept of input focus is tied to that of the *active window* because the active window or a child of the active window always has the input focus. The user makes a window active by clicking the mouse button with the mouse cursor placed inside that window.

Windows sends the WM_SETFOCUS message to a window when it becomes active (and receives the input focus) and the WM_KILLFOCUS message when the window becomes inactive (and loses the focus). As you will see later, you display or hide the cursor or *caret*—the blinking vertical line that marks the location where text is inserted in a window—in response to the WM_SETFOCUS and WM_KILLFOCUS messages. Before discussing text entry, let's consider how to handle the keyboard messages.

Handling Keystrokes

Windows places the keystrokes into two categories: *system keystrokes* and *nonsystem keystrokes*. The system keystrokes are those that are important to Windows because they are used for system functions, such as accessing the pull-down menus or switching the active window. Usually, any key pressed in combination with the Alt key is considered a system keystroke. When the user presses and releases a system key, Windows sends a WM_SYSKEYDOWN message followed by a WM_SYSKEYUP message. Because the system keys are meant for system functions, you do not have to handle these events; Windows takes care of these messages.

Nonsystem keystrokes comprise all other keys besides the system keystrokes. When the user presses and releases any nonsystem key, Windows sends a WM_KEYDOWN message followed by a WM_KEYUP message. If you want to process these keystrokes in your MFC-based Windows application, you have to provide a member function to handle these messages in the main window class. For example, you declare the member function that handles the WM_KEYDOWN messages as follows:

```
afx_msg void OnKeyDown(
    UINT nChar,        // Virtual keycode of key pressed
    UINT nRepCnt,      // Number of times key was pressed
    UINT nFlags);      // An 8-bit scan code of the key
                       // as well as other status bits
```

Additionally, you have to include an appropriate entry in the message map of that window class:

```
// Assume that the window class is MyWindow, derived from
// CFrameWnd

BEGIN_MESSAGE_MAP(MyWindow, CFrameWnd)
    ON_WM_KEYDOWN()
//...
END_MESSAGE_MAP()
```

Interpreting the Keystroke Message

In the handler for the WM_KEYDOWN message, you have to determine which key was pressed. If you use the Windows API directly, Windows provides this information in an encoded form. However, MFC makes it easier to access such information in message handling functions—MFC passes the information through the arguments of the function. For the WM_KEYDOWN message, the three arguments of the OnKeyDown function provide a number of details about the keypress, such as the repeat count (the number of keystrokes in the message) and the virtual keycode identifying the key that the user pressed. The *virtual keycode* is a number assigned to each key on a keyboard. Even the mouse buttons are assigned a virtual keycode. Most of the commonly used virtual keycodes have symbolic names that are defined in the header file <winuser.h>. Table 22.1 shows a list of key names, their numeric keycodes, and the keyboard (or mouse) equivalents.

Table 22.1. Virtual key names.

Symbolic Name	Value (in Hex)	Mouse or Keyboard Equivalent (U.S. English Keyboard)
VK_LBUTTON	01	Left mouse button
VK_RBUTTON	02	Right mouse button

continues

Table 22.1. continued

Symbolic Name	Value (in Hex)	Mouse or Keyboard Equivalent (U.S. English Keyboard)
VK_CANCEL	03	Ctrl+Break key
VK_MBUTTON	04	Middle mouse button (for a three-button mouse)
VK_BACK	08	Backspace key
VK_TAB	09	Tab key
VK_CLEAR	0C	5 on numeric keypad with Num Lock off
VK_RETURN	0D	Enter key
VK_SHIFT	10	Shift key
VK_CONTROL	11	Ctrl key
VK_MENU	12	Alt key
VK_PAUSE	13	Pause key
VK_CAPITAL	14	Caps Lock key
VK_ESCAPE	1B	Esc key
VK_SPACE	20	Spacebar
VK_PRIOR	21	Page Up key
VK_NEXT	22	Page Down key
VK_END	23	End key
VK_HOME	24	Home key
VK_LEFT	25	Left arrow key
VK_UP	26	Up arrow key
VK_RIGHT	27	Right arrow key
VK_DOWN	28	Down arrow key
VK_SELECT	29	*No equivalent key*
VK_EXECUTE	2B	*No equivalent key*
VK_SNAPSHOT	2C	Print Screen key for Windows 3.0 and later
VK_INSERT	2D	Insert key
VK_DELETE	2E	Del key
VK_HELP	2F	*No equivalent key*
VK_0 to VK_9	30–39	0 through 9 above the letter keys
VK_A to VK_Z	41–5A	A through Z
VK_NUMPAD0	60	0 on numeric keypad

Symbolic Name	Value (in Hex)	Mouse or Keyboard Equivalent (U.S. English Keyboard)
VK_NUMPAD1	61	1 on numeric keypad
VK_NUMPAD2	62	2 on numeric keypad
VK_NUMPAD3	63	3 on numeric keypad
VK_NUMPAD4	64	4 on numeric keypad
VK_NUMPAD5	65	5 on numeric keypad
VK_NUMPAD6	66	6 on numeric keypad
VK_NUMPAD7	67	7 on numeric keypad
VK_NUMPAD8	68	8 on numeric keypad
VK_NUMPAD9	69	9 on numeric keypad
VK_MULTIPLY	6A	Multiply key
VK_ADD	6B	Add key
VK_SEPARATOR	6C	*No equivalent key*
VK_SUBTRACT	6D	Subtract key
VK_DECIMAL	6E	Decimal point key
VK_DIVIDE	6F	Divide key
VK_F1	70	F1 key
VK_F2	71	F2 key
VK_F3	72	F3 key
VK_F4	73	F4 key
VK_F5	74	F5 key
VK_F6	75	F6 key
VK_F7	76	F7 key
VK_F8	77	F8 key
VK_F9	78	F9 key
VK_F10	79	F10 key
VK_F11	7A	F11 key
VK_F12	7B	F12 key
VK_F13	7C	*No equivalent key*
VK_F14	7D	*No equivalent key*
VK_F15	7E	*No equivalent key*
VK_F16	7F	*No equivalent key*
VK_F17	80	*No equivalent key*

continues

Table 22.1. continued

Symbolic Name	Value (in Hex)	Mouse or Keyboard Equivalent (U.S. English Keyboard)
VK_F18	81	*No equivalent key*
VK_F19	82	*No equivalent key*
VK_F20	83	*No equivalent key*
VK_F21	84	*No equivalent key*
VK_F22	85	*No equivalent key*
VK_F23	86	*No equivalent key*
VK_F24	87	*No equivalent key*
VK_NUMLOCK	90	Num Lock key
VK_SCROLL	91	Scroll Lock key

In the WM_KEYDOWN message handler, OnKeyDown, you can check for a specific key by testing the nChar field:

```
// Assume MyWindow is the window class
void MyWindow::OnKeyDown(UINT nChar, UINT nRepCnt,
                         UINT nFlags)
{
//...
// Check whether user pressed the F1 function key
    if(nChar == VK_F1)
    {
// Do whatever you had planned to do in response to the F1 key
//...
    }
}
```

Shift and Toggle Keys

Keys such as Shift, Ctrl, Alt, Caps Lock, and Num Lock are known as *modifier keys* because they modify the meanings of other keys. Shift, Ctrl, and Alt are collectively referred to as *shift keys*, and Caps Lock and Num Lock are called *toggles*. Sometimes you may want to know whether any modifier key was down during a specific keystroke. (For example, was the Shift key down when the user pressed the Q key?) The arguments of the OnKeyDown function do not tell you the status of these modifier keys. You have to call the GetKeyState function to determine that. For example, to check whether the Shift key is down during the keystroke being processed now, you write the following:

```
// Call GetKeyState inside the keystroke message handler.
    if(GetKeyState(VK_SHIFT) < 0)
    {
// Shift key was down
//...
    }
```

For the shift keys, the return value from GetKeyState has the high bit set to 1 if the key is down. For the toggles such as the Caps Lock key, GetKeyState sets the low-order bit of the return value to 1 if the toggle key is down.

The *WM_CHAR* Message

So far you have seen how to handle raw keystrokes through the WM_KEYDOWN message. These messages give you information about the user's input at a low level. For example, on a U.S. English keyboard, if the user holds down the Shift key and types 5 (above the letters), Windows sends a WM_KEYDOWN message for the 5 key. It is up to you to call GetKeyState to determine whether the Shift key was pressed. In such situations, all that you might want is a notification from Windows that the user has entered the % symbol (which is what should happen when the user presses the Shift key and types 5 on a U.S. English keyboard). Luckily, Windows provides the WM_CHAR message that directly reports the character entered by the user.

WM_KEYDOWN MESSAGE VERSUS WM_CHAR MESSAGE

The WM_KEYDOWN message reports raw keystrokes, and WM_CHAR provides information on character input. You should be able to handle most keyboard inputs by handling WM_CHAR messages for all alphanumeric input and WM_KEYDOWN messages for noncharacter keys, such as the cursor keys and the function keys.

If you want to handle WM_CHAR messages in your MFC program, you have to include a member function (in the main window class) to handle these messages. The prototype of this member function is the following:

```
afx_msg void OnChar(
    UINT nChar,    // ASCII character code of key pressed
    UINT nRepCnt,  // Number of times key was pressed
    UINT nFlags);  // An 8-bit scan code of the key
                   // as well as other status bits
```

In the OnChar function, you can get the ASCII code of the character in the key argument. Thus, to test for characters such as Backspace, Tab, and the carriage return, include the following code fragment in the OnChar function:

```
void OnChar(UINT nChar, UINT nRepCnt, UINT nFlags)
{
// This is in the WM_CHAR message handler
//...
    switch(nChar)
    {
        case '\r':
// Process carriage return key
            break;

        case '\t':
```

```
// Process TAB key
        break;

     case '\b':
// Process BACKSPACE key
        break;

     default:
// Handle all other keys here (perhaps save in a buffer)
   }
```

The Caret

If you have used any Windows word processor, you have seen the caret. If you are going to accept text input and display the text in a window, you have to display the caret. The caret is a systemwide shared resource—there is only one caret in the system. To use the caret, you have to call CreateCaret first. Then you can position the caret with a call to SetCaretPos and make it visible by calling ShowCaret. Finally, when you no longer need the caret, you have to release it by calling DestroyCaret.

USING THE CARET

If you need the caret, call CreateCaret in the handler for the WM_SETFOCUS message. Release the caret by calling DestroyCaret in the function that handles the WM_KILLFOCUS message. You need the caret only if you plan to accept text input and display the text in a window.

When do you create the caret and when do you destroy it? The answer lies in the way Windows delivers keyboard messages—the keyboard input always goes to the window with the input focus. Thus, you should create the caret when your main window receives input focus and destroy it when the focus moves to some other window.

When you first create the caret, it is hidden. You have to call ShowCaret to make it visible. Additionally, when you draw anything in a window in response to any message other than WM_PAINT, you have to hide the caret first by calling HideCaret and call ShowCaret again when drawing is done.

Mouse Messages

In a graphical user interface such as that in Windows, the mouse is even more important than the keyboard because the essence of a graphical interface is to perform actions by pointing and clicking at graphical objects on the screen. Microsoft Windows supports a mouse with up to three buttons (left, middle, and right). However, most Windows applications assume a mouse with a single button because you can never be sure whether a system has a mouse with more than one button. The lone button is equivalent to the left mouse of a three-button mouse.

As with the keyboard, Windows delivers all mouse inputs through messages. Unlike with the keyboard, there is no confusion over which window gets the mouse input because an on-screen cursor (a small bitmap image) tracks the motion of the mouse. The window with the cursor gets the mouse input. The only exceptions to this rule are the following:

■ A window can capture the mouse (described later) and receive all mouse messages irrespective of the cursor's location.

■ When a system-modal dialog box is on display, no other window can receive mouse messages.

The types of mouse messages depend on the exact area of the window where the cursor lies. Mouse input with the cursor in the client area (the area inside the frame) of a window generates client-area mouse messages. Mouse input with the cursor anywhere else in the window's frame generates nonclient-area mouse messages. Because Windows takes care of the nonclient-area messages, most Windows applications handle the client-area messages only.

DRAG, CLICK, AND DOUBLE-CLICK

The use of the mouse has spawned several new terms. Remember, you *drag* the mouse by moving it while holding down a button. You *click* by pressing and releasing a mouse button without moving the mouse. A *double-click* means two clicks in rapid succession.

Client-Area Mouse Messages

The area of a window inside the borders is referred to as the client area because that's where the application (which Windows views as a client) can draw. Usually applications are concerned with mouse input in this area. There are 10 client-area mouse messages of interest:

■ WM_LBUTTONDOWN

■ WM_MBUTTONDOWN

■ WM_RBUTTONDOWN

■ WM_LBUTTONUP

■ WM_MBUTTONUP

■ WM_RBUTTONUP

■ WM_LBUTTONDBLCLK

■ WM_MBUTTONDBLCLK

■ WM_RBUTTONDBLCLK

■ WM_MOUSEMOVE

As you can surmise from this list, there are three messages (button down, button up, and double-click) per button of a mouse. The tenth event, WM_MOUSEMOVE, tells you the location of the mouse cursor; this message is described in the next section.

One of the commonly handled mouse messages is WM_LBUTTONDOWN. Windows sends the WM_LBUTTONDOWN message when the user presses the left mouse button with the cursor in the client area of a window. A member function, OnLButtonDown is already defined as the WM_LBUTTONDOWN message handler in the CWnd class in MFC. When you derive a new window class from CWnd (or one of the classes derived from CWnd such as CFrameWnd) and you want to handle WM_LBUTTONDOWN messages, you merely declare OnLButton as a member function of your window class:

```
afx_msg void OnLButtonDown(UINT nFlags, CPoint point);
```

Then add the message entry in that window's message map:

```
// Assume that the window class is MyWindow, derived from
// CFrameWnd

BEGIN_MESSAGE_MAP(MyWindow, CFrameWnd)
    ON_WM_LBUTTONDOWN()
//...
END_MESSAGE_MAP()
```

In the OnLButtonDown function's body, you can get the x- and y-coordinates of the cursor position:

```
// Assume that MyWindow is the class derived from CFrameWnd
void MyWindow::OnLButtonDown(UINT nFlags, CPoint point)
{
//...

// Find the x-y position of mouse cursor
    int xpos = point.x;
    int ypos = point.y;
//...
}
```

The x-y coordinates of the cursor are in pixel units with the origin (0,0) at the upper-left corner of the client area. The positive x-axis extends to the right, and the positive y-axis extends down.

You can determine the state of all the mouse buttons as well as that of the Shift and Ctrl keys from the nFlags argument passed to the OnLButtonDown function. Basically, individual bits in the low-order 5 bits of the nFlags argument hold the state of the buttons and the Shift keys. You can test for a specific state by using the bitwise logical operator (&) with a symbolic name. For example, to test whether the Shift key is down, you write the following:

```
void MyWindow::OnLButtonDown(UINT nFlags, CPoint point)
{
//...
```

```
    if(nFlags & MK_SHIFT)
    {
// Yes, the Shift key is down
// Handle the Shift key + Mouse button event
//...
    }
```

To test for the state of the Ctrl key, use similar code, but replace MK_SHIFT with MK_CONTROL.

You can handle the mouse up message, WM_LBUTTONUP, in the same way as you handle WM_LBUTTONDOWN. However, the combination of the button down and button up messages becomes more interesting in combination with WM_MOUSEMOVE messages that are generated when the user moves the mouse.

Handling Mouse Movements

Windows sends WM_MOUSEMOVE messages when the user moves the mouse. To avoid generating too many mouse move messages, Windows does not report every possible position of the mouse. Rather, the WM_MOUSEMOVE messages provide a sampling of the locations that the mouse cursor visits. Yet these reports are good enough to track the position of the mouse.

The most common use of WM_MOUSEMOVE messages is to track the mouse position while the user is moving the mouse and holding down a mouse button. For example, in a drawing program, the user draws a line with the following sequence of steps:

1. Move the mouse cursor to the startpoint of the line and press the mouse button (usually the left button) down.
2. While holding the button down, move to the endpoint of the line.
3. Release the button.

These actions by the user generate a WM_LBUTTONDOWN message followed by a number of WM_MOUSEMOVE events as the user moves the mouse. Finally, when the user releases the button, Windows generates a WM_LBUTTONUP message. If you are writing the drawing program, start by saving the startpoint of the line in the handler for the WM_LBUTTONDOWN message. In the handler for the WM_MOUSEMOVE event, you track the endpoint and provide some visual feedback by drawing a line from the startpoint to the current endpoint. Finally, upon receiving the WM_LBUTTONUP message, you save the endpoint's location and draw the final version of the line.

While the user is drawing the line, you want to ensure that Windows delivers to your application all mouse events, from the starting WM_LBUTTONDOWN event to the final WM_LBUTTONUP event. One way to ensure this is by capturing the mouse. Essentially, you call the SetCapture function upon receiving the WM_LBUTTONDOWN event and call ReleaseCapture when the WM_LBUTTONUP message arrives. SetCapture and ReleaseCapture are member functions of the CWnd class that call similarly named functions from the Windows API.

Controlling the Cursor Shape

In Windows, whenever the user moves the mouse, a cursor tracks the mouse's motions on the display screen. Applications use the cursor's shape to provide feedback. Most of the time, the cursor is an arrow pointing in the upper-left direction. In a text entry area, however, such as a word processor's window or an input field in a dialog box, the cursor changes to an *I-beam*. The I-beam is a thin vertical line with flourishes at the ends that looks like the capital letter I. In drawing programs, a *crosshair cursor* is often used in the drawing area.

Like the stock pens and brushes that you load into a device context, there are stock cursors in Windows. You may have noticed that many applications display an *hourglass cursor* to indicate a possibly lengthy operation. If you want to do the same in your application, here is what you have to do:

1. Load the hourglass cursor in response to the WM_CREATE message:

```
HCURSOR hWait;
//...
// Assume that SampleWindow is our main window class
void SampleWindow::OnCreate(LPCREATESTRUCT lpcs)
{
//...
    hWait = LoadCursor(NULL, IDC_WAIT);
}
```

2. Just before starting the lengthy operation, change the cursor shape by calling the SetCursor function:

```
    HCURSOR hOldCrsr = ::SetCursor(hWait);

// Start lengthy operation
//...

// Change cursor shape when done
    ::SetCursor(hOldCrsr);
```

You could create the cursor on the fly when you need to change it, but preparing the cursor beforehand is faster.

As you can see from the sample code, the hourglass cursor is identified by the symbol IDC_WAIT. The following are some of the other commonly used predefined cursors:

IDC_ARROW   The left-pointing arrow
IDC_IBEAM   The I-beam cursor
IDC_CROSS   A small crosshair

Setting Cursors Based on Location

The previous example of the hourglass cursor is applicable when you change the cursor shape to indicate that the application may take some time before responding to the user again. You may want to change the cursor shape whenever the cursor enters a specific region in your application's main window (as most word processors do when the cursor moves in and out of the text entry area). To do this, you have to handle the WM_SETCURSOR message, which Windows sends when the cursor moves in a window. This gives you a chance to change the cursor shape depending on the location of the mouse.

Assuming that you have loaded the IDC_IBEAM cursor, you can handle the WM_SETCURSOR message as follows:

```
BOOL SampleWindow::OnSetCursor(CWnd* pWnd, UINT nHitTest,
                               UINT message)
{
    if(nHitTest == HTCLIENT)
    {
// Yes, cursor is in the client area
// Now test to see whether cursor is in an area where you want to
// change its shape (this depends on the specific application).

// Assume that change_cursor is TRUE if the cursor should change
// and that c_ibeam is the pointer to a TCursor object that
// is initialized as the I-Beam cursor.
        if(change_cursor)
            SetCursor(hIBeamCrsr);
    }
    else
    {
// Cursor is not in the client area--call message handler
// from base class (assume base class is CFrameWnd)
        return CFrameWnd::OnSetCursor(pWnd, nHitTest, message);
    }
    return TRUE;
}
```

Custom Cursors

Windows API includes the CreateCursor function, which gives you complete control of the cursor shape. For example, you might create a cursor that actually displays the cursor coordinates. You could not define a cursor like this beforehand because the cursor has to change as the user moves it in the window. The solution is to create the cursor on the fly by calling CreateCursor. To create a cursor, you need two monochrome bitmaps:

■ The AND *mask* is a bitmap that is combined with the existing pixels with the bitwise AND operation. The AND mask should be the cursor's shape drawn in black on a white background.

■ The XOR *mask* is a bitmap to be combined with the existing pixels (after the AND mask has been applied) with a bitwise exclusive-OR operation. To get an all-white cursor shape, use an XOR bitmap that is the inverse of the AND bitmap—the cursor shape drawn in white on a black background.

The CreateCursor function expects these two bitmaps as arguments. Here is the prototype of the CreateCursor function:

```
HCURSOR CreateCursor(
    HINSTANCE hinst,       // Handle to application instance
    int       xHot,        // Horizontal position of hot spot
    int       yHot,        // Vertical position of hot spot
    int       nWidth,      // Cursor's width in pixels
    int       nHeight,     // Cursor height in pixels
    const void *ANDmask,   // Pointer to AND mask
    const void *XORmask);  // Pointer to XOR mask
```

The CreateCursor function creates a cursor that has the specified width, height, and bit patterns and returns a handle to the cursor if the function is successful. Otherwise, it returns NULL.

Much of the work in creating a custom cursor is in defining and intializing the AND and XOR bitmaps. Chapter 21, "Displaying Bitmaps in Windows," shows you how to work with bitmaps.

TextIn—A Text Entry Program

To illustrate the techniques for handling keyboard and mouse messages, the rest of this chapter presents TextIn, a simple program that enables the user to enter text in a window. The goal is to show you some sample code that puts to work most of the functions described earlier in this chapter. TextIn enables you to enter text from the keyboard, move the lines of text up and down with the arrow keys, and indicate the text entry point with a click of the mouse. Before you read the code, try running the TextIn program—the companion disk contains the source files and the executable for TextIn. That way you can relate the actions of the program to code that implements those actions.

The *Caret* Class

Although the TextIn class is relatively simple, the example defines a separate class to represent a caret so that it can be used in other projects in the future. Listing 22.1 shows the file CARET.H. This declares the Caret class that creates and manages a caret. The Caret class has the following data members:

■ HWND   hwnd; identifies the window where the caret is displayed.

■ HFONT hfont; is the font being used to display text. The caret's dimensions and position depend on the font.

■ HDC   hdc; is a DC used to get information about the font.

■ short active_flag; indicates whether the caret is active.

- short `cwidth, height`; are the width and height of the caret, respectively.

- short `xref, yref`; denote the starting point of the line of text on which the caret rests.

- short `xpix`; is the x-coordinate of the caret's current position, in pixels.

- char `*line`; is the line of text on which the caret rests.

- short `cpos`; is the character position of the caret.

Listing 22.1. CARET.H. Declaration of the Caret class.

```
//-----------------------------------------------------------------
// File: caret.h
// Declares the Caret class that models and controls the caret.
//-----------------------------------------------------------------
#if !defined(__CARET_H)
#define __CARET_H

#include <afx.h>
#include <afxwin.h>

class Caret
{
public:
    Caret(HWND _hwnd, HFONT _hfont);

    ~Caret();

    virtual void show() { ShowCaret(hwnd);}
    virtual void hide() { HideCaret(hwnd);}

    void xstart(int x) { xref = x;}
    void ystart(int y) { yref = y;}
    int xstart() { return xref;}
    int ystart() { return yref;}

    void charpos(int cp);
    int charpos() { return cpos;}

    void caret_height(int ch) { cheight = ch;}
    int caret_height() { return cheight;}

    void active()
    {
        if(active_flag) return;
        CreateCaret(hwnd, 0, cwidth, cheight);
        SetCaretPos(xpix, yref);
        ShowCaret(hwnd);
        active_flag = 1;
    }
    void inactive()
    {
      if(!active_flag) return;
      DestroyCaret();
        active_flag = 0;
```

continues

Listing 22.1. continued

```
    }
    int is_active() { return active_flag;}

    char *current_line() { return line;}
    void current_line(char *cl) { line = cl;}

    void font(HFONT hf);

protected:
    HWND  hwnd;
    HFONT hfont;
    CDC   *ic;
    int   active_flag;
    int   cwidth;
    int   cheight;
    int   xref;
    int   yref;
    int   xpix;
    char  *line;
    int   cpos;
};

#endif
```

Listing 22.2 shows the file CARET.CPP that implements some of Caret's member functions. Several important member functions, such as show, hide, active, and inactive, are defined directly in the header file CARET.H. In particular, the active function creates the caret and inactive destroys it. Thus, you should call active in response to the WM_SETFOCUS message and call inactive in response to the WM_KILLFOCUS message.

Listing 22.2. CARET.CPP. Implementation of the Caret class.

```
//-----------------------------------------------------------
// File: caret.cpp
// Implements the Caret class that models and controls the caret.
//-----------------------------------------------------------
#include "caret.h"

// -----------------------------------------------------------
// Caret::  C a r e t
// Constructs a caret

Caret::Caret(HWND _hwnd, HFONT _hfont) : hwnd(_hwnd),
    hfont(_hfont), xref(0), yref(0), xpix(0),
    line(NULL), cpos(0), active_flag(0), ic(0)
{
    TEXTMETRIC tm;

// Create an information context (to get font dimensions)
    ic = new CDC;
    ic->CreateIC("DISPLAY", 0, 0, 0);
```

```
    CFont *pOldFont = ic->SelectObject(CFont::FromHandle(hfont));

    ic->GetTextMetrics(&tm);
    ic->SelectObject(pOldFont);

    cwidth = GetSystemMetrics(SM_CXBORDER);
    cheight = tm.tmHeight;
}
//------------------------------------------------------------
// Caret:: ~ C a r e t
// Destroy a caret

Caret::~Caret()
{
    if(active_flag)
    {
        HideCaret(hwnd);
        DestroyCaret();
    }
    delete ic;
}
//------------------------------------------------------------
// Caret:: ch a r p o s
// Set the character position

void Caret::charpos(int cp)
{
    cpos = cp;

// Determine width of string up to specified character position
    CFont *pOldFont = ic->SelectObject(CFont::FromHandle(hfont));
    CSize txtsz = ic->GetTextExtent(line, cpos);
    int width = txtsz.cx;
    ic->SelectObject(pOldFont);

    xpix = xref + width;

// If caret is active, set its position
    if(active_flag) SetCaretPos(xpix, yref);
}
//------------------------------------------------------------
// Caret:: f o n t
// Set a new font

void Caret::font(HFONT hf)
{
    TEXTMETRIC tm;

    hfont = hf;

    CFont *pOldFont = ic->SelectObject(CFont::FromHandle(hfont));

    ic->GetTextMetrics(&tm);
    ic->SelectObject(pOldFont);

    cheight = tm.tmHeight;
}
```

Other TextIn Classes

In addition to the supporting class Caret, TextIn relies on the TextInWindow class for its main window and the TextInApp class to represent the entire application. Listing 22.3 shows the declaration of these classes in the file TEXTIN.H.

As you can see from the declaration of the TextInWindow class, the TextIn application maintains a 512-byte buffer that holds any text entered by the user. The text is stored as a single array of bytes with a single newline character (\n) marking the end of a line. The TextInWindow class has a pointer to a Caret object that represents the caret displayed in the window. Most of the other data members are used to track the number of characters and the number of lines in the buffer.

Listing 22.3. TEXTIN.H. Declaration of the classes in TextIn.

```
//------------------------------------------------------------------
// File: textin.h
//
// Declares classes used in the TextIn application that
// enables the user to enter text in a window.
//------------------------------------------------------------------
#if !defined(__TEXTIN_H)
#define __TEXTIN_H

#include <string.h>
#include <stdio.h>

#include "caret.h"

// Resource identifiers

#define IDM_ABOUT      200
#define IDM_SELFONT    201

const int MAXCHR = 512;

// Declare the main window class

class TextInWindow : public CFrameWnd
{
public:
    TextInWindow(const char far *title);
    ~TextInWindow()
    {
        if(m_pFont) delete m_pFont;
        if(m_pCaret) delete m_pCaret;
    }

    afx_msg void CMSelFont();
    afx_msg void About();
    afx_msg void OnPaint();

    afx_msg int OnCreate(LPCREATESTRUCT lpcs);

    afx_msg void OnChar(UINT key, UINT repeatCount, UINT flags);
```

```
    afx_msg void OnKeyDown(UINT key, UINT repeatCount, UINT flags);
    afx_msg void OnLButtonDown(UINT modKeys, CPoint point);

    afx_msg BOOL OnSetCursor(CWnd *pWnd, UINT nHitTest,
                             UINT message);

    afx_msg void OnSetFocus(CWnd *pOldFocusWnd)
    {
        m_pCaret->charpos(m_CurPos);
        m_pCaret->active();
    }
    afx_msg void OnKillFocus(CWnd *pNewFocusWnd)
    {
        m_pCaret->inactive();
    }
    void reposition_caret()
    {
        m_pCaret->hide();
        m_pCaret->inactive();
        m_pCaret->ystart(m_nLineNum * m_LineHeight);
        m_pCaret->charpos(m_CurPos);
        m_pCaret->active();
    }
private:
    char                    m_aTxtBuf[MAXCHR];
    LOGFONT                 m_LogFont;
    COLORREF                m_FontColor;
    CFont                   *m_pFont;
    HCURSOR                 m_hIBeamCursor;
    Caret                   *m_pCaret;
    int                     m_InPos;
    int                     m_CurPos;
    int                     m_xMargin;
    int                     m_LineHeight;
    int                     m_nLineNum;
    int                     m_nCount;
    int                     m_nTotalLines;

    DECLARE_MESSAGE_MAP()
};

// Declare the application class

class TextInApp : public CWinApp
{
public:
    BOOL InitInstance();
};

#endif
```

Listing 22.4 shows the file TEXTIN.CPP that implements the `TextInWindow` and `TextInApp` classes. Note that the `Caret` object is created and initialized in the `WMCreate` member function of the `TextInWindow` class. The `WMCreate` function handles the `WM_CREATE` message that Windows sends when the window is first created.

Code from the FontSee application in Chapter 20, "Displaying Text in Windows," is reused to enable the user to select a font in the TextIn application as well. You can see this code in the CMSelFont function in Listing 22.4.

You might find the OnPaint function interesting. It displays the text from the buffer one line at a time by looking for the newline character that marks the end of each line (except for the last line, which does not have a newline).

TextIn's text entry capability comes from the OnChar function that handles the WM_CHAR messages. The OnChar function shows code to handle a number of special characters. In particular, look in the OnChar function to see how to delete a character in response to the Backspace key and how to insert a newline when the user presses the Enter key. The deletion of a newline character poses some problems because you have to collapse two consecutive lines into one.

Recall that your application should accept most of the text input through the WM_CHAR messages, but it has to handle the WM_KEYDOWN messages to respond to special keys such as the arrow keys and function keys. To illustrate this concept, TextIn includes the OnKeyDown function that responds to WM_KEYDOWN messages and handles the up and down arrow keys.

The user can move the text insertion point by positioning the cursor on a character and pressing the left mouse button. This event is handled in the OnLButtonDown function that responds to WM_LBUTTONDOWN messages.

Listing 22.4. TEXTIN.CPP. Implementation of the classes in TextIn.

```
//-------------------------------------------------------------
// File: textin.cpp
//
// Implements several classes used in the TextIn application
// that enables the user to enter text in a window.
//-------------------------------------------------------------
#include <afxdlgs.h>
#include "textin.h"

// Define the message map for TextInWindow
BEGIN_MESSAGE_MAP(TextInWindow, CFrameWnd)
    ON_WM_CREATE()
    ON_WM_PAINT()
    ON_WM_CHAR()
    ON_WM_KEYDOWN()
    ON_WM_LBUTTONDOWN()
    ON_WM_SETCURSOR()
    ON_WM_SETFOCUS()
    ON_WM_KILLFOCUS()
    ON_COMMAND(IDM_ABOUT,    About)
    ON_COMMAND(IDM_SELFONT, CMSelFont)
END_MESSAGE_MAP()


//-------------------------------------------------------------
// TextInApp:: I n i t I n s t a n c e
// Initialize the main window of the TextIn application
```

```
BOOL TextInApp::InitInstance()
{
    Enable3dControls();

    m_pMainWnd = new TextInWindow("TextIn");

    m_pMainWnd->ShowWindow(m_nCmdShow);
    m_pMainWnd->UpdateWindow();

    return TRUE;
}
//------------------------------------------------------------
// TextInWindow:: T e x t I n W i n d o w
// Constructor for the TextInWindow

TextInWindow::TextInWindow(const char *title)
    : CFrameWnd(), m_InPos(0), m_CurPos(0), m_nLineNum(0),
      m_nCount(0), m_pFont(0), m_FontColor(RGB(0,0,0))
{
// Create the window

    POINT p;
    p.x = GetSystemMetrics(SM_CXSCREEN) / 10;
    p.y = GetSystemMetrics(SM_CYSCREEN) / 10;

    SIZE s;
    s.cx = p.x * 8;
    s.cy = p.y * 8;

    VERIFY(LoadAccelTable("MainAccelTable"));
    VERIFY(Create(NULL, title, WS_OVERLAPPEDWINDOW, CRect(p, s),
           NULL, "MAINMENU"));

// Initialize the LOGFONT structure m_LogFont
// First zero out the entire structure

    memset(&m_LogFont, 0, sizeof(LOGFONT));

// Now set the needed fields
    m_LogFont.lfHeight = 12;
    m_LogFont.lfWeight = FW_NORMAL;
    m_LogFont.lfCharSet = ANSI_CHARSET;
    m_LogFont.lfOutPrecision = OUT_DEFAULT_PRECIS;
    m_LogFont.lfClipPrecision = CLIP_DEFAULT_PRECIS;
    m_LogFont.lfQuality = PROOF_QUALITY;
    m_LogFont.lfPitchAndFamily = VARIABLE_PITCH;
    strcpy(m_LogFont.lfFaceName, "Helvetica");

    m_pFont = new CFont;
    m_pFont->CreateFontIndirect(&m_LogFont);
}
//------------------------------------------------------------
// TextInWindow:: O n C r e a t e
// Handle the WM_CREATE message.

int TextInWindow::OnCreate(LPCREATESTRUCT lpcs)
{
```

continues

Listing 22.4. continued

```
    if(CFrameWnd::OnCreate(lpcs) == -1) return -1;

// Get dimensions of current font
    CDC ic;
    ic.CreateIC("DISPLAY", 0, 0, 0);
    TEXTMETRIC tm;
    CFont *pOldFont = ic.SelectObject(m_pFont);
    ic.GetTextMetrics(&tm);
    ic.SelectObject(pOldFont);

    m_LineHeight = tm.tmHeight + tm.tmExternalLeading;
    m_xMargin = tm.tmAveCharWidth;

    strcpy(m_aTxtBuf, "Hello...\n123 ");
    m_nCount = strlen(m_aTxtBuf);
    m_nTotalLines = 2;

// Initialize the caret
    m_pCaret = new Caret(GetSafeHwnd(),
                         (HFONT)m_pFont->GetSafeHandle());
    m_pCaret->current_line(m_aTxtBuf);
    m_pCaret->xstart(m_xMargin);
    m_pCaret->ystart(m_nLineNum * m_LineHeight);

// Create an I-Beam cursor for use in the text display area
    m_hIBeamCursor= LoadCursor(NULL, IDC_IBEAM);

    return 0;
}
//--------------------------------------------------------------
// TextInWindow:: C M S e l F o n t
// Display the Font Selection dialog from COMMDLG.DLL and get
// the user's choice of font.

void TextInWindow::CMSelFont()
{
// Activate "choose font" dialog...
    CFontDialog fd(&m_LogFont,
                    CF_INITTOLOGFONTSTRUCT | CF_BOTH |
                    CF_EFFECTS);
    fd.m_cf.rgbColors = m_FontColor;

    if(fd.DoModal() == IDOK)
    {
// Yes, user has chosen a font.
// Make sure window gets redrawn with new font.
        m_FontColor = fd.m_cf.rgbColors;

// Create the new font
        delete m_pFont;
        m_pFont = new CFont;
        m_pFont->CreateFontIndirect(&m_LogFont);

// Get dimensions of characters in this font
        CDC ic;
        ic.CreateIC("DISPLAY", 0, 0, 0);
```

```
        CFont *pOldFont = ic.SelectObject(m_pFont);

        TEXTMETRIC tm;
        ic.GetTextMetrics(&tm);
        ic.SelectObject(pOldFont);

        m_LineHeight = tm.tmHeight + tm.tmExternalLeading;
        m_xMargin = tm.tmAveCharWidth;
        m_pCaret->xstart(m_xMargin);
        m_pCaret->ystart(m_nLineNum * m_LineHeight);
        m_pCaret->font((HFONT)m_pFont->GetSafeHandle());
        m_pCaret->charpos(m_CurPos);
        m_pCaret->hide();
        m_pCaret->inactive();
        m_pCaret->active();

        Invalidate(TRUE);
    }
}
//----------------------------------------------------------------
// TextInWindow:: O n P a i n t
// Draw the window's content

void TextInWindow::OnPaint()
{
    CPaintDC dc(this);

    dc.SetTextColor(m_FontColor);
    dc.SetBkColor(GetSysColor(COLOR_WINDOW));

    CFont *pOldFont = dc.SelectObject(m_pFont);

// Display the lines of text
    int line = 0, nch = 0;
    char  *p_c = m_aTxtBuf;

    while(line < m_nTotalLines-1)
    {
        nch = strcspn(p_c, "\n");
        if(nch <= 0) break;

        dc.TextOut(m_xMargin, line * m_LineHeight, p_c, nch);
        line++;
        p_c = &p_c[nch+1];
    }
// Display the last line
    nch = strlen(p_c);
    if(nch > 0)
        dc.TextOut(m_xMargin, line * m_LineHeight, p_c, nch);

// Restore previous font
    dc.SelectObject(pOldFont);
}
//----------------------------------------------------------------
// TextInWindow:: O n C h a r
// Handle a WM_CHAR message
```

continues

Listing 22.4. continued

```
void TextInWindow::OnChar(UINT key, UINT, UINT)
{
    switch(key)
    {
        case '\b':  // Backspace
// Delete the previous character, if any
            if(m_InPos== 0)
                MessageBeep(0);
            else
            {
                m_InPos--;
                int old_m_InPos= m_InPos;
                if(m_aTxtBuf[m_InPos] == '\n')
                {
                    m_nLineNum--;
                    m_nTotalLines--;
                    int i;
                    for(i = m_InPos-1; i >= 0; i--)
                        if(m_aTxtBuf[i] == '\n') break;
                    m_CurPos= m_InPos- i;
                    m_pCaret->current_line(&m_aTxtBuf[i+1]);
                }
                m_CurPos--;
// Remove a character
                int i;
                for(i = old_m_InPos; i < m_nCount; i++)
                    m_aTxtBuf[i] = m_aTxtBuf[i+1];
                m_nCount--;
// Redraw window
                reposition_caret();
                Invalidate(TRUE);
            }
            break;

        case '\r':  // Enter key
// Insert a new line
            m_nLineNum++;
            m_nTotalLines++;
            m_CurPos= -1;
            m_pCaret->current_line(&m_aTxtBuf[m_InPos]);
            key = '\n';

        default:
// Insert character in buffer and update display
            if(m_nCount >= MAXCHR ||
                (key <= VK_ESCAPE &&
                key != '\n'))
            {
                MessageBeep(0);
                return;
            }
            int i;
            if(m_nCount > m_InPos)
            {
                for(i = m_nCount; i > m_InPos; i--)
                    m_aTxtBuf[i] = m_aTxtBuf[i-1];
```

```
            }
            m_aTxtBuf[m_InPos++] = key;
            m_CurPos++;
            m_nCount++;
            m_aTxtBuf[m_nCount] = '\0';
            reposition_caret();
            Invalidate(TRUE);
            break;
    }
}
//------------------------------------------------------------
// TextInWindow:: O n K e y D o w n
// Handle raw keypresses (for cursor keys).

void TextInWindow::OnKeyDown(UINT key, UINT, UINT)
{
    int caret_has_moved = 0;

    switch(key)
    {
        case VK_UP:
            if(m_nLineNum == 0)
                MessageBeep(0);
            else
            {
                m_nLineNum--;
                int i;
                for(i = m_InPos; i >= 0; i--)
                    if(m_aTxtBuf[i] == '\n') break;

                if(i > 0)
                    for(i--; i >= 0; i--)
                        if(m_aTxtBuf[i] == '\n') break;

                m_InPos= i+1;
                m_CurPos = 0;
                m_pCaret->current_line(&m_aTxtBuf[m_InPos]);
                caret_has_moved = 1;
            }
            break;

        case VK_DOWN:
            if(m_nLineNum >= m_nTotalLines-1)
                MessageBeep(0);
            else
            {
                m_nLineNum++;
                int i;
                for(i = m_InPos; i < m_nCount-1; i++)
                    if(m_aTxtBuf[i] == '\n') break;
                m_InPos= i+1;
                m_pCaret->current_line(&m_aTxtBuf[i+1]);
                m_CurPos = 0;
                caret_has_moved = 1;
            }
            break;
    }
```

continues

Listing 22.4. continued

```
// Reposition caret, if necessary
    if(caret_has_moved)
        reposition_caret();
}
//--------------------------------------------------------------
// TextInWindow:: O n L B u t t o n D o w n
// Handle "mouse button-press" (left button) event.

void TextInWindow::OnLButtonDown(UINT modKeys,
                                 CPoint point)
{
    int x = point.x;
    int y = point.y;

    if(y > m_nTotalLines * m_LineHeight) return;

    int line = y / m_LineHeight;

// See whether x coordinate falls on any character of that line
    char *p_c = m_aTxtBuf;
    int skipped = 0;

    if(line > 0)
    {
// Skip appropriate number of newlines
        int i, nch;
        for(i = 0; i < line; i++)
        {
            nch = strcspn(p_c, "\n");
            p_c = &p_c[nch+1];
            skipped += nch + 1;
        }
    }
    m_nLineNum = line;
    m_CurPos = 0;
    m_InPos= skipped;

// Find extent of line in current font
    CClientDC dc(this);
    CFont *pOldFont = dc.SelectObject(m_pFont);

    int i = 0, wby2prev = m_xMargin, wby2next = 0,
        wtot = m_xMargin;

    while(p_c[i] != '\0' && p_c[i] != '\n')
    {
        CSize extent = dc.GetTextExtent(&p_c[i], 1);
        wby2next = extent.cx / 2;
        if(x >= wtot - wby2prev &&
           x <  wtot + wby2next)
        {
            m_CurPos = i;
            m_InPos+= i;
        }
        wby2prev = wby2next;
```

```
                wtot += extent.cx;
                i++;
        }

    dc.SelectObject(pOldFont);
    m_pCaret->current_line(p_c);
    reposition_caret();
}
//--------------------------------------------------------------
// TextInWindow:: O n S e t C u r s o r
// Handle WM_SETCURSOR messages

BOOL TextInWindow::OnSetCursor(CWnd *pWnd, UINT nHitTest,
                               UINT message)
{
    if(nHitTest == HTCLIENT)
        {
// Yes, cursor is in the client area
// Change cursor to the I-Beam cursor
        ::SetCursor(m_hIBeamCursor);
        }
    else
        {
// Cursor is not in the client area--call message handler
// from base class
        return CFrameWnd::OnSetCursor(pWnd, nHitTest, message);
        }
    return TRUE;
}
//--------------------------------------------------------------
// TextInWindow:: A b o u t
// Display the "About..." box

void TextInWindow::About()
{
    CDialog About("ABOUTTEXTIN", this);
    About.DoModal();
}
//--------------------------------------------------------------
// Create an instance of the application and "run" it.

    TextInApp TextIn;
```

Running TextIn

The accompanying disk contains the source files and the resource file (TEXTIN.RC) necessary to build TextIn. Run Visual C++ 2.0 and use the project file TEXTIN.MAK to build the application. Once you have built the program successfully, you can run TextIn by pressing Shift+F8 in Visual C++ 2.0. Figure 22.1 shows the TextIn application's window after you select the About TextIn... menu item from the Help menu.

FIGURE 22.1.

The TextIn program.

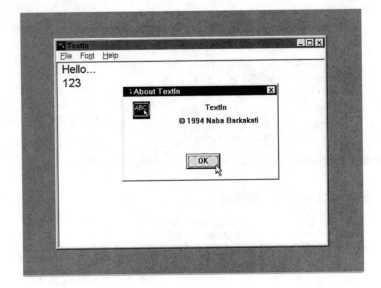

Summary

The mouse and keyboard are important input devices in a graphical user interface such as the one provided by Windows. Like everything else in Windows, both keyboard and mouse inputs are sent to an application through messages. For keyboard, there are raw messages such as WM_KEYDOWN that report the exact key that is down irrespective of the state of the modifier keys, such as Shift and Ctrl. However, for character input, the WM_CHAR message is more suitable because it reports the character entered by the user. The keyboard messages are delivered to the window that has the input focus. The active window, indicated by the user by clicking on it, gets the input focus.

Text display requires the use of a caret to mark the location where text appears. The caret is a systemwide resource that must be created upon receipt of the WM_SETFOCUS message and destroyed at the receipt of the WM_KILLFOCUS message.

The mouse messages usually go to the window that contains the cursor. Most applications handle the WM_LBUTTONDOWN message. If an application supports dragging, the application also handles the WM_MOUSEMOVE and WM_LBUTTONUP messages. The dragging starts with a button down and ends when the button goes up. As soon as the button down message arrives, the application calls SetCapture to ensure that Windows sends all future mouse messages to that application only. The capture ends when the application calls ReleaseCapture in response to the user's releasing the mouse button.

A rudimentary text entry program, TextIn, illustrates how you can handle keyboard and mouse inputs in an MFC program.

23

Printing in Windows

Printing used to be a complicated chore when programmers wrote Windows programs in C using the Windows Software Development Kit (SDK). Although Windows provides an abstraction for all devices—including printers—through the device context (DC), printing was complex because a large amount of ancillary code was required prior to initiating the actual print operation. Visual C++ 2.0 and MFC 3.0 make printing considerably easier, especially if you use MFC AppWizard to generate your application. This chapter describes how to print text and images using MFC classes.

Printing in AppWizard-Generated Applications

MFC AppWizard-generated applications are built around a document-view framework. For these applications, adding support for printing is as easy as selecting the appropriate option during the creation of the application. Specifically, you have to turn on the Printing and Print Preview checkbox in step 4 (see Figure 17.9) of the six-step dialog presented by MFC AppWizard when generating an application's code.

If you do nothing but merely turn on the option for printing and print preview and write the code needed to display output in your application's window, the application automatically can support simple printing by sending output to the printer as if it were a display. What you do not get are the capabilities of printing multipage documents and performing any scaling necesary to account for the higher resolution of the printer compared to the display.

The *OnDraw* Function

The key to supporting printing by MFC AppWizard is the OnDraw member function in the view class of the application. The OnDraw function is responsible for drawing the document on the device identified by the function's argument—a pointer to a device context (CDC) object.

When the application receives a WM_PAINT message, the OnPaint function of the CView class prepares the CDC object for the window and calls the OnDraw function to perform the actual drawing. After MFC AppWizard generates the template for your application, you place the appropriate drawing code in the overridden OnDraw member function of your application's view class. The application framework supports printing essentially by calling OnDraw with a pointer to a CDC object corresponding to a printer.

Printing Protocol in MFC's Document-View Model

Although simple printing is possible by treating the printer as a screen display, there are some significant differences between displaying in a window and printing:

■ Printers generate output on pages of paper; printing requires you to be aware of how a document is divided into pages.

- Factors such as page orientation (portrait or landscape) and size of paper (letter size or legal size) are important in printing.

MFC's document-view application framework cannot predict how your application might want to handle these details of printing, so the application framework specifies a protocol that you can use to support advanced printing in your application. The printing protocol relies on a number of member functions of the view class that the application framework calls at the appropriate times. As the application developer, your job is to override one or more of these functions to meet the printing needs of your application.

Separation of Printing Responsibilities

Before exploring the protocol for printing, consider how the responsibilities for printing are divided between the application's view class (the code you have to write) and the application framework (the code that MFC provides for you). The application framework can execute the following:

- Display the Print dialog box
- Create the CDC object with the printer's device context
- Call StartDoc and EndDoc functions to start and end a print job
- Call StartPage and EndPage for each page and inform the view class which page should be printed
- Call overridable functions (such as OnPreparePrinting, OnBeginPrinting, OnPrepareDC, OnPrint, and OnEndPrinting) of the view class

To fully support printing, your view class has to do the following:

- Paginate the document, compute the number of pages (depending on the page size, orientation, and so on), and inform the application framework how many pages are in the document
- Provide code in the view's OnPrint function to draw the current page (this information is provided in a CPrintInfo structure)
- In the view's OnBeginPrinting function, create any GDI objects, such as fonts, needed for the print job (if you allocate any GDI objects in OnBeginPrinting, you also must deallocate these objects in the OnEndPrinting function)
- If necessary, call the Escape function of the printer's CDC object to include any special programming required by the printer

Steps in Printing

When the user selects the Print... item from the File menu, MFC's document-view application framework goes through the following steps to print the document:

1. Before displaying the print dialog, the framework calls the `OnPreparePrinting` function of the view class. The `OnBeginPrinting` function is declared in the `CView` class:

```
virtual BOOL OnPreparePrinting(CPrintInfo* pInfo);
```

By overriding this function, you can insert values in the Print dialog box. In particular, you can add code to compute the number of pages in the document and provide that information to the framework by calling the `SetMinPage` and `SetMaxPage` member functions of the `CPrintInfo` structure identified by the `pInfo` argument. The `CPrintInfo` structure is defined in MFC 3.0 as follows:

```
struct CPrintInfo // Printing information structure
{
    CPrintInfo();
    ~CPrintInfo();

    CPrintDialog* m_pPD;       // Pointer to print dialog

    BOOL m_bPreview;           // TRUE if in preview mode
    BOOL m_bContinuePrinting;// Set to FALSE to end the
                               // print job prematurely
    UINT m_nCurPage;           // Page number of page being
                               // printed
    UINT m_nNumPreviewPages; // Number of pages to be
                                 shown
                               // in preview window (1 or 2)
    CString m_strPageDesc;     // Format string used to
                               // display the page number
    LPVOID m_lpUserData;       // Pointer to a user-created
                               // structure
    CRect m_rectDraw;          // Rectangle defining the
                               // current usable page area

// Sets page number of first page of document
    void SetMinPage(UINT nMinPage);

// Sets page number of last page of document
    void SetMaxPage(UINT nMaxPage);

// Returns page number of first page of document
    UINT GetMinPage() const;

// Returns page number of last page of document
    UINT GetMaxPage() const;
```

```
// Returns page number of first page to be printed
   UINT GetFromPage() const;

// Returns page number of last page to be printed
   UINT GetToPage() const;
};
```

If you override the OnPreparePrinting function, you should remember to call DoPreparePrinting—the function that displays the Print dialog box and creates the printer device context. A good approach is to end the OnPreparePrinting function's body with this statement:

```
return DoPreparePrinting(pInfo);
```

Another important point is that the page numbers start at 1. Thus, the first page has a page number of 1, not 0.

2. If the OnPreparePrinting function returns TRUE, the framework calls the OnBeginPrinting function of the view class. If you need certain fonts, pens, or other GDI objects for printing, you can allocate these objects in the OnBeginPrinting function (you should deallocate these objects in the OnEndPrinting function). The OnBeginPrinting function has the following prototype:

```
virtual void OnBeginPrinting(CDC* pDC, CPrintInfo* pInfo);
```

3. The application framework calls the StartDoc member function of the printer's CDC object to begin the print job.

4. For each page in the document, the framework performs the following steps:

   a. Calls the OnPrepareDC function of the view class with the following syntax:

   ```
   virtual void OnPrepareDC(CDC* pDC, CPrintInfo* pInfo = NULL);
   ```

   This function is called for both screen display and printing. When it is called for screen display, the pDC argument points to a screen device context and the pInfo argument is NULL. When called during printing, the pInfo argument points to a CPrintInfo structure whose m_nCurPage member contains the page number of the current page being printed. You can override OnPrepareDC if you need to adjust the printer device context—for example, to move the viewport origin and the clipping region to print a portion of the document. Another use of overriding OnPrepareDC is to check for the end of the document (if you are formatting the document on-the-fly) and set the m_bContinuePrinting member variable of the CPrintInfo structure to FALSE when you want the printing to stop.

   b. Calls StartPage function of the printer's CDC object to start printing the page.

   c. Then calls the OnPrint member function of the application's view class to print the current page of the document. By default, OnPrint calls the OnDraw member

function. To print multipage documents, you should override the OnPrint
function, which has the following prototype:

```
virtual void OnPrint(CDC* pDC, CPrintInfo* pInfo);
```

Like most other functions involved in the printing process, OnPrint accepts two
arguments: a pointer to the printer's CDC object and a pointer to a CPrintInfo
structure with information about the page being printed. In particular, your
OnPrint function should draw on the printer's device context the page indicated
by the m_nCurPage variable of the CPrintInfo structure.

    d. Calls the EndPage member function of the printer's CDC object to finish
printing the current page.

5. After printing all the pages, the framework calls the EndDoc function of the printer's
CDC object to end the print job.

6. Finally, the application framework calls the OnEndPrinting member function of the
view class. The OnEndPrinting function has the same calling syntax as its counterpart,
OnBeginPrinting. If you override OnBeginPrinting to allocate GDI objects (such as
fonts and pens) for printing, you should also override OnEndPrinting to deallocate the
GDI objects.

Supporting the Document-View Printing Protocol

As you can surmise from the printing steps, to support the printing protocol of the document-
view application framework, your application needs to override one or more of the following
member functions of the view class:

■ OnPreparePrinting to set the length of the document (by calling the SetMaxPage
function of the CPrintInfo object whose address is the second argument to
OnPreparePrinting) (you must remember to call DoPreparePrinting in
OnPreparePrinting)

■ OnBeginPrinting to allocate GDI objects such as fonts needed for printing

■ OnPrepareDC to adjust the printer's device context

■ OnPrint to render on the printer's device context the current page (indicated by the
m_nCurPage variable of the CPrintInfo object whose address is the second argument to
OnPrint)

■ OnEndPrinting to reverse the effects of what was done in OnBeginPrinting—deallocate
any GDI objects, such as fonts, that were allocated for printing

A Simple AppWizard-Generated Program

To illustrate the simplest way to include printing, consider an MFC AppWizard-generated application that displays and prints text files. Simple single-page printing is nearly effortless,
but multipage printing takes some effort on your part.

Simple Printing

To see printing and print preview in action, generate an application using MFC AppWizard:

1. Create a new AppWizard project (PRNTST) and generate the files for an MDI application with support for printing and print preview. (See Figure 17.9 for the dialog box where you have to enable support for printing and print preview.)

2. After the new project is created, add the following member functions and member variables to the document class (CPrntstDoc):

```
class CPrntstDoc : public CDocument
{
//...
public:

// Operations
    int NumLines() { return m_Contents.GetSize();}
    const CString& Line(int n) { return m_Contents[n];}
//...
protected:
    CStringArray m_Contents;

//...
};
```

The CStringArray m_Contents will be used to store CString objects, each representing a line read from the text file.

3. Choose ClassWizard... from the Project menu. From the ClassWizard's dialog box, add the following OnOpenDocument function to open a text file, read the lines from the file, and store them in the CStringArray member of the document:

```
BOOL CPrntstDoc::OnOpenDocument(LPCTSTR lpszPathName)
{
    if (!CDocument::OnOpenDocument(lpszPathName))
        return FALSE;

// Open file for reading
    ifstream ifs(lpszPathName, ios::in);
    if(!ifs) return FALSE;

// Read and interpret file
    char line[512];
    int i = 0;
```

```
        while(!ifs.eof())
        {
            ifs.getline(line, sizeof(line));
            if(!ifs) break;
            CString cs(line);
            m_Contents.Add(cs);
            i++;
        }

        return TRUE;
    }
```

4. To display the contents of the file in a window, edit the `OnDraw` function of the view class (`CPrntstView`) so that it has the following form:

```
/////////////////////////////////////////////////////////////////
// CPrntstView drawing

void CPrntstView::OnDraw(CDC* pDC)
{
    CPrntstDoc* pDoc = GetDocument();
    ASSERT_VALID(pDoc);

// Get font size
    TEXTMETRIC tm;
    pDC->GetTextMetrics(&tm);

    int LineHeight = tm.tmHeight + tm.tmExternalLeading;
    int xMargin = tm.tmAveCharWidth;

    int y = xMargin;
    int i;
    for(i = 0; i < pDoc->NumLines(); i++)
    {
        pDC->TextOut(xMargin, y, pDoc->Line(i));
        y += LineHeight;
    }
}
```

5. Build the program PRNTST.EXE by selecting Build prntst.exe from the Project menu or by pressing Shift+F8.

That's it. You should be able to run PRNTST and load one or more text files into individual windows. Selecting Print... from the File menu of the PRNTST program displays the Print dialog box as shown in Figure 23.1. Clicking the OK button of the Print dialog box should print a page of text (from the currently active window) on your system's printer. Notice that you get this level of printing support without adding any specific code for printing.

FIGURE 23.1.

The Print dialog box from the PRNTST program.

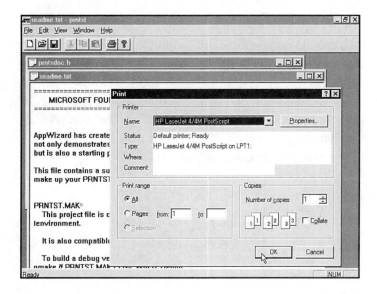

Additionally, you also can preview the appearance of a printed page by selecting the Print Preview item from the File menu of the PRNTST program. Figure 23.2 shows the preview page (after you zoom in by clicking on the preview window).

FIGURE 23.2.

The Print Preview output from the PRNTST program.

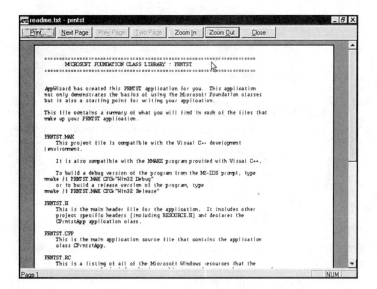

Because you do not add any extra code to handle multipage printing, the application prints only the first page of the document.

Multipage Printing

You can add support for multipage printing easily by following the printing protocol of the document-view application framework. For the PRNTST application, make the following enhancements:

1. Add some member variables in the view class (`CPrntstView`) to store information about number of lines per page, the first line to be printed, and the number of pages in the document:

```
class CPrntstView : public CView
{
//...
protected:
        int m_nLinesPerPage; // Lines per page
        int m_nStartLine;    // Start printing at this line
        int m_nNumPages;     // Pages in the document

//...
};
```

2. Add code in the view's constructor to initialize the newly added member variables:

```
CPrntstView::CPrntstView()
{
        // TODO: add construction code here
        m_nLinesPerPage = 60;
        m_nStartLine = 0;
        m_nNumPages = 0;
}
```

3. Edit the `OnDraw` function to start drawing the text starting at the line number in the member variable `m_nStartLine`. Here are the relevant lines of code:

```
void CPrntstView::OnDraw(CDC* pDC)
{
//...
        int i;
        int end = m_nStartLine + m_nLinesPerPage;

        if(end > pDoc->NumLines()) end = pDoc->NumLines();

        for(i = m_nStartLine; i < end; i++)
        {
```

```
        pDC->TextOut(xMargin, y, pDoc->Line(i));
        y += LineHeight;
    }
}
```

4. In the OnPreparePrinting function, add code to set the maximum number of pages in the document. This information is used by the framework in the Print dialog. The following is the OnPreparePrinting function:

```
BOOL CPrntstView::OnPreparePrinting(CPrintInfo* pInfo)
{
    CPrntstDoc* pDoc = GetDocument();
    ASSERT_VALID(pDoc);
// Compute number of pages using m_nLinesPerPage
    m_nNumPages = (pDoc->NumLines() + m_nLinesPerPage - 1) /
                                        m_nLinesPerPage;

    pInfo->SetMaxPage(m_nNumPages);

    // default preparation
    return DoPreparePrinting(pInfo);
}
```

5. In the OnEndPrinting function, reset the starting line to the first line so that the on-screen display always shows the beginning of the text file:

```
void CPrntstView::OnEndPrinting(CDC* /*pDC*/, CPrintInfo* /*pInfo*/)
{
    m_nStartLine = 0;
}
```

6. Override the OnPrint function and set the starting line number depending on the current page number:

```
void CPrntstView::OnPrint(CDC* pDC, CPrintInfo* pInfo)
{
    m_nStartLine = m_nLinesPerPage * (pInfo->m_nCurPage - 1);
    OnDraw(pDC);
}
```

7. Use the ClassWizard to add an overridden OnPrepareDC function and add code to stop the printing once the page number goes past the last page of the document (this is not necessary when you provide a maximum page number in OnPreparePrinting, but this shows another way to stop the printing prematurely):

```
void CPrntstView::OnPrepareDC(CDC* pDC, CPrintInfo* pInfo)
{
// Stop printing if page number goes beyond last page
```

```
    if(pInfo != NULL && pInfo->m_nCurPage > m_nNumPages)
        pInfo->m_bContinuePrinting = FALSE;


    CView::OnPrepareDC(pDC, pInfo);
}
```

Rebuild the program after making these enhancements. The new version of PRNTST should enable you to print more than one page. As shown in Figure 23.3, the print preview window also will display more than one page.

FIGURE 23.3.

The Print Preview output from the PRNTST program after adding support for multipage printing.

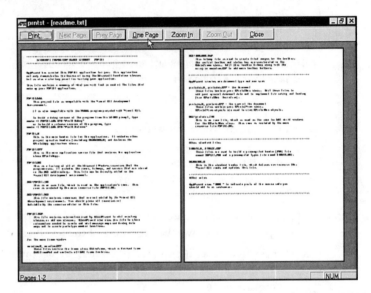

If you need to print header or footer information on each page, you can do so by adding code in the OnPrint function.

Printing in Other MFC Applications

Although the document-view application framework clearly makes printing straightforward and easy, you may sometimes need to support printing in an MFC application that is not generated by MFC AppWizard. The following sections describe how you can add printing support to such MFC applications. As a specific example, you see how to add the capability of printing images to the image display program presented in Chapter 21, "Displaying Bitmaps in Windows."

Print Dialog

Displaying the Print dialog is the first step in printing from a Windows application. In MFC 3.0, the CPrintDialog class encapsulates the Windows common dialog box for printing. CPrintDialog relies on the COMMDLG.DLL dynamic link library that accompanies Windows versions 3.1 or later.

CPrintDialog provides a modal dialog box that you can use to display a standard Print Setup dialog box or a Print dialog box. The first argument to the CPrintDialog constructor controls whether the Print Setup or the Print dialog is displayed. After you create a CPrintDialog object, you can set or modify any values in the PRNTDLG structure named m_pd, which is a member variable of the CPrintDialog object. This PRNTDLG structure holds values that are used to initialize the controls in the dialog box.

After creating and initializing the dialog box, call the DoModal member function to display the dialog box and initiate interaction with the user. The DoModal function returns IDOK if the user selects the OK button. In this case, you can use various member functions of the CPrintDialog class to discover what items the user has selected. In particular, you can call the GetPrinterDC function to get a handle to a Windows DC that you can use directly or associate with a CDC object and use for printing graphics.

The *CPrintDialog* Constructor

The CPrintDialog constructor creates and initializes a CPrintDialog object as specified by the arguments to the constructor:

```
CPrintDialog(
    BOOL bPrintSetupOnly, // TRUE = Print Setup dialog box
                          // FALSE for Print dialog box
    DWORD dwFlags = PD_ALLPAGES ¦        // Flags to customize
                    PD_USEDEVMODECOPIES ¦ // the dialog box
                    PD_NOPAGENUMS ¦
                    PD_HIDEPRINTTOFILE ¦
                    PD_NOSELECTION,
    CWnd* pParentWnd = NULL);  // Pointer to parent window
```

The CPrintDialog constructor only creates the dialog box; you have to call the DoModal function to display the dialog box.

CPrintDialog Operations

In addition to the constructor, the CPrintDialog class provides over a dozen member functions that enable you to access the state or contents of various controls in the dialog box. Here is a summary of the important member functions of the CPrintDialog class:

```
virtual int DoModal(); // Displays dialog box

BOOL GetDefaults();     // Retrieves device settings without
                        // displaying dialog box

int GetCopies() const;        // Number of copies requested
BOOL PrintCollate() const;    // TRUE = collate checked
BOOL PrintSelection() const;  // TRUE = printing a selection
BOOL PrintAll() const;        // TRUE = printing all pages

BOOL PrintRange() const;      // TRUE = printing page range
int GetFromPage() const;      // Starting page and ending
int GetToPage() const;        // page if printing page range

LPDEVMODE GetDevMode() const;    // Returns DEVMODE
CString GetDriverName() const;   // Returns driver name
CString GetDeviceName() const;   // Returns device name
CString GetPortName() const;     // Returns output port name

HDC GetPrinterDC() const;        // Returns HDC that you
                                 // must delete
HDC CreatePrinterDC(); // Creates a printer DC without
                       // displaying the dialog box
```

ImagePrint—An Example Program

To see an example of how to add printing support to an MFC application, consider the ImageView program shown in Chapter 21. Lets create a new program, ImagePrint, that will display images as well as print them. Here are the steps you can follow to add the image printing capability:

1. Add two more menu items, Print... and Print Setup..., in the File menu of the application. Then, declare the functions PrintImage and PrintSetup to handle, respectively, these new menu selections. Add the PrintImage and PrintSetup functions to the message map of the frame window:

```
// Define the message map for ImagePrintFrame

BEGIN_MESSAGE_MAP(ImagePrintFrame, CMDIFrameWnd)
//...
    ON_COMMAND(IDM_PRINT,       PrintImage)
    ON_COMMAND(IDM_PRINT_SETUP, PrintSetup)
//...
END_MESSAGE_MAP()
```

2. To display the Print Setup dialog, define the PrintSetup function as follows:

```
//--------------------------------------------------------------
// ImagePrintFrame:: P r i n t S e t u p
// Allow the user to change printer settings

void ImagePrintFrame::PrintSetup()
```

```
{
// Create and display the printer setup dialog...

    CPrintDialog PrintDlg(TRUE);
    PrintDlg.DoModal();
}
```

Figure 23.4 shows the Print Setup dialog displayed by the code in the `PrintSetup` function.

3. The `PrintImage` function is somewhat more complex because it displays the Print dialog box and when the user clicks on the OK button, it actually performs the printing. The printing itself is performed by copying the image to the printer by calling the `StretchDIBits` function of Windows API.

```
//------------------------------------------------------------
// ImagePrintFrame:: P r i n t I m a g e
// Send the image to the printer

void ImagePrintFrame::PrintImage()
{
    ImagePrintWindow *w = (ImagePrintWindow*)MDIGetActive();
    if(w == NULL) return;

    if(w->current_image() == NULL) return;

// Change cursor shape to an hourglass
    HCURSOR hcursor_old = SetCursor(LoadCursor(NULL, IDC_WAIT));

// Display the print dialogb
    CPrintDialog PrintDlg(FALSE);

    int status = PrintDlg.DoModal();
    if(status != IDOK) return;

// Get the printer device context and check whether it is ok
    HDC hdc_pr = PrintDlg.GetPrinterDC();

    if (hdc_pr == NULL)
    {
        MessageBox("Cannot create printer DC!",
                    "ImageDraw", MB_ICONEXCLAMATION | MB_OK);
        return;
    }
```

```
// Check whether printer supports bitmap block transfers
    if(!(GetDeviceCaps(hdc_pr, RASTERCAPS) & RC_BITBLT))
    {
        MessageBox("Printer cannot BITBLT!",
                    "ImagePrint", MB_ICONEXCLAMATION | MB_OK);
        return;
    }


// Compute the scaling factor needed to ensure that
// the printed graphics look close to how they appear
// on screen
    HDC hdc = ::GetDC(NULL);
    int xscale = ((double)GetDeviceCaps(hdc_pr, HORZRES) /
                GetDeviceCaps(hdc_pr, HORZSIZE)) /
               ((double)GetDeviceCaps(hdc, HORZRES) /
                GetDeviceCaps(hdc, HORZSIZE));

    int yscale = ((double)GetDeviceCaps(hdc_pr, VERTRES) /
                GetDeviceCaps(hdc_pr, VERTSIZE)) /
               ((double)GetDeviceCaps(hdc, VERTRES) /
                GetDeviceCaps(hdc, VERTSIZE));
    ::ReleaseDC(NULL, hdc);

// Now output the drawing on the printer device
    DOCINFO di;
    di.cbSize = sizeof(DOCINFO);
    di.lpszDocName = "ImagePrint";
    di.lpszOutput = NULL;
    StartDoc(hdc_pr, &di);

// Send output to the printer

    short wi = w->current_image()->width(),
          hi = w->current_image()->height();

    short wis = wi * xscale,
          his = hi * yscale;

    DWORD rop_img = SRCCOPY;
```

```
        LPSTR p_image = (LPSTR)(w->current_image()->
                  get_dib()) + sizeof(BITMAPINFOHEADER) +
                  w->current_image()->numcolors() *
                  sizeof(RGBQUAD);
        LPBITMAPINFO p_bi = (LPBITMAPINFO)w->
                            current_image()->get_dib();

// Call StretchDIBits to display the image
        StretchDIBits(hdc_pr, 0, 0, wis, his,
                    0, 0, wi, hi, p_image, p_bi,
                    DIB_RGB_COLORS, SRCCOPY);
// Finish printing
    EndPage(hdc_pr);
    EndDoc(hdc_pr);

    SetCursor(hcursor_old);
}
```

Figure 23.5 shows the Print dialog displayed by the code in the ImagePrint program when the user selects the Print... item from the File menu.

FIGURE 23.4.

The Print Setup dialog from the ImagePrint program.

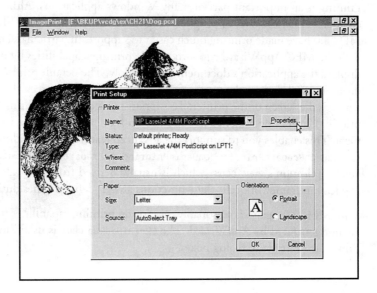

FIGURE 23.5.

*The Print dialog from the
ImagePrint program.*

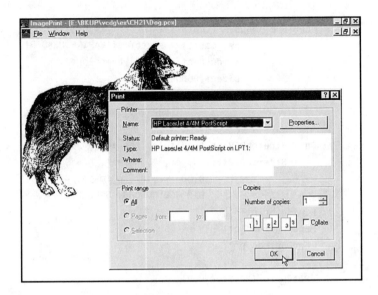

Summary

Printing is an important part of many Windows applications. Although printing used to be cumbersome in the days of programming in C with the Windows SDK, Visual C++ 2.0 and MFC 3.0 have made printing much easier to support. In particular, any application generated with the MFC AppWizard supports simple printing capabilities by using the same code that displays the application's document in a window. The default printing is possible because the document is drawn by the OnDraw function in the view class, regardless of whether the output device is the screen or the printer. To support more complex printing (for example, multipage printing) MFC's document-view application framework follows a well-defined printing protocol. This enables you to support the advanced features by overriding one or more functions (such as OnPreparePrinting, OnBeginPrinting, OnPrepareDC, OnPrint, and OnEndPrinting) in your application's view class (which is usually derived from the CView class). The rest of the application framework calls these functions at well-defined times during printing.

With MFC 3.0, it also is reasonably easy to add printing capabilities to MFC applications that are not generated by AppWizard. The CPrintDialog class is useful in this case to display the Print and Print Setup dialog boxes.

24

Using the Windows Help System

Most Windows applications, including the Visual Workbench, provide context-sensitive on-line help through the Windows Help system. Usually, applications include Help as the rightmost item on the menu bar and provide help through items in the Help pull-down menu. With the Windows API function `WinHelp`, it is easy to include help in any application provided you have the help (HLP) file ready. This chapter starts by showing how to prepare a simple help file and display it in an application. The latter part of the chapter shows how MFC AppWizard can automatically include support for help and generate all the files necessary to build a standard help file.

WINDOWS HELP IS CONTEXT-SENSITIVE

The Windows Help system is called *context-sensitive* because an application can display a different part of the help file depending on the part of the application the user is currently using.

Adding Help to an Application

Most commercial Windows applications include sophisticated help with embedded graphics, hypertext links, and pop-up windows. An application's help system consists of one or more help files with the information about the application. It is easy to activate the Windows Help engine by calling `WinHelp` and then enable the user to traverse through the help information and jump to selected topics. The difficult step in creating an effective help system is in coming up with the content and organization of the help files. It is not unlike planning, organizing, and writing a book.

Although the following sections cannot make you an expert on writing help files, they show you the mechanical aspects of preparing a help file. You see how to write a simple help file with some basic features, "compile" the file into an HLP file, and display it by calling `WinHelp`.

WINDOWS HELP TERMINOLOGY

The following is a review of terms used in the Windows Help system, some of which have already been defined in this book:

A *help topic* is a self-contained body of text and graphics designed to provide information on one or more related items.

Jump text refers to a hypertext link—clicking on this text causes the help system to jump to a new help topic.

A *context string* is the text that uniquely identifies a help topic.

A *build tag* is a text string used to mark a number of help topics so that those topics can be selectively included or excluded when building the help file.

Keywords are text strings that can be used to search for help topics.

A *definition* is a short description of an item that appears in a pop-up window when the user clicks on the text that is linked to the definition.

Secondary windows are separate windows used to display information (such as code or a figure) related to a topic.

A *hypergraphic* is the graphical counterpart of hypertext—a hypergraphic consists of a bitmap or a metafile with one or more hot spots (marked with the Hot Spot Editor, SHED.EXE, which accompanies Visual C++).

Creating the Help File

A typical help file contains a table of contents with each entry showing a jump text. When the user clicks on an item in the table of contents, the help system jumps to the help topic associated with that jump text. Additionally, the help file can include links to pop-up definitions and secondary windows.

When preparing the help file, you have to use character formatting styles such as double-underline and underline to mark the hypertext links—clicking on the link text causes the help system to go to a help topic. Each help topic is identified by a context string; a footnote with a special marking (#) associates a context string to a topic. Keywords and topic titles are also specified through footnotes.

Steps in Preparing a Help File

The basic steps in creating a help file are as follows:

1. Using a word processor capable of producing a Rich Text Format (RTF) output, prepare a file with the help information.
2. Use the Help Compiler (HC31.EXE) to convert the RTF file to a help (HLP) file so that it can be used by the WinHelp function. Essentially, you have to prepare a Help Project (HPJ) file that the Help Compiler reads and then uses to generate the HLP file.

The following sections illustrate these steps through an example.

Rich Text Format (RTF) File

The "source file" of the help system is text files containing various topics and the codes needed to link topics. These topic files must be in rich text format (RTF) files, which can also include graphics. You must have at least one topic file to create a help file.

In theory, you can create an RTF file with a plain text editor because everything in an RTF file, including graphics, is stored as text. In practice, however, you need a word processor that handles RTF to prepare the help topics. I have used Microsoft Word for Windows for this book. There also are commercial Windows Help tools that are especially designed to prepare the RTF files necessary to build help files.

To get an idea of how an RTF file looks, here are a few lines from the beginning of a typical RTF file:

```
{\rtf1\ansi \deff0\deflang1024{\fonttbl{\f0\froman Times New Roman;}
{\f1\froman Symbol;}{\f2\fswiss Arial;}{\f3\froman Tms Rmn;}
{\f4\fswiss Helv;}{\f5\fswiss Helvetica;}{\f6\fswiss MS Sans Serif;}}
```

This is the preamble of an RTF file showing the font table. Codes in RTF files start with a backslash. Luckily, you do not have to learn all these codes because word processors such as Microsoft Word for Windows can create RTF files. When you build the help topic files with Microsoft Word for Windows, you can work in a "what-you-see-is-what-you-get" (WYSIWYG) mode and merely save the document as an RTF file when you are ready to run the Help Compiler.

A Sample Help File

Consider the task of preparing the help file for a simple educational game called SPUZZLE (for Spelling Puzzle) that I created as an example for another book. Here is what you want in the help file:

- A help index showing four entries:
  Playing SPUZZLE
  Overview of SPUZZLE
  Adding a new word to SPUZZLE
  Changing the music
- A topic for each item in the index
- Some embedded bitmap images to illustrate how to play the SPUZZLE game

JUMPING TO A TOPIC IN ANOTHER HELP FILE

From a jump text, you can jump to a topic in another help file. Merely format the context string as follows:

```
Jump TextMyContextString@D:\MYHLP\FILE1.HLP
```

where `Jump Text` is the jump text formatted in double-underline followed (without any intervening space) by the jump destination formatted as hidden text. This example assumes that the topic is to be found in the help file specified by the absolute path D:\MYHLP\FILE1.HLP. You may specify a filename only, in which case the file should be in the directory from which the application starts.

Preparing the Help Topic File

Use Microsoft Word for Windows to prepare the help topic file as follows:

1. Start the Microsoft Word file with the index items. As shown in Figure 24.1, set each index item in double-underline style. Table 24.1 summarizes the other useful text formatting styles.

2. Next to each index item, enter the context string and format it as hidden text. For example, notice the Play_SPUZZLE context string next to the index item Playing SPUZZLE. This specifies that when the user clicks on the Playing SPUZZLE index item, the help system should jump to the help topic identified by the context string Play_SPUZZLE.

3. Write the help topics corresponding to the context strings—you should provide a topic for each context string. Separate each topic from the preceding one by a page break (in Microsoft Word for Windows you can insert a page break with Ctrl+Enter).

4. Assign a context string to each help topic. To assign a context string to a Help topic:

   a. Place the text insertion point (the blinking vertical line) to the left of the topic heading and select Insert | Footnote from the Microsoft Word menu.

   b. In the Footnote dialog, insert the number sign (#) as a custom footnote reference mark and click on the OK button. A superscript number sign (#) will appear next to the heading and a footnote pane will appear. Type the context string as the footnote text.

5. Add other footnotes for topic titles and keywords. Table 24.2 lists the special footnote marks used in help files. Figure 24.2 shows the footnotes for the sample help file.

Table 24.1. Meaning of text formatting styles in help files.

Style	Text Type	Meaning
Strikethrough or double-underline	Jump text	The user can click on this text to jump to another topic.
Underline	Definition	When the user clicks the mouse button or presses Enter, a pop-up window appears.

continues

Table 24.1. continued

Style	Text Type	Meaning
Hidden	Context string	This identifies the help topic that will be displayed when the user selects the text that immediately precedes the context string.

FIGURE 24.1.

A sample help topic file being prepared in Microsoft Word for Windows.

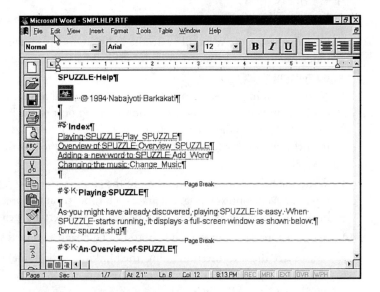

FIGURE 24.2.

Footnotes in the sample help topic file.

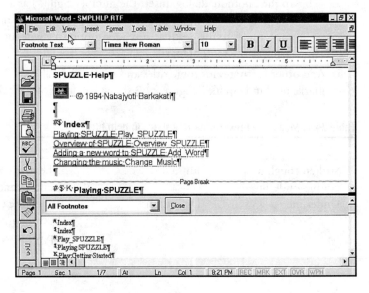

Table 24.2. Meaning of special footnote marks in help files.

Footnote Mark	Name	Meaning
Number sign (#)	Context string	The footnote text is a context string that uniquely identifies a topic. A context string can contain any alphanumeric characters and the period (.) and underscore (_) characters.
Dollar sign ($)	Title	The footnote text is a topic title that appears in a listbox when you use the Search feature in Windows Help. Titles can be up to 128 characters long.
Letter K	Keyword	The footnote text is a keyword that you can use to search for a topic.
Plus sign (+)	Browse sequence number	The number in the footnote text defines a sequence. The Windows Help system uses the sequence to determine the order in which the user can browse through topics.
Asterisk (*)	Build tag	The footnote text specifies one or more strings that mark (or tag) the help topic. The tags are used in the Help Project file specifically to include a selected set of topics in a help file.

Inserting Graphics

The sample help file includes smaller bitmap images (from Windows BMP files), added directly into the help topic file using the Insert | Picture option of Microsoft Word for Windows. You can insert the following types of graphics in a help file:

■ Bitmap images from a Windows bitmap file with the .BMP or .DIB extensions

■ Windows metafiles with vector graphics from files with the .WMF extension

■ Hypergraphics from files with the .SHG extension (recall that a hypergraphic is a bitmap or a metafile to which you add hot spots with the Hot Spot Editor, SHED.EXE)

■ Multiple-resolution bitmaps from files with the .MRB extension (a *multiple-resolution bitmap* is compiled from several bitmaps with different screen resolutions by the Multiple-Resolution Bitmap Compiler, MRBC.EXE)

Although you can insert bitmaps and metafiles directly by using the Insert I Picture command in Microsoft Word for Windows, you have to include the other graphics by reference. For example, to include a hypergraphic from the file SPUZZLE.SHG, you write the following:

```
{bmc spuzzle.shg}
```

where bmc is a command that specifies how to treat the graphics in the help file. You can use one of the following commands to include a graphics by reference:

■ bmc embeds the graphic in the text as if it were a single character.

■ bml aligns the graphic at the left margin with text wrapping along the graphic's right edge.

■ bmr aligns the graphic at the right margin with text wrapping along the graphic's left edge.

After you compile the help topic file with the Help Compiler, the compiled help file contains a single copy of the graphic data separate from the text.

Preparing a Hypergraphic

The idea behind a hypergraphic is to provide a graphical means for jumping to different topics in the help file. You have to use the Hot Spot Editor, SHED.EXE, to prepare the hypergraphic. For SPUZZLE.SHG, you load a Windows bitmap image into the Hot Spot Editor, mark a few hot spots, and assign context strings to each hot spot.

To define a hot spot, merely select a rectangular area of the graphic by pressing down the left mouse button and dragging the mouse as if you were drawing a rectangle. Then select Attributes... from the Edit menu. As shown in Figure 24.3, you have to enter a context string in the Attributes dialog that appears. The hot spot is tied to the help topic through the context string. You should use a context string for a topic in the help file where you plan to insert the hypergraphic.

Compiling the Help Topic Files

After preparing the help topic file in a word processor and saving the file in the Rich Text Format, you have to convert the RTF file into a Windows help file. The Help Compiler (HC31.EXE) takes the RTF file containing help topics and generates a binary HLP file for use by the Windows Help system.

To run the Help Compiler, you need a Help Project (HPJ) file. The help project file looks a bit like the Windows INI files. The file has a number of sections and each section has a number of related options. Although there are many types of sections and options to customize the help file, knowing a few commonly used options is sufficient for most help files.

FIGURE 24.3.

Creating a hypergraphic using the Hot Spot Editor.

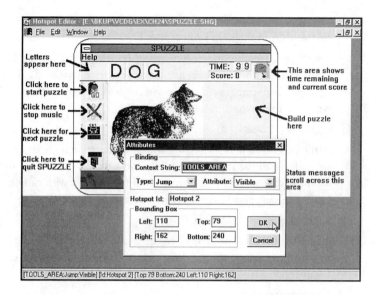

Listing 24.1 shows the Help Project file for the sample help file. The most important section is the FILES section that lists the RTF files to be included in the help file. If you insert graphics by reference, you need to list the names of the graphic files in the BITMAPS section.

Listing 24.1. SMPLHLP.HPJ. Sample help project file.

```
[OPTIONS]
TITLE=SPUZZLE Help
COMPRESS=true
WARNING=2

[FILES]
smplhlp.rtf

[BITMAPS]
spuzzle.shg
```

Once you prepare the project file SMPLHLP.HPJ, enter the following command at a command prompt to generate the help file SMPLHLP.HLP:

```
hc31 smplhlp.hpj
```

Sections in a Help Project File

A help project file can have nine possible sections:

■ [OPTIONS] specifies options that control the operation of the Help Compiler. The [OPTIONS] section is optional, but most help projects use at least a few options, such as

COMPRESS, WARNING, and TITLE. When an [OPTIONS] section is present, it should be the first section in the help project file. There are over a dozen possible options:

BMROOT specifies the directory where the Help Compiler can find the bitmap files referenced through the bmc, bml, and bmr commands in the Help topic files. For example, if all images are in the directories C:\IMAGES and D:\HELP\BMP, you write the following:

BMROOT=C:\IMAGES, D:\HELP\BMP

BUILD lists build tags indicating which topics to include or exclude when building the help file. If all the topics in the help file are tagged with one of two build tags, Beginner or Advanced, and you want to build a help file with only those topics that have both Beginner and Advanced tags, you specify the following:

BUILD=Beginner & Advanced

COMPRESS specifies the type of compression to be used for the help file. You can set it to FALSE, MEDIUM, or TRUE. Thus, to enable maximum compression, you write the following:

COMPRESSION=TRUE

CONTENTS sets the context string of the topic that serves as the table of contents for the help file. If the CONTENTS option is missing, the first topic in the first file listed in the [FILES] section is used as the table of contents.

COPYRIGHT specifies a unique copyright message to be displayed in the About dialog box by WINHELP.

ERRORLOG provides the filename where the Help Compiler saves compilation errors that occur during the build. For example, to save the errors in a file named HLPERR.LOG, set ERRORLOG as follows:

ERRORLOG=HLPERR.LOG

FORCEFONT specifies the font name that will be used by WINHELP to display all topics regardless of the font used to prepare the topics. For example, to display the help file in Arial font, specify FORCEFONT=Arial.

ICON specifies the icon file to be displayed when WINHELP is minimized.

LANGUAGE enables a different sort ordering for help files. You can specify only LANGUAGE=Scandinavian because WINHELP supports only two types of sort ordering.

MAPFONTSIZE maps font sizes in the RTF file to a different font size in the compiled help file. For example, if you want to convert all point fonts to 8- to 12-point/12-point fonts, write MAPFONTSIZE=8-12:12.

MULTIKEY specifies a footnote character to be used for an additional keyword table (in addition to the one built using footnotes marked with K). For example, to use Z as a key, write MULTIKEY=Z.

REPORT controls the display of messages during the help compilation. To turn on reporting, set REPORT=ON.

ROOT lists the directories used to locate topic files listed in the Help Project file. For example, if all help topic files are located in D:\HLPFILES, you set ROOT as ROOT=D:\HLPFILES.

TITLE specifies up to 50 characters of text that WINHELP displays in the title bar of the help window.

WARNING sets the level of error reporting by the Help Compiler. Level 1 reports only extreme errors, 2 reports an intermediate level of errors and warnings, and 3 reports all warnings and errors.

■ [FILES] section lists the names of RTF files that will be combined to form the final help file. The [FILES] section must be present in a help project file. A typical [FILES] section might be the following:

```
[FILES]
hlpmain.rtf
part1.rtf
part2.rtf
```

■ [BUILDTAGS] section specifies build tags—text identifiers used to mark topics—that are used in the help topic file. If the help topic files use two tags, Beginner and Advanced, the [BUILDTAGS] section is the following:

```
[BUILDTAGS]
Beginner    ; Topics for beginners
Advanced    ; Topics for advanced users
```

■ [CONFIG] section lists any author-defined menus and buttons used in the help file and registers any dynamic link libraries (DLLs) and DLL functions used as macros within the help file. For example, to add browse buttons to the WINHELP tool bar, you write the [CONFIG] section as follows:

```
[CONFIG]
BrowseButtons()
```

■ [BITMAPS] section lists all the bitmaps, metafiles, and hypergraphics that are included by the bmc, bml, and bmr commands in the help file. An example [BITMAPS] section might be the following:

```
[BITMAPS]
mainmenu.shg
toolbar.bmp
e:\images\sdump.bmp
```

■ [ALIAS] section instructs the Help Compiler to use one context string in place of another. For example, if you want to map the context strings Play_New_Game and

Repeat_Game to the context string Play_Game, you specify the [ALIAS] section as follows:

```
[ALIAS]
Play_New_Game=Play_Game
Repeat_Game=Play_Game
```

■ [MAP] section associates a context string with a number. Then this number can be used as an argument to the WinHelp function to activate the help topic corresponding to that number. Here is a sample [MAP] section:

```
[MAP]
PUZZLE_AREA    10
TOOLS_AREA     20
STATUS_AREA    30
```

■ [WINDOWS] section specifies the characteristics of the primary help window and any secondary help windows.

■ [BAGGAGE] section lists files to be placed in the HLP file, which has its own internal file system. You can refer to a file listed in the [BAGGAGE] section by prefixing an exclamation point (!) to the filename. A reason for storing data in the help file's internal file system is that WINHELP can access files stored in the help file system more efficiently than files in the normal MS-DOS file system.

Displaying the Help File

There are two ways to display a help file:

■ Run WINHELP.EXE and open the help file from WINHELP.

■ Call the Windows API function WinHelp from your application.

The following sections explore both.

Viewing with the WINHELP program

You can view any Windows help file with the WINHELP program (WINHELP.EXE) that comes with Microsoft Windows—merely run WINHELP and select the sample help file SMPLHLP.HLP. Figure 24.4 shows the initial help screen. Click on any one of the items to view the corresponding help topic. For example, if you click on the Playing SPUZZLE item, WINHELP displays the topic shown in Figure 24.5. Note the hypergraphic displayed in that topic. Try clicking on various areas of the hypergraphic to jump to other parts of the help file.

FIGURE 24.4.

The initial help screen displayed by WINHELP.

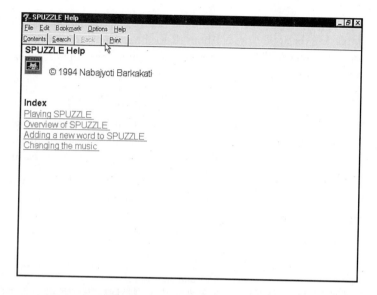

FIGURE 24.5.

A sample help topic with an embedded hypergraphic.

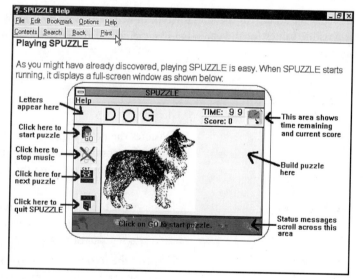

Calling the *WinHelp* Function

Although the WINHELP program provides an easy way to view a help file, your application has to provide its own help menu from which the user can access the application's help file. In most applications, the help menu has items for accessing the help file followed by an item for displaying the application's About dialog box. The first item in the Help pull-down menu is usually Contents. When the user selects this item, the application can display the help table of contents by calling WinHelp as follows:

```
WinHelp(GetSafeHwnd(), "SMPLHLP.HLP", HELP_CONTENTS, 0);
```

where SMPLHLP.HLP is the name of the help file. Assuming that WinHelp is called from a message handling function in the main frame window class of an MFC application, the call to GetSafeHwnd returns the window handle, which is required as the first argument to WinHelp.

The WinHelp function starts Windows Help (WINHELP.EXE), which displays a topic from the specified help file. The calling syntax of WinHelp is as follows:

```
BOOL WinHelp(
    HWND    hwnd,      // Identifies window requesting help
    LPCTSTR lpszHelp,  // Name of the help file
    UINT    uCommand,  // Type of help being requested
    DWORD   dwData);   // Additional data when required by the
                       // uCommand argument
If the WinHelp function is successful, it returns TRUE; otherwise it returns FALSE.
```

The uCommand argument specifies the type of help requested by the application. Table 24.3 lists the possible values for the uCommand parameter and the corresponding formats of the dwData parameter.

Table 24.3. Types of help from WinHelp.

uCommand	Action
HELP_COMMAND	Executes the help macro or macro string specified by the dwData argument. You may specify multiple macro names by separating the names with semicolons.
HELP_CONTENTS	Displays the topic specified by the CONTENTS option in the [OPTIONS] section of the help project file. In this case, you set dwData to 0.
HELP_CONTEXT	Displays the topic identified by the context number in the dwData argument (interpreted as an unsigned long integer). The [MAP] section of the help project file associates the context number to a context string.
HELP_CONTEXTPOPUP	Displays, in a pop-up window, the topic identified by the context number in the dwData argument.
HELP_FORCEFILE	Forces WinHelp to display the correct help file. If the incorrect help file is displayed, WinHelp opens and displays the correct file. In this case, you set dwData to 0.

uCommand	Action
HELP_HELPONHELP	Displays help on how to use Windows Help, provided the WINHELP.HLP file is available. In this case, the dwData argument is ignored; you set it to 0.
HELP_INDEX	Displays the topic as identified by the Index context. The dwData argument is ignored.
HELP_KEY	Displays the topic in the keyword table that matches the keyword specified in the dwData argument, provided there is an exact match. If there is more than one match, displays a list of matching topics and enables the user to select a topic to display.
HELP_MULTIKEY	Displays the topic specified by a keyword in an alternative keyword list. In this case, dwData points to a MULTIKEYHELP structure that specifies a footnote character and a keyword.
HELP_PARTIALKEY	Displays the topic in the keyword list that matches the keyword specified by dwData, provided there is an exact match. If there is more than one match, displays a list of matching topics and enables the user to select a topic to display. If you provide an empty string in dwData, WinHelp displays the Search dialog box.
HELP_QUIT	Informs the WINHELP program that your application no longer needs help. In this case dwData is ignored, so you set it to 0.
HELP_SETCONTENTS	Sets the Contents topic using the context number in the dwData argument.
HELP_SETINDEX	Sets the index topic to the topic identified by the context number in the dwData argument. WINHELP displays the index topic when user selects the index.
HELP_SETWINPOS	Displays the help window with the size and position as specified by the HELPWININFO structure whose address is in the dwData argument.

Help in AppWizard-Generated Applications

You have seen how to prepare a help file and display it using WINHELP—either by running WINHELP from Windows or by calling the Windows API function WinHelp. When you generate your application with MFC AppWizard, you can include context-sensitive help in the application very easily. All you have to do is select the Context Sensitive Help option in step 4 (Figure 17.9) of the six-step dialog presented by MFC AppWizard when generating an application's code. AppWizard generates the necesary help topic files and a help project file; you follow a few steps to create the HLP file for the application. The following sections describe the steps and show you how to add more information to the AppWizard-generated help topics.

Building the Default Help File

When you select Context Sensitive Help, AppWizard generates one or more standard RTF files with the help information for the application. AppWizard also creates the necessary bitmap files and a Help Project (HPJ) file to build the help (HLP) file.

Files for Context-Sensitive Help

As an example, if you use AppWizard (in Visual C++ 2.0) to create an application named TEST, AppWizard generates the following files to support context-sensitive help:

- TEST.HPJ is the help project file used by the Microsoft Help Compiler to create the application's help file.
- MAKEHELP.BAT is the batch file used to create the application's help files. This file invokes the Help Compiler with TEST.HPJ as the help project. The source files for the Help Compiler are located in the HLP subdirectory.
- A HLP subdirectory contains the following Rich Text Format files (RTF) with the help topics for the application. The HLP subdirectory also includes several bitmap files (BMP) that are used in the help file.
- AFXCORE.RTF is the core help topic file with information on all standard menus in the application.
- AFXPRINT.RTF contains the help topics describing printing and print preview features of the application (this help file is generated only if you enable Printing and Print Preview when generating the application).

MAKEHELP

To build the help file, you have to run the MAKEHELP.BAT batch file. After generating the application's files with MFC AppWizard, enter the following command from a command window (such as a DOS window) to build the help file:

```
makehelp
```

For the TEST application, this creates the help file TEST.HLP.

You may have noticed that instead of running the Help Compiler (HC31.EXE) with the help project file you had to use the MAKEHELP batch file. The reason is that AppWizard derives context strings and context numbers for help topics from the application's resource and command IDs. For any resource ID, you can add an H prefix to get the help context string for that resource's help topic. The context number is computed by adding a fixed number to the value of the resource ID. For example, if you have IDD_ABOUTBOX as a resource ID, the help context string for the help topic related to the About box is HIDD_ABOUTBOX and the context number is the value of IDD_ABOUTBOX plus a constant (0x20000).

To use these help context numbers, there has to be a [MAP] section in the help project file that associates the context number to a context string. Visual C++ 2.0 provides the MAKEHM utility program to generate the entries for the [MAP] section of the help project file. MAKEHM reads a header file (usually, RESOURCE.H) containing the resource IDs and applies some rules to convert each resource ID to a help context string and a context number. The MAKEHELP batch file invokes MAKEHM to generate a file containing the [MAP] section entries—the help project file then includes these map entries from the file created by MAKEHM. For example, in the TEST application, the [MAP] section of the help project file TEST.HPJ is as follows:

```
[MAP]
#include <D:\MSVC20\MFC\include\afxhelp.hm>
#include <hlp\test.hm>
```

where afxhelp.hm is the help map file provided with MFC 3.0 and test.hm is the map file generated by MAKEHM for the TEST application.

Viewing the Default Help File

To try out the default help file generated by AppWizard, run the TEST program that was created in Chapter 17, "Windows Programming with Visual C++ 2.0 and MFC 3.0." That test program should include a default help file. Run the application and select Index from the Help menu. Figure 24.6 shows the resulting help window, as well as the menu selection from the TEST application that resulted in the display of the help window.

F1 Help

AppWizard applications provide context-sensitive help when you press F1 in the application. For example, if you press F1 while the TEST application is active, you see the generic application help shown in Figure 24.7. If you press F1 while selecting a menu item (select it but do not release the mouse button), you get help on the selected menu item.

FIGURE 24.6.

Table of contents in the default help file.

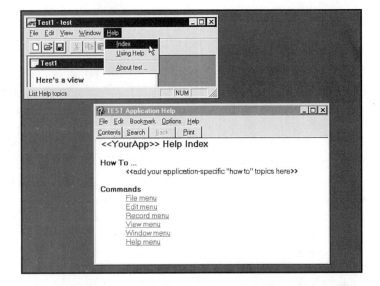

FIGURE 24.7.

F1 help from the default help file.

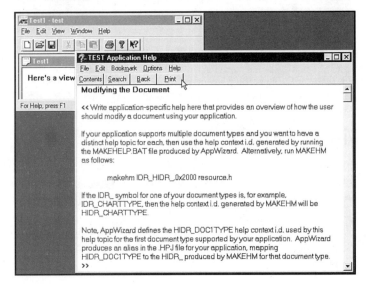

Shift+F1 Help

AppWizard applications provide another type of context-sensitive help that is activated by pressing Shift+F1 or by selecting the help button—the one with the picture of an arrow cursor next to a question mark—on the application's tool bar. When you press that button (or press the keys Shift+F1), the cursor shape changes to a help cursor, which looks like the picture on the help button. If you click on any item with the help cursor, the application provides some relevant help information. For example, Figure 24.8 shows the result of clicking on the Print button (the button with the icon of a printer) with the help cursor.

FIGURE 24.8.

Shift+F1 help on printing.

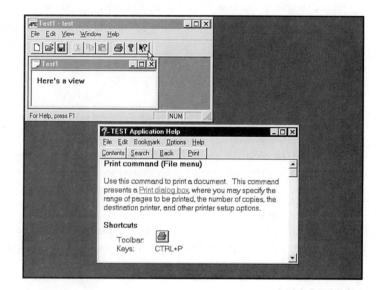

Adding to the Default Help File

The AppWizard-generated default help file is meant to provide a starting point for your application's help file. You have to modify and add to this file to build up your application's help file. From the discussions in the early part of this chapter, you should know how to edit and add topics to the help file.

AppWizard helps you by marking the sections that need editing—you should edit those sections of the help topic files that are enclosed in angular brackets (<< ... >>). For example, wherever the name of the application is needed, the help file uses the string <<YourApp>>. At a minimum, you have to replace the string <<YourApp>> with the name of your application globally.

To edit the help file, open the appropriate RTF file (AFXCORE.RTF or AFXPRINT.RTF) in an RTF-capable word processor such as Microsoft Word for Windows and use the editing capabilities of the word processor.

To see how to add help for a new topic, consider adding a help topic for the application's main frame window. You add a help topic that can be activated with the context HIDR_MAINFRAME. Here are the steps to add the new topic and rebuild the help file:

1. Open the file AFXCORE.RTF in Microsoft Word for Windows. At the end of the file, add a new page break by pressing Ctrl+Enter. Then add some text describing the application's main frame window.

2. Add a footnote with the # mark and associate the string `HIDR_MAINFRAME` as the context string for the new topic.

3. Save the file as the new AFXCORE.RTF file, then close the file.

4. Edit the help project file with a text editor and comment out the following line in the `[ALIAS]` section:

    ```
    [ALIAS]

    ; HIDR_MAINFRAME = main_index
    ```

5. In a command window, change the directory to the project's directory and run HC31 with the help project file.

6. Run the test program, press Shift+F1, and click on an empty part of the main frame window with the help cursor. You should see the newly entered help text in the help window.

To add other jump text and topics to the help files, follow the steps outlined in the early parts of this chapter on building a help file. For example, you should add more jump texts to the table of contents (see Figure 24.6) and provide a corresponding help topic for each jump text.

Summary

Most commercial Windows applications include context-sensitive help with embedded graphics, hypertext links, and pop-up windows. An application's help system consists of one or more help files with the help information organized into help topics that are prepared as Rich Text Format (RTF) files following specific formatting rules. Character formatting styles are used to identify hypertext links. Footnotes associate a context string with a help topic.

The Windows Help system provides a powerful help browser engine in the form of the Windows Help program (WINHELP.EXE). WINHELP enables the user to traverse through the help information and jump to selected topics. The application usually activates the WINHELP program by calling the Windows API function `WinHelp`.

The difficulty in creating an effective help system is in coming up with the content and organization of the help files. This chapter shows you the mechanical aspects of preparing a help file: how to write a simple help file with some basic features, compile the file into a HLP file, and display it by calling `WinHelp`. This chapter also discusses the default help file generated for you when you create your application with MFC AppWizard.

VI

Advanced Windows Programming

25

Multimedia and Game Programming

If you have browsed through the recent issues of any computer magazine lately, you must have noticed the increased coverage of all topics related to *multimedia*—the integration of sound and animated graphic images (including video) on personal computers. You will notice that there is a diversity of multimedia offerings: educational reference material such as dictionaries and encyclopedias on CD-ROMs, computer games with animated graphics and digitized sound generated by a sound board (if the system has one), animated product demonstrations, and business presentations.

Two components—the sound board and the CD-ROM drive—have contributed most to multimedia's popularity. The CD-ROM provides the storage space needed to store the large number of images and sound files in a typical multimedia application. The sound board enables the PC to generate professional quality sound—the other must-have ingredient—in a multimedia application.

Many of the current multimedia offerings, especially computer games, are designed to run under MS-DOS, but more and more multimedia applications are designed to work under Windows. Because of the popularity of Windows, developers see distinct benefits in writing Windows versions of multimedia software. In particular, with the multimedia extensions in Windows versions 3.1 and later, developers can easily make use of CD-ROM media and sound boards to bring a new level of sophistication to their products.

The device-independent manner in which Windows enables an application to handle graphical and sound output is the biggest advantage of writing multimedia applications for Windows. With minimal effort on your part, you can ensure that the same Windows application works properly on a 16-color 640x480 VGA display as well as a 256-color 1,024x768 Super VGA display—for that matter, any display for which Windows offers a graphics driver. This device independence comes at a price; animation under Windows is slower than that designed to work in a specific mode of a video adapter. For example, most interactive DOS-based computer games that display animated graphics scenes do so in a specific video mode of a display adapter, usually mode 13h of the VGA (the 256-color 320x200 resolution mode). When programming in such a specific video mode, the programmer can exploit all nuances of the adapter, including the fact that a 256-color 320x200 image fits in exactly 64,000 bytes—fewer than in the maximum size of a single segment of memory in the older 80x86 processors—which makes image manipulation fast. You cannot use intimate knowledge of the display when programming an application for Windows, but the speed disadvantage of Windows is gradually disappearing as PCs and display adapters become faster. Additionally, Microsoft has released the WinG library to help game developers create Windows games with performance approaching that of MS-DOS games.

WinG (pronounced "win-gee") retains the device independence of Windows graphics but provides performance comparable to that achieved by directly accessing the video card under MS-DOS. Microsoft developed the WinG library to help developers of MS-DOS games port their games to Windows. Microsoft provides the WinG dynamic link library and other support files on a Development Platform CD, which you can get by subscribing to Level 2 of the Microsoft Developer Network.

This chapter shows you some programming techniques needed to develop multimedia applications designed to run under Microsoft Windows. Chapter 21, "Displaying Bitmaps in Windows," shows you how to display and animate bitmap images. Most of this chapter focuses on playing audio and video files using the Windows *Media Control Interface (MCI)*, which offers high- and low-level functions. The last part of this chapter gives an overview of game programming for Windows and describes some common elements of all computer games.

The Media Player

Before learning how to use the MCI functions in your own applications, you should look at the Media Player application that comes with Microsoft Windows. The Media Player can play sound files and video sequences, and it can control other MCI multimedia devices, such as audio compact discs, installed in your system.

When you start the Media Player (it is usually in the Accessories program group), the application displays the main window shown in Figure 25.1. To see the Media Player in action, select File | Open and select a waveform sound file (with .WAV extension) from the Open dialog box (see Figure 25.2). After loading the .WAV file, click on the Play button (the leftmost button at the bottom edge of the Media Player window) to play back the sound waveforms from the file. The other buttons enable you to stop, rewind, and move forward in the currently loaded multimedia data.

FIGURE 25.1.

Main window of the Media Player.

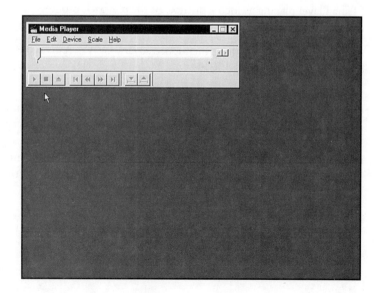

FIGURE 25.2.

Selecting a file to load in the Media Player.

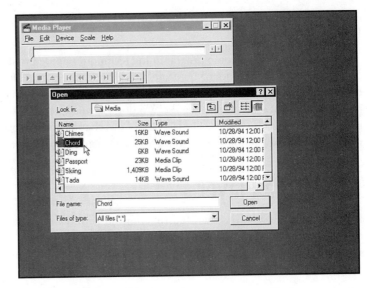

In addition to playing a sound wave file, the Media Player can also play *Musical Instrument Digital Interface (MIDI)* sounds, which are generally stored in files with an .MID or .RMI file extension. As with .WAV files, you open the MIDI file (provided you have one in the system), and click the play button to listen to the music.

Another more exciting type of multimedia file is a video sequence with frames of images stored interleaved with sound in *audio-video interleaved* (.AVI) format files. Figure 25.3 shows the Media Player playing a video sequence. As the playback progresses, the Media Player tracks the current frame in the scale that appears in the middle of the window.

All the multimedia file formats mentioned so far—WAV, AVI, and RMI—are specific instances of a file organization called RIFF.

Resource Interchange File Format (RIFF) is a tagged file format that is designed to store blocks of different types of data in a single disk file. Data types ranging from waveform audio to full-motion video can be stored in RIFF files. The .WAV and .AVI files are examples of RIFF files. The Windows MCI offers high-level functions (such as mciSendCommand and mciSendString) that can work with RIFF files that store several specific types of multimedia data; MCI also includes low-level functions (such as the functions with names starting with mmio) that enable programmers to access blocks of data in any RIFF file.

FIGURE 25.3.

Playing a video sequence in the Media Player.

Sound Under Windows

Compared to the Apple Macintosh, the sound generation capabilities of the IBM-compatible PCs are rather limited. Essentially, all you can do with the PC's speaker is play single notes—you cannot even vary the *volume* (loudness).

One way to improve the sound output under Windows (and DOS) is to install a sound card such as the SoundBlaster that can synthesize a wide range of sounds. These sound cards convert the *analog* (continuously varying) sound waves into 8-bit or 16-bit numbers, sampling the wave at rates from 4 to 44KHz (44,000 times a second). Higher sampling rates and a higher number of bits (16-bit) provide better quality, but you need more disk space to store high-quality sound.

Like any other device under Windows, the sound cards are controlled through drivers. The sound driver provides a standard programming interface for all sound boards.

Once the sound driver is installed, you can use the Windows multimedia API for sound cards as well as other multimedia devices, such as the CD-ROM drive and the video output device. The multimedia API relies on a dynamic link library, WINMM.DLL, which provides the high-level set of commands of the MCI. As a programmer, you can control a multimedia device by sending commands using the `mciSendCommand` function. This chapter describes a few of the MCI functions.

Sound Types

If you open the Device pull-down menu in the Media Player, you will see that the player can play three types of sounds:

- CD audio
- MIDI music
- Waveform (sampled) sound

These are the common types of sounds used in multimedia applications. Before you start programming for sound, it is worth noting the pros and cons of each type.

CD Audio

CD Audio refers to the popular audio compact disc that can be played in the CD-ROM drives. If you decide to use CD audio in your application, the users of your application must have both a CD-ROM drive and a sound card. Although this can be an overkill for simple sounds, the audio CDs can be useful if your application is meant to provide high-quality music.

MIDI Sequence

Most sound cards, including the popular Sound Blaster, support MIDI commands in addition to recording and playing back waveform sound. MIDI is for recording and playing back musical sounds that can be created by a synthesizer (most sound cards have built-in synthesizers). You cannot record or play back other sounds such as voices. MIDI files are reasonably small, so you can use MIDI files to store background music for multimedia applications. However, MIDI does not give you as much flexibility as digitized waveform sound.

MIDI SPECIFICATION

The Musical Instrument Digital Interface (MIDI) protocol is used for computer-assisted music composition. MIDI messages are sent to a synthesizer, including the one built into sound cards such as Sound Blaster, to start and stop musical notes. The Windows MCI functions enable you to write Windows applications that can send and receive MIDI messages. If you plan to work with MIDI, you might want to get copies of the *MIDI 1.0 Detailed Specification* and *Standard MIDI Files 1.0 Specification* from the International MIDI Association (5316 West 57th Street, Los Angeles, CA 90056, USA, 213-649-6364).

Waveform Sound

If you have a sound card installed in your PC, you probably already know about the waveform files with the .WAV extension. These files contain digitized (also known as sampled) sound obtained by taking samples of continuously varying sound waveforms. Although music can be synthesized from a collection of notes, there are many complex sounds (such as a baby's cry or a dog's bark) that cannot be broken down into notes. Digitized waveform sound, on the other hand, can represent any type of sound, no matter how complex. All you have to do is generate the sound waveform and take samples at a fast enough rate. Most sound cards are capable of accepting analog sound waveforms, such as those generated by a microphone, and digitizing them. Microsoft Windows includes the software (the Sound Recorder program) that you can use to create a .WAV file with a microphone hooked up to the sound card.

One problem with digitized waveform sound is that the .WAV files need large amounts of storage space.

Playing Waveform Sound

The Windows MCI makes it very easy to play digitized sounds stored in a .WAV file. You do not have to know how to interpret the contents of the .WAV file. All you have to do is call the sndPlaySound function with the name of the .WAV file as one of the arguments, and Windows MCI takes care of the details.

RESTRICTIONS ON sndPlaySound

To play a sound waveform file with the sndPlaySound function, your system must have a waveform audio device driver installed, and the data format of the sound must be acceptable to the driver. The entire sound waveform must fit in memory.

The *sndPlaySound* Function

The sndPlaySound function is declared in the header file MMSYSTEM.H as the following:

```
BOOL sndPlaySound(
    LPCTSTR lpszSoundName, // Name of sound resource or .WAV file
    UINT    fuOptions);    // Indicates how to interpret sound_
                           // name and how to play the waveform
```

The sndPlaySound function interprets the first argument as the name of an event (with associated sound) listed in the system registry. For example, here is a typical set of sound names:

```
SystemAsterisk
SystemHand
SystemDefault
SystemExclamation
SystemQuestion
SystemExit
SystemStart
```

Each of these entries is associated with a .WAV file. If you specify SystemAsterisk as the first argument, sndPlaySound plays the waveform in the CHORD.WAV file, which is the default sound file associated with SystemAsterisk.

If sndPlaySound cannot find the named sound in the system registry, it assumes that the name refers to a waveform file. To locate the file, sndPlaySound searches the current directory followed by the Windows directory and the SYSTEM subdirectory in the Windows directory. Then sndPlaySound searches through the directories listed in the PATH environment variable. If the function cannot find the file, it plays the SystemDefault sound. The sndPlaySound function returns TRUE if it successfully plays a sound; otherwise, it returns FALSE.

The second argument to sndPlaySound tells the function how to interpret the first argument and how to play the sound. This argument is a bitwise OR combination of one or more of the following constants defined in the header file MMSYSTEM.H:

- SND_SYNC causes the function to play the sound synchronously and return only after the sound ends.

- SND_ASYNC causes the function to play the sound asynchronously and return immediately after beginning the sound. To stop the sound, you must call sndPlaySound with the first argument set to NULL.

- SND_NODEFAULT returns silently without playing the default sound, if sndPlaySound cannot find the specified sound.

- SND_MEMORY indicates that the first argument to sndPlaySound is a pointer to an in-memory image of a waveform sound.

- SND_LOOP causes the sound to play repeatedly until you call sndPlaySound a second time with the first argument set to NULL. Note that the SND_ASYNC flag must accompany the SND_LOOP flag, so you have to specify SND_ASYNC ¦ SND_LOOP to play a waveform repeatedly.

- SND_NOSTOP causes sndPlaySound to return FALSE immediately without playing the requested sound, if a sound is currently playing.

HEADER FILE AND LIBRARY FOR MCI FUNCTIONS

When you use the Windows Media Control Interface (MCI) functions, you must include the MMSYSTEM.H header file in all source code files that call multimedia functions. Because MMSYSTEM.H depends on declarations in the WINDOWS.H header file, you must include WINDOWS.H before MMSYSTEM.H—for MFC applications, you include MMSYSTEM.H after the AFXWIN.H header file.

When building an application that uses MCI functions, you must add the WINMM.LIB import library to the application's project file.

The PLAYWAVE Program

To see how easy it is to play a .WAV file using the sndPlaySound function, build the PLAYWAVE program using the Visual Workbench:

1. Generate an MFC AppWizard application named playwave with a single document interface (see Chapter 17, "Windows Programming with Visual C++ 2.0 and MFC 3.0," for an overview of generating applications with AppWizard). In step 4 of the AppWizard dialogs, click on the Advanced button and set (in the Document Template Strings tab) the Doc Type Name to WAVE and the Document File extension to WAV.

2. Select ClassWizard from the Project menu and add the OnOpenDocument function shown in Listing 25.1 to the CPlaywaveDoc class.

3. Include the header file MMSYSTEM.H in the source file for the CPlaywaveDoc class. Add to the project the multimedia library, WINMM.LIB, from the LIB subdirectory of the Visual C++ 2.0 installation directory.

4. Build the program and run it. When you select File | Open, the program displays a standard file open dialog with a list of all .WAV files in the current directory. Once you select a waveform file from the list of files displayed in this dialog and click on the OK pushbutton, the program opens the selected file and plays the digitized sound.

Listing 25.1. The OnOpenDocument function of the CPlaywaveDoc class.

```
BOOL CPlaywaveDoc::OnOpenDocument(LPCTSTR lpszPathName)
{
    if (!CDocument::OnOpenDocument(lpszPathName))
        return FALSE;

// Open the sound file and play it
    sndPlaySound(lpszPathName, SND_ASYNC);

    return TRUE;
}
```

MCI Command String and Command Message Interfaces

The sndPlaySound function is meant to be a high-level function for playing waveform files. In addition to the simple interface offered by sndPlaySound, Windows 3.1 also includes two general-purpose media control interfaces that can be used for all types of multimedia programming:

■ *Command String Interface.* With this interface, you can use the mciSendString function to send commands in the form of text strings to a multimedia device.

■ *Command Message Interface.* With this interface, you can use the `mciSendCommand` function to send messages (integers that identify various tasks) to the MCI driver for a device.

The *mciSendString* Function

The `mciSendString` function provides as simple an interface as `sndPlaySound` for playing wave-form sound, but `mciSendString` is more general—it also can work with other multimedia devices, such as the MIDI sequencer and the AVI video player.

The `mciSendString` function sends a command string to an MCI device driver, which interprets the command and executes the low-level MCI functions necessary to perform tasks specified by the command. For example, to play the WELCOME.WAV sound file, call the `mciSendString` function as follows:

```
mciSendString("play welcome.wav", NULL, 0, NULL);
```

How does `mciSendString` know which device driver should receive the command? The message is sent to the device associated with the filename extension. The association of a filename extension such as `.wav` to a device such as `waveaudio` is made in the system registry or the WIN.INI file under the `[mci extensions]` section.

If you want to try out the `mciSendString` function in the PLAYWAVE example program, merely replace the call to `sndPlaySound` in Listing 25.1 with the following lines of code:

```
CString mciCmd("play ");
mciCmd += lpszPathName;
mciSendString(mciCmd, NULL, 0, NULL);
```

This shows a simple use of the `mciSendString` function, whose general calling syntax is as follows:

```
MCIERROR mciSendString(
    LPCSTR  lpstrCommand,       // Command string
    LPSTR   lpstrReturnString,  // Buffer for return information
                                // or NULL
    UINT    uReturnLength,      // Size of return buffer
    HWND    hwndCallback );     // Window to be notified if
                                // "notify" is part of command
```

The `mciSendString` function returns zero if there are no errors, otherwise it returns an error code. The command strings depend on the device. Table 25.1 shows a list of some of the commonly supported MCI command strings.

Table 25.1. Some common MCI command strings.

Command Name	*Meaning*
capability	capability device_id parameter [notify] [wait]
	Returns 1 as in `lpstrReturnString` if the device supports

Command Name	Meaning
	the capability identified by `parameter`. For example, to see whether a device can play, here is the command sequence:
	`capability mididev can play`
	where the device is opened with this command:
	`open sequencer alias mididev`
close	`close device_id [notify] [wait]`
	Closes the device. For example, if you open a waveaudio device with the following command:
	`open waveaudio alias wavedev`
	you can close the device with this command:
	`close wavedev`
info	`info device_id parameter [notify] [wait]`
	Returns textual information about specified aspects of the device in the `lpstrReturnString` buffer. For example, this command string:
	`info wavedev product`
	returns information about the manufacturer and model number of the `myinfo` device.
load	`load device_id [filename] [notify] [wait]`
	Loads a specified file into a device. The following loads the file WELCOME.WAV into a waveaudio device opened as `wavedev`:
	`load wavedev welcome.wav`
open	`open device_type [parameters] [notify] [wait]`
	Initializes the device. For example, to open the `waveaudio` device and give it an alias (device ID) of `wavedev`, use this command string:
	`open waveaudio alias wavedev`
pause	`pause device_id [notify] [wait]`
	Pauses the specified device. For example, the following command:
	`pause wavedev`
	pauses the device opened with alias `wavedev`.

continues

Table 25.1. continued

Command Name	Meaning
play	`play device_id [parameters] [notify] [wait]` Plays the device. You can use a device ID or a filename such as WELCOME.WAV or SKIING.AVI.

record	`record device_id [parameters] [notify] [wait]`
	
	Records data using the specified device. For example, to start recording a waveform sound at the current position in the wavedev device, the command string is the following:
	
	`record wavedev`

resume	`resume device_id [notify] [wait]` Resumes playing or recording from where the device was stopped by a previous pause command.

save	`save device_id [filename] [notify] [wait]`
	
	Saves the recorded data in the specified filename. For example, to save a waveform sound in the file NEWSOUND.WAV, use this command:
	
	`save wavedev newsound.wav`

seek	`seek device_id parameter [notify] [wait]`
	
	Moves to the specified position in a device. For example, the following command moves to the beginning of the device:
	
	`move wavedev to start`

set	`set device_id parameters [notify] [wait]`
	
	Sets various parameters of the device driver. For example, to turn off audio output to the right audio channel, use this command:
	
	`set wavedev audio right off`

status	`status device_id parameter [notify] [wait]`
	
	Returns the status information about a specified parameter of the device. Here is an example command string:
	
	`status wavedev mode`
	
	The returned string can be one of the following:
	
	`not ready`
	`paused`
	`playing`
	`stopped`

Command Name	Meaning
stop	stop device_id [notify] [wait]
	Stops the specified device. The command string to stop playing a sound waveform might be this:
	stop wavedev

The *mciSendCommand* Function

Although the mciSendString function provides a simple interface to multimedia devices, application programmers need a more versatile interface. The mciSendCommand function is a message-based interface that gives the application developer more control over the multimedia devices.

As an example of the command message interface, here is how you can recreate the functionality of the sndPlaySound function as it appears in Listing 25.1. To play a waveform file using the mciSendCommand function, you have to replace the single sndPlaySound function in Listing 25.1 with the following block of code:

```
// Use MCI command interface to play sound waveform
   MCI_OPEN_PARMS mci_open;

// Set up parameters and open waveform audio device
   memset(&mci_open, 0, sizeof(mci_open));
   mci_open.lpstrElementName = lpszPathName;

   DWORD err = mciSendCommand(0, MCI_OPEN,
                   MCI_WAIT | MCI_OPEN_ELEMENT,
                (DWORD)(LPMCI_OPEN_PARMS)&mci_open);
   if(err != 0L)
   {
       char errmsg[MAXERRORLENGTH];
       mciGetErrorString(err, errmsg, sizeof(errmsg));
       MessageBox(0, errmsg, "PlayWave",
                MB_OK | MB_ICONEXCLAMATION);
   }
   else
   {
// Play the sound file...
       MCI_PLAY_PARMS mci_play;
       memset(&mci_play, 0, sizeof(mci_play));
       mciSendCommand(mci_open.wDeviceID, MCI_PLAY,
                   MCI_WAIT, (unsigned long)&mci_play);
   }
```

As you can see, playing a waveform file with the mciSendCommand function is more complicated than using the sndPlaySound or the mciSendString function. However, the mciSendCommand interface offers much more control over the multimedia device. You can, for example, stop a device as well as pause it or resume it. Although these capabilities may not be important when playing a short segment of digitized sound, such controls are important for other multimedia devices, such as CD-ROM. CD-ROM can be controlled with the mciSendCommand function just as you would control a waveform audio device.

The mciSendCommand function has the following calling syntax:

```
MCIERROR mciSendCommand(
    MCIDEVICEID mciId,      // Device ID (use NULL when
                            // using MCI_OPEN command)
    UINT        uMessage,   // MCI command ID (see Table 25.2)
    DWORD       dwParam1,   // Flags for the command
    DWORD       dwParam2);  // Pointer to a structure with
                            // data needed by the command
```

The mciSendCommand function returns 0 if successful; otherwise, it returns an error code. In case of error, call mciGetErrorString to get a textual error message corresponding to the returned error code. Table 25.2 lists the MCI commands used with mciSendCommand.

Table 25.2. MCI commands used with mciSendCommand.

Command Name	Action by MCI Device
MCI_BREAK	Sets the break key for the device
MCI_CLOSE	Closes the device (must be supported by all MCI devices)
MCI_COPY	Copies data to the Clipboard
MCI_CUE	Provides advance warning to the device so playback or recording can begin with minimum delay (supported by waveaudio)
MCI_CUT	Removes data and copies it to the Clipboard
MCI_DELETE	Deletes a data segment from the media element, such as disk file (supported by waveaudio)
MCI_ESCAPE	Sends a command string directly to the device (supported by videodisc)
MCI_FREEZE	Freezes motion on video display (supported by overlay)
MCI_GETDEVCAPS	Returns device capabilities, such as the device name and number of inputs and outputs (must be supported by all MCI devices)
MCI_INFO	Returns device information (in string format), such as the product name and the name of the device element currently associated with the device (must be supported by all MCI devices)

Command Name	Action by MCI Device
MCI_LOAD	Loads data from a file
MCI_OPEN	Initializes the device (must be supported by all MCI devices)
MCI_PASTE	Pastes data from the Clipboard into the MCI element (file)
MCI_PAUSE	Pauses the MCI device
MCI_PLAY	Starts playback
MCI_PUT	Sets the location for display windows (supported by animation and overlay)
MCI_REALIZE	Tells the device to select and realize its palette into a display context of the display window (supported by animation)
MCI_RECORD	Starts recording data
MCI_RESUME	Resumes playing or recording on a paused device
MCI_SAVE	Saves data to a file
MCI_SEEK	Moves the current position forward or backward
MCI_SET	Sets device parameters, such as time format, waveform data format, and MIDI sequencer tempo
MCI_SPIN	Starts or stops the spinning of the videodisc (supported by videodisc)
MCI_STATUS	Obtains device status, such as current playback position, media length, media format, time format, record level, CD audio track, and MIDI sequencer tempo (must be supported by all MCI devices)
MCI_STEP	Steps one or more frames forward or reverse (supported by animation and videodisc)
MCI_STOP	Stops playing or recording
MCI_SYSINFO	Returns information about MCI device
MCI_UNFREEZE	Restarts a frozen video display (supported by overlay)
MCI_UPDATE	Redraws the current frame (supported by animation)
MCI_WHERE	Obtains the clipping rectangle for a video device (supported by animation and overlay)
MCI_WINDOW	Specifies the display window and window characteristics such as caption text (supported by animation and overlay)

Video Under Windows

Microsoft's Video for Windows has been around for a while now, but until recently you could get acceptable frame rates only in a 120x160 window. Recently, Microsoft introduced Video for Windows 1.1, which has improved performance so that you can get video output at 15 frames per second in a 240x320 window.

The AVI file format is used to store video clips with the image frames and sampled sound that accompany the images. Generally, you do not need to know the file format because the MCI functions perform the low-level tasks of accessing, extracting, and interpreting the multimedia data from the AVI file. The next few sections briefly show you how to open an AVI file and play a video sequence using the MCI functions.

Playing an AVI File

To play an AVI file, your application has to execute the following actions:

1. Open the AVI file.
2. Set up the window where the video will be played back.
3. Play the AVI sequence.
4. Change the playback state (such as pause), if necessary.
5. Get playback information (such as current frame), if necessary.
6. Close the AVI file.

To execute these tasks, you can use either the mciSendString or the mciSendCommand function. The next few sections describe how a few of these steps are accomplished through the mciSendString interface. Later, an example program (PLAYAVI) shows the same steps implemented by calling mciSendCommand.

Opening an AVI File

To open an AVI file, your application has to send an open command to the MCIAVI driver (the driver that displays video clips). For example, if you use the command string interface, you can open the AVI file SKIING.AVI with this function call:

```
if(mciSendString("open skiing.avi alias movie", NULL, 0, NULL)
    == 0)
{
// File opened successfully
//...
}
```

Of course, if you want to use mciSendString to open a file specified by the user through a file open dialog box, you have to construct a command string. In addition to the filename, you can also specify information about the window to be used for playback. For example, if the filename is in the string `lpszFileName` and the parent window for the playback is `hWnd`, the following code fragment opens the file:

```
char    achCommand[256];
//...
wsprintf((LPSTR)achCommand,"open %s alias movie style child "
                           "parent %d", lpszFileName, hWnd);

// Send the command string to open the file
if (mciSendString((LPSTR)achCommand, NULL, 0, NULL) == 0)
{
// File opened successfully
//...
}
```

If you plan to open multiple AVI files in your applications, an efficient approach is to open the MCIAVI driver initially by specifying the driver identifier and then open each file separately. This saves time because the MCIAVI driver is not loaded for each file open command.

Setting Up the Playback Window

There are several options to define the playback window for playing the AVI sequence. You can use one of the following approaches:

- Use the default pop-up window provided by the driver
- Specify a parent window and window style that the driver can use to create the playback window
- Provide a playback window that the driver uses for playback
- Use the entire screen to play back the AVI sequence

If you do not specify any window options, the MCIAVI creates a default window for playback when your application sends the open command. This default playback window is a pop-up window with a caption, a thick frame, a system menu, and a minimize box.

The playback window is not displayed until your application either plays the sequence or sends a command to display the window. To show the window without playing the video sequence, you can use a command string such as the following:

```
window movie state show
```

where `movie` is the alias used when opening the AVI file.

Playing the AVI Sequence

To play the AVI sequence using the command string interface, use the MCI `play` command. For example, to play the AVI file identified by the alias `movie` and request a notification, you write the following:

```
mciSendString("play movie notify", NULL, 0, hWnd);
```

The notification from MCI is in the form of an `MM_MCINOTIFY` message sent to the window identified by the last argument to `mciSendString`.

The PLAYAVI Program

To see how to open and play an AVI file in an MFC application, build the PLAYAVI program using the Visual Workbench:

1. Generate an MFC AppWizard application named playavi with a single document interface (see Chapter 17 for an overview of generating applications with AppWizard). In step 4 of the AppWizard dialog, click on the Advanced button and set (in the Document Template Strings tab) the Doc Type Name to AVI and the Document File extension to AVI.

2. Insert the following lines at the end of the header file STDAFX.H:

```
#include <mmsystem.h>
#include <digitalv.h>
```

Add the WINMM.LIB library to the project. You will find this library in the LIB subdirectory of the directory where Visual C++ 2.0 is installed.

3. Add the following variables and member functions to the `CPlayaviDoc` class (in the PLAYADOC.H file):

```
class CPlayaviDoc : public Cdocument
{
//...
// Implementation
public:
//...
// Function that returns the AVI file's name as a
// non-const char * variable (that's how the MCI
// function needs it).
    LPTSTR GetAVIFileName()
    {
        return m_AVIFileName.GetBuffer(
                        m_AVIFileName.GetLength());
    }
    BOOL FileToLoad() { return m_fFileToLoad;}
    void FileToLoad(BOOL fB) { m_fFileToLoad = fB;}
//...

    protected:
        BOOL        m_fFileToLoad;
        CString     m_AVIFileName;
```

```
//...
};
```

4. Select ClassWizard from the Project menu and add the following `OnOpenDocument` function to the `CPlayaviDoc` class:

```
BOOL CPlayaviDoc::OnOpenDocument(LPCTSTR lpszPathName)
{
    if (!CDocument::OnOpenDocument(lpszPathName))
        return FALSE;

    m_fFileToLoad = TRUE;
    m_AVIFileName = CString(lpszPathName);

    return TRUE;
}
```

5. Add the following member functions and member variables to the `CPlayaviView` class (in the PLAYAVW.H file):

```
class CPlayaviView : public Cview
{
//...
public:
//...
// Operations
    void CloseAVIDevice();
    void CloseAVIFile();
    void OpenAVIFile(LPTSTR lpszPathName);
    void PlayAVIFile();
//...

protected:
    MCIDEVICEID m_MCIDeviceID;// MCI Device ID for the AVI file
    HWND        m_hwndPlay;   // Window handle of the
                             // playback window
    BOOL        m_fPlaying;   // TRUE == playing
    BOOL        m_fAVIOpen;   // TRUE == AVI file open
//...
};
```

6. Add the following initializations to the `CPlayaviView` constructor:

```
m_MCIDeviceID = 0;
m_hwndPlay = 0;
m_fPlaying = FALSE;
m_fAVIOpen = FALSE;
```

7. Modify the `OnDraw` member function of the `CPlayaviView` class:

```
void CPlayaviView::OnDraw(CDC* pDC)
{
    CPlayaviDoc* pDoc = GetDocument();
    ASSERT_VALID(pDoc);

// Check whether file has to be opened
    if(pDoc->FileToLoad())
    {
        if(m_fAVIOpen)
        {
            CloseAVIFile();
            CloseAVIDevice();
        }
        OpenAVIFile(pDoc->GetAVIFileName());
        pDoc->FileToLoad(FALSE);
    }
}
```

8. Use the ClassWizard to add a function for the `WM_DESTROY` message in the `CPlayaviView` class. This adds the `OnDestroy` member function to the `CPlayaviView` class. Define this function as follows:

```
void CPlayaviView::OnDestroy()
{
// Close the AVI file

    CloseAVIFile();
    CloseAVIDevice();

    CView::OnDestroy();
}
```

9. Write the `OpenAVIFile`, `PlayAVIFile`, `CloseAVIFile`, and `CloseAVIDevice` member functions of the `CPlayaviView` class as shown in Listing 25.2.

10. Build the program and run it. When you select File | Open, the program displays a standard file open dialog with a list of all .AVI files in the current directory. Once you select an AVI file from the list of files displayed in this dialog and click on the OK pushbutton, the program opens the selected file and plays the video (see Figure 25.4).

FIGURE 25.4.

Playing an AVI sequence using PLAYAVI.

Listing 25.2. Member functions of the CPlayaviDoc class for opening and viewing AVI files.

```
//------------------------------------------------------------
// CPlayaviView:: O p e n A V I F i l e
// Opens the specified AVI file

void CPlayaviView::OpenAVIFile(LPTSTR lpszPathName)
{

    MCI_DGV_OPEN_PARMS        mciOpen;
    MCI_DGV_WINDOW_PARMS      mciWindow;
    MCI_DGV_STATUS_PARMS      mciStatus;

// Set up the parameters to open the AVI file
    mciOpen.dwCallback = NULL;
    mciOpen.wDeviceID = 0;
    mciOpen.lpstrDeviceType = NULL;
    mciOpen.lpstrElementName = lpszPathName;
    mciOpen.lpstrAlias = NULL;
    mciOpen.dwStyle = WS_CHILD;
    mciOpen.hWndParent = GetSafeHwnd();

// Try to open the AVI file using MCI
    if(mciSendCommand(0, MCI_OPEN,
                (DWORD)(MCI_OPEN_ELEMENT |
                    MCI_DGV_OPEN_PARENT |
                    MCI_DGV_OPEN_WS),
                (DWORD)(LPMCI_DGV_OPEN_PARMS)&mciOpen) == 0)
    {
```

continues

Listing 25.2. continued

```cpp
// File opened successfully. Save device ID.
        m_MCIDeviceID = mciOpen.wDeviceID;
        m_fAVIOpen = TRUE;

//Set up the playback window
        mciWindow.dwCallback = NULL;
        mciWindow.hWnd = NULL;
        mciWindow.nCmdShow = SW_SHOW;
        mciWindow.lpstrText = (LPSTR)NULL;
        mciSendCommand(m_MCIDeviceID, MCI_WINDOW,
                    MCI_DGV_WINDOW_STATE,
            (DWORD)(LPMCI_DGV_WINDOW_PARMS)&mciWindow);

// Get the window handle of the playback window
        mciStatus.dwItem = MCI_DGV_STATUS_HWND;
        mciSendCommand(m_MCIDeviceID, MCI_STATUS,
                    MCI_STATUS_ITEM,
              (DWORD)(LPMCI_STATUS_PARMS)&mciStatus);
        m_hwndPlay = (HWND)mciStatus.dwReturn;

// Start the playback
        PlayAVIFile();
    }
    else
    {
        MessageBox("PlayAVI", "Failed to open AVI File",
            MB_ICONHAND | MB_OK);
    }
}
//-------------------------------------------------------------
// CPlayaviView:: P l a y A V I F i l e
// Plays the current AVI file

void CPlayaviView::PlayAVIFile()
{
        MCI_DGV_PLAY_PARMS    mciPlay;

// Play the video
        memset(&mciPlay, 0, sizeof(mciPlay));
        m_fPlaying = TRUE;
        mciSendCommand(m_MCIDeviceID, MCI_PLAY, 0,
                    (DWORD)(LPMCI_DGV_PLAY_PARMS)&mciPlay);
}
//-------------------------------------------------------------
// CPlayaviView:: C l o s e A V I F i l e
// Closes the current AVI file

void CPlayaviView::CloseAVIFile()
{
  MCI_GENERIC_PARMS  mciGeneric;

  mciSendCommand(m_MCIDeviceID, MCI_CLOSE, 0L,
                (DWORD)(LPMCI_GENERIC_PARMS)&mciGeneric);
```

```
// Set the flags appropriately
  m_fPlaying = FALSE;
  m_fAVIOpen = FALSE;
}
//-------------------------------------------------------------
// CPlayaviView:: C l o s e A V I D e v i c e
// Closes the current AVI device

void CPlayaviView::CloseAVIDevice()
{
// Get the device ID of the open device type and then close
// the device type.

    MCIDEVICEID   mID;
    MCI_GENERIC_PARMS  mciClose;

    mID = mciGetDeviceID("avivideo");
    mciSendCommand(mID, MCI_CLOSE, 0L,
                  (DWORD)(LPMCI_GENERIC_PARMS)&mciClose);
}
```

Game Programming for Windows

Computer games are one of the popular software categories in the market. Current game offerings run the gamut from simple games, such as Tic Tac Toe, pinball, and puzzles, to sophisticated simulations of real and make-believe worlds. The latter can have animated graphics that depict realistic actions with digitized voices and music generated by a sound board (if the system has one). Until recently, most of the games ran under MS-DOS. This situation is changing as Windows gains popularity and game developers see the benefits of writing Windows versions of their games. In particular, with the multimedia extensions in Windows and recent additions such as the WinG library, game developers can begin using CD-ROM media and sound boards to bring a new level of sophistication to computer games. This chapter has already shown you how to use the Windows MCI functions to control any multimedia device. The next few sections give an overview of computer games, including a classification of the current crop of games and the graphics and sound capabilities that each type of game uses. Then the major steps in developing a game are outlined.

An Overview of Computer Games

The following is a list of the current crop of computer games divided into seven categories:

■ *Educational games.* Slowly the line between educational and entertainment game software is getting blurred because developers of educational games realize that an entertaining educational game is better at teaching than a dull one. The following are some of the popular educational games:

- ■ *Where in the World is Carmen Sandiego?* and *Where in the U.S.A. is Carmen Sandiego?* from BrØderbund Software, Inc. teach geography through a game.
- ■ *New Math Blaster Plus* from Davidson & Associates, Inc. teaches mathematical skills through simple games.
- ■ Learning Company's *Math Rabbit* and *Reader Rabbit* include a variety of activities to teach young children math and reading skills.
- ■ The Living Books series of Windows multimedia software from BrØderbund presents children's books through animated pictures and voices.

■ *Traditional games.* These are the computerized versions of traditional games such as chess, card games (bridge, poker, solitaire), GO, Mah Jongg, and a variety of puzzles.

■ *Arcade games.* An arcade game refers to the games offered in dedicated game machines that you see in places such as shopping center arcades. This category of computer games includes the PC versions of arcade games, such as pinball, Tetris, Pac Man, and a variety of games where you shoot down space invaders. The games in this category use fast-paced animation of small images called sprites. They also include music and other sound effects.

■ *Sports.* This category consists of software implementations of real sports, such as golf, boxing, football, and baseball. These games include a moderate level of animation and sound. Popular sports games include the following:

- ■ *Links 386 Pro* golf game from Access Software, Inc.
- ■ *Jack Nicklaus Signature Edition Golf* from Accolade
- ■ *NFL Pro League Football* from Micro Sports

■ *Adventure and role-playing games.* In these games, you play the role of a character in a specific scenario (usually a dungeon), and move from level to level collecting weapons, potions, and spells. You encounter many nasty characters that you have to defeat using the weapons and spells. Some of the best known games of this genre are *Myst* from BrØderbund, *Doom*, and the Ultima series from Origin Systems, Inc. These games sport continuously moving three-dimensional graphics and realistic sounds, including digitized voice (on PCs equipped with special sound boards).

■ *Real-time action simulations.* These are the fast-paced simulations of airplanes, helicopters, and spaceships with reasonable rendering of 3-D scenarios. When you play one of these games, you are at the controls of the craft (the airplane or the helicopter), and as you manipulate the controls, the craft moves according to the current settings and the 3-D view reflects the motion of the craft. I classify these computer games as real-time action simulations because they simulate the behavior of the airplane or helicopter and the simulation reacts to the player's inputs as the inputs are received (through keyboard, mouse, or joystick), in real time. These games are popular because the real-time feedback makes them exciting. The following are some of the well-known games in this category:

- ■ *Microsoft Flight Simulator* from Microsoft Corporation simulates a number of airplanes.

- ■ *Wing Commander II* from Origin is a space flight simulation game with very good graphics and sound effects.

- ■ *Gunship 2000* from MicroProse Software, Inc. is a simulation of helicopter combat.

■ *Strategic Simulations.* These are simulations of large-scale systems such as cities, railroad systems, naval campaigns, and, in the case of a recent game called SimAnt, even ant colonies. In these simulations, you devise a strategy for the problem at hand and see the entire system evolve as time passes. Viewed from the perspective of time scales, real-time action simulations model systems that change fast—in seconds and minutes. Strategic simulations are concerned with long-term reactions of a system— those occurring in hours, days, and even years. In a strategic simulation game you do not get the thrill of immediate response to your actions, but you will enjoy these games if you like to think through problems and devise strategies. In fact some of the war games, available in this category, have been used to train Naval officers. Most of these games have 2-D graphics and minimal sound effects. Here are some of the popular titles in this category:

- ■ *SimCity for Windows* from Maxis puts you in the role of a city planner.

- ■ *Harpoon* from Three-Sixty Pacific, Inc. is a highly acclaimed naval war game.

- ■ *Great Naval Battles, North Atlantic (1939–43)* from Strategic Simulation, Inc. enables you to command a battleship and participate in one of several naval battles of World War II.

- ■ *Carriers at War* from Strategic Studies Group is another simulation of World War II air and operations in the Pacific ocean.

- ■ *Railroad Tycoon* from MicroProse Software, Inc. enables you to manage a railroad system.

- ■ *SimAnt* by Maxis enables you to control an ant colony that has to fight for its survival in a suburban home's backyard.

Common Themes in Computer Games

All computer games have some common elements: graphics and sound. Simulation games have some of the most demanding graphics, algorithmic, and sound requirements of all games. The details are omitted except for the basic idea and the graphics and sound elements of each game.

Microsoft Flight Simulator

Microsoft Flight Simulator is a best-selling, real-time game that simulates the flight of several types of aircraft from take-off to landing. The simulation takes into account a large number of aircraft characteristics, shows a standardized instrument panel, implements all necessary aircraft controls, and provides a number of 3-D views from different perspectives. As shown in Figure 25.5, the 3-D view is realistic enough to identify specific airports (from landmarks and runway layouts), yet fast enough to work on all Intel 80x86-based MS-DOS PCs with graphics adapters from CGA to VGA.

FIGURE 25.5.

View from the cockpit in Microsoft Flight Simulator.

Gunship 2000

Gunship 2000 is a real-time simulation of helicopter combat from MicroProse Software, Inc. The version of this game designed for the VGA display adapter uses the 256-color 320x200 resolution mode of the VGA to display very realistic 3-D scenery as the helicopter flies. The game accepts input from the keyboard and a joystick. Additionally, *Gunship 2000* can generate digitized sound using one of several popular sound boards, if your system has such a board. Otherwise, *Gunship 2000* uses PC's internal speaker for sound effects.

As you can see from *Gunship 2000*'s opening screen (Figure 25.6), the game emphasizes realistic 3-D graphics within the limits of a typical PC's display system. Although you cannot fly a real helicopter without extensive training, Gunship 2000 provides simplified controls to make flying easy. Once airborne, the helicopter flies within a few hundred feet from the ground or sea and you see a 3-D view of the terrain or water outside. As the at-sea view in Figure 25.7 shows, the 3-D rendering of the scene is reasonably realistic. Note the ship ahead of the helicopter in Figure 25.7.

FIGURE 25.6.

Opening screen of Gunship 2000—a helicopter combat simulation game.

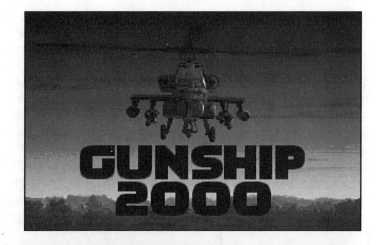

FIGURE 25.7.

View from the cockpit for an at-sea mission in Gunship 2000.

SimCity for Windows

SimCity for Windows is a strategic simulation game—one that runs under Microsoft Windows. Figure 25.8 shows the opening screen of the game. As you can see from the menu options listed on the sign, you can start a simulation of a new city, load an existing city's simulation into the game, or select to start with a predefined city's scenario. Figure 25.9 shows the windows after you load one of the predefined cities—Boston in the year 2010—and continue the simulation for a while.

In SimCity, you play as the planner for a city—you are responsible for setting up residential, commercial, and industrial zones. You also plan and build the roads, the railroads, power plants, power lines, police stations, and fire stations. As you build these, money is expended from a budget. Once the infrastructure is in place, the city's simulation proceeds to build up population, traffic begins to flow on the roads, roads deteriorate, crimes and natural disasters happen. You have to tax the residents to raise money for the upkeep of the city. If you have excess revenues, you can spend the funds to help the city grow. As you might gather from this brief description, you have to attend to numerous details just to keep the infrastructure from collapsing. The game is fun and appears to be popular among strategy enthusiasts.

FIGURE 25.8.

Opening screen in SimCity for Windows.

FIGURE 25.9.

View of Boston in SimCity for Windows.

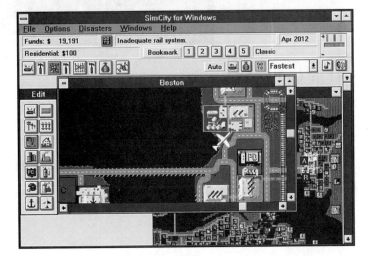

SimCity for Windows has good maplike views, but there are no demanding real-time 3-D graphics in the game. The only aspect of animation is the movement of some sprites representing vehicles such as cars, airplanes, and helicopters.

The game includes some sound effects, but the sound is more of a distraction than an aid to the game.

Harpoon

Harpoon is another game of strategy that simulates naval war games. Harpoon's simulation of large-scale naval scenarios is accurate enough for evaluating naval strategies. As a player, you are given a geo-political scenario with a need for naval intervention and you get to command anything from a single ship to an entire group of ships with a specified mission. Figure 25.10 shows the main screen of Harpoon where you play the game.

FIGURE 25.10.

Main screen of Harpoon.

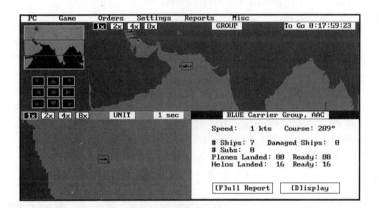

Harpoon is the computer version of a naval war game by Larry Bond that appeared as a board game in 1980. Larry Bond's game gained fame when author Tom Clancy revealed that he used Harpoon as a source of information when writing the novel *The Hunt for Red October*. You use Harpoon's database of information on ships and aircraft to decide how to make the best use of the naval and air units under your command. Figure 25.11 shows a typical screen that shows information on a specific class of ships—in this case, the Arleigh Burke class destroyer of the U.S. Navy. The player can get further information through the menu options at the bottom of the screen shown in Figure 25.11.

FIGURE 25.11.

Displaying information on a ship class in Harpoon.

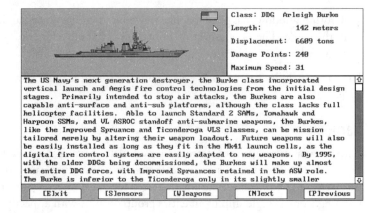

Great Naval Battles, North Atlantic (1939–1943)

Great Naval Battles, North Atlantic (1939–1943) is a recent strategic simulation game depicting naval warfare during World War II, specifically the years 1939 through 1943. In contrast to Harpoon, this game emphasizes realistic graphics and sound as it offers a number of predefined encounters between British and German battleships. The scenarios are historically accurate except that, in the game, you get to command one of the sides and get a chance to change history by blasting the other side with your ship's guns and torpedoes. The game provides a number of views that depict 3-D views of the ships at sea, but there is no real-time animation as in a flight simulator or helicopter simulation. Figure 25.12 shows the opening screen of Great Naval Battles, North Atlantic; Figure 25.13 shows a view from the main gunnery station of one of the ships.

FIGURE 25.12.

Opening screen of Great Naval Battles, North Atlantic (1939–1943).

FIGURE 25.13.
View from the main gunnery station of a ship.

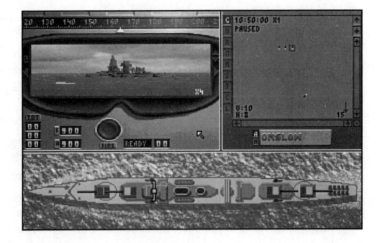

Common Elements of Computer Games

From the brief overview of some of the computer games, you can see the common features of these games: a central theme that tells us what the game does (for example, a naval war game or a helicopter combat simulation), 2-D and 3-D graphics, and sound effects to make the game seem realistic. Additionally, many games include some sort of copy protection scheme to deter unauthorized copying of the game software.

The game's main story line determines the types of programming you have to do to implement the game. For example, realism in graphics and sound effects is very important in a role-playing game. A war game such as Harpoon, however, does not need much realism; a simplified display suffices in a war game that emphasizes strategy over real-time simulation. Even with the differences in the exact requirements, the main story line, the graphics, and the sound effects are definitely the most important components of any game.

Story Line

Before you start developing a game, you must develop the story line, which dictates the details of the other programming requirements of the game. The game's story line should answer the following questions for the prospective player:

■ *What is this game?* This clearly identifies the category of the game. Is it a role-playing adventure game? A real-time flight simulation with 3-D graphics? An educational game that teaches reading skills?

■ *What is the goal of the game?* The answer tells the player what to do to succeed in the game. In an arcade game, the goal might be to shoot down as many space invaders as possible. In an educational game that teaches spelling, the goal is to spell correctly as many words as possible. For a helicopter combat simulation, the goal is to fly into enemy territory, destroy a specified target, and fly back without getting killed.

■ *How does the game provide feedback on the player's performance?* This feature indicates how close the player is to achieving the game's goal. In an arcade game, a total score might indicate performance, whereas a flight simulator might provide feedback through a detailed 3-D view from the cockpit plus a view of the aircraft's instrumentation.

■ *How does the game reward the player?* This tells the player what to expect once the game's goal is met. For a children's game, the reward might be an animation of some cartoon figures with an accompanying musical score. Arcade games maintain a list with names of the high-scoring players and their scores.

■ *How is the game played?* This feature tells the player how to play the game. The story line does not have to provide the full details at this point, but the overall idea should be explained. For example, in many arcade games, you basically point and shoot at targets with your weapons. In most flight simulators, you control the flight of the aircraft through the keyboard. The instrument panel and the outside view tell you whether you are controlling the aircraft properly.

Graphics

All computer games rely on the visual effects of graphics to establish the story line and provide the illusions needed to make the player feel like a part of the game. Computer games employ several different types of graphics techniques:

■ *2-D graphics.* This type of graphics includes points, lines, and outline and filled shapes such as rectangles, polygons, and ellipses—in a plane. Many simple games rely almost solely on simple 2-D figures. The Windows API provides functions for 2-D graphics.

■ *3-D graphics.* This type refers to the techniques used to display 2-D views of 3-D objects. One approach is to specify a 3-D object by many flat surfaces (defined by polygons) that represent the boundaries of the object. Mathematical algorithms are used to derive a 2-D view of the object for a given viewing location. The 2-D view is also a collection of color-filled polygons that are displayed using standard 2-D graphics primitives. Computer games often include many 3-D objects and require that these objects be redrawn many times a second, which may not be possible with a typical PC. Most commercially available games handle this requirement by using a limited number of 3-D objects and by representing each object with as few polygonal surfaces as possible.

■ *Image display and manipulation.* An *image* is a two-dimensional array of points with each point drawn in a specific color. An image can represent a complex drawing. Images are useful because you can use a scanner to digitize detailed pictures and use them as graphical elements in your game's display screens. Image manipulation refers to the scaling and rotation of images. Animation of images—moving one image over another without disturbing the background image—is another technique used in computer games. The Windows API includes functions to display and manipulate bitmaps—rectangular arrays of pixels.

Sound Effects

After graphics, sound is the other element that makes a computer game come alive. Unfortunately, most MS-DOS PCs have very limited hardware support to generate sound. The speaker that is standard on most PCs can generate only a single tone at a time. Although programmers have found ways to generate complex sound with the PC's limited sound hardware, the Windows API supports the capability of generating only one tone at a time on the PC's built-in speaker. However, most computer games can generate more complex sound (including digitized voice and music) using an optional sound board installed in a PC. These sound boards are plug-in cards that include hardware to generate more complex sound. As you have seen through examples presented earlier in this chapter, Windows also supports these additional sound boards.

Summary

There is a diversity of Windows multimedia applications that integrate sound and animated graphic images (including video): educational reference material such as dictionaries and encylopedias on CD-ROMs, computer games with animated graphics and digitized sound generated by a sound board (if the system has one), animated product demonstrations, and business presentations.

Windows provides a device-independent interface to all types of multimedia devices, such as sound cards and digital video through device drivers. Windows makes programming the multimedia devices easier through the Media Control Interface (MCI) of the WINMM.DLL dynamic link library. This chapter describes how to use MCI functions such as `mciSendCommand` and `mciSendString` to play digitized sound waveforms stored in files with the `.WAV` extension. These same functions can also be used to play video clips stored in audio-video interleaved (AVI) files.

Computer games are a popular category of multimedia applications; they use graphics and sound to create the special effects that make the games entertaining. The last part of this chapter provides an overview of the common features of many computer games. Although many popular games run under MS-DOS, Windows offers a unique opportunity to exploit advanced graphics, sound, and video in a device-independent manner.

26

Building and Using Dynamic Link Libraries (DLLs)

Dynamic Link Libraries, or DLLs, are fundamental program units in Windows. A DLL enables several concurrently running programs to share a single copy of a group of functions. Much of the Windows operating system is implemented by a set of DLLs that encapsulates all services (such as user interaction and display) performed by Windows. All Windows applications can then share these functionalities because they are provided through DLLs. This chapter briefly describes how to build and use DLLs in applications created with Visual C++ 2.0 and MFC 3.0.

What Is a DLL?

As a programmer, you are familiar with the concept of a library—an organized collection of one or more object code modules. Applications call functions from the library and a step known as linking enables the application to access and use the object code from the library. There are two ways to link with a library:

- Static linking
- Dynamic linking

DLLs are libraries that are meant for dynamic linking. Most Windows applications use a combination of static and dynamic libraries.

Static Linking

In *static linking*, the linker copies all required object code from the library into the executable file. Figure 26.1 illustrates the process of static linking. This type of linking is referred to as static because all function calls are resolved at the time of linking. The executable file of a statically linked application can run stand-alone because it has all the code required by the application in the executable file.

FIGURE 26.1.
Linking with a static library.

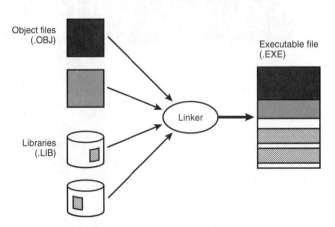

Object files
(.OBJ)

Libraries
(.LIB)

Linker

Executable file
(.EXE)

Figure 26.2 illustrates what happens when two instances of a statically linked application run. Each application instance has its own copy of the code from the static library. As Figure 26.2 shows, when calling a function in the library, each application calls its own copy of the function.

FIGURE 26.2.
Running applications linked with static libraries.

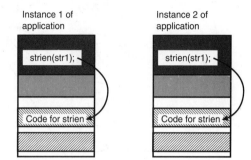

Dynamic Linking

Dynamic linking is a more flexible approach than static linking. In dynamic linking, the application's executable file links with a special import library that acts as an interface to the DLL (there are other ways to access and use a DLL at runtime). When the application runs, the code in the import library loads the DLL and makes it available to the application. The linking is dynamic because all function calls are resolved at runtime. Figure 26.3 illustrates the linking process for an application that uses a DLL.

Figure 26.4 shows the runtime scenario for two instances of an application that uses a DLL. As you can see, there is only one copy of the DLL because a dynamically linked application's executable file does not include the object code from the DLL. The DLL is loaded at runtime and all applications that use the DLL share a single copy of the DLL at runtime.

There are two ways to load and use a DLL:

■ Implicit or load-time dynamic linking
■ Explicit or runtime dynamic linking

Implicit Dynamic Linking

With *implicit linking*, the application is statically linked with an import library that acts as a front end for the DLL. The import library provides stubs for all the DLL's exported functions— the functions that applications can call. When the application runs, the DLL is automatically loaded, and calls to the DLL's functions are automatically resolved at runtime.

FIGURE 26.3.
Linking an application that uses a DLL.

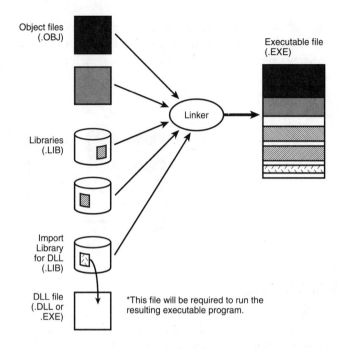

FIGURE 26.4.
Runtime view of applications linked with a DLL.

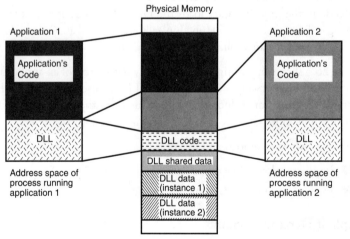

Explicit Dynamic Linking

With *explicit linking*, an application explicitly calls the Windows API function LoadLibrary to load the DLL. After the DLL is loaded, the application can get a pointer to any function in the DLL by calling GetProcAddress with the function's name as an argument. When finished using the DLL, the program calls the FreeLibrary API function to detach the DLL from the application.

When an application uses runtime dynamic linking, it is not necessary to link that application with the DLL's import library. Because the application loads the DLL, it also can detect errors, such as a missing DLL, and either inform the user or take some corrective action. Explicitly taking care of the dynamic linking is, however, somewhat more complex than relying on the implicit approach.

DLLs in Windows

Windows uses DLLs extensively. Not only does Windows use DLLs to provide basic system services such as display and user interaction, most new features in Windows such as Object Linking and Embedding (OLE), Open Data Base Connectivity (ODBC), Messaging Application Programming Interface (MAPI), and Telephony Application Programming Interface (TAPI) are implemented through DLLs. As an example, here is a sampling of DLL files from the Windows SYSTEM directory on a typical system:

```
AVIFIL32.DLL   AVIFILE.DLL    COMCTL32.DLL   COMDLG32.DLL
COMMCTRL.DLL   COMMDLG.DLL    CTL3D.DLL      CTL3D32.DLL
DDEML.DLL      DISPDIB.DLL    GDI32.DLL      KERNEL32.DLL
LZ32.DLL       LZEXPAND.DLL   MAPI32.DLL     MFC30.DLL
MMSYSTEM.DLL   MSNET32.DLL    MSTCP.DLL      NETAPI.DLL
NETAPI32.DLL   NETBIOS.DLL    ODBC32.DLL     OLE2.DLL
OLE32.DLL      REG.DLL        SECURITY.DLL   SHELL.DLL
SHELL32.DLL    TAPI.DLL       TAPI32.DLL     TOOLHELP.DLL
USER32.DLL     VBRUN300.DLL   VERSION.DLL    WIN87EM.DLL
WINASPI.DLL    WINMM.DLL      WOW32.DLL      WSOCK32.DLL
```

The DLL-based architecture has enabled Microsoft to package and add new features to the Windows operating system easily.

Windows Applications and DLLs

Because Windows uses DLLs extensively, all Windows applications implicitly link with many DLLs. Many applications also package a portion of their shared functionality in DLLs. In particular, in Visual C++ 2.0, MFC 3.0 is provided as a set of DLLs:

- MFC30.DLL is the release version of the basic classes (excluding OLE and database classes).
- MFC30D.DLL is the debug version of MFC30.DLL.
- MFCD30.DLL is the release version of the basic classes, including the database classes.
- MFCD30D.DLL is the debug version of MFCD30.DLL.
- MFCO30.DLL is the release version of basic classes including the OLE classes.
- MFCO30D.DLL is the debug version of MFCO30.DLL.

Additionally, there are DLL versions of MFC 3.0 with support for other languages and Unicode. For each version of the DLL, there is an import library with the same name but with a .LIB file extension. When you choose to use the DLL version of MFC in your application, the Visual Workbench links your application with the appropriate import library.

Contents of a DLL

Although the discussions so far have mentioned the use of a DLL as a collection of shared object code modules, DLLs can be used to package anything from code and data to resources such as fonts, bitmaps, and dialogs. For example, the COMDLG32.DLL provides a common set of dialogs (such as File Open and Print) for use in Windows applications.

DLLS IN 16- AND 32-BIT WINDOWS

The code in a DLL is shared by all applications under both 16- (such as Windows 3.1) and 32-bit (such as Windows NT) Windows. However, the behavior differs when it comes to the data in a DLL. In 16-bit Windows, a DLL's data can be accessed and shared by all applications in the system, but in 32-bit Windows, a separate instance of the DLL's data is created for each process that uses the DLL. However, you can create a Win32 DLL with shared sections of data so that all processes using the DLL can share some data.

Changes in DLLs from 16-Bit to 32-Bit Windows

Certain basic properties of DLLs have changed in going from 16-bit Windows (Windows 3.1 and earlier versions) to 32-bit Windows (Win32) such as Windows NT. You need to be aware of the changes if you are porting a DLL from 16-bit Windows to Win32.

DLLs in 16-Bit Windows

In 16-bit Windows, a DLL with all its data appears as a separate entity shared by all applications that use the DLL. You could think of the DLL as a part of the operating system. After the DLL is loaded, all currently running applications immediately have access to the DLL's exported functions.

An application can call the GetModuleHandle API function to determine whether the DLL has been loaded. If the DLL is loaded, GetModuleHandle returns a handle to the DLL; the application can then access the DLL using this handle. If the DLL is not loaded, GetModuleHandle returns NULL, in which case the application can load the DLL using the API function LoadLibrary.

In addition to sharing any DLL in the system, another significant aspect of DLL's behavior under 16-bit Windows is that the DLL has its own data segment wherein the DLL's static and global variables reside. When the DLL allocates memory using LocalAlloc, the memory is allocated from the DLL's own data segment. The result of this design is that all applications can easily share data stored in the DLL.

Even when you design a DLL as a shared service (with data that is common to all users of the DLL), the DLL may have to store information specific to each process that uses its services. For example, consider a DLL that acts as the gateway to a database. In this case, the DLL has to keep track of some state information about each process using the database. The DLL typically has to allocate memory to store and manage the per-process data.

The data sharing behavior of DLLs in 32-bit Windows is exactly the opposite of the behavior under 16-bit Windows.

DLLs in 32-Bit Windows

In Win32, the DLL becomes a part of the process that loads the DLL. There is only one copy of the DLL's code in physical memory—that single copy is mapped into the address space of each process that uses the DLL. However, the DLL's data is replicated in physical memory for each process that uses the DLL. Thus, each application that uses the DLL automatically gets a unique instance of the DLL's data.

Although shared data is not the default in Win32, you can still write a DLL that maintains a shared block of data. The sample DLL presented in the next few sections shows how to maintain shared data in a DLL.

Creating a DLL for Win32

Creating a DLL may have been difficult in the early days of 16-bit Windows when you had to write certain parts of the DLL in assembly language, but today DLLs are simple to write and debug. Visual C++ 2.0 and MFC 3.0 make it easy to build a DLL. The difficult part of writing the DLL is to decide what services the DLL provides and the interface (the functions) that applications use to access the DLL.

A Number Server DLL

As an example, consider a simple DLL that serves a number (you might think of the numbers as tokens). The DLL maintains a "current" number that applications can obtain by calling a function (GetNumber). The DLL automatically increments the number whenever an application gets a number from the DLL. This requires the DLL to share a variable among all processes using the DLL.

Additionally, the DLL is required to store another number on a per-process basis—there is one copy of this number for each process that uses the DLL.

The DLL in the example is called NEXTNUM (for "next number") and is easy to design. You provide a C interface to the DLL so that it can be used by any program even if it is not written using MFC. The interface (in the form of function prototypes) is declared in the header file NEXTNUM.H (Listing 26.1). The important step in defining the interface functions is including a qualifier that identifies these functions as exported functions from a DLL. For example, GetNumber is declared as the following:

```
__declspec(dllexport) int GetNumber();
```

Because the interface is a C-callable one, the interface declarations are embedded in an extern "C" block.

Listing 26.1. NEXTNUM.H. Header file for the NEXTNUM DLL.

```
//------------------------------------------------------------
// File: nextnum.h
//
// Prototypes of functions that are exported from
// the NEXTNUM DLL.

#ifndef __NEXTNUM_H
#define __NEXTNUM_H

#ifdef __cplusplus
extern "C" {
#endif

__declspec(dllexport) int GetNumber();

__declspec(dllexport) void SaveMyID(int id);
__declspec(dllexport) int GetMyID();

#ifdef __cplusplus
}  // extern "C"
#endif

#endif
```

Building NEXTNUM.DLL in Visual C++ 2.0

In Visual Workbench, use the following steps to create the NEXTNUM DLL:

1. When creating the project, select Dynamic-Link Library as the Project Type in the New Project dialog box and specify nextnum as the name of the project.

2. After the project (NEXTNUM.MAK) is created, prepare the NEXTNUM.CPP file (see Listing 26.2) and add it to the project.

3. In the Project Settings dialog, select Not Using MFC from the General tab (if you use MFC in the DLL, you should select Use MFC in a Static Library from the General tab).

4. In the Link tab of Project Settings dialog, add the following in the Project Options area:

```
/SECTION:.shrnum,rws
```

This makes the section named .shrnum a shareable section. Note that in NEXTNUM.CPP, the .shrnum section defines a shared variable as follows:

```
#pragma data_seg(".shrnum")   // Start a new section
                              // Place other shared data
                              // here
int nNumber = 1;              // Data must be initialized
#pragma data_seg()            // End the section
```

5. Build the DLL by selecting the appropriate menu item from the Project menu. The build process creates the following:

- ■ NEXTNUM.DLL, the DLL file
- ■ NEXTNUM.LIB, the import library that can be used by applications for implicit dynamic linking with NEXTNUM.DLL

Listing 26.2. NEXTNUM.CPP. Implementation of the NEXTNUM DLL.

```
//----------------------------------------------------------------
// File: nextnum.cpp
//
// Implementation of the NEXTNUM DLL that serves a number
// to client applications.
//----------------------------------------------------------------
#include "nextnum.h"

// Initialize the number (this part of DLL's data is shared)

#pragma data_seg(".shrnum")

// Place other shared data here...

int nNumber = 1;

#pragma data_seg()

// Room for a single ID (this is on a per-client basis)
int nMyID = 0;

//----------------------------------------------------------------
// G e t N u m b e r
//
// Return the next number

__declspec(dllexport) int GetNumber()
{
    return nNumber++;
}
//----------------------------------------------------------------
// S a v e M y I D
//
// Saves an ID provided by the client application

__declspec(dllexport) void SaveMyID(int nID)
```

continues

Listing 26.2. continued

```
{
    nMyID = nID;
}

//-------------------------------------------------------------
// G e t M y I D
//
// Returns the saved ID

__declspec(dllexport) int GetMyID()
{
  return nMyID;
}
```

A Test Client

You cannot run a DLL alone, so let's use AppWizard to write a test client for the number server DLL. The test program stores its process ID in the NEXTNUM DLL and provides a menu item that enables the user to get a number from the NEXTNUM DLL. Each number received from the DLL is stored in the document class of the application. The view class displays the process ID retrieved from the NEXTNUM DLL and also displays all the numbers that the client has obtained from the DLL.

For the TESTCLNT program, you use AppWizard to generate a single-document interface application that you modify and build as follows:

1. Add the following line to the file TESTCLNT.H:

    ```
    #include "nextnum.h"
    ```

    This declares the NEXTNUM DLL's exported functions that the test client will call.

2. To save the process ID in the NEXTNUM DLL, add the following lines of code to the file TESTCLNT.CPP (in the `CTestclntApp::InitInstance` function before the `return` statement):

    ```
    // Save the process ID in the NEXTNUM DLL
        SaveMyID(GetCurrentProcessId());
    ```

    `GetCurrentProcessId` is a Win32 API function that returns the process identifier of the calling process.

3. Let's use the application's document class to store numbers obtained from the NEXTNUM DLL. To do this, add the following member variables and member functions to the declaration of the `CTestclntDoc` class in the TESTCDOC.H file:

    ```
    class CTestclntDoc : public Cdocument
    {
    //...
    ```

```
// Implementation
public:
//...
    int GetNumber(int i) { return m_Numbers[i];}
    void PutNumber(int n)
    {
        m_Numbers[m_nCount++] = n;
    }
    int GetCount() { return m_nCount;}

protected:
    CDWordArray m_Numbers;
    int         m_nCount;
//...
}
```

4. You also need to add some code to initialize the member variables in the constructor of the CTestclntDoc class in the TESTCDOC.CPP file:

```
// CTestclntDoc construction/destruction

CTestclntDoc::CTestclntDoc()
{
    m_Numbers.SetSize(64, 16);
    m_nCount = 0;
}
```

5. Double-click on the TESTCLNT.RC file to edit the application's resources. Double-click on the item labeled Menu in the window that shows the resources. Then double-click on the item named IDR_MAINFRAME to edit the menu. Delete the menu items that you do not need. All you need is a File menu and a Help menu. Edit the first item of the File menu so that it reads Next number Ctrl+N. You will add code to the view class so that when the user selects the Next number menu item, the application calls the GetNumber function of the NEXTNUM DLL to retrieve a number.

6. Using Class Wizard, add the OnFileNew function to handle the ID_FILE_NEW command, which is tied to the first menu item in the File menu. The body of the OnFileNew function (in the TESTCVW.CPP file) is as follows:

```
void CTestclntView::OnFileNew()
{
    CTestclntDoc* pDoc = GetDocument();
    ASSERT_VALID(pDoc);
```

```
// Get the next number from the NEXTNUM DLL
    int number = GetNumber();

// Store the new number in the document
    pDoc->PutNumber(number);
    pDoc->UpdateAllViews(NULL);
}
```

Essentially, the OnFileNew function (which is called when the user selects Next number from the File menu) gets a number from the NEXTNUM DLL, stores it in the document, and updates the view by calling the UpdateAllViews function of the document class.

7. In an application that uses the document-view architecture, the view is updated by calling the OnDraw member function of the view class. For this application, edit the OnDraw function in the TESTCVW.CPP file as follows:

```
// CTestclntView drawing

void CTestclntView::OnDraw(CDC* pDC)
{
    CTestclntDoc* pDoc = GetDocument();
    ASSERT_VALID(pDoc);

    char buf[80];
    int i, n = pDoc->GetCount();
    int x = 8, y = 10, nc;

// Compute the line height based on current font
    TEXTMETRIC tm;
    pDC->GetTextMetrics(&tm);
    int line_height = tm.tmHeight + tm.tmExternalLeading;

// Display the ID
    nc = wsprintf(buf, "My ID is %x", GetMyID());
    pDC->TextOut(x, y, buf, nc);
    y += 2*line_height;

    if(n == 0)
    {
        nc = wsprintf(buf, "No numbers yet.");
        pDC->TextOut(x, y, buf, nc);
```

```
        }
        else
        {
// Display the numbers retrieved so far
            for(i = 0; i < n; I++)
            {
                nc;
                nc = wsprintf(buf, "Number[%d] = %d", I,
                            pDoc->GetNumber(i));
                pDC->TextOut(x, y, buf, nc);
                y += line_height;
            }
        }
    }
}
```

In this application, the OnDraw function gets the stored numbers from the document and displays them one by one.

8. Now you have to add the NEXTNUM.LIB library to the project. To add this library, select Files from the Project menu. In the resulting dialog box, set the file type to Library files (*.lib), and from the WinDebug subdirectory select the NEXTNUM.LIB file. Then click on the Add button to add the NEXTNUM.LIB library to the project.

9. After making these changes, build the application. To see how the number server DLL works, run a few copies of the application. For example, Figure 26.5 shows three copies of TESTCLNT running on a system. Whenever the user selects Next number from the File menu, the NEXTNUM DLL provides a number. Because the DLL maintains that number as a shared value, each instance of the client application gets the next available value from a single sequence. You can see this from the sequence of numbers displayed in the three instances of the TESTCLNT program shown in Figure 26.5.

Using MFC Classes in a DLL

The NEXTNUM DLL shown in the previous sections does not use any MFC classes. There are two ways to use MFC classes in your DLL:

■ Statically linking your DLL with MFC

■ Dynamically linking your DLL with the MFC DLL

Each approach has its advantages and disadvantages. The following sections describe the two methods.

FIGURE 26.5.

*Three copies of
TESTCLNT
running
on a system.*

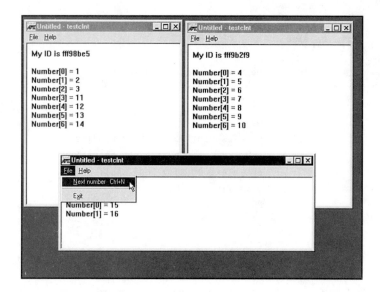

Static Linking with MFC Library

This approach is similar to the one used to build the NEXTNUM DLL. You can build the DLL following the same approach: select Use MFC in a Static Library from the General tab of the Project Settings dialog of the DLL's project. Then you can use MFC classes in the DLL.

Visual C++ 2.0's documentation uses the term "USRDLL version of MFC" to refer to the MFC library that is statically linked with your DLL. The term USRDLL comes from the fact that the preprocessor macro _USRDLL is defined when building a DLL that statically links with the MFC library.

With the USRDLL version of MFC, you can create DLLs that have the following advantages:

■ Any application (including those that do not use MFC or Visual C++ 2.0) can use the DLL as long as the application can call the exported functions of the DLL.

■ The DLL continues to work even if MFC classes change because the DLL is statically linked to its own copy of the MFC library.

A disadvantage of using the UDRDLL version of MFC is that the size of the DLL tends to be large. Additionally, if the application also uses MFC in a static library, the size of the application is large as well.

The process of implementing a DLL using the USRDLL version of MFC involves the following:

■ Declaring the exported functions of the DLL

■ Initializing the DLL when a process attaches itself to the DLL

- Implementing the internal as well as the exported functions of the DLL
- Cleaning up when a process detaches itself from the DLL
- Defining any shared data sections
- Defining the _WINDLL symbol (_USERDLL is defined when you select Use MFC in a Static Library from the General tab of the Project Settings dialog box)

The next few sections summarize these steps, using as an example a DLL that maintains a count of the processes that are currently using the services of the DLL. Let's call this the PCOUNT DLL because it provides a count of processes attached to the DLL.

Declaring the Exported Functions

You should provide a header file that declares the interface to your DLL. The interface is usually a number of functions that can be called from C. For example, in the PCOUNT DLL, an exported function might be GetPCount (that returns the number of processes currently attached to the DLL). In this case, you might provide a header file, PCOUNT.H, as shown in Listing 26.3.

Listing 26.3. PCOUNT.H. Header file with exported functions for a DLL.

```
//----------------------------------------------------------
// File: pcount.h
//
// Prototypes of functions that are exported from
// the PCOUNT DLL.

#ifndef __NEXTNUM_H
#define __NEXTNUM_H

#ifdef __cplusplus
extern "C" {
#endif

__declspec(dllexport) int GetPCount();


#ifdef __cplusplus
}  // extern "C"
#endif

#endif
```

DllMain DOES INITIALIZATION AND CLEANUP IN 32-BIT DLLS

In 16-bit Windows, DLLs provide the LibMain function for initialization and the WEP function for cleanup. In 32-bit Windows, both initialization and cleanup are performed by calling a single function named DllMain that is called whenever a process attaches to or detaches from a DLL. In fact, DllMain is called for each thread of the process as well, so you can perform thread-specific initialization and cleanup also.

Initializing and Cleaning Up

When you write a DLL using the Win32 API functions, the default function for initialization and cleanup is DllMain. When you write a DLL using the USRDLL version of MFC, MFC provides a DllMain. You merely derive a DLL class from CWinApp and provide the InitInstance and ExitInstance functions. The default DllMain function calls the following:

■ InitInstance whenever a process attaches to the DLL

■ ExitInstance whenever a process detaches from the DLL

Thus, you should place any per-process initialization in the InitInstance function and any cleanup code in the ExitInstance function of the DLL class.

For the PCOUNT DLL that maintains a count of the process attached to the DLL, the following steps are a good way to maintain the count:

■ Define a shared data section with an integer variable to store the count.

■ Increment the process count in the InitInstance function of the DLL class.

■ Decrement the process count in the ExitInstance function of the DLL class.

Listing 26.4 shows the file PCOUNT.CPP that implements these steps. The CPCountDLL class is derived from CWinApp, and its InitInstance and ExitInstance functions take care of maintaining the process count. The count is stored in the nProcCnt variable, which resides in a shared data section named .shrnum.

Listing 26.4. PCOUNT.CPP. Implementation of a "process counting" DLL.

```
//------------------------------------------------------------
// File : pcount.cpp
//
// Implementation of the PCOUNT DLL that counts processes
// that are using the DLL.
//------------------------------------------------------------
#include <afxwin.h>
#include "pcount.h"

// Initialize the process count (this part of DLL's data is shared)

#pragma data_seg(".shrnum")

// Place other shared data here...

int nProcCnt = 0;
```

```
#pragma data_seg()

class CPCountDLL : public CWinApp
{
public:

    CPCountDLL(LPCTSTR pszAppName) : CWinApp(pszAppName) {}

    virtual BOOL InitInstance(); // DLL initialization
    virtual int ExitInstance();  // DLL termination
};

// Create an instance of the DLL class
CPCountDLL PCountDLL("pcount.dll");
//-------------------------------------------------------------
// I n i t I n s t a n c e
//
// DLL Initialization (called when a process attaches to DLL)

BOOL CPCountDLL::InitInstance()
{
// Put any DLL initialization code here
    nProcCnt++;
    return TRUE;
}
//-------------------------------------------------------------
// E x i t I n s t a n c e
//
// Called when a process detaches from the DLL

int CPCountDLL::ExitInstance()
{
// Put any DLL termination code here
    nProcCnt--;
    return CWinApp::ExitInstance();
}
//-------------------------------------------------------------
// G e t P C o u n t
//
// Returns the total number of processes that are using the
// DLL

__declspec(dllexport) int GetPCount()
{
  return nProcCnt;
}
```

Dynamic Linking with the MFC DLL

When you dynamically link your DLL to MFC DLL, your DLL can be called only by MFC applications that also dynamically link with the MFC DLL. A DLL that dynamically links with the MFC DLL is called an *MFC Extension DLL* (or extension DLL, for short) because such a

DLL adds new classes, which are usually derived from other MFC classes. You could think of extension DLLs as a way of packaging your own document-view classes for shared use.

Visual C++ 2.0 makes it easy to generate the template for an extension DLL. All you have to do is create a new project and select MFC AppWizard (dll) as the Project Type in the New Project dialog. For example, if you create a project EXTDLL with a Project Type of MFC AppWizard (dll), AppWizard generates the EXTDLL.CPP file shown in Listing 26.5.

As you can see, there is an explicit `DllMain` function where you can add initialization and cleanup codes. If you check the Project Settings of the EXTDLL.MAK project, you will notice that in the General tab, the Microsoft Foundation Classes option is set to Use MFC in a Shared Dll (mfc30.(d)dll). That is how you have to set the option if you prepare the project file manually.

For an example of an extension DLL, see the DLLHUSK sample program in the \MSVC20\SAMPLES\MFC\DLLHUSK directory. This directory contains two extension DLLs—TESTDLL1.CPP and TESTDLL2.CPP—that you should examine to see how classes are added to an extension DLL.

Listing 26.5. Source file for an MFC Extension DLL generated by AppWizard.

```
// extdll.cpp : Defines the initialization routines for the DLL.
//

#include "stdafx.h"
#include <afxdllx.h>

#ifdef _DEBUG
#undef THIS_FILE
static char BASED_CODE THIS_FILE[] = __FILE__;
#endif

static AFX_EXTENSION_MODULE extdllDLL = { NULL, NULL };

extern "C" int APIENTRY
DllMain(HINSTANCE hInstance, DWORD dwReason, LPVOID lpReserved)
{
    if (dwReason == DLL_PROCESS_ATTACH)
    {
        TRACE0("EXTDLL.DLL Initializing!\n");

        // Extension DLL one-time initialization
        AfxInitExtensionModule(extdllDLL, hInstance);

        // Insert this DLL into the resource chain
        new CDynLinkLibrary(extdllDLL);
    }
    else if (dwReason == DLL_PROCESS_DETACH)
    {
        TRACE0("EXTDLL.DLL Terminating!\n");
    }
    return 1;   // ok
}
```

Summary

Dynamic Link Libraries (DLLs) are an integral part of Windows software architecture. When an application links with a static library, the linker copies all required object code from the library into the application. When an application uses a DLL, the DLL stays as a separate entity. At runtime, the application either implicitly or explicitly loads the DLL, and calls functions and uses data embedded in the DLL. The implicit loading mechanism requires the application to link with an import library that serves as a front-end for the DLL. For explicit loading, Windows provides API functions such as `LoadLibrary`, `GetProcAddress`, and `FreeLibrary` to load a DLL into memory, get the address of functions in the DLL, and detach the application from the DLL, respectively.

As a packaging mechanism, a DLL can store not only code, but data and resources as well. For example, you can store resources such as fonts, icons, bitmaps, and dialogs in a DLL. DLLs are widely used as an efficient mechanism to share code as well as to break up an application into components that can be easily upgraded.

The basic properties of DLLs have changed some in going from 16-bit Windows (Windows 3.1 and earlier versions) to 32-bit Windows (Win32) such as Windows NT. In 16-bit Windows, the DLL with all its data appears as a separate entity shared by all applications that use the DLL. In Win32, the DLL becomes part of the process that loads the DLL. Although there is only one copy of the DLL's code in both 16- and 32-bit Windows, the data is replicated for each process in Win32. Thus, in 16-bit Windows, it is easy to share data, but you have to add code to store per-process data. In Win32, the opposite is true: the DLL's data is automatically stored on a per-process basis, and you have to do some work to share data among processes.

Using Visual C++ 2.0, you can prepare a Win32 DLL easily. This chapter shows a sample DLL that illustrates how to implement data sharing in Win32 DLLs. You can also use MFC classes in DLLs—either as a statically linked library or with MFC itself in a shared DLL.

27

Using Dynamic Data Exchange (DDE)

There are times when a Windows application may need to exchange data with another Windows application. For example, your application may need to obtain some data from a spreadsheet automatically or acquire real-time data such as stock quotes from a communications program. You may even design a large application as a number of smaller, specialized applications that communicate with each other. For these needs, Dynamic Data Exchange (DDE) is the data exchange protocol of choice. To affect a DDE transfer, you need cooperating applications—both the sender and the receiver must support DDE. When it was first introduced, DDE had a reputation of being hard to program. Now, however, Microsoft provides the DDE Management Library (DDEML), which is an Application Programming Interface (API) designed for DDE. This chapter describes how to use the DDEML API in your MFC-based Windows applications.

What Is DDE?

DDE is an *interprocess communication mechanism (IPC)* that uses Windows messages and shared memory to enable cooperating applications to exchange data. There is a protocol underlying DDE that both the sending and receiving application must follow when exchanging data.

DDE is suitable for transferring data from one application to another, especially if the receiving application has to manipulate the data. In client-server terminology, the provider of the data is the DDE server and the recipient of the data is the DDE client. In DDE, both the client and the server applications must have knowledge of the data format.

As you will see in Chapter 28, "OLE 2.0 Programming with MFC 3.0," object linking and embedding provides a more comprehensive approach to using the data from a server application in a client program. In OLE, the client application provides a display area for the server's data; the client does not have to understand or manipulate the data—the server manages the display of the data. As a data exchange mechanism, DDE is at a lower level than OLE—in fact, OLE 1.0 depended on DDE for the data transport.

A DDE server also can accept commands from a client. For example, the Windows Program Manager accepts DDE commands that applications can use to create, display, and modify groups. Many Windows installation programs use these commands to install the application's icon in a group.

DDE Programming with DDEML

Originally, programmers had to implement the DDE protocol by a set of Windows messages. Programmers had to use Windows API functions `SendMessage` or `PostMessage` to send messages and include code to handle various types of messages. More recently, Microsoft introduced the DDEML API, which hides much of the complexity of the DDE protocol from the programmer. Rather than sending Windows messages directly, programmers call DDEML functions that are more intuitive and easier to use. In addition to simpler programming, another benefit of using the DDEML API to implement DDE is that the underlying mechanism of data exchange between client and server can be changed in the future without breaking applications that support DDE.

The basic idea of DDEML programming is to require both the server (the provider of data and services) and client (the requester of data and services) applications to provide a callback function (known as a DDE callback). The server and client call DDEML functions for various tasks. DDEML calls the callback functions to transfer information from one side to the other. Figure 27.1 shows the general idea of DDEML acting as an intermediary in DDE-based client-server communications.

FIGURE 27.1.

Client-server communication using DDEML.

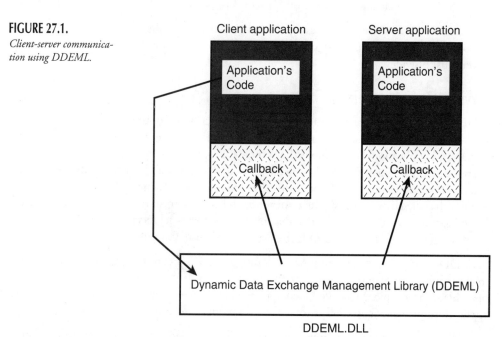

The following sections briefly describe how you can add DDE support to your own applications using the DDEML API, which is supported through a DLL called DDEML.DLL. If you use the DDEML functions, you have to include the DDEML.H header file in your appplication's source files and link with the DDEML.LIB import library.

DDE Terminology

Before diving into DDE programming, you should become familiar with some terms that have special meaning in DDE.

Client and Server

A *DDE client* is an application that initiates a data exchange operation or sends a command to a DDE server. The *server* is the application that responds to the client either with the requested data or by executing the command sent by the client. An application can be both client and server if it requests data from some applications and provides data to others.

Conversations and Transactions

A DDE client is said to have established a *conversation* with a DDE server when the client connects to the server for the purpose of exchanging data or requesting the execution of a command. Servers and clients can have multiple conversations.

The term *transaction* refers to a message exchanged between a client and a server. As you will see soon, transactions are processed by the DDE callback function that both the client and the server must provide.

Services, Topics, and Items

A DDE server provides one or more services with each service identified by a *service name.* Usually, a server provides a single service and the name of that service is the same as the name of the server application. For example, the Windows Program Manager provides a service named Progman and the service names for Microsoft Word for Windows and Microsoft Exel are WinWord and Excel, respectively. A benefit of having the service name the same as the server application's name is that the client can easily determine which program to start if a server is not available for the required service. For example, if a client needs the Excel service and no server is available, the client can run EXCEL.EXE (by using the WinExec function).

Each DDE service supports a number of topics. A *topic* is a common set of data that clients might request. For example, Microsoft Excel and Microsoft Word for Windows consider each open file to be a topic. Most file-based applications treat each open file as a topic, but other applications may choose to define topics in a different manner.

A DDE topic has one or more items. An *item* refers to a piece of data that clients can obtain from the server. For example, in Microsoft Excel, an item is a range of spreadsheet cells expressed in row-column coordinates. Thus, if you want to access the single cell at the intersection of the first row and the second column, you write the item's name as r1c2:r1c2.

The System Topic

To assist the client applications, a DDE server should always support a specific topic called the *System topic.* If a DDE server includes the System topic, DDE clients can easily find out information, such as the list of topics currently available from the server, the data formats that the server supports, the status of the server, and some help information.

Table 27.1 shows a few System topic items that a DDE server should support. Each entry shows the constant identifier from DDEML.H together with the current string equivalent in quotation marks. Use the defined constants in your application rather than the actual string to ensure portability. System topics that return lists (for example, the SZDDESYS_ITEM_SYSITEMS item) return tab-delimited text items.

Table 27.1. Typical System topic items for DDE servers.

Defined Constant	*Name*	*Description*
SZDDESYS_ITEM_SYSITEMS	"SysItems"	A tab-delimited list of items in the System topic. DDE servers should, at a minimum, include the following items in the System topic: SZDDESYS_ITEM_SYSITEMS, SZDDESYS_ITEM_TOPICS, SZDDE_ITEM_ITEMLIST, and SZDDESYS_ITEM_FORMATS.
SZDDESYS_ITEM_TOPICS	"Topics"	A tab-delimited list of the currently available topics.
SZDDESYS_ITEM_FORMATS	"Formats"	A tab-delimited list of names of all the formats supported by the server. All DDE servers should support the CF_TEXT format (the format name is "TEXT"). On Windows NT, the server should also support CF_UNICODETEXT.
SZDDE_ITEM_ITEMLIST	"TopicItemList"	A tab-delimited list of items for each topic other than the System topic.
SZDDESYS_ITEM_HELP	"Help"	Text that briefly explains how to use the DDE server.
SZDDESYS_ITEM_STATUS	"Status"	An indication of the current status of the server. The server should return either Busy or Ready, as appropriate.

DDE Links

When a DDE client initiates a conversation with a DDE server, the client forms a *link* with the server. There are three types of links:

■ *Cold Link* refers to the situation wherein a client establishes a conversation, makes a one-time request for data from the server, and terminates the conversation after the transaction. In this case, if the server's data changes, the client will not be aware of the changes.

■ *Hot Link* refers to the case wherein, after the client establishes a conversation, the server continues to retransmit the data whenever it changes. A hot link is useful for maintaining a continual data stream from one application to another.

■ *Warm Link* is like a hot link, but rather than retransmitting the new data, the server notifies the client whenever the data changes. After receiving the notification, the client has to request the new data explicitly.

DDE Commands

In addition to providing data, a DDE server can also execute a command sent by the client. A DDE command is a special type of transaction (the XTYP_EXECUTE transaction) that clients use to send commands to a DDE server.

DDE Handles

In DDEML, strings and data are identified by handles. Data transferred between a server and a client is identified by an HDDEDATA handle. Strings identifying service, topic, and item names are represented by HSZ handles.

There are other handles as well. For example, the DDE conversation is identified by an HCONV handle.

Event Sequence in a DDE Conversation

Table 27.2 shows a sequence of events for a simple DDE transaction wherein a client establishes a conversation with a server, requests data, and, after completing the necessary transactions, ends the conversation.

Table 27.2. Sequence of events in a typical DDE conversation.

Step Action by Client	Action by Server
1. Initializes DDEML by calling DdeInitialize. Provides a DDE callback function.	Initializes DDEML by calling DDEInitialize. Provides a DDE callback function.
2. Connects to server by calling DdeConnect or DdeConnectList.	Server's callback function receives an XTYP_CONNECT transaction. Callback function returns TRUE if topic and item are available.

Step	Action by Client	Action by Server
3.	Initiates transaction by calling DdeClientTransaction (assume synchronous for this example).	Server's callback function receives an XTYP_REQUEST transaction. If server can provide data, it creates a memory block by calling DdeCreateDataHandle, copies requested data to that memory, and returns the HDDEDATA handle.
4.	DdeClientTransaction returns the HDDEDATA handle with the data from the server. Client reads the data by calling DdeAccessData and uses data according to its needs. (In an asynchronous transaction, client's callback function is called with an XTYP_XACT_COMPLETE transaction.)	Server waits for more transactions.
5.	Repeats steps 3 and 4 to get more data if necessary.	Server handles transactions, if any.
6.	Closes the conversation by calling DdeDisconnect or DdeDisconnectList.	Server's callback function gets an XTYP_DISCONNECT transaction, which tells the server that the conversation has ended.
7.	Calls DdeUninitialize to indicate that it no longer needs the DDEML DLL.	Server may also call DdeUninitialize if it does not need DDEML anymore.

The next few sections briefly describe some of these steps.

Initialization

When an application uses DDEML, it must call the DdeInitialize function before calling any DDEML functions. For ASCII text, the DdeInitialize function is declared in DDEML.H as follows (a different function is provided for wide-character text, which is used to support UNICODE):

```
UINT DdeInitialize(
    LPDWORD     pidInst,     // Location where DDE instance
                             // handle is returned.
    PFNCALLBACK pfnCallback, // DDE callback function
    DWORD       afCmd,       // Indicates type of application
                             // and types of transactions the
                             // application wants to receive.
    DWORD       ulRes);      // Must be set to zero.
```

This function returns DMLERR_NO_ERROR if there are no errors; otherwise, it returns one of the following error codes: DMLERR_DLL_USAGE, DMLERR_INVALIDPARAMETER, or DMLERR_SYS_ERROR.

The first argument (pidInst) to the DdeInitialize function should be a DWORD initialized to zero. On return, this DWORD holds the DDE instance handle—an identifier that you have to provide as an argument when calling many of the DDEML functions.

The afCmd argument is a bitwise OR combination of APPCLASS_, APPCMD_, CBF_, and MF_ flags that respectively tell DDEML the class of application, type of application, the types of transactions to be filtered by DDEML, and any monitoring activity to be performed. For example, if you want to write a DDE client application, you might use the following flag:

APPCMD_CLIENTONLY

If you do not have a callback function, you can filter out all transactions by providing the following as afCmd:

APPCMD_CLIENTONLY ¦ CBF_SKIP_ALLNOTIFICATIONS

The pfnCallback argument is the address of the callback function. If you do not have a callback function, set this argument to NULL.

DDE Callback Function

DDEML calls the DDE callback function to notify the application of various events such as the beginning and end of conversation and the arrival of data. The DDE callback function should have the following prototype:

```
HDDEDATA CALLBACK DdeCallback(
    UINT      uType,   // Transaction type (see Table 27.3)
    UINT      uFmt,    // Format in which data is sent or received
    HCONV     hConv,   // Conversation associated with the
                       // transaction
    HSZ       hsz1,    // String handles whose meaning
    HSZ       hsz2,    // depends on the type of transaction
    HDDEDATA  hData,   // DDE data (meaning depends on
                       // type of transaction)
    DWORD     dwData1, // Transaction-specific data
    DWORD     dwData2);// Transaction-specific data
```

There are many arguments because the DDE callback transfers much more than simple messages. The meaning of the arguments depends on the value of the first argument, which indicates the transaction type. Table 27.3 shows a list of 15 transactions with a brief description of each transaction.

Table 27.3. DDEML Transactions.

Transaction	Description
XTYP_ADVDATA	Notifies a client that the value of a data item has changed. The arguments hsz1 and hsz2 are the topic name and item name, respectively. The data is in hData. The callback function should return DDE_FACK if it processes this transaction, DDE_FBUSY if it is too busy to process this transaction, or DDE_FNOTPROCESSED if it does not want to process the transaction.
XTYP_ADVREQ	Notifies a server that an advise transaction is outstanding (this occurs when the server application calls the DDEML function DdePostAdvise). The topic name and item name are in the arguments hsz1 and hsz2, respectively. The callback function should call the DdeCreateDataHandle function to create a data handle that identifies the changed data and then should return the handle. If the server is unable to complete the transaction, it should return NULL.
XTYP_ADVSTART	Notifies a server that a client is starting an advise loop with the server on the topic and item identified by the string handles hsz1 and hsz2, respectively. The server's DDE callback function should return TRUE to enable the advise loop or FALSE to deny the advise loop.
XTYP_ADVSTOP	Notifies a server that a client is ending an advise loop with the server on the topic and item identified by the string handles hsz1 and hsz2, respectively. This transaction does not require any return value.
XTYP_CONNECT	Notifies a server that a client has requested connection for a topic and service identified by the string handles hsz1 and hsz2, respectively. The dwData1 argument should point to a CONVCONTEXT structure that contains context information for the conversation. The dwData2 argument is 1 if the client is the same application instance as the server; otherwise, this argument is 0. The callback function should return TRUE to enable the client to establish a conversation, or the function should return FALSE to deny the conversation.

continues

Table 27.3. continued

Transaction	Description
XTYP_CONNECT_CONFIRM	Confirms to the server that a conversation has been established for the topic and service identified by the string handles hsz1 and hsz2, respectively. The dwData2 argument is 1 if the client is the same application instance as the server; otherwise, this argument is 0. This transaction does not require a return value.
XTYP_DISCONNECT	Notifies a client or a server that the other party of a conversation has terminated the conversation. The dwData2 argument is 1 if the client is the same application instance as the server; otherwise, this argument is 0. This transaction does not require a return value.
XTYP_ERROR	Notifies a client or a server that a critical error has occurred. The low-order word of dwData1—LOWORD(dwData1)— contains the error code. This transaction does not require a return value.
XTYP_EXECUTE	Notifies a server that a client has sent a command string for execution by the server. The hsz1 argument specifies the topic. The callback function should return DDE_FACK if it processes this transaction, DDE_FBUSY if it is too busy to process this transaction, or DDE_FNOTPROCESSED if it does not want to process the transaction.
XTYP_MONITOR	Notifies a DDE debugging application that a DDE event has occurred. The hData argument identifies the DDE data object that contains information about the DDE event. The application must have specified the APPCLASS_MONITOR flag when it called the DdeInitialize function. The callback function should return 0 if it processes this transaction.
XTYP_POKE	Notifies a server that a client has sent unsolicited data for a conversation on the topic and item identified by the string handles hsz1 and hsz2, respectively. The callback function should return DDE_FACK if it processes this transaction, DDE_FBUSY if it is too busy to process this transaction, or DDE_FNOTPROCESSED if it does not want to process the transaction.

Transaction	Description
XTYP_REGISTER	Notifies an application that a DDE server has called the DdeNameService function to register a service name or that a non-DDEML application that supports the System topic has started. The hsz1 and hsz2 arguments respectively identify the base service name and the instance-specific service name being registered. The callback function does not have to return a value for this transaction.
XTYP_REQUEST	Notifies a server that a client has requested data for a topic and item identified by the string handles hsz1 and hsz2, respectively. The server's callback function should call the DdeCreateDataHandle function to create a data object, copy the requested data into that data object, and return that handle. The callback function should return NULL if it is unable to complete the transaction. If the function returns NULL, DDEML sends a DDE_FNOTPROCESSED acknowledgment flag to the client.
XTYP_UNREGISTER	Notifies a DDEML application that a DDEML server application has used the DdeNameService function to unregister a service name or a non-DDEML application that supports the System topic has terminated. The hsz1 and hsz2 arguments respectively identify the base service name and the instance-specific service name being unregistered. This transaction does not require a return value.
XTYP_WILDCONNECT	Notifies a server that a client is requesting conversation with any server that provides the topic and service identified by the string handles hsz1 and hsz2, respectively. If these handles are NULL, the client is a conversation on all topic names that the server supports. The dwData1 argument points to a CONVCONTEXT structure that contains context information for the conversation. The dwData2 argument is 1 if the client is the same application instance as the server; otherwise, this argument is 0. The callback function should return an array of HSZPAIR structures. There should be one structure for each topic-service pair that matches the topic-service requested by the client. A NULL string handle should terminate the array. To refuse the XTYP_WILDCONNECT transaction, the callback function should return NULL.

continues

Table 27.3. continued

Transaction	Description
XTYP_XACT_COMPLETE	Notifies a client that an asynchronous transaction, initiated by the client by calling the DdeClientTransaction function, has completed. The hsz1 and hsz2 string handles identify the topic and item name, respectively. The data sent by the server, if any, is in the hData argument. (The callback function should call DdeGetData to copy the data.) The dwData1 argument has the transaction identifier for the completed transaction. This transaction does not require a return value.

A typical DDE callback function uses a switch statement to handle different types of transactions. For example, the callback function for a DDEML client application might be as follows:

```
//-------------------------------------------------------------
// DDE callback function for a DDEML client
//

HDDEDATA CALLBACK DDECallback(UINT uType, UINT uFmt,
    HCONV hConv, HSZ hsz1,HSZ hsz2, HDDEDATA hDDEData,
    DWORD dwData1, DWORD dwData2)
{
    switch (uType)
    {
        case XTYP_REGISTER:
// New server available
//...
        break;

        case XTYP_DISCONNECT:
// Server terminated conversation
//...
        break;

        case XTYP_ADVDATA:
// Data (requested by an earlier asynchronous transfer
// request) has arrived from server
    {
            BYTE *pData;
            DWORD dwLength;
            pData = DdeAccessData(hDDEData, &dwLength);

            if (pData)
            {
// Process data as necessary
//...
            }

// When done with the data, call DdeUnaccessData.
// No need to free the data handle.
```

```
            DdeUnaccessData(hDDEData);
            return (HDDEDATA) DDE_FACK;
        }

        case XTYP_XACT_COMPLETE:
// Asynchronous transaction has completed
//...
        return NULL;

        default:
// Call default transaction handler, if any.
//...
    }

    return NULL;
}
```

Starting a DDE Conversation

After calling DdeInitialize, a client application can attempt to start a conversation with a server by calling DdeConnect. (This step does not apply to a server because the server handles as requests for conversations arrive via its DDE callback function.) For example, to start a conversation with a server that provides a service named Excel and a topic named AWIPS96.XLS, the client application calls this:

```
    HSZ hszService, hszTopic;
    HCONV hConv;  // store this for later use
//...
// Assume that dwDDEInst is the DDE instance returned
// by DdeInitialize
    hszService = DdeCreateStringHandle(dwDDEInst, "Excel",
                                    CP_WINANSI);
    hszTopic = DdeCreateStringHandle(dwDDEInst, "AWIPS96.XLS",
                                    CP_WINANSI);
// Establish conversation and save hConv for later use
    hConv = DdeConnect(dwDDEInst, hszService, hszTopic, NULL);

    if(!hConv)
    {
// Error connecting to a server. Handle error by trying to
// start the server application (see later in this section).
//...
    }

// Free the string handles now

    DdeFreeStringHandle(dwDDEInst, hszService);
    DdeFreeStringHandle(dwDDEInst, hszTopic);
```

DDEML sets up the conversation by sending an XTYP_CONNECT transaction to each DDE server's DDE callback function. The server's callback usually checks whether it supports the specified service and topic and returns TRUE to accept the connection.

A client can connect to multiple servers by calling the DdeConnectList function, which returns the conversation handles in an HCONVLIST list. You can walk through the list of conversations and examine the details of each conversation using DdeQueryNextServer.

If DdeConnect returns NULL, you may want to start the server by calling WinExec. For example, if connection to a service and topic identified by the strings lpszService and lpszTopic fails, you might start the server application as follows:

```
// Assume that hConv is the conversation handle that
// DdeConnect returned (and it's NULL because the service
// was not found.)

    if(!hConv)
    {
// Construct command line for WinExec (assume that server
// application's name is the same as the service name).

        char buf[256];
        wsprintf(buf, "%s.EXE %s", lpszService, lpszTopic);

        UINT status = WinExec(buf, SW_SHOWNOACTIVATE);

// Check status for error (If successful, WinExec returns
// a value greater than 31).
        if(status < 32)
        {
// Handle error (probably display a MessageBox with an
// appropriate message and return an error value).
//...
        }
    }
```

Requesting Data

After a conversation is established (DdeConnect has returned a non-NULL conversation handle), a DDE client application can begin requesting data from the server. To request data, the client application calls DdeClientTransaction to send transactions to the server. For example, to make a single request for a data item, the client application might use the following code fragment:

```
// Local buffer to hold data
    BYTE dbuf[256];

// Assume that hConv is the conversation handle returned by
// DdeConnect
    if(hConv)
    {
// Prepare a string handle for the item being requested
// from the server (in this case, the application is
// requesting a range of cells from an Excel spreadsheet).
// (Assume that dwDDEInst is the DDE instance returned
// by DdeInitialize).

        HSZ hszItem = DdeCreateStringHandle(dwDDEInst,
                                            "r1c1:r10c4",
                                            CP_WINANSI);
```

```
// Request data from server
      HDDEDATA hData = DdeClientTransaction(
                           NULL,     // Address of data to server
                           0,        // Length of data
                           hConv,    // Conversation handle
                           hszItem, // Item name handle
                           CF_TEXT, // Data format
                           XTYP_REQUEST, // Transaction type
                           1000,        // Timeout in milliseconds
                           &dwResult); // Local for returned
                                       // result
// Free the string handle because it is no longer needed.
      DdeFreeStringHandle(dwDDEInst, hszItem);

// Process received data. Here we show how to copy up to
// 256 bytes from the returned data into a local buffer
//...
      if(hData)
      {
// Copy data into local buffer dbuf
         DdeGetData(
            hData, // DDE object containing data
            dbuf,  // Copy into this buffer
            256,   // Maximum number of bytes to copy
            0);    // Offset to beginning of data
                   // within the DDE object

// Now free the data object
         DdeFreeDataHandle(hData);
      }
   }
```

DDEML calls the server's callback function with this transaction. The server's callback function processes the transaction by calling the DDEML function DdeCreateDataHandle to set up the data and return an HDDEDATA handle. Eventually, the HDDEDATA handle makes its way to the client as a return value from the DdeClientTransaction function.

Setting Up Links

When a client makes a request for data using the XTYP_REQUEST transaction, it establishes a cold link.

Setting up a hot link is also referred to as setting up an advise loop. To set up a hot link, the client application sends an XTYP_ADVSTART transaction. When the server has new data, DDEML sends the data to the client by calling the client application's callback function with an XTYP_ADVDATA transaction.

With a warm link, the client receives notification of data availability without the actual data. To set up a warm link, the client application calls DdeClientTransaction with a transaction type of XTYP_ADVSTART ¦ XTYP_NODATA.

Ending a DDE Conversation

When a client wants to end a DDE conversation, it calls DdeDisconnect or DdeDisconnectList. To completely shut down all DDE activity, the application calls DdeUninitialize. Usually, a client calls before DdeUninitialize exiting. Thus, if a DDE client is ending a DDE conversation and terminating, it does so as follows:

```
// Assume hConv is the conversation handle

    DdeDisconnect(hConv);

// Assume that dwDDEInst is the DDE instance that was
// returned by DdeInitialize

    DdeUninitialize(dwDDEInst);
```

DDEML Functions

In going through the steps of DDEML programming, you have seen a number of DDEML functions mentioned in the earlier sections. Table 27.4 lists all 28 DDEML functions in alphabetical order. You will see some of these functions used again in the example programs later in this chapter.

Table 27.4. DDEML Functions.

Function	Description
DdeAbandonTransaction	Stops a specified asynchronous transaction in progress
DdeAccessData	Locks a DDE data object (specified by HDDEDATA handle) and provides access to the data by returning a pointer to the first byte of data (or NULL if the data cannot be accessed)
DdeAddData	Adds data to a specified HDDEDATA object
DdeClientTransaction	Begins a DDE transaction with a specified server (identified by a handle to the conversation)
DdeCmpStringHandles	Compares two string handles and returns zero if they are equal (this amounts to a case-insensitive comparison of the two strings)
DdeConnect	Establishes a DDE conversation with a server that supports the specified service and topic
DdeConnectList	Establishes DDE conversations with all servers that support the specified service and topic
DdeCreateDataHandle	Allocates a block of memory for a DDE data object and returns an HDDEDATA handle

Function	Description
DdeCreateStringHandle	Creates and returns an HSZ handle for a specified null-terminated string
DdeDisconnect	Terminates a DDE conversation started by DdeConnect or DdeConnectList
DdeDisconnectList	Terminates all DDE conversation started by a previous call to DdeConnectList
DdeEnableCallback	Enables or disables transactions for a specified DDE conversation (or all conversations)
DdeFreeDataHandle	Releases the memory associated with the DDE data object identified by an HDDEDATA handle
DdeFreeStringHandle	Frees the specified HSZ handle
DdeGetData	Copies data from a DDE object identified by an HDDEDATA handle to a buffer provided by the application
DdeGetLastError	Returns the last error value and resets the error value to DMLERR_NO_ERROR
DdeImpersonateClient	Impersonates a DDE client (identified by a conversation handle)
DdeInitialize	Registers an application with DDEML by providing a DDE callback function that DDEML calls to handle DDE transactions (this must be the first step in starting a DDE conversation)
DdeKeepStringHandle	Increments the usage count of a string (for use in DDE callback functions to ensure that the string is not released when the callback function returns)
DdeNameService	Registers a service name with DDEML
DdePostAdvise	Called by a server whenever the data associated with a topic-item pair changes (calls the server's DDE callback function with an XTYP_ADVREQ transaction)
DdeQueryConvInfo	Fills in an application-provided structure with information about a DDE transaction
DdeQueryNextServer	Returns the next conversation handle (HCONV) in the specified conversation list
DdeQueryString	Copies the string associated with an HSZ handle to a buffer provided by the application

continues

Table 27.4. continued

Function	Description
DdeReconnect	Attempts to reestablish a conversation with a service that has terminated the conversation
DdeSetUserHandle	Associates a 32-bit value with a conversation handle or transaction identifier
DdeUnaccessData	Unlocks the DDE data object identified by an HDDEDATA handle that was locked by a previous call to DdeAccessData
DdeUninitialize	Ends a DDE session that uses DDEML (this frees all DDEML resources associated with the calling application)

Sample Applications with DDEML

The following sections present two simple MFC-based applications that use the DDEML functions for DDE. The first program enables the user to connect to a specified DDE service and obtain a data item. The second example shows how an installation program might add a new program group by sending DDE commands to the PROGMAN service (Windows Program Manager).

Getting Data from a DDE Server

To show how to access a DDE server from an MFC application, consider an application that offers a menu option through which the user can connect to a specified DDE service and request a data item. The application needs a dialog box to prompt the user for the names of a service, a topic, and an item as required for a DDE conversation. You can build such an application easily with MFC AppWizard. Here are the steps:

1. Generate a Single Document Interface AppWizard application named DDECLNT (for DDE Client) without the tool bar, status bar, and any printing or print preview support.

2. After the application's files are generated, double-click on the resource file, DDECLNT.RC. Double-click on the item labeled Menu in the window that shows the resources. Then double-click on the item named IDR_MAINFRAME to edit the menu. Remove the unnecessary menu items. Change the first entry in the File menu to Connect to DDE Server.... While editing the resources, add a new dialog with three combo boxes and two buttons labeled OK and Cancel (see Figure 27.2). This dialog box will be used to prompt the user for the service name, topic name, and item name.

3. Add a new class, `DDEDlg`, for the Connect to DDE Server dialog needed by this application. Listings 27.1 and 27.2 show the files DDEDLG.H and DDEDLG.CPP, respectively, that define and implement the `DDEDlg` class.

To create the `DDEDlg` class, first prepare the dialog's resource (by editing the resource file) and then use ClassWizard to create a new class derived from `CDialog`. Specify the resource ID of the Connect to DDE Server dialog in the input area labeled Dialog (this appears only when you add a class derived from `CDialog`) in ClassWizard's Add Class dialog box.

After the class is added, add member variables `m_Service`, `m_Topic`, and `m_Item` to hold values specified through the three combo boxes in the newly defined dialog box, using the Member Variables tab of the ClassWizard's tab dialog. ClassWizard automatically generates the code needed to transfer values from the dialog box into these member variables.

The only part of the `DDEDlg` class that you have to write is the `OnInitDialog` member function that is called to initialize the dialog box before it is displayed. As you can see in Listing 27.2, you connect to all available DDE services and list them in the combo box that shows the service names. If the PROGMAN service is available, you set up the topic to be PROGMAN and the item as GROUPS so that users have a default choice when the dialog first appears.

In the `OnInitDialog` function, you have to access the DDE instance stored in the `dwDDEInst` variable of the application class. You can use a global variable to access the single instance of the application as follows:

```
extern CDdeclntApp theApp;
```

Listing 27.1. DDEDLG.H. Declaration of the `DDEDlg` dialog class.

```
// ddedlg.h : header file
//

/////////////////////////////////////////////////////////////////
// DDEDlg dialog

class DDEDlg : public CDialog
{
// Construction
public:
    DDEDlg(CWnd* pParent = NULL);    // standard constructor

// Dialog Data
    //{{AFX_DATA(DDEDlg)
    enum { IDD = IDD_DIALOG1 };
    CString    m_Service;
    CString    m_Topic;
    CString    m_Item;
```

continues

Listing 27.1. continued

```
    //}}AFX_DATA


// Overrides
    // ClassWizard generated virtual function overrides
    //{{AFX_VIRTUAL(DDEDlg)
    protected:
    virtual void DoDataExchange(CDataExchange* pDX);    // DDX/DDV support
    //}}AFX_VIRTUAL

// Implementation
protected:

    // Generated message map functions
    //{{AFX_MSG(DDEDlg)
    virtual BOOL OnInitDialog();
    //}}AFX_MSG
    DECLARE_MESSAGE_MAP()
};
```

Listing 27.2. DDEDLG.CPP. Implementation of the DDEDlg dialog class.

```
// ddedlg.cpp : implementation file
//

#include "stdafx.h"
#include "ddeclnt.h"
#include "ddedlg.h"

#ifdef _DEBUG
#undef THIS_FILE
static char BASED_CODE THIS_FILE[] = __FILE__;
#endif

extern CDdeclntApp theApp;

/////////////////////////////////////////////////////////////////
// DDEDlg dialog


DDEDlg::DDEDlg(CWnd* pParent /*=NULL*/)
    : CDialog(DDEDlg::IDD, pParent)
{
    //{{AFX_DATA_INIT(DDEDlg)
    m_Service = _T("");
    m_Topic = _T("");
    m_Item = _T("");
    //}}AFX_DATA_INIT
}


void DDEDlg::DoDataExchange(CDataExchange* pDX)
{
    CDialog::DoDataExchange(pDX);
    //{{AFX_DATA_MAP(DDEDlg)
```

```
    DDX_CBString(pDX, IDC_COMBO1, m_Service);
    DDV_MaxChars(pDX, m_Service, 256);
    DDX_CBString(pDX, IDC_COMBO2, m_Topic);
    DDV_MaxChars(pDX, m_Topic, 256);
    DDX_CBString(pDX, IDC_COMBO3, m_Item);
    DDV_MaxChars(pDX, m_Item, 256);
    //}}AFX_DATA_MAP
}


BEGIN_MESSAGE_MAP(DDEDlg, CDialog)
    //{{AFX_MSG_MAP(DDEDlg)
    //}}AFX_MSG_MAP
END_MESSAGE_MAP()


/////////////////////////////////////////////////////////////////
// DDEDlg message handlers

BOOL DDEDlg::OnInitDialog()
{
    CDialog::OnInitDialog();

// Initialize contents of the dialog
    HCONVLIST hConvList;
    DWORD dwDDEInst = theApp.dwDDEInst;

    hConvList = DdeConnectList(dwDDEInst,
                        NULL, // Any service
                        NULL, // Any topic
                        NULL, // New conversation list
                        NULL);// Default context

// Walk through the returned list and fill in the Service list
    if(hConvList)
    {
        HCONV hConv = NULL;
        CONVINFO cinfo;
        cinfo.cb = sizeof(CONVINFO);
        CComboBox *pCB = (CComboBox*)GetDlgItem(IDC_COMBO1);
        TCHAR buf[256];

        while (hConv = DdeQueryNextServer(hConvList, hConv))
        {

            UINT status = DdeQueryConvInfo(hConv,QID_SYNC,
                                      &cinfo);

// Get the name of the server
            DdeQueryString(dwDDEInst, cinfo.hszSvcPartner,
                        buf, sizeof(buf), CP_WINANSI);

// Add the name to the service list
            pCB->AddString(buf);
        }

// Close all conversations
        DdeDisconnectList(hConvList);
```

continues

Listing 27.2. continued

```
// Select PROGMAN as the default service
        if(pCB->SelectString(0, "progman") != CB_ERR)
        {
// Add topic "progman" and item "groups"
            CComboBox *pCBT = (CComboBox*)
                                GetDlgItem(IDC_COMBO2);
            pCBT->AddString("Progman");
            pCBT->SetCurSel(0);

            pCBT = (CComboBox*)GetDlgItem(IDC_COMBO3);
            pCBT->AddString("Groups");
            pCBT->SetCurSel(0);
        }
    }

    return TRUE;  // return TRUE unless you set the focus to a control
                  // EXCEPTION: OCX Property Pages should return FALSE
}
```

Now continue the steps:

4. Add the DDEML.H header file to STDAFX.H:

   ```
   #include <ddeml.h>    // For DDEML functions
   ```

5. In the application class, CDdeclntApp, add the member variable dwDDEInst to store the DDE instance handle (in the DDECLNT.H file):

   ```
   class CDdeclntApp : public CWinApp
   {
   public:
       CDdeclntApp();

   // DDE Instance handle
       DWORD dwDDEInst;

   //...
   }
   ```

   In the CDdeclntApp class constructor (in the DDECLNT.CPP file), initialize the dwDDEInst variable to zero:

   ```
   CDdeclntApp::CDdeclntApp()
   {
       dwDDEInst = 0;
   }
   ```

6. In the InitInstance function of the CDdeclntApp class, add the following code to initialize DDEML:

```
// Place this near the beginning of the DDECLNT.CPP file
// DDE Callback Function
HDDEDATA CALLBACK DDECallback(UINT uType, UINT uFmt, HCONV hConv,
                             HSZ hsz1, HSZ hsz2, HDDEDATA hData,
                             DWORD dwData1, DWORD dwData2);
//...


// CDdeclntApp initialization
BOOL CDdeclntApp::InitInstance()
{
//...


// Initialize DDEML (DDECallback is declared above)

    DdeInitialize(&dwDDEInst, DDECallback,
                  APPCMD_CLIENTONLY, 0);
//...


    return TRUE;
}
```

Add the following `ExitInstance` function to the `CDdeclntApp` class (in the DDECLNT.CPP file):

```
int CDdeclntApp::ExitInstance()
{
// Uninitialize DDEML
    DdeUninitialize(dwDDEInst);
    return CWinApp::ExitInstance();
}
```

7. Note that the `DdeInitialize` function call in step 6 specifies a callback function named `DDECallback`. This example program does not really need a callback function, but it includes the function to show how to define a DDE callback function. For this example, add the following definition of `DDECallback` function to the DDECLNT.CPP file:

```
        // DDE callback
    HDDEDATA CALLBACK DDECallback(UINT uType, UINT uFmt, HCONV hConv,
                                  HSZ hsz1, HSZ hsz2, HDDEDATA hData,
                                  DWORD dwData1, DWORD dwData2)

    {
        return NULL;
    }
```

8. You will use the document class to retrieve and store the requested DDE data. In the header file for the document, DDECLDOC.H, add the following member variable and member functions:

```
class CDdeclntDoc : public Cdocument
{
//...

// Implementation
public:
//...

// DoDDE carries out the DDE transaction
    void DoDDE(CString& service, CString& topic, CString& item);

// GetDDEdata provides access to the retrieved DDE data stored
// in the document object
    CString& GetDDEdata() { return m_DDEdata;}

protected:
    CString m_DDEdata;  // To store retrieved DDE data
//...
};
```

Initialize the m_DDEdata string in the CDdeclntDoc class constructor (in the DDECLDOC.CPP file):

```
CDdeclntDoc::CDdeclntDoc()
{
    m_DDEdata = "Select 'Connect to DDE Server...' from File menu";
}
```

9. In the DDECLDOC.CPP file that implements the document class, add the code for the DoDDE function as shown in Listing 27.3.

Listing 27.3. Implementation of the DoDDE function in the document class.

```
extern CDdeclntApp theApp; // Need this to access the DDE instance

void CDdeclntDoc::DoDDE(CString& service, CString& topic,
                        CString& item)
{
    m_DDEdata = "Service: ";
    if(service.GetLength() > 0)
        m_DDEdata += service;
    else
        m_DDEdata += "(None)";
```

```
    m_DDEdata += " Topic: ";
    if(topic.GetLength() > 0)
        m_DDEdata += topic;
    else
        m_DDEdata += "(None)";

    m_DDEdata += " Item: ";
    if(item.GetLength() > 0)
        m_DDEdata += item;
    else
        m_DDEdata += "(None)";
    m_DDEdata += "\n------------------------------------\n";

// Establish a DDE conversation
    DWORD dwDDEInst = theApp.dwDDEInst;

    HSZ hszService = DdeCreateStringHandle(dwDDEInst,
                            service.GetBuffer(256),
                                    CP_WINANSI);
    service.ReleaseBuffer(-1);

    HSZ hszTopic = DdeCreateStringHandle(dwDDEInst,
                            topic.GetBuffer(256),
                                    CP_WINANSI);
    topic.ReleaseBuffer(-1);
    HCONV hConv = DdeConnect(dwDDEInst, hszTopic,
                            hszService, NULL);

// Free the HSZs now
    DdeFreeStringHandle(dwDDEInst, hszService);
    DdeFreeStringHandle(dwDDEInst, hszTopic);

    if(!hConv)
    {
        m_DDEdata += "Could not connect to server\n";
        return;
    }

// Try to get the specified item in CF_TEXT format

    HSZ hszItem = DdeCreateStringHandle(dwDDEInst,
                            item.GetBuffer(256),
                                    CP_WINANSI);
    item.ReleaseBuffer(-1);
    DWORD dwResult;
    HDDEDATA hDDEData = DdeClientTransaction(NULL,
                                0,
                                hConv,
                                hszItem,
                                CF_TEXT,
                                XTYP_REQUEST,
                                1000, // timeout
                                &dwResult);

    DdeFreeStringHandle(dwDDEInst, hszItem);

    if(hDDEData)
    {
```

continues

```
// Lock the data so we can parse it
     DWORD dwLength;
     BYTE *pData = DdeAccessData(hDDEData, &dwLength);
     m_DDEdata += pData;

// Done with the data. Unlock and free the data handle.
     DdeUnaccessData(hDDEData);
     DdeFreeDataHandle(hDDEData);
    }

// Disconnect the conversation
    DdeDisconnect(hConv);
}
```

The process continues with the following steps:

10. All that remains now is to add code in the view class, CDdeclntView, to enable the user to initiate a DDE transaction and display the data retrieved during the transaction. Using ClassWizard, add the OnFileNew message handler to handle the menu selection Connect to DDE Server... in the File menu (this menu item is usually labeled New, hence the function name: OnFileNew). Define OnFileNew (in the DDECLVW.CPP file) as follows:

    ```
    #include "ddedlg.h"

    /////////////////////////////////////////////////////////////
    // CDdeclntView message handlers

    void CDdeclntView::OnFileNew()
    {
    // Display the "Connect to DDE Server" dialog
        DDEDlg dlg;

        int status = dlg.DoModal();
        if(status == IDOK)
        {
            CDdeclntDoc* pDoc = GetDocument();
            ASSERT_VALID(pDoc);
            pDoc->DoDDE(dlg.m_Service,
                        dlg.m_Topic,
                        dlg.m_Item);
            pDoc->UpdateAllViews(NULL);
        }
    }
    ```

    This function displays the dialog box that enables the user to select a DDE service, a topic, and an item to be used for a DDE transaction from a server, if available.

11. In the view class, edit the OnDraw member function to match Listing 27.4. This function obtains the retrieved DDE data (in text format) from the document class and displays the result in separate lines (the function looks for carriage returns and newlines).

Listing 27.4. Implementation of the OnDraw function of the view class.

```
//////////////////////////////////////////////////////////////
// CDdeclntView drawing

void CDdeclntView::OnDraw(CDC* pDC)
{
    CDdeclntDoc* pDoc = GetDocument();
    ASSERT_VALID(pDoc);

    CString& data = pDoc->GetDDEdata();
    int x = 8, y = 10, nc = data.GetLength();

// Compute the line height based on current font
    TEXTMETRIC tm;
    pDC->GetTextMetrics(&tm);
    int line_height = tm.tmHeight + tm.tmExternalLeading;
    LPCTSTR pc = (LPCTSTR)data;

    int np = 0, nl = 0;

    while(np < nc)
    {
// Expand tabs and break up text into lines
        for(nl = 0; nl < nc-np; nl++)
        {
            if(pc[nl] == '\t')
            {
                pDC->TextOut(x, y, pc, nl);
                x += nl * tm.tmAveCharWidth;
                pDC->TextOut(x, y, "    ", 4);
                nl++;
                np += nl;
                pc = &pc[nl];
                break;
            }
            if(pc[nl] == '\r' || pc[nl] == '\n')
            {
                pDC->TextOut(x, y, pc, nl);
                nl++;
                y += line_height;

// Skip the line feed (\n) following a carriage return (\r)
                if(nl < nc-np-1 && pc[nl-1] == '\r' &&
                    pc[nl] == '\n') nl++;

                np += nl;
                pc = &pc[nl];
                break;
            }
        }
```

continues

Listing 27.4. continued

```
        }
// Display last line (which may not have a newline)
        if(nl >= nc-np)
        {
            pDC->TextOut(x, y, pc, nc-np);
            break;
        }
    }
}
```

You are now ready for the final step:

12. Build the DDECLNT.EXE program and try it out. Figure 27.2 shows the Connect to
    DDE Server dialog box through which the user specifies the DDE service, topic, and
    item. Figure 27.3 shows the result of a transaction with the PROGMAN service with
    the topic Progman and the Groups item. Figure 27.4 shows the contents of the
    Accessories group obtained from the Progman service by specifying the Progman topic
    and the Accessories item.

FIGURE 27.2.

*DDECLNT displaying the
Connect to DDE Server
dialog.*

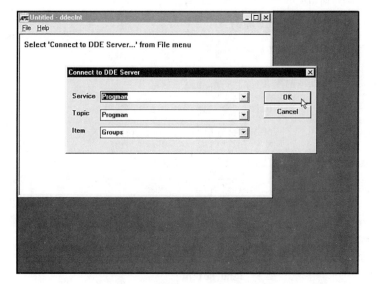

FIGURE 27.3.

Listing groups obtained from PROGMAN.

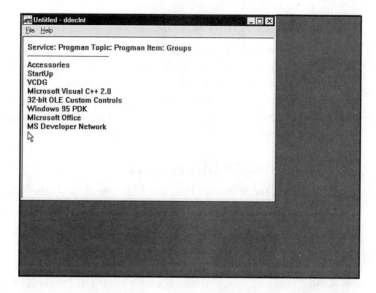

FIGURE 27.4.

Contents of the Accessories group obtained from PROGMAN.

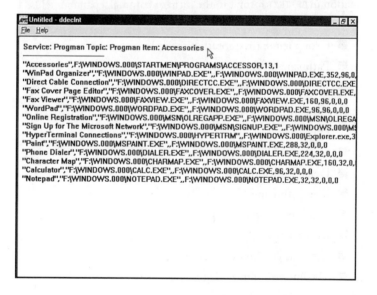

Adding New Program Group

A Windows-based installation program usually has to install a new program group and add the icon for one or more applications in the new group. The Windows Program Manager, PROGMAN, provides a DDE command interface through which an application such as an installation program can set up new groups and add items to a group. The following sections describe the Program Manager's DDE interface and present a simple MFC application that illustrates the use of the command interface.

The Program Manager DDE Interface

As a DDE server, the Windows Program Manager supports the PROGMAN service and the PROGMAN topic. A client application can obtain the names of all the groups by requesting the item named GROUPS. Program Manager provides the group names separated by carriage returns.

A client application can also request detailed information about a specific group by using a group name as an item name when requesting data. The Program Manager provides this information in CF_TEXT format in the form of comma-separated fields. The first line of the information contains the following information separated by commas:

- Group name (in quotation marks)
- Pathname of the group file
- Number of items in the group

Each subsequent line contains the following comma-separated information about an item in the group:

- Command line (in quotation marks)
- Default directory
- Icon pathname
- Item's position in the group
- Icon's index
- Shortcut key (in numeric form)
- Maximize/minimize flag

The Program Manager also responds to a number of DDE commands that applications can use to execute the following: create, display, delete, and reload groups; add items to groups; replace items in groups; delete items from groups; and close Program Manager. Each command must be enclosed in square brackets with command arguments appearing in parentheses. If a command accepts multiple arguments, these are separated by commas. For example, to add a new item named HELLO.EXE to a new group named Visual C++ DevGuide, you send the following commands (using the XTYP_EXECUTE transaction) to the Program Manager:

```
[CreateGroup(Visual C++ DevGuide)]
[ShowGroup(Visual C++ DevGuide,1)]
[AddItem(HELLO.EXE,Visual C++ DevGuide)]
```

Table 27.5 shows the eight DDE command strings accepted by the Program Manager through examples.

Table 27.5. Program manager's DDE command interface.

Sample Command	Description
`[CreateGroup(My Group)]`	Creates a new group named `My Group`
`[ShowGroup(My Group,1)]`	Activates and displays the group window named `My Group`
`[DeleteGroup(My Group)]`	Deletes the group named `My Group`
`[Reload(My Group)]`	Removes and reloads the group named `My Group`
`[AddItem(HELLO.EXE,Hello)]`	Adds the icon for HELLO.EXE with the title `Hello` to the currently active group
`[ReplaceItem(Hello)]`	Removes the icon for the item named `Hello` and uses this location to insert the next item
`[DeleteItem(Hello)]`	Deletes the item named `Hello`
`[ExitProgMan(1)]`	Exits the Program Manager and saves the group information (if argument is `0`, exits without saving group information)

PMGROUP—A Program to Add a New Group

With the Visual Workbench it is easy to write a simple dialog-based application that enables the user to add a new program manager group and insert a single item into that group. To build the application, create a new project named PMGROUP and follow these steps:

1. Select MFC AppWizard(exe) as the Project Type when creating the project. In step 1 of the AppWizard's dialog, specify that you want to build a dialog-based application (see Figure 17.6).

2. After AppWizard generates the source files and the project file (PMGROUP.MAK), edit the resource file (PMGROUP.RC) and add a dialog resource. This dialog is what the user sees when the PMGROUP application runs (see Figure 27.5).

3. Using ClassWizard, add member variables m_GroupName, m_ItemName, and m_FileName to hold the three items entered by the user. ClassWizard adds the code necessary to copy the values from the dialog box into these variables.

4. In the header file STDAFX.H, add the following line:

```
#include <ddeml.h>    // For DDEML functions
```

5. In the `InitInstance` function of the application class (in file PMGROUP.CPP), add the following code shown in boldface:

```
BOOL CPmgroupApp::InitInstance()
{
//...

// Initialize DDEML
    DdeInitialize(&dwDDEInst, NULL,
                  APPCMD_CLIENTONLY, 0);

    CPmgroupDlg dlg;
    m_pMainWnd = &dlg;
    int nResponse = dlg.DoModal();
    if (nResponse == IDOK)
    {
        if(!AddPMGroup(dlg.m_GroupName, dlg.m_ItemName,
                    dlg.m_FileName))
        {
            ::MessageBox(NULL, "PMGroup: DDE Error",
                "Error adding group and item.",
                MB_ICONHAND | MB_OK);
        }
    }
    else if (nResponse == IDCANCEL)
    {
        // TODO: Place code here to handle when the dialog is
        //  dismissed with Cancel
    }
//...
}
```

You also have to add a member variable `dwDDEInst` to the `CPmgroupApp` class:

```
DWORD dwDDEInst; // Used to store the DDE instance handle
```

Because it is a dialog-based application, PMGROUP does all its work in `InitInstance`. After displaying the dialog, if the user clicks on the OK button, the `AddPMGroup` function is called to add the new group. You have to add the `AddPMGroup` member function to the `CPmgroupApp` class and define the function as shown in Listing 27.5. As you can see from Listing 27.5, `AddPMGroup` establishes a DDE conversation with the PROGMAN service and, if successful, sends it the necessary DDE commands to add the new group, activate the group, and then add the new item to that group.

Listing 27.5. The AddPMGroup function for adding a new group.

```
int CPmgroupApp::AddPMGroup(CString& group, CString& item,
                            CString& file)
{
// Establish a DDE conversation with the PROGMAN service
    HSZ hszService = DdeCreateStringHandle(dwDDEInst,
                                           _T("PROGMAN"),
                                           CP_WINANSI);

    HSZ hszTopic = DdeCreateStringHandle(dwDDEInst,
                                         _T("PROGMAN"),
                                         CP_WINANSI);

    HCONV hConv = DdeConnect(dwDDEInst, hszTopic,
                             hszService, NULL);

// Free the HSZs now
    DdeFreeStringHandle(dwDDEInst, hszService);
    DdeFreeStringHandle(dwDDEInst, hszTopic);

    if(!hConv)
    {
        return FALSE;
    }

// Send DDE commands to add group and add the item to
// the group. First create the new group.

    CString cmd = "[CreateGroup(" + group + ")]";
    DWORD dwResult;
    LPCTSTR data = (LPCTSTR)cmd;
    DdeClientTransaction((LPBYTE)data, cmd.GetLength(),
                         hConv, NULL, CF_TEXT,
                         XTYP_EXECUTE, 1000,
                         &dwResult);

// Make this the active group
    cmd = "[ShowGroup(" + group + ",1)]";
    data = (LPCTSTR)cmd;
    DdeClientTransaction((LPBYTE)data, cmd.GetLength(),
                         hConv, NULL, CF_TEXT,
                         XTYP_EXECUTE, 1000,
                         &dwResult);

// Add the item to the new group
    cmd = "[AddItem(" + file + "," + item + ")]";
    data = (LPCTSTR)cmd;
    DdeClientTransaction((LPBYTE)data, cmd.GetLength(),
                         hConv, NULL, CF_TEXT,
                         XTYP_EXECUTE, 1000,
                         &dwResult);

    return TRUE;
}
```

Continue the process with the following steps:

6. Using ClassWizard, add an `ExitInstance` function to the application class, `CPmgroupApp`. Define the `ExitInstance` function as follows:

```
int CPmgroupApp::ExitInstance()
{
    DdeUninitialize(dwDDEInst);
    return CWinApp::ExitInstance();
}
```

7. Build and test the program PMGROUP.EXE. Figure 27.5 shows the dialog displayed by the application. As shown in Figure 27.5, the user has filled in the name of a new group and an item to be added to the new group. Figure 27.6 shows the resulting new group (with the new item) added by PMGROUP after the user clicks on the OK button in the dialog.

FIGURE 27.5.

Dialog displayed by PMGROUP.

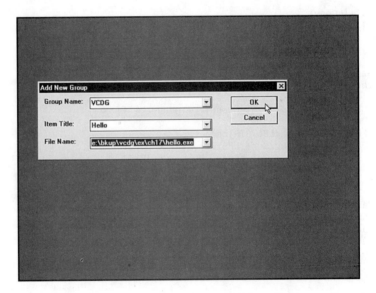

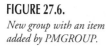

FIGURE 27.6.

New group with an item added by PMGROUP.

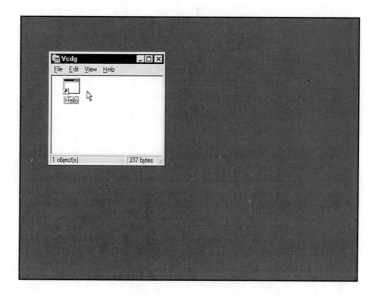

Summary

Dynamic Data Exchange (DDE) is an interprocess communication protocol that relies on Windows messages and shared memory to enable cooperating Windows applications to exchange information. DDE is based on a client-server model wherein a DDE server offers one or more services. Each service comprises one or more topics and there are one or more items in each topic. A DDE client requests a conversation with a DDE server for a specific topic. Once a conversation is established, the client can initiate DDE transactions to obtain values of specific items from the server. If the client wants to get the value of an item continually whenever the value changes, it can establish a DDE advise loop for that item.

In addition to data exchange, an application may use DDE to send a DDE command to another application. For example, the Windows Program Manager or Shell (the provider of the PROGMAN service) provides a DDE command interface that applications can use to add new program groups and add new program items to a group. Windows-based installation programs use the PROGMAN service's DDE interface to add new program groups and icons when installing applications.

Earlier, adding DDE support to an application was complicated because the programmer had to keep track of various shared memory locations and send Windows messages to accomplish DDE data exchanges. Now, however, Microsoft provides the DDE Management Library (DDEML), which provides a standard Application Programming Interface (API) for adding DDE capability in an application.

This chapter describes the DDEML and shows how to use DDEML functions to write applications with DDE capability.

28

OLE 2.0 Programming
with MFC 3.0

Although DDE is a powerful interprocess communication mechanism that enables the application developer to tie together multiple applications, DDE requires a client to manipulate the data received from the server. Thus a DDE client can handle only data that it is programmed to handle.

Object Linking and Embedding (OLE) provides a higher-level abstraction than DDE and enables a server to manipulate the data in a client's window. OLE 1.0 started as a way of creating *compound documents*—documents composed of data from a variety of sources, including applications other than the one displaying and manipulating the document. For example, when you embed (paste) a drawing created in Paintbrush and some parts of a spreadsheet created in Microsoft Excel into a document being prepared with Microsoft Word for Windows, you create a compound document containing Word, Paintbrush, and Excel objects. Each object can be manipulated by the application that created the object. In this case, Microsoft Word acts as the OLE container (or client), and Paintbrush and Excel are OLE servers that display and edit the Paintbrush and Excel objects, respectively.

From its roots as a mechanism for creating compound documents, OLE has evolved into a more comprehensive component object model that provides a standard way to package objects—to store them in files; support drag-and-drop, copy, and paste operations; and manipulate objects through scripting languages.

Although OLE has a reputation for being difficult to program, the object model of OLE can be conveniently encapsulated in C++ classes. In Visual C++ 2.0, MFC 3.0 provides a whole set of classes for OLE programming. This chapter describes the OLE object model and shows how to use the MFC 3.0's OLE classes to write OLE containers (or clients) and servers. Chapter 29, "Building OLE Custom Controls (OCX)," describes the software components, or controls, that can be embedded in OLE 2.0 control containers.

OLE WITHOUT VERSION NUMBERS

Although OLE started as Object Linking and Embedding version 1.0 and evolved to OLE 2.0, Microsoft has recently started referring to this strategic object technology as simply OLE, without spelling it out. Furthermore, Microsoft states that version numbers will no longer be used with OLE because OLE is the official name of a technology. Thus, OLE 2.0 will become OLE. This book continues to refer to OLE with version numbers when referring to a specific OLE implementation.

What Is OLE?

Microsoft first introduced Object Linking and Embedding version 1.0 (OLE 1.0) in Microsoft Windows version 3.1 as a standard way of sharing data among various Windows applications.

In the context of OLE 1.0, *sharing* is the capability of embedding objects from one application into documents created in another application. For example, incorporating a drawing in a word processing document is an example of this type of sharing. Although sharing was possible with cut-and-paste even before OLE 1.0 arrived in Windows version 3.1, OLE 1.0 provided a more powerful and standardized way of sharing data.

OLE 1.0

With OLE 1.0, when you embed a drawing from Paintbrush, for example, into a Microsoft Word for Windows (version 6.0) document, you can edit that drawing without leaving Word for Windows. Merely double-click the drawing to launch the Paintbrush application with that drawing loaded for editing. Of course, the applications must follow certain rules to enable this to happen. OLE 1.0 provides the rules and conventions for creating compound documents— documents consisting of parts created by multiple Windows applications.

Figure 28.1 shows a Paintbrush picture embedded (by cutting and pasting) in a Microsoft Word document. Figure 28.2 shows what happens when you double-click on the Paintbrush picture. Paintbrush is automatically started with the embedded picture loaded and ready for the user to edit. When the user exits Paintbrush, the embedded picture is automatically updated and the user can continue working in Microsoft Word. This is an illustration of a compound document created using the capabilities provided by OLE 1.0.

FIGURE 28.1.

A Microsoft Word document with an embedded Paintbrush picture.

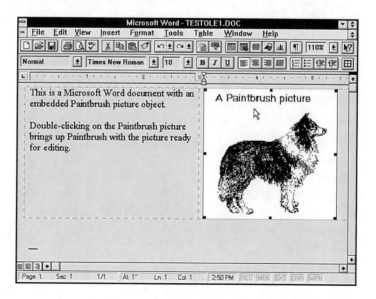

FIGURE 28.2.

Editing the embedded
Paintbrush picture.

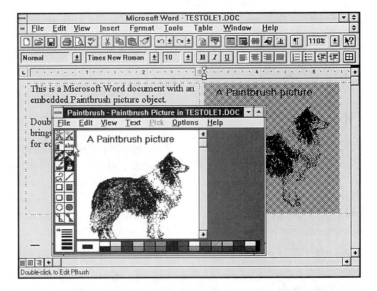

OLE TERMINOLOGY

OLE introduced a number of new terms to the world of Windows programming, some of which have already been defined in this book. The following reviews those and introduces new terms that are used extensively in this chapter:

Object is data, such as a drawing, a block of formatted text, a range of cells from a spreadsheet—anything that can be displayed and manipulated and is defined as an object in a Windows application that uses OLE. The Microsoft Foundation Class Library uses the term *item* to refer to OLE objects (to avoid confusing them with C++ objects).

A *client application* is a Windows application that can accept, display, and store objects from servers. A *client document* is a document that displays OLE objects. Because the client application contains OLE objects from servers, clients are also referred to as *containers* in OLE 2.0.

The *server application* is a Windows application that creates and edits objects. A *server document* is the specific file from which the OLE objects are pasted into a client document.

Embedding is the process of placing a complete representation of an object in the client document. You embed objects through the normal cut-and-paste operations or by selecting the Object... option from the Insert menu of the client application.

Linking is the process of storing a description of the object (for example, the file where the object resides and the name of the server application) in the client document. You establish a link to an object by selecting that object in the server document and picking the Paste Special... option from the Edit menu of the client application. If you edit a linked object, the changes are automatically available in the client document.

Essentially, OLE 1.0 provided a protocol (that OLE 2.0 continues to support) between two applications—a client and a server—for the following:

- The client can embed objects from the server inside a document being created in the client application.
- The client can request the server to manipulate that object when the user selects the embedded object.

In addition to the concept of embedding, linking is integral to OLE 1.0. In the process of linking, the client application remembers the full pathname of the server document from which an object is being pasted into the client. For example, if you link a range of spreadsheet cells to a word processing document, any changes to those cells are reflected in the information that appears in the word processing document. The disadvantage of linking is that the spreadsheet information becomes unavailable if you move or destroy the spreadsheet from which the spreadsheet cells were originally linked.

OLE 2.0

OLE 1.0 was aimed at creating compound documents, but OLE 2.0 goes beyond compound documents and provides a more comprehensive object model with associated programming interfaces that enable applications to interact and interoperate. OLE 2.0 is based on the Component Object Model (COM), which is the foundation of Microsoft's vision of "Windows Objects."

OLE 2.0 continues to support all the capabilities offered by OLE 1.0. In the area of editing embedded objects, OLE 2.0 enhances the editing capability in a significant manner. As with OLE 1.0, you can insert an object into a document. For example, Figure 28.3 shows a Microsoft Word document with an embedded Microsoft Excel spreadsheet.

You will notice the difference in behavior between OLE 1.0 and OLE 2.0 when you double-click on the spreadhsheet object, however. Instead of bringing up Excel in a separate window, OLE 2.0 provides the facilities that enable Excel essentially to take over the Microsoft Word document's window. Figure 28.4 shows the appearance of the document window with the Excel spreadsheet activated in place. If you compare the menu bar and tool bar shown in Figure 28.4 with those in Figure 28.3, you will realize that the menus and tools reflect those of Excel and not Word. Essentially, the document window takes on the personality of a spreadsheet when the spreadsheet object is active. For example, if you select the Help menu item from the menu bar, you can clearly see that the items belong to Excel (see Figure 28.5). The term *visual editing* is used to refer to the OLE 2.0-supported capability of editing embedded objects in place.

FIGURE 28.3.

A Microsoft Word document with an embedded Excel spread-sheet.

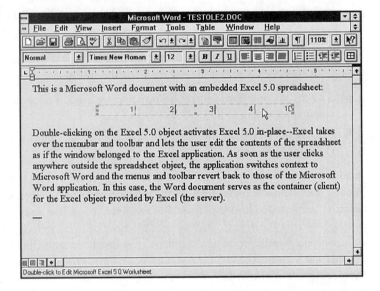

FIGURE 28.4.

The embedded Excel 5.0 spreadsheet object activated in place.

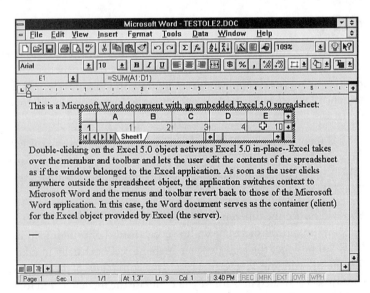

FIGURE 28.5.

Menus belong to Excel 5.0 when the Excel 5.0 spreadsheet object is activated in place.

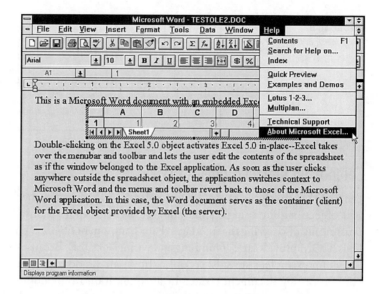

As noted, unlike OLE 1.0, OLE 2.0 supports the creation of compound documents through the Compound Object Model, which specifies compound objects with well-defined interfaces that an application can call. Essentially, OLE 2.0 provides the runtime facilities (through DLLs) and the protocols that enable applications to exchange data and invoke each other's services. OLE 2.0 also provides the protocols for sharing a display window and accessing various components in a compound file—a standard file format for storing compound documents. The important point is that these interfaces and the protocols are designed so that independently developed applications, developed without prior knowledge of each other, can interoperate and collaborate at runtime.

Figure 28.6 shows an abstract view of OLE 2.0 with its components. As you can see from Figure 28.6, OLE 2.0 has the following constituent elements:

- Component Object Model (COM)
- Compound files
- Uniform data transfer
- Compound documents
- Automation

FIGURE 28.6.

Components of OLE 2.0.

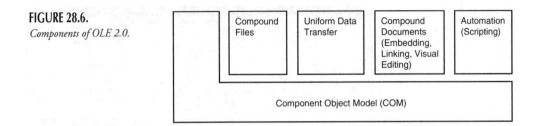

Component Object Model (COM)

The COM forms the basis of OLE technology. COM specifies the interfaces between component objects within a single application or between applications. There is a mechanism for dynamically discovering the interfaces that a component object exports and for invoking them. Thus, COM provides the "plumbing and wiring" of OLE. Because of the interfaces defined by COM, for example, a spreadsheet object from one vendor can be seamlessly embedded into a word processing document created by an application from another vendor. The spreadsheet and word processor do not need to know anything about each other's implementation; they need to know only how to connect through the interface provided by the component object model.

Each interface to a component object is the array of function pointers known as a virtual table (VTBL). This is the part of an OLE object that programmers see. Figure 28.7 shows a pictorial representation of an OLE object (a component object) with its interface. Many articles and books on OLE show a shorthand representation of an OLE object and its interface as shown in Figure 28.8.

FIGURE 28.7.

A component object in OLE.

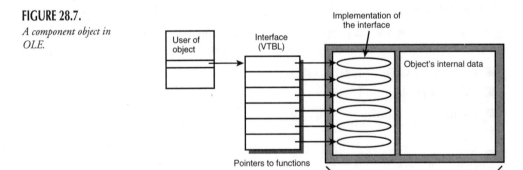

FIGURE 28.8.
Shorthand representation of an OLE object and its interface.

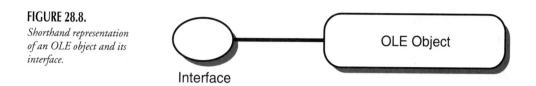

Interface

Compound Files

Compound files provide a standard file format for structured storage of compound documents for OLE applications. Within a compound file, storages have many features of directories, and streams have many features of files.

Uniform Data Transfer

Uniform data transfer refers to a standard mechanism for all types of data transfers, whether through cut-and-paste, drag-and-drop, or by API calls.

Drag-and-drop transfers data as the cut-and-paste operation does, except that you do not need to use the menus for drag-and-drop. You merely select the data to be transferred and drag the selection to the desired destination. OLE 2.0's drag-and-drop approach moves only a pointer to the data object from the source application to the destination (target) application. So you can easily move large amounts of data through drag-and-drop.

Compound Documents

Recall that compound documents are documents in a container application that seamlessly integrate various types of data (items), such as spreadsheets, bitmaps, sound clips, or video clips. Each item in a compound document is created and maintained by the item's object application (the OLE Server).

Linking and embedding are the two mechanisms used in compound documents to incorporate items created in another application. These features of compound documents are the same as they were in OLE 1.0. Linking enables an application to be linked to data objects in another application. For example, if you link a spreadsheet into a word processing document, any changes made to the spreadsheet automatically update the word processing document. Embedding occurs when you paste a data object directly into a document. An embedded object does not maintain a link to the object's data source. In both object linking and object embedding, applications supplying objects are called OLE servers. Applications containing objects are called OLE containers. An application can be both an OLE container and an OLE server.

Visual editing or in-place activation is a powerful new feature of compound documents in OLE 2.0. Recall that when you double-click on a spreadsheet embedded in a word processing document, the only changes that you see are the new tool bars and menu commands for the spreadsheet. As soon as you click on some text outside of the spreadsheet, the word processor's tool bars and menu commands instantly reappear. With visual editing, you can edit the embedded or linked object in the context of the document, without worrying about activating and switching to another application.

Automation

Automation enables the use of a macro or scripting language to activate the verbs (or commands) that any OLE 2.0 application can expose. For example, a user can invoke a command from a word processing program that sorts a range of cells in a spreadsheet created by a different application.

You might say that OLE automation enables one application to control (or "drive") another application. The *automation client* is the controlling application and the *automation server* is the application being controlled. Most automation servers support verbs such as OPEN and EDIT.

LEARNING MORE ABOUT OLE

OLE is a significantly large addition to Microsoft Windows, and as such, this chapter cannot do justice to the amount of information that you need to include support for OLE fully in your applications. There are, however, many sources of information about programming OLE. Here are a few ways you can learn more about including OLE support in your Windows application:

■ Read articles on OLE in programmers magazines. For example, the *Microsoft Systems Journal* (published monthly by Miller Freeman, Inc., 600 Harrison St., San Francisco, CA 94107) includes many articles about OLE programming, complete with sample code.

■ Study the sample programs in the SAMPLES subdirectory of the Visual C++ 2.0 install directory. In particular, study the programs in SAMPLES\MFC\ CONTAIN, SAMPLES\MFC\DRAWCLI, SAMPLES\MFC\OCLIENT, SAMPLES\MFC\HIERSVR, and SAMPLES\MFC\SUPERPAD. These examples show you how to use OLE classes such as COleServerDoc, COleServerItem, COleDocument, and COleClientItem that are part of MFC 3.0.

■ Consult books on OLE. An example is *Inside OLE 2* by Kraig Brockschmidt (Microsoft Press, Redmond, WA, 1994) that includes detailed information on OLE programming in C++ (the examples in that book do not use the MFC 3.0 classes, however).

The Registration Database

When you click on an embedded or linked OLE object, the object's application is automatically activated to edit the object. You might wonder: "How does Windows know where to find the embedded object's application?" The answer lies in the registration database, which contains a listing of the OLE-enabled component objects available on a system. The registration database is updated whenever an OLE object is installed or executed. OLE container applications know what objects are available by looking at the object registry.

You can examine and modify the registration database by running the REGEDIT.EXE program (it should be in your system's Windows directory). Run the program with the /V option to see detailed information. Figure 28.9 shows REGEDIT displaying information related to Microsoft Excel Worksheets. The Microsoft Excel installation program adds this information to the registration database when you first install Excel.

FIGURE 28.9.

The registration database editor.

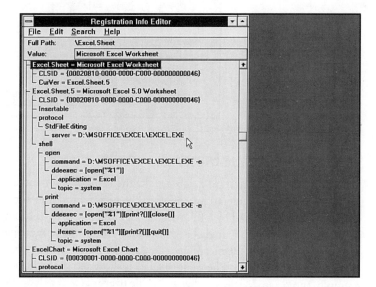

As you can see in Figure 28.9, Excel worksheets support the protocol StdFileEditing, which is a standard protocol for all OLE applications. The server for the StdFileEditing protocol is the full pathname of Excel's executable file. This is how Windows finds Excel to update links or edit embedded worksheets.

The section under the keyword shell specifies the DDE commands that Excel supports. The DDE service is Excel (listed under the key named application) and the topic for the DDE conversation is System. You may want to consult Chapter 27, "Using Dynamic Data Exchange (DDE)," for more information.

The Win32 version of the Registration Editor (REGEDT32.EXE in Windows NT) sports a different user interface. Figure 28.10 shows the appearance of the Win32 Registration Editor displaying the same information as that in Figure 28.9. Instead of showing the value of a key next to the key, the Win32 version of the Registration Editor requires the user to click on a key to see its value.

FIGURE 28.10.

Win32 version of the Registration Editor.

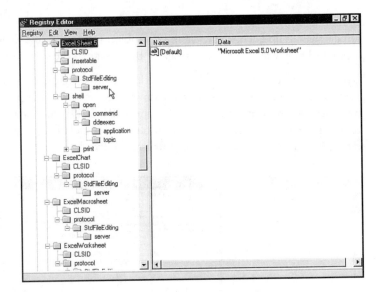

Registration Database Entries

The entries in the registration database take the form of a key and a corresponding value. The keys are organized in a hierarchy similar to the hierarchical directory structure in a file system. In fact, a key is identified by a full pathname much like a file. The keys start with a single root key, which is shown as a single backslash character (\). The meaning of keys depends on the application. However, the meaning of keys used for OLE are standard. In Figure 28.9, you can see many key-value pairs. The value of a key is shown to the right side of an equal sign (=). For example, the \Excel.Sheet key has the value Microsoft Excel Worksheet and this key:

```
\Excel.Sheet.5\protocol\StdFileEditing\server
```

has the following value:

```
D:\MSOFFICE\EXCEL\EXCEL.EXE
```

This key-value pair specifies the full pathname of the Excel application as the OLE server for editing a Microsoft Excel Worksheet OLE item.

Programming the Registration Database

Windows applications usually have to add entries to the registration when they are installed. OLE server and container applications also rely on the registration database for information needed to handle OLE objects properly. Windows provides an API for adding, deleting, and changing entries in the registration database. You have to include the header file SHELLAPI.H in programs that use the registration database. All the registration database functions use key handles (HKEY data type) to keep track of keys in the database.

To create a new key for your application, call the `RegCreateKey` function. For example, to add the key `MyServer` attached to the root key and set it to a descriptive string, you write the following:

```
char  value = "My OLE Server";
int   nchar = strlen(value);
HKEY hKeyMyRoot;

if(RegCreateKey(
        HKEY_CLASSES_ROOT, // Handle of parent key
        "MyServer",        // Name of key to create
        &hKeyMyRoot)       // Handle returned here
    == ERROR_SUCCESS) // Returns ERROR_SUCCESS if successful
{
    RegSetValue(
        hKeyMyRoot, // Handle of root key
        NULL,       // Name of subkey or NULL
        REG_SZ,     // Type (should be set to REG_SZ)
        value,      // The value string
        nchar);     // Number of characters in "value"
}
```

After you create a key, you can add other subkeys to that key by calling `RegCreateKey` followed by `RegSetValue`. For example, the following sets the subkey `protocol\StdFileEditing\server` to `C:\MYSERVER\MYSERVER.EXE`:

```
char  srvrexe = "C:\\MYSERVER\\MYSERVER.EXE";
nchar = strlen(srvrexe);
HKEY hKeySrvr;

if(RegCreateKey(
        hKeyMyRoot,                        // Parent key
        "protocol\\StdFileEditing\\server", // Key to create
        &hKeySrvr)                         // Returned handle
    == ERROR_SUCCESS) // Returns ERROR_SUCCESS if successful
{
    RegSetValue(
        hKeySrvr,  // Handle of root key
        NULL,      // Name of subkey or NULL
        REG_SZ,    // Type (should be set to REG_SZ)
        srvrexe,   // The value string
        nchar);    // Number of characters in value string
}
```

After you create all the keys and set their values, you must close all open keys. The registration database is updated when all open keys are closed. For this example, you have to close the two keys `hKeyMyRoot` and `hKeySrvr`:

```
RegCloseKey(hKeyMyRoot);
RegCloseKey(hKeySrvr);
```

REGLIST—A Program to List Keys

To illustrate the use of the registration database access functions, let's build a simple dialog-based application (REGLIST.EXE) that lists the top-level keys in a system's registration database. To build the application, you create a new project named REGLIST in Visual C++ 2.0 and follow these steps:

1. Select MFC AppWizard(exe) as the Project Type when creating the project. In step 1 of the AppWizard's dialog, specify that you want to build a Dialog-based application (see Figure 17.6 in Chapter 17, "Windows Programming with Visual C++ 2.0 and MFC 3.0").

2. After AppWizard generates the source files and the project file (REGLIST.MAK), edit the resource file (REGLIST.RC) and add appropriate controls to the dialog identified by IDD_REGLIST_DIALOG. This dialog is what the user sees when the REGLIST application runs (see Figure 28.11).

3. In the header file STDAFX.H, add the following line:

```
#include <shellapi.h>  // For registration database functions
```

4. Edit the OnInitDialog function of the dialog class (in file REGLIDLG.CPP) and add the following code (shown in boldface):

```
BOOL CReglistDlg::OnInitDialog()
{
//...

// Fill in the listbox with names of top-level keys
    CListBox *pLB = (CListBox*)GetDlgItem(IDC_LIST1);
    HKEY hKeyRoot;
    char szKey[80], szValue[80], szBuf[160];
    int nStatus, nChar;
    long nSize;
    DWORD dwKey = 0;

    if(RegOpenKey(HKEY_CLASSES_ROOT, NULL, &hKeyRoot)
        == ERROR_SUCCESS)
    {
// Get the keys
        do
        {
            nSize = 80;
            nStatus = RegEnumKey(hKeyRoot, dwKey++, szKey, 80);
```

```
                RegQueryValue(hKeyRoot, szKey, szValue, &nSize);
                nChar = wsprintf(szBuf, "%s = %s", szKey, szValue);
                pLB->AddString(szBuf);
            } while(nStatus == ERROR_SUCCESS);

// Close all open keys
        RegCloseKey(hKeyRoot);

// Set the label for the list of keys
        wsprintf(szBuf,
            "%d Top-Level Keys in the Registration Database",
            dwKey);
        CStatic *pLabel = (CStatic*)GetDlgItem(IDC_STATIC_LABEL);
        pLabel->SetWindowText(szBuf);
    }
    else
    {
        ::MessageBox(NULL,
            "Cannot access registration database.",
            "RegList", MB_ICONHAND | MB_OK);
    }


        return TRUE;   // return TRUE  unless you set the focus to a control
}
```

This code uses the registration database access functions RegOpenKey, RegEnumKey, RegQueryValue, and RegCloseKey to obtain the names and values of the top-level keys in the registration database and populate the listbox in the application's main dialog box.

5. Build and test the program REGLIST.EXE. Figure 28.11 shows the dialog displayed by the application. As shown in Figure 28.11, the listbox shows the key-value pairs for the top-level keys, and the label above the listbox shows the total number of top-level keys in the system's registration database. You can exit the application by clicking the OK button.

FIGURE 28.11.
List of top-level keys displayed by REGLIST.

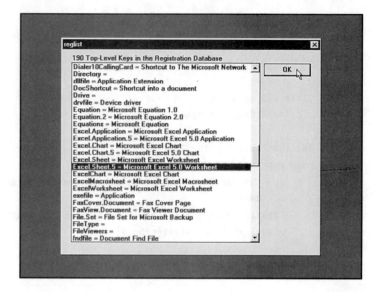

OLE Classes in MFC 3.0

Adding OLE support in your Windows application can be complicated, especially when you use the OLE 2.0 API directly. Luckily for Visual C++ programmers, MFC 3.0 includes more than two dozen classes specifically intended for implementing OLE capabilities in a Windows application. Figure 18.1 shows the OLE classes (most have names that start with the COle prefix) together with the rest of the MFC 3.0 classes intended for Windows programming. The OLE classes in MFC 3.0 can be organized into six categories:

■ *OLE Base Classes.* The three classes in this category serve as base classes for more specialized OLE classes in the other categories:

CDocItem is an abstract base class from which the COleClientItem and COleServerItem classes are derived. Objects of these classes represent parts of a document.

COleDispatchDriver encapsulates the capability of calling automation servers from an automation client. ClassWizard uses this class to create type-safe classes for automation servers that provide a type library.

COleDocument implements an OLE compound document and serves as an OLE container for classes derived from CDocItem. The COleServerDoc class is derived from COleDocument and you can use COleDocument as the base class for other container documents.

■ *OLE Visual Editing Container Classes.* The two classes in this category are used by container applications. Both COleLinkingDoc and COleDocument manage collections of COleClientItem objects:

`COleLinkingDoc`, derived from `COleDocument`, provides the necessary support for linking. If you want the documents in your container application to support links to OLE items, you should derive the document classes from the `COleLinkingDoc` class.

`COleClientItem` encapsulates the client's side of the connection to an embedded or linked OLE item. The client items in your application should be derived from this class.

■ *OLE Visual Editing Server Classes.* OLE servers use the following six classes to handle various required tasks:

`COleObjectFactory` serves as the base class for more specific object factories such as `COleTemplateServer`. The factory classes are used to create OLE items in response to requests from OLE containers.

`COleTemplateServer` uses an associated `CDocTemplate` object to create documents using MFC's document-view architecture.

`COleServerDoc` provides most of the necessary server capabilities support through interactions with `COleServerItem` objects. `COleServerDoc` uses MFC's document-view architecture to support visual editing. `COleServerDoc` is used as the base class for a server application's document classes.

`COleServerItem` encapsulates the OLE interface to `COleServerDoc` objects. Usually, one `COleServerItem` object represents the entire server document for an OLE item embedded in an OLE container.

`COleIPFrameWnd` represents the frame window for a view when an OLE server item is being edited in place.

`COleResizeBar` is used in conjunction with `COleIPFrameWnd` objects to provide the standard user interface for in-place resizing.

■ *OLE Data Transfer Classes.* The following four classes are used in OLE data transfers between applications by using the Clipboard or drag-and-drop:

`COleDropSource` is responsible for starting a drag operation, providing feedback (by displaying a specific cursor shape) during the drag-and-drop operation, and ending the drag-and-drop.

`COleDropTarget` corresponds to a window representing the target of a drag-and-drop operation. A `COleDropTarget` object determines whether to accept any data dropped onto the associated window and implements the actual drop operation.

`COleDataSource` acts as a cache into which an OLE application places data during data transfers through the Clipboard or drag-and-drop operations.

`COleDataObject` is used in the recipient of a data transfer operation to access the data contained in a `COleDataSource` object.

■ *OLE Dialog Box Classes.* A number of OLE classes are meant to handle the user interaction needs during OLE operations. The following eight classes implement a number of standard OLE dialog boxes:

`COleDialog` serves as the abstract base class from which all other OLE dialog box classes are derived.

`COleInsertDialog` implements the Insert Object dialog box, which prompts the user to insert new embedded or linked OLE items.

`COleConvertDialog` displays the Convert dialog box that enables the user to convert OLE items from one type to another.

`COleChangeIconDialog` represents the Change Icon dialog box that enables the user to change the icon associated with an embedded or linked OLE item.

`COlePasteSpecialDialog` implements the Paste Special dialog box that is activated through the Edit|Paste Special command.

`COleLinksDialog` displays the Edit Links dialog box that enables the user to modify information about linked items.

`COleUpdateDialog` provides the Update dialog box used when updating all links in a document. This dialog box contains a progress indicator that shows the progress of the update procedure.

`COleBusyDialog` implements the Server Busy and Server Not Responding dialog boxes that are used when the server does not respond. These dialogs are usually displayed automatically by the `COleMessageFilter` class.

■ *Miscellaneous OLE Classes.* The remaining five classes provide a number of different OLE services, ranging from file I/O to exception handling:

`COleException` is used in both containers and servers to represent an exception resulting from a failure in an OLE operation.

`COleDispatchException` represents an exception resulting from an error during OLE automation that is thrown by the automation server and expected to be caught by the automation client.

`CRectTracker` is used when moving and resizing in-place OLE items.

`COleStreamFile` is derived from `CFile` and uses the OLE 2.0 `IStream` interface to provide access to OLE compound files. `COleStreamFile` enables MFC serialization to use OLE 2.0's structured storage.

`COleMessageFilter` manages the concurrency during interactions between OLE applications.

In addition to the OLE support classes, the Microsoft Foundation Class (MFC) library includes a number of global functions that support OLE programming. These global functions have names with the `AfxOle` prefix. When you generate OLE applications using MFC AppWizard, you do not have to call these `AfxOle` functions explicitly. The only function call that is visible to you is the call to `AfxOleInit` in the `InitInstance` member function of an AppWizard-generated OLE application.

Building OLE Applications with MFC AppWizard

The easiest way to support OLE in your application is to use MFC AppWizard to generate a "bare bones" application with the type of OLE support you want. You will be pleasantly surprised by the level of OLE support you can get by merely clicking on a few buttons.

The overall steps for creating an OLE application using Visual C++ 2.0 and MFC AppWizard are as follows:

1. Start a new project by selecting File|New as usual. Specify MFC AppWizard(exe) as the Project Type, provide the project name, and select the location of the project's files.

2. Continue with steps and 1 and 2 of MFC AppWizard's six-step dialog. The key step in adding OLE support to your application is step 3 (see Figure 28.12). In step 3, select the type of OLE support you want from one of the following choices:

   ■ *None.* Select this option if you do not want any OLE support in your application. This is the default choice.

   ■ *Container.* Select this option if you want your application to incorporate embedded and linked OLE items.

   ■ *Mini-server.* Mini-servers are OLE applications that cannot run standalone—they can provide embedded OLE items and run only when an embedded item is edited. Microsoft Word for Windows includes a number of mini-servers such as Microsoft Graph and Microsoft WordArt. Select this option if you want your application to be a mini-server providing some embedded items to OLE container applications.

   ■ *Full-server.* A full server is a stand-alone application that can provide both embedded and linked OLE items to OLE containers. Select this option if you want your application to be a stand-alone OLE server.

   ■ *Both container and server.* Select this option if you want your application to be a container as well as a full server.

   You also have the option of adding support for OLE Automation in step 3 (Figure 28.12). If you enable this option, your application becomes an automation server so that automation clients can control your application through command strings. OLE automation is described later in this chapter.

3. Work through the other steps of MFC AppWizard dialog as usual and generate the application's code.

FIGURE 28.12.
*Selecting the level of OLE
support in MFC
AppWizard.*

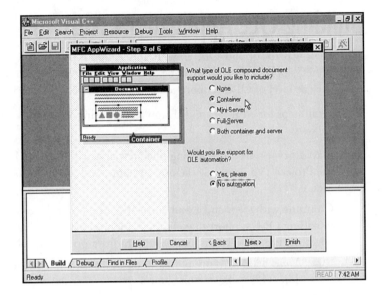

After MFC AppWizard has created the source files and the project for your application, you can proceed to add application-specific code to complete your application's desired functionality. The next few sections describe how to create three specific types of OLE applications:

■ OLE container

■ OLE server

■ OLE automation server

Building an OLE Container Application

An OLE container application can incorporate embedded or linked OLE items into its own document. The container application should be able to store and display OLE items as well as items created by the application itself. The application also should enable the user to insert new OLE items and delete existing items.

The AppWizard-Generated Container

With MFC AppWizard, it is easy to generate the skeleton of an OLE container. To see what you can get with the default container application, create a new project named CONAPP (for Container Application) and select the Container option in step 3 of the MFC AppWizard dialog (Figure 28.12). Accept the default choices for all the other options. At the final step, AppWizard displays the New Project Information dialog showing the classes to be generated. As you can see from Figure 28.13, AppWizard generates a Container Item class `CConappCntrItem` for the OLE container application. This is an additional item that AppWizard generates because the application is an OLE container. Choose OK in the New Project Information dialog to enable AppWizard to create the files and open the project in Visual Workbench.

FIGURE 28.13.

MFC AppWizard's New Project Information dialog for an OLE container application.

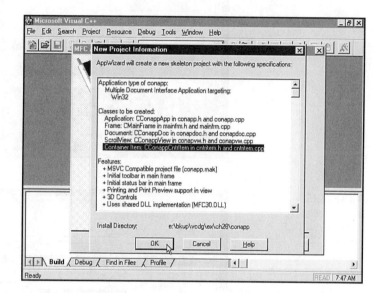

In addition to the new Container Item class (`CConappCntrItem`) derived from `COleClientItem`, the OLE container's document class (`CConappCntrItem`) is derived from `COleDocument`. In a non-OLE application, the document class is derived from `CDocument`.

After AppWizard generates the project files, select the Build conapp.exe option from the Project menu to generate the CONAPP.EXE program. Try running the program. Select the Edit menu. You will notice that the AppWizard-generated container application already has the Insert New Object option in the Edit menu (see Figure 28.14). Selecting this option brings up the standard Insert Object dialog shown in Figure 28.15. The application's code uses an instance of the `COleInsertDialog` class to display the Insert Object dialog.

FIGURE 28.14.

The Insert New Object option in the OLE container's Edit menu.

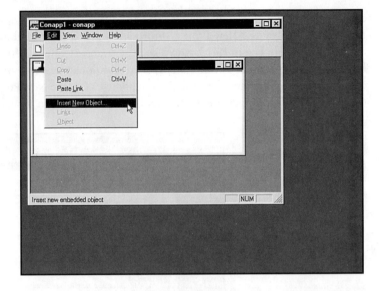

FIGURE 28.15.

The Insert Object dialog displayed by the OLE container.

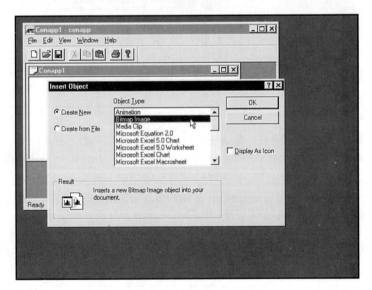

From the Insert Object dialog, you can select an OLE object for insertion into the container's document. The Insert Object dialog lists OLE objects for the servers listed in the registration database. Try selecting the Bitmap Image object. A frame containing an empty bitmap image appears in the container application's document. The paint application becomes active, enabling you to edit the bitmap image in place. Figure 28.16 shows the result after some scribbling with a drawing tool.

FIGURE 28.16.

A bitmap image being edited in place in the OLE container.

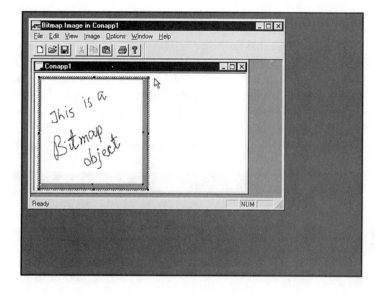

You even can save the document with the bitmap in a file and retrieve it later. Additionally, when you load a document containing an embedded object such as the bitmap image, the Edit menu offers options that make sense for the image (see Figure 12.17). For example, if you select Open from the cascading menu in Figure 12.17, the paint program is launched with the bitmap image loaded and ready to be edited. On the other hand, if you select Edit from the cascading menu, you can edit the bitmap image in place inside the container's window.

FIGURE 28.17.

Entries in the Edit menu when the document has an embedded bitmap image object.

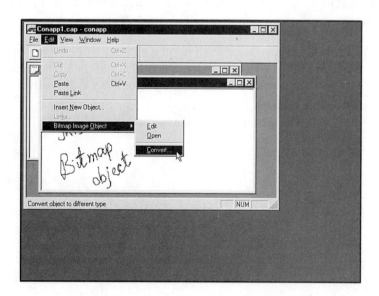

Customizing the Container

You have to admit that the AppWizard-generated OLE container application already has a lot of functionality, but it still needs many basic functionalities that you have to add. For example, you cannot click on the embedded object to select it; nor can you move the item. In addition, when you insert more than one OLE item into the container, only the last one is visible and available for interactions. All these shortcomings can be fixed easily by modifying one or more member functions of the client item class and the view class. The next few sections show a few specific customizations of the container application generated by MFC AppWizard.

CONTAINERS ARE CLIENTS

What used to be clients in OLE 1.0 are called containers in OLE 2.0. Although most new documentation attempts to refer to clients as containers, both terms are used to mean the same entity—the recipient of an OLE item. The client-side representation of an OLE item is the client item and represented by a class derived from COleClientItem.

Positioning a Client Item

In the CONAPP application, each client item is represented by an instance of the application's client item class, CConappCntrItem, which is derived from COleClientItem. The application's document class, CConappDoc (derived from COleDocument) maintains the client items corresponding to the OLE items inserted into the OLE container. In fact, the facilities for managing the client items are built into the CConappDoc's base class—COleDocument.

To keep track of the position of a client item, follow these steps:

1. Add a member variable m_rect of type CRect to the CConappCntrItem class in CNTRITEM.H, as shown by the bold line of code. This variable holds the location and size of the client item within the container's document:

```
// In CNTRITEM.H
class CConappCntrItem : public COleClientItem
{
//...
public:
//...
    CRect m_rect; // Item's position within document
//...
};
```

Initialize the rectangle in the constructor of the CConappCntrItem class in CNTRITEM.CPP:

```
CConappCntrItem::CConappCntrItem(CConappDoc* pContainer)
    : COleClientItem(pContainer)
{
    m_rect.SetRect(10, 10, 210, 210);
}
```

2. In CNTRITEM.CPP, change the implementation of the `OnGetItemPosition` position as shown by the bold line of code:

```
void CConappCntrItem::OnGetItemPosition(CRect& rPosition)
{
    ASSERT_VALID(this);
// Return correct rectangle (in pixels) in rPosition
    rPosition = m_rect;
}
```

The AppWizard-generated code always returned a fixed rectangle. Here, you return the current rectangle, whatever it may be.

3. During in-place activation, the client item's `OnChangeItemPosition` function is called whenever position of the item changes within the document window. The AppWizard-generated code does not do anything in this case. You have to update the `m_rect` variable and ensure that the document gets redrawn. The code shown in boldface accomplishes this:

```
BOOL CConappCntrItem::OnChangeItemPosition(const CRect& rectPos)
{
    ASSERT_VALID(this);

    if (!COleClientItem::OnChangeItemPosition(rectPos))
        return FALSE;

// Store the rectangle, update the views, and
// mark the document dirty
    m_rect = rectPos;
    GetDocument()->UpdateAllViews(NULL);
    GetDocument()->SetModifiedFlag();

    return TRUE;
}
```

4. Add code in the `Serialize` function of the `CConappCntrItem` class to store and retrieve the `m_rect` member variable:

```
    if(ar.IsStoring())
    {
        ar << m_rect;
```

```
    }
    else
    {
        ar >> m_rect;
    }
```

Drawing All Client Items

As generated by AppWizard, the CONAPP application displays only one OLE item—the current selection—in the view window. Modify the OnDraw function of the view class, CConappView, as shown by the code in boldface, to draw all client items in the document:

```
void CConappView::OnDraw(CDC* pDC)
{
    CConappDoc* pDoc = GetDocument();
    ASSERT_VALID(pDoc);

// Draw all items except the selection
    POSITION pos = pDoc->GetStartPosition();
    while(pos != NULL)
    {
        CConappCntrItem *pItem =
            (CConappCntrItem*)pDoc->GetNextClientItem(pos);
        if(pItem != m_pSelection)
            pItem->Draw(pDC, pItem->m_rect);
    }

// Draw the current selection
    if (m_pSelection != NULL)
    {
        m_pSelection->Draw(pDC, m_pSelection->m_rect);

// Draw a tracker rectangle for the current selection
        CRectTracker tracker;
        PutTracker(m_pSelection, &tracker);
        tracker.Draw(pDC);
    }
}
```

The strategy is to draw all the items except the current selection, then draw the current selection last. The actual drawing of a client item is done by calling the Draw member function of the client item class—all you have to do is provide the device context and the rectangle where the drawing should appear. In this example, the client item is drawn in the rectangle stored in the item's m_rect member variable.

Selecting and Activating a Client Item

In an OLE container application, the user selects an item with a click and activates an item with a double-click. To support selecting and activating client items in CONAPP, make the following changes:

1. In the view class, add a helper function, PutTracker, to draw a rectangle that tracks the movement of the mouse when the user drags the mouse. Add the function declaration to the file CONAPVW.H, as shown in boldface:

```
class CConappView : public CScrollView
{
//...
// Operations
public:
    void PutTracker(CConappCntrItem* pItem,
                    CRectTracker* pTracker);
//...
};
```

Then add the PutTracker function's definition to the file CONAPVW.CPP:

```
void CConappView::PutTracker(CConappCntrItem* pItem,
                            CRectTracker* pTracker)
{
    pTracker->m_rect = pItem->m_rect;

// For current selection, show resize handles
    if(pItem == m_pSelection)
        pTracker->m_nStyle |= CRectTracker::resizeInside;

    if(pItem->GetType() == OT_LINK)
        pTracker->m_nStyle |= CRectTracker::dottedLine;
    else
        pTracker->m_nStyle |= CRectTracker::solidLine;

    if(pItem->GetItemState() == COleClientItem::openState ||
        pItem->GetItemState() == COleClientItem::activeUIState)
    {
        pTracker->m_nStyle |= CRectTracker::hatchInside;
    }
}
```

2. To enable the user to select an item by clicking on it, you have to handle the WM_LBUTTONDOWN event. Use ClassWizard to add a handler for the WM_LBUTTONDOWN event in the view class. ClassWizard adds the OnLButtonDown function as the handler for the WM_LBUTTONDOWN event. From ClassWizard, select that function and click on the Edit Code button to edit the function. You should define the OnLButtonDown function as follows:

```
void CConappView::OnLButtonDown(UINT nFlags, CPoint point)
```

```
    {
// Find the item at the cursor location
    CConappDoc* pDoc = GetDocument();
    CConappCntrItem* pItemHit = NULL;
    POSITION pos = pDoc->GetStartPosition();
    while(pos != NULL)
    {
        CConappCntrItem* pItem =
            (CConappCntrItem*)pDoc->GetNextItem(pos);
        if (pItem->m_rect.PtInRect(point))
                pItemHit = pItem;

    }

// Now set the current selection as this item
    if(pItemHit == NULL || m_pSelection != pItemHit)
    {
        COleClientItem* pActiveItem =
            GetDocument()->GetInPlaceActiveItem(this);
        if (pActiveItem != NULL && pActiveItem != pItemHit)
            pActiveItem->Close();
    }
    Invalidate();
    m_pSelection = pItemHit;

// Display a tracker rectangle
    if(pItemHit != NULL)
    {
        CRectTracker tracker;
        PutTracker(pItemHit, &tracker);
        UpdateWindow();
        if(tracker.Track(this, point))
        {
            Invalidate();
            pItemHit->m_rect = tracker.m_rect;
            GetDocument()->SetModifiedFlag();
        }
    }

    CScrollView::OnLButtonDown(nFlags, point);
}
```

In OnLButtonDown, the first step is to determine whether the mouse click occurred on an item. That item is then made the currently selected item (if the mouse click is not on any item, the current selection is set to NULL). Finally, a tracker rectangle is displayed around the item by calling the PutTracker helper function. The document also is marked dirty and the view is updated. This approach causes the view to be updated every time the user clicks on an item. You could use a smarter approach that redraws only those parts of the view window that need redrawing.

3. To activate an item when the user double-clicks on an item, use ClassWizard to add a handler for the WM_LBUTTONDBLCLK event. Edit the handler OnLButtonDblClk:

```
void CConappView::OnLButtonDblClk(UINT nFlags, CPoint point)
{
// First, handle a single click
    OnLButtonDown(nFlags, point);

// If the double-click is on a valid item, activate it
    if(m_pSelection != NULL)
    {
        m_pSelection->DoVerb(GetKeyState(VK_CONTROL) < 0 ?
            OLEIVERB_OPEN : OLEIVERB_PRIMARY, this);
    }

    CScrollView::OnLButtonDblClk(nFlags, point);
}
```

The OnLButtonDblClk function first calls OnLButtonDown to handle the single button down event. Then, if the double-click is on an item, that item's DoVerb function is called to activate the item. If the Ctrl key is down during the double-click, the OPEN verb is invoked; otherwise, the primary verb of the item's server is invoked.

4. Last, but not the least, you should add a handler for the WM_SETCURSOR event. This enables the cursor shape to change as the user moves the cursor over a selected item. All you have to do is create a tracker rectangle over the current selection and call the tracker's SetCursor function:

```
BOOL CConappView::OnSetCursor(CWnd* pWnd, UINT nHitTest,
                            UINT message)
{
    if(pWnd == this && m_pSelection != NULL)
    {
        CRectTracker tracker;
        PutTracker(m_pSelection, &tracker);
        if(tracker.SetCursor(this, nHitTest))
            return TRUE;
```

```
    }

        return CScrollView::OnSetCursor(pWnd, nHitTest, message);
    }
```

Testing the Improved Container

After making the changes shown in the previous sections, build the CONAPP.EXE program again and run it. Now you should be able to insert multiple objects and position them in the view. You also can select an item by clicking or edit it in place by double-clicking. Figure 28.18 shows the improved container application with two embedded bitmap images, one of them selected by a click.

FIGURE 28.18.

Improved container with two embedded bitmap image objects.

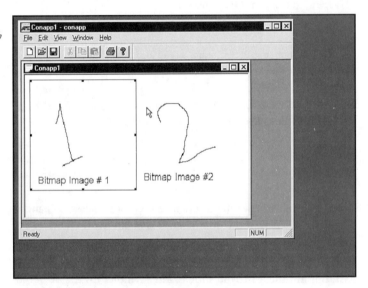

Building an OLE Server Application

An OLE server application acts as the provider of OLE items for use by OLE containers. Some server applications support creation of embedded items only; some can create both linked and embedded items. An application can be both an OLE server and an OLE container; in this case, it can both incorporate OLE items from other servers and provide OLE items for use in other containers.

Recall that there are two types of OLE servers:

■ A mini-server is a special type of OLE application that can be launched only from an OLE container; mini-servers cannot run standalone. A mini-server cannot save documents in files; it can work only with items obtained from a client's document. Thus, a mini-server can support only embedding and not linking.

■ A full-server can run stand-alone or can be launched from a container. A full-server supports all forms of OLE: embedding alone, linking alone, or both embedding and linking.

With MFC AppWizard, you can easily build either type.

A Timestamp Server

It is reasonably easy to build an OLE server if you start from scratch and enable MFC AppWizard to generate the server application's template. To see how to create an OLE server, consider a simple application that creates a timestamp—the application creates a document with the current date and time. The idea is that an OLE container can insert an item from this server to place a timestamp string in the container's document. To implement this simple server, create a new project named DTMSRV (for Date-Time Server) and select the Full-Server option in step 3 of the MFC AppWizard dialog (see Figure 28.12). Accept the default choices for all the other options. At the final step, AppWizard displays the New Project Information dialog showing the classes to be generated. As you can see from Figure 28.19, AppWizard generates a Server Item class and an In-Place Frame class for the OLE server application. These two are additional items that AppWizard generates because the application is an OLE server. Choose OK in the New Project Information dialog. AppWizard creates the files and opens the project in Visual Workbench.

FIGURE 28.19.

MFC AppWizard's New Project Information dialog for an OLE server application.

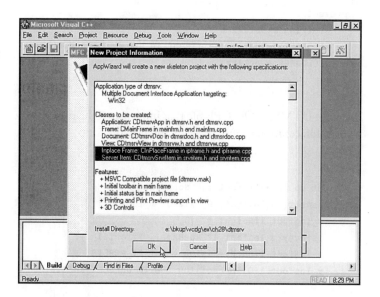

In addition to the new server item class (CDtmsrvSrvrItem) derived from COleServerItem and the in-place frame window class (CInPlaceFrame) derived from COleIPFrameWnd, the OLE server's document class (CDtmsrvDoc) is derived from COleServerDoc. In a non-OLE application, the document class is derived from CDocument.

After AppWizard generates the project files, make the following changes to add the timestamp capability (unlike an OLE container that can do something useful without any additional code, you have to add some visual items to see the server in action):

1. The first change has to do with initializing and storing the current date and time in a CString variable in the document class of the server. In the document class, CDtmsrvDoc, add a member variable (m_DateTime) to store the date-time string and two helper functions: one named Draw to display the string and another named GetExtent to compute the extent of the string. Add member variables m_logfont and m_crtext to store the font and text color. In the DTMSRDOC.H file, make the additions shown in boldface:

```
class CDtmsrvDoc : public COleServerDoc
{
// Implementation
public:
//...
    void CDtmsrvDoc::Draw(CDC *pDC) const;
    void CDtmsrvDoc::GetExtent(CDC *pDC, CSize &size) const;
//...
protected:
    CString m_DateTime;
    LOGFONT m_logfont;  // Font to use for the document
    COLORREF m_crText;
//...
};
```

2. In the DTMSRDOC.CPP file that implements the document class, add code (shown in boldface) in the constructor to initialize the font:

```
CDtmsrvDoc::CDtmsrvDoc()
{
// Set up default font for document
    memset(&m_logfont, 0, sizeof m_logfont);
    m_logfont.lfHeight = -10;
    lstrcpy(m_logfont.lfFaceName, _T("Arial"));
    m_logfont.lfOutPrecision = OUT_TT_PRECIS;
    m_logfont.lfClipPrecision = CLIP_DEFAULT_PRECIS;
```

```
    m_logfont.lfQuality = PROOF_QUALITY;
    m_logfont.lfPitchAndFamily = FF_SWISS | VARIABLE_PITCH;

// Use default window text color
    m_crText = COLOR_WINDOWTEXT+1;
}
```

3. In the OnNewDocument function of the document class (in the DTMSRDOC.CPP file), add the code shown in boldface (to set up the date and time string):

```
BOOL CDtmsrvDoc::OnNewDocument()
{
    if (!COleServerDoc::OnNewDocument())
                return FALSE;

// Get current date and time
    time_t tnow;
    time(&tnow);
    char *tstr = ctime(&tnow);

// Get rid of newline character at the end of string
    tstr[strlen(tstr)-1] = '\0';

// Save in CString variable
    m_DateTime = tstr;

    return TRUE;
}
```

Also in the DTMSRDOC.CPP file, add definitions of the Draw and GetExtent member functions as shown in Listing 28.1. The Draw function is called whenever the server's document needs drawing, whether it is in stand-alone mode or is an embedded item that is activated in place in a container application. Similarly, GetExtent is called whenever there is a need to calculate the display extent of the server's document (which, in this example, is the date-time string).

4. Add the following call (shown in boldface) to the document's Draw function in the OnDraw function of the view class (in DTMSRVW.CPP file):

```
void CDtmsrvView::OnDraw(CDC* pDC)
{
    CDtmsrvDoc* pDoc = GetDocument();
    ASSERT_VALID(pDoc);
```

```
    pDoc->Draw(pDC);
}
```

This takes care of displaying the date-time string when the server application runs stand-alone.

5. In the implementation of the server item class (in the SRVRITEM.CPP file), add the following code (shown in boldface) to the OnGetExtent function to compute properly the extent of the string displayed by the server:

```
BOOL CDtmsrvSrvrItem::OnGetExtent(DVASPECT dwDrawAspect,
                                  CSize& rSize)
{
//...
    CDtmsrvDoc* pDoc = GetDocument();
    ASSERT_VALID(pDoc);

    CClientDC dc(NULL);
    dc.SetMapMode(MM_ANISOTROPIC);
    pDoc->GetExtent(&dc, rSize);
    dc.LPtoHIMETRIC(&rSize); // convert pixels to HIMETRIC

    return TRUE;
}
```

Add code to the server item's OnDraw function to display the date-time string (by setting the mapping mode and the extent and calling the Draw function of the document class). The new code is shown in boldface:

```
BOOL CDtmsrvSrvrItem::OnDraw(CDC* pDC, CSize& rSize)
{
    CDtmsrvDoc* pDoc = GetDocument();
    ASSERT_VALID(pDoc);

// Set mapping mode and extent.
// (The extent is usually the same as the size returned
// from OnGetExtent)

    OnGetExtent(DVASPECT_CONTENT, rSize);
    pDC->SetMapMode(MM_ANISOTROPIC);
    pDC->SetWindowOrg(0,0);
    pDC->SetWindowExt(rSize.cx, rSize.cy);

// All drawing takes place in the metafile device context (pDC).
    pDoc->Draw(pDC);
```

```
        return TRUE;

    }
```

Listing 28.1. **Draw** and **GetExtent** member functions of the server's document class.

```
//-----------------------------------------------------------------
// CDtmsrvDoc:: D r a w
// Displays the date-time string

void CDtmsrvDoc::Draw(CDC *pDC) const
{
// Display the date+time string using default font
// Convert fontsize in points (in m_logfont.lfHeight)
// to logical extent

    LOGFONT logfont = m_logfont;
    logfont.lfHeight = -::MulDiv(-logfont.lfHeight,
                pDC->GetDeviceCaps(LOGPIXELSY), 72);

// Set the text color
    pDC->SetTextColor(m_crText);

// Create the font
    CFont font;
    if (!font.CreateFontIndirect(&logfont))
    {
// Select the font
        CFont* pOldFont = pDC->SelectObject(&font);
        pDC->TextOut(0, 0, m_DateTime,
                            m_DateTime.GetLength());
// Restore the DC
        pDC->SelectObject(pOldFont);
    }
    else
        pDC->TextOut(0, 0, m_DateTime,
                            m_DateTime.GetLength());
}
//-----------------------------------------------------------------
// CDtmsrvDoc:: G e t E x t e n t
// Return the extent of the string

void CDtmsrvDoc::GetExtent(CDC *pDC, CSize &size) const
{
// Set up the font
    LOGFONT logfont = m_logfont;
    logfont.lfHeight = -::MulDiv(-logfont.lfHeight,
                pDC->GetDeviceCaps(LOGPIXELSY), 72);

    CFont font;
    if (!font.CreateFontIndirect(&logfont))
    {
// Select the font
        CFont* pOldFont = pDC->SelectObject(&font);
```

continues

Listing 28.1. continued

```
// Compute the line height and extent
        TEXTMETRIC tm;
        pDC->GetTextMetrics(&tm);
        size.cy = tm.tmHeight + tm.tmExternalLeading;
        size.cx = m_DateTime.GetLength() * tm.tmAveCharWidth;

// Restore the DC
        pDC->SelectObject(pOldFont);
    }
    else
    {
// Compute the line height and extent based on default font
        TEXTMETRIC tm;
        pDC->GetTextMetrics(&tm);
        size.cy = tm.tmHeight + tm.tmExternalLeading;
        size.cx = m_DateTime.GetLength() *
                        tm.tmAveCharWidth;
    }
}
```

Testing the Timestamp Server

After making the suggested changes to the AppWizard-generated server application, select the Build dtmsrv.exe option from the Project menu to generate the DTMSRV.EXE program. Run the program once—you will see a new window with a date and time string. Running the server application also registers the application in the system's registration database. Once the server is registered, you do not have to keep it running to try embedding a timestamp in an OLE container application. Quit the server application.

To see the server in action, you need an OLE container application. Run the container application, CONAPP.EXE, developed earlier in this chapter. Select the Insert New Object option of the Edit menu. In the resulting standard Insert Object dialog, you should see the entry Dtmsrv Document—that is the name of the timestamp object (AppWizard provides it as the default name). If you select that item, the DTMSRV server inserts a timestamp into the container. You also can insert other OLE items (such as a bitmap image) to the container. Figure 28.20 shows the container application with two inserted objects—a bitmap image and a timestamp object. The timestamp object shows the date and time when the item was inserted into the container.

FIGURE 28.20.

The OLE container displaying a bitmap image and a timestamp object.

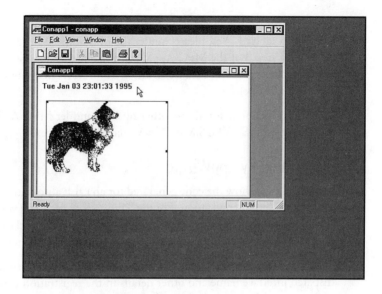

Building an OLE Automation Server

An OLE automation server provides a programmable interface that other applications use to manipulate OLE objects within the automation server. In OLE terminology, this interface is referred to as the dispatch interface or, more precisely, the IDispatch interface, which exposes objects, methods, and properties from an OLE automation server to OLE automation clients (also known as OLE automation controllers). OLE automation enables the automation server to be controlled through a programming language such as Microsoft Visual Basic.

The best way to understand OLE automation is to see an example. The following sections show how to create a simple OLE automation server using Visual C++ 2.0 and MFC 3.0 and how to test the automation server using the DISPTEST program that accompanies Visual C++ 2.0.

A Status Display Automation Server

You can build a simple OLE automation server easily in Visual Workbench. As an idea for a server, consider a status display of the kind commonly used by many installation programs—the kind that shows a horizontal gauge that gets filled as the installation progresses (see Figure 28.21). The next example builds such a status display with some external interfaces for controlling the label that appears above the gauge and the "percent completed" value used to show the amount of the gauge filled. The idea is that the automation client will set the label and change the value to show the current status of some operation in progress.

To implement this simple automation server, create a new project named STATUS and click on the checkbox labeled "Yes, please" under the question, "Would you like support for OLE automation?" in step 3 of the MFC AppWizard dialog (see Figure 28.12). Do not check the boxes for OLE client or server because an automation server does not have to be an OLE server (although it can be one).

Accept the default choices for all the other options and let MFC AppWizard create the files and open the project (STATUS.MAK) in Visual Workbench.

Code Generated By AppWizard

It is educational to see how the code generated for an OLE automation server differs from that for a regular AppWizard application. For the STATUS project, you will find source and header files for the usual document, view, main frame, and application classes. There are two additional files that are generated specifically because STATUS is an automation server:

■ STATUS.REG is a text file with information that can be used to register the OLE dispatch interface name and other details in the registration database. Note that the same information is used within the program to register itself when you first run the program. If you want to load the registration information directly without running the program, you may do so by using REGEDIT:

```
REGEDIT STATUS.REG
```

■ STATUS.ODL is another text file that contains the Object Description Language (ODL) source code defining the dispatch interfaces offered by the STATUS application. STATUS.ODL serves as input to the MKTYPLIB program that converts it to a type library file named STATUS.TLB. The type library is used by OLE automation clients to obtain information about the interfaces exposed by the automation server. ClassWizard maintains this file as you add automation methods and expose member variables for outside access; therefore, you do not have to learn the syntax of the ODL file.

Implementing the Basic Behavior of STATUS.EXE

After AppWizard generates the shell of the automation server application, implement the basic behavior of STATUS.EXE—display a label with a gauge underneath the label—and test the program stand-alone. Here are the steps:

1. Add member variables in the document class, CStatusDoc, to store the current label and the current value (reflecting the "percent complete" amount). Add the necessary member functions so that the view class can access these values. To do this, add the declarations shown in boldface to the file STATUDOC.H:

```
class CStatusDoc : public CDocument
{
```

```
//...
// Implementation
public:
//...
    WORD GetValue(void) { return m_nValue;}

    void SetValue(int n)
    {
        if(n != m_nValue)
        {
            if(n < 0) n = 0;
            if(n > 100) n = 100;
            m_nValue = n;
            Refresh();
        }
    }

    CString& GetLabel() { return m_Label;}
    void SetLabel(LPCTSTR lpszNewLabel)
    {
        CString s(lpszNewLabel);
        SetLabel(s);
    }
    void SetLabel(CString& s)
    {
        if(s == m_Label) return;
        m_Label = s;
    }

protected:

    WORD        m_nValue;
    CString     m_Label;
//...
};
```

2. In the implementation of the CStatusDoc class in the STATUDOC.CPP file, add code to initialize the newly added member variables:

```
CStatusDoc::CStatusDoc()
{
    EnableAutomation();
```

```
    m_nValue = 0;
    m_Label = _T("Status");

    AfxOleLockApp();
}
```

Note that the calls to EnableAutomation and AfxOleLockApp (in the document class constructor) are necessary because this application is an OLE automation server.

Implement the Refresh function (used later as part of the dispatch interface) in file STATUDOC.CPP as follows:

```
void CStatusDoc::Refresh()
{
    UpdateAllViews(NULL);
    SetModifiedFlag();
}
```

3. In the application's view class, CStatusView, define the OnDraw function (in the STATUVW.CPP file) as follows:

```
// Some constants
const int Extent = 300;
const int Thickness = 10;

//...
void CStatusView::OnDraw(CDC* pDC)
{
    CStatusDoc* pDoc = GetDocument();
    ASSERT_VALID(pDoc);

// Fill window with blue color
    CRect rect;
    GetClientRect(&rect);
    CBrush brush;
    brush.CreateSolidBrush(RGB(0,0,255));
    pDC->FillRect(&rect, &brush);

// Set up font to display label
// Set up default font for document
    LOGFONT lf;
    memset(&lf, 0, sizeof lf);
    lf.lfHeight = -::MulDiv(24,
                pDC->GetDeviceCaps(LOGPIXELSY), 72);
    lstrcpy(lf.lfFaceName, _T("Arial"));
```

```
        lf.lfOutPrecision = OUT_TT_PRECIS;
        lf.lfClipPrecision = CLIP_DEFAULT_PRECIS;
        lf.lfQuality = PROOF_QUALITY;
        lf.lfPitchAndFamily = FF_SWISS ¦ VARIABLE_PITCH;

// Display label in the desired font
// Create the font
        CFont font;
        if (font.CreateFontIndirect(&lf))
        {
// Select the font
            CFont* pOldFont = pDC->SelectObject(&font);

// Compute the character height
            TEXTMETRIC tm;
            pDC->GetTextMetrics(&tm);
            int cheight = tm.tmHeight + tm.tmExternalLeading;
            int x = (rect.right - Extent) / 2;
            int y = (rect.bottom - cheight - 10) / 2;

// Set the text color black and display the label
            COLORREF old_colr = pDC->SetTextColor(RGB(0,0,0));
            int oldmode = pDC->SetBkMode(TRANSPARENT);
            pDC->TextOut(x, y, pDoc->GetLabel(),
                            pDoc->GetLabel().GetLength());

// Display again in white, with a little shift to
// upper-left corner
            pDC->SetTextColor(RGB(255,255,255));
            pDC->TextOut(x - cheight/8, y - cheight/8,
                        pDoc->GetLabel(),
                        pDoc->GetLabel().GetLength());

// Restore the DC
            pDC->SetTextColor(old_colr);
            pDC->SelectObject(pOldFont);
            pDC->SetBkMode(oldmode);

// Draw the status bar
            y += (cheight * 3) / 2;
            CRect r(x, y, x + Extent, y + Thickness);
            CBrush b;
```

```
       b.CreateSolidBrush(RGB(255,255,255));
       pDC->FillRect(&r, &b);

// Now fill in the part corresponding to current value
       WORD value = pDoc->GetValue();
       CRect rv(x, y, x + (value*Extent)/100, y + Thickness);
       CBrush bv;
       bv.CreateSolidBrush(RGB(255, 0, 0));
       pDC->FillRect(&rv, &bv);
   }
}
```

This code first fills the window with a blue color. Then it displays the label twice—once in black and the next time in white, but shifted up a bit to give the appearance of a shadow. Finally, the "percent complete" gauge is displayed by filling rectangles.

4. Select Build status.exe from the Visual Workbench's Project menu to build the program. Figure 28.21 shows the resulting display when you run the program.

FIGURE 28.21.

The Status automation server running stand-alone.

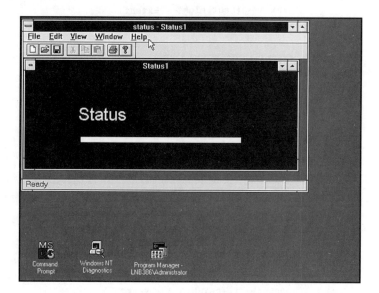

Exposing a Dispatch Interface

The basic capabilities of the STATUS application do not include any user interface element (such as menu selection or dialog box) to change the label or alter the value used to display the gauge. You provide a dispatch interface to manipulate these items so that an OLE automation client can control the status display through a Visual Basic program.

For the STATUS application, you expose a dispatch interface that enables an OLE automation client to execute the following:

- Set and get the label string
- Set and get the "percent complete" value
- Redraw the contents of the window
- Make the frame window visible (by default, AppWizard-generated automation servers do not show the frame window)

In OLE automation terminology, variables are exposed through *properties,* and actions (to be performed by the automation server) are exposed through *methods.*

In Visual Workbench, all these interfaces are specified through the ClassWizard dialog. Here are the steps for defining the dispatch interface for the STATUS automation server:

1. Select ClassWizard from the Project menu and choose the OLE Automation tab from the resulting dialog.

2. Specify CStatusDoc as the class name.

3. To provide access to the variable m_nValue, click on the Add Property button (see Figure 28.22). In the Add Property dialog box, type percent as the external name and select Get/Set Methods under Implementation. In the Type box, select short to indicate that the property named percent is of type short integer. Later on you will see that the external name is used when referring to the property in Visual Basic code. For example, here is how Visual Basic refers to the Percent property of the StatDisp object, which is an instance of a Status.Document (the AppWizard-assigned dispatch name for the document class of the STATUS application):

```
Dim StatDisp As object


Sub Form_Load ()
    Set StatDisp = CreateObject("Status.Document")
    StatDisp.ShowWindow
End Sub


Sub SetPercent_Click ()
    StatDisp.Percent = Percent.Text
End Sub
```

Choosing OK in the Add Property dialog box brings you back to the OLE Automation tab. The Implementation box shows the following:

```
short GetPercent();
void SetPercent(short nNewValue);
```

4. Click on the Edit Code button and implement the `GetPercent` and `SetPercent` functions:

```
short CStatusDoc::GetPercent()
{
        return m_nValue;
}

void CStatusDoc::SetPercent(short nNewValue)
{
    SetValue(nNewValue);
}
```

5. Repeat steps 3 and 4 to add a property named `text` corresponding to the `m_Label` variable; you should select BSTR as the Type for the `m_Label` variable (in the Add Property dialog box). This adds two more Get/Set functions:

```
BSTR GetText();
void SetText(LPCTSTR lpszNewValue);
```

Click on the Edit Code button and define these functions:

```
BSTR CStatusDoc::GetText()
{
        return m_Label.AllocSysString();
}

void CStatusDoc::SetText(LPCTSTR lpszNewValue)
{
    SetLabel(lpszNewValue);
}
```

Note that BSTR is a type of null-terminated string prefixed with a count of the characters in the string. To return a BSTR, the `GetText` function calls the `AllocSysString` member function of the `CString` class to allocate a BSTR and copy the contents of the `CString` object into the BSTR.

6. The STATUS automation server exposes two methods: one to refresh the window and the other to make the main frame window visible. To add the method to redraw the window, click on the Add Method button in the OLE Automation tab of the ClassWizard's dialog (see Figure 28.22). In the Add Method dialog box, enter

RefreshWindow in the External Name box. This is the name that the OLE automation clients will use to invoke the method from a scripting language such as Visual Basic:

```
Dim StatDisp As object
...
Sub RefreshDisplay_Click ()
    StatDisp.RefreshWindow
End Sub
```

In the Internal Name box of the Add Method dialog, enter Refresh as the internal name of the function. Set the Return Type box to void and click on the OK button. This returns you to the OLE Automation tab. Now you can click on the Edit Code button and define the Refresh function as follows:

```
void CStatusDoc::Refresh()
{
    UpdateAllViews(NULL);
    SetModifiedFlag();
}
```

7. Repeat step 6 and add another method; use ShowWindow as both the external and internal names. Define the ShowWindow function as follows:

```
void CStatusDoc::ShowWindow()
{
    POSITION pos = GetFirstViewPosition();
    CView* pView = GetNextView(pos);
    if (pView != NULL)
    {
        CFrameWnd* pFrameWnd = pView->GetParentFrame();
        pFrameWnd->ActivateFrame(SW_SHOW);
        pFrameWnd = pFrameWnd->GetParentFrame();
        if(pFrameWnd != NULL)
            pFrameWnd->ActivateFrame(SW_SHOW);
    }
}
```

This code gets the view object associated with the document and activates the frame window for that view.

FIGURE 28.22.

The OLE Automation tab in the ClassWizard dialog.

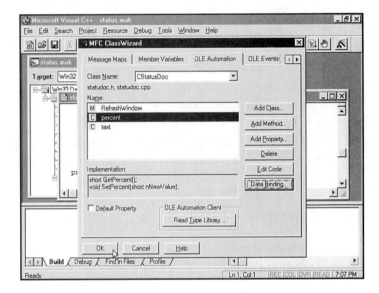

After defining the dispatch interface properties and methods, choose `Build status.exe` from the `Project` menu to build the program again. If you run STATUS.EXE again, you will not see any change in behavior because all you did was add the dispatch interface. To see how STATUS works as an automation server, you need an OLE automation client with support for a scripting language such as Visual Basic.

BASIC 3.0 IS AN OLE AUTOMATION CONTROLLER

In addition to the DISPTEST program that comes with Visual C++ 2.0, you can use Visual Basic 3.0 to test your OLE automation server. With Visual Basic 3.0, you can create stand-alone .EXE files that use automation servers.

Testing the Automation Server with DISPTEST

DISPTEST.EXE is an OLE automation client program that comes with Microsoft Visual C++ 2.0. DISPTEST enables you to design a form with buttons and text fields and attach Visual Basic code to handle user actions such as button clicks. The Visual Basic code can create automation objects, get and set properties, and invoke methods of the automation objects.

To test the STATUS automation server using DISPTEST, follow these steps (remember to run STATUS.EXE once to ensure that it is registered properly):

1. Start DISPTEST (you may do so by typing `start disptest` in the Windows NT command window or by selecting File|Run from the Program Manager).

2. Using the graphical tools, lay out a form with a number of buttons and text fields. Figure 28.23 shows the appearance of DISPTEST when you are designing a form. In the figure, the form appears with the title `Status Display Driver`. The properties of the form are displayed in a window on the right side of the form. The window at the bottom of the screen shows the Visual Basic code to load a form. As you can see, an object of type `Status.Document` is created when loading the form. This starts the STATUS automation server when the form is loaded.

3. Add Visual Basic code to handle events for all other buttons. For example, the button labeled Set All is assigned the name `SetAll` (in that button's property sheet) and the Visual basic code to handle a mouse click on that button is as follows:

```
Sub SetAll_Click ()
    StatDisp.Text = Text.Text
    StatDisp.Percent = Percent.Text
End Sub
```

Note that `Percent` and `Text` are the names of the text fields labeled Percent and Text, respectively. This code sets the `Percent` and `Text` properties of the `StatDisp` object to the text contained in the text fields of same name in the form. If you know Visual Basic (or learn it in a hurry), you will see how to write the event handling code for the form.

4. After writing the event procedures for all components of the form, you can try it out by selecting Start from the Run menu in DISPTEST. Figure 28.24 shows the STATUS automation server being driven from the form created using DISPTEST. Try setting the Percent field to 88 (denoting 88%) and the Text field to Percent Complete. Then click on the Set All button. Figure 28.24 shows the resulting output in the STATUS automation server's window.

FIGURE 28.23.

A form, its properties, and the Visual Basic code in DISPTEST.

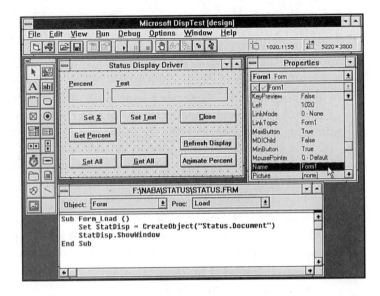

FIGURE 28.24.

Testing the STATUS automation server using DISPTEST.

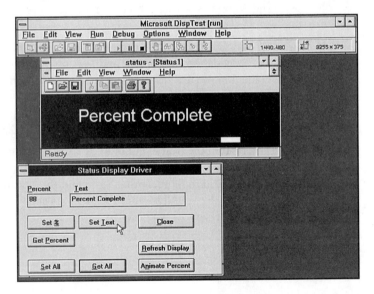

As you can see, OLE automation offers a powerful way for a programmer to access the capabilities of an application through a language such as Visual Basic. In fact, the programmer can assemble completely new applications from OLE automation objects using Visual Basic.

Summary

Object Linking and Embedding (OLE) started as OLE version 1.0, which focused on the mechanisms required to create compound documents. A compound document contains parts created by different applications. An OLE container supports a compound document containing OLE items provided by one or more OLE servers. The OLE container is sometimes referred to as an OLE client. The OLE items appearing in a container's document are displayed and manipulated by the OLE servers that provide the items. The container application does not have to know anything about the items embedded in the container. Embedding refers to the incorporation of an OLE item in the container's document; linking implies storing a reference to an OLE item but not its actual data. When the user edits a contained item, the server application is launched and used to edit the item.

OLE 2.0 continues to support creation of compound documents, but OLE 2.0 is also a collection of features and supporting technologies that forms the basis of Microsoft's strategy for supporting Windows objects. OLE 2.0 is built on the foundation of the Component Object Model (COM), which defines the structure of an object, its interface, and the protocols for defining and accessing these interfaces. Compound files provide a structured storage mechanism for storing OLE objects. Uniform data transfer mechanisms enable all types of data exchanges, through either the Clipboard or drag-and-drop. OLE automation enables an application (called the automation server) to expose a programmable interface. Other applications (known as automation clients) can use a scripting language or Visual Basic to manipulate OLE objects within the automation server.

OLE 2.0 also supports visual (or in-place) editing, which enables the OLE server to take over the display window of the OLE container temporarily when the user edits an embedded item. To see an example of this, insert an Excel spreadsheet into a Microsoft Word document and double-click on the spreadsheet to edit it. You will notice that the Word document takes on the personality of Excel (by changing the menus and the tool bar) while you edit the spreadsheet.

Although OLE has a reputation of being difficult to program, the object-oriented design of OLE enables C++ classes to encapsulate OLE objects easily. MFC 3.0 includes more than 25 classes for OLE programming. MFC AppWizard in the Visual Workbench also automatically generates all necessary code to create a shell application with a variety of OLE capabilities, including full-server, mini-server, container, and OLE automation support.

This chapter shows you how to write an OLE container, an OLE server, and an OLE automation server. The sample programs illustrate how to use AppWizard and ClassWizard to create OLE applications easily.

29

Building OLE Custom Controls (OCX)

Object-based technologies such as OLE aim to facilitate building *component software*—software packaged in a self-contained unit with well-defined external interfaces. Before OLE came along, Microsoft had implemented the Visual Basic Custom Control (VBX) architecture in Visual Basic. Although originally designed for custom controls (user interface components such as dialog boxes), enterprising software developers discovered that they could use the VBX architecture to package a variety of software. Thus, you can now find VBXs as software building blocks providing add-on capabilities, such as text editing, image processing, database access, facsimile (FAX) send/receive, and various types of graphing and charting. Although VBX has proven successful, the VBX architecture is closely tied to 16-bit Windows. OLE Custom Controls (OCX) is the successor to VBX in the 32-bit Windows world. The OCX architecture is based on OLE and is expected to be as popular as VBX with software developers building component software for 32-bit Windows.

This chapter provides an overview of OLE Custom Controls and shows how to build an OCX using Microsoft's OLE Custom Control Developer's Kit (CDK), which is available as an add-on to Visual C++ 2.0.

LEARNING MORE ABOUT OLE CUSTOM CONTROLS

OLE Custom Controls (OCX) are relatively new, but there is considerable interest in information about OCX because Microsoft has positioned it as a successor to the highly successful Visual Basic Custom Control (VBX) technology. Although this chapter provides a good starting point for prospective OCX developers, the limited space is not enough to present the detailed information that you need to build a complex OCX. Luckily, there are many sources of information about OCX. Here are a few ways you can learn more about building OCXs:

■ Read articles on OCX in programmers' magazines. A good source is the *Microsoft Systems Journal* (published monthly by Miller Freeman, Inc., 600 Harrison St., San Francisco, CA 94107), which has regular articles about OCX programming, complete with sample code.

■ Consult the *CDK Books Online*—the online book that comes with the OLE Custom Control Development Kit (CDK). The online information describes how to use the various development tools and new classes provided with the CDK.

■ Study the sample programs in the CDK32\SAMPLES subdirectory of the Visual C++ 2.0 install directory. This is where the OCX samples are placed when you install the OLE Custom Control Development Kit that is available as an add-on to Microsoft Visual C++ 2.0.

■ Subscribe to the Microsoft Developer Network (MSDN)—the official source of software development kits, operating systems, and information on developing applications for Microsoft Windows and Windows NT. There are levels of membership and you get the information on CD-ROMs. The listings of the current contents for the Development Library and the Development Platform are available via ftp (file transfer protocol) from the Internet site `ftp.microsoft.com` in the files `/msdn/proginfo/libctnt.txt` and `/msdn/proginfo/platctnt.txt`, respectively. The `ftp.microsoft.com` site also has archives of code from the Microsoft Systems Journal.

What Is an OLE Custom Control (OCX)?

An OLE Custom Control is a reusable software component, implemented as an OLE object and designed to work in OLE control containers. Usually, an OCX has a graphical appearance, but you can have an OCX that does not have any visible output. As you might expect, as a reusable software component, an OCX has many similarities with a VBX because the basic philosophy of the OCX is the same as that for a VBX; however, the underlying architecture of the OCX is based on the object model of OLE 2.0 (see Chapter 28, "OLE 2.0 Programming with MFC 3.0," for more information on OLE). For a VBX, the container is the Visual Basic application that accesses the VBX's properties, invokes the VBX's methods, and processes events sent from the VBX. An OCX is controlled similarly through its attributes.

OCX Attributes

Like a VBX, an OCX has the following attributes:

■ *Properties* are named variables representing characteristics (such as caption, font, background color, and so forth) of the OCX.

■ *Methods* are functions (implemented within the OCX) that can be called from external code to manipulate the control's behavior and characteristics.

■ *Events* are actions triggered by the control in response to user input, such as mouse clicking or a keypress.

Figure 29.1 shows the use of these OCX attributes in interactions between the OCX and the OLE control container. Essentially, the control container can get and set properties and invoke methods, and the OCX can "fire" (send) events to the control container.

FIGURE 29.1.

Interaction between an OCX and an OLE control container.

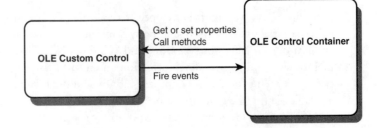

Properties

Properties are externally accessible variables of the OCX. Each property represents a variable that the OCX designer provides for the use of the OCX user—the developer who uses OCX components in an OLE control container. Visual characteristics, such as background color, caption, or font, are typical examples of properties.

There are four categories of OCX properties:

■ *Stock properties* are standard properties that most controls need. Some examples of stock properties are: BorderStyle, Caption, Text, and hWnd. These properties are defined in the COleControl class—the base class for an OCX implemented in MFC. You can use the stock properties without writing any code.

■ *Custom properties* are properties that are unique to your OCX and that you have to implement yourself.

■ *Ambient properties* are container-wide properties that your control can read and use. Ambient properties provide information about the container that the control can use to synchronize its appearance with that of the control container. For example, the control might read and use the BackColor property and use the value to display itself in the same color as the form in which it is embedded.

■ *Extended properties* are managed and held by the control's container, but the control can get access to them, if necessary. Examples of extended properties are the position and size of the control in the container.

A VBX has stock and custom properties only; the ambient and extended properties were introduced in OCX.

Methods

Methods are functions within the OCX that can be called from the OLE control container. An OCX can have stock or custom methods. The stock methods implement the common behavior of all OCXs. For example, the stock method named Refresh draws the contents of the OCX. Custom methods depend on the purpose of the control. Essentially, the custom methods are the external interfaces through which the OCX is controlled.

Events

Events are the key difference between the OCX and an embedded OLE item provided by an OLE server (see Chapter 28 for an example). The purpose of most controls is to send event notification to a parent window so that some action can be initiated. OCXs and OLE control containers have extended OLE interfaces that enable the OCX to trigger events and the control container to receive and respond to those events.

OCX Architecture

An OCX is an OLE object with a set of well-defined interfaces. Specifically, an OCX is a compound document object with the following special characteristics:

■ An OCX has control interfaces in addition to the interfaces that support OLE automation and visual editing.

■ Currently, an OCX is implemented as an *in-process server* DLL (so called because the DLL is in the same process space as the control container). This enables the control container to communicate with the control using fast function calls rather than the slower Lightweight Remote Procedure Call (LRPC) that other OLE containers and servers use.

■ Unlike other embedded OLE items, an OCX is active when visible and responds to a single mouse click (as opposed to a double-click required to activate other embedded OLE items). The term *inside-out object* is used to refer to this characteristic of an OCX.

Conceptually, you can view the OCX architecture as shown in Figure 29.2. The control container provides a site object (also referred to as a *client site*) for each control in the container. Both the client site object and the control expose control-specific interfaces besides the standard compound document interfaces.

FIGURE 29.2.
*OLE Custom Control
architecture.*

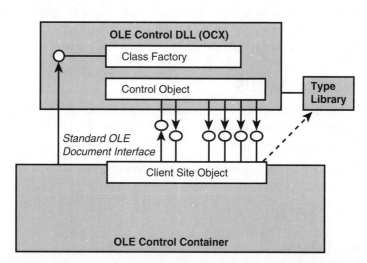

The control container application is an executable program (EXE) that supports the following control-specific interfaces:

- ■ IOleControlSite is the interface that a control uses to communicate with its client site.
- ■ IPropertyNotifySink is used by the control to notify the container of changes in its property.
- ■ IDispatch (events) is used by the control to fire its events.
- ■ IDispatch (ambient properties) is the interface through which a control accesses the ambient properties of the container.

The control itself is a DLL with an .OCX extension (when built with the OLE CDK). The control supports the following control-specific interfaces:

- ■ IOleControl is used by the container to communicate with the control.
- ■ IDispatch exposes the control's properties and methods to the container.
- ■ IConnectionPointContainer provides access to the control's connection points. Typically, there are two connection points—one for events and one for property notifications.
- ■ ISpecifyPropertyPages is used as the container to get the class IDs of the property pages that can be used to enter values for the control's properties.

When you use the OLE CDK to build an OCX, you do not have to know about these interfaces; the COleControl base class takes care of the details for you.

OLE Custom Control Developer's Kit (CDK)

The OLE CDK is provided as an add-on to Visual C++ 2.0 (you can also install it with Visual C++ 1.5). The CDK includes a number of classes that extend the MFC and provide you with all the ingredients necessary to build OLE controls in a straightforward manner. In addition to the new MFC classes, the CDK includes a new wizard—the ControlWizard—to generate the source and header files that constitute the template of an OCX.

Installing the CDK

To use the CDK, you should install it separately after you finish installing Microsoft Visual C++ 2.0. Merely run SETUP from the Visual C++ 2.0 CD-ROM and select the OLE CDK button to install the CDK.

The OLE CDK includes the following components to help you develop OCXs:

- ControlWizard for creating an initial OLE Custom Control project or porting an existing VBX control to the new OLE control architecture. ControlWizard generates all the files necessary to build an OCX, including header files, source files, resource files, a project file, an object-description language (ODL) file, and a project makefile.
- A set of OLE control classes built on top of MFC 3.0 for implementing 32-bit OLE controls. These classes encapsulate the OLE interfaces, event maps, and property pages. These classes enable you to write only those parts of the code that implement the unique behavior of your control without having to worry about the mechanics of using the OLE interfaces.
- ClassWizard extensions to support OLE Custom Controls. These extensions enable ClassWizard to support stock properties, stock events, and stock methods.
- An OLE Test Container program (TSTCON32.EXE) to enable you to test a 32-bit OLE control's look, events, properties, and property pages.
- Full online documentation.
- Samples of OLE Custom Controls with source code.

When you install the OLE CDK, the setup program creates a CDK32 subdirectory (in the directory where you have installed Visual C++ 2.0) and places all header files, binaries, source code, and samples in that subdirectory. A few necessary runtime DLLs are copied to the Windows system directory. The CDK setup program also adds several new entries (such as ControlWizard) in the Visual C++ Tools menu. You will learn more about these tools when you go through the process of building an OCX.

MFC OLE Control Classes

The new OLE control classes are at the heart of the OLE CDK. One of the most important classes is the COleControl class, which implements all necessary functionality of an OLE control. COleControl serves as the base class for any OCX built using the CDK. Another important class is COlePropertyPage, which implements the property pages—dialogs through which the control's properties can be viewed or set.

Table 29.1 lists the OLE control classes in the OLE CDK. You have to include the AFXCTL.H file when using these classes (the OLE CDK does this for you when you build a control using the ControlWizard tool).

Figure 29.3 shows the class hierarchy of the new classes. As you can see, these classes are designed to fit into the existing MFC 3.0 classes. The COleControlModule class, representing the main module of the control, is derived from CWinApp. The base class of OCXs, COleControl, is derived from CWnd and the property page class, COlePropertyPage, is derived from CDialog.

FIGURE 29.3.
*MFC OLE control
class hierarchy.*

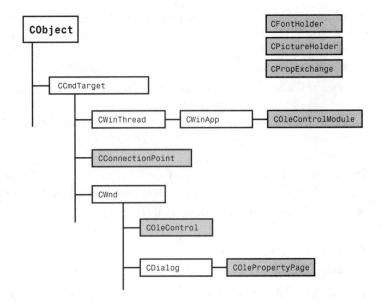

Table 29.1. MFC OLE control classes in the OLE CDK.

Class	Derived From	Description
COleControlModule	CWinApp	This class provides the main module of the OLE control DLL (this class is similar to the application class in other MFC applications).
CConnectionPoint	CCmdTarget	This class represents a connection point, which is a special type of OLE interface for initiating actions on other objects such as firing events and sending property change notifications.
COleControl	CWnd	This is the base class for all OLE Custom Controls. This class represents a Windows window object that has additional functionality specific to OLE controls, such as support for properties and methods and the capability of firing events.
COlePropertyPage	CDialog	This is the base class for the control-specific dialog boxes through which the control's properties can be examined and set.

Class	Derived From	Description
COleObjectFactoryEx	COleObjectFactory	This class extends the functionality of its base class, COleObjectFactory, by enforcing licensing and registering the control object factories in the system registry. The licensing approach enables only licensed developers to use the control at design-time and licensed applications at runtime.
CPropExchange		A CPropExchange object is used when an OLE control's properties are to be loaded from or stored to persistent storage.
CFontHolder		This class encapsulates the functionality of a Windows font object and the IFont interface. You can use this class to store custom font properties in your control.
CPictureHolder		This class implements a Picture property, which can be used to display a picture in your control. The stock Picture property enables the developer to specify a bitmap, icon, or metafile for display in the control. You can use the CPictureHolder class for custom picture properties in your control.

Building an OCX

Writing an OCX using the OLE CDK is quite simple—as long as you do not feel the urge to understand how everything works behind the scenes. The best way to start on the path to becoming an OCX developer is to begin creating simple OCXs using the tools and classes provided by the OLE CDK. As you progress toward more complex controls and study the CDK's online documentation, you will, no doubt, learn about the OLE mechanisms that make the OCX possible. The following sections go through the steps involved in building a simple OCX.

A ControlWizard-Generated OCX

If you have used MFC AppWizard to build Windows applications, you will feel right at home with the ControlWizard tool that enables you to create an OCX. Unlike AppWizard, which is tightly integrated with Visual C++ 2.0's Visual Workbench, ControlWizard is a separate executable (MFCCTLWZ.EXE in the CDK32 subdirectory) that is accessible through the Tools menu. The first step in building an OCX is to run ControlWizard.

Generating the OCX Project

To create the OCX project and all necessary support files, select ControlWizard from the Tools menu (see Figure 29.4) in the Visual Workbench. Note that three tools following ControlWizard in the menu—Register Control, Unregister Control, and Test Container—are all installed by the OLE CDK. These tools register the control and activate a sample OLE container that you can use to test your OCX.

FIGURE 29.4.

Activating ControlWizard from the Tools menu.

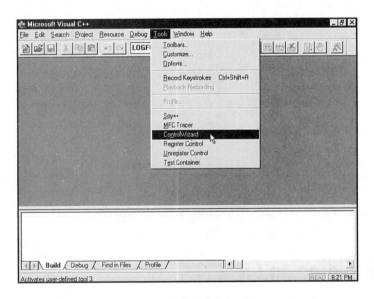

When ControlWizard runs, it displays a dialog box (see Figure 29.5) through which you can set various options of the OCX project. You have to specify the project's name and the path for the project's files. Figure 29.5 shows a project named TEST (which results in an OCX named TEST.OCX).

FIGURE 29.5.

*The MFC
ControlWizard dialog.*

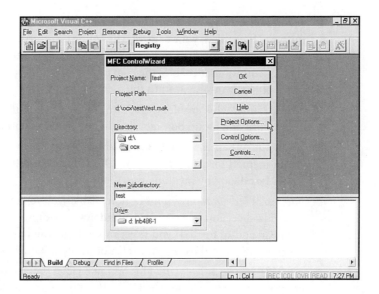

In the MFC ControlWizard dialog box of Figure 29.5, there are three buttons that enable you to specify various options:

- *Project Options...* dialog (see Figure 29.6) has four options. The first three options—Context Sensitive Help, External Makefile, and Source Comments—serve the same purpose as in AppWizard. The last option, License Validation, is specific to OLE controls. If you turn this option on (by clicking on the checkbox), ControlWizard creates a license file (with a .LIC extension) and adds the necessary code to enforce licensing. The licensing scheme is based on the license file; a purchaser of the control (who presumably builds applications using your control) gets both the control's DLL file (with the .OCX extension) and the license file. However, the purchaser is legally allowed to distribute only the control's DLL with an application. Without the license file, applications built with the control continue to work, but no new instances of the control can be created for use in a new application. This limits the use of the control to runtime and enables design-time use only with a valid license file.

- *Control Options...* dialog provides seven checkboxes (see Figure 29.7):
    - *Activate when visible.* This enables the control to be activated whenever it is visible.
    - *Show in Insert Object dialog.* When enabled, the name of your control will be included in the list of objects that can be inserted into an OLE container.

- *Invisible at runtime.* This option controls whether your control is displayed at runtime. If enabled, your control will not be displayed. This option is useful for controls that do not have any visible output, such as a timer control or a spell-checker control that enables the container application to decide how to present the spell-check information to the user.

- *Simple Frame.* This enables the control to contain a number of other controls visually just as a group box can contain and manage a number of radio buttons.

- *About box.* When enabled, ControlWizard generates an About box and an About method for your control. An OLE control container can display the About box dialog by invoking the About method.

- *Subclass Windows control.* This option enables you to create an OCX that is a customized version of a standard Windows control, such as pushbutton, scrollbar, and so forth. If you select this option, you have to select a Windows control class from the drop-down list of the combo box next to this option.

- *Use VBX control as template.* This option enables you to specify an existing VBX control as the template for the OCX. If you have an existing VBX control that you want to migrate to the OCX architecture, this option will be of interest to you. When you select this option, you have to specify the .VBX file for the VBX control. ControlWizard then builds an OCX with the same interfaces as the specified VBX; however, you are responsible for implementing all the interfaces.

- *Controls...* dialog is for viewing and changing the class names, filenames, or programmatic ID of the control. You can also use this dialog to add more controls to an OCX file. Just like VBXs, an OCX file can contain more than one control. Figure 29.8 shows the default settings for the TEST OLE control.

CONVERTING A VBX TO AN OCX

ControlWizard's Control Options dialog gives you the option of using an existing VBX as a template for an OCX. Using this option, you can create an OCX with most of the features of the VBX. After you specify a VBX as a template for an OCX, ControlWizard uses the information in the .VBX file and creates a Visual C++ project file, as well as the source code files for an equivalent OLE control. The first step is to compile and link these files to produce a working skeleton of the OCX.

Once the skeleton OCX is built and tested, you can begin inserting code from the VBX source files into appropriate places in the ControlWizard-generated source files. You may have to edit the code to make everything work, but ControlWizard gives you a good start by creating the skeleton OCX with most of the functionality of the existing VBX.

FIGURE 29.6.
The Project Options dialog in ControlWizard.

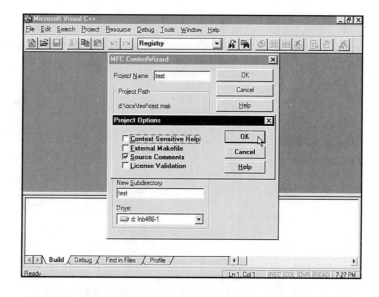

FIGURE 29.7.
The Control Options dialog in ControlWizard.

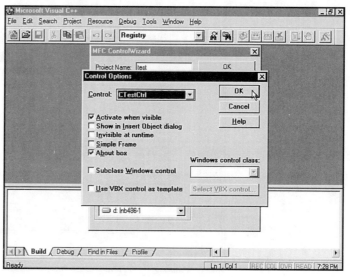

After specifying the options, click on the OK button in the main MFC ControlWizard dialog. This brings up the New Control Information dialog (see Figure 29.9) that summarizes information about the control to be created. Although the dialog in Figure 29.9 shows TEST.DLL as the name of the DLL to be generated, the project is set to create a DLL named TEST.OCX.

FIGURE 29.8.

The Controls dialog in ControlWizard.

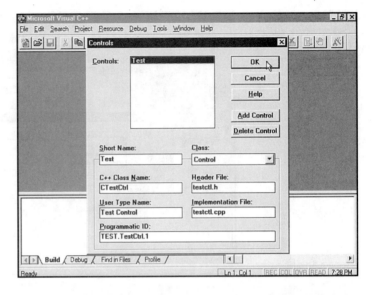

FIGURE 29.9.

The New Control Information dialog in ControlWizard.

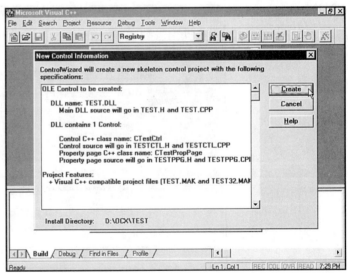

Click on the Create button to enable ControlWizard to generate the files and load the project into Visual Workbench. Listing 29.1 shows the ControlWizard-generated README.TXT file that describes all the files that it creates. By studying the listing you will get a feel for the kinds of files required to build an OCX.

ControlWizard generates project files (.MAK) for both 16-bit and 32-bit OLE controls. For the TEST OLE control, ControlWizard generates two project files: TEST.MAK to build a 16-bit control and TEST32.MAK to build the 32-bit version of the OLE control.

Listing 29.1. README.TXT file describing files generated by ControlWizard.

```
=========================================================================
          OLE Custom Control DLL : TEST
=========================================================================

ControlWizard has created this project for your TEST OLE Custom
Control DLL, which contains 1 Control.

This skeleton project not only demonstrates the basics of writing an OLE
Custom Control, but is also a starting point for writing the specific
features of your control.

This file contains a summary of what you will find in each of the files
that make up your TEST OLE Custom Control DLL.


TEST.MAK
    The project makefile for building your 16-bit OLE Custom Control.
    This project file is compatible with the Visual C++ 1.5 Workbench.
    It is also compatible with NMAKE.

TEST32.MAK
    The project makefile for building your 32-bit OLE Custom Control.
    This project file is compatible with the Visual C++ 2.0 Workbench.
    It is also compatible with NMAKE.

MAKEFILE
    A makefile that makes it easy to run NMAKE from the command prompt.
    Use the following parameters with NMAKE:
        DEBUG=0     Builds retail version
        DEBUG=1     Builds debug version (default)
        WIN32=0     Builds 16-bit version (default)
        WIN32=1     Builds 32-bit version
        UNICODE=0   Builds ANSI/DBCS version (default for WIN32=0)
        UNICODE=1   Build Unicode version (default for WIN32=1)

TEST.H
    This is the main include file for the OLE Custom Control DLL.  It
    includes other project-specific includes such as RESOURCE.H.

TEST.CPP
    This is the main source file that contains the OLE DLL initialization,
    termination, and other bookkeeping.

TEST.RC
    This is a listing of the Microsoft Windows resources that the project
    uses.  This file can be directly edited with the Visual C++ resource
    editor.

TEST.RC2
    This file contains resources that are not edited by the resource editor.
    Initially, this contains a VERSIONINFO resource that you can customize
    for your OLE Custom Control DLL, and a TYPELIB resource for your DLL's
    type library.  You should place other manually maintained resources in
    this file.
```

continues

Listing 29.1. continued

TEST.DEF
>   This file contains information about the OLE Custom Control DLL that
>   must be provided to run with Microsoft Windows. It defines parameters
>   such as the name and description of the DLL, and the size of the initial
>   local heap. The numbers in this file are typical for OLE Custom Control
>   DLLs.

TEST32.DEF
>   This is a version of TEST.DEF for building a 32-bit version of
>   the OLE Custom Control DLL.

TEST.CLW
>   This file contains information used by ClassWizard to edit existing
>   classes or add new classes. ClassWizard also uses this file to store
>   information needed to generate and edit message maps and dialog data
>   maps and to generate prototype member functions.

TEST.ODL
>   This file contains the Object Description Language source code for the
>   type library of your OLE Control.

TEST.ICO
>   This file contains an icon that will appear in the About box. This icon
>   is included by the main resource file TEST.RC.

//

TESTCTL.H
>   This file contains the declaration of the CTestCtrl C++ class.

TESTCTL.CPP
>   This file contains the implementation of the CTestCtrl C++ class.

TESTPPG.H
>   This file contains the declaration of the CTestPropPage C++ class.

TESTPPG.CPP
>   This file contains the implementation of the CTestPropPage C++ class.

TESTCTL.BMP
>   This file contains a bitmap that a container will use to represent the
>   CTestCtrl control when it appears on a tool palette. This bitmap
>   is included by the main resource file TEST.RC.

//
Other standard files:

STDAFX.H, STDAFX.CPP
>   These files are used to build a precompiled header (PCH) file
>   named STDAFX.PCH and a precompiled types (PCT) filenamed STDAFX.OBJ.

RESOURCE.H
>   This is the standard header file, which defines new resource IDs.
>   App Studio reads and updates this file.

//

```
Other notes:

ControlWizard uses "TODO:" to indicate parts of the source code you
should add to or customize.
```

///

Trying Out the Default OCX

After the project is created, build the control (TEST.OCX) by selecting Build test.ocx from the Project menu. Although you have not added any code yet, ControlWizard adds a bit of graphics code in the control, so you can try out the control.

The first step in trying out the OCX is to register the control. To do this, select the Register Control option from the Tools menu (see Figure 29.10). If all goes well, a confirmation dialog should inform you that the control has been successfully registered.

FIGURE 29.10.

Registering the control in Visual C++ 2.0.

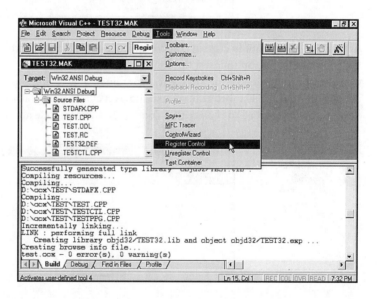

Now you need an OLE control container to test the control. From the Tool menu (Figure 29.10), select the Test Container option to launch the test container. The Edit menu of the test container application provides an option to insert a selected OLE control into the container. Figure 29.11 shows the test container application with the Insert OLE Control dialog displayed.

FIGURE 29.11.

Inserting the control into the test container.

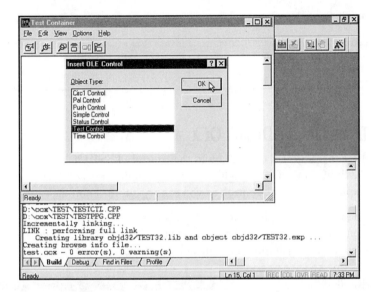

As you can see, the newly created control appears as the Test Control in the list—select it and click on the OK button to insert the control into the container. Figure 29.12 shows the result with the test control embedded in the test container. The reason the control displays an ellipse is ControlWizard—it embeds the code to draw an ellipse in the OnDraw function of the control class. You are supposed to replace that code with drawing code appropriate for your control.

FIGURE 29.12.

The test container with the test OLE control.

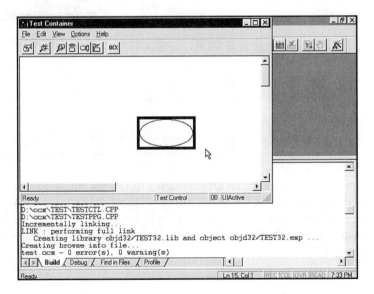

There you have it—a "do nothing" OLE control without having to write a single line of code. Granted, the ControlWizard-generated code does not do anything interesting yet, but you now have the entire framework for an OCX. All that remains is to customize the OCX to meet your needs.

Customizing the OCX

The steps in customizing the OCX depend on what you have in mind for the control. Here are the typical customization steps that most OCXs have to follow:

■ Add properties and implement necessary access functions through which the property values can be obtained or set.

■ Add the code in the OnDraw function of the control's class to draw the control.

■ Define one or more dialog resources to be used as property pages through which the control's user (the application developer who uses the control as a component) can view and specify values for the properties.

■ Add member variables for the property page for storing the values of properties.

■ Add and implement methods that the container can invoke to initiate specific actions.

■ Add events to be sent to the control's container when the user presses a key or clicks on the control.

The following sections show how to customize the TEST OLE control so that it displays an on/off indicator with a label next to the indicator. The idea is to make the control look like one of those switches that has a small (rectangular) green light that glows when the switch is on. Also, the control should send ("fire") an event to the container when the user clicks on the control.

Adding Properties

The control container accesses internal variables of an OCX through that OCX's properties. OLE automation servers also provide access to internal variables through properties (see Chapter 28 for an example of an OLE automation server). As with OLE automation servers, you can add properties through the OLE Automation tab of MFC ClassWizard.

For the TEST control, Figure 29.13 shows the Add Property dialog (displayed when you click on the Add Property button in the ClassWizard's main dialog box) being used to add a custom property to the control. To add a custom property, which is a property unique to your control, you have to specify the following:

■ *External Name.* Indicates the name by which the control container refers to the property. In this case, the variable is named On (to indicate the state of the control).

- *Type.* Specifies the type of the variable. For the On variable, the type is BOOL (for Boolean).

- *Implementation.* Specifies the way the property is implemented. There are three types of implementation:

    - *Stock implementation* is used when you select a stock property (from the list in the combo box labeled External Name).

    - *Member Variable implementation* creates a member variable to store the property's value. A suggested variable name (m_on in Figure 29.13) appears in the Variable Name field. You also can specify a notification function (for example, the function OnOnChanged in Figure 29.13) that will be called after the property value has changed. This enables you to handle any redrawing of the control that may be necessary when a property changes value.

    - *Get/Set Methods implementation* is the most general way of handling properties. In this case, you provide Get and Set functions that the control's container may call to get or set the value of a property. You have to take care of any member variables needed to store the value of the property. You might also use this approach when the value of a property is computed at runtime or when you want to validate a value before changing the property.

FIGURE 29.13.

Adding a custom property to the test OLE control.

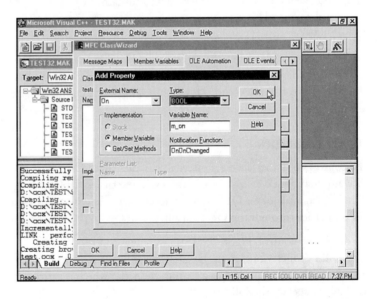

For the TEST OLE control, we also use some custom properties. For example, we can use the Caption property to refer to the label that appears in the TEST control. To add a stock property, all you have to do is select the stock property's name from the drop-down list of the combo box labeled External Name. Figure 29.14 shows the Caption property being added to the control.

FIGURE 29.14.

Adding a stock property to the test OLE control.

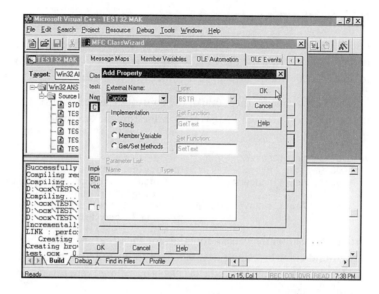

After adding the properties, you return to the main dialog of MFC ClassWizard (see Figure 29.15). In the OLE Automation tab of the ClassWizard's dialog, you will see all the properties that you have added so far. Click on the OK button to complete the process of adding the properties.

FIGURE 29.15.

MFC ClassWizard dialog showing the properties being added.

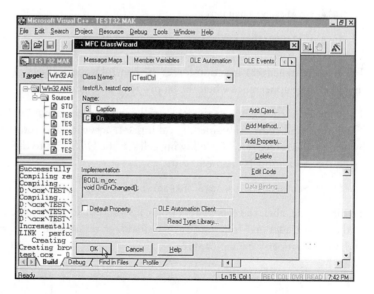

Drawing the Control

Usually, a control's properties affect its appearance on the screen. After adding the necessary properties, you can write the code to draw the control. You are supposed to provide the code to draw the control in the OnDraw member function of the control class.

For the TEST control, the name of the control's class is CTestCtrl and the implementation is in the file TESTCTL.CPP. If you examine this file, you will see that the OnDraw function's prototype is as follows:

```
void CTestCtrl::OnDraw(
    CDC*        pdc,          // The device context
    const CRect& rcBounds,    // Rectangular area of the control
                              // including the border
    const CRect& rcInvalid);  // Rectangular area of the control
                              // that needs redrawing
```

Listing 29.2 shows the OnDraw function for the CTestCtrl class. First, OnDraw gets the current background color by calling GetBackColor—this function returns a value of type OLE_COLOR, which you have to translate into COLORREF (by calling TranslateColor) before using it to fill the control's rectangle.

The on/off indicator is a small rectangle, which is filled with green color if the m_on variable is TRUE. Recall that the m_on is the member variable for the property named On. When the control's container sets On to TRUE, the m_on variable is also set to TRUE and the notification function OnOnChanged is called. That function is defined as follows to ensure that the control is redrawn:

```
void CTestCtrl::OnOnChanged()
{
    InvalidateControl();
}
```

The InvalidateControl function forces the control to be redrawn. Thus, the on/off indicator should change appearance when the On property changes value.

The OnDraw function displays the label in the current foreground color and the current font. The foreground color is obtained by calling GetForeColor and translated to a COLORREF value by using TranslateColor. The following call sets the DC's font to the current font corresponding to the stock property named Font:

```
    CFont *pOldFont = SelectStockFont(pdc);
```

To display the label, the OnDraw function calls TextOut to display the CString object returned by the InternalGetText function. InternalGetText returns the CString representing the value of the stock property named Caption.

Listing 29.2. OnDraw function of the test control class in the TESTCTL.CPP file.

```
void CTestCtrl::OnDraw(CDC* pdc, const CRect& rcBounds,
                       const CRect& rcInvalid)
{
// Fill control with background color
    CBrush bgBrush;
    COLORREF crBGColor = TranslateColor(GetBackColor());
    bgBrush.CreateSolidBrush(crBGColor);
    pdc->FillRect(rcBounds, &bgBrush);

// Draw the on/off indicator
    CRect r(CPoint(rcBounds.left+8, rcBounds.top+8),
            CSize(24, 8));
    CBrush b;
    if(m_on)
        b.CreateSolidBrush(RGB(0,255,0));
    else
        b.CreateSolidBrush(RGB(0,0,0));
    pdc->FillRect(&r, &b);

// Display caption in foreground color
    pdc->SetBkMode(TRANSPARENT);
    COLORREF oldTextColor = pdc->SetTextColor(
                                TranslateColor(GetForeColor()));
    CFont *pOldFont = SelectStockFont(pdc);
    pdc->TextOut(rcBounds.left + 34, rcBounds.top + 8,
                 InternalGetText());

// Reset the device context
    pdc->SetTextColor(oldTextColor);
    pdc->SelectObject(pOldFont);
}
```

Defining the Property Page Dialog

Users need a way to set the properties of an OLE control to configure it for use in an application. The OLE control technology introduces a user interface item called property page through which the user can view or modify the control's properties. A *property page* is a dialog that is integrated into a tabbed dialog box along with other property pages to provide a consistent and easy-to-use user interface for manipulating properties of an object.

As an OCX developer, your responsibility is to implement one or more property pages through which the user can access the properties of the OCX. A property page is a dialog resource. At the time of generating the template for an OCX, the ControlWizard creates a blank property page. To modify the property page, double-click on the resource file (TEST.RC for the TEST control) from the project window. From the resulting window, select the Dialog resource type and double-click on the resource named IDD_PROPPAGE_TEST. The dialog will appear in a window and you will be able to edit it. Use the Controls palette to place controls on the dialog. For the TEST control, place a static text control named `Caption`. To the right of the static text control, place an edit control where the user can enter the caption. To the right of the edit control, place a checkbox. When you double-click on the checkbox, the Check Box Properties dialog appears. As shown in Figure 29.16, enter the caption `On` for the checkbox. Because the TEST OCX has only two custom properties, this dialog is adequate to serve as the property page for this control.

FIGURE 29.16.

Preparing the dialog resource for the test control's property page.

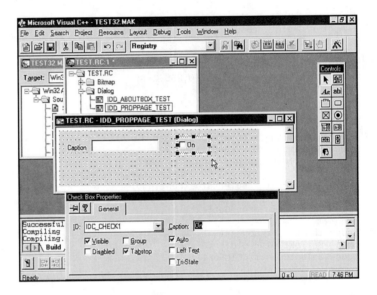

If your control uses stock properties such as `Font` and `BackColor` and you want to provide property pages to alter these stock properties, you can do so without having to prepare any dialog resources. There are stock property pages available to handle the stock properties. To add these stock property pages to your control's tabbed dialog, locate the line that starts with `BEGIN_PROPPAGEIDS` in the source file for the control. You have to add extra lines indicating the stock property pages you want to use. For example, to use the font and color stock property pages in the TEST control, you should add the code shown in boldface:

```
//
// In file TESTCTL.CPP: Implementation of the CTestCtrl OLE
//                      control class.

/////////////////////////////////////////////////////////////////
// Property pages

// TODO: Add more property pages as needed.
// Remember to increase the count!
BEGIN_PROPPAGEIDS(CTestCtrl, 3)
        PROPPAGEID(CTestPropPage::guid)
        PROPPAGEID(CLSID_CColorPropPage) // Color property page
        PROPPAGEID(CLSID_CFontPropPage)  // Font property page
END_PROPPAGEIDS(CTestCtrl)
```

Adding Member Variables for the Property Page

The values that the user sets in the property pages have to be communicated to the control class. To make this happen, you define member variables for the property page class (the CTestPropPage class for the TEST control) and associate each variable with a property name.

Use the ClassWizard to add the member variables for the property page. Figure 29.17 shows the addition of a member variable to store the setting of the checkbox labeled On. Here are the steps to add the member variable for the checkbox:

1. Start by selecting ClassWizard from the Project menu.
2. From MFC ClassWizard's main dialog box, select the Member Variables tab.
3. In the Class Name combo box, select the class for the property page (CTestPropPage in this case).
4. The listbox titled Control IDs will show the IDs of the controls in the dialog resource for the property page. Click on the control ID for the checkbox (IDC_CHECK1), then click on the Add Variable button.
5. The Add Member Variable dialog box (see Figure 29.17) appears. Enter the name of the member variable and its type. In the Optional OLE Property Name field, enter the name of the property whose value is being set through this checkbox. In this case, the On property is being set through the checkbox. This last step is important because it associates a value entered in the property page to a property of the control.

Repeat these steps for other member variables needed by the property page. For the TEST control, you need another member variable for the text string entered in the edit control—this string is to be used as the value of the stock property named Caption. Figure 29.18 shows a CString variable being added for the edit control and being associated with the Caption property.

After adding all the member variables, review the list of variables in the Member Variables page of the MFC ClassWizard dialog (see Figure 29.19). Click on the OK button to enable ClassWizard to complete the process of adding member variables.

Adding Methods

Methods are functions that the control's container can call. The process of adding methods is similar to the process of adding properties. Start with the OLE Automation tab in MFC ClassWizard's main dialog (see Figure 29.20), select the control class (CTestCtrl), and click on the Add Method button. This brings up the Add Method dialog box where you can add the method. Figure 29.20 shows the stock method Refresh being added to the control class.

FIGURE 29.17.

Adding member variables for the test control's property page.

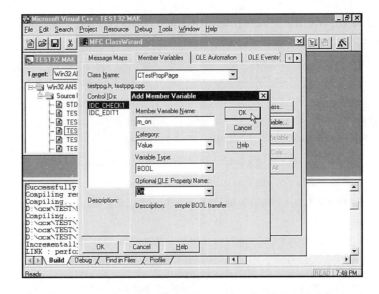

FIGURE 29.18.

Associating a property page member variable to a stock property.

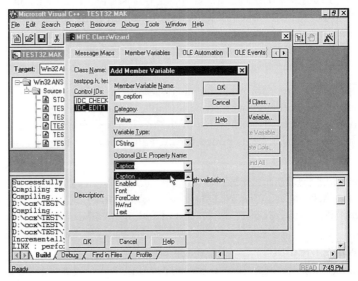

FIGURE 29.19.

*MFC ClassWizard's
Member Variables page.*

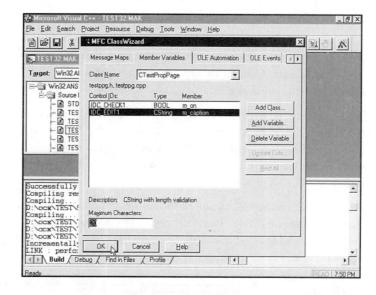

FIGURE 29.20.

*Adding a method
to the test control.*

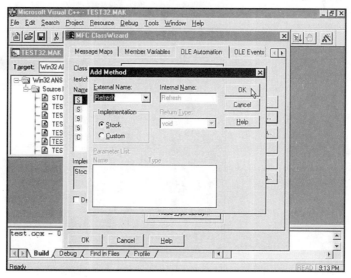

Firing Events

An important difference between a control and other embedded OLE items is the control's capability of firing events to the control container. Adding an event is straightforward with MFC ClassWizard. As an illustration, consider how to make the TEST control send a mouse click event to the container.

To add an event, go to the OLE Events tab of the MFC ClassWizard dialog. Select the control class in the Class Name combo box. Then click on the Add Event button. This brings up the Add Event dialog (see Figure 29.21). As with properties and methods, a control can have stock events or custom events. Figure 29.21 shows a stock event named Click being added to the test control.

After you click on the OK button in the Add Event dialog box, you will be back at the MFC ClassWizard's main dialog. The OLE Events tab (see Figure 29.22) will now show the events that have been added to the control. Click on the OK button to complete the process of adding the events.

FIGURE 29.21.

Adding an event to the test control.

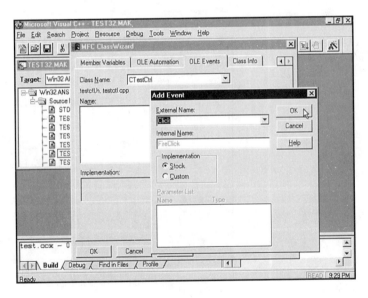

FIGURE 29.22.

*List of events added
to the test control.*

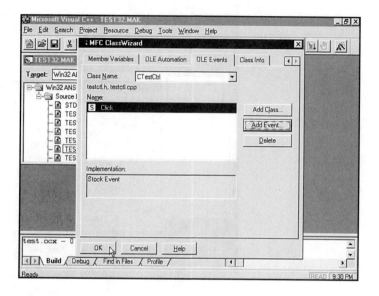

Trying Out the Customized Control

After customizing the control as described in the previous sections, select Build test.ocx from the Project menu to build a new version of the control.

Start the Test Container from the Tools menu of Visual Workbench and insert the Test Control into the container (select Insert OLE Control from the Edit menu).

The modified control has property pages to enable you to choose the label, the on/off state, the colors, and the font. To view the property pages, click once on the control and activate the Edit menu and bring the cursor into the item labeled Test Control Object in the Edit menu. A cascading menu appears; select the Properties item from that menu.

Figure 29.23 shows the appearance of the control after setting a label, foreground color, and font. Figure 29.23 also shows the custom property page (the one you added by editing the IDD_PROPPAGE_TEST dialog resource) in the tabbed dialog titled Test Control Properties. To set the color or the font, click on the appropriate page (or tab) in the tabbed dialog. Figures 29.24 and 29.25 show the property pages for selecting a font and the background and foreground colors, respectively.

FIGURE 29.23.

The test control showing its custom property page.

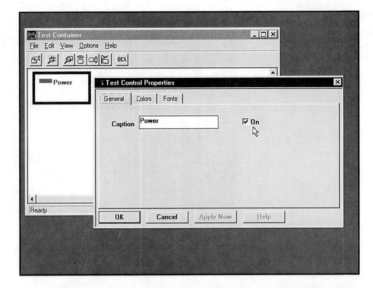

FIGURE 29.24.

The stock property page for selecting font.

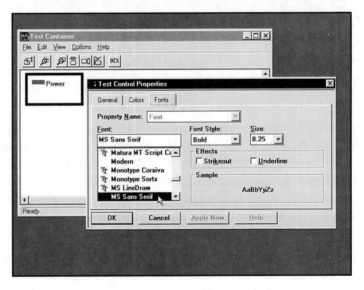

To test the event firing mechanism, select Event Log... from the View menu of the Test Container—an event log window appears (see Figure 29.26). Click anywhere on the test control with the left mouse button. This generates a Click stock event, which the event log window displays. In the event log window, the event report is prefixed with a two-digit value and the control's name. This is necessary because the test container can support more than one control as well as multiple copies of the same control. The two-digit value enables you to distinguish between multiple copies of the same control.

FIGURE 29.25.

The stock property page for selecting colors.

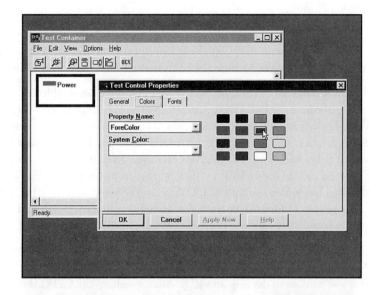

FIGURE 29.26.

Viewing events being sent by the test control.

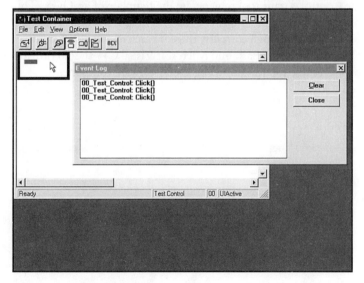

Summary

Microsoft's Visual Basic Custom Controls (VBX) architecture, originally designed for custom controls (user interface components such as pushbuttons and dialog boxes), has proven very useful as a software packaging approach. The VBX architecture has created a viable market for component software—software packaged in a self-contained unit with well-defined external interfaces. VBXs, however, are designed specifically for 16-bit Windows and lack the extensibility and interoperability that OLE is designed to achieve. Microsoft has designed the OLE Custom Controls (OCX) as a successor to the VBX technology. Because OCXs rely on OLE as the foundation, OCXs should work in all environments where OLE is supported. In particular, OCXs will become the equivalent of VBXs in 32-bit Windows.

An OCX is like other OLE objects (items) that can be embedded in an OLE container. However, embedded OLE items are generally provided by stand-alone OLE servers and they can be viewed or edited only by double-clicking. To function as a control, an OCX needs to respond to single clicks and it must activate much more quickly than what is possible with a stand-alone OLE server. The OCX architecture overcomes these shortcomings by adding new interfaces that enable the control to "fire" events to its container. The efficiency of activation is achieved by implementing the OCX as an in-process sever—a DLL that is part of the container process. This enables the interface between the container and the control to be a function call rather than the slower Lightweight Remote Procedure Call (LRPC) used by other OLE servers and containers.

Microsoft Visual C++ 2.0 includes an add-on OLE Custom Control Developer's Kit (CDK) that you can use to develop an OCX. After installing the CDK, it is only a matter of running the ControlWizard tool to generate the template of an OCX. This chapter goes through the process of building a simple OCX and testing it with the Test Container that comes with the OLE CDK. Although currently there is a lack of good OLE control containers, future versions of Microsoft Visual Basic and Microsoft Visual C++ should provide the containers required to build and test applications using OCX software components.

30

Current Windows Programming Considerations

We are at a crossroads when it comes to developing applications for Windows—most users still use the 16-bit Windows 3.1 (or Windows for Workgroups), some users are moving to the 32-bit Windows NT 3.5, and the 32-bit Windows 95 is on the horizon. For 32-bit Windows, you are supposed to use the Win32 Application Programming Interface (API)—a 32-bit API that runs on multiple platforms including Windows NT. This book implicitly covers 32-bit Windows programming by virtue of its focus on Microsoft Visual C++ 2.0, because Visual C++ 2.0 and MFC 3.0 are meant for developing 32-bit applications only. However, if you have a 16-bit application developed with Visual C++ 1.5 or earlier and MFC 2.5 or earlier, you can migrate that application to 32-bit Windows with minimal effort. This chapter describes the steps you should follow to port a 16-bit MFC application to 32-bit Windows. Additionally, it points out some of the unique features of the Win32 API and describes some operating system-specific capabilities such as the OpenGL 3-D graphics API that is a part of Windows NT version 3.5.

DIFFERENCES BETWEEN 16-BIT AND 32-BIT SOFTWARE

Although 80386, 80486, and Pentium processors have 32-bit registers and are capable of processing data items 32 bits at a time, 16-bit applications (including 16-bit Windows such as Windows 3.1) use only 16 low-order bits of the 32-bit registers and work with data items in 16-bit chunks. Thus, 16-bit C and C++ compilers (such as Microsoft Visual C++ 1.5) generate code that uses only the low-order 16 bits of the processor's registers. In a 16-bit compiler, int variables are 16 bits or 2 bytes.

32-bit applications (including operating systems such as Windows NT) exploit the 32-bit registers and process data 32 bits at a time. 32-bit C and C++ compilers (such as Microsoft Visual C++ 2.0) generate code that makes use of the 32-bit registers and performs all operations in 32-bit blocks. In a 32-bit C or C++ compiler, the size of an int variable is 32 bits or 4 bytes.

Even though it is a 16-bit operating system, Windows 3.1 supports a 32-bit extension, Win32s, that can run 32-bit applications.

32-Bit Programming

There is nothing magical about 32-bit programming—all the examples in this book are 32-bit programs. You do, of course, need a compiler such as Visual C++ 2.0 capable of generating 32-bit code. In a 32-bit compiler, the size of an int variable is 32 bits as opposed to 16 bits in a compiler such as Visual C++ 1.5 that generates 16-bit code. One benefit of moving to a 32-bit environment is that all pointers are 32 bits. This makes 32-bit programming easier than 16-bit programming because you no longer have to worry about near and far pointers when writing 32-bit code. You work with a flat 32-bit address space in 32-bit code.

In addition to the uniform 32-bit pointers and the `int` variables being 32 bits, there are many nuances of 32-bit programming that become important when you write Windows applications using the Win32 API. Moving from older 16-bit versions of MFC to the 32-bit MFC 3.0 also requires some changes. The following sections summarize some of these—starting with the guidelines for porting a 16-bit MFC application to the 32-bit environment, using Visual C++ 2.0 and MFC 3.0.

Porting 16-Bit MFC Applications to 32-Bit Windows

If you used MFC for your 16-bit application, you are already ahead of the game when it comes to porting the application to 32-bit Windows. To port most 16-bit MFC applications, you merely load the project into Visual C++ 2.0 and rebuild the executable to create the 32-bit version.

Use the following steps when porting a 16-bit MFC program to a 32-bit environment:

1. Open the old project files in Visual C++ 2.0. Visual C++ 2.0 automatically converts the project files from Visual C++ 1.0 and 1.5 to Visual C++ 2.0 format.

2. Get rid of features that are not supported in 32-bit Windows applications. These include the following:

   ■ *Visual Basic Controls (VBX)*. VBXs are not supported in the 32-bit environment. If you use the `CVBControl` class or other VBX-related features, such as the `ON_VBXEVENT` macro, you have to replace these controls with standard Windows controls. In the future, you may be able to replace the VBXs with functionally equivalent OLE Custom Controls (OCX).

   ■ *Windows for Pen Computing*. Win32 does not support classes such as `CHEdit` and `CBEdit` that implement Windows for Pen Computing.

   ■ *Unnecessary MFC Functions*. The MFC functions `CGdiObject::UnrealizeObject` and `CDC::QueryAbort` are not needed in Win32. `CDC::QueryAbort` has been deleted; `CGdiObject::UnrealizeObject` is retained for backward compatibility but it does not do anything.

3. Replace any assembly-language functions or MS-DOS calls with stubs. Later on, you have to rewrite these functions in C or C++ and replace the MS-DOS system calls with Win32 equivalents.

4. Build the program in Visual C++ version 2.0 (at warning level 3) and note any errors or warnings, such as use of `near`, `far`, and `huge` pointers, use of wrong argument types in GDI functions, or use of unsupported functions. Correct each problem appropriately. For example, get rid of the near and far pointers and use the correct forms of Win32 GDI functions.

5. Rebuild until the program compiles and links without errors.

6. Implement any functions that you may have replaced with stubs in step 4. Replace any file I/O, using MS-DOS calls with the new Win32 file I/O functions. A better choice is to use the CFile class from MFC or use the C++ streams.

7. To ensure that your program is linked with the correct version of MFC libraries, do not explicitly specify any MFC libraries; rather, let Visual C++ 2.0 automatically link in the appropriate libraries.

Of course, these are only the general steps in porting a 16-bit MFC application to Win32. The details in each step depend on the features that your program implements. For example, if your program uses GDI functions for graphic output, you may have to change some function calls to take advantage of new capabilities of the Win32 GDI.

Some Porting Tips

The seemingly simple change in the size of integer variables—from 16-bit integers to 32-bit integers—had considerable impact on Windows programming with the Win32 API. In 16-bit Windows, most integers are 16-bit wide, which means that most integer types such as int, short, and WORD, and various handle types (HANDLE, HWND, HMENU, HMODULE, HICON, HCURSOR, and HBITMAP) are all 16 bits. Among integer types, long and DWORD are 32-bit wide in 16-bit Windows.

In 32-bit Windows (Win32), on the other hand, most integer values are 32-bit wide; only short and WORD values are still 16 bits. In particular, all handles are 32-bit values, but WORD is still a 16-bit type. Even if you write your application using MFC, you should be aware of these differences because most MFC applications also call various Windows API functions that use arguments of type WORD, DWORD, and various handles.

The following sections highlight things you should watch out for when porting 16-bit Windows applications to Win32.

Data Sizes

The differences in the sizes of basic data types is one of the significant changes in going from 16-bit Windows to Win32. Table 30.1 shows the size (in bits) of some C++ and Windows data types in 16-bit Windows and in Win32.

One common problem is that 16-bit Windows programs often use the WORD data type interchangeably with types such as HWND and HANDLE. In Win32, WORD stays 16 bits, but the handles are 32 bits wide. The Visual C++ compiler will warn you when you assign a handle to a WORD; you replace the WORD type with an appropriate handle data type (such as HWND, HPEN, HBRUSH, and so forth).

Table 30.1. Changes in data types from 16-bit to 32-bit Windows.

Type	Size in 16-Bit Windows	Size in Win32
BOOL	16	32
BYTE	8	8
DWORD	32	32
HANDLE	16	32
HWND	16	32
int	16	32
long	32	32
short	16	16
UINT	16	32
WORD	16	16

Data Alignment in Structures

In 16-bit Windows programs, structures are usually packed at byte boundaries—all the items in the structure are packed one after another in memory without any gaps. Although this may appear to be an efficient way to lay out structures in memory, there is a performance penalty due to the way 32-bit processors access memory. For each basic data type, there is a natural alignment that is most efficient for the processor. For example, on most 32-bit processors (such as Intel 80486 or Pentium), a 4-byte data member should have an address that is a multiple of 4.

Table 30.2 shows the alignment boundaries for various data types. When defining structures, you should align structure members at addresses that are natural for the data type and the processor involved. For example, consider the following structure:

```
struct MyStruct          // Total size = 9 bytes
{
    char  flag1;         // 1 byte
    short s_value;       // 2 bytes
    char  b_value[2];    // 2 bytes
    long  l_value;       // 4 bytes
};
```

This structure has several problems:

■ The short integer s_value needs a 2-byte alignment, but it appears at an offset of a single byte from the beginning of the structure. The long integer l_value is also misaligned—it should be aligned at a 4-byte boundary.

■ The entire structure should be aligned at a 4-byte boundary because that's the largest byte alignment required by the structure's member variables. This implies that the structure's size should be a multiple of 4 bytes.

To correct the problems, you can rearrange the members to meet the alignment needs of the short and long data types. Add extra padding bytes to make the total size of the structure a multiple of 4 by redefining the structure as follows:

```
struct MyStruct          // Total size = 12 bytes
{
    char   flag1;        // 1 byte
    char   b_value[2];   // 2 bytes
    char   reserved[3];  // 3 padding bytes
    short  s_value;      // 2 bytes
    long   l_value;      // 4 bytes
};
```

A 32-bit compiler usually adds filler bytes to meet the alignment needs of various data types, but it is good practice to define structures with proper data alignments.

Table 30.2. Natural alignment of data types in Win32.

Type	Alignment
char	Align on byte boundaries.
short	Align on even byte boundaries.
int	Align at an address that is a multiple of 4.
long	Align at an address that is a multiple of 4.
float	Align at an address that is a multiple of 4.
double	Align at an address that is a multiple of 8.
structure	Align according to the data member with largest boundary requirement.
union	Align according to the requirement of the first data member.

Binary File I/O

If your program stores structures and other data types in files in binary form, the program might be affected by the changes in size of data items and the alignment of items in a structure. The following are some potential problems:

■ Data files previously prepared by a 16-bit version of the program may no longer be read correctly by the 32-bit version of the program.

■ Data files generated by the same 32-bit code may not work in a different environment where the Win32 API is supported (for example, Win32 programs should work after recompilation on MIPS RISC systems).

To ensure that a data file is compatible between several Win32 platforms, follow these guidelines:

■ Use data types that do not change size from one environment to another. For example, WORD, short, and LONG are better choices than int, which changes size from 16-bit Windows to Win32. WORD, short, and LONG stay the same size in both 16- and 32-bit Windows.

■ Store a multibyte structure and any multibyte data one byte at a time.

Changes to API Functions

Although header files and MFC hide most of the differences in the Windows API between 16- and 32-bit Windows, you may need to revise code if you call certain API functions for graphics and text output. Most of the Windows API functions that have to be revised in Win32 are those returning x- and y-coordinates. In 16-bit Windows, the x- and y-coordinates are 16 bits each and are packed into a single 32-bit (DWORD) return value.

In Win32, neither x- nor y-coordinates can be returned in a single return value because each coordinate is 32 bits. Each Windows API function requiring change is replaced by a Win32 function with the same name, but with an Ex suffix added. The revised functions pass the x- and y-coordinates using an additional argument rather than a return value.

Table 30.3 shows the 16-bit Windows API functions with their Win32 replacements. Note that both Win32 and 16-bit Windows support these new functions. In addition, the GetTextExtent function needs a Point suffix because there is already an extended function GetTextExtentEx in 16-bit Windows API. The Point suffix has been added to both GetTextExtent and GetTextExtentEx to name the new versions of the functions.

Table 30.3. Win32 replacements for some older API functions.

16-Bit Windows API	*Equivalent Win32 API*
GetAspectRatioFilter	GetAspectRatioFilterEx
GetBitmapDimension	GetBitmapDimensionEx
GetBrushOrg	GetBrushOrgEx
GetCurrentPosition	GetCurrentPositionEx
GetTextExtent	GetTextExtentPoint
GetTextExtentEx	GetTextExtentExPoint
GetViewportExt	GetViewportExtEx
GetViewportOrg	GetViewportOrgEx
GetWindowExt	GetWindowExtEx
GetWindowOrg	GetWindowOrgEx
MoveTo	MoveToEx

continues

Table 30.3. continued

16-Bit Windows API	*Equivalent Win32 API*
OffsetViewportOrg	OffsetViewportOrgEx
OffsetWindowOrg	OffsetWindowOrgEx
ScaleViewportExt	ScaleViewportExtEx
ScaleWindowExt	ScaleWindowExtEx
SetBitmapDimension	SetBitmapDimensionEx
SetMetaFileBits	SetMetaFileBitsEx
SetViewportExt	SetViewportExtEx
SetWindowExt	SetWindowExtEx
SetWindowOrg	SetWindowOrgEx

You must replace the old function call (from the first column in Table 30.3) with the new extended function. The old functions are not supported in Win32.

If you compare the old API functions with the extended API functions (the Ex functions), you will notice that each Ex function includes an additional argument that points to a location to receive data. After the function call, you can find the returned information in this location. For example, in 16-bit Windows, you can get the extent of a line of text by calling GetTextExtent and extracting the x- and y-extents from a DWORD return value as shown by the following code fragment that highlights a line of text:

```
DWORD    dwExt;

dwExt = GetTextExtent(hDC, szString, strlen(szString));

RECT    rect;
rect.left = 0;
rect.bottom = 0;
rect.right = LOWORD(dwExt);
rect.top = HIWORD(dwExt);
InvertRect(hDC, &rect);
```

The Ex version GetTextExtent (called GetTextExtentPoint) returns the value in SIZE structure whose address you provide. Now the same code fragment looks like this:

```
SIZE s;

GetTextExtentPoint(hDC, szString, strlen(szString), &s);

RECT    rect;
rect.left = 0;
rect.bottom = 0;
rect.right = s.cx;
rect.top = s.cy;
InvertRect(hDC, &rect);
```

For some functions, you may not care about the return value. In this case, you can provide NULL as the last argument to the Ex functions. For example, in 16-bit Windows, a call to the MoveTo function might be written as follows:

```
// Move to the point (x,y)
MoveTo(hDC, x, y);
```

where the return value is being ignored. With the Ex version of the function, the call is changed as follows:

```
// Move to the point (x,y)
MoveToEx(hDC, x, y, NULL);
```

By specifying NULL as the last argument to MoveToEx, you are still ignoring the return value.

Reading and Writing Profile Strings

In 16-bit Windows, .INI files (such as WIN.INI and SYSTEM.INI) store various settings for programs and device drivers. In Windows NT, the information in .INI files is replaced by a registration database. Use of a database provides security controls that prevent an application from corrupting system information and facilitates remote administration of workstation software. Thus, code that directly accesses .INI files will not work when ported to Windows NT. If your 16-bit Windows program directly accesses the .INI file, replace that code with calls to the WriteProfileString and GetProfileString API functions. These functions work in both 16- and 32-bit Windows—they use the available underlying mechanism (.INI file or registration database) to store and retrieve information.

MORE INFORMATION ABOUT WIN32 AND WINDOWS NT

Although this chapter summarizes some issues in porting 16-bit MFC applications to Win32 and provides an overview of Win32 features, the detailed information about Win32 is too voluminous to fit into a single chapter. There are, however, many sources of information about Win32 and porting to Win32. Here are a few suggested ways to gather further information:

■ Read articles about Win32 in programmers' magazines. For example, the *Microsoft Systems Journal* (published monthly by Miller Freeman, Inc., 600 Harrison St., San Francisco, CA 94107) has printed articles on porting 16-bit Windows applications to Win32.

■ Consult books on Windows NT programming, such as *Advanced Windows NT*, Microsoft Press, 1994, by Jeffrey Richter. Most books on Windows NT cover all aspects of Win32 programming.

■ For information on developing for international markets using Unicode, see the *Win32 Programmer's Reference*, Volume 2. Detailed information on Unicode can be found in *The Unicode Standard: Worldwide Character Encoding*, Version 1.0, Volumes 1 and 2, Addison-Wesley, 1992.

New Features in Windows NT

In addition to the differences in API functions, Win32 in general and Windows NT in particular also include many new features. This section summarizes the new features, which you may want to use in your 32-bit Windows applications.

Processes and Threads

Windows NT views a process as a combination of the following elements:

■ The code and data of an executable program

■ A 4G virtual address space where the code and data resides

■ System resources, such as files, communication ports, and threads (see next item), belonging to the process

■ At least one *thread of execution,* or *thread,* which constitutes a stack, a set of CPU registers, and the sequence of CPU instructions that Windows NT schedules for execution by a processor (Windows NT can support more than one processor)

In Windows NT, a process can have multiple threads, with each thread scheduled CPU time by the operating system. Thus, you can have multitasking within a single process. Multiple threads can be very useful in an event-driven program (such as any Windows program) to process events from multiple sources without hanging up while awaiting events from one of the sources. You can merely set up separate threads for each event source. You can, for example, set up one thread to poll a network connection while another thread continually processes Windows messages.

Although support for multiple threads gives you an easy way to set up a program that handles multiple tasks, an application that uses multiple threads must ensure that the threads are synchronized with respect to one another. For example, if two threads share a common data area, you must ensure that each thread completes its operation on the data before the other can access the data. Windows NT provides several ways for synchronizing threads:

■ *Critical sections* enable you to implement exclusive access to a section of code. To use a critical section, you call InitializeCriticalSection, then EnterCriticalSection to block other threads, and LeaveCriticalSection when you are finished.

■ *Mutexes* are used to synchronize data among multiple threads. A thread calls CreateMutex to create a mutex with a specified name. Any thread can call OpenMutex to open a specified mutex (identified by the name or a handle). When the thread is finished changing the data, it calls ReleaseMutex to enable other threads to use the mutex.

■ *Semaphores* are like mutex—they enable multiple threads to gain access to an object, but a semaphore also keeps a reference count. Semaphores are created by calling CreateSemaphore, accessed with OpenSemaphore, and released by calling ReleaseSemaphore.

■ *Events* are used to signal completion of an operation. The API functions for using events are `CreateEvent`, `OpenEvent`, and `CloseHandle`.

MFC 3.0 enables you to create multithreaded applications. In MFC 3.0, the `CWinThread` class represents a thread. Usually, you do not have to create `CWinThread` objects explicitly; merely call the `AfxBeginThread` function, which creates the `CWinThread` object.

MFC organizes threads in two categories:

■ *User-interface threads* that handle user input and respond to events and messages generated by the user

■ *Worker threads* that perform other tasks, such as recalculating a spreadsheet, that do not require user input

The Win32 API does not distinguish between types of threads—each thread is characterized by the starting address, which is used to begin executing the thread. MFC treats a user-interface thread specially by providing a message handling mechanism for user-interface events. The `CWinApp` class, derived from `CWinThread`, represents a user-interface thread because `CWinApp` handles events and messages generated by the user.

Even with MFC support for multithreading, you are still responsible for synchronizing access to objects that are shared by multiple threads. For this, you have to call directly various Win32 multithreading functions that use critical sections, mutexes, semaphores, and events.

For further information on using multiple threads and thread synchronization functions, please consult other books on Windows NT.

Memory-Mapped Files

Win32 supports memory-mapped files, which enable you to allocate a block of memory and associate a disk file with that memory. After you associate a file with some memory, you can access the file as if that file's contents are completely residing in memory. The operating system takes care of the messy details, such as opening the file, buffering the contents in memory, and closing the file when you are done.

Memory-mapped files are important in Windows NT because they provide the way to share blocks of memory between processes. You can name the block of memory to which a file has been mapped—such a block of memory is known as a *named shared memory*.

There are only a small number of Win32 API functions for using memory-mapped files:

■ `CreateFile` to open or create a file and get back a file handle

■ `CreateFileMapping` to create a file-mapping object using the handle returned by a successful call to `CreateFile` (use `0xffffffff` as the file handle to share data between processes when the data is not on disk)

■ `MapViewOfFile` to create a pointer to the file view using the handle to the file-mapping object returned by `CreateFileMapping`

■ `OpenFileMapping` to access the shared memory using the pointer returned by `MapViewOfFile`

■ `FlushViewOfFile` to force the operating system to write all the modified data back to the disk

Use the `CloseHandle` function to close the file-mapping object as well as the file object identified by the handle returned by `CreateFile`.

Win32 GDI Extensions

Windows NT extends the Graphic Device Interface of 16-bit Windows with the following major additions:

■ *Bézier splines.* A Bézier spline is a curve drawn from the startpoint to an endpoint with the shape of the curve controlled by two control points between them. In addition to the current point, a Bézier spline needs three more points—the endpoint and the two control points. The Win32 GDI provides the `PolyBezier` and `PolyBezierTo` functions to draw Bézier splines. In MFC 3.0, the CDC class provides `PolyBezier` and `PolyBezierTo` member functions for this purpose.

■ *Paths.* Paths are used to define arbitrarily shaped outlines, irregular shapes, and filled areas. A path consists of straight lines or curves that can be drawn outlined, filled, or both filled and outlined. To define a path, start by calling `BeginPath`. Then you can define the rest of the path using any of the following functions:

AngleArc	LineTo	Polyline
Arc	MoveToEx	PolylineTo
ArcTo	Pie	PolyPolygon
Chord	PolyBezier	PolyPolyline
CloseFigure	PolyBezierTo	Rectangle
Ellipse	PolyDraw	RoundRect
ExtTextOut	Polygon	TextOut

Call `EndPath` to finish defining the path. The path can then be drawn by calling `StrokePath`, `FillPath`, or `StrokeAndFillPath`. You can also create a region from the path by calling `PathToRegion` or set a path as a clipping region by calling `SelectClipPath`. In MFC 3.0, the CDC class provides member functions with the same names as the Win32 GDI's path manipulation functions.

■ *Matrix Transforms.* The Win32 GDI provides a new coordinate transformation called the world transform that can be used to perform skewing, reflection, rotation, and shearing in addition to scaling and offsetting that were available with the 16-bit Windows API. Supporting world transform requires three new API functions: `SetWorldTransform`, `ModifyWorldTransform`, and `GetWorldTransform`. The world transform also introduces a new structure called `XFORM`, which is defined as follows:

```
typedef struct
{
    FLOAT eM11; // x scale
    FLOAT eM12; // y skew
    FLOAT eM21; // x skew
    FLOAT eM22; // y scale
    FLOAT eDx;  // x offset
    FLOAT eDy;  // y offset
}
XFORM;
```

The six members of the XFORM structure correspond to six elements of a 3x3 matrix that defines the world transform. In matrix notation, the world transform modifying a coordinate (x,y) to produce a coordinate (x',y') can be expressed as follows:

```
              ¦ eM11   eM12   0 ¦
[x  y  1]  *  ¦ eM21   eM22   0 ¦  =  [x'  y'  1]
              ¦ eDx    eDy    1 ¦
```

For translation, the terms eDx and eDy specify the horizontal and vertical offsets, respectively. For scaling, the terms eM11 and eM22 specify the horizontal and vertical scalings, respectively. For a clockwise rotation angle of A radians and with the y-axis pointing downwards as in the MM_TEXT mapping mode, the relationships are as follows:

```
eM11 = cos(A)        eM12 = -sin(A)
eM21 = sin(A)        eM22 = cos(A)
```

■ *Bitmap Operations*: Win32 provides two new bitmap functions that complement BitBlt, PatBlt, and StretchBlt (available in 16-bit Windows):

■ MaskBlt extends the functionality of BitBlt by adding a mask bitmap that enables you to display nonrectangular bitmap images. If you do not provide a mask bitmap, MaskBlt behaves exactly like BitBlt. Before using MaskBlt, you should call GetDeviceCaps to determine whether the device context supports MaskBlt.

■ PlgBlt ("Parallelogram Blt") transfers the bits of a bitmap from a rectangle to a parallelogram. If a mask bitmap is supplied, PlgBlt also masks the destination parallelogram. With PlgBlt, you can rotate or skew bitmaps.

In MFC 3.0, the CDC class provides MaskBlt and PlgBlt member functions for these enhanced bitmap operations.

Although this book does not cover these new Win32 GDI capabilities in detail, now that you know about them, you may wish to look up the details in the online documentation and use these GDI functions in your Win32 applications.

Unicode

Many languages, such as Japanese and Chinese, have large character sets. To support programming for these markets, MFC 3.0 offers two approaches to handling large character sets:

■ *Unicode* is a 16-bit character encoding, which provides a range of values for the character sets of all languages. All ASCII characters are included in Unicode as "widened" characters.

■ *Double-Byte Character Sets* (DBCS) characters are composed of one or two bytes. Some ranges of bytes are used as *lead bytes*. A lead byte and the following *trail byte* comprise a single 2-byte-wide character.

DBCS is supported on 16-bit and 32-bit Windows. Unicode is supported on Windows NT.

MFC 3.0 directly supports Unicode characters and strings. Except for database class member functions, all MFC functions are Unicode-enabled, including the `CString` class. `CString` also provides Unicode to ANSI conversion functions (and vice versa).

Here are some tips that will help you take advantage of MFC 3.0 and C runtime library's support for Unicode:

■ Define the `_UNICODE` symbol before you build your program.

■ When using Unicode, specify the proper entry point for your program. To do this, select the Output category in the Link page of the Project Settings dialog box and set the Entry Point Symbol to `wWinMainCRTStartup`.

■ Rather than using the string manipulation functions (the `str` family of functions), use the `wcs` family of functions or the macros prefixed with `tcs`.

Use `_TCHAR` and the following related portable data types:

Nonportable type	*Portable type*
char	TCHAR
char*, LPSTR	LPTSTR
const char*, LPCSTR	LPCTSTR

■ Specify all literal strings properly. For example, to specify a string of Unicode characters, use the following syntax:

```
L"This is a literal string in Unicode."
```

Use the `_T` macro to specify literal strings in a more portable manner, so that the strings are treated as Unicode strings when Unicode is enabled or as ASCII strings (including MBCS) when Unicode is not enabled. For example, rather than writing the following:

```
SetWindowText("Visual C++");
```

use this:

```
SetWindowText(_T("Visual C++"));
```

Note that the _T macro is identical to the _TEXT macro.

◼ Functions that require string lengths can be a problem when Unicode is used. Some functions want the number of characters in a string; others want the number of bytes. If you have a Cstring object, use the Length function when a function requires count of characters. When a function expects the number of bytes, use the following expression (str is a CString):

```
UINT nbytes = str.Length( ) * sizeof(_TCHAR )  // count of bytes
```

Networking

Built-in networking support is a strong point of 32-bit Windows such as Windows NT 3.5. As a Win32 programmer, you can use one of the following means to write programs that access the network:

◼ Win32 Network (WNet) API provides functions such as WNetAddConnection, WNetCancelConnection, and WNetGetConnection for connecting to browsing remote file systems.

◼ NetBIOS API provides backward compatibility with existing MS-DOS or 16-bit Windows applications that send data directly on the network using a low-level system call.

◼ Windows Socket API is a standard set of Berkeley Sockets functions, which is common in UNIX systems. There are additional Windows-specific functions that start with a WSA prefix. The Windows Sockets API supports communications using TCP/IP protocol.

◼ Win32 Named Pipes and Mailslot APIs provide the mechanisms necessary to support the LAN Manager API set. Both named pipes and mailslots provide peer-to-peer communication mechanisms with mailslots useful for broadcasting messages to any number of processes.

◼ The Remote Procedure Call (RPC) facility enables a program to call procedures located on another computer.

Consult Chapter 32, "Network Programming with Visual C++ 2.0," for further details about Win32 network programming.

3-D SCREEN SAVERS IN WINDOWS NT 3.5

To see an example of 3-D graphics with OpenGL, take a look at the 3-D screen savers (3-D Flying Objects and 3-D Pipes) that accompany Windows NT 3.5. These 3-D screen savers were implemented using OpenGL.

3-D Graphics with OpenGL in Windows NT 3.5

A unique feature of Windows NT 3.5 is the OpenGL graphics library, which provides an API for displaying 3-D graphics. OpenGL is a portable procedural software interface. OpenGL is based on GL, which was developed by Silicon Graphics, Inc. (SGI) as a 3-D graphics library for the Silicon Graphics IRIS workstations. Enhancements and changes to OpenGL are controlled by the OpenGL Architecture Review Board (ARB), whose founding members are Digital Equipment Corporation, IBM, Intel, Microsoft, and Silicon Graphics.

Because OpenGL comes with Windows NT 3.5, if you are using Visual C++ 2.0 on Windows NT 3.5, this is your chance to try out 3-D graphics on your PC. The following sections provide a brief overview of OpenGL and show an example OpenGL program. The sample program shows how to make OpenGL calls in an application created with Visual C++ 2.0 and MFC 3.0. You can follow the steps shown for the sample program to add 3-D graphics to your MFC applications.

OpenGL Overview

OpenGL is basically a library of functions for drawing and rendering 3-D shapes. OpenGL functions are portable, but because OpenGL programs rely on the underlying operating system for the output window, an OpenGL program will require some changes when ported from one implementation of OpenGL to another. By the same token, each implementation of OpenGL, including the one in Windows NT 3.5, requires support functions to display the output in that windowing environment. Windows NT 3.5 includes five categories of API functions to support OpenGL:

- A core OpenGL library with 115 OpenGL functions with names that have the gl prefix. The core functions provide drawing primitives (for points, lines, and polygons), matrix transformation, lighting, shading, coloring, texturing, clipping, and more. The core library functions are portable across all implementations of OpenGL.

- The OpenGL Utility (GLU) library with 43 functions that have names with the glu prefix. These functions perform a variety of tasks including texture support; coordinate transformation; polygon tessellation; rendering spheres, cylinders and disks; curves and surfaces; and error handling.

- The OpenGL Auxiliary library with 31 functions that have names with the aux prefix. These functions provide a simple way to manage windows, handle input events, and draw some predefined 3-D objects. This library gives you a quick and dirty way to get started with OpenGL programming.

- Six new support functions with names that have the wgl prefix—these functions are referred to as the "wiggle" functions because of the prefix. These six functions connect OpenGL to the Windows NT windowing system by managing rendering contexts and font bitmaps.

■ Five new Win32 functions: `ChoosePixelFormat`, `DescribePixelFormat`, `GetPixelFormat`, `SetPixelFormat`, and `SwapBuffers` that support per-window pixel formats and double-buffering needed for smooth rendering of OpenGL graphics in Win32 systems.

The key to displaying 3-D graphics in a Windows NT window is the rendering context, which is tied to a Windows device context (DC). However, before you associate a DC with a rendering context, you have to specify the pixel format—the organization of the OpenGL *frame buffer* (the drawing surface consisting of pixels with a specified number of bits) for the DC.

Pixel Formats

A pixel format characterizes the organization of the OpenGL frame buffer, which you can think of as a collection of bit planes used to render the 3-D graphics. The OpenGL frame buffer is the combination of all the buffers utilized by OpenGL:

■ *Color buffer* holds pixel data that is either color-indexed or RGBA values (RGBA stands for red-green-blue and alpha, where alpha denotes opacity).

■ *Depth buffer* holds the depth values for the pixels. A pixel with a smaller depth overwrites one with a larger depth.

■ *Stencil buffer* restricts drawing to specific areas.

■ *Accumulation buffer* is meant for accumulating many images into a single composite image.

The *PIXELFORMATDESCRIPTOR* Structure

In Windows NT 3.5, the pixel format is represented by the `PIXELFORMATDESCRIPTOR` structure, which is defined as follows:

```
typedef struct tagPIXELFORMATDESCRIPTOR
{
    WORD  nSize;             // Size of this structure
    WORD  nVersion;          // Version number (1)
    DWORD dwFlags;           // Pixel buffer property flags
    BYTE  iPixelType;        // Pixel type (RGBA or color-indexed)
    BYTE  cColorBits;        // Number of color bitplanes
    BYTE  cRedBits;          // Number of red bitplanes
    BYTE  cRedShift;         // Shift count for red bitplanes
    BYTE  cGreenBits;        // Number of green bitplanes
    BYTE  cGreenShift;       // Shift count for green bitplanes
    BYTE  cBlueBits;         // Number of blue bitplanes
    BYTE  cBlueShift;        // Shift count for blue bitplanes
    BYTE  cAlphaBits;        // Number of alpha bit planes
    BYTE  cAlphaShift;       // Shift count for alpha bitplanes
    BYTE  cAccumBits;        // Number of accumulation buffer
                             // bitplanes
    BYTE  cAccumRedBits;     // Number of red bitplanes in
                             // the accumulation buffer
    BYTE  cAccumGreenBits;   // Number of green bitplanes in
```

```
                                // the accumulation buffer
    BYTE   cAccumBlueBits;    // Number of blue bitplanes in
                                // the accumulation buffer
    BYTE   cAccumAlphaBits;   // Number of alpha bitplanes in
                                // the accumulation buffer
    BYTE   cDepthBits;        // Number of bits per pixel
                                // in the depth (z) buffer
    BYTE   cStencilBits;      // Number of bits per pixel in
                                // the stencil buffer
    BYTE   cAuxBuffers;       // Number of auxiliary buffers
    BYTE   iLayerType;        // Type of layer
    BYTE   bReserved;         // Reserved (must be 0)
    DWORD  dwLayerMask;       // Specifies the layer mask
    DWORD  dwVisibleMask;     // Specifies the visible mask
    DWORD  dwDamageMask;      // Specifies the damage mask
} PIXELFORMATDESCRIPTOR;
```

Table 30.4 lists the meanings of the members of the `PIXELFORMATDESCRIPTOR` structure in Microsoft's generic implementation of OpenGL version 1 (generic implementation implies the implementation is all in software and is independent of graphics hardware).

Table 30.4. Members of the `PIXELFORMATDESCRIPTOR` structure.

Member	Description
nSize	Size of this data structure in bytes. Should be set to `sizeof(PIXELFORMATDESCRIPTOR)`.
nVersion	Version of this data structure. Should be set to 1.
dwFlags	A set of bit flags that specify properties of the pixel buffer. Use a bitwise OR combination of the following bit flag constants:
	PFD_DRAW_TO_WINDOW to enable drawing to a window or device surface
	PFD_DRAW_TO_BITMAP to enable drawing to a memory bitmap
	PFD_SUPPORT_GDI to support GDI drawing (in the generic implementation, you cannot use this flag if PFD_DOUBLEBUFFER is also set)
	PFD_SUPPORT_OPENGL to support OpenGL drawing
	PFD_GENERIC_FORMAT to indicate that the pixel format is supported by the generic software-based implementation (if this bit is clear, the pixel format is supported by a device driver or hardware)
	PFD_NEED_PALETTE to indicate that the buffer uses RGBA pixels on a palette-managed device (the application should use a logical palette for best results)
	PFD_DOUBLEBUFFER to indicate that double-buffering is enabled (in the release 1.0 generic implementation, you cannot set

Member	Description
	PFD_SUPPORT_GDI if this flag is on)
	PFD_STEREO to indicate that the buffer is stereoscopic (not supported in the release 1.0 generic implementation)
	PFD_NEED_SYSTEM_PALETTE to indicate that the OpenGL hardware supports only one hardware palette
iPixelType	Type of pixel values. Can be one of PFD_TYPE_RGBA for RGBA pixels and PFD_TYPE_COLORINDEX for color index pixels.
cColorBits	Number of color bits per pixel. This is normally 4, 8, 16, 24, or 32 (for a 256-color display, cColorBits is 8).
cRedBits	Number of red bits in each pixel of type RGBA. For an 8-bit color display in RGBA mode, each pixel is organized in 3-3-2 format—three bits each of red and green and two bits of blue.
cRedShift	Shift count for red bitplanes in an RGBA color buffer. For an 8-bit device context in 3-3-2 format, the shift counts for red, green, and blue are 0, 3, and 6, respectively.
cGreenBits	Number of green bits in each pixel of type RGBA.
cGreenShift	Shift count for green bitplanes in an RGBA color buffer.
cBlueBits	Number of blue bits in each pixel of type RGBA.
cBlueShift	Shift count for blue bitplanes in an RGBA color buffer.
cAlphaBits	Number of alpha bitplanes in an RGBA color buffer. (Alpha bitplanes are not supported in release 1.0 generic implementation of OpenGL in Windows NT 3.5.)
cAlphaShift	Shift count for alpha bitplanes in an RGBA color buffer.
cAccumBits	Number of bitplanes in the accumulation buffer.
cAccumRedBits	Number of red bitplanes in the accumulation buffer.
cAccumGreenBits	Number of green bitplanes in the accumulation buffer.
cAccumBlueBits	Number of blue bitplanes in the accumulation buffer.
cAccumAlphaBits	Number of alpha bitplanes in the accumulation buffer.
cDepthBits	Number of bitplanes in the depth (z-axis) buffer.
cStencilBits	Number of bitplanes in the stencil buffer.
cAuxBuffers	Number of auxiliary buffers. (Auxiliary buffers are not supported in release 1.0 of the generic implementation of OpenGL in Windows NT 3.5.)

continues

Table 30.4. continued

Member	Description
iLayerType	Type of layer. The value can be one of the following (however, only PFD_MAIN_PLANE is supported in release 1.0 of the generic implementation of OpenGL in Windows NT 3.5):
	PFD_MAIN_PLANE to indicate that the layer is the main plane
	PFD_OVERLAY_PLANE to indicate that the layer is the overlay plane
	PFD_UNDERLAY_PLANE to indicate that the layer is the underlay plane
bReserved	Reserved. Must be 0.
dwLayerMask	Layer mask, which is used in conjunction with the visible mask to determine whether one layer overlays another.
dwVisibleMask	Visible mask, which is used in conjunction with the layer mask to determine whether one layer overlays another. If the visible mask is 0, the layer is opaque.
dwDamageMask	Mask specifying whether more than one pixel format shares the same frame buffer. If the result of the bitwise AND of the damage masks of two pixel formats is nonzero, they share the same buffers.

Associating a Pixel Format with a DC

A given device, represented by a DC, can support several pixel formats. The supported pixel formats are identified by index values (1, 2, 3, 4, and so on). When you use a DC for OpenGL output, you have to first associate it with a single pixel format chosen from the set of pixel formats it supports.

To display OpenGL output on a device, an application typically obtains a DC, sets the DC's pixel format to one of the supported formats, and then creates an OpenGL rendering context suitable for that device.

There are four new Win32 functions to manage pixel formats:

■ ChoosePixelFormat provides a DC's pixel format that is the closest match to a specified pixel format specified through a filled-in PIXELFORMATDESCRIPTOR structure.

■ DescribePixelFormat fills in a PIXELFORMATDESCRIPTOR data structure with information about a DC's pixel format, identified by an index number.

■ SetPixelFormat sets a DC's pixel format to the pixel format specified by a pixel format index.

■ GetPixelFormat returns the pixel format index of a device context's current pixel format.

To set up a DC's pixel format, you have to first get a DC. Then set up a PIXELFORMATDESCRIPTOR structure with a desired set of values and call ChoosePixelFormat to obtain that DC's best match to the pixel format specified by the structure. The ChoosePixelFormat function returns the index of the pixel format that best matches the specified pixel format.

Next, call SetPixelFormat to set DC's current pixel format to the one returned by ChoosePixelFormat. You should set the pixel format of a DC only once. Here is a typical example of setting the pixel format of a DC (identified by the handle hdc):

```
static PIXELFORMATDESCRIPTOR pfd =
{
    sizeof(PIXELFORMATDESCRIPTOR),   // Size of this structure
    1,                               // Version number
    PFD_DRAW_TO_WINDOW |             // Flags
    PFD_SUPPORT_OPENGL |
    PFD_DOUBLEBUFFER,
    PFD_TYPE_RGBA,                   // Use RGBA pixel values
    24,                              // Try to use 24-bit color
    0, 0, 0, 0, 0, 0,                // Don't care about these
    0, 0,                            // No alpha buffer
    32, 0, 0, 0, 0,                  // 32-bit accumulation buffer
    32,                              // 32-bit depth buffer
    0,                               // No stencil buffer
    0,                               // No auxiliary buffers
    PFD_MAIN_PLANE,                  // Layer type
    0,                               // Reserved (must be 0)
    0, 0, 0                          // No layer masks
};
//...

    int nPixelFormat;

    nPixelFormat = ChoosePixelFormat(hdc, &pfd);
    SetPixelFormat(hdc, nPixelFormat, &pfd);
```

After setting the pixel format, you should call GetPixelFormat to obtain information about the pixel format. If the pixel format requires a palette, you should set up the logical palette at this point. Here is the code fragment showing the logic:

```
DescribePixelFormat(hdc, nPixelFormat,
                    sizeof(PIXELFORMATDESCRIPTOR),
                    &pfd);

    if(pfd.dwFlags & PFD_NEED_PALETTE)
    {
        nColors = 1 << pfd.cColorBits;

// Code to create palette and initialize it
//...


// Assume hPalette is handle of palette
// Realize the color palette
        if(hPalette != NULL)
        {
            SelectPalette(hdc, hPalette, FALSE);
```

```
        RealizePalette(hdc);
    }
}
```

REQUIRED WINDOW STYLES FOR OPENGL OUTPUT

SetPixelFormat successfully sets a window's pixel format *only if* the window's style has the WS_CLIPCHILDREN and WS_CLIPSIBLINGS bits set. If you are using MFC, remember to override the PreCreateWindow member function of the window class and set the WS_CLIPCHILDREN and WS_CLIPSIBLINGS style bits. Otherwise, OpenGL output will not appear in the window.

Rendering Context

Just as drawing in a Win32 window requires a device context (DC), displaying OpenGL graphics requires a rendering context. The DC contains information necessary to display text and graphics in Windows; the rendering context contains information pertinent to displaying OpenGL output. The rendering context links OpenGL to the Windows NT windowing system. Once you have a DC with a specified pixel format, you are ready to create a rendering context and associate the rendering context with that DC.

To create and manage rendering contexts, Windows NT 3.5 provides the following six functions with the wgl prefix in their names:

- BOOL wglUseFontBitmaps(HDC, DWORD, DWORD, DWORD);

- HGLRC wglCreateContext(HDC hdc); creates a new rendering context and associates the rendering context with the specified DC. You must set the DC's pixel format before creating the rendering context. The DC must support at least 16 colors.

- BOOL wglMakeCurrent(HDC hdc, HGLRC hglrc); binds the rendering context with the specified DC and makes that rendering context the current one.

- HGLRC wglGetCurrentContext(void); returns a handle to the current rendering context. If there is no current rendering context, wglGetCurrentContext returns NULL.

- HDC wglGetCurrentDC(void); returns a handle to the device context associated with the current rendering context. If there is no current rendering context, wglGetCurrentDC returns NULL.

- BOOL wglDeleteContext(HGLRC hglrc); deletes the specified rendering context.

- BOOL wglUseFontBitmaps(HDC hdc, DWORD dwFirst, DWORD dwCount, DWORD dwBase); creates a series of display lists that draw bitmaps depicting a specified range of characters in the DC's current font. You then can use these display lists to draw text (in that font) in the current OpenGL rendering context. The hdc argument identifies the DC whose current font is used to generate the display lists. The dwFirst argument specifies the character code of the first character and `dwCount` specifies the number of consecutive characters to be converted into a series of display lists with `dwBase` as the ID code of the first display list. After the display lists are created, you can draw text by executing the display lists—call OpenGL's `glCallList` or `glCallLists` function.

There are two approaches to associating a rendering context with a DC for use in OpenGL programming:

■ The first approach, illustrated in Figure 30.1, gets the window's DC at the time of creation of the window, sets the pixel format of the DC, and creates a rendering context with that DC. Then, to handle `WM_PAINT` messages, the program merely calls OpenGL functions, which automatically use the current rendering context and DC. When the window is about to be destroyed, the DC is released and the rendering context is destroyed.

■ The second approach also gets the window's DC at the time of creation of the window, sets the pixel format of the DC, and creates a rendering context with that DC (see Figure 30.2). From this point on, the second approach differs from the first. The DC is released after creating the rendering context. When a `WM_PAINT` message is received, the program calls `wglMakeCurrent` to bind the window DC to the rendering context, draws 3-D graphics by calling OpenGL functions,and makes the rendering context not current by a call `wglMakeCurrent(NULL, NULL)`. When the window is about to be destroyed, the rendering context is destroyed.

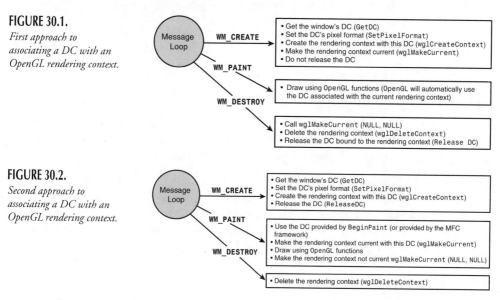

FIGURE 30.1.

First approach to associating a DC with an OpenGL rendering context.

FIGURE 30.2.

Second approach to associating a DC with an OpenGL rendering context.

The first approach is more efficient because it binds the rendering context to a DC once and uses that rendering context throughout the life of the program. The second approach incurs the performance penalty associated with binding the rendering context to the DC every time 3-D graphics are drawn.

MORE INFORMATION ON OPENGL

With the information presented in this chapter, you should be able to experiment with 3-D graphics programming using OpenGL. For more substantial 3-D graphics applications, you will find detailed information on OpenGL in the following references:

■ *OpenGL Programmer's Reference* in the Win32 SDK for Windows NT 3.5.

■ *OpenGL Programming Guide* by Jackie Neider, Tom Davis, and Mason Woo, Addison-Wesley, 1992.

■ *OpenGL Reference Manual,* OpenGL Architecture Review Board, Addison-Wesley, 1992.

You also need to become familiar with all aspects of 3-D graphics including normalized coordinates, transformation matrix, and lighting and shading models. For these and other computer graphics topics, you may want a copy of the following classic textbook:

■ *Computer Graphics Principles and Practice, Second Edition,* James D. Foley, Andries van Dam, Steven K. Feiner, and John D. Hughes, Addison-Wesley, 1990.

OpenGL Programming

The basic idea in OpenGL programming is to draw a scene using OpenGL calls and then display that scene in a window managed by the underlying operating system. The scene is animated by simply drawing and displaying the scene in rapid succession.

After you select a pixel format for a DC and create a rendering context for that DC, you can begin generating 3-D output in that DC's window. For this, you have to learn how to set up the viewing parameters, set up the objects in a scene, and call appropriate OpenGL functions to render the scene. Detailed coverage of this topic requires a book by itself. The following sections highlight the major steps in building and rendering a 3-D scene.

Setting Up a Perspective View

To view a scene, you have to set up a projection transformation that generates the 2-D representation of the scene by transforming 3-D coordinates into 2-D. The simplest projection is orthographic projection, which merely drops the z-coordinates (assuming that the z-axis of the view coordinate system is along the viewing direction).

Unfortunately, orthographic projection does not provide a sense of depth. Our visual system shows us what is known as a perspective projection of the 3-D world around us. A good example of perspective projection is the view of a straight stretch of railroad tracks. Even though the railroad tracks are parallel lines, they seem to meet at a distance. The perspective projection provides this view.

In addition to the projection transformation, you also need to specify the viewport, which defines how the projected 2-D image is mapped to the window.

In a Windows program, you should set up the projection matrix and the viewport in response to a WM_SIZE message for these reasons:

■ The view should be redefined whenever the window's size changes.

■ The first WM_SIZE message always precedes the first WM_PAINT message, thus guaranteeing that the viewing parameters will be set before the scene is drawn for the first time.

You have to use gl and glu functions to set the viewing parameters. Here is a typical set of function calls to set up a perspective view:

```
// Redefine the viewing volume and viewport once when the program
// starts and again any time the window size changes.

// Assume cx = window width, cy = window height

    m_glnWidth = (GLsizei) cx;
    m_glnHeight = (GLsizei) cy;
    m_gldAspect = (GLdouble) m_glnWidth / (GLdouble) m_glnHeight;

    glMatrixMode(GL_PROJECTION);
    glLoadIdentity();
    gluPerspective(
        45.0,          // Field-of-view angle in y
                       // direction (in degrees)
        m_gldAspect,   // Ratio of x (width) to y (height)
        1.0,           // z-coord of near clipping plane
        100.0);        // z-coord of far clipping plane

    glViewport(0, 0, m_glnWidth, m_glnHeight);
```

OpenGL maintains three transformation matrices:

■ *ModelView matrix* for converting coordinates from object coordinates to eye coordinates

■ *Projection matrix* for transforming coordinates from eye coordinates to clip coordinates that are subsequently converted to screen coordinates

■ *Texture matrix* for use in applying textures to objects (the texture matrix is unrelated to ModelView and Projection matrices)

When you call any coordinate transformation functions such as glTranslate, glScale, or glRotate, the operation affects the current transformation matrix. That is why, before calling `gluPerspective` to set up a perspective view, you have to call `glMatrixMode` to indicate that the subsequent changes to the coordinate transformation matrix should affect the projection matrix.

Figure 30.3 shows what a typical perspective view looks like and also illustrates the meaning of the arguments to the `gluPerspective` function. Note the orientation of the coordinate axes located at the eye:

■ The eye is looking at the 3-D scene down the negative z-axis.

■ From the eye's vantage point, the x-axis extends to the right and the y-axis points up.

As you can see, the visible region (the *viewing volume*) is defined by the field-of-view angles along y- and x-axes and the locations of the near and far clipping planes. The clipping planes are parallel to the x-y plane; thus only their z-coordinates are needed to locate and orient the clipping planes.

FIGURE 30.3.

Defining a perspective viewing volume.

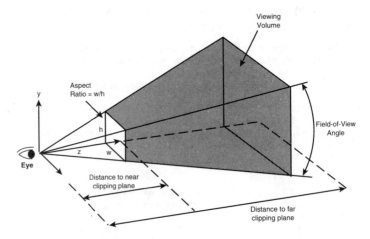

Setting Up the ModelView Transformation

When drawing a scene, the first step is to position the scene with respect to the eye. This is done by setting up the ModelView transformation, which manipulates the local coordinate system in which the 3-D objects are drawn. Essentially, you start with an identity matrix and use translation and rotation operations to position and orient the local coordinate system. Then define the 3-D objects in that local coordinate system. For example, suppose you place a scene 64 units away from the eye along the z-axis and rotate the scene to view it at a depression angle of 30 degrees. You would then set up the ModelView matrix as follows:

```
glMatrixMode(GL_MODELVIEW);
glLoadIdentity();
glTranslatef(0.0f, 0.0f, -64.0f);
glRotatef(30.0f, 1.0f, 0.0f, 0.0f);
```

Drawing a 3-D Scene

To draw the 3-D objects in a scene, you have to remember that the eye (the viewing point) remains fixed and you move the local coordinate system around, rotate it as needed, and draw the object in the local coordinate system. Call glTranslate and glRotate, respectively, to translate and rotate the local coordinate frame. There are many OpenGL drawing primitives to draw 3-D shapes. You will find it helpful to write your own functions to draw specific shapes. For example, you might define a DrawSphere function that calls various OpenGL functions to draw a sphere:

```
//----------------------------------------------------------------
//  D r a w S p h e r e
//
//  Draws a sphere using OpenGL calls.

void DrawSphere(GLdouble gldRadius,
                GLint glnSlices, GLint glnStacks)
{
    GLUquadricObj *glquad;

    glquad = gluNewQuadric();
    gluSphere(glquad, gldRadius, glnSlices, glnStacks);
    gluDeleteQuadric(glquad);
}
```

That way, you can simply call DrawSphere whenever you need to draw a sphere.

When composing a scene with many 3-D objects, you may want to start with a common reference location and orientation for the local coordinate frames. To do this, you can use glPushMatrix and glPopMatrix to enclose the steps involved in drawing each individual object in the scene. For example, suppose you are drawing a scene with the following:

```
// Draw first object.

    glPushMatrix();
       // Call glTranslate and glRotate to set up local
       // coordinateframe
       //...
       // Draw the object
       //...
    glPopMatrix();

// Draw second object.

    glPushMatrix();
       // Call glTranslate and glRotate to set up local
       // coordinateframe
       //...
       // Draw the object
       //...
    glPopMatrix();
```

The idea is that you save the state of the ModelView matrix, mess around with the local coordinate frame, draw the object, and then revert back to the original ModelView matrix.

Lighting

OpenGL also enables you to add up to eight light sources and define each source's characteristics, such as color and intensity of the diffuse, ambient, and specular components of the light. For example, the following code adds a single light source:

```
// Define Red, Green, Blue intensities of ambient, diffuse,
// and specular components of the lights
    GLfloat glfLightAmbient[] = { 0.1f, 0.1f, 0.1f, 1.0f };
    GLfloat glfLightDiffuse[] = { 0.7f, 0.7f, 0.7f, 1.0f };
    GLfloat glfLightSpecular[] = { 0.0f, 0.0f, 0.0f, 1.0f };
//...
// Add a light to the scene and activate it.
    glLightfv(GL_LIGHT0, GL_AMBIENT, glfLightAmbient);
    glLightfv(GL_LIGHT0, GL_DIFFUSE, glfLightDiffuse);
    glLightfv(GL_LIGHT0, GL_SPECULAR, glfLightSpecular);
    glEnable(GL_LIGHTING);
    glEnable(GL_LIGHT0);
```

The eight lights are identified by constants GL_LIGHT0 through GL_LIGHT7.

Material Properties

The color of an object depends on the light striking the object and the reflective properties of the material that makes up the object. In OpenGL, you can specify the reflective properties of an object (or a surface in an object) by calling the glMaterialfv function. For example, to define a material that reflects red color (and thus appears in various shades of red), you may use the following code:

```
// Define a color. In OpenGL, RGB values are specified as
// floating-point numbers between 0.0 and 1.0.
    GLfloat glfRed[] = { 1.0f, 0.0f, 0.0f, 1.0f };
//...
// Set properties of the material
    glMaterialfv(GL_FRONT, GL_AMBIENT_AND_DIFFUSE, glfRed);
```

32-BIT WINDOWS WITH OPENGL SUPPORT

You need a 32-bit Windows environment with OpenGL support to run the sample OpenGL program. Currently, only Windows NT 3.5 supports OpenGL. However, in the near future, other versions of Windows, such as Windows 95, may also support 3-D graphics with OpenGL.

A Sample OpenGL Program

Once you understand the steps involved in setting up the pixel format for a window's DC and associating a DC with a rendering context, it is straightforward to display some rudimentary 3-D graphics in an MFC application. To see how this is done, let's generate a project named TEST3D for a single-document-interface application using MFC AppWizard. You add code to this project so that it renders a 3-D scene consisting of a sphere at the end of two cylindrical links. The scene is animated by using the Windows timer—the cylindrical links move up and down while the entire scene rotates around (see Figure 30.4). To build this program, enhance the TEST3D project as follows:

1. Add the following lines to the file STDAFX.H:

   ```
   #include <GL/gl.h>
   #include <GL/glu.h>
   ```

2. For the sample program, let's place all 3-D graphics calls in the view class of the application. Accordingly, add some member variables and member functions to the CTest3dView class (in the file TEST3VW.H) as shown in boldface in the following listing:

   ```
   class CTest3dView : public Cview
   {
   //...
   // Operations
   public:

   // Functions to draw 3-D objects and a scene
       void DrawScene(UINT nAngle, UINT nBaseAngle);
       void DrawCone(GLdouble gldBaseRadius, GLdouble gldTopRadius,
                   GLdouble gldHeight, UINT nDivisions);
       void DrawSphere(GLdouble gldRadius, GLint glnSlices,
                   GLint glnStacks);

   // Initialize the rendering context
       void InitRC();

   // Set a DC's pixel format
       void SetDCPixelFormat(HDC hdc);


   //...


   // Implementation
   //...


   protected:
       GLdouble    m_gldAspect;  // Aspect ratio
       GLsizei     m_glnWidth;   // Width of window
       GLsizei     m_glnHeight;  // Height of window
       BOOL        m_bUp;        // TRUE = up, FALSE = down
       UINT        m_nUpAngle;   // Up-down angle
   ```

```
        UINT        m_nBaseAngle;  // Angle of the base
        UINT        m_nTimer;      // Timer ID
        HPALETTE    m_hPalette;    // Logical palette
//...
};
```

3. In the implementation of the CTest3dView class (in the file TEST3VW.CPP), initialize the member variables in the class constructor:

```
CTest3dView::CTest3dView()
{
    m_bUp = TRUE;
    m_nUpAngle = 0;
    m_nBaseAngle = 270;
    m_hPalette = NULL;
}
```

4. Using ClassWizard, override the PreCreateWindow function for CTest3dView class and define that function:

```
BOOL CTest3dView::PreCreateWindow(CREATESTRUCT& cs)
{
// The SetPixelFormat function requires a window style of
// WS_CLIPSIBLINGS and WS_CLIPCHILDREN

    cs.style |= WS_CLIPSIBLINGS | WS_CLIPCHILDREN;

    return CView::PreCreateWindow(cs);
}
```

It is very important to set the window style in this manner because the SetPixelFormat function will fail if the window associated with the DC does not have the styles WM_CLIPSIBLINGS and WS_CLIPCHILDREN.

5. To initialize the DC, set its pixel format, and create a rendering context, define the OnCreate function (use ClassWizard to add this function) of the CTest3dView class as follows:

```
int CTest3dView::OnCreate(LPCREATESTRUCT lpCreateStruct)
{
    if(CView::OnCreate(lpCreateStruct) == -1)
        return -1;

// Create a rendering context, associate it with the window's
// DC, and set a timer.

    HDC hdc = ::GetDC(GetSafeHwnd());
```

```
    SetDCPixelFormat(hdc);

    HGLRC hrc = wglCreateContext(hdc);
    wglMakeCurrent(hdc, hrc);

    InitRC();

    m_nTimer = ::SetTimer(GetSafeHwnd(), 1, 50, NULL);

    return 0;
}
```

This step also sets up a timer, which you use to animate the scene by changing certain angles upon receipt of timer (WM_TIMER) events.

Listing 30.1 shows the functions SetDCPixelFormat and InitRC that are used to set up the DC and initialize the rendering context.

6. Using ClassWizard, add a handler for the WM_SIZE event and define the OnSize function as follows:

```
void CTest3dView::OnSize(UINT nType, int cx, int cy)
{
    CView::OnSize(nType, cx, cy);

// Redefine the viewing volume and viewport once when the program
// starts and again any time the window size changes.

    m_glnWidth = (GLsizei) cx;
    m_glnHeight = (GLsizei) cy;
    m_gldAspect = (GLdouble) m_glnWidth / (GLdouble) m_glnHeight;

    glMatrixMode(GL_PROJECTION);
    glLoadIdentity();
    gluPerspective(45.0, m_gldAspect, 1.0, 100.0);

    glViewport(0, 0, m_glnWidth, m_glnHeight);
}
```

7. Edit the OnDraw function so that it is defined as follows:

```
//------------------------------------------------------------
// CTest3dView:: O n D r a w

void CTest3dView::OnDraw(CDC* pDC)
{
```

```
        DrawScene(m_nUpAngle, m_nBaseAngle);
}
```

Listing 30.2 shows the DrawScene function and the helper functions DrawCone and DrawSphere that are used to draw the 3-D scene.

8. Using ClassWizard, add the handler OnTimer for WM_TIMER events and define that function as follows:

```
void CTest3dView::OnTimer(UINT nIDEvent)
{
// Update various rotation angles and force a repaint.

    if(m_bUp)
    {
        m_nUpAngle += 4;
        if(m_nUpAngle >= 90)
            m_bUp = FALSE;
    }
    else
    {
        m_nUpAngle -= 4;
        if(m_nUpAngle <= 0)
            m_bUp = TRUE;
    }

    if((m_nBaseAngle +=2) >= 360)
            m_nBaseAngle = 0;

    InvalidateRect(NULL, FALSE);

    CView::OnTimer(nIDEvent);
}
```

9. To handle the logical color palettes, add handlers for WM_QUERYNEWPALETTE and WM_PALETTECHANGED messages. Unfortunately, you have to add these functions manually to the message map of the CTest3dView class. First, add the two lines shown in boldface to the declaration of the CTest3dView class in file TEST3VW.H:

```
class CTest3dView : public Cview
{
//...

// Generated message map functions
protected:
    //{{AFX_MSG(CTest3dView)
```

```
    afx_msg int OnCreate(LPCREATESTRUCT lpCreateStruct);
    afx_msg void OnSize(UINT nType, int cx, int cy);
    afx_msg void OnTimer(UINT nIDEvent);
    afx_msg BOOL OnQueryNewPalette();
    afx_msg void OnPaletteChanged(CWnd* pFocusWnd);
    //}}AFX_MSG
    DECLARE_MESSAGE_MAP()
};
```

Then add two more lines to the message map definition of the `CTest3dView` class in file TEST3VW.CPP:

```
BEGIN_MESSAGE_MAP(CTest3dView, Cview)
    //{{AFX_MSG_MAP(CTest3dView)
    ON_WM_CREATE()
    ON_WM_SIZE()
    ON_WM_TIMER()
    ON_WM_QUERYNEWPALETTE()
    ON_WM_PALETTECHANGED()
    //}}AFX_MSG_MAP
END_MESSAGE_MAP()
```

Finally, define the `OnQueryNewPalette` and `OnPaletteChanged` functions in file TEST3VW.CPP as follows:

```
//-------------------------------------------------------------
BOOL CTest3dView::OnQueryNewPalette()
{
    HDC hdc = wglGetCurrentDC();
    int n = 0;

    if(m_hPalette != NULL && hdc)
    {
        if((n = RealizePalette (hdc)))
            InvalidateRect(NULL, FALSE);
    }
    return n;
}
//-------------------------------------------------------------
void CTest3dView::OnPaletteChanged(CWnd* pFocusWnd)
{
    if((m_hPalette != NULL) && (pFocusWnd != this))
    {
        HDC hdc = wglGetCurrentDC();
        if(hdc && RealizePalette (hdc))
```

```
                      UpdateColors (hdc);

        }

    }
```

10. Define the destructor of the CTest3dView so that it performs all necessary cleanup chores:

```
CTest3dView::~CTest3dView()
{
// Get the current rendering context
    HGLRC hrc = wglGetCurrentContext();


    if(hrc)
    {
// Get the DC associated with the rendering context
        HDC hdc =  wglGetCurrentDC();
        wglMakeCurrent(NULL, NULL);


// Delete rendering context and release DC
        wglDeleteContext(hrc);
        ::ReleaseDC(GetSafeHwnd(), hdc);

    }
    if(m_hPalette != NULL)
            DeleteObject(m_hPalette);
    ::KillTimer(GetSafeHwnd(), m_nTimer);

}
```

Listing 30.1. Functions to set up a DC's pixel format and initialize the rendering context.

```
//-----------------------------------------------------------
//  SetDCPixelFormat sets the pixel format for a device context in
//  preparation for creating a rendering context.

void CTest3dView::SetDCPixelFormat(HDC hdc)
{

    HANDLE       hHeap;
    int          nColors, i;
    LPLOGPALETTE lpPalette;
    BYTE         byRedMask, byGreenMask, byBlueMask;

    static PIXELFORMATDESCRIPTOR pfd =
    {
        sizeof(PIXELFORMATDESCRIPTOR), // Size of this structure
        1,                             // Version number
        PFD_DRAW_TO_WINDOW |           // Flags
        PFD_SUPPORT_OPENGL |
        PFD_DOUBLEBUFFER,
        PFD_TYPE_RGBA,                 // Use RGBA pixel values
```

```
        24,                                // Try to use 24-bit color
        0, 0, 0, 0, 0, 0,                  // Don't care about these
        0, 0,                              // No alpha buffer
        32, 0, 0, 0, 0,                    // 32-bit accumulation buffer
        32,                                // 32-bit depth buffer
        0,                                 // No stencil buffer
        0,                                 // No auxiliary buffers
        PFD_MAIN_PLANE,                    // Layer type
        0,                                 // Reserved (must be 0)
        0, 0, 0                            // No layer masks
    };

    int nPixelFormat;

    nPixelFormat = ChoosePixelFormat(hdc, &pfd);
    SetPixelFormat(hdc, nPixelFormat, &pfd);


    DescribePixelFormat(hdc, nPixelFormat,
                        sizeof(PIXELFORMATDESCRIPTOR),
                        &pfd);

    if(pfd.dwFlags & PFD_NEED_PALETTE)
    {
        nColors = 1 << pfd.cColorBits;
        hHeap = GetProcessHeap();

        lpPalette = (LPLOGPALETTE) HeapAlloc(hHeap, 0,
                        sizeof(LOGPALETTE) + (nColors *
                                    sizeof(PALETTEENTRY)));

        lpPalette->palVersion = 0x300;
        lpPalette->palNumEntries = nColors;

        byRedMask = (1 << pfd.cRedBits) - 1;
        byGreenMask = (1 << pfd.cGreenBits) - 1;
        byBlueMask = (1 << pfd.cBlueBits) - 1;

        for(i = 0; i < nColors; i++)
        {
            lpPalette->palPalEntry[i].peRed =
                (((i >> pfd.cRedShift) & byRedMask) * 255) /
                                            byRedMask;
            lpPalette->palPalEntry[i].peGreen =
                (((i >> pfd.cGreenShift) & byGreenMask) * 255) /
                                            byGreenMask;
            lpPalette->palPalEntry[i].peBlue =
                (((i >> pfd.cBlueShift) & byBlueMask) * 255) /
                                            byBlueMask;
            lpPalette->palPalEntry[i].peFlags = 0;
        }

// Create the palette and free the allocated memory
        m_hPalette = CreatePalette(lpPalette);
        HeapFree(hHeap, 0, lpPalette);

// Realize the color palette
```

continues

Listing 30.1. continued

```
        if(m_hPalette != NULL)
        {
            SelectPalette(hdc, m_hPalette, FALSE);
            RealizePalette(hdc);
        }
    }
}
//------------------------------------------------------------
//  InitRC initializes the current rendering context.

void CTest3dView::InitRC()
{
    GLfloat glfLightAmbient[] = { 0.1f, 0.1f, 0.1f, 1.0f };
    GLfloat glfLightDiffuse[] = { 0.7f, 0.7f, 0.7f, 1.0f };
    GLfloat glfLightSpecular[] = { 0.0f, 0.0f, 0.0f, 1.0f };

// Initialize state variables.

    glFrontFace(GL_CCW);
    glCullFace(GL_BACK);
    glEnable(GL_CULL_FACE);

    glDepthFunc(GL_LEQUAL);
    glEnable(GL_DEPTH_TEST);

// Set background color to white
    glClearColor(1.0f, 1.0f, 1.0f, 0.0f);

// Add lights to the scene.
    glLightfv(GL_LIGHT0, GL_AMBIENT, glfLightAmbient);
    glLightfv(GL_LIGHT0, GL_DIFFUSE, glfLightDiffuse);
    glLightfv(GL_LIGHT0, GL_SPECULAR, glfLightSpecular);
    glEnable(GL_LIGHTING);
    glEnable(GL_LIGHT0);
}
```

Listing 30.2. Functions to draw the 3-D scene.

```
//------------------------------------------------------------
//  CTest3dView:: D r a w C o n e
//
//  DrawCone draws a capped cone around the z axis.
//  The base of the cone is drawn at z=0, the top at z=gldHeight.
//  Note that when base radius equals top radius, the cone
//  becomes a cylinder.

void CTest3dView::DrawCone(GLdouble gldBaseRadius,
                           GLdouble gldTopRadius,
                           GLdouble gldHeight, UINT nSlices)
{
    GLUquadricObj *glquad;

    glquad = gluNewQuadric();
```

```
        gluCylinder(glquad, gldBaseRadius, gldTopRadius,
                    gldHeight, nSlices, 1);

// Draw the end caps for the cone
        gluQuadricOrientation(glquad, GLU_INSIDE);
        gluDisk(glquad, 0.0, gldBaseRadius, nSlices, 1);

        glTranslatef(0.0f, 0.0f, (GLfloat) gldHeight);
        gluQuadricOrientation(glquad, GLU_OUTSIDE);
        gluDisk(glquad, 0.0, gldTopRadius, nSlices, 1);

        gluDeleteQuadric(glquad);
}
//----------------------------------------------------------------
// CTest3dView:: D r a w S p h e r e
//
// Draws a sphere using OpenGL calls.

void CTest3dView::DrawSphere(GLdouble gldRadius,
                             GLint glnSlices, GLint glnStacks)
{
    GLUquadricObj *glquad;

    glquad = gluNewQuadric();
    gluSphere(glquad, gldRadius, glnSlices, glnStacks);
    gluDeleteQuadric(glquad);
}
//----------------------------------------------------------------
// CTest3dView:: D r a w S c e n e
//
// DrawScene uses OpenGL commands to draw a number of
// objects in a scene.

void CTest3dView::DrawScene(UINT nAngle, UINT nBaseAngle)
{
// Define a few colors. In OpenGL, RGB values are specified as
// floating-point numbers between 0.0 and 1.0.

    GLfloat glfBlue[] = { 0.0f, 0.0f, 1.0f, 1.0f };
    GLfloat glfYellow[] = { 1.0f, 1.0f, 0.0f, 1.0f };
    GLfloat glfGreen[] = { 0.0f, 1.0f, 0.0f, 1.0f };
    GLfloat glfRed[] = { 1.0f, 0.0f, 0.0f, 1.0f };
    GLfloat glfCyan[] = { 0.0f, 1.0f, 1.0f, 1.0f };

// Clear the color and depth buffers.
    glClear(GL_COLOR_BUFFER_BIT | GL_DEPTH_BUFFER_BIT);

// Set up the viewpoint
// Note coordinate system is:
//
//          y
//
//          ^
//          |    z-axis points out
//          |
//          |
//          |
//      z (.)----------> x
//
```

continues

Listing 30.2. continued

```
//

    glMatrixMode(GL_MODELVIEW);
    glLoadIdentity();
    glTranslatef(0.0f, 0.0f, -64.0f);
    glRotatef(30.0f, 1.0f, 0.0f, 0.0f);
    glRotatef((GLfloat) nBaseAngle, 0.0f, 1.0f, 0.0f);

// Draw a cylindrical base.

    glPushMatrix();
    glRotatef(90.0f, 1.0f, 0.0f, 0.0f);
    glMaterialfv(GL_FRONT, GL_AMBIENT_AND_DIFFUSE, glfRed);
    DrawCone(6.0, 6.0, 2.0, 24);
    glPopMatrix();

// Next a cylindrical cone on top of the base.
    glPushMatrix();
    glRotatef(-90.0f, 1.0f, 0.0f, 0.0f);
    glMaterialfv(GL_FRONT, GL_AMBIENT_AND_DIFFUSE, glfYellow);
    DrawCone(4.0, 1.0, 4.0, 12);
    glPopMatrix();

// A cylindrical arm
    glPushMatrix();
    glMaterialfv(GL_FRONT, GL_AMBIENT_AND_DIFFUSE, glfBlue);
    glTranslatef(0.0f, 4.0f, 0.0f);
    glRotatef(-((GLfloat) nAngle), 1.0f, 0.0f, 0.0f);
    DrawCone(1.0, 1.0, 10.0, 6);

// Next cylindrical segment
    glRotatef(((GLfloat) nAngle) / 2.0f, 1.0f, 0.0f, 0.0f);
    DrawCone(1.0, 1.0, 10.0, 6);

// A sphere at the end of the second cylindrical segment
    glMaterialfv(GL_FRONT, GL_AMBIENT_AND_DIFFUSE, glfCyan);
    DrawSphere(2.0, 8, 8);
    glPopMatrix();

// Render the scene in the window's DC
    SwapBuffers(wglGetCurrentDC());
}
```

After executing these steps, build the executable TEST3D.EXE and give it a try. Figure 30.4 shows a snapshot of the 3-D scene animated by TEST3D. Try experimenting with the program by replacing the 3-D objects with other OpenGL function calls that draw other 3-D shapes.

FIGURE 30.4.

A snapshot of the scene animated by the TEST3D program.

Summary

The Windows environment is moving from 16-bit to 32-bit—the basic unit of integer variables is changing from 16 to 32 bits. This change has forced us to consider the key aspects of 32-bit programming and how to port existing 16-bit Windows applications to 32-bit Windows, such as Windows NT 3.5 and Windows 95, that support the Win32 application programming interface (API). This chapter starts with an overview of 32-bit programming and provides some guidelines for moving from 16-bit Windows to 32-bit Windows. Descriptions are presented for the new features of Win32 and Windows NT, which is an implementation of Win32.

Finally, the chapter describes how to display 3-D graphics with OpenGL in Windows NT 3.5. An example program shows how to use OpenGL in an MFC application created using Visual C++ 2.0.

VII

Extending Visual C++ 2.0

31

Using MFC 3.0 Database Classes for ODBC Programming

Most business applications access and use databases. In the not-too-distant past, database programming and database management systems (DBMS) were in the realm of mainframe computers. More recently, however, information systems are being implemented using the client-server architecture wherein the data is managed centrally by a server, and users access the data through client systems. PCs running Windows have become a common choice for the client systems. On these systems, you generally find Windows applications that enable the user to access data through graphical front-ends. This is where Open Database Connectivity (ODBC) and the MFC 3.0's database classes come into play.

ODBC provides a way for applications to access data stored in many different databases using the Structured Query Language (SQL, often pronounced as Se-quell) as the standard. ODBC includes several components, one of which is the SQL-based Application Programming Interface (API) that you can use to access and query databases. MFC 3.0 includes database classes that simplify ODBC programming and hide some of the details of SQL that form the basis of the ODBC API.

This chapter briefly describes the ODBC architecture and then shows how to use the ODBC API and MFC 3.0's database classes to write Windows applications that access databases through ODBC.

ODBC and Databases

As the name Open Database Connectivity implies, ODBC provides a common framework for applications accessing many disparate databases using a standard API. Traditionally, database applications have been written to access a specific database, often using an API specific to the database. In recent years, embedded SQL has been used to standardize the application's code. Although embedded SQL makes the application code portable, the source code must be compiled for each database because the usual method for compiling embedded SQL is to use a preprocessor that converts the embedded SQL statements into a database-specific code.

As you will see in the following sections, ODBC uses a layered architecture that isolates applications from database-specific code by providing a standard SQL-based API and placing the database-specific code in ODBC drivers.

ODBC and the Relational Database Model

ODBC's standard view of data is based on the *relational database management system* (RDBMS) where data is organized in tables. The columns in the table represent attributes (such as name, identification number, and salary in an employee database) that apply to the rows. Each row in the table is a database record (for example, the record of a specific employee in an employee database). Figure 31.1 shows how employee information might be organized in a number of tables—note that the employee ID ties the two tables together.

Consistent with the table-oriented view of data, ODBC's API is based on the SQL, which also treats a database as a collection of tables.

FIGURE 31.1.

Employee information organized in tables.

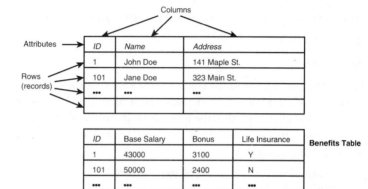

The following standards apply to Structured Query Language (SQL):

■ Database Language—SQL with Integrity Enhancement, American National Standards Institute (ANSI), 1989 ANSI X3.135-1989

■ X/Open and SQL Access Group (SAG) SQL Common Applications Environment (CAE) specification (1992)

■ Database Language—SQL: ANSI X3H2 and ISO/IEC JTC1/SC21/WG3 9075:1992 (SQL-92) (the latest SQL standard)

In addition to these standards and the SQL guides that accompany most databases, there are many books that describe SQL including C. J. Dates *A Guide to the SQL Standard*, published by Addison-Wesley in 1989—a following classic reference on SQL.

SQL and Call Level Interface

Because SQL plays an important role in ODBC, this section provides a brief description of SQL. SQL originated from the relational data model, which is based on organizing data into tables. By now, SQL is a widely accepted industry standard for defining, manipulating, and managing tables. Even databases that do not use the relational data model support SQL.

A Taste of SQL

SQL is not a programming language. It lacks flow control (such as the `if-else` statements in C++). Essentially, SQL provides operators for manipulating tables. For example, the SQL `SELECT` statement queries tables with the following general syntax:

```
SELECT attributes
FROM table1, table2, ...
WHERE condition
```

Here, `attributes` refers to the columns you want to retrieve from the tables (identified by the names `table1, table2, ...`). The `FROM` clause identifies the tables with the specified columns, and the `WHERE` clause specifies the rows you want to see. The `SELECT` query returns the rows for which the `condition` is true. Here is a typical query from a database (with two tables named `employees` and `benefits`):

```
SELECT employees.name, benefits.base_salary
FROM employees, benefits
WHERE employees.id = benefits.id
and benefits.base_salary > 45000
```

The `SELECT` statement can have many other clauses, such as `GROUP BY` and `ORDER BY`.

1989 SQL Standard

SQL was first standardized by the American National Standards Institute (ANSI) in 1986. In the first ANSI standard, SQL was defined as a query language independent of any programming language. In the 1989 revision of the ANSI standard for SQL, three programming interfaces were defined:

- *Module language* enables the definition of procedures in compiled programs (modules). These procedures are then called from programs written in traditional programming languages.
- *Embedded SQL* enables SQL statements to be placed directly inside a program written in a standard programming language. The 1989 SQL standard defines embedded statements for COBOL, FORTRAN, Pascal, and PL/1.
- *Direct invocation* provides access that is implementation-dependent.

Embedded SQL has been the most popular programming interface for applications that need to access databases with SQL. The 1989 SQL standard supported the embedding of static SQL statements; the 1992 SQL standard enables embedding of dynamic SQL. These are briefly described in the following sections.

1992 SQL Standard

The 1992 SQL standard (or SQL-92, for short) is the most recent ANSI standard for SQL. SQL-92 is now an international standard adopted by the International Standards Organization (ISO). SQL-92 defines three levels of functionality:

- Entry
- Intermediate
- Full

SQL-92 added many new features to the 1989 SQL standard, including the following:

- Additional data types such as date and time
- The notion of a connection to a database environment to address the needs of client-server architectures
- Support for dynamic SQL so that applications can generate and execute SQL statements at runtime
- Scrollable cursors (that keep track of records) for access to result sets (available only in the full level of functionality)
- Outer joins that enable you to combine rows from two tables regardless of whether there is a matching row between the tables (available only in intermediate and full levels of functionality)

Embedded SQL

Databases supporting SQL offer an interactive mode where the user can use SQL statements to access the data. Applications, however, need another way to send SQL statements to the DBMS. Embedded SQL enables you to place SQL statements into a program written in a standard programming language, such as COBOL, Pascal, or FORTRAN (you can have embedded SQL statements in C and C++ as well, but these were not part of the SQL standard). The SQL standard refers to the programming language used to write the application as the *host language*.

The embedded SQL approach is to use specific starting and ending statements of the host language to delimit SQL statements placed in an application's source code. Source files with embedded SQL statements are compiled in a two-step process:

1. A precompiler translates the SQL statements into equivalent host language source code.
2. The host language compiler compiles the resulting source code.

Static SQL

The ANSI 1989 SQL standard enabled embedding of static SQL statements only. Embedding static SQL statements is executed as follows:

- Define each SQL statement as well as the number of result columns and their data types within the program source code.

■ Host variables (that are fully defined prior to compilation) are accessible to both the host-language code and to SQL statements. However, host variables cannot be used for table names or column names.

■ For SQL statements that are expected to return more than one row of data, define a cursor that points to one row of results at a time.

■ Declare standard data storage areas for status and error information.

Static SQL requires definition of all SQL statements before the application runs. This approach is efficient because all SQL statements can be precompiled prior to execution and run multiple times without recompiling. However, there are drawbacks to static SQL:

■ Because the table names and column names are fixed, the application becomes bound to a particular DBMS when it is compiled.

■ The application cannot create queries on-the-fly and provide the flexibility needed in client-server architecture where there is often a need to connect to a database dynamically.

Dynamic SQL

The most recent ANSI specification, SQL-92, includes dynamic SQL, which enables an application to generate and execute SQL statements at runtime. SQL-92 supports the notion of a database environment that is responsible for handling dynamic SQL statements. When a SQL statement is prepared at runtime, the database environment generates an access plan and a description of the result set. To retain the efficiency advantages of static SQL, a dynamic SQL statement can be executed multiple times with the previously generated access plan, thus minimizing the processing overhead of parsing and generating the access plan.

Dynamic SQL statements can accept arguments. When embedding a dynamic SQL statement, the arguments are in the form of host variables to which you assign values prior to executing the SQL statement. Although dynamic SQL is not as efficient as static SQL, it is very useful because it enables an application to do the following:

■ Construct SQL statements at runtime

■ Connect to a database at runtime

Call Level Interface

Although embedded SQL (especially with support for dynamic SQL statements) provides a powerful mechanism for writing database applications, embedded SQL does not provide a standard callable API. The Call Level Interface (CLI) for SQL consists of a library of functions that support execution of dynamic SQL statements. As you will learn in later sections of this chapter, the ODBC API is a CLI for SQL.

The industry standards groups X/Open and SQL Access Group's SQL Common Application Environment (CAE) specification (1992) are defining a CLI for SQL that is straightforward to use because of the function call interface. The function call interface does not require concepts from embedded SQL such as host variables or need for a precompiler.

The SQL CLI enables you to place a SQL statement in a text buffer and execute that SQL statement by providing the text buffer as an argument in a function call. The CLI function's return values indicate the status of execution of the submitted SQL statement.

ODBC Overview

Figure 31.2 illustrates the ODBC architecture that enables you to write a database application capable of accessing any database for which an ODBC driver is available. ODBC makes the application independent of the specific details of the database by providing an API that presents a standard table-oriented view of the underlying data, regardless of how the data is actually stored in the database.

FIGURE 31.2.
ODBC architecture.

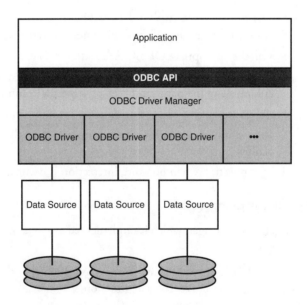

The ODBC architecture consists of the following major components:

■ *ODBC Applications* store and retrieve data by calling the ODBC API functions. Usually, applications process and display the data in various formats that make the data more useful to the user.

■ *ODBC API* provides a standard set of functions that applications can call to access data. The access method is similar to that provided by SQL.

■ *ODBC driver manager* loads drivers on behalf of the application.

■ *ODBC driver* is a Dynamic Link Library (DLL) that processes ODBC function calls, sends SQL statements to a specific database, and returns results to the application. If the DBMS does not support SQL, the driver translates the SQL statements into requests that conform to the syntax supported by the DBMS.

■ *Data sources* represent the files or database tables accessed by a driver.

ODBC Applications

Here, the term "ODBC applications" refers to applications that use the ODBC API to access a database. Typically, such applications provide a front-end through which the user accesses and views data stored in a database. The application performs the following basic steps to get the data:

1. Connect to a data source by calling appropriate API functions.

2. Process SQL statements as follows:

   a. Prepare text buffer with SQL statement.

   b. Assign a cursor name if the SQL statement returns a result set.

   c. Call the appropriate ODBC API function to execute the statement.

   d. If necessary, inquire about the attributes of the result set such as the number of columns and the name and type of a specific column.

   e. Assign storage for each column in the result set and fetch the results.

   f. In case of error, retrieve error information from the driver and take appropriate action.

2. End the connection when no more interaction is needed with the data source.

ODBC Driver Manager

The ODBC Driver Manager, which is implemented as a dynamic link library (DLL), performs the following tasks:

■ Load an ODBC driver DLL when the application calls the `SQLBrowseConnect`, `SQLConnect`, or `SQLDriverConnect` function.

■ Process some ODBC API calls such as `SQLDataSources` and `SQLDrivers` (that are generally for information requests) wihout passing them on to the driver.

■ Pass ODBC API calls to the appropriate driver.

■ Perform some error checking.

■ Optionally, log function ODBC API calls made by applications.

ODBC Drivers

An ODBC driver is a DLL that implements the ODBC API functions and interacts with a data source. The ODBC driver performs the following typical functions in response to an application's calls to the ODBC API functions:

- Establish a connection to a specified data source.
- Submit data storage and retrieval requests to the data source.
- If necessary, declare and manipulate cursors.
- If necessary, translate data to or from other formats.
- In case of error, return standard error codes to the application.
- Return result sets to the application.

There are two basic types of ODBC drivers:

- *Single-tier* drivers process both ODBC calls and the SQL statements. Such drivers are used when the data source does not directly support SQL.
- *Multiple-tier* drivers process only the ODBC calls and pass the SQL statements to the data source. Multitier drivers are used when the data source supports SQL or there is a separate SQL engine available to handle the SQL requests.

Data Sources

A data source is an abstraction of the data that a user wants to access. A data source can be a database file with a number of tables or a directory with a number of text files, for example. A sophisticated data source might be a DBMS with a SQL front-end. The amount of work done by an ODBC driver depends on the sophistication of the data source. If a data source is a file, the driver has to act as the DBMS, but if the data source is a DBMS, the driver merely acts as an agent transferring SQL requests to the data source.

ODBC Conformance Levels

ODBC drivers are expected to follow specified conformance levels in two areas:

- *ODBC SQL grammar,* which defines the standard SQL data types and the syntax for SQL statements supported by the driver
- *ODBC API,* which defines the set of functions that applications can call

Applications can use the conformance levels to determine the standard sets of functionality that a driver provides. Although applications may check for the conformance level of a driver, Microsoft encourages application developers to determine the exact functionality supported by a driver by calling `SQLGetInfo`, `SQLGetFunctions`, and `SQLGetTypeInfo`. This is necessary because an ODBC driver may not fully conform to a level, but implement some functionality at that level instead.

SQL Conformance Levels

ODBC defines three levels of conformance to the SQL grammar:

- *Minimum SQL Grammar* requires support for the following:
    - Data Definition: CREATE TABLE and DROP TABLE statements
    - Data Manipulation: simple SELECT, INSERT, UPDATE SEARCHED, and DELETE SEARCHED statements.
    - Expressions: simple expressions, such as X > Y + Z
    - Data types: CHAR, VARCHAR, or LONG VARCHAR
- *Core SQL Grammar* roughly corresponds to the X/Open and SAG CAE specification of 1992. Conformance to the core grammar requires the following:
    - Support for the Minimum SQL grammar and data types
    - Data Definition: ALTER TABLE, CREATE INDEX, DROP INDEX, CREATE VIEW, DROP VIEW, GRANT, and REVOKE statements
    - Data Management: complete syntax of the SELECT statement
    - Expressions: subquery and set functions, such as SUM and MIN
    - Data types: DECIMAL, NUMERIC, SMALLINT, INTEGER, REAL, FLOAT, DOUBLE PRECISION
- *Extended SQL Grammar* provides for some common extensions to SQL. Conformance to the extended SQL grammar requires the following:
    - Support for Minimum and Core SQL grammar and data types
    - Data Management: outer joins, positioned UPDATE, positioned DELETE, SELECT FOR UPDATE, and unions

API Conformance Levels

The ODBC API has three conformance levels: Core, Level 1, and Level 2, which are summarized in the following list:

- Core ODBC API corresponds to the functions in the X/Open and SAG CLI specification. Core API conformance provides functions to execute the following:
    - Allocate environment, connection, and statement handles and free these handles
    - Connect to one or more data sources and use one or more SQL statements on a connection
    - Prepare and execute SQL statements (if necessary, immediately)
    - Assign storage for parameters in a SQL statement and the result columns
    - Retrieve information about a result set and retrieve data from a result set
    - Commit or roll back transactions
    - Retrieve error information

- Level 1 ODBC API provides extended capability beyond the Core API. Conformance to the Level 1 API includes functions to execute the following:
    - Support Core API capability
    - Connect to data sources with driver-specific dialog boxes
    - Set values of options for statement and connection handles and inquire about these values
    - Send part of a parameter value to a data source, which is a useful capability to have for lengthy data types
    - Retrieve part of a column value from a result set
    - Retrieve catalog information (such as table names and column names) about a data source
    - Retrieve information about driver and data source capabilities, such as supported data types, scalar functions, and ODBC API functions
- Level 2 ODBC API provides further extensions beyond the Level 1 API. Conformance to the Level 2 API implies availability of functions to execute the following:
    - Support Core and Level 1 API capabilities
    - Browse information about a connection to a data source and list available data sources
    - Send arrays of parameter values and retrieve arrays of column values from a result set
    - Retrieve the number of parameters and descriptions of individual parameters
    - Use a scrollable cursor
    - Retrieve the form of a SQL statement as presented by the driver to the data source
    - Retrieve catalog information about privileges, keys, and procedures
    - Call a translation DLL to convert data from one format to another

ODBC API

The ODBC API consists of a function library that provides a standard SQL syntax (based on the X/Open and SQL Access Group's SQL CAE specification of 1992) for accessing data from a variety of data sources. Each ODBC API function has a name that starts with the SQL prefix. Visual C++ programs that call ODBC functions must include the SQL.H and SQLEXT.H header files so that various data types, constants, and function prototypes are defined properly.

The ODBC provides considerable flexibility because you can do the following:

- Create and execute strings containing SQL statements on the fly at runtime
- Use the same program to access different databases

■ Ignore underlying data communications protocols between the application and the DBMS

■ Send and receive data values in a format convenient to the application

There are two broad categories of ODBC API functions:

■ *Core functions* that conform to the X/Open and SQL Access Group (SAG) Call Level Interface (CLI) specification for SQL

■ *Extended functions* that were added by Microsoft to provide additional functionality, such as scrollable cursors and asynchronous processing; there are two levels of extended functions: *Level 1* and *Level 2*.

Table 31.1 lists the ODBC API functions grouped by task. The table also briefly describes each function and shows the conformance level (Core, Level 1, or Level 2) of the function.

Because an ODBC driver's level of conformance to the SAG CLI specification may vary, the application should call the SQLGetInfo function to obtain conformance information about a driver. To obtain information about a driver's support for a specific function, the application can call SQLGetFunctions.

Table 31.1. ODBC API functions grouped by task.

Function	Conformance	Description
Connecting to Data Source		
SQLAllocConnect	Core	Returns a connection handle.
SQLAllocEnv	Core	Returns an environment handle that can be used for one or more connections.
SQLBrowseConnect	Level 2	Returns successive levels of connection attributes and valid attribute values. After a value has been specified for each connection attribute, this function connects to the data source identified by the attribute values.
SQLConnect	Core	Connects to a data source identified by name, user ID (optional), and password (optional).
SQLDriverConnect	Level 1	Connects to a specific driver identified by a connection string or requests that the Driver Manager and driver display connection dialog boxes for the user.
Retrieving Information About Driver and Data Source		
SQLDataSources	Level 2	Returns Data Source Names (DSNs) identifying the available data sources.

Function	Conformance	Description
SQLDrivers	Level 2	Returns descriptions of installed drivers and their attributes.
SQLGetFunctions	Level 1	Returns information about API functions supported by driver.
SQLGetInfo	Level 1	Returns information about a specific driver and data source.
SQLGetTypeInfo	Level 1	Returns information about SQL data types supported by the driver.
Setting and Retrieving Driver Options		
SQLGetConnectOption	Level 1	Returns the current setting of a connection option.
SQLGetStmtOption	Level 1	Returns the current setting of a statement option.
SQLSetConnectOption	Level 1	Sets an option for a connection.
SQLSetStmtOption	Level 1	Sets an option for a SQL statement.
Preparing SQL Statements		
SQLAllocStmt	Core	Allocates a handle for a SQL statement.
SQLBindParameter	Level 1	Associates a buffer to a parameter marker in a SQL statement.
SQLGetCursorName	Core	Returns the name of a cursor associated with a statement handle.
SQLParamOptions	Level 2	Specifies multiple values for the set of parameters assigned by SQLBindParameter.
SQLPrepare	Core	Prepares a SQL statement for execution.
SQLSetCursorName	Core	Associates a cursor name with an active statement handle.
SQLSetScrollOptions	Level 2	Sets options that control the behavior of a cursor.
Submitting SQL Statements		
SQLDescribeParam	Level 2	Returns the description of a parameter marker in a statement.
SQLExecDirect	Core	Executes a statement.
SQLExecute	Core	Executes a prepared SQL statement.
SQLNativeSql	Level 2	Returns the SQL statement as translated by the driver.

continues

Table 31.1. continued

Function	Conformance	Description
Submitting SQL Statements		
SQLNumParams	Level 2	Returns the number of parameters in a statement.
SQLParamData	Level 1	Used with SQLPutData to supply parameter value at the time of executing a SQL statement.
SQLPutData	Level 1	Sends all or part of a parameter value. (Useful for lengthy parameter values.)
Retrieving Results and Information About Results		
SQLBindCol	Core	Associates a buffer with a column in a result set and specifies the data type.
SQLColAttributes	Core	Returns information about a column in a result set.
SQLDescribeCol	Core	Returns the descriptor—column name, type, precision, scale, and nullability—for a column in a result set.
SQLError	Core	Returns error or status information.
SQLExtendedFetch	Level 2	Returns multiple rows for a result set.
SQLFetch	Core	Returns a row of data from a result set.
SQLGetData	Level 1	Returns all or part of result data for a single column in the current row of a result set (useful for lengthy data values).
SQLMoreResults	Level 2	Determines whether there are more results available on a statement containing SELECT, UPDATE, INSERT, or DELETE requests and, if so, initializes processing for those results.
SQLNumResultCols	Core	Returns the number of columns in a result set.
SQLRowCount	Core	Returns the number of rows affected by an UPDATE, INSERT, or DELETE statement.
SQLSetPos	Level 2	Positions a cursor within a block of data.
Obtaining Catalog Information		
SQLColumnPrivileges	Level 2	Returns a list of column names and the associated privileges for a specified table.
SQLColumns	Level 1	Returns the list of column names in the specified tables.

Function	Conformance	Description
SQLForeignKeys	Level 2	Returns a list of foreign keys (columns in the table that refer to primary keys in other tables) in a specified table.
SQLPrimaryKeys	Level 2	Returns the column names that comprise the primary key for a table.
SQLProcedureColumns	Level 2	Returns the list of input and output parameters and the columns of the result set for the specified procedures.
SQLProcedures	Level 2	Returns the list of procedure names stored in a specific data source.
SQLSpecialColumns	Level 1	Returns information about the optimal set of columns that uniquely identifies a row in a specified table or the columns that are automatically updated when any value in the row is updated by a transaction.
SQLStatistics	Level 1	Returns a list of statistics about a single table and the list of indexes associated with the table.
SQLTablePrivileges	Level 2	Returns a list of tables and the privileges associated with each table.
SQLTables	Level 1	Returns a list of table names associated with a specific data source.
Terminating a Statement		
SQLCancel	Core	Cancels the processing of a SQL statement.
SQLFreeStmt	Core	Stops processing of a specific SQL statement, closes any open cursors associated with the statement, discards pending results, and (if requested) frees all resources associated with the statement handle.
SQLTransact	Core	Performs a commit or rollback operation for all active operations on all SQL statements associated with a connection.
Terminating a Connection		
SQLDisconnect	Core	Closes the connection (identified by a connection handle).

continues

Table 31.1. continued

Function	Conformance	Description
Terminating a Connection		
SQLFreeConnect	Core	Releases a specified connection handle and frees all memory associated with the handle.
SQLFreeEnv	Core	Releases a specified environment handle and frees all memory associated with the environment handle.

Steps in an ODBC Application

A typical ODBC application performs the following sequence of steps when accessing a database and executing a SQL query:

1. Allocate the environment.
2. Allocate the connect handle.
3. Connect to a data source.
4. Allocate the statement handle.
5. Set up the SQL statement and execute the statement.
6. Retrieve the result.
7. Free the statement handle.
8. Disconnect from the data source.
9. Free the connection handle.
10. Free the environment.

In C++ pseudocode, this sequence of steps can be presented as follows:

```
HENV  hEnv;
HDBC  hDbc;
HSTMT hStmt;

SQLAllocEnv(&hEnv);
    SQLAllocConnect(hEnv, &hDbc);
    SQLConnect(hDbc, szDSN, cbDSN, ...);

        SQLAllocStmt(hDbc, &hStmt);

        // Set up SQL statement and execute
        SQLExecuteDirect(hStmt, szSqlStr, cbSqlStr);

        // Bind variables to each column
        SQLNumResultCols(hStmt, &nCols);

        for each column
        {
```

```
            SQLDescribeCol(hStmt, icol, szColName, ...);
            SQLBindCol(hStmt, icol, ...);
        }

        // Retrieve the rows
        while(SQLFetch(hStmt) != SQL_NO_DATA_FOUND)
        {
            // Process the column variables...
        }

        // Clean up...
        SQLFreeStmt(hStmt, SQL_DROP);

    SQLDisConnect(hDbc);
    SQLFreeConnect(hDbc);
SQLFreeEnv(hEnv);
```

Calling the ODBC API from MFC Applications

Although the Microsoft Foundation Classes include several classes that encapsulate the ODBC API, you can call ODBC API functions directly from an MFC application (in fact from any C++ program). The following sections show simple examples of using the ODBC API directly in sample programs built using the MFC application framework.

DBSRC—Finding the Data Sources

Let's start with a simple example that gets the names of the data sources that are currently known to the ODBC driver manager. To create the example program, follow these steps:

1. Use MFC AppWizard to generate a single-document interface application named DBSRC based on AppWizard's document-view model. Select the checkbox labeled Only include header files in step 2 of the AppWizard dialog where you have to respond to the level of database support the application needs. This ensures that the required ODBC header files are included (otherwise, you have to include SQL.H and SQLEXT.H header files directly in STDAFX.H).

2. Add the ODBC calls in the body of the OnNewDocument function in the document class(CDbsrcDoc in file DBSRCDOC.CPP) so that opening a new document is equivalent to getting the names of data sources. The steps in getting the data source names require allocating an environment and calling the SQLDataSources function. You store the data source names in a CStringList (a list of CString objects) member variable (named m_strList) in the document class. Here is the code for the OnNewDocument function of the document class:

```
BOOL CDbsrcDoc::OnNewDocument()
{
    if (!CDocument::OnNewDocument())
        return FALSE;
```

```
// Remove all elements from list (RemoveAll does not
// generate error if list is already empty)

    m_strList.RemoveAll();


// Allocate SQL environment

    HENV hEnv;
    if(SQLAllocEnv(&hEnv) != SQL_SUCCESS)
        return FALSE;

    CString sDSN;
    SWORD   cbDSN;
    UCHAR   szDescr[256];
    SWORD   cbDescr;
    RETCODE ret;

// Get the names of data sources by calling
// SQLGetSources in a loop

    while(1)
    {
        ret = SQLDataSources(hEnv, SQL_FETCH_NEXT,
                    (UCHAR*)sDSN.GetBuffer(40), 40, &cbDSN,
                    szDescr, 256, &cbDescr);

        if(ret == SQL_ERROR ¦¦ ret == SQL_NO_DATA_FOUND)
            break;

        sDSN.ReleaseBuffer();
        m_strList.AddTail(sDSN);
    }

// Free the environment
    SQLFreeEnv(hEnv);

    return TRUE;
}
```

3. Declare the member variable m_strList and provide an access function in the document class. Add the lines shown in boldface to the declaration of the document class (CDbsrcDoc in file DBSRCDOC.H):

```
class CDbsrcDoc : public CDocument
{
//...
public:
    CStringList& GetStringList() { return m_strList;}

protected:
    CStringList m_strList;

//...
};
```

4. In the OnDraw function of the view class (CDbsrcView), retrieve the CStringList and display each CString by calling the text output function, TextOut. Here is the OnDraw class from the file DBSRCVW.CPP:

```
void CDbsrcView::OnDraw(CDC* pDC)
{
    CDbsrcDoc* pDoc = GetDocument();
    ASSERT_VALID(pDoc);

    CStringList& strList = pDoc->GetStringList();
    int x = 8, y = 10;

    if(strList.IsEmpty())
    {
        CString msg("No data source found!");
        pDC->TextOut(x, y, msg);
        return;
    }

    TEXTMETRIC tm;
    pDC->GetTextMetrics(&tm);
    int nLineHeight = tm.tmHeight + tm.tmExternalLeading;

    POSITION posNext = strList.GetHeadPosition();
    while(posNext != NULL)
    {
        CString str = strList.GetNext(posNext);
        pDC->TextOut(x, y, str);
        y += nLineHeight;
    }
}
```

5. Build the DBSRC.EXE program and run it. Figure 31.3 shows a typical output (the names of the data sources appear as you typed them when adding the data source, so these names depend on the data sources that you explicitly added using the ODBC control panel application).

ADDING ODBC DATA SOURCES

You have to add data sources before an application using the ODBC API can access the data. To add a data source, start the Control Panel and double-click on the 32-bit ODBC icon. Click on the Add button, select an installed ODBC driver, then enter information about a data source (such as the name of a Microsoft Access or dBASE file) from the driver-specific dialog that appears.

FIGURE 31.3.

Listing the names of available data sources.

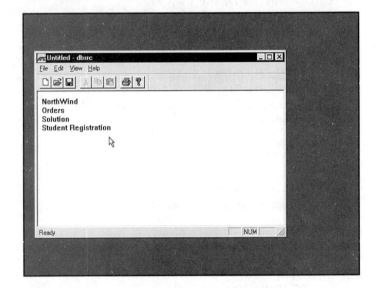

DBINFO—Getting Information About Tables and Columns

The next example goes a step beyond DBSRC, which merely lists the names of available data sources. DBINFO is a dialog-based MFC application that enables you to browse the tables in a data source and view the names and data types of the columns in a selected table. Figure 31.4 shows the main dialog window of the DBINFO program. As Figure 31.4 shows, the dialog box consists of three listboxes that display data source names, table names, and column names from left to right, in that order. The basic idea behind the DBINFO application is as follows:

■ When DBINFO starts, it fills the leftmost listbox with the names of available data sources.

■ When the user selects the name of a data source, Windows sends an `LBN_SELCHANGE` event to the parent of the listbox. You install a handler for this event and in that handler, connect to the selected data source, get the names of the tables (by calling `SQLTables`), and fill the middle listbox with names of the tables.

■ When the user selects the name of a table, you can again connect to the current data source, get the names of the columns (by calling `SQLColumns`) for the currently selected table, and fill the rightmost listbox with the names of the columns in the selected table. You also can provide information about the data type of the columns because the `SQLColumns` function returns this information.

Thus, DBINFO enables the user to select a data source, then select a table, and view the names of the columns in the selected table. The rightmost listbox in Figure 31.4 shows the names of the columns (and their types) for the Catalog table of the NorthWind data source (this happens to be a sample database that comes with Microsoft Access 2.0, but you can try the program with any other data source that may be available on your system).

FIGURE 31.4.

DBINFO displaying the columns of a selected table in a data source.

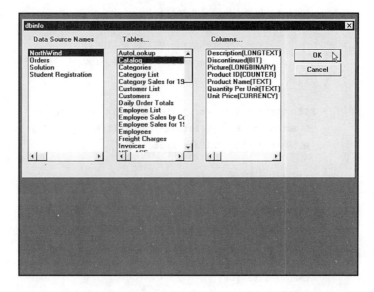

To implement DBINFO, generate a dialog-based application in Visual C++ 2.0. After MFC AppWizard generates the DBINFO.MAK project, make the following changes to build the program:

1. Design the dialog box (see Figure 31.4) by editing the resource file DBINFO.RC.

2. Add the following lines to STDAFX.H (these header files are necessary when you call ODBC functions):

```
#include <sql.h>
#include <sqlext.h>
```

3. Modify the OnInitDialog function by adding the lines shown in boldface:

```
BOOL CDbinfoDlg::OnInitDialog()
{
    CDialog::OnInitDialog();
    CenterWindow();

    // Add "About..." menu item to system menu.

    // IDM_ABOUTBOX must be in the system command range.
    ASSERT((IDM_ABOUTBOX & 0xFFF0) == IDM_ABOUTBOX);
    ASSERT(IDM_ABOUTBOX < 0xF000);

    CMenu* pSysMenu = GetSystemMenu(FALSE);
    CString strAboutMenu;
    strAboutMenu.LoadString(IDS_ABOUTBOX);
    if (!strAboutMenu.IsEmpty())
    {
        pSysMenu->AppendMenu(MF_SEPARATOR);
        pSysMenu->AppendMenu(MF_STRING, IDM_ABOUTBOX, strAboutMenu);
    }

// Fill the first listbox with names of data sources
    CListBox *pLB = (CListBox*)GetDlgItem(IDC_LIST1);
    pLB->SetHorizontalExtent(800);

// Allocate SQL environment

    HENV hEnv;
    if(SQLAllocEnv(&hEnv) != SQL_SUCCESS)
        return FALSE;

    char    szDSN[60];
    SWORD   cbDSN;
    UCHAR   szDescr[256];
    SWORD   cbDescr;
    RETCODE ret;

// Get the names of data sources by calling
// SQLGetSources in a loop

    while(1)
```

```
    {
        ret = SQLDataSources(hEnv, SQL_FETCH_NEXT,
                        (UCHAR*)szDSN, 60, &cbDSN,
                        szDescr, 256, &cbDescr);

        if(ret == SQL_ERROR ¦¦ ret == SQL_NO_DATA_FOUND)
            break;

        pLB->AddString(szDSN);
    }


// Free the environment
    SQLFreeEnv(hEnv);



    return TRUE;  // return TRUE  unless you set the focus to a control
}
```

4. Using ClassWizard, add a handler for the LBN_SELCHANGE event for the leftmost listbox (whose ID is IDC_LIST1) and define it as follows:

```
void CDbinfoDlg::OnSelchangeList1()
{
// User has selected a different data source name.
// Update the list of table names

// Clear the table name and column name listboxes
    CListBox *pLBTN = (CListBox*)GetDlgItem(IDC_LIST2);
    pLBTN->ResetContent();
    pLBTN->SetHorizontalExtent(1280);

    CListBox *pLBCN = (CListBox*)GetDlgItem(IDC_LIST3);
    pLBCN->ResetContent();
    pLBCN->SetHorizontalExtent(1280);

    HENV hEnv;
    if(SQLAllocEnv(&hEnv) != SQL_SUCCESS)
        return;

    CListBox *pLB = (CListBox*)GetDlgItem(IDC_LIST1);
    char  szDSN[120];
    int   cbDSN;
    cbDSN = pLB->GetText(pLB->GetCurSel(), szDSN);
```

```
// Connect to selected data source
   HDBC hDbc;
   if(SQLAllocConnect(hEnv, &hDbc) != SQL_SUCCESS) return;

   int ret;

   ret = SQLConnect(hDbc, (UCHAR*)szDSN, cbDSN,
                    NULL, 0, NULL, 0);
   if(ret == SQL_SUCCESS || ret == SQL_SUCCESS_WITH_INFO)
   {
// Get names of tables and populate the second listbox

// Allocate a statement handle
       HSTMT hStmt;
       if(SQLAllocStmt(hDbc, &hStmt) == SQL_SUCCESS)
       {
// Call SQLTables to get the table names

           UCHAR any[] = "%";
           ret = SQLTables(hStmt, NULL, 0, NULL, 0,
                           any, 1, NULL, 0);
           if(ret == SQL_SUCCESS ||
              ret == SQL_SUCCESS_WITH_INFO)
           {
// Get the result, which is in the form of a table with
// the following columns:
//
//      1              2              3              4              5
//   TABLE_QUALIFIER, TABLE_OWNER, TABLE_NAME, TABLE_TYPE, REMARKS
//
// So, column 3 is the table's name—it's of type Varchar(128)

               char szTName[128];
               SDWORD cbTName;
               ret = SQLBindCol(hStmt, 3, SQL_C_CHAR,
                                szTName, 128, &cbTName);
               if(ret == SQL_SUCCESS ||
                  ret == SQL_SUCCESS_WITH_INFO)
               {
                   while(SQLFetch(hStmt) != SQL_NO_DATA_FOUND)
                   {
                       pLBTN->AddString(szTName);
```

```
                                }
                        }
                }
// Free the statement
                SQLFreeStmt(hStmt, SQL_DROP);
        }
    }
    else
    {
        char szMsg[80];
        wsprintf(szMsg, "Error connecting to: %s", szDSN);
        pLBTN->AddString(szMsg);
        SQLFreeConnect(hDbc);
        return;
    }


// Disconnect and free connection handle
    SQLDisconnect(hDbc);
    SQLFreeConnect(hDbc);


// Free the environment
    SQLFreeEnv(hEnv);
}
```

5. Using ClassWizard, add a handler for the LBN_SELCHANGE event for the middle listbox (whose ID is IDC_LIST2) and define it as follows:

```
void CDbinfoDlg::OnSelchangeList2()
{
// User has selected a different table name.
// Update the lists of column names

// Clear the column name listbox
    CListBox *pLBCN = (CListBox*)GetDlgItem(IDC_LIST3);
    pLBCN->ResetContent();

    HENV hEnv;
    if(SQLAllocEnv(&hEnv) != SQL_SUCCESS)
        return;

// Start by connecting to currently selected table

    CListBox *pLB = (CListBox*)GetDlgItem(IDC_LIST1);
```

```
      char  szDSN[120];
      int   cbDSN;
      cbDSN = pLB->GetText(pLB->GetCurSel(), szDSN);

// Connect to selected data source
      HDBC hDbc;
      if(SQLAllocConnect(hEnv, &hDbc) != SQL_SUCCESS) return;

      int ret;

      ret = SQLConnect(hDbc, (UCHAR*)szDSN, cbDSN,
                       NULL, 0, NULL, 0);
      if(ret == SQL_SUCCESS ¦¦ ret == SQL_SUCCESS_WITH_INFO)
      {
// Get the name of the currently selected table
          CListBox *pLBTN = (CListBox*)GetDlgItem(IDC_LIST2);
          char  szTN[128];
          int   cbTN;
          cbTN = pLBTN->GetText(pLBTN->GetCurSel(), szTN);


// Get column names for this table
// First, allocate a statement handle
          HSTMT hStmt;
          if(SQLAllocStmt(hDbc, &hStmt) == SQL_SUCCESS)
          {
// Call SQLColumns to get the column names

              UCHAR any[] = "%";
              ret = SQLColumns(hStmt, NULL, 0, NULL, 0,
                               (UCHAR*)szTN, SQL_NTS, NULL, 0);
              if(ret == SQL_SUCCESS ¦¦
                 ret == SQL_SUCCESS_WITH_INFO)
              {
// The result itself is in the form of a table with
// the following columns:
//
//    1              2           3           4
//  TABLE_QUALIFIER, TABLE_OWNER, TABLE_NAME, COLUMN_NAME,
//
//    5         6        7          8        9
//  DATA_TYPE, TYPE_NAME, PRECISION, LENGTH, SCALE,
//
```

```
//    10         11        12
//  RADIX,  NULLABLE, REMARKS
//
// So, column 4 is the column name—it's of type Varchar(128) and
// column 6 is the name of the column's data type.
// Bind variables to these columns and call SQLFetch to get their
// values.

                char szCName[128], szCType[128], szNT[256];
                SDWORD cbCName, cbCType;
                int ret1 = SQLBindCol(hStmt, 4, SQL_C_CHAR,
                                szCName, 128, &cbCName);
                int ret2 = SQLBindCol(hStmt, 6, SQL_C_CHAR,
                                szCType, 128, &cbCType);

                if((ret1 == SQL_SUCCESS ¦¦
                   ret1 == SQL_SUCCESS_WITH_INFO) &&
                   (ret2 == SQL_SUCCESS ¦¦
                   ret2 == SQL_SUCCESS_WITH_INFO))
                {
                    int ret3 = SQLFetch(hStmt);
                    while(1)
                    {
                        if(ret3 == SQL_STILL_EXECUTING) continue;

                        ret3 = SQLFetch(hStmt);
                        if(ret3 == SQL_NO_DATA_FOUND) break;

                        wsprintf(szNT, "%s(%s)",
                                szCName, szCType);
                        pLBCN->AddString(szNT);
                    }
                }
            }
        }
        else
        {
            char szMsg[80];
            wsprintf(szMsg, "SQLTables: Error return %d",
                    ret);
            pLBCN->AddString(szMsg);
            wsprintf(szMsg, "Cannot get columns for: %s",
                    szTN);
```

```
                        pLBCN->AddString(szMsg);
                }
// Free the statement
                SQLFreeStmt(hStmt, SQL_DROP);
            }
        }
        else
        {
            char szMsg[80];
            wsprintf(szMsg, "Error connecting to: %s", szDSN);
            pLBCN->AddString(szMsg);
            SQLFreeConnect(hDbc);
            return;
        }

// Disconnect and free connection handle
        SQLDisconnect(hDbc);
        SQLFreeConnect(hDbc);

// Free the environment
        SQLFreeEnv(hEnv);
}
```

6. Build the DBINFO.EXE program and run it. Figure 31.4 shows a sample output from DBINFO.

Accessing Results Returned by ODBC API Functions

An aspect of the DBINFO program that is worth studying is the way you retrieve the results returned by the ODBC API functions. Whether you are submitting a database query or using an API function to determine the structure of a database, the results are themselves organized in a table, and there is a specific procedure for retrieving individual rows from this result table (often called the result set). For example, in DBINFO, when we call SQLTables, the information about the tables is in a table with five columns:

TABLE_QUALIFIER, TABLE_OWNER, TABLE_NAME, TABLE_TYPE, REMARKS

Each row of this table will have information about a table in the database. When retrieving information from the result set, follow these steps:

1. Allocate storage for each column that you want to retrieve. You can call SQLDescribeCol to obtain information about the data type of each column. In some cases, such as the tables returned by SQLTables and SQLColumns, you can find out information about the column types from the function's documentation.

2. Call `SQLBindCol` to associate storage for the columns (you do not have to bind a variable to each column, only the columns that you need).

3. Call `SQLFetch` repeatedly until it returns `SQL_NO_DATA_FOUND`. Each call to `SQLFetch` copies a row of information from the table—values are copied for only those columns that have bound variables (see Figure 31.5). Thus, after each call to `SQLFetch` you get one set of values that you should save before calling `SQLFetch` again. In DBINFO, the values are simply inserted into a listbox. In some other application, you may save them in some other manner.

FIGURE 31.5.

Retrieving results from database queries.

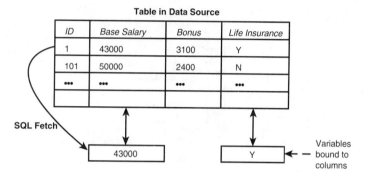

MFC 3.0 Database Classes

The previous sections provide an overview of ODBC and show how to use the ODBC API directly in an MFC application. MFC 3.0 also includes some classes that are designed to hide much of the details of the ODBC API and enable you to focus on the task of presenting the data to the user. The following sections describe these database classes and show some simple example programs that use these classes.

Overview of Database Classes

MFC 3.0's database classes are meant to simplify writing database applications with ODBC. There are six classes for database programming of which the following three are the most important:

■ `CDatabase` represents a connection to a data source.

■ `CRecordset` models the tables in which results are returned by the ODBC driver.

■ `CRecordView` is a forms-based view of individual rows of the table represented by `CRecordSet`.

These classes are well supported by the MFC AppWizard and ClassWizard, so much so that for most applications you do not even have to use these classes explicitly—the wizards do all the work for you.

Table 31.2 lists the database classes in MFC 3.0. You have to include the AFXDB.H file when using these classes (the AppWizard does this for you when you enable database support when building an application).

Figure 31.6 shows the class hierarchy of the database classes. As you can see, the database classes fit right into the rest of the MFC 3.0 class hierarchy. In particular, the CRecordView class, which provides a forms-based view of a record from a database table, is derived from CFormView.

FIGURE 31.6.
MFC 3.0 database class hierarchy.

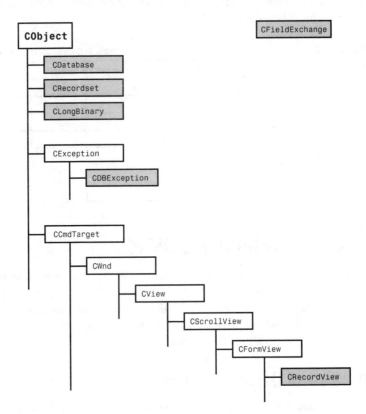

Table 31.2. Database classes in MFC 3.0.

Class	Derived From	Description
CDatabase	CObject	This class represents a connection to a data source, through which you can operate on the data source. An application can have one or more CDatabase objects active at a time.
CDBException	CException	This class is used to represent an exception condition arising in one of the database classes.

Class	Derived From	Description
CFieldExchange		This class is used to implement the record field exchange (RFX) functions used to exchange data between the data members of a recordset object and the corresponding fields of the current row on the data source.
CLongBinary	CObject	This class is meant to be used when working with very large binary data objects, often called BLOBs. For example, a CLongBinary object might be used to receive the contents of a database field that stores a bitmap image.
CRecordset	CObject	This class represents a set of records selected from a data source. The collection of records are known as *recordsets* and are available in two forms: *snapshots* and *dynasets*. A snapshot is a static recordset that reflects the state of the database at the time the snapshot was taken. A dynaset is a dynamic recordset that always reflects any updates to the database records made by other users.
CRecordView	CFormView	This class provides a view to display database records in a dialog box. The view is created from a dialog resource and is directly connected to a CRecordset object whose fields appear in various controls of the dialog.

Creating Database Applications with MFC AppWizard

When you use MFC AppWizard to generate your database application, you can see how the MFC classes simplify the problem of accessing and retrieving data from a ODBC data source. In most cases, you can follow a cookbook approach to write a database application using the MFC 3.0 database classes. The following sections outline the basic steps.

Setting Up the ODBC Data Source

Before you use AppWizard to generate an application with database support, ensure the following:

■ ODBC manager and drivers are installed.

■ One (or more) ODBC data sources is set up with the ODBC manager (start the control panel, double-click on the 32-bit ODBC icon, select an ODBC driver, and then pick a data source from the dialog box displayed by the driver).

Generating the Application with Database Support

After a ODBC data source is set up, use AppWizard and generate an application with database support. When you generate the project, select single document interface in the first step of the MFC AppWizard dialog. In step 2 (see Figure 17.7), the dialog prompts you for the level of database support. The following options are available:

■ *None.* This is the default option; it means you do not want AppWizard to provide any database support (of course, you can still call ODBC API functions directly).

■ *Only include header file.* Selecting this option causes AppWizard to include the header file AFXDB.H (the #include directive placed in STDAFX.H) and make your application link with the ODBC library (ODBC32.LIB). With this option, you can use any of the database classes, macros, global functions, and other items defined in AFXDB.H. However, AppWizard does not create any database-related classes for you (but you can create such classes later with ClassWizard).

■ *A database view, without file support.* Selecting this option provides the following support for the AppWizard-generated application:

   ■ A view class derived from CRecordView rather than CView, which is commonly used for non-database applications. You have to provide a dialog box, whose controls can be tied to specific columns of a database table so that the view can be used to browse the rows (records) in the table. (The application automatically provides only a single-document interface when this option is selected.)

   ■ A class derived from CRecordset that stores the rows (records) from a database table. The view class derived from CRecordView stores a pointer to a recordset object (instances of classes derived from CRecordset are called *recordset objects*).

   ■ No support for serialization (to store data in files) because database applications usually manage data stored in a database, rather than working with files.

   ■ No menu commands for opening and saving files.

■ *Both a database view and file support.* Selecting this option causes AppWizard to provide the same support for database view as the previous option. Additionally, AppWizard provides support for serialization and file menu entries for opening and saving disk files.

When you select one of the last two options, the button labeled Data Source... becomes active (see Figure 17.7). Clicking on this button brings up a list of data sources from which you should select one. For the selected data source, you also have to select a table. Then, AppWizard binds all columns of the selected table to the recordset class. That means that operations on the table occur through the objects of the recordset class.

Complete the remaining steps of AppWizard's dialog and let AppWizard generate the project for the application.

Editing the Dialog Resource for the RecordView

The view class of an AppWizard-generated database application is derived from the CRecordView class. Essentially, this view enables the user to look at one database record at a time. The appearance of the view depends on the dialog resource associated with the view. After generating the database application, you have to open the application's resource (.RC) file and edit the dialog resource. You should add controls to display specified fields of a database record (such as edit controls to display text strings). You do not have to provide controls to display every field of a record, just the ones that your application should display.

TIP

You can associate a control with a member of the recordset as you build the dialog resource. Select a control, press Ctrl, and double-click the mouse. This brings up ClassWizard's Add Member Variables dialog box, where you can associate (bind) a recordset data member to the control.

If you place a static text label ahead of each control and use a meaningful label, ClassWizard even preselects the most likely recordset member to associate with that control.

Associating the Recordset to the RecordView

Use the ClassWizard to associate the fields of a database record to the controls that appear in the dialog resource (that forms the basis of the record view). To do this, follow these general steps:

1. From ClassWizard's Member Variables tab, select the record view class. The IDs of the controls will appear.

2. Select a control and click on Add Variable button. A dialog box pops up. Click on the arrow in the drop-down combo box labeled Member Variable Name. You will see a list of names, each with an m_pSet-> prefix and then a name that has a resemblance to the name of a column in the database table that you associated with the recordset class. Pick the appropriate variable for the selected control.

3. Repeat step 2 for each control in the dialog box.

Figure 31.7 illustrates how a database table is associated with a recordset through the record field exchange (RFX) mechanism for transferring data between a table in a data source and a `CRecordset` object. That figure also shows how dialog data exchange (DDX) is used to transfer data from the `CRecordset` object to the `CRecordView` object that provides the visual display of individual records in a form (whose design is provided by a dialog resource).

FIGURE 31.7.

Mapping database tables to the view.

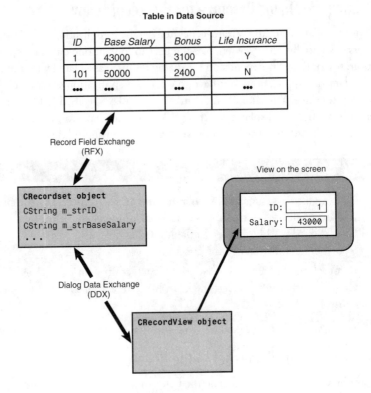

Calling ODBC API Directly

If necessary, you may call ODBC API functions directly from an AppWizard-generated database application. MFC provides two macros that you can use to call ODBC API directly:

■ `AFX_SQL_ASYNC(pRecordset, SQLFunction);`

Use this macro to call any ODBC API function that may return `SQL_STILL_EXECUTING` (a return code from ODBC API functions).

■ `AFX_SQL_SYNC(SQLFunction);`

Use this macro to call ODBC API functions that do *not* return `SQL_STILL_EXECUTING`.

These macros use a variable named `nRetCode` of type `RETCODE` that you must declare before using these macros.

The first argument of the AFX_SQL_ASYNC macro, *pRecordSet*, is a pointer to a CRecordset or CDatabase object. The macro uses this argument to yield control to other processes while the asynchronous database transaction identified by the *SQLFunction* argument is completed.

The *SQLFunction* argument is a complete ODBC API function call. For example, if you are calling the SQLColumns function to get the names of columns in a table, you write the following:

```
// pRS is a pointer to a CRecordset object, which is
// defined elsewhere.

RETCODE nRetCode;  // Must declare

AFX_SQL_ASYNC(pRS, ::SQLColumns(pRS->m_hstmt,
    NULL, SQL_NTS, NULL, SQL_NTS,
    strTableName, SQL_NTS, NULL, SQL_NTS));

// Check for error return by calling the Check member
// function of the CRecordSet class
if (!pRS->Check(nRetCode))
{
// An error occurred. Throw a database exception...
    AfxThrowDBException(nRetCode, pRS->m_pdb, pRS->m_hstmt);
}
```

DBMFC—Viewing Records in a Database

You can easily write a database application by following the steps outlined in the previous sections. To show the ease with which you can write database applications with MFC AppWizard, this section presents DBMFC—an application for viewing successive records in a database table. Here are the steps for writing the DBMFC application:

1. Use MFC AppWizard to generate an application with support for a database view. In step 2 of the AppWizard dialog, select a data source and a table. The sample DBMFC application on the enclosed disk is meant for the Products table in the North Wind sample data base—stored in the file named NWIND.MDB—that comes with Microsoft Access 2.0. If you do not have Microsoft Access 2.0, you have to create your own sample program from scratch.

2. Create the dialog resource, providing a control for each field you want to display. For each control, select the control and double-click while pressing Ctrl to bring up ClassWizard's Add Member Variable dialog box. From that dialog, associate a member of the recordset with that control (see Figure 31.8).

3. Build and run the program.

That's it! You get a database application without writing a single line of code. All you have to do is design the "form" (through the dialog resource) and associate fields from the database record with controls on the form's dialog resource.

Figure 31.9 shows the DBMFC application showing a record from the database—in this case, the Products table of the North Wind sample database (NWIND.MDB) that comes with Microsoft Access 2.0. As you can see from Figure 31.9, for a database application, MFC AppWizard automatically provides a tool bar that includes buttons (the arrow buttons) to browse through the records in the recordset.

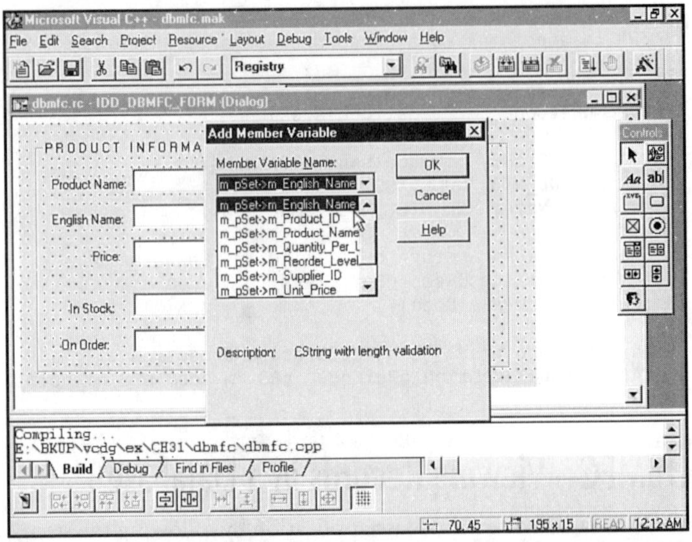

FIGURE 31.8.

Associating a control with a recordset member variable for DBMFC.

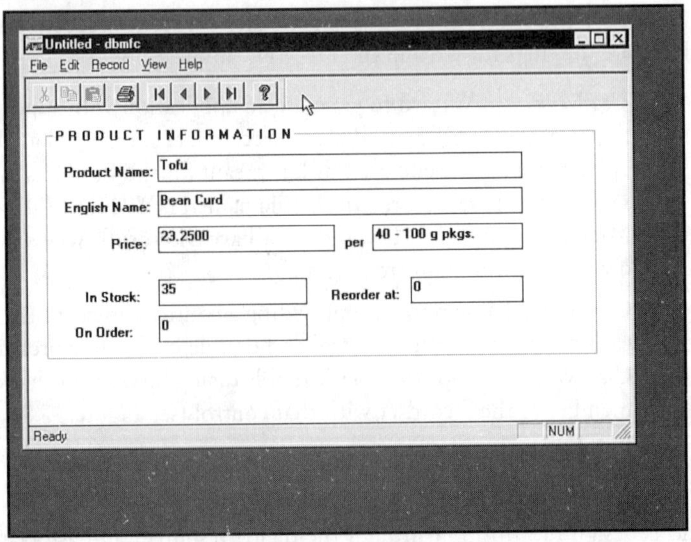

FIGURE 31.9.

A database record being displayed by DBMFC.

Summary

Nowadays, the trend in information systems is to use client-server architectures that manage data at a central server while users access the data through client applications running on desktop PCs. Increasingly, these data access clients run under Windows because of the graphical user interface that Windows offers. Microsoft's Open Database Connectivity (ODBC) architecture is designed to ease the task of writing database applications under Windows 3.*x* and Windows NT.

ODBC enables database applications to access many different databases in a standard manner by calling API functions that provide a unified model of the data (viewed as relational tables). The ODBC API is based on the X/Open and SQL Access Group (SAG) Call Level Interface for SQL. When you write a database application using the ODBC API, your application can access any database that provides an ODBC driver.

Although you can directly call the ODBC API in Windows applications that use MFC classes, MFC 3.0 also includes a number of classes designed specifically to support database programming with the ODBC API. In particular, the CDatabase class represents a connection to a data source, CRecordset represents a table, and CRecordView provides a forms-based view for a single row (record) from the database table.

This chapter provides an overview of the ODBC API and shows how to use MFC AppWizard to generate database applications that make use of the database classes in MFC 3.0.

32

Network Programming with Visual C++ 2.0

Client-server and peer-to-peer architectures are gaining popularity as approaches for implementing distributed information systems. These architectures consist of a collection of computers connected by a communication network. The functions of the information system are performed by processes (computer programs) that run on these computers and communicate through the network.

In recent years, the client-server architecture has become commonplace as the mechanism that brings the centralized corporate databases to desktop PCs on a network. Recall that in a client-server environment, one or more servers manage the centralized database and clients gain access to the data through the server. Peer-to-peer architecture does away with the classification of applications as servers and clients. Instead, the peer-to-peer model enables an application to be both a server (a provider of services) and a client (a user of services) and assume these roles as necessary.

Both client-server and peer-to-peer models require applications that communicate over a network. Thus, network programming has become an increasingly important part of an application developer's job because distributed computing architectures depend on interprocess communications over a network.

Visual C++ 2.0 does not include any built-in facility to help you with network programming. However, you can write distributed applications (that require network programming) using Visual C++ 2.0. This chapter introduces you to network programming under Windows NT with Visual C++ 2.0, using a versatile Application Programming Interface (API) for network programming—the Windows Sockets API.

Windows NT Network Programming

Network programming refers to the programming tasks that have to be performed in an application that communicates with other applications running on various systems on a network. The following sections describe the network programming options available in Windows NT. The latter part of the chapter focuses on network programming with the Windows Sockets API.

MORE INFORMATION ON NETWORK PROGRAMMING

This chapter introduces you to network programming under Windows NT, but there is too much information to cover in a single chapter. In fact, there are entire books devoted to the subject. In particular, you might want to consult the following books for more information on network programming:

■ *Windows NT Network Programming*, by Ralph Davis, Addison-Wesley, 1994. This book covers several networking APIs (such as NetBIOS, Named Pipes, Remote Procedure Calls, and Windows Sockets) available under Windows NT.

■ *UNIX Network Programming,* by W. Richard Stevens, Prentice-Hall, 1990. Although this book covers network programming under UNIX, the information on Berkeley Sockets is relevant to Windows Sockets programming. You will also find this book to be a good source for information about networks in general and TCP/IP in particular.

Network Programming Model

Network programming relies on a layered model where each layer is responsible for providing particular functionality. The best known of networking models is the 7-layer Open Systems Interconnection (OSI) reference model developed by the International Standards Organization (ISO).

The OSI 7-Layer Model

As shown in Figure 32.1, the OSI reference model describes the flow of data between the physical connection to the network and the end-user application. The OSI layers are numbered from bottom to top. Basic functions, such as physically sending data bits through the network cable, are at the bottom, and functions dealing with higher-level abstractions of the data are at the top. The purpose of each layer is to provide services to the next higher layer in a manner such that the higher layer does not have to use any knowlege of how the services are actually implemented.

FIGURE 32.1.
OSI 7-layer model.

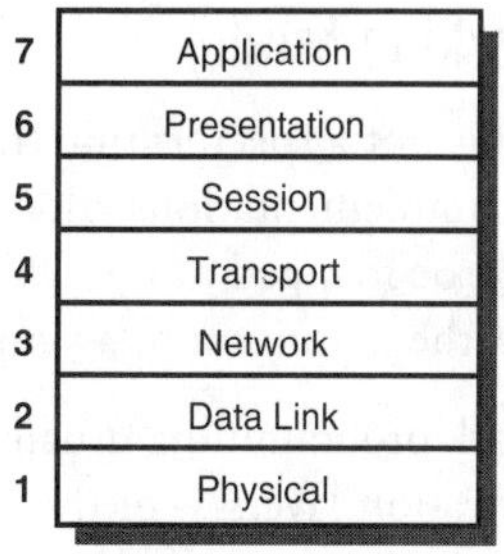

7	Application
6	Presentation
5	Session
4	Transport
3	Network
2	Data Link
1	Physical

The seven layers in the OSI reference model are as follows:

1. *Physical Layer* is responsible for transmitting raw bits of data across the physical medium (the networking cable or electromagnetic waves, in case of wireless networks). This layer carries the data generated by all the higher layers. The physical layer deals with three physical components:

   ■ Network topology (such as bus or star)

   ■ Transmission Medium (RG-58 coaxial cable, shielded or unshielded twisted pair, fiber-optic cable, microwave, and so forth)

■ Transmission technique (such as Carrier Sense Multiple Access with Collision Detection—CSMA/CD—used by Ethernet, token-based techniques in Token Ring, and so forth)

2. *Data Link Layer* deals with logical packets (or frames) of data. This layer packages raw bits from the Physical Layer into frames, the exact format of which depends on the type of network (such as Ethernet or Token Ring). The frames used by the Data Link layer contain the physical addresses of the sender and the receiver of data.

3. *Network Layer* knows about the logical network addresses and how to translate logical addresses to physical ones. At the sending end, the Network Layer converts larger logical packets into smaller physical data frames. At the receiving end, the Network Layer reassembles the data frames into their original logical packet structures.

4. *Transport Layer* is responsible for the reliable delivery of messages originating at the Application Layer. At the sending end, this layer divides long messages into several packets. At the receiving end, the Transport Layer reassembles the original messages and sends an acknowledgment of receipt.

5. *Session Layer* enables applications on different computers to initiate, use, and terminate a connection called a *session*.

6. *Presentation Layer* manages the format used to exchange data between networked computers.

7. *Application Layer* is the gateway through which application processes access network services. This layer represents services that directly support applications, such as file transfers, database access, and electronic mail.

A Simplified Networking Model

The OSI 7-layer model is not a specification; rather, it provides guidelines for organizing the network services. Most implementations adopt a layered model for networking services and these layered models can be mapped to the OSI reference model. As an example of a different layered model, consider the definition of a simplified model.

Application-level network programming usually deals with the topmost three layers—Session, Presentation, and Application layers— of the OSI 7-layer reference model. We can combine these three layers into a single layer called the Application Layer.

The bottom two layers—Physical and Data Link layers—in the OSI model can also be combined into a single Physical Layer. This gives us a simplified 4-layer model as shown in Figure 32.2. A further simplification combines the Network and Transport layers into a single layer.

FIGURE 32.2.
*Simplified 4-layer
networking model.*

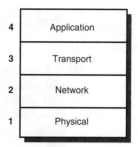

4	Application
3	Transport
2	Network
1	Physical

Information can be exchanged at each of these layers through network protocols.

Network Protocols

A network protocol refers to the method agreed upon by the sender and receiver for exchanging data at a specific layer of the networking model. Thus, the simplified network model of Figure 32.2 can have the following protocols:

- Physical Layer protocols, such as Ethernet and Token Ring
- Network Layer protocols, such as the Internet Protocol (IP), which is part of the TCP/IP protocol suite
- Transport Layer protocols, such as the Transmission Control Protocol (TCP) and User Datagram Protocol (UDP) that are part of the TCP/IP protocol suite
- Application Layer protocols, such as the File Transfer Protocol (FTP) and Simple Mail Transfer Protocol (SMTP)

A *protocol suite* is a collection of two or more protocols from these layers that form the basis of a network. The following are some of the well-known protocol suites:

- IPX/SPX (Internet Packet Exchange/Sequenced Packet Exchange) protocol suite used by Novell Netware
- TCP/IP protocol suite
- NetBIOS and NetBEUI (Network BIOS Extended User Interface)

Windows NT Networking Model

Like most other operating systems, Windows NT uses a layered model for the networking services. Figure 32.3 illustrates the Windows NT networking model and shows the relationship of the layers to those in the OSI reference model.

FIGURE 32.3.
Windows NT networking model.

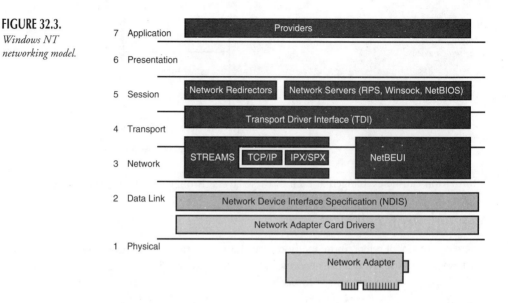

As Figure 32.3 shows, the Windows NT networking model has the following features:

■ *Network Adapter Card Drivers* are at the lowest layer. Windows NT supports multiple network adapter cards on a single computer.

■ *Network Device Interface Specification (NDIS)*—current version is NDIS 3.0—is a standard interface through which the higher-level transport protocols access the network adapter card drivers.

■ *Transport Protocols* implement various network protocols, such as TCP/IP, NWLink (Microsoft's implementation of Novell's IPX/SPX protocol), and NetBEUI.

■ *Transport Driver Interface (TDI)* is another interface through which all higher-level services access the transport protocols.

■ *Network Redirectors* take requests for network resources and send the requests to the machine responsible for processing them.

■ *Providers* are the gateway through which an application request is sent to the redirectors. A Multiple Provider Router (MPR) determines the appropriate provider that should receive an application request.

Network Programming APIs in Windows NT

Windows NT offers several APIs for network programming:

■ NetBIOS API over NetBEUI or TCP/IP

■ Windows Socket API over TCP/IP or NWLink

■ Named Pipes using NetBEUI

■ Remote Procedure Call (RPC) over any available protocol

The following sections provide summary descriptions of these APIs; the Windows Sockets API is covered in detail in the latter part of the book.

NetBIOS

NetBIOS stands for Network Basic Input/Output System—an interface used by applications to communicate with network transports such as NetBEUI. NetBIOS was originally developed by Sytek, Inc., and introduced by IBM with its PC network cards. Later, Microsoft developed a NetBIOS interface for its MS-Net and LAN Manager products and also included this interface with Windows for Workgroups.

NetBIOS uses a unique alphanumeric name (up to 15 characters long) to identify each node (computer) on the network. NetBIOS can establish a logical connection, or session, between two nodes and provides for reliable data transfer between two computers after establishing a session.

The NetBIOS API started out as an assembly language interface—under MS-DOS and Windows 3.*x*, you request NetBIOS services by setting 80x86 registers and issuing the INT 5CH assembly language instruction. In Windows NT, you access the NetBIOS services by calling the Netbios API function with the following prototype:

```
UCHAR Netbios(
    PNCB pncb); // Pointer to Network Control Block (NCB)
```

This is the only function in the NetBIOS API. To perform specific functions, you have to set up a Network Control Block (NCB) and provide a pointer to that NCB structure as the sole argument to the Netbios function. The NCB structure is declared in the nb30.h header file:

```
#define NCBNAMSZ        16    // Absolute length of a net name

// Network Control Block

typedef struct _NCB
{
    UCHAR    ncb_command;            // Command code
    UCHAR    ncb_retcode;            // Return code
    UCHAR    ncb_lsn;                // Local session number
    UCHAR    ncb_num;                // Number of our network name
    PUCHAR   ncb_buffer;            // Address of message buffer
    WORD     ncb_length;            // Size of message buffer
    UCHAR    ncb_callname[NCBNAMSZ]; // Blank-padded name of remote
    UCHAR    ncb_name[NCBNAMSZ];    // Our blank-padded netname
    UCHAR    ncb_rto;                // Rcv timeout/retry count
    UCHAR    ncb_sto;                // Send timeout/sys timeout
    void (CALLBACK *ncb_post)( struct _NCB * ); // POST routine
                                    // (called when asynchronous
                                    // operation completes)
    UCHAR    ncb_lana_num;          // LANA (adapter) number
    UCHAR    ncb_cmd_cplt;          // 0xff => commmand pending
    UCHAR    ncb_reserve[10];       // reserved, used by BIOS
```

```
    HANDLE  ncb_event;              // HANDLE to Win32 event which
                                    // will be set to the signalled
                                    // state when an ASYNCH command
                                    // completes
} NCB, *PNCB;
```

Windows Sockets

Windows Sockets is a Windows implementation of the Berkeley Sockets, which is a popular interface for network programming in TCP/IP networks. Because TCP/IP is popular in the Internet, Windows Sockets provides the best connectivity for wide-area networks. If you are writing Internet tools such as World Wide Web (WWW) browsers (like the well-known Mosaic) for Windows NT, Windows Sockets is the API to use. The Windows Sockets API is described in detail later in this chapter.

Named Pipes

Named pipes are based on the OS/2 API calls for communications. Named pipes are implemented as file systems, so the sending and receiving data use standard Win32 file I/O calls.

To use named pipes, a connection must be established between the communicating applications. A server typically performs the following tasks:

1. Call CreateNamedPipe to create a named pipe and obtain a handle to the pipe. The pipe is identified by a name in the UNC format. Because CreateNamedPipe can create only a named pipe in the current machine, the UNC for the pipe must have a single period (.) as the machine name (to indicate that it is the local machine) and PIPE as the share name followed by the name of the pipe. For example, use UNC \\.\PIPE\dataread to open a pipe named dataread.

2. Call ConnectNamedPipe to wait for clients requesting connections.

A client application using named pipes requests a connection to a named pipe server by calling CreateFile with a full UNC name. For example, use the UNC \\LNB486\PIPE\dataread to connect to the pipe named dataread on the LNB486 machine. If successful, CreateFile returns a handle to the pipe.

After the pipe is connected, the client and server applications can use the Win32 file I/O functions ReadFile and WriteFile to exchange data. If a client writes some data by calling WriteFile and then waits to read a response (by calling ReadFile), it can accomplish the two operations by a call to a single function: TransactNamedFile.

To end a named pipe connection, the client application calls CloseHandle with the pipe handle that it obtained by a previous successful call to CreateFile. When the client closes the handle, the server detects a failure and calls DisconnectNamedPipe to put the pipe back in a listening state. When the pipe is no longer needed, the named pipe server calls CloseHandle to close the pipe.

UNIVERSAL NAMING CONVENTION (UNC)

Windows NT supports the Universal Naming Convention (UNC), which specifies a standard way to refer to files in a network. The syntax is as follows:

```
\\<Machine Name>\<Share Name\<Path Name>\<File Name>
```

For example, if the machine named LNB486 is sharing the `c:\` directory under the share name C$, you access the file TEST.C in the C:\MYDIR directory with the UNC name:

```
\\LNB486\C$\MYDIR\TEST.C
```

Remote Procedure Call

As the name implies, Remote Procedure Call (RPC) enables an application to call a procedure that physically resides on another machine on a network. RPC enables you to write distributed applications using the conventional procedural model with the added twist that a procedure call can cross machine boundaries.

In the RPC approach, applications do not have to deal with the network communications explicitly. RPC automatically handles all data exchanges, error handling, and necessary format conversions (required by differences in data representation on different systems on the network).

RPC is not covered in this chapter; rather, the focus of this chapter is on the Windows Sockets API, which provides a standard way of developing networking applications for Windows NT.

Windows Sockets API

TCP/IP is popular as the wide-area networking protocol of choice in the global Internet. Much of TCP/IP programming is done using the Berkeley Sockets API (so named because the socket interface was introduced in Berkeley UNIX around 1982). The Windows Sockets API was modeled after the Berkeley Sockets API to provide a standard API that Windows programmers can use to write network applications. The Windows Sockets API is consistent with release 4.3 of the Berkeley Software Distribution (4.3BSD) UNIX.

Before Windows Sockets became available, the programming interface for developing TCP/IP-based networking applications depended on the TCP/IP networking software vendor. For the following reasons, the Windows Sockets API greatly eases the task of writing TCP/IP applications for Windows:

- The API is same for all TCP/IP vendors.
- Programmers experienced with Berkeley Sockets API under UNIX can migrate their code easily to Windows.

The next few sections introduce you to the Windows Sockets API and show a simple example program written with the API.

WINDOWS SOCKETS SPECIFICATION

The Windows sockets specification is available from the following sources:

■ Anonymous FTP from `rhino.microsoft.com`

■ The Microsoft Software Library forum (GO MSL) on Compuserve

The online help in Windows NT SDK also includes the Windows sockets API.

Basic Sockets

A *socket* is an abstraction that represents a bidirectional endpoint of a connection. Because a socket is bidirectional, data can be sent as well as received through a socket. A socket has three attributes:

■ The network address (known as the IP address in a TCP/IP network) of the system

■ The port number identifying the process that exchanges data through the socket

■ The type of socket (such as stream or datagram) identifying the protocol for data exchange

Essentially, the IP address identifies a network node, the port number identifies a process on the node, and the socket type determines the manner in which data is exchanged—through a connection-oriented or a connectionless service.

Connection-Oriented Service

Connection-oriented data exchange requires both the sending and the receiving processes to establish a connection before data exchange can begin. In the TCP/IP protocol suite, the TCP protocol provides connection-oriented service with reliable, two-way, byte stream for a process.

TCP is useful for applications that plan to exchange large amounts of data at a time. Applications that need reliable data exchange also should use TCP.

In the sockets model, a socket that uses TCP is referred to as a *stream socket*.

Connectionless Service

Connectionless data exchange does not require the sender and receiver to establish a connection explicitly. In the TCP/IP protocol suite, the User Datagram Protocol (UDP) provides connectionless service for sending and receiving packets known as datagrams. Unlike TCP,

UDP does not guarantee that datagrams ever reach their intended destination. Nor does UDP ensure that datagrams are delivered in the order they are sent.

UDP is used by applications that exchange small amounts of data at a time, or by applications that do not need the reliability and sequencing of data delivery.

In the sockets model, a socket that uses UDP is referred to as a *datagram socket*.

Sockets and the Client-Server Model

It takes two sockets to complete a communication path. When two processes communicate, they typically use the client-server model to establish the connection. The server application listens on a specific port on the system (identified by an IP address). The client initiates connection from any available port and tries to connect to the server (identified by the IP address and port number). Once the connection is established, the client and the server can exchange data according to their own protocol.

The typical sequence of events in sockets-based data exchanges depends on whether the transfer is connection-oriented or connectionless.

Figure 32.4 shows the typical sequence of events for a connection-oriented data transfer using sockets. Each step shows the names of sockets functions that are called (there are Windows-specific functions in the Windows Sockets API that you will see later in the chapter). As Figure 32.4 shows, the server "listens" on a specific port, waiting for clients to request connection. Data transfers begin only after a connection is established.

FIGURE 32.4.

Connection-oriented data transfer with sockets.

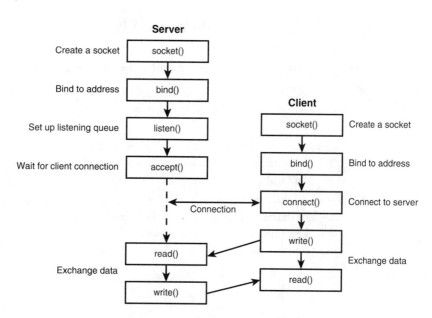

For connectionless data transfers, the server waits for a datagram to arrive at a specified port. The client does not wait to establish a connection; it merely sends a datagram to the server. As you can see from Figure 32.5, the client and the server use the socket calls `sendto` and `recvfrom` to send and receive data. When the server reads a datagram by calling `recvfrom`, the `recvfrom` function returns the datagram as well as the network address of the client that sent the datagram. This enables the server to send a response to the correct client process.

FIGURE 32.5.

Connectionless data transfer with sockets.

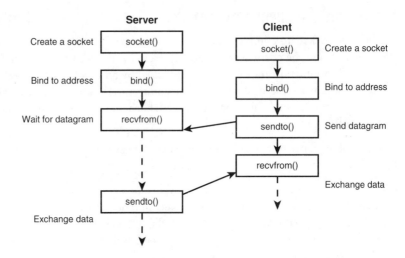

Taking Stock of the Windows Sockets API

Like many other APIs designed to provide a specific type of functionality, the Windows Sockets API consists of a number of data structures and three broad categories of functions:

■ *Database Functions.* These functions enable you to retrieve information, such as host name, service name, and network address of a host. These functions exist in Berkeley Sockets API.

■ *Sockets Functions.* These functions (that are the same as the ones in Berkeley Sockets API) provide the mechanism to establish a network connection and transmit and receive data using the socket model.

■ *Windows Sockets Extension Functions.* These functions are unique to the Windows version of the Sockets API. Most of these extension functions were added to ensure that sockets function calls that may wait for data (block) do not render the Windows 3.*x* system unresponsive.

Data Structures

The Windows Sockets API declares the following structures in the header file WINSOCK.H:

- `fd_set` stores information about sockets.
- `hostent` holds host information.
- `in_addr` represents the Internet address.
- `ip_mreq` holds arguments for `IP_ADD_MEMBERSHIP` and `IP_DROP_MEMBERSHIP`.
- `linger` is used for manipulating the linger option that controls whether a socket should stay around (even after being closed by an application) if data is available.
- `netent` holds network information.
- `protoent` contains information about a protocol such as TCP or UDP.
- `servent` holds information about a service and the port number associated with the service.
- `sockaddr` is a general structure for storing the endpoint address to connect to a socket.
- `sockaddr_in` is used to specify the address for the Internet address family.
- `sockproto` is for storing protocol information for raw sckets (type `SOCK_RAW`).
- `timeval` is a structure (denoting time) used as an argument for the select function.
- `WSAData` holds information about a Windows Sockets implementation.

Of these, only a few are required by all Windows Sockets applications. In particular, most applications use `sockaddr_in`, `hostent`, `protoent`, `servent`, and `WSAData` structures. These structures are described in the Windows Sockets documentation that accompanies the Windows NT Software Development Kit (SDK).

Database Functions

The database functions enable applications to convert names of hosts and services to numbers. Here, the term database refers to text files that list host names and services available on a system. Table 32.1 lists the database functions provided by Windows Sockets API.

Table 32.1. Database functions in Windows Sockets API.

Function	Description
gethostbyaddr*	Returns a `hostent` structure containing information about a host identified by its network address
gethostbyname*	Returns a `hostent` structure containing information about a host identified by a name
gethostname	Retrieves the name of the local host

continues

Table 32.1. continued

Function	Description
getprotobyname*	Returns a protoent structure with information about a protocol identified by name
getprotobynumber*	Returns a protoent structure with information about a protocol identified by a protocol number
getservbyname*	Returns a servent structure with information about a service identified by name
getservbyport*	Returns a servent structure with information about a service identified by a port number

*These function calls may block for a blocking socket.

Socket Functions

The socket functions are the ones that you can use to establish a connection between sockets and carry out the data transfer operations. Table 32.2 lists the socket functions in Windows Sockets API; these functions are the same ones that Berkeley Sockets provides for network communication.

In addition to the functions for establishing communication and exchanging data, Table 32.2 also lists several functions, such as htonl, htons, ntohl, and ntohs, that are meant for converting between network byte order and host byte order.

Recall that byte order refers to the way the bytes of 2-byte and 4-byte integers are laid out in consecutively addressed memory. In the little-endian order used by Intel 80x86 and Pentium processors, the low-order byte is at the lowest address and the highest-order byte is at the highest address. Big-endian byte order (used by Motorola processors) reverses the layout with the highest-order byte at the lowest address.

On the network, the TCP/IP protocol uses the big-endian byte order. To ensure portability of the networking software, you should use functions such as ntohs and ntohl to convert short and long integers from network byte order to host byte order.

Table 32.2. Socket functions in Windows Sockets API.

Function	Description
accept	Acknowledges an incoming connection, creates a socket, and associates the connection with the newly created socket
bind	Assigns a local name with a socket; for TCP/IP, the name has three parts: an IP address, the protocol type, and a port number

Function	Description
closesocket	Closes a socket (blocks if SO_LINGER is set)
connect	Establishes a connection to a peer socket
getpeername	Retrieves the name of the peer connected to a specified socket descriptor
getsockname	Retrieves the current name of a specified socket
getsockopt	Retrieves options associated with a specified socket descriptor
htonl	Converts a 32-bit quantity from host byte order to network byte order
htons	Converts a 16-bit quantity from host byte order to network byte order
inet_addr	Converts a character string representing a number in the Internet standard dot notation for IP address (such as 140.90.23.100) to an Internet address value
inet_ntoa	Converts an Internet address value to an ASCII string in dot notation, such as 143.90.23.100
ioctlsocket	Controls the modes of a socket
listen	Listens for incoming connections on a specified socket
ntohl	Converts a 32-bit quantity from network byte order to host byte order
ntohs	Converts a 16-bit quantity from network byte order to host byte order
recv*	Receives data from a connected socket
recvfrom*	Receives data from either a connected or unconnected socket
select*	Determines the status of one or more sockets
send*	Sends data to a connected socket
sendto*	Sends data to either a connected or unconnected socket
setsockopt	Sets options for a specified socket descriptor
shutdown	Disables reception or transmission of data over a specified connection
socket	Creates a socket and returns a socket descriptor

*These functions may block for a blocking socket.

Windows Sockets Extension Functions

One of the problems with network programming is that some operations can take an indeterminate amount of time. For example, when a server calls accept, the function does not return until a client establishes connection with the server. This is known as a blocking function call because the function waits rather than returning and consequently blocks all further processing.

If the server is a Windows 3.*x* application, this causes a problem, because the program stops processing Windows messages and the whole system stops responding to users' input until the blocking function returns. Although Windows 3.*x* can handle multiple tasks, the multitasking is not preemptive (meaning multitasking is not under the control of a separate scheduling process). Windows 3.*x* uses cooperative multitasking, which relies on each program processing Windows messages. As soon as one program (task) calls a blocking function, processing for all tasks comes to a halt. This, however, is not a problem in preemptive multitasking operating systems such as UNIX and Windows NT. Because Windows NT provides threads, you can merely start a thread that takes care of the blocking calls while the main thread of your NT application continues to respond to Windows messages.

Windows Sockets API provides a number of functions (see Table 32.3) that provide alternatives to the blocking function calls. These functions are unique to Windows Sockets and are extensions to the Berkeley Sockets. The extension functions have names that start with the prefix WSA, which stands for Windows Sockets API.

These functions typically handle network transactions asynchronously by using a Windows message-based scheme. Essentially, your application calls one of the extension functions to initiate the operation; the extension function returns immediately, thus enabling your application to continue processing messages. When the operation is completed, your application receives a message.

In addition to the functions for asynchronous operations, there are two WSA functions—WSAStartup and WSACleanup—that a Windows Sockets application cannot avoid. As you will see in the next section, these two functions set up a Windows Sockets application and clean up after the application exits.

Table 32.3. Windows Sockets extension functions.

Function	Description
WSAAsyncGetHostByAddr,	Asynchronous versions of the
WSAAsyncGetHostByName,	standard Berkeley get... functions
WSAAsyncGetProtoByName,	(for example, WSAAsyncGetHostByName
WSAAsyncGetProtoByNumber,	provides an asynchronous-message-
WSAAsyncGetServByName,	based implementation of the
WSAAsyncGetServByPort	gethostbyname function)
WSAAsyncSelect	Asynchronous version of select

Function	Description
WSACancelAsyncRequest	Cancels an outstanding instance of a WSAAsyncGet... function
WSACancelBlockingCall	Cancels an outstanding blocking API function call
WSACleanup	Ends the use of the Windows Sockets DLL
WSAGetLastError	Returns error status for the last Windows Sockets API function that failed
WSAIsBlocking	Returns TRUE if a blocking call is in progress
WSASetBlockingHook	Sets up an application-specific hook function for use by the Windows Sockets DLL during blocking calls
WSASetLastError	Sets the error code to be returned by a subsequent call to WSAGetLastError
WSAStartup	Initializes the underlying Windows Sockets DLL
WSAUnhookBlockingHook	Restores the original blocking function

Windows Sockets Programming

The basic event sequences shown in Figures 32.4 and 32.5 indicate the Windows Sockets API functions that a client or server typically calls. Although the exact set of function calls depends on the type of socket (stream or datagram) and whether the application is a server or a client, the basic steps are as follows:

1. Initialize.
2. Create a socket.
3. Bind a machine address and port to the socket.
4. Listen for connections if the application is a server using a stream socket.
5. Establish a connection if the application is a client using a stream socket.
6. Exchange data.
7. Clean up.

These steps are summarized in the next few sections.

Initializing a Windows Sockets Application

Before calling any Windows Sockets functions, you must call WSAStartup to initialize the Windows Sockets DLL. When calling WSAStartup, you have to specify the version of Windows

Sockets API that your application needs. For example, to start up Windows Sockets with a version number of 1.1, you write the following:

```
#include <winsock.h>

int     status;    // Status Code
WSADATA wsaData;   // Structure to hold information
                   // about Sockets DLL

if((status = WSAStartup(MAKEWORD(1,1), &wsaData)) == 0)
{
    // Success
    // wsaData contains information about the Windows
    // Sockets DLL
    //...
}
else
{
    // Failed. Handle error.
    //...
}
```

WSAStartup returns 0 if successful. Otherwise, it returns a nonzero error code.

The first argument to the WSAStartup function is a WORD containing the version of Windows Sockets DLL you need. The low-order byte specifies the major version number, and the high-order bytes have the minor version number. The second argument to WSAStartup is a pointer to a WSADATA structure that is declared in <winsock.h>:

```
#define WSADESCRIPTION_LEN    256
#define WSASYS_STATUS_LEN     128

typedef struct WSAData
{
    WORD            wVersion;
    WORD            wHighVersion;
    char            szDescription[WSADESCRIPTION_LEN+1];
    char            szSystemStatus[WSASYS_STATUS_LEN+1];
    unsigned short  iMaxSockets;
    unsigned short  iMaxUdpDg;
    char*           lpVendorInfo;
} WSADATA;

typedef WSADATA *LPWSADATA;
```

On return from WSAStartup, the structure is filled with information about the Windows Sockets DLL. You should interpret the members of the WSADATA structure as follows:

wVersion	The Windows Sockets DLL conforms to this version of the Windows Sockets specification.
wHighVersion	This is the highest version of the Windows Sockets specification that this DLL can support.

szDescription	This is a null-terminated string, up to 256 characters long, containing a description of the Windows Sockets implementation, including identification of the vendor.
szSystemStatus	This is a null-terminated string with status or configuration information.
iMaxSockets	This is the maximum number of sockets that a single process is allowed to open.
iMaxUdpDg	This is the size (in bytes) of the largest UDP datagram that can be sent or received by a Windows Sockets application. A zero value means that the implementation imposes no limit on the size of a datagram. (All Windows Sockets implementations are expected to provide 512 bytes as the minimum value of iMaxUdpDg.)
lpVendorInfo	This is a pointer to a vendor-specific data structure. (You have to consult vendor-supplied documentation for the definition of this structure, if any.)

After a successful WSAStartup call, you can begin calling other Windows Sockets API functions as needed. When you no longer need the services of the Windows Sockets DLL, you must call WSACleanup:

```
WSACleanup();
```

Creating a Socket

After initializing the Windows Sockets API by calling WSAStartup, you can create a socket by calling the socket function. When calling a socket, you have to specify the address family, the socket type (stream or datagram), and, in some cases, the protocol family, as illustrated by the following example:

```
#include <winsock.h>
//...

SOCKET sock1;
sock1 = socket(
    AF_INET,      // Address family (AF_INET = Internet)
    SOCK_STREAM,  // Socket type (SOCK_STREAM or SOCK_DGRAM)
    0);           // Protocol family (0 = use default for
                  // specified socket type
if (sock1 == INVALID_SOCKET)
{
    int errNo = WSAGetLastError();
//Report error (perhaps through a message box)
//...
}
```

The socket function returns a SOCKET value, which is an integer value like a Windows handle. You should save the SOCKET because it is needed as an argument in many Windows Sockets functions.

Binding a Socket to an Address and a Port

Before using a socket, you have to bind it to the local system's network address and a port. The network address identifies the machine, and the port identifies the process using the socket. To bind a socket to an address, call the bind function as illustrated by the following code fragment wherein a socket is being bound to a specific address for a server application:

```
// Port associated with this server
#define SRV_PORT 5050

// Set up the address structure
SOCKADDR_IN sa;
sa.sin_family = AF_INET;           // Internet address family
sa.sin_addr = htonl(INADDR_ANY);   // Use any appropriate address
sa.sin_port = htons(SRV_PORT)      // Can be 0 for clients

// Bind the socket to the address
if(bind(sock1,(PSOCKADDR)&sa, sizeof(sa))
        == SOCKET_ERROR)
{
// Error binding socket to address
    WSAGetLastError();
    closesocket(sock1);
}
```

In this example, the port number is uniquely specified because a server must be listening on a well-known port so that clients can connect to that port to access the server. For a client application, the process of binding a socket to the local address is the same, but you can use zero as the port number—Windows Sockets will use an unused port number between 1025 and 5000.

Listening for Connections at the Server

The communicating applications have to establish a connection only for a connection-oriented stream socket. The exact steps for establishing a connection depend on whether the application is a server or a client.

In the client-server model, the server has to be up and running before the client can run. For a server, after creating a socket and binding the socket to a port, you have to call the listen function to set up a queue of connections, which determines how many clients can connect to the server. Windows Sockets currently allows from one to five connections. After setting up the listening queue, the server calls the accept function to wait for a connection from a client. The following code fragment illustrates how a server waits for connection requests from clients:

```
// Maximum backlog of connections
    const int MAX_PENDING_CONNECTS = 4;
//...

// Listen for incoming connections
    if(listen(sock1, MAX_PENDING_CONNECTS) == SOCKET_ERROR)
    {
// Handle error
        WSAGetLastError();
        closesocket(sock1);
// Do anything else needed to handle the error
```

```
//...
    }

// Call accept to wait for a connection (blocks until
// a client connects.

// Note: Normally, you would place the accept call in a
// separate thread so that the main thread can continue
// processing Windows messages

    SOCKADDR saClnt;
    int saClntLen = sizeof(saClnt);
    SOCKET  sockClnt = accept(sock1, &saClnt, &saClntLen);
    if(sockClnt == INVALID_SOCKET)
    {
// Handle error
        int err = WSAGetLastError();
// ...
    }
// At this point, a connection has been established
// and data exchange can begin

// Call closesocket(sockClnt) when done
```

Establishing the Connection from the Client

Establishing the connection from the client side is somewhat simpler. After creating a socket and binding the socket to a network address, the client has to call the connect function to establish connection with the server. To call connect, the client needs to know the network name or address of the server as well as the port on which the server process accepts connection. For example, to connect to port number 23—a standard port for the popular Internet service called telnet that is used for logging into remote systems—on the system with IP address 140.90.23.100, you write the following:

```
// Host address and port number of server
#define SRV_HOST "140.90.23.100"
#define SRV_PORT 23
//...

// Set up the server's address structure
SOCKADDR_IN saSrv;
saSrv.sin_family = AF_INET;
saSrv.sin_addr = inet_addr(SRV_HOST);
saSrv.sin_port = htons(SRV_PORT)

// Assume that mySocket is the SOCKET created by the client
if(connect(mySocket,(PSOCKADDR)&saSrv,sizeof(saSrv)) ==
        SOCKET_ERROR)
{
// Handle error
        int err = WSAGetLastError();
// ...
}
// At this point, a connection to the server has been
// established and data exchange can begin

// Call closesocket(mySocket) when done
```

Data Exchange with Stream Sockets

After a client establishes connection to a server using a connection-oriented stream socket, the client and server can exchange data by calling the send and recv functions. As with a conversation between two persons, the server and client alternately send and receive data—the meaning of the data depends on the message protocol used by the server and the clients. Usually, a server is designed for a specific task, and inherent in that design is a message protocol that the server and clients use to exchange the necessary data.

As an example of data exchange, consider a server that merely echoes back whatever data it receives. The server calls accept to wait for a connection from a client. After returning from the accept call, the server can fall into an endless loop that receives and sends data:

```
// The call to "accept" that receives the connection
// where sock1 is the local server socket
SOCKET  sockClnt = accept(sock1, &saClnt, &saClntLen);

// Receive and send data in a loop

char buf[1024];  // Receive buffer
char *p_c;
int   count;
int   numchr;

while(1)
{
//---------------------------------------------------------------
// First receive all outstanding data on socket sockClnt
    p_c = buf;
    count = sizeof(buf);
    numchr = 0;

    do
    {
        numchr = recv(sock1, p_c, count, 0);
        if(numchr == SOCKET_ERROR)
        {
// Handle error
            int err = WSAGetLastError();
//...
        }
        else
        {
            p_c += numchr;
            count -= numchr;
        }
    } while(count > 0);

//---------------------------------------------------------------
// Now send the received data back to the client
    p_c = buf;
    count = sizeof(buf);
    numchr = 0;
```

```
      do
      {
          numchr = send(sock1, p_c, count, 0);
          if(numchr == SOCKET_ERROR)
          {
// Handle error
              int err = WSAGetLastError();
//...
          }
          else
          {
              p_c += numchr;
              count -= numchr;
          }
      } while(count > 0);
}
```

Note the use of the do-while loops to receive and send data. These are necessary because in stream-oriented data transfers, the send and recv functions may not transfer all the data at once.

On the client's side, a similar loop can be used for the data exchange; only the order of recv and send are reversed—the client starts by sending data and then it proceeds to receive data echoed back by the server. In addition, the client does not call accept; instead, it calls connect, and after connect returns, it starts the data exchange.

Data Exchange with Datagram Sockets

When using connectionless datagram sockets, the server does not have to call listen and accept; nor does the client need to call connect to establish a connection. Clients and servers use the sendto and recvfrom functions to exchange datagrams.

Data exchange with datagrams differs from stream-based data exchange in one significant way: datagrams are message-oriented—each datagram is treated as a message and sent all at once. Thus, there is a one-to-one correspondence between sendto amd recvfrom calls. Because of the message-oriented nature of datagrams, you should make sure that the size of each message does not exceed the maximum IP packet size, which is given by the iMaxUdpDg element in the WSAData structure returned by WSAStartup.

As an example of datagram-based message exchange, consider a server that echoes back each message it receives. The server creates a socket, binds it to an address and a port, and falls into a loop where it calls recvfrom to await a datagram from a client. When a datagram arrives, the recvfrom function returns the data as well as the address of the sender (the client). The server can then call sendto to echo the datagram back to the client. Here is how such a datagram-based server's data exchange code might be implemented:

```
// Assume the server has created SOCKET sock1 and bound
// it to local address and port

SOCKADDR_IN  saClnt;     // Socket address of client
int          saClntLen;  // Size of the address structure
char         buf[512];   // Buffer for message
```

```
while(1)
{
    int numchr = 0;
    saClntLen = sizeof(saClnt);

// Receive a message
    numchr = recvfrom(sock1, buf, sizeof(buf), 0,
                      (PSOCKADDR)&saClnt, &saClntLen);

// If there are no errors, send the message back
    if(numchr != SOCKET_ERROR)
    {
        if(sendto(sock1, buf, numchr, 0,
               (PSOCKADDR)&saClnt, saClntLen) ==
                SOCKET_ERROR)
        {
// Error sending message.
// Handle error (perhaps break the loop)...
//...
        }
    }
}
```

As with the example for connection-oriented data transfer, the client side of this datagram example can use a similar loop. The client begins by calling sendto with the address of the server as the destination. Then it calls recvfrom to receive data from the server.

Locating Hosts and Services

From the steps in Windows Sockets programming, you may have noticed that clients have to know the address of a host system and the port number where a specific service is located. Generally, hosts and services are identified by descriptive names. Text files store the database of host names and services and the database functions in Windows Sockets API enable you to translate the names into machine-readable formats required by other sockets API functions.

Host Names

In the TCP/IP protocol suite, hosts are identified by 4-byte IP addresses. There is a well-known "dot" format for IP addresses in which the bytes are expressed as decimal values separated by periods (.). Thus, you often see references to IP addresses such as 140.90.23.100 or 129.79.20.84.

Usually, you can refer to a host by a name rather than the IP address. Recall that the host file associates each host name to an IP address. The location of the host file depends on the operating system:

■ On UNIX systems, the host file is /etc/hosts.

■ In Windows NT, the host file is
%SystemRoot%\SYSTEM32\DRIVERS\ETC\HOSTS
where the environment variable SystemRoot denotes the installation directory of
Windows NT.

The entries in the host file are of the following form:

```
# This is a comment

140.90.23.100   addlab
140.90.23.101   addlabx    # X Terminal
```

Each line has an IP address in dot notation followed by the name associated with that IP address.

The Windows Sockets API functions `gethostbyname` and `gethostbyaddr` access the host file to retrieve information about a host. These functions return a pointer to a `hostent` structure that is declared in WINSOCK.H:

```
struct  hostent
{
    char    *h_name;        // Official name of host
    char    **h_aliases;    // Aliases (other names)
    short   h_addrtype;     // Host address type
    short   h_length;       // Length of address
    char    **h_addr_list;  // List of addresses
#define h_addr  h_addr_list[0] // address, for backward compat
};
```

Services

The TCP/IP protocol suite has become the common language of the Internet because there are quite a few standard services available on systems that support TCP/IP. These services make the Internet tick by enabling the transfer of mail and news and also remote logins. Like the hosts, these services go by well-known names such as the following:

- ftp (File Transfer Protocol)
- smtp (Simple Mail Transfer Protocol)
- nntp (Network News Transfer Protocol)
- snmp (Simple Network Management Protocol)
- tftp (Trivial File Transfer Protocol)
- nfs (Network File System)

Each of these services has a well-known port associated with it. Like the association between host names and IP addresses, the association between a service name and a port number (and protocol—stream or datagram) is stored in another text file whose location depends on the operating system:

- On UNIX systems, the file is /etc/services.
- In Windows NT, the file is
  %SystemRoot%\SYSTEM32\DRIVERS\ETC\SERVICES
  where the environment variable `SystemRoot` denotes the installation directory of
  Windows NT.

As an example, here is a portion of the SERVICES file for Windows NT 3.5:

```
# Copyright (c) 1993 Microsoft Corp.
#
# This file contains port numbers for well-known services as
# defined by RFC 1060 (Assigned Numbers).
#
# Format:
#
# <service name> <port number>/<protocol> [aliases...] [#<comment>]
#

echo            7/tcp
echo            7/udp
discard         9/tcp       sink null
discard         9/udp       sink null
systat         11/tcp
systat         11/tcp       users
daytime        13/tcp
daytime        13/udp
netstat        15/tcp
qotd           17/tcp       quote
qotd           17/udp       quote
chargen        19/tcp       ttytst source
chargen        19/udp       ttytst source
ftp-data       20/tcp
ftp            21/tcp
telnet         23/tcp
smtp           25/tcp       mail
time           37/tcp       timserver
time           37/udp       timserver
rlp            39/udp       resource      # resource location
name           42/tcp       nameserver
name           42/udp       nameserver
whois          43/tcp       nicname       # usually to sri-nic
domain         53/tcp       nameserver    # name-domain server
domain         53/udp       nameserver
nameserver     53/tcp       domain        # name-domain server
nameserver     53/udp       domain
mtp            57/tcp                     # deprecated
bootp          67/udp                     # boot program server
tftp           69/udp
```

As you can see, each entry starts with the name of the service followed by a port number, a slash, and then a protocol name (tcp or udp). The tcp protocol refers to stream sockets, and udp means a datagram socket is used. The two protocols can use the same port numbers without any conflict. Often, a service listens to the same port number, using both tcp and udp protocols. Some services, however, use only one type of protocol.

The Windows Sockets API functions getservbyname and getservbyport use the SERVICES file to provide information about a service. These functions return a pointer to a servent structure that is declared in WINSOCK.H:

```
struct  servent
{
    char    *s_name;            // Official service name
    char    **s_aliases;        // Aliases (other names)
    short   s_port;             // Port number
    char    *s_proto;           // Protocol to use (tcp or udp)
};
```

Windows Sockets Sample Applications

Now that you know the basics of Windows Sockets programming, it's time to try out some examples. The following sections present two example programs that show how to use the Windows Sockets API functions from an MFC-based application. The first example is a simple client that gets the date and time from a specified host by establishing connection to the daytime server. The second example shows a connectionless datagram protocol used for exchanging messages between a server and one or more clients.

To test these examples, you need, at a minimum, a Windows NT system. To see the programs work in a distributed manner with the server and client running on separate systems, you need at least two networked systems running the TCP/IP protocols.

DAYTIME—A Simple Client

Because a Windows Sockets client application is easier to write than a server, start with a simple client that connects to the daytime service at a specified host (identified by an IP address), gets the date and time, and reports the results.

Designing DAYTIME

Let's use a standard MFC AppWizard-generated document-view application that enables the user to start a connection by selecting the File | Open menu item. This displays a dialog box that prompts the user for the IP address of a host. You can display the dialog box in the command handler for the File | Open command in the application's view class.

After the user enters a host address and clicks the OK button in the dialog, the File | Open command handler can call a member function of the document class to take care of the sockets-based communications. After receiving the data, the document class can store it in a CString object. The view is updated by calling the UpdateAllViews function.

The OnDraw member function of the view class parses the text contained in the display text in the view window.

Generating and Building DAYTIME

Start by creating a new project named DAYTIME in Visual C++ 2.0. Select MFC AppWizard(exe) as the project time. Accept all default options except the interface style—use single document interface (SDI) rather than multiple document interface (MDI).

After the project is created, follow these steps to modify the template and build the Windows Sockets client application DAYTIME.EXE:

1. To use the Windows Sockets API, you need to include the header file WINSOCK.H. To take care of this, add the following line to the header file STDAFX.H:

   ```
   #include <winsock.h>
   ```

2. To prompt the user for the IP address of a host, create a new dialog box by double-clicking on the DAYTIME.RC file in the project window and adding a dialog by selecting Resource | New. Figure 32.6 shows the appearance of the dialog box.

3. Select ClassWizard from the Project menu and select the Add Class button from one of the tabs in the ClassWizard dialog. Specify a class name of CConDlg and select a class type of CDialog. This enables you to select a dialog resource to be associated with the resource—pick the resource ID of the dialog you created in step 2.

4. Without exiting from ClassWizard, go to the Member Variables tab and add a CString member variable named m_HostAddress for accepting the value in the IDC_EDIT1 control (this is where the user enters the host's IP address). Close the ClassWizard dialog by clicking on the OK button at the bottom of the dialog box.

5. Using ClassWizard, add a member function named OnFileOpen in the view class (CDaytimeView) to handle the ID_FILE_OPEN and ID_FILE_NEW commands. Click on the Edit Code button and define the OnFileOpen function as follows:

   ```
   void CDaytimeView::OnFileOpen()
   {
       CConDlg conDlg;
       conDlg.DoModal();

   // Call the TalkTo function of the document class
       CDaytimeDoc* pDoc = GetDocument();
       ASSERT_VALID(pDoc);

       if(!pDoc->TalkTo(conDlg.m_HostAddress, DAYTIME_PORT))
       {
           MessageBox("Cannot talk to server", "Client");
       }
   }
   ```

6. In the source file for the CDaytimeView class (DAYTIVW.CPP), add the following lines:

```
#include "condlg.h"

// Port number of 'daytime' server
const UINT DAYTIME_PORT = 13;
```

7. Edit the OnDraw function of the view class so that it parses the text maintained by the document class and displays the lines in the window:

```
/////////////////////////////////////////////////////////////////
// CDaytimeView drawing

void CDaytimeView::OnDraw(CDC* pDC)
{
    CDaytimeDoc* pDoc = GetDocument();
    ASSERT_VALID(pDoc);

// Get the text from the document
    CString& data = pDoc->GetData();
    int x = 8, y = 10, nc = data.GetLength();

// Compute the line height based on current font
    TEXTMETRIC tm;
    pDC->GetTextMetrics(&tm);
    int line_height = tm.tmHeight + tm.tmExternalLeading;
    LPCTSTR pc = (LPCTSTR)data;

    int np = 0, nl = 0;

    while(np < nc)
    {
// Expand tabs and break up text into lines
        for(nl = 0; nl < nc-np; nl++)
        {
            if(pc[nl] == '\t')
            {
                pDC->TextOut(x, y, pc, nl);
                x += nl * tm.tmAveCharWidth;
                pDC->TextOut(x, y, "    ", 4);
                nl++;
                np += nl;
                pc = &pc[nl];
                break;
```

```
            }
            if(pc[nl] == '\r' || pc[nl] == '\n')
            {
                pDC->TextOut(x, y, pc, nl);
                nl++;
                y += line_height;

// Skip the line feed (\n) following a carriage-return
                (\r) if(nl < nc-np-1 && pc[nl-1] == '\r' &&
                  pc[nl] == '\n') nl++;

                np += nl;
                pc = &pc[nl];
                break;
            }
        }
// Display last line (which may not have a newline)
        if(nl >= nc-np)
        {
            pDC->TextOut(x, y, pc, nc-np);
            break;
        }
    }
}
```

8. In the header file (DAYTIDOC.H) for the document class (CDaytimeDoc), add the following member variables and member functions (shown in boldface):

```
class CDaytimeDoc : public Cdocument
{
//...

// Implementation

public:
//...

    CString& GetData() { return m_data;}
    BOOL TalkTo(CString& address, UINT port);

protected:
    CString m_data;        // Text received from server
    BOOL    m_bInitialized; // TRUE = Winsock initialized
//...
};
```

9. Initialize the `m_data` and `m_bInitialized` variables in the `CDaytimeDoc` class constructor:

```
CDaytimeDoc::CDaytimeDoc()
{
    m_data = "Select 'Open...' from File menu\n";
    m_bInitialized = FALSE;
}
```

10. The DAYTIME client application's work is done in the `TalkTo` member function of the `CDaytimeDoc` class. This function initializes the Windows Sockets API, establishes a connection to the specified host address and port number, and reads data from the server. The `TalkTo` function is defined as follows:

```
BOOL CDaytimeDoc::TalkTo(CString& address, UINT port)
{
    m_data  += "----------------------------------------------\n";
    m_data  += "Connecting to" + address + "\n";
    UpdateAllViews(NULL);

    if(!m_bInitialized)
    {
        int      status;   // Status Code
        WSADATA wsaData;   // Structure to hold information
                           // about Sockets DLL

        m_data += "Initializing Windows Sockets DLL...";
        UpdateAllViews(NULL);

        if((status = WSAStartup(MAKEWORD(1,1), &wsaData)) == 0)
        {
// Success
// wsaData contains information about the Windows
// Sockets DLL
//...
            m_data += "Succeeded\n";
            m_bInitialized = TRUE;
        }
        else
        {
// Failed. Handle error.
//...
            m_data += "Falied\n";
            return FALSE;
        }
```

```
        }

        m_data += "Creating socket...";
        UpdateAllViews(NULL);

// Create socket
    SOCKET s = socket(AF_INET, SOCK_STREAM, 0);

    if (s == INVALID_SOCKET)
    {
        m_data += "Failed\n";
        return FALSE;
    }

// Bind socket to address
    m_data += "Succeeded\nBinding socket...";
    UpdateAllViews(NULL);
// Set up the address structure
    SOCKADDR_IN sa;
    sa.sin_family = AF_INET;              // Internet address family
    sa.sin_addr.s_addr = htonl(INADDR_ANY);  // Use any appropriate address
    sa.sin_port = htons(0);      // Can be 0 for clients

    if(bind(s,(PSOCKADDR)&sa, sizeof(sa)) == SOCKET_ERROR)
    {
// Error binding socket to address
        m_data += "Failed\n";
        closesocket(s);
        return FALSE;
    }

    m_data += "Succeeded\nCalling connect()...";
    UpdateAllViews(NULL);

// Call connect to establish a connection
// Set up the server's address structure
    SOCKADDR_IN saSrv;
    saSrv.sin_family = AF_INET;
    saSrv.sin_addr.s_addr = inet_addr(address);
    saSrv.sin_port = htons(port);
```

```
    if(connect(s,(PSOCKADDR)&saSrv,sizeof(saSrv)) ==
            SOCKET_ERROR)
    {
// Handle error
        m_data += "Failed\n";
        closesocket(s);
        return FALSE;
    }
    m_data += "Succeeded\n";
    UpdateAllViews(NULL);

// At this point, a connection to the server has been
// established and data exchange can begin

// Exchange data...

    char buf[512] = "\n";
    char *p_c;
    int  count;
    int  numchr;

// The daytime server sends the date and time immediately
// after connection is established. So, we begin by reading
// from the socket. Other clients may start by sending
// data to the server.

// Receive all outstanding data on socket
    p_c = buf;
    count = sizeof(buf);
    numchr = 0;

    do
    {
        numchr = recv(s, p_c, count, 0);
        if(numchr == 0 || numchr == SOCKET_ERROR)
        {
            closesocket(s);
            break;
        }
        else
        {
```

```
            p_c += numchr;
            count -= numchr;
        }
    } while(count > 0);
    m_data += "Report: ";
    m_data += buf;
    UpdateAllViews(NULL);

    return TRUE;
}
```

11. Add a call to WSACleanup in the destructor for the CDaytimeDoc class:

```
CDaytimeDoc::~CDaytimeDoc()
{
    if(m_bInitialized)
    {
        WSACleanup();
    }
}
```

12. Select the Files... item from the Project menu and add the Windows Sockets import library (WSOCK32.LIB) to the project.

13. Build the DAYTIME.EXE program by pressing Shift+F8.

Testing DAYTIME

After successfully building DAYTIME.EXE, run it from the Visual Workbench by pressing F5 (or selecting Go from the Debug menu). The view window will display a line asking you to select File | Open. When you do, DAYTIME displays a dialog prompting for the IP address of a server. Figure 32.6 shows the initial view window with the dialog.

After you enter a host address and click the OK button, the DAYTIME program establishes a connection with the daytime server at port 13 of that host and displays the date and time. As Figure 32.7 shows, the program also displays some detailed information about the steps involved in establishing a connection.

You can contact another host, if you want. Figure 32.8 shows the dates and times obtained from the DAYTIME server at two different hosts.

FIGURE 32.6.
DAYTIME prompting for a host address.

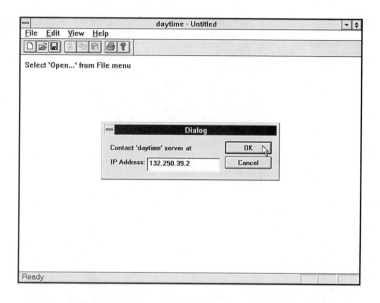

FIGURE 32.7.
Date and time displayed by DAYTIME.

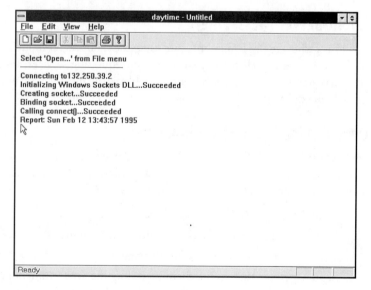

FIGURE 32.8.

Date and time from multiple hosts.

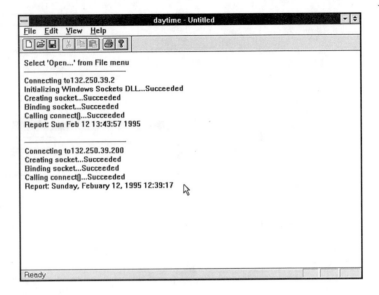

Client-Server Messaging

To illustrate how to implement software using the client-server model, consider a simple server that enables multiple clients to send messages requesting services. In this example, the messages may not do much, but in a real-life problem, the messages are more complex—the messages define the protocol between the server and its clients.

Designing the Client-Server Example

Let's use a standard MFC AppWizard-generated document-view application for both the server and the client. The server will create a socket, bind it to the local address and a well-known port, and start a thread that performs the following tasks:

1. Read a datagram by calling `recvfrom`.
2. Interpret the message code—use a short integer value as the message code.
3. Process the message in a `switch` statement.
4. Send a message back to the client by calling the `sendto` function. (Recall that the `recvfrom` function also returns the address of the sending client.)

On the client side, the user initiates a session with a host by selecting the File | Open menu item. This displays a dialog box that prompts the user for the IP address of the host. This dialog box is activated in the command handler for the File | Open command in the application's view class.

After the user enters a host address and clicks the OK button in the dialog, the File | Open command handler creates a socket, binds it to the local address and port (selected by Windows Sockets API), and starts a thread to listen to messages arriving from the server. That way the client's main thread can continue to react to user input and display received messages in the view window.

The listening thread in the client stores all received data (which is textual in this example) in a CString object. The OnDraw member function of the view class parses this text and displays the lines of text in the view window. The listening thread updates the display by calling the InvalidateRect member function of the view.

For both the server and the client, you use the same OnDraw function as that used by the view class of the DAYTIME example program.

Building the Server

Start by creating a new MFC AppWizard(exe) project named SRVR in Visual C++ 2.0. After MFC AppWizard creates the project, use the following steps to complete the server:

1. In the header file SRVRVIEW.H for the CSrvrView class, add the following member variables (make them public):

   ```
   CString m_data;
   SOCKET  m_sock;
   HANDLE  m_hListenerThread;
   ```

2. At the beginning of the file SRVRVIEW.CPP, add the following to define some messages and the port number for the server:

   ```
   #define ATTACH   100
   #define DETACH   200
   #define ECHO     300
   #define TIME     400


   const UINT SRV_UDP_PORT = 5050;
   ```

3. Initialize Windows Sockets and create and bind the socket in the view class constructor:

   ```
   CSrvrView::CSrvrView()
   {
       m_hListenerThread = NULL;

       int     status;    // Status Code
       WSADATA wsaData;    // Structure to hold information
                           // about Sockets DLL

       m_data = "Initializing Windows Sockets DLL...";
   ```

```
        if((status = WSAStartup(MAKEWORD(1,1), &wsaData)) == 0)
        {
// Success
// wsaData contains information about the Windows
// Sockets DLL
//...
            m_data += "Succeeded\n";
            m_bInitialized = TRUE;
        }
        else
        {
            m_bInitialized = FALSE;
        }

        m_data += "Creating socket...";

// Create socket
        m_sock = socket(AF_INET, SOCK_DGRAM, 0);

        if (m_sock == INVALID_SOCKET)
        {
            m_data += "Failed\n";
        }

// Bind socket to address
        m_data += "Succeeded\nBinding socket...";

// Set up the address structure
        SOCKADDR_IN sa;
        sa.sin_family = AF_INET;
        sa.sin_addr.s_addr = htonl(INADDR_ANY);
        sa.sin_port = htons(SRV_UDP_PORT);

        if(bind(m_sock,(PSOCKADDR)&sa, sizeof(sa)) == SOCKET_ERROR)
        {
// Error binding socket to address
            m_data += "Failed\n";
            closesocket(m_sock);
        }

        m_data += "Succeeded\nCreating listener thread...";
```

```
        unsigned long idThread;
        m_hListenerThread = CreateThread(NULL,0,
                            (LPTHREAD_START_ROUTINE)Listener,
                            (void *)this, 0, &idThread);
        if(m_hListenerThread)
            m_data += "Succeeded\nListening...\n";
        else
            m_data += "Failed\n";
    }
```

4. Perform necessary cleanups in the destructor of the view class:

```
    CSrvrView::~CSrvrView()
    {
        if(m_bInitialized)
            WSACleanup();

        closesocket(m_sock);

        if(m_hListenerThread)
            ::TerminateThread(m_hListenerThread, 0);
    }
```

5. Define the thread that receives and processes messages:

```
    long WINAPI Listener(CSrvrView* pView)
    {
    // This thread is terminated by calling TerminateThread when
    // the view is destroyed

        SOCKADDR_IN saClnt;
        char msg[MSGSIZE];
        int saClntLen, nchar, msglen;

        while(1)
        {
            saClntLen = sizeof(saClnt);
            nchar = recvfrom(pView->m_sock, msg, MSGSIZE, 0,
                                (PSOCKADDR)&saClnt, &saClntLen);

            if(nchar < 0)
            {
                pView->m_data += "Error in recvfrom\n";
                pView->InvalidateRect(NULL);
```

```
            }
            else
            {
                msglen = nchar;

                short *p_code = (short*)msg;
                short code = ntohs(*p_code);

                switch(code)
                {
                    case ATTACH:
                        wsprintf(msg, "Client from %s attached\n",
                                inet_ntoa(saClnt.sin_addr));
                        msglen = strlen(msg);
                        pView->m_data += msg;
                        pView->InvalidateRect(NULL);
                        break;

                    case DETACH:
                        wsprintf(msg, "Client from %s detached\n",
                                inet_ntoa(saClnt.sin_addr));
                        msglen = strlen(msg);
                        pView->m_data += msg;
                        pView->InvalidateRect(NULL);
                        break;

                    case TIME:
                        time_t tnow;
                        time(&tnow);
                        sprintf(msg, "Time now: %s\n", ctime(&tnow));
                        msglen = strlen(msg);
                        break;

                    case ECHO:
// Read the next message and echo it back
                        saClntLen = sizeof(saClnt);
                        msglen = recvfrom(pView->m_sock, msg, MSGSIZE, 0,
                                (PSOCKADDR)&saClnt, &saClntLen);
                        break;

                    default:
                        wsprintf(msg,
```

```
                                "Don't understand message: %d\n",
                                code);
                        msglen = strlen(msg);


                }
        }


    // Send the reply back to the client
            sendto(pView->m_sock, msg, msglen, 0,
                                (PSOCKADDR)&saClnt, saClntLen);
    }


        return(0);
}
```

6. Add WSOCK32.LIB to the project and build the server executable, SRVR.EXE.

Building the Client

Create a new MFC AppWizard(exe) project named CLNT in Visual C++ 2.0. After the project is created, follow these steps to build the client:

1. Add a new dialog box to the resource file. This dialog box (see Figure 32.10) prompts the user for the IP address of the host. Using the ClassWizard, add a dialog class (CEchoDlg) associated with the newly added dialog resource and a member variable m_HostAddress to hold the host address entered by the user.

2. In the header file CLNTVIEW.H for the CClntView class, add the following member variables (make them public):

```
    CString      m_data;
    HANDLE       m_hListenerThread;
    SOCKET       m_sock;
    SOCKADDR_IN  m_saSrvr;
    BOOL         m_bInitialized;
```

3. At the beginning of the file CLNTVIEW.CPP, add the following to define the message codes and the port number of the server:

```
#define ATTACH   100
#define DETACH   200
#define ECHO     300
#define TIME     400


#define MSGSIZE 512


const UINT SRV_UDP_PORT = 5050;
```

4. Using ClassWizard, add the OnFileOpen member function to the CClntView class to handle the File | Open and File | New messages. In the OnFileOpen function, display the dialog box that prompts the user for a host address and then set up the sockets appropriately. Define the OnFileOpen function as follows:

```
void CClntView::OnFileOpen()
{
    if(m_bInitialized)
    {
        MessageBox("Already connected", "Client",
                     MB_ICONHAND | MB_OK);
        return;
    }

    CConDlg condlg;
    condlg.DoModal();

// Set up the server's address structure
    m_saSrvr.sin_family = AF_INET;
    m_saSrvr.sin_addr.s_addr = htonl(INADDR_ANY);
    m_saSrvr.sin_addr.s_addr = inet_addr(condlg.m_HostAddress);
    m_saSrvr.sin_port = htons(SRV_UDP_PORT);

    int     status;   // Status Code
    WSADATA wsaData;  // Structure to hold information
                      // about Sockets DLL

    m_data = "Initializing Windows Sockets DLL...";

    if((status = WSAStartup(MAKEWORD(1,1), &wsaData)) == 0)
    {
// Success
// wsaData contains information about the Windows
// Sockets DLL
//...
        m_data += "Succeeded\n";
        m_bInitialized = TRUE;
    }
    else
    {
        m_bInitialized = FALSE;
        return;
```

```
    }

    m_data += "Creating socket...";

// Create socket
    m_sock = socket(AF_INET, SOCK_DGRAM, 0);

    if (m_sock == INVALID_SOCKET)
    {
        m_data += "Failed\n";
        return;
    }

// Bind socket to address
    m_data += "Succeeded\nBinding socket...";

// Set up the address structure
    SOCKADDR_IN sa;
    sa.sin_family = AF_INET;              // Internet address family
    sa.sin_addr.s_addr = htonl(INADDR_ANY);   // Use any appropriate address
    sa.sin_port = htons(0);

    if(bind(m_sock,(PSOCKADDR)&sa, sizeof(sa)) == SOCKET_ERROR)
    {
// Error binding socket to address
        m_data += "Failed\n";
        closesocket(m_sock);
    }

    m_data += "Succeeded\nCreating listener thread...";

    unsigned long idThread;
    m_hListenerThread = CreateThread(NULL,0,
                            (LPTHREAD_START_ROUTINE)Listener,
                            (void *)this, 0, &idThread);
    if(m_hListenerThread)
        m_data += "Succeeded\nWaiting...\n";
    else
        m_data += "Failed\n";

    InvalidateRect(NULL);
}
```

5. Define the Listener function (representing the thread that listens to the server) as follows:

```
long WINAPI Listener(CClntView* pView)
{
// This thread is terminated by calling TerminateThread when
// the view is destroyed

    pView->m_data += "Sending ATTACH command\n";
    pView->InvalidateRect(NULL);

// Send an ATTACH command to the server
    short cmd = htons(ATTACH);
    sendto(pView->m_sock, (char*)&cmd, sizeof(cmd), 0,
                (PSOCKADDR)&pView->m_saSrvr,
                sizeof(pView->m_saSrvr));

    char msg[MSGSIZE];
    int saSrvrLen, nchar;

    while(1)
    {
        saSrvrLen = sizeof(pView->m_saSrvr);
        nchar = recvfrom(pView->m_sock, msg, MSGSIZE, 0,
                    (PSOCKADDR)&pView->m_saSrvr, &saSrvrLen);

        if(nchar < 0)
        {
            pView->m_data += "Error in recvfrom\n";
        }
        else
        {
            pView->m_data += msg;
        }
        pView->InvalidateRect(NULL);
    }

    return(0);
}
```

6. To enable the user to send specific messages to the server, add a new Transactions menu to the menu bar and provide menu items to send a TIME or ECHO message to the server. Implement these command handlers as follows:

```
void CClntView::OnTransactionsTime()
{
// Send a TIME transaction to the server
    m_data += "Sending TIME command\n";
    InvalidateRect(NULL);

    short cmd = htons(TIME);
    sendto(m_sock, (char*)&cmd, sizeof(cmd), 0,
                (PSOCKADDR)&m_saSrvr,
                sizeof(m_saSrvr));

}


void CClntView::OnTransactionsEcho()
{
    CEchoDlg echodlg;
    echodlg.DoModal();

// Send an ECHO transaction to the server
    m_data += "Server should echo: ";
    m_data += echodlg.m_EchoString;
    m_data += "\n";
    InvalidateRect(NULL);

    short cmd = htons(ECHO);
    sendto(m_sock, (char*)&cmd, sizeof(cmd), 0,
                (PSOCKADDR)&m_saSrvr,
                sizeof(m_saSrvr));

// Now send the message to echo
    sendto(m_sock, echodlg.m_EchoString,
                echodlg.m_EchoString.GetLength(), 0,
                (PSOCKADDR)&m_saSrvr, sizeof(m_saSrvr));
}
```

7. Add WSOCK32.LIB to the project and build the client executable, CLNT.EXE.

Testing the Server and the Client

After successfully building the server and the client, you can test them using the following steps:

1. Run the server (SRVR.EXE). It displays the view shown in Figure 32.9 and waits for a client to send messages.

2. Start the client (CLNT.EXE) and select File | Open. It displays a dialog box prompting for the host's address as shown in Figure 32.10. Enter the host address and click the OK button.

3. Figure 32.11 shows the resulting server and client windows. As the server window indicates, the client has sent an ATTACH message to the server. Figure 32.11 also shows the Transactions menu in the client application. In this case, the client and server are running on the same system.

4. If you happen to have another system on the network (or you could do this from the same system as the one where the server is running), start another copy of the client (CLNT.EXE) on the other system and specify the server's host address. These clients can then send specific messages (by using the Transactions menu). For example, when the client sends a TIME message, the server returns the current time just as the standard daytime server does. Figure 32.12 shows the server connected to two clients (as indicated by the message in the server's window).

FIGURE 32.9.

Server waiting for clients.

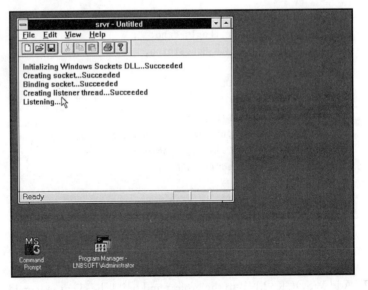

FIGURE 32.10.

Client application prompting for a server's address.

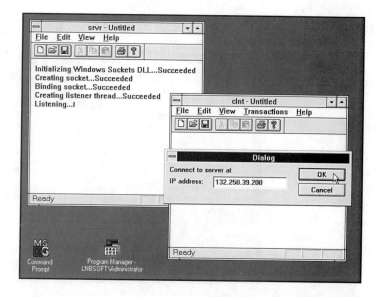

FIGURE 32.11.

Client sending an ATTACH message to the server.

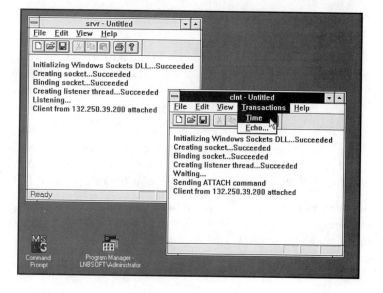

FIGURE 32.12.
Two clients exchanging messages with the server.

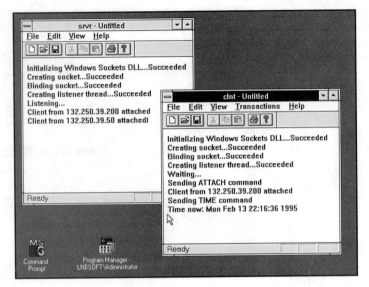

Summary

With the increasing popularity of networks and the Internet, network programming is becoming an increasingly important part of application development. When the client-server model is used to implement corporate information systems, the information is managed by servers with desktop PCs running Windows playing the role of clients. This makes network programming under Windows a necessity for many business applications.

There are many network programming options available for Windows NT, including NetBIOS, named pipes, RPC, and the Windows Sockets API. The Windows Sockets API is ideal for writing network applications that support the popular Internet protocol TCP/IP.

Although Visual C++ 2.0 does not include any built-in facility to help you with network programming, you can write distributed applications (that require network programming) using the Windows Sockets API. This chapter introduces you to the Windows Sockets API and presents example programs that show how to write MFC-based client and server applications that call Windows Sockets API functions.

B

Bibliography

C++ and object-oriented programming (OOP) are steadily gaining popularity, and the number of books and articles on these topics reflect this trend. Here is a list of resources that will help you learn more about C++ and OOP. The list, organized by category, also includes a number of references for other topics, such as Microsoft Windows programming and ANSI Standard C. This bibliography is by no means exhaustive; it's just a sample of the numerous books and journals that cover C++ and object-oriented programming.

C++ and Object-Oriented Programming

Most books on C++ cover object-oriented programming. One recent book, *Data Abstractions and Object-Oriented Programming in C++*, by Keith Gorlen, Sanford Orlow, and Perry Plexico, does a good job of teaching data abstraction and OOP using C++. Much of the book focuses on showing how to exploit reusable software components from class libraries such as the NIH Class Library developed by the authors.

For an official description of C++, check out a copy of *The C++ Programming Language*, Second Edition, by Bjarne Stroustrup, the inventor of C++. Another source of official description of C++ is *The Annotated C++ Reference Manual*, (often referred to as the *ARM*) by Margaret Ellis and Bjarne Stroustrup. The annotations in this book can help you understand the motivation behind the choices made during the design and improvement of the C++ programming language.

The book by Mark Mullin, *Object-Oriented Program Design with Examples in C++*, is worth noting because it covers object-oriented techniques with a single, large-scale program example in C++. Jerry Smith's book, *Reusability & Software Construction: C & C++*, also covers the design and implementation of a single program—in this case, a window-based text editor.

There are a host of other books by authors such as Lippman, Pohl, Dewhurst, Swan, and Weiskamp that cover the C++ programming language. Some offer insights into OOP, but focus mainly on teaching the C++ language without much emphasis on object-orientation.

To keep up with recent developments on how others are using C++ and how the ANSI standard for C++ is progressing, you should consult journals such as *The C++ Report*, published by SIGS Publications, New York, NY.

Dewhurst, Stephen C., and Kathy T. Stark. *Programming in C++*. Prentice Hall, Inc., Englewood Cliffs, NJ, 1989.

Ellis, Margaret A., and Bjarne Stroustrup. *The Annotated C++ Reference Manual*. Addison-Wesley Publishing Company, Reading, MA, 1990.

Gorlen, Keith E., Sanford M. Orlow, and Perry S. Plexico. *Data Abstractions and Object-Oriented Programming in C++*. John Wiley & Sons, Ltd., Chichester, West Sussex, England, 1990.

Lippman, Stanley B. *C++ Primer*, Second Edition. Addison-Wesley Publishing Company, Reading, MA, 1991.

Mullin, Mark. *Object-Oriented Program Design with Examples in C++*. Addison-Wesley Publishing Company, Reading, MA, 1989.

Pohl, Ira. *C++ for C Programmers*. The Benjamin/Cummings Publishing Company, Redwood City, CA, 1989.

Smith, Jerry D. *Reusability & Software Construction: C & C++*. John Wiley & Sons, Inc., New York, NY, 1990.

Stroustrup, Bjarne. *The C++ Programming Language,* Second Edition. Addison-Wesley Publishing Company, Reading, MA, 1991.

Swan, Tom. *Learning C++*. Sams Publishing, Carmel, IN, 1992.

Weiskamp, Keith, and Bryan Flamig. *The Complete C++ Primer*. Academic Press, Inc., San Diego, CA, 1990.

Object-Oriented Design and Programming

As a topic, object-oriented programming is still in the evolutionary stage—its very definition is a subject of debate among experts. Still, the basic concepts of OOP have been covered in many books and journal articles.

Bertrand Meyer's book, *Object-Oriented Software Construction,* has a good description of the object-oriented approach. For a high-level overview of object-oriented concepts, terminology, and software, consult the recent books by Setrag Khosafian and Razmik Abnous (*Object Orientation: Concepts, Languages, Databases, User Interfaces*) and by Ann Winblad, Samuel Edwards, and David King (*Object-Oriented Software*).

Other good sources of information on recent developments in OOP include the proceedings of the annual *Object-Oriented Programming Systems, Languages, and Applications (OOPSLA)* conference sponsored by the Association for Computing Machinery and the *Journal of Object-Oriented Programming* published bimonthly by SIGS Publications, Inc. of New York, NY.

OBJECT-ORIENTED ANALYSIS, DESIGN, AND PROGRAMMING

Object-oriented programming (OOP) refers to the implementation of programs using objects, preferably in an object-oriented programming language such as C++. Although this book focuses on OOP using C++, the analysis and design phases of the software development process are even more important than the language used. *Object-oriented analysis (OOA)* refers to methods of specifying the requirements of the software in terms of real-world objects, their behavior, and their interactions.

Object-oriented design (OOD), on the other hand, turns the software requirements into specifications for objects and derives class hierarchies from which the objects can be created. OOD methods usually use a diagramming notation to represent the class hierarchy and to express the interaction among objects.

Despite a recent surge in books and articles on object-oriented design, this topic remains an elusive one to grasp. Because no single approach works for all problems, most descriptions of object-oriented design are, of necessity, a collage of case studies and extrapolations based on the experience of programmers in the field. You have to work through many examples before you can arrive at a set of guidelines for the software design approach that best suits a specific problem. Here is a selection of reading material to help you achieve that goal. Although this is a short list, each of these sources will, in turn, provide you with numerous other references on object-oriented design.

Grady Booch first described object-oriented design in his 1983 book on the Ada programming language. In his 1990 book, *Software Engineering with Ada,* he presents a more refined description of the incremental and iterative nature of object-oriented software design.

Brad Cox, the originator of the *Objective-C* language, describes his view of object-oriented programming in his 1986 book, *Object-Oriented Programming—An Evolutionary Approach.* He promotes the idea of packaging software in modular units, which he calls *Software-ICs* (software integrated circuits).

Bertrand Meyer, author of an object-oriented language named *Eiffel,* describes object-oriented design as supported by the Eiffel language in his book, *Object-Oriented Software Construction.* One of his ideas is the notion of *programming by contract*—the idea that for correct operation, a software module and its consumers must, in some way, formally express the rights and obligations of each side.

The recent book by Rebecca Wirfs-Brock, Brian Wilkerson, and Lauren Wiener, *Designing Object-Oriented Software*, presents a detailed example of object-oriented design using a "responsibility-driven" approach. The idea is to identify the classes, their responsibilities, and their collaborators. In this approach, you lay out the design on a set of index cards, called CRC cards, where CRC stands for Class, Responsibility, and Collaboration. This seems to be a promising step-by-step approach to object-oriented design of software.

The September 1990 issue of *Communications of the ACM*—the flagship magazine of the Association for Computing Machinery—is a special issue on object-oriented design. Consult this issue for a good assortment of articles on the object-oriented approach. In another article in the May 1989 issue of this journal, "An Object-Oriented Requirements Specification Method," Sidney Bailin presents a method for specifying the requirements for object-oriented software.

Notational schemes are another important tool because they enable you to express your design in a concise, yet descriptive manner. Although Booch, Meyer, and Cox have used some form of notation in their books, there is no universally accepted convention. For a sampling of some proposed notational schemes, see the recent journal articles.

Another interesting idea is to mix conventional function-oriented design with object-oriented concepts in a hybrid design strategy. Larry Constantine, one of the pioneers of structural techniques, discusses such an approach in a *Computer Language* article called "Objects, Functions, and Program Extensibility."

For a description of SmallTalk-80's Model-View-Controller (MVC) architecture, see Adele Goldberg's recent article in *Dr. Dobb's Journal,* "Information Models, Views, and Controllers." For another good discussion of the MVC model as well as some other examples of practical applications of object-oriented methods, see the compendium of essays edited by Lewis Pinson and Richard Wiener, *Applications of Object-Oriented Programming.*

Beck and Cunningham's article in *Proceedings of OOPSLA 1989,* "A Laboratory for Teaching Object-Oriented Thinking," describes the use of index cards to record initial class designs. This tool is used by Wirfs-Brock and colleagues in their responsibility-driven design approach.

The book by James Rambaugh and his colleagues at the General Electric Research and Development Center at Schenectady, New York, is another recommended source of material on object-oriented modeling and design. This book covers the entire development life cycle—analysis, design, and implementation—using a graphical notation and methodology developed by the authors.

Bailin, Sidney. "An Object-Oriented Requirements Specification Method," *Communications of the ACM.* Vol. 32, No. 5, (May 1989), pages 608–23.

Beck, K., and H. Cunningham. "A Laboratory for Teaching Object-Oriented Thinking," *Proceedings of OOPSLA 1989.* New Orleans, LA, October 1989, pages 1–6.

Booch, Grady. *Object-Oriented Design with Applications.* The Benjamin/Cummings Publishing Company, Redwood City, CA, 1991.

———. *Software Engineering with Ada.* The Benjamin/Cummings Publishing Company, Redwood City, CA, 1991.

Communications of the ACM. Special Issue on Object-Oriented Design, Vol. 33, No. 9, (September 1990), pages 38–159.

Constantine, Larry L. "Objects, Functions, and Program Extensibility," *Computer Language.* Vol. 7, No. 1, (January 1990), pages 34–54.

Cox, Brad. *Object-Oriented Programming—An Evolutionary Approach.* Addison-Wesley Publishing Company, Reading, MA, 1986.

Goldberg, Adele. "Information Models, Views, and Controllers," *Dr. Dobb's Journal.* July 1990, pages 54–61.

Khosafian, Setrag, and Razmik Abnous. *Object Orientation: Concepts, Languages, Databases, User Interfaces.* John Wiley & Sons, Inc., New York, NY, 1990.

Meyer, Bertrand. *Object-Oriented Software Construction.* Prentice Hall International (U.K.) Ltd., Hertfordshire, Great Britain, 1988.

Pinson, Lewis J., and Richard S. Wiener, Editors. *Applications of Object-Oriented Programming.* Addison-Wesley Publishing Company, Reading, MA, 1990.

Rambaugh, James, Michael Blaha, William Premerlani, Frederick Eddy, and William Lorensen. *Object-Oriented Modeling and Design.* Prentice-Hall, Inc., Englewood Cliffs, NJ, 1991.

Winblad, Ann L., Samuel D. Edwards, and David R. King. *Object-Oriented Software.* Addison-Wesley Publishing Company, Reading, MA, 1990.

Wirfs-Brock, Rebecca, Brian Wilkerson, and Lauren Wiener. *Designing Object-Oriented Software.* Prentice Hall, Inc., Englewood Cliffs, NJ, 1990.

ANSI Standard C

There are many books on C, and all recent books cover the ANSI standard for C. If you are familiar with C as defined in Kernighan and Ritchie's original book, *The C Programming Language,* First Edition, and want to learn about the changes wrought by the ANSI standardization of C, you can get the second edition of Kernighan and Ritchie's book. Other good references to ANSI Standard C are the books by authors such as Plauger (*Standard C*) and Kochan (*Programming in ANSI C*).

Kernighan, Brian W., and Dennis M. Ritchie. *The C Programming Language*, First Edition. Prentice Hall, Inc., Englewood Cliffs, NJ, 1978.

————. *The C Programming Language*, Second Edition. Prentice Hall, Inc., Englewood Cliffs, NJ, 1988.

Kochan, Stephen G. *Programming in ANSI C.* Hayden Books, Carmel, IN, 1988.

Plauger, P.J., and Jim Brodie. *Standard C.* Microsoft Press, Redmond, WA, 1989.

Visual C++ and Windows Programming

Like C++, Microsoft Windows programming is a favorite topic of computer book authors. Among the available books, the ones by Myers and Doner, Conger, and Schulman are very useful.

Brian Myers and Chris Doner provide very good tutorial coverage of graphics programming with the Windows API and Microsoft C. Although Myers and Doner do not cover Windows programming with C++, you can readily adapt the information from their book for use in your Visual C++ programs. For reference information on Windows API functions, you will find James Conger's books handy. Charles Petzold's classic book is another good tutorial on Windows programming in C with the Windows API.

There are a host of books on Windows programming with Visual C++. David Kruglinski's book covers programming with MFC. Nancy Nicolaisen's recent book is a good reference guide for the MFC classes in Visual C++ 2.0. Michael Young's book focuses exclusively on Windows programming with MFC and Visual C++.

Popular programming journals are a good source of information on programming with Windows Multimedia Control Interface (MCI). Chapter 15 of the book by Brian Myers and Chris

Doner shows a sample application, written in C, that plays sound waves using the MCI commands of the MMSYSTEM.DLL. James Conger's book includes a concise description of the MCI commands.

Conger, James L. *The Waite Group's Windows API Bible.* Waite Group Press, Corte Madera, CA, 1992.

———. *Windows API New Testament.* Waite Group Press. Corte Madera, CA, 1993.

Kruglinski, David. *Inside Visual C++.* Microsoft Press, Redmond, WA, 1993.

Myers, Brian, and Chris Doner. *Programmer's Introduction to Windows 3.1.* SYBEX, Alameda, CA, 1992.

Nicolaisen, Nancy. *The Visual Guide to Visual C++.* Ventana Press, Chapel Hill, NC, 1994.

Petzold, Charles. *Programming Windows.* Microsoft Press, Redmond, WA, 1992.

Schulman, Andrew, David Maxey, and Matt Pietrek. *Undocumented Windows.* Addison-Wesley Publishing Company, Reading, MA, 1992.

Young, Michael J. *Mastering Microsoft Visual C++ Programming.* SYBEX, Alameda, CA, 1993.

Imaging and Animation

For information on displaying and manipulating Windows DIB files (the ones commonly known as the BMP files), consult the book by Brian Myers and Chris Doner (listed in the previous section).

Steve Rimmer has written several books that explain many popular file formats, such as MacPaint, PCX, GIF, TIFF, Truevision Targa, and Microsoft Windows BMP. Rimmer's books include source code in C and 80x86 assembly language to interpret image files. He also provides code to display images on display adapters such as EGA, VGA, and super VGA.

David Kay and John Levine have recently written a book on graphics file formats. Their book describes a large number of image file formats, including PCX, TIFF, JPEG, Windows DIB, Truevision Targa, GIF, MacPaint, and Macintosh PICT. This is the book to consult if you have questions about any of the image file formats described in this chapter.

Craig Lindley's books also cover a number of image file formats, most notably, PCX, TIFF, and GIF. Additionally, one of his books describes the public domain ray tracing program, DKBTrace, which you can use to create computer-generated imagery.

For information on LZW data compression techniques, consult the articles by Ziv and Lempel, by Welch, and by Nelson.

If you are interested in cel animation, you might want to try out the animation studio software from The Walt Disney Company. It runs under DOS and includes the tools necessary to create the cels for an animation.

For a general discussion of animation, consult Chapter 21 of the classic graphics textbook by Foley, van Dam, Feiner, and Hughes.

The Animation Studio. Walt Disney Computer Software, Inc., Burbank, CA, 1991.

Foley, James D., Andries van Dam, Steven K. Feiner, and John F. Hughes. *Computer Graphics Principles and Practice,* Second Edition. Addison-Wesley Publishing Company, Reading, MA, 1990.

Kay, David C., and John R. Levine. *Graphics File Formats.* Windcrest/McGraw-Hill, Blue Ridge Summit, PA, 1992.

Lindley, Craig A. *Practical Image Processing in C.* John Wiley & Sons, Inc., New York, NY, 1991.

———. *Practical Ray Tracing in C.* John Wiley & Sons, Inc., New York, NY, 1992.

Nelson, M. R. "LZW Data Compression," *Dr. Dobb's Journal.* October 1990.

Rimmer, Steve. *Bit-Mapped Graphics.* Windcrest/McGraw-Hill, Blue Ridge Summit, PA, 1990.

———. *Supercharged Bit-Mapped Graphics.* Windcrest/McGraw-Hill, Blue Ridge Summit, PA, 1992.

Welch, T. "A Technique for High-Performance Data Compression," *Computer.* June 1984.

Ziv, J., and A. Lempel. "A Universal Algorithm for Sequential Data Compression," *IEEE Transactions on Information Theory.* May 1977.

OLE Programming

OLE is a significantly large addition to Microsoft Windows, and as such, there are many sources of information about OLE programming. Kraig Brockschmidt's book has detailed information about all aspects of OLE programming in C++ (the examples in that book do not use the MFC 3.0 classes, however). The book by Al Williams is another succinct source of information about OLE 2.0 and Dynamic Data Exchange.

You should also read articles about OLE in programmers' magazines. For example, the *Microsoft Systems Journal* (published monthly by Miller Freeman, Inc., 600 Harrison St., San Francisco, CA 94107) includes many articles about OLE programming, complete with sample code.

Brockschmidt, Kraig. *Inside OLE 2.* Microsoft Press, Redmond, WA, 1993.

Williams, Al. *OLE 2.0 and DDE Distilled.* Addison-Wesley Publishing Company, Reading, MA, 1994.

I

Index

Symbols

Q

R

Add to Your Sams Library Today with the Best Books for Programming, Operating Systems, and New Technologies

The easiest way to order is to pick up the phone and call

1-800-428-5331

between 9:00 a.m. and 5:00 p.m. EST.
For faster service please have your credit card available.

ISBN	Quantity	Description of Item	Unit Cost	Total Cost
0-672-30279-9		C++ Programming PowerPack (book/disk)	$24.95	
0-672-30493-7		What Every Visual C++ 2 Programmer Should Know	$29.99	
0-672-30030-3		Windows Programmer's Guide to Serial Communications (book/disk)	$39.95	
0-672-30097-4		Windows Programmer's Guide to Resources (book/disk)	$34.95	
0-672-30226-8		Windows Programmer's Guide to OLE/DDE (book/disk)	$34.95	
0-672-30364-7		Win32 API Desktop Reference (book/CD)	$49.95	
0-672-30236-5		Windows Programmer's Guide to DLLs and Memory Management (book/disk)	$34.95	
0-672-30295-0		Moving into Windows NT Programming (book/disk)	$39.95	
0-672-30338-8		Inside Windows File Formats (book/disk)	$29.95	
0-672-30299-3		Uncharted Windows Programming (book/disk)	$44.95	
0-672-30239-X		Windows Developer's Guide to Application Design (book/disk)	$34.95	

❏ 3 ½" Disk
❏ 5 ¼" Disk

Shipping and Handling: See information below.		
TOTAL		

Shipping and Handling: $4.00 for the first book, and $1.75 for each additional book. Floppy disk: add $1.75 for shipping and handling. If you need to have it NOW, we can ship product to you in 24 hours for an additional charge of approximately $18.00, and you will receive your item overnight or in two days. Overseas shipping and handling adds $2.00 per book and $8.00 for up to three disks. Prices subject to change. Call for availability and pricing information on latest editions.

201 W. 103rd Street, Indianapolis, Indiana 46290

1-800-428-5331 — Orders   1-800-835-3202 — FAX   1-800-858-7674 — Customer Service

Book ISBN 0-672-12345-6

PLUG YOURSELF INTO...

The MCP Internet Site

Free information and vast computer resources from the world's leading computer book publisher—online!

Find the books that are right for you!

A complete online catalog, plus sample chapters and tables of contents give you an in-depth look at *all* our books. The best way to shop or browse!

✦ **Stay informed** with the latest computer industry news through discussion groups, an online newsletter, and customized subscription news.

✦ **Get fast answers** to your questions about MCP books and software.

✦ **Visit** our online bookstore for the latest information and editions!

✦ **Communicate** with our expert authors through e-mail and conferences.

✦ **Play** in the BradyGame Room with info, demos, shareware, and more!

✦ **Download software** from the immense MCP library:
   - Source code and files from MCP books
   - The best shareware, freeware, and demos

✦ **Discover hot spots** on other parts of the Internet.

✦ **Win books** in ongoing contests and giveaways!

Drop by the new Internet site of Macmillan Computer Publishing!

To plug into MCP:

World Wide Web: http://www.mcp.com/
Gopher: gopher.mcp.com   **FTP:** ftp.mcp.com

GOING ONLINE DECEMBER 1994!

Installing Your Disk

Installing the Companion Disk

The source code files on the companion disk are compressed into a single archive file. To install the files to your hard drive, insert the disk into your floppy disk drive and follow these steps. You'll need at least 4M of free space on your hard drive.

1. Start Windows, if it's not already running.
2. From Windows File Manager or Program Manager, choose **File+R**un from the menu.
3. Type **B:\INSTALL** and press Enter. If the disk is in your A drive, type **A:\INSTALL** instead.
4. A dialog box appears that enables you to change where the files will be installed. To accept the default destination of **C:\VC2DG**, click the **U**nzip button.
5. The files will be decompressed and installed to your hard drive. This will take a while, so be patient. When the installation is complete, a text file will be displayed that contains information about the files and programs that were installed.